ECONOMIC, SOCIAL, AND CULTURAL RIGHTS IN INTERNATIONAL LAW

Economic, Social, and Cultural Rights In International Law

Contemporary Issues and Challenges

Edited by
EIBE RIEDEL, GILLES GIACCA,
and
CHRISTOPHE GOLAY

OXFORD
UNIVERSITY PRESS

OXFORD
UNIVERSITY PRESS

Great Clarendon Street, Oxford, OX2 6DP,
United Kingdom

Oxford University Press is a department of the University of Oxford.
It furthers the University's objective of excellence in research, scholarship,
and education by publishing worldwide. Oxford is a registered trade mark of
Oxford University Press in the UK and in certain other countries

First published 2014
First published in paperback 2016

Published in the United States of America by Oxford University Press
198 Madison Avenue, New York, NY 10016, United States of America

British Library Cataloguing in Publication Data
Data available

Library of Congress Cataloging in Publication Data
Data available

ISBN 978–0–19–968597–4 (Hbk.)
ISBN 978–0–19–879474–5 (Pbk.)

Acknowledgments

This book was developed based upon an experts meeting organized at the Villa Moynier in Geneva on 10 and 11 February 2011. The initiative was part of the Swiss Human Rights Chair's projects supported by the Swiss Department of Foreign Affairs (FDFA) and implemented by the Geneva Academy of International Humanitarian Law and Human Rights (the Geneva Academy). For this purpose, a blend of academic and practitioners' perspectives was sought to cover a variety of contemporary issues and challenges in the realization of economic, social, and cultural rights.

The book is the product of tenacity and patience. In part, this is due to the number of contributors to this volume, but also to the fact that it is never a simple or straightforward undertaking to have legal scholars and practitioners—all extremely busy people—commit themselves to providing their work for publication. The journey has thus been rather a long one, with many twists and turns, and not without its challenges at various points along the way. Even though a great variety of topics has been touched upon, it is clear that in the area of economic, social, and cultural rights more challenges lie in wait, for which future research is desirable, but we are convinced that the book has singled out particularly pressing ones. Accordingly, we are deeply grateful and indebted to all those who contributed their work for publication in this edited volume.

This book would not have been possible without the support and assistance of many talented and dedicated individuals. For superb assistance in the editorial process, we are greatly indebted to Binesh Hass, whose capacity to work under tight deadlines and provide excellent editing has been admirable. We should also like to thank Dr Stuart Casey-Maslen, Head of Research of the Geneva Academy, for his support in editing a number of chapters.

We are most grateful to the Directors of the Geneva Academy, Professor Paola Gaeta and Professor Andrew Clapham, for having supported the project throughout, as well as to the Executive Manager, Kamelia Kemileva, for her support and assistance. Naturally, such a research initiative would not have been possible without the generous financial support of key donors. We thus should like to thank the Swiss FDFA, in particular Ambassador Ralf Heckner and Ambassador Thomas Greminger, Human Security Division, as well as Mirko Guilietti and Nathalie Erard, Section for Human Rights Policy, Human Security Division. We are also most grateful to the Law Faculty of Oxford University and the Oxford Martin School for funding our project. A special thank you to Sandra Fredman, Dapo Akande, and Professor Simon Caney, the Co-Directors of the Oxford Human Rights for Future Generations programme for their undivided support, as well as to our colleagues Dr Jaakko Kuosmanen, Dr Dominic Roser, and Zoe Davis-Heaney.

Furthermore, we are grateful to Dr Takhmina Karimova for her advice and suggestions throughout the project, as well as to our colleagues of the Geneva Academy Dr Annyssa Bellal, Dr Sharon Weill, Daniela Renggli, Dr Ioana Cismas, Ivona Tuscan, Antonella Ghio, Nathalie Staffler, Antoine Kaboré, Tatiana Avanthay, Jean-Baptiste Maillart, and Antonio Coco.

We also acknowledge the important contribution of Claire Mahon who started the project with us and whose expertise helped shape the book. We dedicate this book to Claire.

Special thanks are due to the team at Oxford University Press for their support and work on this book, in particular Merel Alstein, Anthony Hinton, and John Louth, as well as to Anto Aroshini and his team from the Newgen Publishing & Data Services for their great work on the final manuscript. We are also most grateful to the talented Yashka Steiner who designed the cover of the book.

Our hope is that our work will make some useful contributions to the important subject matter to which this volume is dedicated: the implementation and realization of economic, social, and cultural rights.

Professor Eibe Riedel, Dr Gilles Giacca, and Dr Christophe Golay
Geneva/Oxford, March 2014

Contents

Detailed Contents

VI. TRENDS IN THE JUSTICIABILITY AND MONITORING OF ESC RIGHTS AT THE NATIONAL AND INTERNATIONAL LEVEL

Table of Cases

AFRICAN COMMISSION ON HUMAN AND PEOPLES' RIGHTS

EUROPEAN COMMISSION ON HUMAN RIGHTS

EUROPEAN COMMITTEE OF SOCIAL RIGHTS

EUROPEAN COURT OF HUMAN RIGHTS

EUROPEAN COURT OF JUSTICE

INTER-AMERICAN COURT ON HUMAN RIGHTS

INTERNATIONAL CENTRE FOR SETTLEMENT OF INVESTMENT DISPUTES

INTERNATIONAL CRIMINAL COURT

INTERNATIONAL CRIMINAL TRIBUNAL FOR THE FORMER YUGOSLAVIA

INTERNATIONAL CRIMINAL TRIBUNAL FOR RWANDA

INTERNATIONAL COURT OF JUSTICE

UNITED NATIONS COMMITTEE AGAINST TORTURE

UNITED NATIONS COMMISSION ON INTERNATIONAL TRADE LAW

UNITED NATIONS HUMAN RIGHTS COMMITTEE

NATIONAL COURTS

Argentina

Bangladesh

Canada

India

Ireland

Kenya

Nepal

Philippines

South Arica

Table of Treaties, Legislation, and Other Relevant Instruments

NATIONAL LEGISLATION

List of Abbreviations

ACP	African, Caribbean, and Pacific
ACHR	American Convention on Human Rights
AfCHPR	African Commission on Human and Peoples' Rights
ANSA	Armed non-state actors
APs	Additional Protocols
ATS	Alien Tort Statute
BITs	Bilateral investment treaties
CAFTA	Central American Free Trade Agreement
CEDAW	Convention on the Elimination of All Forms of Discrimination against Women
CESCR	Committee on Economic, Social and Cultural Rights
CHRAJ	Commission on Human Rights and the Administration of Justice
CHRP	Commission on Human Rights of the Philippines
CHRT	Canadian Human Rights Tribunal
CP	Civil and political
CRPD	Convention on the Rights of Persons with Disabilities
CRC	Convention on the Rights of the Child
DIME	Dense Inert Metal Explosive
DSU	Dispute Settlement Understanding
EAA	Ecumenical Advocacy Alliance
ECHR	European Convention on Human Rights
ECtHR	European Court of Human Rights
ECOSOC	Economic and Social Council
EIA	Environmental impact assessment
EPA	Economic Partnership Agreement
ERRC	European Roma Rights Centre
ESC	Economic, social, and cultural
ETO	Extra-territorial obligations
EU	European Union
FAO	Food and Agriculture Organization
FDI	Foreign direct investment
FET	Fair and equitable treatment
FIO	Federation of Ibero-American Ombudspersons
FTA	Free trade agreements
GA	United Nations General Assembly
GATS	General Agreement on Trade in Services
GATT	General Agreement on Tariffs and Trade
GCIV	Fourth Geneva Convention of 12 August 1949 relative to the Protection of Civilian Persons in Time of War
GDP	Gross Domestic Product
GFC	Global Financial Crisis
HeRWAI	Health Rights of Women Assessment Instrument
HRA	Human Rights Act
HRC	Human Rights Council

HRIA	Human rights impact assessment
IACtHR	Inter-American Court on Human Rights
IBSA	Indicator-Benchmarking-Scoping-Assessment
ICC	International Criminal Court
ICCtee	International Coordinating Committee
ICCPR	International Covenant on Civil and Political Rights
ICESCR	International Covenant on Economic, Social and Cultural Rights
ICHRP	International Council on Human Rights Policy
ICJ	International Court of Justice
ICRC	International Committee of the Red Cross
ICSID	International Centre on the Settlement of Investment Disputes
ICTR	International Criminal Court for Rwanda
ICTY	International Criminal Court for the Former Yugoslavia
IDA	International Disability Allowance
IEL	International economic law
IFAD	International Fund for Agricultural Development
IHL	International humanitarian law
ILC	International Law Commission
ILO	International Labour Organization
IMF	International Monetary Fund
IPR	Intellectual property rights
KFOR	Kosovo Force
KNCHR	Kenya National Commission on Human Rights
MDGs	Millennium Development Goals
NAAECE	North American Agreement for Environmental Cooperation
NAFTA	North American Free Trade Association
NGO	Non-governmental organizations
NHRIs	National human rights institutions
NIHE	Northern Ireland Housing Executive
NIEO	New International Economic Order
NZHRC	New Zealand Human Rights Commission
OECD	Organisation for Economic Cooperation and Development
ODA	Official development assistance
OHCHR	Office of the UN High Commissioner for Human Rights
OP	Optional Protocol
OPT	Occupied Palestinian Territories
PPACA	Patient Protection and Affordable Care Act
PPP	Public-private partnership
PSAC	Public Service Alliance of Canada
QALYs	Quality-adjusted life-years
QUB	Queen's University Belfast
RAI	Responsible Agricultural Investment
RBS	Royal Bank of Scotland
SAHRC	South African Human Rights Commission
SDGs	Sustainable development goals
SEM	Submissions on Enforcement Matters
STIs	Sexually transmitted infections
SWAps	Sector-wide approaches to development

TBT	Technical Barriers to Trade
TRIMS	Trade-Related Investment Measures
TRIPS	Trade-Related Aspects of Intellectual Property
UDHR	Universal Declaration of Human Rights
UN	United Nations
UNCLOS	United Nations Convention on the Law of the Sea
UNECE	United Nations Economic Commission for Europe
UNICEF	United Nations Children's Fund (formerly United Nations International Children's Emergency Fund)
UNMIK	United Nations Interim Administration Mission in Kosovo
VCLT	Vienna Convention on the Law of Treaties
VgT	Verein gegen Tierfabriken
WHO	World Health Organization
WTO	World Trade Organization

List of Contributors

EDITORS

Eibe Riedel is Emeritus Professor of German and Comparative Public Law, European and International Law at the University of Mannheim/Germany, and a former member of the UN Committee on Economic, Social and Cultural rights, Geneva. He is a judge at the Hague Permanent Court of Arbitration, chairs the Board of Trustees of the German Institute of Human Rights, Berlin, and is a director of the Institute of Medical Law, Bioethics and Public Health of the Universities of Mannheim and Heidelberg, as well as a director and founder of the Mannheim Institute of Transport Law, Inland Navigation Law. Prof. Riedel was Swiss Chair of Human Rights and is presently a visiting Professor at the Geneva Academy of International Humanitarian Law and Human Rights. He also is honorary adjunct Professor at the University of Adelaide. He has written widely on human rights, most recently on the Optional Protocol to the ICESCR in *Essays in Honour of Judge Bruno Simma* (OUP 2011); on 'Global Human Rights at the Crossroads: 'Strengthening' or 'Reforming' the System', in *Festschrift Eckart Klein*, (Berlin 2013); and on 'ESC-Rights in Armed Conflict' in Andrew Clapham (ed.), *Oxford Handbook on International Law*, OUP 2014).

Dr Gilles Giacca is a Research Fellow at the Law Faculty of Oxford University, Co-ordinator of the Oxford Martin School of Human Rights for Future Generations programme and Research Associate, Oxford Institute for Ethics, Law and Armed Conflict. Gilles has advised states, international organizations, and NGOs on matters of international law, including the Swiss FDFA on humanitarian access. His main research interests lie in the field of public international law, collective security, international humanitarian law, human rights law, and refugee law as well as weapons law. He has contributed to a number of legal commentaries, including the *UN Charter Commentary* (OUP 2012) as well as the forthcoming *Geneva Conventions Commentary* (OUP 2014) and the *Commentary on the Rio Declaration on Environment and Development* (OUP 2014). He is currently co-authoring *A Commentary on the UN Arms Trade Treaty* that will be published by OUP in 2015 and publishing a book entitled *Economic, Social and Cultural Rights in Armed Conflict* (OUP 2014),

Dr Christophe Golay is Research Fellow and Coordinator of the Project on Economic, Social and Cultural Rights at the Geneva Academy of International Humanitarian Law and Human Rights. He is Lecturer at the Geneva Centre for Education and Research in Humanitarian Action. In 2013, he was Visiting Fellow at the McGill University Centre for Human Rights and Legal Pluralism. From 2001 to 2008, he was the Legal Advisor to the first UN Special Rapporteur on the Right to Food. His most recent publications include *The Fight for the Right to Food. Lessons Learned*, with Jean Ziegler, Claire Mahon, and Sally-Anne Way (Palgrave Macmillan 2011), and *Droit à l'alimentation et accès à la justice* (Bruylant 2011).

CONTRIBUTORS

Christine Chinkin is Professor of International Law at the London School of Economics, a barrister, and a member of Matrix Chambers.

Stéphanie Chuffart is Visiting Fellow at the Columbia University School of Law (Centre for Climate Change Law) and PhD Candidate at Graduate Institute of International and Development Studies, Geneva.

Dr Ioana Cismas is law clinic coordinator, Geneva Academy of International Humanitarian Law and Human Rights and consultant, Office of the High Commissioner for Human Rights, working on the mandate of the UN Special Rapporteur on the promotion of truth, justice, reparation, and guarantees of non-recurrence.

Larissa van den Herik is Professor of Public International Law and programme director of the Grotius Centre for International Legal Studies at Leiden University.

Allison Corkery is researcher at Center for Economic and Social Rights, New York.

Olivier De Schutter is Professor at the University of Louvain (Belgium) and at the College of Europe. Since 2008 he has been the United Nations Special Rapporteur on the right to food.

Dr Mary Dowell-Jones is a Research Fellow in international financial law at the University of New South Wales, and a fellow of the Human Rights Law Centre at the University of Nottingham.

Hans Morten Haugen is Associate Professor, Diakonhjemmet University College, Oslo.

Priv Doz Dr Holger P. Hestermeyer is a Référendaire at the Court of Justice of the European Union.

Frank Haldemann is a Swiss National Science Foundation Professor at the Law Faculty of the University of Geneva and teaches Transitional Justice at the Geneva Academy for International Humanitarian Law and Human Rights.

Dr Takhmina Karimova is Research Fellow and Coordinator of the Project on Economic, Social and Cultural Rights at the Geneva Academy of International Humanitarian Law and Human Rights.

Rachelle Kouassi is a PhD Candidate at the Law Faculty of the University of Geneva. She currently works as a research and teaching assistant at the Geneva Academy of International Humanitarian Law and Human Rights.

Dr Malcolm Langford is a Research Fellow at the Norwegian Centre for Human Rights (NCHR), Faculty of Law, University of Oslo.

Nicholas Lusiani is Senior Researcher at the Center for Economic and Social Rights, New York.

Aoife Nolan is Professor of International Human Rights Law, School of Law, Nottingham University.

Ignacio Saiz is Executive Director of the Center for Economic and Social Rights, New York.

Sandra Ratjen is Senior Legal Adviser and Head of Programme, Economic, Social and Cultural Rights at the International Commission of Jurists.

Manav Satija is currently employed as a solicitor and barrister for an Indigenous Legal Aid Organisation in Central Australia.

Jorge E. Viñuales is the Harold Samuel Professor of Law and Environmental Policy at the University of Cambridge.

Dr Simon Walker works in the Human Rights Treaty Division at the UN Office of the High Commissioner for Human Rights (OHCHR) as section chief dealing with the Committee on Economic, Social and Cultural Rights, the Human Rights Committee, and three other committees.

Sally-Anne Way is Human Rights Officer at the UN Office of the High Commissioner for Human Rights (OHCHR).

Duncan Wilson is Head of Strategy and Legal, Scottish Human Rights Commission, Edinburgh.

I

INTRODUCTION

1

The Development of Economic, Social, and Cultural Rights in International Law

Eibe Riedel, Gilles Giacca, and Christophe Golay

1. Introduction

The field of economic, social, and cultural (ESC) rights is growing at a fast pace. Scholars and advocates around the world are increasingly focusing their energy and attention on poverty eradication, sustainable development, dignity, and their realization through the implementation of the rights to housing, education, food, water, health, social security, work, and culture. Over the last 20 years, this movement has gained great strength, leading to an impressive development of tools and resources at national, regional, and international level, as well as consolidation of doctrine on ESC rights.[1]

[1] These include P. Alston and K. Tomasevski (eds.), *The Right to Food* (The Hague: Martinus Nijhoff Publishers, 1984); A. Eide, *Food as a Human Right* (Tokyo: The United Nations University, 1984); K. Tomasevski (ed.), *The Right to Food: Guide through Applicable International Law* (Dordrecht: Martinus Nijhoff, 1987); A. Eide, W. Barth Eide, S. Goonatilake, and J. Gussow, Omale (eds.), *Food as a Human Right*, 2nd printing (Singapore: United Nations University, 1988) (1st printing 1984); R. Beddard, and D.M. Hill (eds.), *Economic, Social and Cultural Rights: Progress and Achievement* (New York: St.Martin's Press, 1992); M.C.R. Craven, *The International Covenant on Economic, Social and Cultural Rights: A Perspective on its Development* (Oxford: Clarendon Press, 1995); P. Hunt, *Reclaiming Social Rights: International and Comparative Perspectives* (Dartmouth: Ashgate, 1996); K. Arambulo, *Strengthening the Supervision of the International Covenant on Economic, Social and Cultural Rights: Theoretical and Procedural Aspects* (Antwerp: Intersentia, 1999); I. Merali, and V. Oosterveld (eds.), *Giving Meaning to Economic, Social and Cultural Rights* (Philadelphia: University of Pennsylvania Press, 2001); A. Eide, C. Krause, and A. Rosas (eds.), *Economic, Social and Cultural Rights: A Textbook*, 2nd rev. edn (The Hague: Kluwer Law International, 2001); A. Chapman and S. Russell (eds.), *Core Obligations: Building a Framework for Economic, Social and Cultural Rights* (Antwerp: Intersentia, 2002); B.K. Goldewijk, A.C. Baspineiro, and P.C. Carbonari (eds.), *Dignity and Human Rights: The Implementation of Economic, Social and Cultural Rights* (Antwerp, Oxford, New York: Intersentia, 2002); M. Sepúlveda Carmona, *The Nature of the Obligations under the International Covenant on Economic, Social and Cultural Rights*, School of Human Rights Research Series, Vol. 18 (Antwerp: Intersentia, 2003); Y. Ghai and J. Cottrell (eds.), *Economic, Social and Cultural Rights in Practice* (London: Interights, 2004); J. Squires, M. Langford, and B. Thiele, *The Road To A Remedy: Current Issues in the Litigation of Economic, Social and Cultural Rights* (Sydney: Australia Human Rights Centre, 2005); P. Alston, *Labour Rights as Human Rights* (Oxford: Oxford University Press, 2005); R.E Howard-Hassmann and C.E. Jr. Welch (eds.), *Economic Rights in Canada and the United States*

At the United Nations (UN) and in regional and national human rights systems, new mechanisms have been established to monitor implementation of these rights. As judges and lawyers are being asked to address more legal claims related to these rights, and as non-governmental organizations (NGOs) and UN agencies expand their programmes in these areas, universities and professional trainers are responding to the demand by introducing courses to train lawyers, development workers, policymakers, and diplomats in these areas.

These activities have culminated in the adoption of the Optional Protocol to the International Covenant on Economic, Social and Cultural Rights (ICESCR or Covenant) in December 2008 and its entry into force in May 2013. For the first time, individuals and groups can bring complaints about violations of ESC rights before the treaty monitoring body of the Covenant, namely the UN Committee on Economic, Social and Cultural Rights (CESCR). This significant development also forges an optimistic view about the future clarification and development of aspects of the ESC rights that hitherto were controversial.

From the review of progress achieved, it follows that, on the one hand, the broad normative framework of ESC rights has attained a high degree of specificity in terms of content as well as efficacy of implementation mechanisms, most importantly at the national level. On the other hand, the project of ESC rights is saddled with serious, sometimes persistent and emerging challenges that first relate to its structural approach to human rights realization, hinged largely but not exclusively upon economic issues. Legal theory, as is known, always faces constraints when it is 'entangled with the shifting and unruly facts of international politics, economics and social justice'.[2]

(Philadelphia: University of Pennsylvania Press, 2006); S. Leckie and A. Gallagher (eds.), *Economic, Social and Cultural Rights: A Legal Resource Guide* (Philadelphia: University of Pennsylvania Press, 2006); M. Langford and A. Nolan, *Litigating Economic, Social and Cultural Rights: Legal Practitioners Dossier*, 2nd edn (Geneva: COHRE, 2006); E. Palmer, *Judicial Review, Socio-Economic Rights and the Human Rights Act* (Portland: Hart Publishing, 2007); M.E. Salomon, *Global Responsibility for Human Rights: World Poverty and Development of International Law* (Oxford: Oxford University Press, 2007); D. Bilchitz, *Poverty and Fundamental Rights: The Justification and Enforcement of Socio-Economic Rights* (Oxford: Oxford University Press, 2007); D. Barak-Erez and A.M. Gross, *Exploring Social Rights: Between Theory and Practice* (Oxford: Hart, 2007); M. Foster, *International Refugee Law and Socio- Economic Rights* (Cambridge: Cambridge University Press, 2007); S. Hertel and L. Minkler, *Economic Rights: Conceptual, Measurement, and Policy Issues* (Cambridge: Cambridge University Press, 2007); V. Gauri and D.M. Brinks, *Courting Social Justice: Judicial enforcement of Social and Economic Rights in the Developing World* (Cambridge: Cambridge University Press, 2008); M. Langford, *Social Rights Jurisprudence: Emerging Trends in International and Comparative Law* (Cambridge: Cambridge University Press, 2008); C. Mbazira, *Litigating Socio-Economic Rights in South Africa* (Pretoria: Pretoria University Law Press, 2009); S. Liebenberg, *Socio-Economic Rights: Adjudication Under a Transformative Constitution* (Cape Town: Juta Press, 2010); M. Langford, W. Vandenhole, M. Scheinin, and W. van Genugten (eds.), *Global Justice, State Duties: The Extraterritorial Scope of Economic, Social and Cultural Rights in International Law* (Cambridge: Cambridge University Press, 2013); M. Langford, A. Sumner, and A. Ely Yamin (eds.), *Millennium Development Goals and Human Rights: Past, Present, and Future* (New York: Cambridge University Press, 2013); A Nolan (ed.), *Economic and Social Rights after the Global Financial Crisis* (Cambridge: Cambridge University Press, forthcoming 2014).

[2] O. Schachter, 'The Evolving International Law of Development', 15 *Columbia Journal of Transnational Law* 1 (1976), 1–16, at 1.

Second, armed conflict, environment, gender issues, social development, and security are among a range of other dimensions that clearly have to be factored into an assessment of the realization of ESC rights, but their relationship with those rights is not yet precisely articulated. Debates on these topics have occurred in a fragmented manner within respective disciplinary fields with little attempt being made to bridge them with ESC rights and particularly how these diverse contexts affect implementation of these rights. In recognition of these challenges, it is important to continue to be innovative in our thinking about ESC rights and their operationalization in practice. International law provides a rich framework through which human dignity can be upheld based on improvements in education, health, and standards of living.

But prior to more in-depth discussion of these topics, this introductory chapter will chart the development of ESC rights in international law. This will provide the appropriate backdrop for the issues engaged in this work. It begins with the historical setting in which the protection of ESC rights developed since the adoption of the Universal Declaration of Human Rights (UDHR) in 1948. The focus is on the work of its main driver, the CESCR. The aim is to define ESC rights and the nature of states' obligations under the ICESCR, before analysing the future role of the Optional Protocol to the ICESCR. The concluding part of this introductory chapter provides an outline of the present volume, structured around the main issues and challenges confronting ESC rights today.

2. Historical Setting

In 1945, shattered by the cruelties, brutality, and inhumanity of two World Wars, and feeling the repercussions of devastating economic and social crises like the Great Depression of the 1930s, world leaders united in the newly created United Nations and decided to lay the foundation for the universal protection of a set of rights fundamental to the life of every individual.[3] It was, however, not possible at that time to reach agreement on the details of that UN purpose.[4] Instead, only

[3] A. Clapham, *Brierly's Law of Nations*, 7th edn (Oxford: Oxford University Press, 2012), 235–242; P. Alston and R. Goodman, *International Human Rights* (Oxford: Oxford University Press, 2013), 3 and 58; E. Riedel and J. Arend, 'Art. 55(c)', in B. Simma, D.E. Khan, G. Nolte, and A. Paulus (eds.), *The Charter of the United Nations, A Commentary*, Vol. II, 3rd edn (Oxford: Oxford University Press, 2012), 1565–1602; C. Tomuschat, *Human Rights. Between Idealism and Realism*, 2nd edn (Oxford: Oxford University Press, 2008), 7; W. Kälin and J. Künzli, *The Law of International Human Rights Protection* (Oxford: Oxford University Press, 2009), 3–26; E. Bates, 'History', in D. Moeckli, S. Shah, and S. Sivakumaran (eds.), *International Human Rights Law* (Oxford: Oxford University Press, 2010), 17–37; M.A. Baderin and M. Ssenyonjo, *International Human Rights Law: Six Decades after the UDHR and Beyond* (Farnham: Ashgate, 2010), 3–27; H. Hannum, 'United Nations and Human Rights Law', in C. Krause and M. Scheinin (eds.), *International Protection of Human Rights: A Textbook*, 2nd edn (Turku: Abo Akademi University, 2012), 61–78; O. De Schutter, *International Human Rights Law: Cases, Materials, Commentary* (Cambridge: Cambridge University Press, 2010), 48–58.

[4] See R.B. Russell and J.E. Muther, *A History of the United Nations Charter* (Washington: The Brookings Institution, 1958), 303.

the preamble and a few general Articles mentioned in the text of the Charter took note of this function and it was decided to leave the elaboration of a Universal Bill of Rights to the newly created Commission on Human Rights. By 1948, however, it became clear that agreement on such a treaty was not possible. The beginning of the Cold War and East–West ideological disputes prevented that. As a compromise, it was decided in 1948 to first formulate a legally non-binding, but standard-setting UDHR, to be supplemented by a subsequent treaty that would translate the UDHR standards into legally binding obligations.

The UDHR contained civil and political (CP), and ESC rights in a single instrument, and in remarkably concise terminology. Apart from rights of the first generation—or, better, first dimension[5]—(understood as freedom rights) it also includes rights of the second dimension that belong to the catalogue of inalienable human rights, ultimately flowing from human dignity. Without minimum claim rights in working life, health protection, and education systems, and without the guarantee of an adequate standard of living, flowing from human dignity, guaranteeing a 'survival kit' that sets a minimum existence protection standard, the overall picture of human rights would be incomplete, missing out crucial dimensions of protection for the most needy, in particular marginalized and disadvantaged persons and groups of persons.[6] Thus, freedom of opinion alone makes no sense to a starving person. The preamble of the UN Charter had made this abundantly clear when naming the core main purposes and functions of the UN, namely: peacekeeping, guaranteeing the rule of law (including human rights), and furthering social progress, and achieving better standards of life in a larger freedom. This third function has often been overlooked. But member states of the UN could not, as yet, agree on how to implement those rights in a binding treaty. The Commission on Human Rights was, however, empowered to elaborate such a human rights treaty.[7] By 1952, however, it became evident that growing ideological disputes in the wake of the Cold War between East and West prevented the adoption of a unified treaty, comprising all UDHR rights. By the so-called Separation Resolution of 1952,[8] the Commission on Human Rights split the UDHR guarantees into two separate draft treaties. Negotiations over these two drafts continued until 1966.

This fundamental rift between categories of rights took more than 40 years to overcome. Western States, led by the United States of America—in contradiction

[5] See E. Riedel, 'Menschenrechte der dritten Dimension' (1989) 16 *Europäische Grundrechte Zeitschrift*, 9–21, on the need to replace 'generations' by 'dimensions'.

[6] See generally E. Riedel, 'Monitoring the 1966 ICESCR', in G.P. Politakis (ed.), *Protecting Labour Rights: Present and Future of International Supervision* (Geneva: International Labour Organization, 2007), 3–13, at 10; on poverty and the right to food, see J. Ziegler, C. Golay, C. Mahon, and S.-A. Way, *The Fight for the Right to Food: Lessons Learned* (London: Palgrave Macmillan, 2011).

[7] UN General Assembly Resolution, Draft International Covenant on Human Rights and Measures to Implementation: Future Work of the Commission of Human Rights, 4 December 1950, UN Doc. A/RES/421 (V). See generally E. Riedel and G. Giacca, 'Article 68', in B. Simma, D.E. Khan, G. Nolte, and A. Paulus (eds.), *The Charter of the United Nations: A Commentary*, Vol. II, 3rd edn (Oxford: Oxford University Press, 2012), 1753–1761.

[8] UN General Assembly Resolution, Preparation of Two Drafts International Covenants on Human Rights, 5 February 1952, UN Doc. A/RES/543 (VI). See also E. Riedel, *Theorie der Menschenrechtsstandards* (Berlin: Duncker & Humblot, 1986), 25–64.

with the Four Freedoms Speech of Franklin D. Roosevelt of 1941 and with his Economic Bill of Rights Speech of 1944[9]—favoured the concept of two separate treaties maintaining that CP rights and ESC rights were and are inherently of a different legal nature, insofar as the latter would lack judicial enforceability. Contrary to this position, the so-called Eastern bloc as well as many non-aligned states supported and demanded equal treatment for ESC rights.[10] At the final count, the supporters of one comprehensive treaty had to compromise and accept two separate treaties, adopted simultaneously on 16 December 1966, both entering into force in 1976.[11]

At the level of implementation, the two Covenants displayed marked differences, still reflecting the ideological divide of the 1950s and 1960s: while the International Covenant on Civil and Political Rights (ICCPR) provided for three monitoring devices at global level, namely state reporting, individual communications, and state complaint procedures, the ICESCR merely foresaw a state reporting obligation. Furthermore, to underline the different treatment of these categories of rights, the ICESCR did not establish a separate supervisory committee in the text, but entrusted that task to the Economic and Social Council (ECOSOC). The CESCR was only set up later by a resolution of ECOSOC,[12] and started its work with independent experts in 1987.[13] Since then, CESCR receives in principle one comprehensive state report per member state every five years, with sectorial reporting having been tried but found to be less effective in the early 1990s.

Nearly thirty years after the adoption of the two Covenants, at the Vienna World Conference on Human Rights of 1993, states emphasized in the Vienna Declaration and Plan of Action that ESCR form one of the two pillars of international human rights law and stressed the universality, indivisibility, inter-dependence, and inter-relatedness of all human rights. The Conference concluded that '[t]he international community must treat human rights globally in a fair and equal manner, on the same footing, and with the same emphasis'.[14] This objective has been at least

[9] See President R.D. Roosevelt, *State of the Union Address*, 6 January 1941, available at <http://www.ourdocuments.gov/doc.php?flash=true&doc=70&page=transcript> (last accessed 24 November 2013) and President R.D. Roosevelt, *State of the Union Address*, 11 January 1944, available at <http://www.gutenberg.org/dirs/etext04/sufdr11.txt> (last accessed 24 November 2013).

[10] See I. Cismas, 'The Intersection of Economic, Social, and Cultural Rights and Civil and Political Rights', ch. 16 in this book.

[11] UN General Assembly Resolution, 16 December 1966, UN Doc. A/RES/2200 (XXI).

[12] Originally, ECOSOC set up a Sessional Working Group on the Implementation of the ICESCR, through the adoption of ECOSOC Decision 1978/10 on 3 May 1978. This Sessional Working Group was later renamed CESCR with the adoption of ECOSOC Decision 1985/17 on 28 May 1985.

[13] In the monitoring practice of the treaty bodies, however, this procedural difference has not played a significant role. In fact, the Commission on Human Rights and its successor, the Human Rights Council, have treated all treaty bodies alike, and states parties have similarly treated the reporting mechanisms of all treaty bodies alike. One could even say that difference in the establishment of the treaty body has given the CESCR quite a degree of independence, which has led to introducing new methodologies where other committees remained more hesitant, such as allowing contributions from non-governmental organizations (NGOs). This has helped to focus and prioritize discussions with states parties, and the other treaty bodies soon followed suit.

[14] UN World Conference on Human Rights, Vienna Declaration and Plan of Action, 12 July 1993, UN Doc. A/CONF.157/23, Part I, para. 5. The Vienna declaration and plan of action was adopted by 173 states.

partially reached today if we look at the number of ratifications, as by December 2013, 161 states had ratified the ICESCR and 167 the ICCPR. However, original ideological positions did not totally disappear, and the United States of America has still not ratified the ICESCR.

The CESCR had also propagated from the early 1990s the adoption of an Optional Protocol (OP), similar to the OP to the ICCPR, to introduce individual communications alongside the state reporting procedure, and to emphasize the equal importance of CP and ESC rights. But that venture took another two decades to be realized.

3. The Practice of the Committee on Economic, Social and Cultural Rights

Since the beginning of its work in 1987, the CESCR has been by far the main driver of the development of ESCR in international law.[15] It has been particularly effective in defining the notion of ESC rights and in monitoring ESC rights in states parties to the ICESCR.

A. The notion of ESC rights

In defining ESC rights, it seems logical to distinguish three main categories. The first category, economic rights, embraces the guarantees and claims to participation in the economic life of the community.[16] Within this category of ESC rights is to be found the right to property, which is contained in Article 17 of the UDHR, but dropped from the ICESCR Draft in 1954.[17] Other examples are elements of the right to housing (Article 11 (1)),[18] and the right to freely chosen or accepted work (Article 6 (1)).[19] The second category, social rights, by contrast, usually relates to

[15] For a detailed presentation on the impact of other international monitoring mechanisms on the development of ESC rights, with a particular focus on UN Special Procedures, see C. Golay, C. Mahon, and I. Cismas, 'The impact of the UN Special Procedures on the development and implementation of economic, social and cultural rights' (2010), 15 *The International Journal of Human Rights*, 299–318.

[16] See F. Coomans, *Economic, Social and Cultural Rights* (Utrecht: Netherlands Institute of Human Rights, 1995), 3.

[17] E. Riedel, *Theorie der Menschenrechtsstandards (Theory of Human Rights Standards)* (Berlin: Duncker & Humblot, 1986), ch. 2, 25–147; E. Riedel, 'Farewell to the Sources Triad in International Law?' (1991) 2 *European Journal of International Law*, 58–84. For a recent study on the right to property see C. Golay and I. Cismas, *The Right to Property From a Human Rights Perspective* (Montreal, Geneva: Rights and Democracy, Geneva Academy of International Humanitarian Law and Human Rights, 2010).

[18] CESCR, General Comment No. 4: The Right to Adequate Housing (Art. 11(1) of the Covenant), 1 January 1992, UN Doc. E/1992/23 ('General Comment No. 4'); CESCR, General Comment No. 7: The Right to Adequate Housing (art. 11, para. 1, of the Covenant): Forced Evictions, adopted on 14 May 1997, UN Doc. E/1998/22, E/C.12/1997/10, Annex IV ('General Comment No. 7').

[19] CESCR, General Comment No. 18: The Right to Work (Art. 6 of the Covenant), 6 February 2006, UN Doc. E/C.12/GC/18 ('General Comment No. 18').

aspects of employment and, in particular, to the conditions under which people live.[20] Thus, Articles 6 to 9 of the ICESCR cover specific rights of employment, or rather rights in employment, including technical and vocational guidance and training programmes (Article 6 (2)), just and favourable conditions of work, including equal remuneration for work of equal value (Article 7 (a)), safe and healthy working conditions (Article 7 (b)), limitation of working hours, etc. (Article 7 (d)), trade union rights (Article 8), and the right to social security, including social insurance, usually related to employment conditions,[21] and social assistance (Article 9). Yet a large part of social rights is not specifically employment-related, and instead refers to actual living conditions of people, irrespective of their being employed. Such social rights comprise family rights, the rights to food, housing, clothing, and health, and are to be found in Articles 10 to 12 ICESCR. The third category of ESC rights embraces cultural rights, usually those embodied in Articles 13 to 15, ICESCR, such as the right to education (Articles 13 and 14), to one's cultural identity, to be able to participate freely in cultural life, to enjoy the benefits of scientific progress and its applications, authors' rights, and to conduct scientific research (Article 15). While Part III of the Covenant—Articles 6 to 15 ICESCR—points towards certain obligations a state party has to honour with particular relevance to the respective rights, Part II (Articles 2 to 5 ICESCR) outlines cross-cutting state obligations of a general nature applicable to all individual rights, such as issues of non-discrimination and equality. These general obligations have been elucidated over the years by the CESCR in its monitoring practice, complemented by a variety of international expert opinions, and by workshops and conferences.

To date, the CESCR has adopted 21 General Comments in which it defined ESC rights and correlative states' obligations,[22] and principles and standards proposed by expert conferences, such as the Limburg Principles on the Implementation of the ICESCR of 1987 and the Maastricht Guidelines on Violations of ESC rights of 1997, have been adopted outside the work of the CESCR.[23] And yet, it does not

[20] Classification examples abound. For an overview see E. Riedel, 'The examination of State reports', in E. Klein (ed.), *The Monitoring System of Human Rights Treaty Obligations* (Berlin: Verlag Spitz, 1998), 95–105.

[21] CESCR, General Comment No. 19: The Right to Social Security (Art. 9 of the Covenant), 4 February 2008, UN Doc. E/C.12/GC/19 ('General Comment No. 19'). See also E. Riedel, 'The Human Right to Social Security: Some Challenges', in E. Riedel (ed.), *Social Security as a Human Right* (Berlin/Heidelberg/New York: Springer, 2007), 17–28.

[22] Like the other United Nations treaty bodies, the CESCR adopts General Comments—also called 'General Recommendations' by the Committee on the Elimination of all Forms of Discrimination of Women (CEDAW). The General Comments of the CESCR are authoritative interpretations of the rights enshrined in the ICESCR. Their purpose is to assist states parties in the carrying out of their obligations and to give greater clarity to the object, the purpose and the content of the ICESCR. See P. Alston, 'The Historical Origins of the Concept of "General Comments" in Human Rights Law', in L. Boisson De Chazournes and V. Gowland-Debbas (eds.), *The International Legal System in Quest of Equity and Universality: Liber Amicorum Georges Abi-Saab* (The Hague: Martinus Nijhof, 2001), 763–776. Regarding the CESCR's interpretation in its general comments as being generally accepted by states parties as authoritative, see M. Sepúlveda Carmona, *The Nature of the Obligations under the International Covenant on Economic, Social and Cultural Rights*, School of Human Rights Research Series, Vol. 18 (Antwerp, Oxford, New York: Intersentia, 2003), 40–42.

[23] Limburg Principles on the Implementation of the ICESCR ('Limburg Principles'). The Limburg Principles were drafted during a meeting of experts on ESC rights in Limburg (Maastricht,

seem adequate to differentiate strictly among these interrelated rights. Economic and social rights are different sides of the same coin. In the practice of the CESCR, no strict division of rights has been followed, apart from the fact that the textual order of rights has been adhered to in the monitoring practice, by clustering rights monitoring topics into general issues, Articles 6 to 9, Articles 10 to 12, and Article 13 to 15 ICESCR.[24]

B. Nature of ESC rights monitoring

While at regional level in Europe, Africa, and the Americas a judicial approach has been developed for human rights implementation, at the universal level this has not been possible. In international law, three modalities of implementation are possible: the judicial, quasi-judicial, and political. The judicial avenue leads to a court or tribunal decision in the form of a declaratory judgment, imposing on states parties to human rights treaties an obligation to execute the judgments at national level. At the Council of Europe level with 47 member states the judgments of the European Court of Human Rights have generally been followed, with few exceptions, and this has meant that complainants have often found redress for their grievances for the alleged human rights violations. While under the African system the range of rights subject to judicial review is larger because it embraces ESC rights, the European Convention on Human Rights (ECHR) merely deals with CP rights, with few exceptions, such as Protocol 1 to the ECHR, which deals with the rights to property and education.[25] It was felt in 1950/51 that other ESC rights ought to be dealt with under a different monitoring system, as developed in the European Social Charter 1960, and the Revised Social Charter of 1996 which precluded judicial review and instead merely opted for quasi-judicial and political monitoring devices.[26]

Netherlands) in June 1986. They were published in *Human Rights Quarterly*, Vol. 9, 1987, 122–135. They have also been submitted to the CESCR, Background paper submitted by the International Commission of Jurists, 2 October 2000, UN Doc. E/C.12/2000/13, 3–15. The Maastricht Guidelines on Violations of ESC Rights ('Maastricht Guidelines') were drafted during a meeting of experts on ESC rights in Maastricht, Netherlands, in January 1997. Like the Limburg Principles, they appeared in *Human Rights Quarterly*, Vol. 20, 1998, 691–704, and have been submitted to CESCR, Background paper submitted by the International Commission of Jurists, 2 October 2000, UN Doc. E/C.12/2000/13, 16–25.

[24] This tendency of the CESCR is likely to be maintained, considering the recent reduction of dialogue time with state party delegations from nine to six hours, reserving nine hours only for initial reports. With the reduction of dialogue time, and the increase in the number of reports to be covered during one session, and further time constraints in relation to dealing with communications under the new Optional Protocol which are likely to be forthcoming relatively soon, the whole monitoring procedure in the state reporting process will have to be changed. It may involve stricter prioritizing in periodic reports, thus limiting the issues to be covered, and/or developing smaller Committee working groups dealing with a particular state report, the plenary only endorsing concluding observations *en bloc* without discussion, unless the working group wishes a plenary discussion or cannot agree on issues.

[25] On the justiciability question see M. Langford, 'Judicial Review in National Courts: Recognition and Responsiveness', ch. 15 in this book.

[26] See R. Brillat, 'The European Social Charter', in G. Alfredsson et al. (eds.), *International Human Rights Monitoring Mechanisms: Essays in honour of Jackob Th. Möller* (The Hague: Martinus Nijhoff

The quasi-judicial approach foresees monitoring by the treaty body of individual communications or complaints, leading to a recommendation in the form of opinions. Individuals and groups of individuals can thus allege violations of their individual rights, but the treaty body does not hand down decisions in the form of judgments, but merely 'views', which only have recommendatory force. The practice under the Human Rights Committee over the last 40 years has shown, however, that member states of the ICCPR normally treat these legally non-binding views as if they were judgments. The advantages of such individual communications procedures are obvious: it is much easier to understand the scope and extent of a particular right when measured against a specific case. Such cases contribute best to the definitional and interpretation function of the treaty body concerned and will influence future application of the Covenant guarantees in a convincing manner. Thus, the generally phrased provisions of the treaties will gradually, on a case-by-case method, be concretized and the proper meaning of a particular right will be made clearer progressively.

C. The political monitoring procedure

The political approach of monitoring was one that all human rights treaties at the international level have adopted, namely the state reporting procedure, whereby in the case of the ICESCR each state party provides a report on the domestic realization of ESC rights over the five-year reporting period. That report is then examined by a pre-sessional working group of CESCR which formulates additional questions to the state, the so-called 'list of issues', to which the government concerned has to provide specific answers. Subsequently, a dialogue between the CESCR and a state party delegation takes place, where the report and the answers to the list of issues are discussed in public session. At the end, CESCR adopts concluding observations in private session, containing suggestions and recommendations, and during the monitoring of the next periodic report the dialogue begins with follow-up questions on the previous report, before dealing with the current one. This ensures that there is some degree of assessing implementation of recommendations. That follow-up process is gradually being expanded and increasingly states parties are aware that they will face difficult questions on the application of the previous recommendations made.

However, it must be stressed that the conclusions of the CESCR and of all other treaty bodies in this procedure merely represent legally non-binding recommendations to the state party, not judicial pronouncements. The value of such concluding observations—if well drawn—lies in elucidating the meaning and content of particular rights under the Covenant, but also in shaping discussion at the national level as to how such recommendations and suggestions can be implemented in domestic law. This may be by influencing the legislative process, bringing in policy changes and administrative practices, and, above all, influencing judges in changing the domestic case law along the lines of the human rights guarantees that the state has accepted in international law.

4. The Nature of Obligations under the ICESCR

States' obligations under the ICESCR are articulated in Part II—Articles 2 to 5—of the Covenant and in particular in its Articles 2 and 3. Since the adoption of the ICESCR, they have been further defined through the work of the CESCR.[27]

A. Article 2(1), ICESCR

From the beginning of its work the CESCR has taken great pains to explain to states parties in concluding observations that Article 2(1) of the Covenant is of prime importance to a full understanding of the ICESCR and is to be seen as having a dynamic relationship with all of the other provisions of the Covenant. Article 2(1), on a superficial reading, seems to suggest that the whole Covenant merely lays down programmatic statements as to how ESC rights are to be implemented, leaving it entirely up to the states parties how they will implement these guarantees.[28] Article 2(1) states:

> Each State Party to the present Covenant undertakes to take steps, individually and through international assistance and cooperation, especially economic and technical, to the maximum of its available resources, with a view to achieving progressively the full realization of the rights recognized in the present Covenant by all appropriate means, including particularly the adoption of legislative measures.

While the ICCPR refers to 'every human being', 'no one', 'everyone', 'all persons', indicating that the rights enunciated in that Covenant are directly applicable to everyone, ESC rights were couched in much more indirect language, speaking of 'States parties recognizing' and 'undertake to ensure'. On a narrow reading the use of the formulations 'undertakes to take steps', 'to the maximum of its available resources', and 'with a view to achieving progressively the full realization of the rights' in Article 2(1)—language not found in the ICCPR—supports the view that ESC rights guarantees are merely programmatic statements whose realization rests entirely in the hands of states parties. For this reason, commentators mainly from Western states for a long time concluded—and a few still support that view—that

Publishers, 2001), 601–606; N. Prouvez, 'The European Social Charter, an Instrument for the Protection of Human Rights in the 21st Century?' (1997) 58/59 *The Review*, International Commission of Jurists, 30–44; E. Riedel, 'Der Einfluss internationaler und europäischer Menschenrechte auf das deutsche Kündigungsrecht' (the Influence of International and European Human Rights on the German Law of Termination of Employment) in F. Maschmann (ed.) *Kündigungsrecht: alte und neue Fragen* (Baden-Baden: Nomos, 2013), 13–35.

[27] On the contribution of UN Special Procedures in the definition of states' obligations in relation to ESC rights, see C. Golay, C. Mahon, and I. Cismas, 'The impact of the UN Special Procedures on the development and implementation of economic, social and cultural rights' (2010), 15 *The International Journal of Human Rights*, 299–318.

[28] The original state position and probably the prevalent one is that the progressive implementation standard entailed a mere promotional type of commitment to enhance certain objectives set by the Covenant without requiring the attainment of specific results.

only the ICCPR imposes direct legal obligations on states parties, while the ICESCR merely lays down indirect legal obligations, needing implementation steps at the national level, before becoming fully operative.

To support this view, stemming from the ideology divide of the 1950s and 1960s, the literature frequently used the notion of self-executing and non-self-executing treaty obligations. While this is perfectly correct in relation to typical international treaty law, where the reciprocity element of obligations is responsible for the distinction of directly and indirectly applicable norms, thus requiring further national steps before becoming directly applicable, this treaty law notion should not be applied strictly to human rights treaties where the obligations of each member state primarily refers not to the treaty partners. It should rather refer to the general population inside state parties themselves. The reciprocity notion of traditional treaty law cannot operate in the same way: human rights treaties form a separate treaty category, as representing integral treaties[29] or regime treaties[30] that, once ratified and set in motion, take on a life of their own, operating against even those states that ratified them.

The CESCR has maintained that while there are undoubtedly some aspects of the individual rights enshrined in the Covenant which realistically cannot be fully realized in a short period of time, thus leaving room for governmental discretion, every single Covenant right does, however, contain elements lending themselves to immediate implementation that must be honoured by the states parties without delay or restrictions.

Although discussion persists as to whether a set of minimum core obligations under the ICESCR should be identified, as the CESCR has done since its General Comment No. 13 on the right to education,[31] or whether that cuts down the progressive development dimension of rights realization, the view that in each Covenant right certain elements exist which lend themselves to immediate implementation, such as in relation to the right to food and the freedom from hunger, seems more convincing. This notion has been adopted by CESCR in its constant practice since it adopted General Comment No. 3 on the nature of states parties' obligations (Article 2, paragraph 1 of the Covenant) in 1990.[32]

The most important example in this regard, inherent in each of the rights, is the principle of non-discrimination under Article 2(2), ICESCR, which each

[29] Integal treaties are also called treaties with integral fulfilment structure. See E. Klein, *Statusverträge im Völkerrecht* (Berlin, Heidelberg, New York: Springer-Verlag, 1980), 234.

[30] See R. Wolfrum, *Die Internationalisierung staatsfreier Räume* (Berlin, Heidelberg, New York, Tokyo: Springer-Verlag, 1984), 688; E. Riedel, 'The progressive development of international law at the universal and regional level', in R. Wolfrum (ed.), *Strengthening the World Order: Universalism v Regionalism* (Berlin: Duncker & Humblot, 1990), 115–144, at 128; E. Riedel, 'Global Human Rights Protection at the Crossroads: Strengthening or Reforming the System', in M. Breuer A. Epiney, A. Haratsch. S. Stahl, and N. Weiss (eds.), *Der Staat im Recht: Festschrift für Eckart Klein zum 70. Geburtstag* (Berlin: Duncker & Humblot, 2013), 1289–1306.

[31] CESCR, General Comment No. 13: The Right to Education (Art. 13 of the Covenant), 8 December 1999, UN Doc. E/C.12/1999/10 ('General Comment No. 13').

[32] CESCR, General Comment No. 3: The Nature of States Parties Obligations (Art. 2, para.1), 1 January 1991, UN Doc. E/1991/23(SUPP) ('General Comment No. 3').

state party is capable of implementing without further ado because it is not essentially resource-dependent, but rather requires making policy choices in line with internationally agreed obligations.[33] As the CESCR has consistently held since the adoption of General Comments Nos. 3 and 20,[34] and more recently still in the CESCR Statement No. 16 on resource allocation,[35] that states parties, in order not to render the Covenant provisions devoid of any meaning, must at all times guarantee the minimum core obligation as a matter of priority, that is, ensuring essential foodstuffs, equal access to primary health care, basic shelter and housing, access to potable water, work and social security, basic education, and access to culture.

Any failure by a state to guarantee these essential prerequisites for leading an adequate and dignified life, ensuring the 'survival kit' as a minimum, automatically amounts to a violation of the Covenant, unless the state party can show that it was practically impossible to guarantee even these minimal rights, due to resource constraints, armed conflict, tsunamis, earthquakes, or other catastrophes. It means essentially that the state party has the burden of proof to demonstrate that it was unable to fulfil even the minimum basic survival rights requirements.[36] Thus, even in a situation of armed conflict where vulnerable groups can find themselves in urgent need of food and medical care, states are required to take immediate action, including the duty to accept humanitarian assistance offered by the international community. The CESCR in its Concluding Observations to state reports by Israel remarked that:

> The Committee repeats its position that even in a situation of armed conflict, fundamental human rights must be respected and that basic economic, social and cultural rights, as part of the minimum standards of human rights, are guaranteed under customary international law and are also prescribed by international humanitarian law.[37]

It should be noted that in looking at the state party's obligations, the CESCR from the beginning has taken a country-by-country approach, avoiding misleading comparisons with other states. As the state reporting procedure foreseen by the Covenant and ECOSOC resolution setting up the CESCR closely envisage, this approach follows the philosophy of constructive dialogue, believing that more can be achieved by this softer approach than by a violations approach, focusing more

[33] See generally section 4.B that follows. See also M. Langford and J.A. King, 'Committee on Economic, Social and Cultural Rights, Past, Present and Future', in M. Langford (ed.), *Social Rights Jurisprudence: Emerging Trends in International and Comparative Law* (New York: Cambridge University Press, 2009), 477–516, at 492–495.

[34] CESCR, General Comment No. 20: Non-Discrimination in Economic, Social and Cultural Rights (Art. 2, para. 2 of the Covenant), 2 July 2009, UN Doc. E/C.12/GC/20 ('General Comment No. 20').

[35] CESCR, Statement No. 16.

[36] On this issue, Limburg Principle No. 25 refers to the obligation 'to guarantee respect for the minimum rights of survival for all', independent of available resources.

[37] CESCR, Concluding Observations: Israel, 26 June 2003, UN Doc. E/C.12/1/Add.90, para. 31. See further G. Giacca, 'The Relationship between Economic, Social, and Cultural Rights and International Humanitarian Law', ch. 11 in this book.

on states' failures to guarantee the rights recognized under the Covenant.[38] Over the years, the Committee has refined this method, and in its concluding observations details concerns and recommendations which reflect the degree to which the state party in the opinion of the CESCR has met its obligations or not. Sometimes, however, when gross and massive violations of ESC rights have occurred and been reliably attested, the Committee has called a spade a spade, particularly when the state has done nothing on previous CESCR recommendations, then stated that particular Covenant obligations were and still are being violated. But these are relatively rare occasions. Usually the constructive dialogue approach has yielded measurable results, reflected in the following periodic report of that state party.

Another overarching feature that is considered to be essential in the context of 'progressive realization' of Covenant obligations is the principle of non-retrogression which prohibits any deliberate step backwards that cannot be justified with severe economic difficulties, *force majeure*, or the like.[39] Aware of the economic realities prevalent in today's world, the CESCR nevertheless regards the principle of 'progressive realization' as a legally binding flexibility device, necessary and useful for the implementation of human rights at the national level. Accordingly, the Article 2(1) reference to the 'maximum available resources' weighs heavily in this context, on the one hand leaving room for different economic and financial capacity and budgetary discretion for member states, and, on the other requiring them to 'strive to ensure the widest possible enjoyment of the relevant rights under the prevailing circumstances'.[40]

As Article 2(1) ICESCR clearly stipulates, these maximum available resources may be obtained through requesting international cooperation and assistance.[41] Thus, in order to reach the goal of the highest possible standard in terms of ESC rights, every state that cannot meet its obligations owing to resources constraints, by virtue of the Covenant, remains under the concurrent obligation to seek technical assistance from other, more developed states that are in a position to help, or from the international community as such. Conversely, Article 2(1) imposes a legal obligation to render such assistance on the developed states parties, who thus have a dual obligation: to fulfil the Covenant obligations at home, and to render assistance to other states needing such assistance. In this regard, Article 2(1) ICESCR is closely linked to Articles 22 and 23 ICESCR, which encourage the involvement of all relevant UN organs, their subsidiary organs, and the specialized agencies in the implementation of the Covenant.[42]

[38] See A. Chapman and S. Russell (eds.), *Core Obligations: Building a Framework for Economic, Social and Cultural Rights* (Antwerp/Oxford/New York: Intersentia, 2002), 18. See also C. Courtis, *Courts and the Legal Enforcement of ESC rights* (Geneva: International Commission of Jurists, 2008), 23–28.

[39] See generally A. Nolan, 'Budget Analysis and Economic and Social Rights', ch. 13 in this book.

[40] CESCR, General Comment No. 3, para. 11; CESCR, Statement No. 16.

[41] See generally T. Karimova, 'The Nature and Meaning of "International Assistance and Cooperation" under the International Covenant on Economic, Social, and Cultural Rights', ch. 6 in this book.

[42] For details, see E. Riedel and G. Giacca, 'Article 68', in B. Simma, D.E. Khan, G. Nolte, and A. Paulus (eds.), *The Charter of the United Nations. A Commentary*, vol. II, 3rd edn (Oxford: Oxford University Press, 2012), marginal notes 104–106.

B. Non-discrimination (Articles 2(2) and 3 ICESCR)

Of equal importance for the implementation of the Covenant as a whole is Article 2(2) that incorporates the principle of non-discrimination found in most international human rights instruments.[43] This principle, in conjunction with Article 3 on equal rights for men and women, belongs to the very core elements of the Covenant, and calls for immediate and unconditional implementation. Unlike other specific ESC rights guarantees whose implementation to some extent depends on availability of resources, non-discrimination issues are less resource-related and usually only require governmental will to apply the obligations undertaken by ratifying the Covenant. Even the least developed countries do not need to discriminate against the most marginalized and disadvantaged individuals and groups of society when legislating new norms, or applying and interpreting existing legislation.

All it requires is the political will to implement obligations undertaken at the international legal level. That does not mean that the state party has no scope of action, apart from one particular action, but the standard of evaluation is one of reasonableness and proportionality of aims sought to be achieved by legislative or administrative acts, measured against the effects and means undertaken. In its General Comment No. 20 of 2009, the CESCR has dealt with these issues extensively. Read together with General Comment No. 16 on Equality,[44] it entails that these Covenant provisions are cross-cutting and overarching principles that are to be applied in conjunction with these rights.[45]

These provisions are not stand-alone rights like Article 26 ICCPR. General Comment No. 20 is quite explicit on the issue of differential treatment based on prohibited grounds.[46] This will be viewed by the CESCR as discriminatory, unless the justification for differentiation is reasonable and objective. This will include an assessment as to whether the aim and effects of the measures or omissions are legitimate, compatible with the nature of the Covenant rights, and applied solely for the purpose of promoting the general welfare in a democratic society. In addition, there must be a clear and reasonable relationship of proportionality between the aim sought to be realized and the measures or omissions and their effects.[47]

The CESCR has summarized in General Comment No. 20 its previous approach in nearly all other General Comments on specific rights. It has also dealt extensively with questions of discrimination in practically all its concluding observations addressed to states parties.

When addressing the prohibited grounds of discrimination mentioned in Article 2(2), ('race, colour, sex, language, religion, political or other opinion, national or

[43] See E. Riedel and J. Arend, 'Art. 55(c)', in B. Simma, D.E. Khan, G. Nolte, and A. Paulus (eds.), *The Charter of the United Nations, A Commentary*, Volume II, 3rd edn (Oxford: Oxford University Press, 2012), marginal notes 17–19.

[44] CESCR, General Comment No. 16: The Equal Right of Men and Women to the Enjoyment of All Economic, Social and Cultural Rights (Art. 3 of the Covenant), 11 August 2005, UN Doc. E/C.12/2005/4 ('General Comment No. 16').

[45] See in this regard S. Ratjen and M. Satija 'Realizing Economic, Social, and Cultural Rights for All', ch. 4 in this book.

[46] CESCR, General Comment No. 20.

[47] CESCR, General Comment No. 20, para. 13.

social origin, property, birth or other status'), General Comment No. 20 devotes nine extensive paragraphs to interpretation of 'other status' and begins its analysis by stating that discrimination 'varies according to context and evolves over time',[48] thus needing a flexible approach to the ground of 'other status'. The list of newer categories of 'other status' that have been developed over the years include disability, age, nationality, marital and family status, health status, place of residence, economic and social situation, and after extensive discussion in the CESCR, also the category of sexual orientation and gender identity.[49] While some commentators have criticized this particular category, it reflects changed societal attitudes towards these sexual orientation issues all over the world, albeit rejected by some states and religious denominations. Same-sex marriages or partnerships, adoption rights, social security benefits, and other status questions are now regularly discussed under this heading in dialogue with states parties, and there are marked tendencies towards changing national legislation in that respect. It is an example of human rights treaties representing living instruments of evolving practice, not merely reflecting static normative settings at the time of adoption of the text. Positivists, of course, will query this position taken by CESCR and other treaty bodies, by civil society organizations and by increasing numbers of states parties. However, even those states that object to this dynamic and evolving interpretation method will fully engage in discussions with the CESCR during the constructive dialogue and will present the resulting concluding observations at the domestic level, and may thus prepare the way for new policies, strategies, legislation, and administrative practices, and may, moreover, influence the reasoning of the judicial dicta as persuasive authority.

The realities of disadvantaged and marginalized individuals and groups of society provide one exception to the principle of non-discrimination, namely the concepts of reverse discrimination, affirmative action, or temporary special measures, as found, for example, in CEDAW.[50] In 1986, the Limburg Principles acknowledged that temporary special measures taken for the sole purpose of securing adequate advancement of certain groups or individuals requiring such protection 'shall not be deemed discrimination, provided that such measures do not, as a consequence, lead to the maintenance of separate rights for different groups',[51] and that such measures will be discontinued once their objectives have been achieved. All this shows that the principles laid down in Articles 2(1), 2(2), and 3 of the Covenant in their cross-cutting effect neatly shape the content of specific ESC rights found in Part III of the Covenant, in Articles 6 to 15 ICESCR.

[48] CESCR, General Comment No. 20, para. 27.

[49] CESCR, General Comment No. 20, para. 32. See generally C. Chinkin, 'Gender and Economic, Social, and Cultural Rights', ch. 5 in this book.

[50] Convention on the Elimination of All Forms of Discrimination against Women (CEDAW), Article 4. CEDAW was adopted through UN General Assembly Resolution 34/180 of 18 December 1979. It entered into force on 3 September 1981.

[51] Limburg Principle No. 39.

C. The obligations to respect, protect, and fulfil ESC rights

In parallel with the definition of obligations contained in Articles 2 and 3 ICESCR by the CESCR, philosophical and legal reflections led to the creation of a new framework describing states' obligations—both negative and positive—in relation to ESC rights.[52] According to this framework, states have obligations to respect, protect, and fulfil ESC rights.[53]

While this typology has been widely acclaimed in the literature,[54] followed by the CESCR in its consistent practice, and by many NGOs and national human rights institutions (NHRIs), it does not form part of the text of the Covenant.[55] There are voices in the literature that are sceptical and prefer a different typology, just differentiating between obligations of result and obligations of conduct,[56] to capture the notions of immediate obligations and obligations only to be realized progressively over a longer period of time. The commentators suggest that this should be left to the Committee practice, or even to state practice. The CESCR, at any rate, has used the triad of respect, protect, and fulfil in all its General Comments since General Comment No. 12 on the right to food and regards it as a useful analytical tool.

The obligation to respect prohibits infringements by state authorities of the enjoyment of ESC rights of citizens under the state's jurisdiction. For instance, if a state party passes legislation discriminating certain groups of society, this violates the obligation to respect, unless justifications can be mustered that do not infringe Covenant rights. The CESCR will point out in its concluding observations that such legislation contravenes Covenant obligations and will recommend action

[52] The same typology in the ambit of civil and political rights is equally valid and is treated as such in the literature. See M. Nowak, *UN Covenant on Civil and Political Rights. CCPR Commentary*, 2nd rev. edn (Kehl am Rhein: Engel, 2005), 37–41.

[53] Maastricht Guideline No. 6.B. Originally espoused by H. Shue where he distinguished between the duties to avoid depriving; duties to protect from deprivation; and duties to aid the deprived, H. Shue, *Basic Rights: Subsistence, Affluence and US Foreign Policy* (Princeton: Princeton University Press, 1980). This typology was further developed within the framework of a study on the normative content of the right to adequate food by the former member of the Sub-Commission on Human Rights, A. Eide. See Report of Asbjorn Eide, The Right to Adequate Food as a Human Right, 7 July 1987, UN Doc. C/CN.4/Sub.2/1987/23. It was then systematically applied to ESC rights by the CESCR. See CESCR, General Comment No. 12: The Right to Adequate Food (Art. 11 of the Covenant), 12 May 1999, UN Doc. E/C.12/1999/5 ('General Comment No. 12'); CESCR, General Comment No. 13; CESCR, General Comment No. 15: The Right to Water (Arts. 11 and 12 of the Covenant), 20 January 2003, UN Doc. E/C.12/2002/11 ('General Comment No. 15').

[54] See M. Sepúlveda Carmona, *The Nature of the Obligations under the International Covenant on Economic, Social and Cultural Rights*, School of Human Rights Research Series, Vol. 18 (Antwerp, Oxford, New York: Intersentia, 2003), 13–14, 115–156.

[55] See the comparison to Article 2(1), ICCPR which reads that '[e]ach State Party to the present Covenant undertakes to respect and to ensure to all individuals within its territory and subject to its jurisdiction'. M. Nowak interprets the verb 'to ensure' in Article 2(1) ICCPR as incorporating the positive obligations to protect and to fulfil. M. Nowak, *UN Covenant on Civil and Political Rights, CCPR Commentary*, 2nd rev. edn (Kehl am Rhein: Engel, 2005), 37.

[56] On a critical note, see M. Langford and J.A. King, 'Committee on Economic, Social and Cultural Rights, Past, Present and Future', in M. Langford (ed.), *Social Rights Jurisprudence* (New York: Cambridge University Press, 2008), 484–489.

to be taken by the state party to bring its legislation in line with the Covenant obligations.

The obligation to protect requires states parties to protect their citizens against infringements of rights by private third parties, such as, for example, employers. A state thus acts in violation of the Covenant, if it fails to ensure that private employers comply with basic labour standards as detailed in the Covenant articles, particularly Articles 6 and 7 ICESCR. In fact, while the obligation to respect mirrors a state's direct obligation to meet its own Covenant duties, in the case of the obligation to protect, the responsibility of the state changes to an indirect one, seeing to it that others do not violate human rights obligations to which the state party has agreed internationally. Here the state may redress the violation by legislation enjoining private firms to respect basic human rights parameters, and omission to provide remedies for individuals and groups of society affected by the activities of such private persons represents a clear violation of Covenant obligations resting on the state party.[57]

More than the other two obligations, the obligation to fulfil demands an active role by the state, be it in the form of legislation, administrative, budgetary, judicial, or other measures. Here a state does not meet its obligation if, for example, it fails to provide the population with an adequate, appropriate, and efficient primary health care system or primary schooling. That obligation to fulfil can be subdivided into obligations to facilitate, promote and provide that the CESCR has elaborated fully from General Comment No. 12 onwards.

Under the obligation to promote, public information campaigns or other means of informing the general population can be seen as fulfilment obligations, where the state party retains quite a large margin of discretion as to how it implements this obligation. In General Comment No. 14 on the right to health the CESCR has described this obligation in some detail, requiring for example states parties:

> to undertake actions that create, maintain and restore the health of the population. Such obligations include (1) fostering recognition of factors favouring positive health results, e.g. research and provision of information; (2) ensuring that health services are culturally appropriate and that health care staff are trained to recognize and respond to the specific needs of vulnerable or marginalized groups; (3) ensuring that the State meets its obligations in the dissemination of appropriate information relating to healthy lifestyles and nutrition, harmful traditional practices and the availability of services; (4) supporting people in making informed choices about their health.[58]

Under the obligation to facilitate, the state party is required, for example, 'to take positive measures that enable and assist individuals and communities to enjoy the right to health'.[59] The CESCR devoted much time and space to detailing such

[57] On the application of human rights law to non-state actors see O. De Schutter, 'Corporations and Economic, Social, and Cultural Rights', ch. 7 in this book.

[58] CESCR, General Comment No. 14: The Right to the Highest Attainable Standard of Health (Art. 12 of the Covenant), 11 August 2000, UN Doc. E/C.12/2000/4 ('General Comment No. 14'), para. 37: See also E. Riedel, 'The Human Right to Health: Conceptual Foundations', in A. Clapham, M. Robinson, C. Mahon, and S. Jerbi (eds.), *Realizing the Right to Health* (Zürich: Rüffer and Rub, 2009), 21–39.

[59] CESCR, General Comment No. 14, para. 37.

facilitation and promotion measures as subcategories of the obligation to fulfil, and it did so in order to rebut the criticism that the obligation to fulfil is generally cost-intensive. In fact, cost-intensive measures only arise to a greater extent with the obligation to provide.

Under the obligation to provide, the state party is bound to fulfil a specific right contained in the Covenant when individuals or groups are unable, for reasons beyond their control, to realize that right themselves by the means at their disposal. Providing access to essential medicines, to schools, and sufficient teaching staff for elementary schooling are relevant examples. Another example would be to establish non-contributory schemes or provide social assistance for those unable to cope with the issues involved themselves. This the CESCR elaborated in detail in its General Comment No. 19 on the right to social security.[60] Under this obligation the state party has to allocate adequate funds with the available resources and, as shown, to seek international assistance and cooperation where even that minimum fulfilment obligation cannot be met.[61]

Some of the criticism levelled against the triad respect-protect-fulfil is based on the assumption that no clear delineations between the categories are possible, and that consequently it remains doubtful whether the respect, protect, or fulfilment level is addressed. The CESCR has refuted this criticism by stating that all three types of violations can occur individually or in combination, which the following example illustrates: if housing legislation is changed regarding the execution of forced eviction orders without provision of minimal alternative housing, this involves a violation of the 'respect' obligation. If private actors such as owners of houses obtain eviction orders ultimately rendering the tenants homeless, the obligation to 'protect' of the state authorities (administrators or judges) are involved, and the CESCR will argue that the state party, despite privatization, remains responsible to provide alternative housing, either by itself or via the private owners of the property, or to enact restricting housing control legislation. The obligation to fulfil may therefore exist, for instance, involving the set-up of social housing programmes for homeless people. In that case, the provision of alternative housing involves either direct provision of tenements or the development of new housing policies, strategies, and plans of action to be realized progressively. Overall, this illustrates that the state party's obligations to respect, protect, and fulfil may well exist side by side, but usually only one of the three obligation types will be used.

5. Sources of ESC Rights other than Treaties

Since the initial phases of CESCR practice in 1987, most of the emphasis has been placed on diligently interpreting the provisions of the treaty law, the ICESCR. Under the traditional sources of international law, as applied by the International

[60] CESCR, General Comment No. 19, para. 51.

[61] See generally T. Karimova, 'The Nature and Meaning of "International Assistance and Cooperation" under the International Covenant on Economic, Social, and Cultural Rights', ch. 6 in this book.

Court of Justice (ICJ), laid down in Article 38 (1) ICJ Statute, the ICESCR is regarded as an international treaty to which the VCLT applies.[62] But as mentioned, the international treaty modality does not easily fit the human rights treaties that represent regime treaties or integral treaties rather than normal treaties where the state interests are exchanged on a reciprocal basis.[63] In regime treaties the obligations are set in motion by ratification and then take on their own life, usually with implementation mechanisms that are directed against the states themselves that have ratified the human rights treaty, with the object of protecting the rights of individuals under their jurisdiction. Therefore, the traditional treaty approach has to be supplemented.

In recent decades, following extensive literature debates, the treaty category has been supplemented by *ius cogens* and erga omnes obligations, and has gradually been introduced into the reasoning of textual treaty interpretation in the human rights sphere. As Alston and Simma have convincingly shown,[64] some of the core obligations contained in the ICESCR by now can be regarded as part of customary international law, or as general principles of law that apply universally, even for states not party to the Covenant. These principles can be deduced from extensive state practice, such as adoption of the UDHR or parts of it in national constitutions, which many states have done on gaining independence in the post-colonial period. The human rights minimum standards of protection[65] that have evolved under the UN Charter system can also be counted in this category of customary law.[66]

In relation to Covenant rights, further general principles of law have evolved in the past half-century. These include the so-called PANTHER principles, that is, participation, accountability, non-discrimination, transparency, human dignity, empowerment, and the rule of law.[67] These principles partially go beyond the actual wording of the Covenant text, but help to shape further developments of the treaty

[62] E. Riedel, 'Standards and Sources: Farewell to the Exclusivity of the Sources Triad in International Law?' (1991) 2 *European Journal of International Law*, 58–84; E. Riedel, *Theorie der Menschenrechtsstandards* (Berlin: Duncker & Humblot, 1986) ch. VII, 260; A. Clapham, *Brierly's Law of Nations*, 7th edn (Oxford: Oxford University Press, 2012), 74–77.

[63] See E. Klein, *Statusverträge im Völkerrecht* (Berlin, Heidelberg, New York: Springer-Verlag, 1980), 234.

[64] B. Simma and P. Alston, 'The Sources of Human Rights Law: Custom, *Jus Cogens*, and General Principles' (1992), 12 *Australian Yearbook of International Law*, 82.

[65] The minimum standards of human rights protection comprise, inter alia, acquired rights of aliens, protection against expropriation and nationalization which is only permissible under certain conditions, access to justice for foreigners, protection of *habeas corpus* rights, in particular legal hearing, and protection of life, liberty, property, and dignity of aliens. It is only a small step to extend these customary rules to all citizens, see E. Riedel, 'Der internationale Menschenrechtsschutz. Eine Einführung', in E. Riedel (ed.), *Menschenrechte. Dokumente und Deklarationen* (Bonn: Bundeszentrale für politische Bildung, 2004), 13–14.

[66] E. Riedel, 'Der internationale Menschenrechtsschutz. Eine Einführung', in E. Riedel (ed.), *Menschenrechte. Dokumente und Deklarationen* (Bonn: Bundeszentrale für politische Bildung, 2004), 13.

[67] See for example O. De Schutter, *Countries tackling hunger with a right to food approach. Significant progress in implementing the right to food at national scale in Africa, Latin America and South Asia*, Briefing Note No.1 of the UN Special Rapporteur on the Right to Food, May 2010, available at <http://www.srfood.org/images/stories/pdf/otherdocuments/20100514_briefing-note-01_en.pdf>

text in a progressive manner. To pick out just one example, to guarantee conditions of work under Article 7, ICESCR depends heavily on participatory processes of employers and employees alike. The danger, of course, is that the monitoring body exceeds its treaty powers and legislates or creates new obligations that the treaty text did not foresee. The line to be drawn between legitimate interpretation and illegitimate legislation by treaty bodies is thin, and states parties will stress that legislation remains their own exclusive domain. So the CESCR, like other treaty bodies, has to steer a careful course in its interpretation task that it has done with its General Comments.

In the practice of the CESCR under the Covenant, increasing use has been made of legal standards which may be applied, but do not have to be applied. They serve as interpretation aids, just like non-binding persuasive authority utilized in court decisions. The decisions themselves rest on the often vague and generally phrased text of a Covenant provision, but in the judges' reasoning these standards can help to convincingly support the arguments chosen by the judges. Such standards and also combination standards or 'zebras'—bringing together binding but abstractly formulated norms and non-binding concrete standards, such as for example, codes of conduct—have also influenced the interpretation of the ICESCR.

The classical positivist position of literal treaty text interpretation, that will only accept the actual wording of a norm, even if it produces defective solutions to problems, can be contrasted with the 'zebra' approach containing binding and non-binding 'soft law' standards. It may include declarations of the General Assembly adopted with near universal acceptance, like the UDHR, or legally non-binding conference documents like the Vienna Declaration of Human Rights of 1993 which read together with particular human rights treaty provisions produce convincing reasoning for dynamic treaty interpretation.

For instance, the strictly speaking non-binding 'Anti-Apartheid Code of Conduct' that European ministers developed to control European firms operating in South Africa at the time of the apartheid regime effectively led to a liberalization of employment of coloured people in those firms.[68] The reason why those firms ultimately complied with the strictly speaking non-binding code of conduct was the following: if they contravened to this code, they would no longer be entitled to receive discretionary export risk guarantees. This shows that these legally non-binding norms can have great relevance on their own in some cases. In others, if read together with existing, but rather vaguely formulated binding human rights norms, the combination standards or 'zebras' play an increasing role to take on board newer developments, particularly when many decades have passed since the adoption of the treaty provisions.

(last accessed 24 November 2013). See also FAO, *Right to Food: Making it Happen: Progress and Lessons Learned through Implementation* (Rome: FAO, 2011) 6–7.

[68] See C. Smith, *The Impact of the EEC Code of Conduct on the Behavior of European Corporations in South Africa*, Paper presented at the International Conference on South Africa in Transition, New York, 29 September to 2 October 1987, available at <https://dspace.lib.cranfield.ac.uk/retrieve/753/SWP0894.pdf> (last accessed 24 November 2013).

With the establishment of the Human Rights Council and particularly the Universal Periodic Review inter-governmental monitoring, the discussion on human rights non-treaty sources has increased.[69] The policy orientation of inter-governmental processes increasingly makes use of combination standards, blending UN Charter-based and treaty-based arguments in defining human rights positions. Sometimes, the development of such standards is very progressive, and then calls for new human rights treaties or amendments to existing ones are made. Considering, however, that it takes many years and provision of substantial financial means, states now are quite reluctant to create new human rights treaties, also because the existing system is already suffering from overburdening, overlaps, and unwieldiness. In this context, careful progressive realization through human rights standards and combination standards applied in the interpretation practice of monitoring bodies would appear to be the best approach.

6. Using Indicators in Monitoring ESC Rights

The development of indicators to monitor the progressive realization of ESC rights can be seen as a response to the relative vagueness of Article 2(1) of the Covenant. And in that field too, the CESCR has been one of the main actors. For a number of years the CESCR has attempted to use indicators and benchmarks in its monitoring practice when reviewing state party reports on the realization of Covenant rights. It soon emerged that many different ideas about the use of indicators and benchmarks were proposed. After having reviewed more than 200 state party reports, the time has come for the CESCR to systematically assess the value of indicators and benchmarks in the monitoring of state party obligations under the ICESCR.

Numerous expert workshops have been conducted, and scientific studies on indicators published, focusing on particular rights such as the rights to education, health, and food.[70] In that process it soon emerged that the existing method of monitoring was suffering from a series of flaws. In the reporting practice it transpired that some states presented qualitatively deficient reports which were either incomplete, or evaded direct answers to CESCR questions, or frequently only superficially addressed material issues, or only provided isolated data which did not explain how the human rights situation actually developed during the reporting cycle. Moreover, reports were often dated and did not take into account recent developments.

[69] See generally E. Riedel and G. Giacca, 'Article 68', in B. Simma, D.E. Khan, G. Nolte, and A. Paulus (eds.), *The Charter of the United Nations: A Commentary*, Vol. II, 3rd edn (Oxford: Oxford University Press, 2012), 1753–1761. On the contribution of UN Special Procedures to the creation of soft-law instruments, see C. Golay, C. Mahon, and I. Cismas, 'The impact of the UN Special Procedures on the development and implementation of economic, social and cultural rights', 15 *The International Journal of Human Rights* (2010), 299–318.

[70] For an overview, see E. Riedel, 'Measuring Human Rights Compliance. The IBSA Procedure as a Tool of Monitoring', in A. Auer, A. Flückiger, and M. Hottelier (eds.), *Les droits de l'homme et la constitution. Etudes en l'honneur du Professeur Giorgio Malinverni* (Geneva: Schulthess, 2007), 251–271.

This finding, in fact, regrettably describes the situation of all human rights treaty bodies, and also applies to the UN Charter-based procedures, such as the Universal Periodic Review of the Human Rights Council (HRC). Moreover, in monitoring the Millennium Development Goals, similar problems arise in using indicators.[71] The expert workshops on human rights indicators gradually overcame the inter-disciplinary difficulties of defining precisely what indicators mean. Economists, political scientists, and human rights lawyers each had their own tradition, and it took a number of years before substantial agreement on some basic common parameters was reached: to start with, quantitative and qualitative indicators had to be distinguished in the human rights context for which they are to be used. While many economists and statisticians initially insisted on operating only with data-based quantitative indicators that can be assessed objectively, political scientists and human rights lawyers stressed the need for finding suitable qualitative indicators in line with the normative frameworks for which indicators were to be used. Following protracted discussions agreement was finally reached to use both quantitative and qualitative data in the human rights context. Indicators are to be distinguished into structural, process, and outcome indicators. Structural indicators will measure the constitutional and other legal settings in relation to particular human rights, whether a particular right is actually legally guaranteed, or intended to be introduced in the foreseeable future, at the domestic law level.

Process indicators can both reflect (objective) quantitative data and qualitative data, flowing from the components of a particular human right, involving some (subjective) value judgments about the realization of a particular right, that is, measuring whether and to what extent action (plans, policies, programmes, laws, administrative, or judicial action) has been taken during the monitoring period, and for this purpose process indicators alongside structural indicators can be used.

Outcome indicators, by contrast, will simply address concrete results achieved, giving a 'yes' or 'no' answer to specific data, such as, for example, actual changes in the maternal death rate in right to health or occupational safety issues. Yet it must be remembered that these indicators can only represent tools for evaluating the performance of states in meeting their international human rights obligations. The agreed indicators help to find a common human rights language, and help to focus on measurable results, enabling a better and proper assessment of the fulfilment of human rights obligations resting on states.

Against this background the CESCR began to develop a monitoring tool that offers to overcome these challenges. The method to be applied embraces the idea of indicator-guided monitoring, where such indicators exist, and since General Comment No. 14 on the right to the highest attainable standard of physical and mental health has consistently proposed to engage in a four-step application of (i) human rights indicators, (ii) nationally set benchmarks on a voluntary basis, (iii)

[71] See C. Golay, I. Biglino, and I. Truscan, 'The Contribution of the UN Special Procedures to the Human Rights and Development Dialogue', 17 *SUR International Journal of Human Rights* (2013), 15–37.

scoping suggested benchmarks, and (iv) assessments of such agreed benchmarks by the CESCR (Indicator-Benchmarking-Scoping-Assessment (IBSA) process).

In relation to the first element—human rights indicators—the state party uses a list of relevant indicators for each right that the CESCR has already identified in close cooperation with UN specialized agencies and other actors from the UN system, such as special procedures.

The second element encourages states parties to identify country-specific problem areas or issues which may be reflected in specific indicators, and to set concrete targets or benchmarks for improving the human rights situation during the next reporting cycle, and to suggest such benchmarks to the CESCR.

The third element of this procedure—scoping—involves the state party and the CESCR discussing the state proposals and agreeing on final benchmarks that are reasonable, realistic, and sufficiently ambitious. When benchmarks are agreed, the state party will use them in its next periodic report, devoting more time on them than on other individual Covenant rights. If no agreement on a particular benchmark can be reached, the CESCR remains free to raise this issue during the dialogue on the state party's report.

During the fourth element of the IBSA procedure, the CESCR assessment, a close analysis of the state party report and the dialogue on the report will take place. The main advantage of this four-elements procedure lies in the truly voluntary, cooperative, and interactive spirit between states parties and the CESCR. It allows for more focused and more meaningful discussion of the relevant issues.

The CESCR consequently began to develop a list of indicators for one particular right, the right to food,[72] and lists of indicators for other rights are planned. Under the IBSA procedure, existing lists of indicators can be used, while the traditional procedure continues to be applied for all other rights. Meanwhile, the Office of the UN High Commissioner for Human Rights (OHCHR) proposed a table of indicators for 14 rights in 2008,[73] which may serve as the basis for the development of specific lists of indicators to be elaborated for each Covenant right. The OHCHR has since published a comprehensive guide on indicators for measurement and implementation of human rights that extends the application of indicators to a broader range of human rights, including the right to development and Millennium Development Goals. It bases its analysis on the normative setting of the UDHR rather than merely focusing on treaty-based monitoring.[74] It thus extends the indicators methodology to Charter-based monitoring, such as the Universal Periodic Review of the HRC.

[72] See E. Riedel, A.M. Suarez Franco, and J.M. Arend (eds.), *The IBSA Procedure: A new mechanism for measuring international compliance with economic, social and cultural rights* (Mannheim: 2014), forthcoming; E. Riedel, 'New Bearings to the State Reporting Procedure: Practical Ways to Operationalize Economic, Social and Cultural Rights—the Example of the Right to Health', in S. von Schorlemer, *Praxishandbuch UNO* (Heidelberg: Springer, 2003), 345–358.

[73] UN International Human Rights Instruments, Report on Indicators for Promoting and Monitoring the Implementation of Human Rights, 6 June 2008, UN Doc. HRI/MC/2008/3.

[74] UN OHCHR, *Human Rights Indicators. A Guide to Measurement and Implementation* (New York and Geneva: OHCHR, 2012).

The benchmarking by states parties for a particular right for which a list of indicators exist, or for which no such list exists so far, highlights issues which the state party considers to be of immediate importance at the domestic level and for which it intends to set concrete targets. In submitting its next periodic report, the state party assesses its own targets to be achieved during the reporting cycle, outlining whether those targets have been met, or the reasons for non-fulfilment. By describing the actual country situation in the state report, the state party may also analyse how improvement of existing conditions might be achieved, either by legislative, executive, or administrative measures. The benchmarking in practice, however, might entice the state party to set benchmarks too low, so as to avoid admitting at the end of the reporting cycle that the targets set have not been or could not be realized, or only to a limited and insufficient extent. Occasionally the benchmarks may be set too high, and this could lead to rather unnecessary apologies or explanations in the subsequent state report. Nevertheless, the main advantage of benchmarking lies in enabling the state party to address priority concerns that it itself considers to represent particularly important human rights problems.

The scoping process that ensures benchmarking may require that the country rapporteur who until now is mainly concerned with the elaboration of the list of issues and drafting concluding observations for the CESCR may, through the Secretariat of the Committee, inform specialized agencies and other relevant stakeholders about the state party proposals and request their comments. The country rapporteur will take up such comments, look at the selected problem areas and the corresponding benchmarks, and make his/her own proposals to the CESCR, suggesting that the proposals may be confirmed as acceptable, or that modifications should be suggested to the state party. At this stage of the procedure, both components of a state party proposal—the identified general problem area, as well as the target level contained in the benchmark—may be modified. The country rapporteur will then proceed to transmit the CESCR's position to the state party. In case the scoped benchmark is accepted, step three of the IBSA procedure would be complete, that is, the yardstick for the examination of the next state report is fixed. If the state party would not accept the newly identified or targeted benchmark, further consultation would have to take place. If no agreement can be reached, either on the problem area selected or on the specific targets set, the CESCR may, nevertheless, pick up the issue during the next dialogue with the state party. Obviously, this process will be subject to a certain time limit, so that sufficient time remains for the drafting of the state report. Ideally, the scoped benchmarks will be set within two years after the previous report was examined and discussed at the respective CESCR session.

In the assessment phase following the submission of the state report the scoped benchmarks, as reflected in that report and in the written answers to the list of issues, will be evaluated, prior to the actual dialogue with the state party delegation, by the CESCR which will take into account information received from specialized agencies and accredited NGOs. This process will also generate additional comments from country desk officers of the OHCHR and other UN actors. During the constructive dialogue with the state party CESCR members will look carefully at the scoped benchmarks and may recommend different or more differentiated problem areas and/or benchmarks for the next periodic report. One advantage of this process lies in the possibility to involve specific governmental experts in the scoped benchmark issues.

The IBSA process thus has a Janus-type appearance: it looks back in order to assess the past reporting period, and it also looks forward in order to target future developments in the fuller realization of rights. By looking back, it may impress the state party to assess candidly the record for itself, why certain targets have not been met, or could not be met, and this will enable the state party to set realistic new benchmarks for the next reporting period.

At the same time, it must not be overlooked that while the four-step IBSA procedure represents an attempt to render the state party reporting mechanism more effective and easier to administer for states parties and for the relevant treaty body, this cooperative mechanism contains obvious limits. For instance, many developing countries already complain about copious reporting obligations surpassing their means. Such states should seek cooperation and assistance from the OHCHR or from other states prepared to render support. Furthermore, the necessary indicators sometimes are simply not practicable or are too expensive in their application, in which case the state party may have to resort to the traditional mode of reporting.

The advantages of employing indicators and benchmarks in relation to more effective monitoring and implementation of ESC rights are, however, self-evident: in using these tools, the role of state parties in relation to variable obligations of conduct and process would clearly be strengthened. The IBSA procedure is designed to simplify and streamline the task of state reporting by prioritizing a select few problem areas where in-depth indicator analysis is foreseen, while the remaining traditional article-by-article reporting may be substantially condensed. IBSA would also serve to show that varying circumstances, specific to each reporting state, prevail. By employing indicators and benchmarks, the CESCR as monitoring body may also enhance its own effectiveness. Moreover, it would provide a standardized procedure capable of being applied nationally, thus substantially contributing to better implementation of Covenant obligations at the domestic level.

Other actors involved in monitoring state compliance under the ICESCR may also have a keen interest in the application of the IBSA procedure: specialized agencies and other UN actors may get more involved in the assessment of state reports. The expertise of specialized agencies in their particular fields of specialization supplied to the CESCR could render the Committee's work easier. In return, cooperation with the CESCR may help the specialized agencies to further develop their expertise with regard to human rights dimensions of their policies, strategies, and programmes, in an attempt at 'mainstreaming human rights' in their work. Finally, for NGOs the use of indicators and benchmarks opens up the possibility to participate in a more focused manner in the discussion of the state reports under review.

The IBSA procedure should begin with a closer analysis of elaborated indicators on the right to food, for which substantial information from country piloting already exists, while the examination of other ESC rights would still follow the traditional monitoring methodology. However, it should not be forgotten that IBSA is based on a voluntary mechanism to which states parties have agreed. If not, the traditional monitoring practice will continue. The voluntary character of the IBSA process also entails that no new legislative steps or treaty amendments are required. Whether rules of procedure would have to be changed can be decided by the CESCR, once sufficient piloting practice with IBSA has evolved.

7. International Adjudication of ESC Rights: the OP-ICESCR

As we have seen, the CESCR has for a long time advocated the establishment of a communications procedure similar to the one that exists for decades for other treaties, including the ICCPR. Since the Vienna World Conference on Human Rights in 1993, calls for an OP allowing individual and/or collective complaints analogous to the OP-ICCPR increased. CESCR itself produced a draft OP in 1996, largely based on the OP-ICCPR,[75] but this draft was shelved until a working group of the Commission on Human Rights/Human Rights Council eventually produced a draft OP, adopted by consensus in April 2008, which was then approved by the HRC and finally adopted by the General Assembly (GA) on 10 December 2008, on the 60th anniversary of the UDHR.[76] On 5 May 2013 that OP entered into force three months after the deposit of the 10th ratification. With that step the aim of protecting all human rights as foreseen in the UDHR was eventually reached.[77]

During the negotiation of the OP-ICESCR, the CESCR strongly argued in favour of a fully comprehensive approach to such a new procedure, meaning that all Covenant rights can be raised in a communications procedure under the OP, while a number of states, mostly from Common Law jurisdictions and Switzerland, had favoured an 'à la carte', 'opt-in', or 'opt-out' procedure,[78] whereby states might pick those rights which they would subject to the individual complaints/communication

[75] CESCR, Contributions Submitted by the Committee on Economic, Social and Cultural Rights, 26 March 1993, UN Doc. A/CONF.157/PC/62/Add.5.

[76] For an account of the *travaux péparatoires*, see the careful analyses by I. Biglino and C. Golay, *The Optional Protocol to the International Covenant on Economic, Social and Cultural Rights*, Geneva Academy In-Brief No. 2 (Geneva: Geneva Academy of International Humanitarian Law and Human Rights, 2013); C. Mahon, 'Progress at the Front: The Draft Optional Protocol to the ICESCR' (2008), 8 *Human Rights Law Review*, 617–646; E. Riedel, 'New Bearings in Social Rights? The Communications Procedure under the ICESCR', in U. Fastenrath et al. (eds.), *From Bilateralism to Community Interest: Essays in Honour of Judge Bruno Simma* (Oxford: Oxford University Press, 2011), 574–589.

[77] With the exception of the right to property that was not recognized in the 1966 Covenants. See E. Riedel, *Theorie der Menschenrechtsstandards* (Berlin: Duncker & Humblot, 1986), 25–147; E. Riedel, 'Farewell to the Sources Triad in International Law?', 2 *European Journal of International Law* (1991), 58–84. See also C. Golay and I. Cismas, *The Right to Property From a Human Rights Perspective* (Montreal and Geneva: Rights and Democracy, Geneva Academy of International Humanitarian Law and Human Rights, 2010).

[78] E. Riedel, 'New Bearings in Social Rights? The Communications Procedure under the ICESCR', in U. Fastenrath et al. (eds.), *From Bilateralism to Community Interest. Essays in Honour of Judge Bruno Simma* (Oxford: Oxford University Press, 2011), 576.

procedure, and those they would prefer to exclude from such scrutiny. Experience gained in the European context shows, however, that the European Social Charter of 1961 that allowed such a selective approach has resulted in patchwork ratification practice, whereby states parties have tended to exclude important rights guarantees from review. At the introduction of that system it had been argued that states parties would, at a later stage, gradually opt for more rights under that European Social Charter, once domestic law had been changed accordingly. This, however, did not happen. Even the Revised European Social Charter of 1996 has only been ratified by about half of the European Union member states. Most states remained only at the level of their initial pledges. To the uninformed public the impression was given that economic and social rights would be adhered to, while in reality only some rights were accepted. It is submitted that the argument that it would be better to allow such selectivity, to get as many ratifications as possible, was too high a price to be paid. In reality, the status quo in relation to ESC rights was hardly ruffled by the European Social Charter. And even now, the Revised European Social Charter has not brought about substantial change. The OP-ICESCR eventually settled for the comprehensive and radical approach: states have the choice to 'take it or leave it'.

A. Specificities of the OP-ICESCR

To a large extent the OP-ICESCR follows the examples given by the OP-ICCPR, like all other communications procedures, and particularly the parameters of OP-CEDAW.[79] The following remarks will be restricted to those issues that are specific to ESC rights.[80]

1. Individual or collective complaints

Much discussion in the open-ended working group of the Human Rights Council had centred on the issue of whether only individuals or also groups and NGOs could bring cases themselves. After much dispute, a subtle compromise was reached, whereby individuals and groups of individuals could have locus standi, but not NGOs by themselves (Article 2). By allowing groups of individuals to bring cases, participation of NGOs was not excluded, but their participation requires the consent of individuals or groups of individuals, unless the author of the communication can justify acting on their behalf without such consent.[81] Thus NGOs may assist individuals and groups of individuals in cases of asylum seekers,

[79] The Optional Protocol to CEDAW was adopted through UN General Assembly Resolution 54/4, 15 October 1999, UN Doc. A/RES/54/4. It entered into force on 22 December 2000.

[80] For further details on the procedure, see in particular I. Biglino and C. Golay, *The Optional Protocol to the International Covenant on Economic, Social and Cultural Rights*, Geneva Academy In-Brief No. 2 (Geneva: Geneva Academy of International Humanitarian Law and Human Rights, 2013).

[81] See CESCR, Rules of Procedure of the Optional Protocol to the ICESCR, 3 December 2012, UN Doc. E/C.12/49/3, Rules 1(3) and 4.

disabled persons, older persons, homeless people, and other marginalized or disadvantaged groups and minorities, as long as the linkage to particular individuals can be made out. The initial draft of the working group had contained a specific article on collective communications, but that provision was ultimately deleted.

Article 2 OP-ICESCR also provides that there must be a link of jurisdiction of the state party concerned. A specific restriction to the territory of states was not required. Thus, extraterritorial application of the OP-ICESCR is likely to be considered admissible, but if one hazards a guess, in the beginning of the CESCR practice under the OP, the cases examined will most likely concentrate on typical cases where the territorial link will be in the foreground.[82]

2. *Admissibility criteria*

A number of states delegates at the working group sessions had feared that the CESCR might be swamped by cases, even though that had not occurred in the Human Rights Committee over the last decades. To prevent that from happening, Article 4 OP-ICESCR provides that communications may be declined where it 'does not reveal that the author has suffered a clear disadvantage'. While some warned that this might become a normal procedural step for denying admissibility, the CESCR most likely will only exceptionally rely on Article 4 OP, particularly as the text qualifies the utilization at the end. The provision was included as a safety valve, in case of the CESCR actually being overloaded, as happened in the European Convention on Human Rights system. But there, actual court decisions are at stake, while at the universal level only views are involved, and the danger of seeing the CESCR overburdening is far less likely. The idea that ultimately the deciding body should be able to prioritize cases, if a flood of complaints arose, seems a sensible idea, and reflects judicial practice in many constitutional courts (the iudex ad quem system).[83]

3. *Resource allocation and the issue of reasonableness*

One of the most heatedly discussed issues was the question of resource allocation under Article 2(1) ICESCR and individual complaints, and whether such 'macro' questions could be raised in individual communications. Macro questions of poverty reduction, or alleviation, environment protection, or contributions of development assistance meeting the Gross Domestic Product (GDP) aim of 0.7 per cent, even though clearly very relevant causes of specific rights violations, in the view of many participants of the working group should not be part of individual cases brought under the OP-ICESCR, but should be reserved for the state reporting procedure.

[82] On this issue, see generally, M. Langford, W. Vandenhole, M. Scheinin, and W. van Genugten (eds.), *Global Justice. States Duties, The Extraterritorial Scope of Economic, Social and Cultural Rights in International Law* (Cambridge: Cambridge University Press, 2013).

[83] Such as, for example, in the United States of America.

The CESCR also took this view and had been requested to draft a General Comment on how it might treat resource allocation questions under the OP- ICESCR. CESCR in response produced a Committee Statement on resource allocation.[84] It did not formulate a General Comment that always reflects actual Committee practice, and is intended as an interpretation aid for specific Covenant provisions, not answering moot questions of a hypothetical nature. So, the CESCR drafted its Statement by analogy to the actual state reporting practice instead, how it might view such issues in the context of an individual communications procedure.[85] In paragraph 11 of that Statement, CESCR emphasized that while each state party has a margin of appreciation to take steps and adopt measures more suited to its specific circumstances, the CESCR would look whether a transparent and participative decision-making process at the national level existed or not. CESCR would fully respect the separation of powers, meaning that major policy choices are left to parliaments and to the executive, reserving for the judicial power purely controlling functions, not making judicial policy choices. The Statement then goes on to outline the criteria to be applied in concluding observations, recommending, for example, remedial action such as compensation to a victim or victims; calling on the state party to remedy the circumstances leading to a violation of a right; suggesting low-cost and case-by-case measures; always leaving it up to the state party concerned to adopt its own alternative measures; and recommending a follow-up mechanism at the domestic level to ensure accountability, for instance, requiring that in its next periodic report the state party explain the steps taken to redress the violation.[86] On the question of reasonableness, the CESCR is likely to take into consideration, inter alia:

(a) the extent to which the measures taken were deliberate, concrete and targeted towards the fulfilment of ESC-rights; [87]
(b) whether the state party exercised its discretion in a non-discriminatory and non-arbitrary manner (para. 8);
(c) thus showing that many issues are not resource-dependent but matters of political will;
(d) where several policy options are available, whether the state party adopts the option that least restricts Covenant rights;[88]
(e) the time frame in which steps were taken; and
(f) whether the steps had taken into account the precarious situation of disadvantaged and marginalized individuals or groups and whether they were non-discriminatory, and whether they prioritized grave situations or situations of risk.[89]

[84] E. Riedel, 'New Bearings in Social Rights? The Communications Procedure under the ICESCR', in U. Fastenrath et al. (eds.), *From Bilateralism to Community Interest. Essays in Honour of Judge Bruno Simma* (Oxford: Oxford University Press, 2011), 581.

[85] CESCR, Statement No. 16, para. 2.

[86] CESCR, Statement No. 16, para. 13.

[87] The Statement No.16 takes up many parameters of General Comment No. 3, but develops them in relation to communications.

[88] This, in fact, is the proportionality principle.

[89] CESCR, Statement No. 16, para. 8.

To illustrate this issue by two examples in relation to the right to water and the right to housing, the CESCR will most likely not decide the actual policy choice of public, private, or public–private partnership water management models,[90] but if the public management model is chosen, the state will be directly responsible under the obligation to respect. If a private management model is preferred, then the state remains indirectly responsible under an obligation to protect, to regulate the water management so that the right to water remains guaranteed. If a mixed public–private partnership (PPP) model is chosen, the state party remains responsible directly for the public component of the PPP, and indirectly for the private management section of the model. The actual choice of management model will be left to the state parties. The CESCR might merely point out that the state party should select those models that least infringe individual rights. The standard of review will be a reasonableness test under Article 8(4), OP-ICESCR. In cases of forced evictions under the right to housing,[91] the state party might be asked to provide alternative housing following legal forced evictions, and that reasonable notice ought to be given prior to eviction, and that such measures should be carried out in stages. Here the experience of national jurisprudence ought to be taken into account.[92]

4. *The trust fund*

The OP-ICESCR also contains a provision on a trust fund (Article 14) that has no parallel in the OP-ICCPR. Since it depends on voluntary contributions, adoption of this provision met with little resistance. Sceptics had warned that on no account should states where massive human rights violations were alleged be allowed 'rewards' by receiving funds from the trust fund. Article 14(3) OP therefore specified a carefully drafted compromise that the fund would only be available 'for the enhanced implementation of the rights contained in the Covenant, thus contributing to building national capacities in the area of economic, social and cultural rights', for instance helping in the creation of a national human rights institution. Misuse of funds for the benefit of violators of human rights is thus excluded.

Article 14 (4) OP sets out that seeking international assistance and cooperation under Article 2(1) ICESCR is without prejudice to the primary obligations under the Covenant that each state party, whether rich or poor, must fulfil. While

[90] See CESCR, General Comment No. 15; E. Riedel, 'The Human Right to Water and General Comment No.15', in E. Riedel and P. Rothen (eds.), *The Human Right to Water* (Berlin: Berliner Wissenschaftsverlag, 2006), 19–36, 29–30.

[91] See CESCR, General Comment No. 4; CESCR, General Comment No. 7.

[92] S. Leckie, 'The Human Right to Housing', in A. Eide, C. Krause, and A. Rosas (eds.), *Economic, Social and Cultural Rights: A Textbook*, 2nd rev. edn (The Hague: Kluwer Law International, 2001), 149–168; S. Leckie (ed.), *Returning Home: Housing and Property Restitution Rights of Refugees and Displaced Persons* (New York: Transnational Publishers, 2003); S. Marks and A. Clapham, 'Housing', in *International Human Rights Lexicon* (Oxford: Oxford University Press, 2005), 209–221; see also the recent study of M. Krennerich, *Soziale Menschenrechte zwischen Recht und Politik* (Schwalbach:Wochenschau Verlag, 2013), 230–248.

such a provision is not found in any other human rights treaty, it emphasizes that each state has a dual obligation under Article 2(1) ICESCR: on the one hand doing everything possible 'within the available means' itself to meet its Covenant obligations, and on the other hand the obligation to seek international cooperation and assistance from other states when it lacks sufficient own resources to fulfil its human rights obligations under Article 2(1) ICESCR. The donor states thus have this additional obligation to render assistance beyond meeting their own internal human rights obligations. The ESC rights-specific text of Article 14(4) OP reflects the unique formulation of Article 2(1) ICESCR. The inclusion of Article 14 OP enhanced the acceptance of the whole Protocol by the African and Asian delegation groups, facilitating the acceptance of the entire OP by consensus in the end.

5. *Reservations*

The final provisions of the OP-ICESCR are similar to other communications procedures. Unlike the OP-CEDAW, however, no express reservations clause was included. This issue has been left to be determined by general international treaty law. Under Articles 19 to 23 of the Vienna Convention on the Law of Treaties (VCLT) no reservation to a provision forming part of the object and purpose of the treaty would be valid, even though no procedure exists to determine when that is the case. Arguably, all human rights issues immediately fall under the category of 'object and purpose of the treaty', thus negating the possibility of a reservation. The Human Rights Committee in its General Comment No. 24 had assumed the role of deciding such an issue, but met with much criticism from states parties.[93]

The question of reservations to human rights treaty provisions can be problematized, because any exception immediately touches on the core substance of the treaty, and would thus be invalid. The usual treaty law escape hatch—lodging an interpretative declaration instead of a formal reservation—would appear to be possible only in exceptional circumstances, because under the VCLT each such declaration would have to be assessed as to its substance, and might turn out to be, in fact, just another mode of reservation, according to Article 2(d), VCLT. By 'declaring' an issue, the real nature of the declaration would not be changed, and if that were to be a reservation, it would be invalid. But it is submitted that this objective invalidity of these declarations could not be decided by the CESCR or other treaty body, nor by the state party concerned—for whom the 'declaration' would merely represent its subjective view—but would remain an open question, until objectively tested and decided by the International Court of Justice, or by another dispute settlement procedure.[94] In the meantime, it is submitted that the better view would be that

[93] Human Rights Committee, General Comment No. 24: Issues Relating to Reservations Made Upon Ratification or Accession to the Covenant or the Optional Protocols Thereto, or in Relation to Declarations Under Article 41 of the Covenant, 11 November 1994, UN Doc. CCPR/C/21/Rev.1/Add.6 ('General Comment No. 24').

[94] E. Riedel, 'New Bearings in Social Rights? The Communications Procedure under the ICESCR', in U. Fastenrath et al. (eds.), *From Bilateralism to Community Interest: Essays in Honour of Judge Bruno Simma* (Oxford: Oxford University Press, 2011), 585.

CESCR can merely state in its concluding observations that the reservation is contrary to the ICESCR provisions, but that would only be a recommendation, although of course with considerable persuasive authority.

B. Future role of the OP-ICESCR

The OP-ICESCR marks several achievements in the realization of ESC rights generally. After decades of leading a shadow or second-class life alongside civil and political rights, ESC rights now rank equally alongside CP rights. Until 2008 it was easy to maintain the ideological divides of the 1950s and 1960s that ESC rights, if rights at all, merely stood for political or programmatic statements, leaving it in the hands of states parties how and to what extent they would be put into effect at the domestic level.

While the CESCR state reporting practice during the last 20 years had already disproved this position to a large extent, the new OP-ICESCR now emphasizes that the community of states regards ESC rights as an inseparable part of the fundamental guarantees first spelled out fully in the UDHR, and that rights to work, social security, food, housing, health, water, education, and participation in culture have to be seen in conjunction with the freedom rights, of CP rights. Both Covenants' rights are interdependent, indivisible, interrelated and universally applicable. While up to now this mantra of human rights was merely reflected in declarations, conclusions of world human rights conferences, and in the overwhelming academic and civil society literature, it is now mirrored as part of treaty law in the OP-ICESCR, standing side by side to the OP-ICCPR and other Optional Protocols.

The preamble to the OP-ICESCR is explicit in that regard: it notes that all human beings are born free and equal in dignity and rights, and recalls that the UDHR and the two Covenants recognize that the 'ideal of free human beings enjoying freedom from fear and want can only be achieved if conditions are created whereby everyone may enjoy civil, cultural, economic, political and social rights'. At last, international human rights protection has come full circle from the beginnings of the UDHR of 1948.

The OP-ICESCR has also paved the way for greater publicity and greater public awareness, because it is easier to attract attention when dealing with individual cases, rather than having to cope with complex and interconnected structural rights issues generally, as in the state reporting procedure. There the concluding observations often remain abstract and general, on which it is difficult to report nationally in the media. Under the communications procedure NGOs and NHRIs can put much more immediate pressure on decision-makers at the national level, and may often encourage or plead for reconsideration of existing or projected legislation or administrative practices that are in violation of ESC rights guaranteed internationally, by pointing at glaring violations of an individual's right. This is what happened under the OP-ICCPR that greatly enhanced the visibility and credibility of the Human Rights Committee's work.

The OP-ICESCR procedure will undoubtedly also contribute to building up a kind of 'committee jurisprudence' or 'case law' which will help to crystallize the normative content and scope of each Covenant right at the universal level, and will assist in interpreting specific and vague or ambiguous provisions of the Covenant, if any, but will also serve as concrete interpretation aids in similar cases pending before courts of law.

Last, but not least, the case law under the OP-ICESCR will probably greatly influence the debates on proper implementation of all ESC rights at the national level. This will be done through civil society organizations, most particularly by NHRIs, as happened with the OP-ICCPR.[95] NHRIs have already begun to refocus their general work programme, by devoting more time to the views and concluding observations developed at the international level, in order to draw specific conclusions for implementation at the national law level, when the governments concerned have done little or nothing to implement those treaty body recommendations and views. CESCR in General Comment No. 10 on the role of NHRIs has highlighted that function.[96] At the present time, however, awareness of ESC rights is still not as visible as it should be, but the debate on the adoption of the OP-ICESCR and its entry into force in 2013 produced quite a new momentum to all ESC rights questions, and certainly the literature on the topic is quickly expanding.[97]

8. Outline of the Book: Contemporary Issues and Challenges

As noted at the outset of this chapter, the potential scope of an analysis dealing with ESC rights is almost boundless. The approach taken in this book is clearly of a legal character and centres on how the fundamental ESC rights that are enshrined in international law are defined, interpreted, understood, and implemented. The aim is to review critically their conceptual and practical applications. The analysis thus seeks to bring a fresh perspective to some of the main challenges facing the implementation of ESC rights by examining five cross-cutting themes.

A. Challenges in the protection of ESC rights in times of crisis

That the enduring economic crisis can have adverse consequences on the protection and fulfilment of ESC rights is wholly unsurprising. Its relevance to these rights

[95] In this regard, see A. Corkery and D. Wilson, 'Building Bridges: National Human Rights Institutions and Economic, Social, and Cultural Rights', ch. 17 in this book.

[96] CESCR, General Comment No. 10: The Role of National Human Rights Institutions in the Protection of Economic, Social and Cultural Rights, 10 December 1998, UN Doc. E/C.12/1998/25 ('General Comment No. 10').

[97] I. Biglino and C. Golay, *The Optional Protocol to the International Covenant on Economic, Social and Cultural Rights*, Geneva Academy In-Brief No. 2 (Geneva: Geneva Academy of International Humanitarian Law and Human Rights, 2013); E. Riedel,'New Bearings in Social Rights? The Communications Procedure under the ICESCR', in U. Fastenrath et al. (eds.), From *Bilateralism to Community Interest. Essays in Honour of Judge Bruno Simma* (Oxford: Oxford University Press, 2011), 576.

can be understood in a number of ways, including harsh austerity measures, such as forced public budget cuts across health, education, housing, social protection, and unemployment benefits. The current debt problems and austerity programmes across Europe as well as the wider impact of the ongoing crisis in the financial markets and the debt situation of the United States of America have challenged in a significant manner not only the way we think about socio-economic rights but also how we go about implementing them.

The contributions in Part II of this book address some of these challenges, which have brought not only economic and social hardship in their wake, but also a further diminution of the role of the state in the protection of economic and social rights. As Saiz noted in 2009, 'despite the obvious human rights dimensions of the crisis, human rights have barely figured in the diagnoses or prescriptions proposed by the international community'.[98] As will become clear in the discussions throughout this book, the current financial crisis and financial assistance conditions imposed by the European Union on Greece, Portugal, and Spain, are cases in point.[99] In order to receive credits to avoid national bankruptcy and to be able to remain within the Euro area, the government of Greece, for instance, had to agree to make sizeable cuts in social spending and to dismiss large numbers of public servants as part of a comprehensive austerity programme.[100] The High Commissioner for Human Rights, Ms Navinathem Pillay, in her recent report on 'Social and Human Rights Questions' has stressed that when austerity measures have to be imposed, fundamental human rights compliance criteria have to be met. States, thus, should demonstrate the following:

(1) the existence of a compelling state interest;
(2) the necessity, reasonableness, temporariness, and proportionality of the austerity measures;
(3) the exhaustion of alternative and less restrictive measures;
(4) the non-discriminatory nature of the proposed measures;
(5) protection of a minimum core content of the rights; and
(6) genuine participation of affected groups and individuals in decision-making processes.[101]

These criteria should be taken into account before austerity measures are agreed and applied. Thus, for example, when austerity measures have led to cutbacks in employment in the state sector and state-sponsored projects, the state party is under

[98] I. Saiz, 'Rights in Recession? Challenges for Economic and Social Rights Enforcement in Times of Crisis' (2009), 1 *Journal of Human Rights Practice*, 277–293, 280.

[99] Other member states of the European Monetary Union face similar problems, but to a lesser degree.

[100] See for instance, G. Giacca and T. Karimova, 'Implications for Arms Acquisitions of Economic, Social and Cultural Rights', in S. Casey-Maslen, *Weapons under International Human Rights Law* (Cambridge: Cambridge University Press, 2014), ch. 16.

[101] Report of Navinathem Pillay, High Commissioner for Human Rights, Social and Human Rights Questions: Human Rights ('HC Report'), 7 May 2013, UN Doc. E/2013/82, para. 15.

the obligation to formulate policies and to implement them, taking into account the six compliance criteria, in order to reduce the employment rate without discrimination, especially with regard to women and other disadvantaged and marginalized people.[102] All these human rights compliance criteria are based on the relevant General Comments and Statements of the CESCR, read together.[103]

States, accordingly, have a positive obligation to ensure adequate financial regulation that is necessary to guarantee human rights and, moreover, must justify austerity measures by showing that they actually protect Covenant rights, particularly the rights of the most vulnerable. States ultimately have to demonstrate that all other less incursive alternatives have been exhausted and that the measures taken are necessary, proportionate, and non-discriminatory.[104] The CESCR, therefore, will have to analyse carefully which measures it is to recommend to the states parties in order to improve the rights situation of all affected persons, even in such crisis situations.

In this context, Mary Dowell-Jones casts a critical eye on the scant progress that has been made in addressing the gap between international human rights law standards and the realities of macroeconomic, fiscal, and social policy.[105] In 2004, Dowell-Jones noted that only recently the doctrine of socio-economic rights has started to place the meaning of ESC rights obligations within the broader global economic context. For her:

> As economic conditions continually mutate it is imperative that the Covenant is conceptualised dynamically in light of evolving possibilities and needs, rather than statically as a linear progression of implementation according to the level of development of any particular economy. This is not to sacrifice core human rights to economic expediency, but rather to advocate a pragmatic approach to the Covenant which is responsive to its changing context.[106]

The author further points out that:

> Commentary on the Covenant has so far failed to address the Covenant holistically as an interlinked package of socio-economic measures, nor as part of a broader economic programme. The difficult economic policy choices involved in implementing the Covenant has so far not figured in theoretical analysis of the normative framework of the Covenant.[107]

Taking the view that the current sovereign debt and austerity crisis in the advanced economies represents one of the most serious contemporary challenges to the

[102] Report of Navinathem Pillay ('HC Report'), 7 May 2013, UN Doc. E/2013/82, para. 28.

[103] They were discussed at length during the May 2012 session of CESCR and contained in a Chairperson's letter to the High Commissioner for Human Rights. See CESCR, Report on the forty-eighth and forty-ninth sessions 30 April to 18 May 2012, 12–30 November 2012, ECOSOC Official Records 20113, Supp. No.2, E/2013/22, E/C.12/2012/3, 87–90.

[104] HC Report, paras. 69–71.

[105] M. Dowell-Jones 'The Sovereign Bond Markets and Socio-Economic Rights: Understanding the Challenge of Austerity', ch. 2 in this book.

[106] M. Dowell-Jones, *Contextualising the International Covenant on Economic, Social and Cultural Rights: Assessing the Economic Deficit* (Leiden/Boston: Martinus Nijhoff Publishers, 2004), 8.

[107] M. Dowell Jones, *Contextualising the International Covenant on Economic, Social and Cultural Rights: Assessing the Economic Deficit* (Leiden/Boston: Martinus Nijhoff Publishers, 2004), 38.

effective implementation of socio-economic human rights, the author examines in chapter 2 the backdrop to austerity by scrutinizing its key contributory factors, including the over-reliance by states on using sovereign debt to fund the expansion of public services over the last two decades, and also considers the implications of austerity for international human rights law. The author explains that part of the crisis stems from 'the steady expansion of the state into public services that can be linked to human rights such as education, healthcare, and social welfare, coupled with the demands of an ageing population and the failure to fund existing services on a fully sustainable basis'.[108] The chapter investigates the dynamics of public debt, deficit financing, and socio-economic rights realization and discusses the role and responsibilities of private financial institutions in the current austerity crisis from the perspective of the Guiding Principles on Business and Human Rights endorsed by the UN Human Rights Council in 2011.[109]

Despite the obvious human rights dimensions of the crisis, little attention has been given to the extent to which human rights should guide policy responses at the national or international level. In this regard, chapter 3 by Sally-Anne Way, Nicholas Lusiani, and Ignacio Saiz provides an innovative antidote to this dearth of scholarship.[110] In examining the evidence of the impact on economic and social rights of the successive waves of financial and economic crisis, the authors consider the crisis as a historic opportunity to reshape the discourse of the role of the state in the economy. They point out ways of operationalizing a human rights-based approach to macroeconomic policymaking (in terms of both fiscal and monetary policy) to re-envision the regulatory and redistributive roles of the state in the economy, not merely to facilitate economic growth simply, but to guarantee economic and social rights for all. This chapter thus aims to contribute to the emerging scholarship on human rights and economics, particularly on the application of human rights standards to the design, implementation, monitoring, and review of economic policy more generally.[111]

As we have seen, from the perspective of the ICESCR, equal treatment and non-discrimination are critical components in securing ESC rights for all, especially in times of economic crisis. In chapter 4, 'Realizing Economic, Social, and Cultural Rights for All', Sandra Ratjen and Manav Satija reflect on the contribution to the normative advances in the area of ESC rights made by the struggle for non-discrimination and substantive equality. Faced with the socio-economic upheavals and growing inequalities prevailing in contemporary societies, this study appositely explores the challenges of a non-discrimination and equality approach to the general exercise of ESC rights. In particular, Ratjen and Satija confront the difficulties inherent in the adequacy of the judicial standards of review related

[108] M. Dowell Jones, 'The Sovereign Bond Markets and Socio-Economic Rights: Understanding the Challenge of Austerity', ch. 2 in this book.

[109] Human Rights Council Resolution 17/4, adopted on 16 June 2011.

[110] S.-A. Way, N. Lusiani, and I. Saiz, 'Economic and Social Rights in the "Great Recession": Towards a Human Rights-Centred Economic Policy in Times of Crisis', ch. 3 in this book.

[111] See for instance A. Nolan (ed), *Economic and Social Rights after the Global Financial Crisis* (Cambridge: Cambridge University Press, 2014).

to discrimination for the legal enforcement of ESC rights. Lastly, this chapter examines the possible tensions between the universality of human rights and their individual nature on the one hand, and the defence of specific groups' rights and aspirations for socio-economic equality and justice on the other.

In chapter 5, Christine Chinkin examines the impact and relevance of a gender perspective on ESC rights.[112] Challenging the assumption that gender analysis is only relevant to address issues relating to women, rather than to appraise relations between women and men, the author rightly argues that women's equal enjoyment of ESC rights with men is core to their relationships with the state, their community, private employers, and within their family. In this context, the author traces the evolution of the concept of 'gender' that began to enter the international agenda in the 1980s. She analyses how this development has taken place along with the important role played by UN human rights treaty bodies in seeking an appreciation of ESC rights that takes account of women's as well as men's live.

Chinkin then addresses a number of challenges and obstacles that arise in relation to women's enjoyment of ESC rights. She begins by considering how gender-based violence has been a particular obstacle. Reference here is made to a wide range of practices, including some that occur in all countries, such as domestic violence. Another set of challenges addressed is those of economic inequalities and the feminization of poverty, where the author emphasizes how the current international economic order and the economic crisis have contributed to gender inequality in the enjoyment of these rights. The final category considered relates to the gendered dimensions of armed conflict and the political economy of conflict as contributing to unequal enjoyment of economic and social rights.[113]

B. International dimension of ESC rights obligations

Two central questions lie at the heart of the debates on the international dimension of human rights obligations in the area of economic, social, and cultural rights. The first flows directly from the wording of the Covenant, viz. the application of Article 2(1) and specifically its designation of international cooperation and assistance as the *means* to implement the ESC rights. In effect, while the international community has assigned a high priority to Millennium Development Goals as well as the broader poverty eradication agenda, the legal nature of international action, on which achievement of these objectives are largely based, has been very controversial.[114]

The second question addresses one of the most challenging questions of human rights law: how to ensure that factors and practices of external origins do not interfere with the enjoyment of human rights. It is, however, not clear how Article 2(1)

[112] C. Chinkin, 'Gender and Economic, Social, and Cultural Rights', ch. 5 in this book.

[113] See also G. Giacca, 'The Relationship between Economic, Social, and Cultural Rights and International Humanitarian Law', ch. 11 in this book.

[114] M. Langford, A. Sumner, and A. Ely Yamin (eds.), *Millennium Development Goals and Human Rights: Past, Present, and Future* (New York: Cambridge University Press, 2013).

resolves the issue of a state's capacity to fulfil the human rights of persons under its jurisdiction in view of the dramatic impact external economic processes have on national efforts, including but not limited to foreign economic policies, global financial institutions, and activities of transnational corporations.[115] These two questions have received considerable attention under different rubrics in the contemporary literature: extraterritorial obligations, transnational obligations, global responsibilities, third state obligations, and so on.[116] The two chapters that make up Part III seek to systematize these issues through the analysis of two distinct yet interrelated topics.

Takhmina Karimova's chapter examines the nature and meaning of concept of international cooperation and assistance under the ICESCR.[117] The highly disputed macro- and micro-parameters of the concept under the Covenant are carefully contrasted through the analysis of, first, the various forays that treaty bodies have made in this sphere and, second, state practice. The author concludes that while an obligation to cooperate on human rights issues exists, not all elements of the obligation to cooperate are equally recognized. The author also finds that international law in general as yet does not provide answers to some of the important questions raised in the context of international cooperation and assistance. Even in situations of severe distress, such as armed conflict or disaster situations, the rights that current rules of international law generate for the state in need of assistance are imperfect.

In the following chapter, the claim made by Adolf A. Berle and Gardiner C. Means in *The Modern Corporation and Private Property*[118] is the backdrop to a broader assessment by Olivier De Schutter on whether and how international human rights law applies to corporations.[119] The author raises a number of stimulating questions as to whether economic and social rights as stipulated in international human rights law can be fittingly applied to corporations: are rules set out for states in international human rights law too vague and indeterminate, or simply unsuitable for application to corporate actors, or is such a transposition possible?

The chapter builds on the considerable progress that was achieved in recent years in clarifying the human rights responsibilities of companies, notably through the endorsement by the UN Human Rights Council of the 2011 Guiding Principles

[115] See Chapter VI. Only recently, the doctrine of the socio-economic rights has started to read within the notion of 'maximum available resources' the question of economic capacity situated within the broader global economic context. M. Dowell Jones, *Contextualising the International Covenant on Economic, Social and Cultural Rights: Assessing the Economic Deficit* (Leiden/Boston: Martinus Nijhoff Publishers, 2004).

[116] M. Langford, W. Vandenhole, M. Scheinin, and W. van Genugten (eds.), *Global Justice. States Duties: The Extraterritorial Scope of Economic, Social and Cultural Rights in International Law* (Cambridge: Cambridge University Press, 2013).

[117] T. Karimova, 'The Nature and Meaning of "International Assistance and Cooperation" under the International Covenant on Economic, Social, and Cultural Rights', ch. 6 in this book.

[118] A.A. Berle and G.C. Means, *The Modern Corporation and Private Property* (originally published in 1932 by Harcourt, Brace & World, reprinted in New York: Transaction Publishers, 1991), in particular ch. VI.

[119] O. De Schutter, 'Corporations and Economic, Social, and Cultural Rights', ch. 7 of this book.

on Business and Human Rights.[120] The chapter questions whether imposing positive duties on corporations poses any specific problems, and how these can be addressed. It then moves on to consider how such positive duties can be identified and defined. Finally, noting that courts have routinely imposed on corporations certain duties that correspond to economic and social rights, De Schutter traces the role of courts in enforcing such duties.

C. The relationship between ESC rights and other legal regimes

One of the greatest complexities within international law is its fragmented character.[121] Indeed, the bulk of international law stems from bilateral or multilateral treaties between states covering a vast variety of different fields. In this context, Part IV of the book argues that with the increased fragmentation arising from the diversification and expansion of international law and legal disciplines, the protection of ESC rights should be examined in a broader sense and on the basis of the different but complementary branches of international law (for example, environmental law, economic law, trade and investment law, humanitarian law, UN Charter law, and criminal law).

The ICESCR and International economic law are instances of this fragmented system. In this regard, Hans Morten Haugen examines how these rights are actually taken into account when arbitration or adjudicating bodies (panels or tribunals) seek to solve disputes arising under investments and trade law.[122] International economic law encompasses both the conduct of sovereign states in international economic relations, and the conduct of private parties involved in cross-border economic and business transactions. While it covers a wide range of fields, this chapter places emphasis on trade and investment. In this context, the author explains how currently there is stronger emphasis on states maintaining a proper policy space in order to meet their human rights obligations when entering into international investment treaties. He discusses new instruments that are being developed for this purpose, such as the Guiding principles on human rights impact assessments of trade and investment, formulated by the UN Special Rapporteur on the right to food.[123] Haugen shows how investment tribunals can receive submissions of non-disputing parties and can apply all relevant rules of international law, which is said to be more inclusive than the World Trade Organization (WTO) dispute settlement. He thus proposes an analysis of some of the prominent cases from international investment disputes in light of interpretative principles, including how to justify measures by their relationship to legitimate policy objectives, the

[120] Human Rights Council Resolution 17/4, adopted on 16 June 2011.

[121] International Law Commission (ILC), Fragmentation of International Law: Difficulties Arising from Diversification and Expansion of International Law: Report of the Study Group of the International Law Commission, 13 April 2006, UN Doc. A/CN.4/L.682.

[122] H.M. Haugen, 'Trade and Investment Agreements: What Role for Economic, Social, and Cultural Rights in International Economic Law?' ch. 8 in this book.

[123] See also S. Walker, 'Human Rights Impact Assessments: Emerging Practice and Challenges', ch. 14 in this book.

essence of the proportionality test, and what is legitimately included in the fair and equitable treatment standard under international investment law. The chapter also identifies whether states have a duty to give more weight to their human rights obligations when agreements under International Economic Law (IEL) are negotiated, implemented, and enforced.

Holger P. Hestermeyer discusses how the distinct legal regimes of the WTO Agreements and of the ICESCR seem to drift apart and risk imposing contradictory obligations on states parties.[124] While the Covenant, with currently 161 states parties, relies on a quasi-judicial system for its enforcement, the WTO, an international organization with its roots in the 1947 General Agreement on Tariffs and Trade (GATT) and with 159 members as of March 2013,[125] represents in the view of the author a highly ambitious and successful dispute settlement mechanism for states, with proceedings that can ultimately allow trade retaliation for violations of the WTO Agreements. As pointed out by Hans Morten Haugen in chapter 9, the WTO Agreements do not contain explicit references to human rights, nor does the ICESCR make references to international trade law. The two regimes thus 'seemingly live entirely separate lives'. Hestermeyer highlights a 'factual hierarchy' of regimes:

> The strength of the WTO regime raises a haunting spectre for human rights: a country choosing which obligation to follow may, irrespective of the normative relationship between the two regimes, choose to follow WTO law, because a failure to implement WTO obligations entails more severe consequences than a failure to properly implement the ICESCR. I have referred to this phenomenon elsewhere as a 'factual hierarchy' of regimes.[126]

His contribution discusses the institutional aspects involved by first analysing the legal obligations of the WTO under the ICESCR as well as the possibility of applying the ICESCR in WTO dispute settlement, and second, by empirically examining how and when the ICESCR is referred to in the different bodies of the WTO. In this regard, his chapter shows that the impact of the Covenant has been rather limited, even though 84 per cent of all WTO members are parties to the ICESCR. Hestermeyer challenges the prevailing myth that the WTO as an organization is to blame for a culture hostile to human rights, noting that it is the representatives of the states that fail to bring up considerations based on the ICESCR. Despite this state of affairs, Hestermeyer examines some realistic approaches that can remedy this deficit.

Stéphanie Chuffart and Jorge E. Viñuales in chapter 10 discuss the intersection between ESC rights and the environment 'from the other shore', that is, from

[124] H.P. Hestermeyer, 'Economic, Social, and Cultural Rights in the World Trade Organization: Legal Aspects and Practice', ch. 9 in this book.

[125] Current membership data is available at <http://www.wto.org/english/thewto_e/whatis_e/tif_e/org6_e.htm> (last accessed 4 August 2013).

[126] H. Hestermeyer, 'Economic, Social, and Cultural Rights in the World Trade Organization: Legal Aspects and Practice', ch. 9 in this book. See generally H. Hestermeyer, *Human Rights and the WTO* (Oxford: Oxford University Press, 2007).

an international environmental law perspective. The authors explain that this relationship between these legal regimes is usually approached from the perspective of human rights, which is still the prevailing standpoint: 'The "dependent variable" is thus international environmental law whereas human rights are the independent or "explanatory variable".'[127]

The authors note that although a number of legitimate reasons, including the significant contribution made by human rights' adjudicatory and quasi-adjudicatory bodies to environmental protection, are legitimate, it is important to understand what international environmental law as a mature branch of international law has to offer in this context. This chapter thus takes the reverse perspective on the relationship between human rights and international environmental law and shows how the impact of international environmental law, with its own approaches and mechanisms, can broaden the scope of human rights law in a variety of ways that, in turn, can suggest a new perspective for their implementation.

In chapter 11, Gilles Giacca reminds us that the general articulation between human rights law and international humanitarian law (IHL) has been a matter of controversy among scholars and governmental experts for quite some time.[128] Different strands of doctrine have claimed that these two legal regimes are concurrent, convergent, confluent, complementary, contradictory, or even in conflict. In turn, it is suggested that the rules belonging to both regimes can indeed be applied and interpreted in the light of one another when they provide rules in areas that are common to both. As a matter of cross-interpretation, not only could human rights law be construed in the light of IHL, as observed by the ICJ in the *Nuclear Weapons Advisory Opinion*,[129] but IHL could also be interpreted in light of human rights law. Alternatively, it has been suggested that one legal regime can displace, replace, or curtail the other.

Despite the rich vein of subject matter and the scholarly attention paid separately to both ESC rights and IHL we are still faced by a relatively underplayed hand when it comes to considering the two regimes together. This chapter by Giacca thus looks at the importance of this relationship and examines whether such a close interaction between human rights law and IHL impacts on their complementary protection when it comes to ESC rights.[130] The author seeks to

[127] S. Chuffart and J.E. Viñuales, 'From the Other Shore: Economic, Social, and Cultural Rights from an International Environmental Law Perspective', ch. 10 in this book.

[128] See also S. Sivakumaran, *The Law of Non-International Armed Conflict* (Oxford: Oxford University Press, 2012), 87.

[129] The oft-quoted famous passage of the Court is worthy of reproduction:

> [i]n principle, the right not arbitrarily to be deprived of one's life applies also in hostilities. The test of what is an arbitrary deprivation of life, however, then falls to be determined by the applicable *lex specialis*, namely, the law applicable in armed conflict which is designed to regulate the conduct of hostilities. Thus whether a particular loss of life, through the use of a certain weapon in warfare, is to be considered an arbitrary deprivation of life contrary to Article 6 of the Covenant, can only be decided by reference to the law applicable in armed conflict and not deduced from the terms of the Covenant itself.

ICJ, Legality of the Threat or Use of Nuclear Weapons, Advisory Opinion, 8 July 1996, para. 25.

[130] G. Giacca, 'The Relationship between Economic, Social, and Cultural Rights and International Humanitarian Law', ch. 11 in this book.

demonstrate that there is no one-size-fits-all answer to questions about the relationship between these legal regimes, or more specifically between some of the apparently conflicting norms within each branch.

Another area that is of particular relevance is the intersection between international criminal law and ESC rights, a topic that has not yet been fully addressed in the literature.[131] In this light, Larissa van den Herik seeks to revisit the theoretical explanation for the disconnect between international criminal law and ESC rights.[132] Taking into account the alleged limited normative substance of ESC rights, the author traces and revisits the theoretical explanation for this disconnect. A number of concrete examples and case scenarios in which international crimes prosecution could have a socio-economic or cultural dimension are examined. This allows the author to provide a number of critical thoughts on the instrumentality of international criminal justice as a means of protecting ESC rights.

D. Concepts and tools to measure the progressive realization of ESC rights

Part V of this book encompasses new ways that have been developed in both theory and practice to measure the level of implementation of and compliance with ESC rights. As we have seen with regard to human rights indicators, the emphasis on new concepts and approaches is guided by the consideration to promote an objective assessment of the realization of ESC rights that can, importantly, be monitored. In this regard, the chapter on budget analysis and socio-economic rights by Aoife Nolan looks at macroeconomic and domestic economic policies.[133] In an effort to clarify the focus of the chapter, the author begins by defining the meaning and contours of 'ESR-based budget analysis'—a term that has been accorded multiple definitions in the literature. The author argues that the increased focus on, and employment of, rights-based budget analysis is merely one manifestation of a broader move towards the integration of human rights and economics discourse at the academic, advocacy, and policy levels. As noted by the author, the emergent interaction between these respective disciplines has accelerated as a result of the current economic crisis. This is explained by the role played in causing the crisis by certain macroeconomic and domestic economic policies as well as by the concern

[131] On the question of whether ESC rights abuses can give rise to individual criminal responsibility under the accepted definitions of international and transnational crimes, See E. Schmid, 'War Crimes Related to Violations of Economic, Social and Cultural Rights' (2011) 71(3) *Heidelberg Journal of International Law*, 523–540; E. Schmid, *Violations of Economic, Social and Cultural Rights in International and Transnational Criminal Law* (Geneva: IHEID, 2012); S. Skogly, 'Crimes against Humanity—Revisited: Is There a Role for Economic and Social Rights?' (2001) 5(1) *International Journal of Human Rights*, 58–80; D. Marcus, 'Famine Crimes in International Law (2003) 97(2) *AJIL*, 245–281; M. Drumbl, *Accountability for Property and Environmental War Crimes: Prosecution, Litigation, and Development* (New York: ICTJ, November 2009), 1–33;

[132] L. van den Herik, 'Economic, Social, and Cultural Rights: International Criminal Law's Blind Spot?', ch. 12 in this book.

[133] A. Nolan, 'Budget Analysis and Economic and Social Rights', ch. 13 in this book.

about the implications of national and supranational responses for human rights. The author then addresses a number of challenges that arise in relation to human rights budget work, one of them being of a practical or logistical nature faced by practitioners seeking to carry out budget analysis in the performance of such work.

The chapter 'Human Rights Impact Assessments: Emerging Practice and Challenges' by Simon Walker advances a new approach to make free trade work for all people by developing a step-by-step process to identify the human impacts of trade before trade agreements are finalized.[134] The chapter discusses this emerging practice with a particular focus on impact assessments of policies and projects that affect ESC rights. It shows how the growing interest in such rights has naturally led practitioners towards developing tools that can clarify which policies and projects have positive impacts on them and which policies and projects should be better avoided. After identifying a general methodology for human rights impact assessment, Walker illustrates the methodology through a case study of a right to health impact assessment. Most importantly, Walker contends that human rights practitioners should build a body of impact assessment practice so as to move from theory to practice and so better understand the benefits and challenges of impact assessment as a means of promoting ESC rights.

E. Trends in the justiciability and monitoring of ESC rights at the national and international level

The question of the justiciability of ESC rights has occupied a central position in the discussions on these rights since their recognition at the international level. During the preparatory work of the ICESCR, certain states, such as India, proposed explicitly writing into the ICESCR the non-justiciability of ESC rights. These proposals were subsequently rejected,[135] but in practice, ESC rights continued, as we have seen, to be considered non-justiciable throughout the Cold War. Today, in spite of the opposition of certain states during the negotiations of the Optional Protocol to the ICESCR,[136] the existence of an abundance of jurisprudence and the adoption of the Optional Protocol make it more difficult to credibly maintain that these rights are not at all justiciable.[137] For the former High Commissioner for Human Rights Louise Arbour, '[t]he simplified division between justiciable

[134] S. Walker, 'Human Rights Impact Assessments: Emerging Practice and Challenges', ch. 14 in this book.

[135] Commission on Human Rights, 10 July 1951, UN Doc. E/CN.4/SR.248. See also OHCHR, in cooperation with the International Bar Association, *Human Rights in the Administration of Justice: A Manual on Human Rights for Judges, Prosecutors and Lawyers* (New York and Geneva: OHCHR, 2003), 691.

[136] M.J. Dennis and D.P. Stewart, 'Justiciability of Economic, Social and Cultural Rights: Should There Be and International Complaints Mechanism to Adjudicate the Rights to Food, Water, Housing, and Health?' (2004), 98 *American Journal of International Law*, 462–515, 471–476.

[137] See for example C. Golay, *The Right to Food and Access to Justice: Examples at the National, Regional and International Levels* (Rome: FAO, 2009); C. Golay, *Droit à l'alimentation et accès à la justice* (Bruxelles, Bruylant, 2011).

and non-justiciable rights does not stand up to closer scrutiny. It is contradicted by reality and is contrary to the unified vision of human rights underlying the international human rights system'.[138]

In this regard, it should be noted that over the last 50 years, the ICESCR has fulfilled at least four major functions at the domestic law level: first, it has led to the adoption of specific constitutional law provisions, mirroring ICESCR provisions directly; second, it has served as an interpretation aid for structural principles in those constitutions that prefer to use umbrella provisions like the directive principles of state policy in India, or utilize human dignity in conjunction with notions of solidarity, as is the case in Germany, Switzerland, Spain, Portugal, and Greece; third, the ICESCR has been used generally as a judicial interpretation aid for statutory provisions at the internal law level; fourth, it has also been used as a yardstick *de lege ferenda*, offering rights formulations from the international level for application at the national level, when it comes to developing new legislation. Generally, it is submitted that courts at all levels ought to be bolder when it comes to realizing ESC rights: states parties, after all, have committed themselves internationally, and should be held to account nationally on that score, and internal law should meet the standards that have been agreed upon internationally. In relation to ESC rights generally, one is not talking about a grand, extravagant bouquet of every conceivable social blessing, but of no more than minimum subsistence levels, necessary for survival—the minimum for existence.

In chapter 15, 'Judicial Review in National Courts: Recognition and Responsiveness', Malcolm Langford seeks to temper the outbreak of optimism over the future role of ESC rights adjudication by highlighting an array of issues and challenges faced by the current emerging practice in jurisprudential developments in the field of ESC rights. The chapter focuses mainly on two of them. The first is termed 'recognition', which is the degree to which ESC rights are formally enforceable. Noting an explosion of constitutional guarantees, Langford examines more closely the significant variance in legal opportunity structures for claimants, its causes, and possible solutions. The second challenge Langford engages with is 'responsiveness'; an idea that designates the extent to which courts entertain petitions in good faith. Despite the existence of many progressive judgments, the author echoes the criticism that too many courts are unresponsive to ESC rights in general, or to disadvantaged claimants and distributive justice in particular. The chapter then investigates the theoretical contestation over the causes of judicial responsiveness, the lessons learned from a century-long arc of state-level right to education litigation in the United States of America, and the contemporary comparative picture of judicial responsiveness.

In the following chapter, Ioana Cismas examines the various interactions of ESC rights and civil and political rights.[139] The characteristics of ESC rights can no longer

[138] Human Rights Council, *Statement by Ms Louise Arbour, High Commissioner for Human Rights to the Open-ended Working Group on an optional protocol to the International Covenant on Economic, Social and Cultural Rights*, 31 March 2008.

[139] I. Cismas, 'The Intersection of Economic, Social, and Cultural Rights and Civil and Political Rights', ch. 16 in this book; D. Mzikenge Chirwa, 'African Regional Human Rights System', in

be understood in terms of dimensions or generations of rights. As she explains, the evolution of international human rights law departs from its traditional or historical foundations that rights can be neatly compartmentalized into two broad categories. Starting from the premise that ESC and civil and political rights intersect at normative-theoretical level, as well as in practice through litigation, monitoring, and advocacy, this chapter analyses the consequences of such interactions. In grappling with this question, the author draws on the concept of intersectionality rooted in gender studies and demonstrates how it can result in the advancement of both ESC and civil and political rights. In turn, the chapter reveals the risk of weakening the human rights regime because of an over-reliance on intersectional litigation strategies, given the impossibility or unwillingness to directly adjudicate ESC rights.

In their contribution, Allison Corkery and Duncan Wilson trace the role of national human rights institutions (NHRIs)—independent bodies with a specific mandate to promote and protect human rights—in monitoring ESC rights.[140] The authors critically challenge the prevalent assumption that NHRIs are considered to be less effective in relation to ESC rights than civil and political rights. Noting that national institutions play a series of unique 'bridging' roles, which position them well to address these rights, Corkery and Wilson argue that NHRIs do play a strategic role in ensuring states' compliance not only with their obligations to respect and protect ESC rights but also increasingly in addressing the obligation to fulfil them. The chapter also investigates how the particularities of local context impact on an institution's ability to effectively address ESC rights and discuss the need to develop new approaches to pragmatically address broader issues of resource allocation and socio-economic policy.

The chapter by Frank Haldemann and Rachelle Kouassi questions whether ESC rights are an integral, rather than marginal, part of the transitional justice agenda.[141] Throughout the 1990s, the marginalization of ESC rights has been perceptible from debates over how to deal with the aftermath of civil wars or authoritarian regimes. A few voices over the last decade have regretted the fact that ESC rights abuses have rarely been included within transitional justice processes and mechanisms.[142] There is now a rapidly growing discourse concerned with integrating socio-economic and cultural rights into the transitional justice framework.

M. Langford, *Social Rights Jurisprudence: Emerging Trends in International and Comparative Law* (New York: Cambridge University Press, 2008), 323–338; T.J. Melish, 'The Inter-American Court of Human Rights', in M. Langford, *Social Rights Jurisprudence: Emerging Trends in International and Comparative Law*, (New York: Cambridge University Press, 2008), 372–408; I.E. Koch, *Human Rights as Indivisible Rights: The Protection of Socio-Economic Demands under the European Convention on Human Rights* (Martinus Nijhoff: The Hague, 2009).

140 A. Corkery and D. Wilson 'Building Bridges: National Human Rights Institutions and Economic, Social, and Cultural Rights', ch. 17 in this book.

141 F. Haldemann and R. Kouassi 'ESC Rights and Transitional Justice without Economic, Social, and Cultural Rights?', ch. 18 in this book.

142 Commission on Human Rights, Final Report on the Question of the Impunity of Perpetrators of Human Rights Violations (Economic, Social and Cultural Rights), prepared by Mr. El Hadji Guissé, Special Rapporteur, pursuant to Sub-Commission resolution 1996/24, 27 June 1997, UN Doc. E/CN.4/Sub.2/1997/8; R. Mani, *Beyond Retribution: Seeking Justice in the Shadows of War*

In this context, Haldemann and Kouassi critically engage with this emerging discourse, referred to as the 'ESC rights thesis'. While sympathetic to the call for an expanded understanding of transitional justice, the authors warn against one-dimensional thinking—the temptation of fitting transitional justice into one single, central system called 'human rights'. Through the metaphor of the hedgehog and the fox made famous by Isaiah Berlin,[143] the authors argue that viewing the world exclusively through the prism of human rights does not come without costs, as we risk losing sight of its complexity: 'the human rights activist is tempted to rely on "one single system", human rights, to answer any moral and political question; and it is this search for a universal, unitary vision that reduces the possibility for a larger, more nuanced, "fox-like" view of political action and the context of action'.[144] Such a 'hedgehog-like' vision, the authors argue, cannot do justice to the depth and persistence of conflicts and hard choices in societies emerging from large-scale violence.

9. Conclusion

This introduction sets the scene for the various studies that follow. In particular it has sought to review the development of ESC rights in international law. The progress made in advancing the universal respect for ESC rights since their recognition in the UDHR in 1948 is notable. After a slow start during the Cold War, this movement accelerated with the 1993 World Conference on Human Rights in Vienna. Twenty years later, some important objectives of the Vienna Declaration and Plan of Action have been reached. Symbolically, the most important one might be the adoption of the Optional Protocol to the ICESCR and its entry into force in 2013.

It is clear from this book that the challenges to implementation and realization of ESC rights remain important, maybe more important than ever, given the persistent deprivation of basic ESC rights for the majority of the world's population. It is opportune to recall that, while this book was being written, a wave of protests around the world—the Arab Spring, the 'Western winter of discontent' in Greece, Spain, Italy, Chile, the United Kingdom,[145] and the Occupy Movement emerged in response to socio-economic inequalities—all of which effectively bear witness to the importance of the ideals of the International Covenant on Economic, Social and Cultural Rights on social progress and better standards of living for all.

(Cambridge: Polity Press, 2002). For more recent views, see L. Arbour, 'Economic and Social Justice for Societies in Transition', Center for Human Rights and Global Justice, New York University School of Law, Working Paper No. 10, 2006; C. Chinkin, 'The Protection of Economic, Social and Cultural Rights Post-Conflict' paper series commissioned by the Office of the High Commissioner for Human Rights, 2009.

[143] I. Berlin, 'The Hedgehog and the Fox: An Essay on Tolstoy's View of History', in H. Hardy and A. Kelly (eds.), *Russian Thinkers*, 2nd edn (London: Penguin Classics, 2008), 24–92.

[144] F. Haldemann and R. Kouassi, 'Transitional Justice without Economic, Social, and Cultural Rights?', Ch. 18, section 4.A.

[145] Opening Statement by Navi Pillay United Nations High Commissioner for Human Rights, in Panel discussion 'The Relevance of the Right to Development in the context of global challenges', Geneva, 6 December 2011.

II

CHALLENGES IN THE PROTECTION OF ESC RIGHTS IN TIMES OF CRISIS

2

The Sovereign Bond Markets and Socio-Economic Rights

Understanding the Challenge of Austerity

Mary Dowell-Jones

1. Introduction

The current debt problems and austerity programmes in the European economies as well as the wider impacts of the ongoing crisis in the financial markets and the US debt situation all combine to challenge significantly our understanding of fundamental socio-economic human rights that are enshrined in international law. Such rights are by their essence designed to protect the basic needs of people while also supplying the basic essential goods necessary to function in modern society. As such, they are a fluid part of any economic system that is open to renegotiation as economic structures shift and mutate around them. Failing to recognize this ossifies human rights over time and robs them of their ongoing relevance to the economic and social issues of the people who need them. Contemporary fiscal problems which stem from a variety of causes—the ongoing effects of financial crisis, the changing nature of welfare provision, changing demographics, and problems in the way state finances have been managed over the last 20 years, including an over-reliance on the sovereign bond markets to fund a growing proportion of state spending—present both an opportunity and a challenge for defenders of socio-economic rights. The opportunity is to reinvent, reformulate, and reinterpret international legal standards relating to socio-economic rights in light of the redrawing of the boundaries of the welfare state. The challenge is to do this effectively and publicly in a way that enhances the protection of socio-economic rights by making them a more visible presence in public policy debates, and also relevantly by defining standards and methodologies which will work in the context of today's financial, economic, and public policy problems. The depth of this challenge should not be underestimated because, despite increased attention to socio-economic rights by human rights lawyers over the last 10 years, very little progress has been made in addressing the gap between international legal standards and the realities of macroeconomic, fiscal, and social policy, as debates around Europe's austerity crisis have made clear.

This chapter will explore some of these issues and examine the challenges they raise for international human rights law. It will begin by reviewing the reality facing public finances in the advanced economies, and why austerity is a challenge to the functional utility of human rights law in the face of very difficult and long-term public policy problems. It will then examine the role that financial institutions and financial crisis have played in the current situation, and will consider whether the UN Guiding Principles on Business and Human Rights could or should be relevant to the current situation. It will go on to discuss some of the core issues for international human rights law and make suggestions for how human rights law could be used in the current context.

2. The Noticeable Absence of Human Rights in the Age of Austerity

'[N]o Geneva Convention exist[s] to mitigate the cruelty of the financial war'.[1]

Although this was written to describe the victims of market abuses in the years leading up to the 1929 Wall Street crash, it can easily be applied to the wider victims of all great financial panics and crashes. Of these there have been many throughout history as financial disasters are a perennial feature of financial markets, although they have increased in frequency over the last 20 years as markets have globalized.[2] The current financial crisis that has had such a devastating and ongoing impact on human rights around the world began in the structured credit markets back in 2007, engulfed global financial markets in turmoil in 2008, and has now morphed into a sovereign debt crisis that threatens years of austerity, recession, and broad-based negative impacts on the whole range of socio-economic human rights. The price of austerity is likely to be a fundamental restructuring of the welfare state in the Western economies over the coming years as states face up to current budgetary challenges and an ageing population. This is and will undoubtedly be highly contested due to the conflicting interests and rights of the broad range of stakeholders involved—from those dependent on benefits, to the unemployed, to taxpayers, to public service employees, to pensioners, to consumers of the whole range of public services. A wide range of people are being affected by the current economic and public policy challenges, and their human rights claims are often in conflict with each other when the state faces inexorable budgetary pressures.

This makes it all the more remarkable just how absent international human rights law has been in the unfolding distress. If any area of law could and should provide the needed Geneva Convention for protecting ordinary citizens from the dangers of financial manias and panics and the hardships of recession, it should

[1] J. Brooks, *Once in Golconda: A True Drama of Wall Street 1920–1938* (London: Victor Gollancz, 1970), 28.

[2] C. Kindleberger and R. Aliber, *Manias, Panics and Crashes: A History of Financial Crises* 6th edn (New York: Palgrave Macmillan, 2011); C. Reinhart and K. Rogoff, *This Time is Different: Eight Centuries of Financial Folly* (Princeton: Princeton University Press, 2011).

be human rights law. This has as broad a remit as could be wanted—covering all aspects of basic human dignity and need—and as wide an international reach as is required, with the core treaties of the International Bill of Human Rights now covering the vast majority of states on earth.[3] The International Covenant on Economic, Social and Cultural Rights[4] (ICESCR) in particular provides a list of the basic economic and social rights that modern economies are expected to provide.[5] It reads like an economic charter for those goods which human beings require to function as economic agents, and is simultaneously a list of those issues of ordinary life that are most heavily impacted by economic and financial crisis. With the costs of bailing out financial institutions and the economic costs of recession borne largely by ordinary citizens, it is surprising that human rights law has not been a more visible feature of the debates on how to tackle the current situation of high debts, austerity, and low growth.

With the growth of the business and human rights agenda over recent years, many of the financial institutions at the heart of the financial crisis (either as entities needing bailouts or as holders of sovereign debt and/or assets that are exposed to crisis-hit economies) have also made their own commitments to upholding these international human rights.[6] This commitment is further strengthened by the UN Guiding Principles on Business and Human Rights (the Guiding Principles), endorsed by the UN General Assembly in 2011, which state that the responsibility to respect human rights is now 'a global standard of expected conduct for all business enterprises wherever they operate'.[7] It is not yet clear exactly how the Guiding Principles will apply across the vast operations of the financial services industry as there is currently a significant gap in theory and practice between human rights aspirations and current areas of operational application, and the broad-based

[3] The database of the Office of the High Commissioner for Human Rights contains statistics on ratification by instrument of the core human rights treaties and is available at <http://www.ohchr.org/EN/ProfessionalInterest/Pages/InternationalLaw.aspx> (last accessed 18 November 2013).

[4] 993 UNTS 3, 16 December 1966.

[5] It is often surprising how much the objectives of economic theory and socio-economic rights can overlap in principle, even if in practice the two debates rarely engage with each other. See for example J.K. Galbraith, *The Good Society: The Humane Agenda* (London: Sinclair-Stevenson, 1996), and S. Brittan, *Capitalism With a Human Face* (London: Fontana, 1996).

[6] The website of major banks, asset managers, and insurers now have sections devoted to corporate social responsibility, as a part of which there will generally be a commitment to human rights. See for example Barclays Group Statement on Human Rights, available at <http://tinyurl.com/oouzmgz> (last accessed 18 November 2013); Citigroup Statement on Human Rights, available at <http://www.citigroup.com/citi/citizen/humanrights/index.htm> (last accessed 18 November 2013); JP Morgan Statement on Human Rights, available at <http://www.jpmorganchase.com/corporate/Corporate-Responsibility/human-rights.htm> (last accessed 18 November 2013); UBS Statement on Human Rights, available at <http://www.ubs.com/1/e/about/corp_responsibility/commitment_strategy/policies_guidelines/human_rights.html> (last accessed 18 November 2013).

[7] *Guiding Principles on Business and Human Rights: Implementing the United Nations 'Protect, Respect and Remedy' Framework*, UN Doc. A.HRC/17/31, 21 March 2011, Part II, A, Principle 11 and Commentary. For analysis see R. Mares (ed.) *The UN Guiding Principles on Business and Human Rights: Foundations and Implementation* (Leiden: Martinus Nijhoff, 2012). See also Committee on the Rights of the Child, General Comment No. 16 on State obligations regarding the impact of the business sector on children's rights, 17 April 2013.

impacts of financial activities on human rights.[8] Notably, financial institutions have made very few references to human rights in debates on the unfolding crisis, and it is difficult to find any acknowledgement that the problems of austerity, bank bailouts, and sovereign (over)indebtedness in the Euro area may have anything to do with their human rights commitments (the problem being seen largely as one of budgetary responsibility/profligacy on the part of states, and financial market stability).[9] It is largely as if human rights/sustainability issues are ring-fenced in corporate social responsibility departments where they sit as entirely separate issues to bond market exposures, reckless lending, unsustainable risk taking, contagion, and the ongoing need for extra capital to bolster weak balance sheets and to comply with post-crisis regulatory reforms.[10]

In an interview in the autumn of 2012, Barclays' General Counsel listed the following as the 'top five human rights issues currently affecting the financial sector':

- Operating responsibly and consistently in high-risk environments (by which is inferred countries such as Sudan and Burma);
- Support for inclusive economic development in emerging markets;
- Access to banking;
- Corruption prevention; and
- Gender diversity within the workforce.[11]

This rather anodyne list is truly surprising in the current economic climate, particularly in a UK context, as it makes no mention of the socio-economic impacts of the catastrophic bank failures of 2008 and the continuing consequences of the taxpayer-funded bailouts.[12] It does, however, provide slightly more detail than the bank's Corporate Citizenship Report, which provides a mere half-page, 200-word paragraph on 'Respecting Human Rights'.[13] In a similar vein, Citigroup notes in

[8] These issues are explored in M. Dowell-Jones, 'Financial Institutions and Human Rights', in L. Blecher, G. Bellamy, and N. Stafford (eds.) *Corporate Accountability for Human Rights Impacts: New Paradigms and Expectations* (Chicago: American Bar Association Publishing, 2013) (forthcoming); and M. Dowell-Jones and D. Kinley, 'The Monster Under the Bed: Financial Services and the Ruggie Framework', in R. Mares, *supra* note 7, 193–216.

[9] R. McCormick, 'What Makes a Bank a "Sustainable Bank"?', 1 *Law and Economics Yearly Review* (2012), 77–104.

[10] International requirements for the amount of capital banks need to hold have been increased since the crisis, when existing regulations did not prevent the near collapse of the international banking system. The international regulations are enacted through national law, and certain jurisdictions such as Switzerland have chosen to impose even higher levels in order to prevent the taxpayer from having to fund another bailout of major financial institutions. For the international framework of capital adequacy regulation see Basel Committee on Banking Supervision, *Basel III: A global regulatory framework for more resilient banks and banking systems* (Basel, Bank for International Settlements, 2011).

[11] M. Harding, 'Banking on Human Rights', 1 *The Business and Human Rights Review* (Autumn 2012), 4–7, Allen & Overy LLP Human Rights Working Group.

[12] Although Barclays wasn't bailed out by the UK Treasury, it tapped Sovereign Wealth Funds of Middle Eastern States instead for emergency funding to prevent its collapse. This included a transaction of £6.1 billion with Qatar Holding, a subsidiary of the Qatar Investment Authority, which is now under investigation by the Serious Fraud Office. See Barclays Plc, *Annual Report 2012* (London: Barclays Plc, 2013) at 113. Barclays was also as much a part of the activity in financial markets that led to the economic and financial collapse as any other major banking group.

[13] Barclays Plc, *Citizenship Report 2011* (London: Barclays Plc, 2012) at 50. This is the latest Citizenship report available at the time of writing.

its 2011 Corporate Citizenship Report that only 13 of its transactions that year were deemed relevant to its Human Rights Statement, across 200 million client accounts, 280,000 employees worldwide and operations in 140 countries. Of these 13, five transactions related to resettlement; four to indigenous rights; three to security risks; and two to labour risks.[14] This is despite the fact that Citigroup received the largest government bailout of all the US banks—US$476.2 billion worth of cash and asset guarantees[15] —and it has agreed to pay a settlement of US$730 million over claims that it misled investors in its subprime mortgage-backed bonds.[16] Citigroup has also been implicated in the London InterBank Offered Rate-rigging scandal (LIBOR-rigging), and will contribute US$2 billion to the National Mortgage Settlement, a mechanism established by US State Attorney Generals and the Federal Government to compensate homeowners who were mis-sold mortgages during the subprime boom and/or those who have been illegally foreclosed on since the collapse.[17]

While this level of transparency in its Corporate Citizenship Report is encouraging, it demonstrates how limited an understanding of international human rights issues such international banks have. They tend to view them as issues of egregious violations, like forced resettlement, but to have little understanding of socio-economic rights and how they may apply as broad principles to all their operations, particularly given the key role that financial institutions play in the global economy. The Guiding Principles are clear that the corporate responsibility to respect applies to the whole range of human rights, including as a minimum those set out in the International Bill of Rights and the International Labour Organization's (ILO) Declaration on Fundamental Principles and Rights at Work,[18] and that it applies right across their operations, not just to a small fragment of them. And yet despite the human wreckage of the financial crisis and the economic and social meltdown in the southern European countries like Greece, Ireland, Portugal, and Spain, it is as if the storms of crisis swirling around banks have somehow not intruded upon the hallowed world of financial institutions' human rights commitments. This is evidence of a cognitive gap and limited thinking in the financial sector around their human rights commitments and what they actually mean in terms of banks' broader role in society. This is a gap that is begging to be bridged as the Guiding Principles gain more operational relevance and as the social consequences of the financial crisis continue to bite.

[14] Citigroup, *2011 Global Citizenship Report* (New York: Citigroup, 2012), at 48. One transaction was counted under two headings.

[15] Congressional Oversight Panel, *The Final Report of the Congressional Oversight Panel* (Washington DC: US Government Printing Office, 16 March 2011), at 23, Fig. 7, 'Total Federal Government Exposure to SCAP Bank Holding Companies'.

[16] 'Citi to pay $730m in subprime settlement', *Financial Times* (London, 18 March 2013).

[17] For details of the joint settlement, see information available at <http://www.nationalmortgagesettlement.com/about> (last accessed 18 November 2013) and <https://www.citimortgage.com/Mortgage/displayHomeOwnerAssistance.do?page=settlement> (last accessed18 November 2013).

[18] *Guiding Principles on Business and Human Rights, supra* note 7, Principle 11.

3. The Challenges Facing Public Finances in the Advanced Economies

First, no-one should doubt the seriousness of the fiscal challenges facing the advanced economies. Current borrowing requirements across the OECD countries stand at US$10 trillion per year[19]—that is, governments in the OECD countries are collectively spending US$10 trillion a year more on public services than they receive in taxes and have to raise this money from private investors/financial institutions (or their own central banks) via sovereign bond issues or direct lending in order to fund their spending commitments. Government debt-to-GDP ratios have reached an average of 111.4 per cent of GDP across the OECD, a level that is unprecedented for peacetime and significantly higher than the levels of sovereign indebtedness that plunged Latin America into crisis in the early 1980s and resulted in their 'lost decade'.[20] Although the question of when sovereign debt becomes unsustainable is 'a matter of judgement not "hard science"'[21] because it can depend on a range of economic and financial factors, the build-up of such heavy debt loads across the advanced economies creates significant risks for economies and human rights. These include the risk of another banking crisis, the risk of another global financial crisis on the scale of 2007–9, slow economic growth and lack of economic opportunity for years to come and, of course, prolonged austerity and public service cuts as deficits are brought under control and debt loads reduced. There are significant underlying problems with the way states have been funding public services which pre-date the financial crisis.

Although human rights lawyers are keen that austerity should not be used to undermine the rights of the vulnerable which should be protected at times of crisis,[22] one of the underlying triggers of the current sovereign debt crisis is the steady expansion of the welfare state and public services over the last two decades. This, combined with the future strain that ageing populations which will place on public resources, particularly in relation to health, social care, and pension provision, which are key factors of the current situation:

> As bad as these [current] fiscal problems may appear, relying solely on these official [debt] figures is almost certainly very misleading. Rapidly ageing populations present a number

[19] OECD, *OECD Sovereign Borrowing Outlook 2013* (Paris: OECD, 27 February 2013). See also R. Nelson, *Sovereign Debt in Advanced Economies: Overview and Issues for Congress* (Washington DC: Congressional Research Service, 31 January 2013), available at <http://www.fas.org/sgp/crs/misc/R41838.pdf> (last accessed 18 November 2013).

[20] G. Bootheway: 'The Symbolic Value of the Euro in the Eurozone Crisis', 19 *Proceedings of the American Society of Business and Behavioural Sciences Annual Conference* (February 2012), 77–83. For information on the Latin American debt crisis see: B. Eichengreen and P. Lindert (eds.), *The International Debt Crisis in Historical Perspective* (London: MIT Press, 1989); J. Sachs, *New Approaches to the Latin American Debt Crisis* (Princeton: Princeton Studies in International Economics, 1989).

[21] H. Tran, 'The Role of Markets in Sovereign Debt Crisis Detection, Prevention and Resolution', Speech delivered at the BIS Seminar: 'Sovereign Risk: A World Without Risk-Free Assets?' (Basel: 8–9 January 2013).

[22] Committee on Economic, Social and Cultural Rights, General Comment No. 3: The nature of States parties obligations (Art. 2, para. 1 of the Covenant, 1990), para. 12.

of countries with the prospect of enormous future costs that are not wholly recognised in current budget projections. The size of these future obligations is anybody's guess. As far as we know, there is no definite and comprehensive account of the unfunded, contingent liabilities that governments currently have accumulated.[23]

Research published in 2006 showed that the United States government was already technically insolvent (even before the financial crisis) once its unfunded future liabilities were taken into account—mainly healthcare and social security.[24] Since then its debt has doubled from US$8.5 trillion to US$16 trillion as entitlements have been expanded and the economic situation has stagnated.[25] The study cited a figure of US$65.9 trillion as the projected size of the 'fiscal gap' (that is, a calculation of the cost of future spending promises set against estimated future government income)—a figure that is clearly heavily dependent upon the assumptions used to calculate it but it nevertheless gives an insight into the future cost of funding the state.[26] What the scale of this figure also indicates is that the fiscal problems facing the US go beyond anything that could be addressed simply by raising taxes on the rich or on corporations. US national debt was US$10.6 trillion when President Obama was inaugurated in January 2009, and he has added another US$6 trillion to that figure in just four years—more than any other president has done.[27]

The UK government has similarly built up an unprecedented peacetime debt load of £1.1 trillion, and is now spending £47 billion a year (3 per cent of GDP) on meeting the interest payments, as well as currently borrowing a further £120 billion per year to fund existing spending. Interest payments are forecast to rise to £68 billion a year by 2017–18,[28] and the deficit is forecast to double over the next 30 years, thanks to pressures of an ageing population, according to Bank for International Settlements projections.[29] Although the UK appears to have done a lot in terms of trimming public spending and cutting entitlements, with, for example, controversial changes to Disability Living Allowance and Housing Benefit, in reality the country has barely begun to cut its deficit. In the financial year 2012–13, public sector net borrowing was £120.6 billion, which is only £300 million lower

[23] S. Cecchetti, M. Mohanty, and F. Zampali, *The Future of Public Debt: Prospects and Implications* (Basel: Bank for International Settlements Working Paper no. 300, March 2010), at 1.

[24] L. Kotlikoff, 'Is The United States Bankrupt?', 88 *Federal Reserve of St. Louis Review* (2006), 234–249.

[25] Figures from the US Treasury, available at <http://www.treasurydirect.gov/govt/reports/pd/histdebt/histdebt_histo5.htm> (last accessed 18 November 2013).

[26] The fiscal gap is defined as measuring: 'the present value difference between all future government expenditures, including servicing official debt, and all future receipts'. Kotlikoff, *supra* note 24, at 239.

[27] Figures from the US Treasury, 'The Daily History of the Debt Results', available at <http://www.treasurydirect.gov/NP/debt/search?startMonth=01&startDay=15&startYear=2009&endMonth=06&endDay=14&endYear=2013> (last accessed 18 November 2013).

[28] D. Webb and J. Bardens, *Government borrowing, debt and debt interest payments: historical statistics and forecasts*, UK Parliamentary Briefing Note SN/EP/5745, 13 March 2013, House of Commons Library.

[29] Cecchetti et al., *The Future of Public Debt, supra* note 23, at 9.

than the figure for the previous year.[30] The country borrowed £15.1 billion in March 2013 alone, indicating just how quickly the country's debt load is mounting even when 'austerity' policies are apparently being pursued.[31] In reality all the country has done so far is trim the rate of growth of public spending, rather than make noticeable net cuts to actual expenditure. While the task of implementing austerity is complicated by a sluggish economy, which means lower tax revenue and higher numbers of people claiming welfare support, the country will have to make far greater cuts in public spending before state borrowing is brought under control. Similar scenarios are being played out across the developed countries.

Much of the current problems in the European and other industrial countries have come about through a structural 'deficit bias'

> These debts were not accumulated due to wars or exogenous disasters. Instead, debt financing was regarded as a convenient way of providing ever-increasing public services and transfers.[32]

Despite concerns during the 1990s that neoliberal ideology was leading to a withering-away of the state,[33] there was no great retrenchment of the state from the commanding heights of the economy in industrial countries over the last 20 years.[34] State spending as a proportion of GDP has not altered much in the intervening years. In the UK it fell slightly in the 1990s, started to rise in 2000, and is now 45 per cent of GDP (roughly back to where it was in the mid-1990s).[35] This has been accompanied by a steady growth in government debt[36] and a steady rise in social spending commitments and services which can in one way or another be linked to the state's human rights commitments—for example health, education, social welfare, and public sector employment.[37] In 2013 the UK government is projected to spend £478.5 billion out of a total government budget of £683.6 billion on services directly linked to socio-economic rights: pensions, healthcare, education, and social welfare. This is before services linked to other human rights,

[30] Office for National Statistics, *Statistical bulletin: Public Sector Finances, March 2013*, available at <http://www.ons.gov.uk/ons/rel/psa/public-sector-finances/march-2013/stb—march-2013.html> (last accessed 19 October 2013).

[31] Office for National Statistics, *Statistical ((should itt be Bulletin??))bulletin: Public Sector Finances, March 2013*, available at <http://www.ons.gov.uk/ons/rel/psa/public-sector-finances/march-2013/stb—march-2013.html> (last accessed 19 October 2013).

[32] B. Eichengreen et al., *Public Debts: Nuts, Bolts and Worries*, Geneva Reports on the World Economy No. 13 (Geneva: International Center for Monetary and Banking Studies, 2011), 48.

[33] A seminal report on the idea of transferring State functions to the market was World Bank, *World Development Report 1997: The State in a Changing World* (Washington DC: World Bank, 1997); see also J. Gray, *False Dawn: The Delusions of Global Capitalism* (London: Granta Press, 1998); L. Weiss, *The Myth of the Powerless State: Governing the Economy in a Global Era* (Cambridge: Polity Press, 1998).

[34] A phrase used in the title of a well-known book about the reformulation of the State: D. Yergin and J. Stanislaw, *The Commanding Heights: The Battle for the World Economy* (2nd edn, New York: Simon & Schuster, 2002).

[35] Data from the UK Treasury, *Statistical Bulletin: Public Spending Statistics February 2013* (London: HM Treasury, 2013), Chart 2 'Trends in Public spending since 1991–2', at 8.

[36] Eichengreen et al., *supra* note 32, see Figure 4.1 'Public debt of the US and of the Eurozone (% of GDP)', at 49.

[37] *Statistical Bulletin: Public Spending Statistics, supra* note 35, Chart 1 'Real term trends in Public Spending'. The chart shows that since 1991–2, health, education, and social protection have seen the largest increase in spending.

like peace and security, the rule of law, development/foreign aid, and public sector employment, are taken into account.[38] From a human rights point of view, it is interesting to note that if the current budgets for pensions, healthcare, education, and social welfare (£478.5 billion) were ring-fenced, and the existing deficit (£120.6 billion) eliminated entirely from the remainder, this would only leave a total of £84.5 billion in the pot to fund all the remaining government services including defence and development. £84.5 billion may sound like a lot of money, but in terms of the UK government's budget it is less than the annual running cost of the National Health Service and less than half of what the country spends on the welfare state.[39] It also does not leave any fiscal room for making provision for growing future claims on pension, healthcare, and social budgets as the population ages, or for paying off some of the state's enormous debts.

Public spending data for other advanced economies show a similar trend, with social expenditures as a percentage of GDP growing over the last few decades.[40] Across the 27 member countries of the European Union, state spending as a proportion of GDP is 49.1 per cent of GDP, and of that health, education, and social protection account for roughly 65 per cent of outlays. Broken down by country, healthcare, education, and social protection account for 68.2 per cent of state spending in Germany; 62.4 per cent in Ireland; 68.1 per cent in France; 64.2 per cent in Italy; and 63.4 per cent in Portugal.[41] While it may be argued that this is positive for human rights protection and indicates that these countries have taken steps towards fulfilling the obligation to devote the 'maximum available resources' to the realization of economic, social, and cultural rights (Article 2(1) ICESCR), the problem with the statistics is threefold: (a) long-term structural fiscal deficits underlie them which implies an ongoing need for borrowing to fund part of this spending; (b) the ageing population and rising costs of pensions and healthcare means that the cost to the state of continuing to provide existing services will only grow, and (c) it is very difficult to roll back such public services both politically and without negatively affecting people's rights, even where states have overstretched themselves financially to provide them. People come to rely on them so that cutting them can cause hardship and there is a presumption against retrogression in the provision of socio-economic rights under the ICESCR.[42]

[38] *United Kingdom Central Government and Local Authority Spending Fiscal Year 2013*, available at <http://www.ukpublicspending.co.uk/total_spending_2013UKbn> (last accessed 18 November 2013).

[39] In the financial year 2011–12, expenditure for the Department of Health was £101.6 billion, compared to £100.3 billion for the previous financial year. UK Department of Health, *Annual Report and Accounts 2011–12* (London: The Stationary Office, 18 October 2012).

[40] See the OECD Social Expenditures Database (SOCX), available at <http://www.oecd.org/els/soc/socialexpendituredatabasesocx.htm> (last accessed 18 November 2013).

[41] L. Freysson and L. Wahrig, *General government expenditure in 2011: Focus on the functions 'social protection' and 'health'* (Luxembourg: Eurostat, 2013), Table 1 'Total general government expenditure by main function and country (2011), at 2, available at <http://epp.eurostat.ec.europa.eu/cache/ITY_OFFPUB/KS-SF-13-009/EN/KS-SF-13-009-EN.PDF> (last accessed 18 November 2013).

[42] Committee on Economic, Social and Cultural Rights, General Comment No. 3, *supra* note 22, para. 9.

The current crisis of sovereign borrowing and austerity, therefore, is at its heart a crisis of socio-economic rights, almost by definition. Globalization and the triumph of neoliberal ideas were about the state retreating from the commanding heights of the economy, leaving business to run the economy. The state would instead focus on its role in providing social welfare/health functions and targeted support to business, such as appropriate regulation. This was the ethos around which the concept of the state has been rebuilt in the post-communist era and it had socio-economic rights at its heart (even if it was not framed in terms of rights). However, the state did not simply decline into atrophy, providing social support to those unable to participate in the economy. The state in industrialized countries has instead used the good economic years of the financial boom to expand its remit in these target areas and increase spending in many areas of social policy beyond what was truly sustainable on a long-term basis.

In doing so, it was reasonably easy to ignore the cost when tax receipts were high and it was easy for the state to borrow from the financial markets at declining rates of interest, and in doing so to sidestep the issue of future provision of these benefits to an ageing population. Political argument and social claims could focus around the expansion of service provision for particular interest groups, rather than collective analysis of overall cost; that is to say that it is politically easier to expand services and benefits than it is to restrict them. This has led to an incremental expansion of public services and benefits. The only people left scrutinizing the state's books and analysing the long-term cost were the Treasury, accountants/economists, or investors who care to wade through the national balance sheet, and statisticians working for the Office for National Statistics or the Bank of England. Few people/voters have bothered themselves with watching the state's bottom line and in the circumstances it has proven easy for an incumbent government to make promises to voters and simply issue sovereign bonds to fill the funding gap—especially when financial regulation has meant that there is an avid demand in the financial markets for these instruments.[43] This has resulted in a debate about the 'crisis of the welfare state' that is now several decades old,[44] and which has been brought to a head by the financial crisis of 2007–9.

This is the underlying story that has now come back to haunt the state—it is a crisis of the failure to effectively define what the political, social, and financial boundaries of the state are in these areas. Thus the current crisis of austerity is in essence a crisis of socio-economic rights—it is a crisis that revolves around the role, scope, and appropriate limits to the state's provision of these rights. What should it provide and to whom and in what volume? What should the limits be on how it funds them? What happens to individual claims on state services when a crisis erupts—can claims be prioritized? How can they be cut in a manner that

[43] Credit ratings were introduced as a key pillar of bank capital requirements in the 1990s. Banks and insurance companies were forced to hold assets with a particular credit rating to satisfy regulations, which led to avid demand from institutions for sovereign bonds and other AAA-rated assets. This, of course, was one of the key dynamics of the credit crisis.

[44] See P. Pierson, 'The New Politics of the Welfare State', 48 *World Politics* (1996), 143–179 and research cited therein.

is compliant with human rights law? The austerity crisis is bringing into focus important issues in the theory and definition of the socio-economic rights that are set out in international law which have so far largely been under the radar: what are they, what are their boundaries, who should claim them, and how? What do they guarantee? How should the state fund them? What are the limits to their provision in the advanced economies? While these are core questions in the practical definition of socio-economic rights, austerity has revealed a clear deficit in the theory and practice of international human rights where answers should be. Currently it appears that human rights scholarship has few, if any, clear answers to these key questions because they have not been rigorously and systematically studied, not least because they require an in-depth understanding of the macroeconomic and fiscal framework of rights. They are questions that cannot be answered by relying solely on legal principle.

4. Austerity and the ICESCR

It is within the context of these debt and deficit statistics that it is interesting to consider the letter sent by the Chairperson of the Committee on Economic, Social and Cultural Rights (the Committee) to States Parties in 2012, on the subject of Covenant rights and austerity.[45] In it the Chairperson reminds states that:

> under the Covenant all States Parties should avoid at all times taking decisions which might lead to the denial or infringement of economic, social and cultural rights.

And that:

> the Covenant [...] provides certain important guideposts which can help States Parties to adopt appropriate policies that deal with the economic downturn while respecting economic, social and cultural rights.[46]

For an economist, politician, or financier negotiating the current debt crisis, the problem with the Covenant is precisely that it has failed to do this. We still only have vague legal principles of what these rights mean, which may make sense in legal theory but which have little quantitative specification or fiscal meaning in the context of insolvent governments trying to fund a £120 billion deficit, to avoid economic stagnation, and financial market contagion.[47] There is no clarity

[45] 'Letter dated 16 May 2012 addressed by the Chairperson of the Committee on Economic, Social and Cultural Rights to States parties to the International Covenant on Economic, Social and Cultural Rights', UN Doc. CESCR/48th/SP/MAB/SW available at <http://www2.ohchr.org/english/bodies/cescr/statements.htm> (last accessed 19 October 2013).

[46] 'Letter dated 16 May 2012 addressed by the Chairperson of the CESCR to States parties to the International Covenant on Economic, Social and Cultural Rights', UN Doc. CESCR/48th/SP/MAB/SW available at <http://www2.ohchr.org/english/bodies/cescr/statements.htm> (last accessed 19 October 2013).

[47] See M. Dowell-Jones, *Contextualising the International Covenant on Economic, Social and Cultural Rights: Assessing the Economic Deficit* (Leiden: Martinus Nijhoff, 2004); M. Dowell-Jones, 'The Committee on Economic, Social and Cultural Rights: Assessing the Economic Deficit', 1 *Human*

as to how a state that has been using the bond markets for years to finance an unsustainable expansion of state spending on welfare rights or social services provision—the current reality in Europe—can hope to undo the excess in a manner that is in compliance with international human rights law. For example, which areas of the £100 billion budget for the National Health Service should be protected under the right to health, and which areas of spending could be considered for cuts that would not impact on human rights? The letter provides no substantive guidance on how this may be achieved, nor does the Committee's General Comment on the right to health.[48] Ultimately, the Covenant and those tasked with implementing it still do not have the rudimentary technical tools that they require for the task of budgetary analysis and providing a rights-based framework for fiscal, monetary, and financial sector policy, which would be readily useful to people having to make those difficult decisions.[49] Private discussions that this author has had with public sector decision-makers revealed that they would welcome such guidance were it available.

The Committee goes on to remind states parties that 'at the heart of the Covenant' is an obligation to progressively achieve the socio-economic rights it sets out:

> This requires States to adopt and implement laws and policies that aim to achieve incremental improvements in universal access to basic goods and services such as health care, education, housing, social security and cultural life.[50]

The standard of progressive achievement, which is a cornerstone of the ICESCR, is understood by scholars to demand: 'that after achieving the minimum core obligations, states have to take appropriate steps to ensure "the continuous improvement of living conditions" necessary to live an adequate standard of living'.[51] This is largely wishful thinking in the industrial countries given the scale of today's sovereign debt problems as it may be argued instead that in trying to achieve this goal—the continuous improvement of living standards—states have undermined the

Rights Law Review (2001), 11–33. Compare this with recent work on art. 2(1) ICESCR, which continues to seek legal principles for the clarification of what is a complex challenge in the economic and budgetary sphere. Resort to legal principle alone will never resolve the contradictions inherent in this provision. While budget analysis is seeking a broader understanding of the fiscal potential of ESC rights, it is still in the process of development.

[48] Committee on Economic, Social and Cultural Rights, General Comment No. 14: The right to the highest attainable standard of health (Art. 12 of the International Covenant on Economic, Social and Cultural Rights), UN Doc. E/C.12/2000/4, 11 August 2000.

[49] The application of socio-economic rights to budgetary analysis is in an ongoing state of development, but not yet refined enough to provide clear guidelines on today's tough budgetary situation. See C. Harvey and E. Rooney, 'Integrating Human Rights? Socio-Economic Rights and Budget Analysis', 3 *European Human Rights Law Review* (2010), 266–279; A. Nolan and M. Dutschke, 'Article 2(1) ICESCR and States Parties Obligations: Whither the Budget?', 3 *European Human Rights Law Review* (2010), 280–289.

[50] 'Letter dated 16 May 2012 addressed by the Chairperson of the Committee on Economic, Social and Cultural Rights', *supra* note 45.

[51] M. Ssenyonjo, 'Reflections on state obligations with respect to economic, social and cultural rights in international human rights law', 15 *The International Journal of Human Rights* (2011), 969–1012, 978.

sustainability of welfare states and socio-economic rights enjoyment by mortgaging themselves and their economies to the hilt and are now having to deal with the consequences. The existence of such large debt loads and persistent fiscal deficits is a clear threat to states parties' ability to provide this 'continuous improvement in living conditions' as it not only dampens economic activity but also threatens the future viability of public services. It is critically important to understand that the state is currently able to finance these debts and deficits because it can continue to borrow at low interest rates (the UK currently only pays 2 per cent on its two-year bonds), but a sharp rise in interest rates—as happened in Greece—could plunge the advanced economies into severe economic crisis that would arguably have worse consequences for human rights than the current austerity cuts. Failing to tackle these deficits and debts will most likely lead to a future crisis scenario where socio-economic rights are extensively denied and infringed. Given the close integration of the world economy, any negative human rights impacts of a debt-induced meltdown in the advanced economies would most likely be felt around the world.

Another of the clearest and most longstanding legal principles of the ICESCR is that of non-retrogression. This requires that once any given level of enjoyment of a Covenant right has been reached, there is a presumption that this level cannot then be reduced by a state without the most stringent consideration.[52] Although the Committee has recognized in the context of the current crisis that 'some adjustments in the implementation of some of these Covenant rights are at times inevitable';[53] which would appear to be a softening of the principle of non-retrogression, this simply does not help a state decide where or how cuts should be made in order to balance the books, and how the human rights of different individuals and groups should be ordered in terms of priority for state spending. Increasing demand on health services as populations age means that an existing entitlement to a service under the right to health becomes steadily more costly to fund. Even calling for any retrogressive measures to be temporary, 'covering only the period of crisis', would seem to be overly optimistic in the current context.[54]

It would be easier to implement this principle in the context of austerity if we had a clear framework setting out the specifics of what each ESC right entitled a person to—which could then be protected from retrogressive measures—but we do not have this beyond the requirements of the minimum core content of Covenant rights. The Committee's General Comments which provide normative guidance on the content of Covenant rights have to be drafted at the high level of principle, and in such a way that the normative guidance is relevant to all states parties. This means that it is difficult to identify from them precise quantitative measures of the content of each right even across a reasonably coherent grouping of states like the Euro area. In considering the implications of non-retrogression in the context of austerity, the holistic nature of ICESCR rights also needs to be

[52] Committee on Economic, Social and Cultural Rights, General Comment No. 3, *supra* note 22, para. 9.

[53] 'Letter dated 16 May 2012', *supra* note 45.

[54] 'Letter dated 16 May 2012', *supra* note 45.

borne in mind. As the Committee recognized in its General Comment on the right to health: 'the right to health must be understood as a right to the enjoyment of a variety of facilities, goods, services and conditions necessary for the realization of the highest attainable standard of health'.[55] Protecting the budget for the health service, therefore, could lead to impacts on the right to health if cuts are implemented in other areas of public services instead.

The choice facing the industrialized countries now is not human rights versus austerity, but austerity that can hopefully be implemented in such a way as to minimize the inevitable negative social, human rights, and economic impacts. Guidance from the Committee on how this could be achieved in practice would undoubtedly be very useful. As the figures cited have highlighted, it is in practice very difficult to identify areas for spending cuts that cannot in some way be linked to internationally guaranteed human rights. For example, should library or museum services be cut (right to education, right to culture) or funding for hip replacements or cancer treatment (right to health)? Or should jobs be cut from administrative functions (impacting the right to work, right to an adequate standard of living, and possible other rights of the employees affected and potentially other rights through affecting service delivery)? Should leisure services bear the brunt of cuts (right to health)? Should leisure services be cut so as to protect the budget for social care (right to health, right to social security, right to privacy?) Should front-line policing be cut (rule of law, access to justice, right to security of person)? Should legal aid be cut (right to a fair trial, right to access to justice)? Should the budget for road maintenance be cut, including jobs (undermining the right to work not only for road workers, but eroding public access to other services via roads that are safe to use) in order to provide funding for educational material for schools?

Even where there may seem to be only a very limited link to human rights, one can nevertheless be found. Rural bus routes are an expensive cost to local councils in the UK, but they provide a lifeline to elderly and disabled people living in remote villages who may have no other means of transport or ready way of accessing health services, shops, or community activities. Should these services be reduced in order to protect other services that are used by more people? In its General Comment No. 6 on 'The economic, social and cultural rights of older persons', the Committee on Economic, Social and Cultural Rights affirmed that in accordance with the principle of independence for older people, 'national policies should help elderly persons to continue to live in their own homes as long as possible' and that as part of this, policies should 'facilitate mobility and communication through the provision of adequate means of transport'.[56] This would seem to raise a human rights presumption in favour of protecting such services, highlighting how difficult it is for states to find areas of spending that can be cut

[55] Committee on Economic, Social and Cultural Rights, General Comment No. 14, *supra* note 48, para. 9.

[56] Committee on Economic, Social and Cultural Rights, General Comment No. 6: The economic, social and cultural rights of older persons, 1995, para. 33.

back without somehow touching upon the broad range of internationally protected human rights.

Similarly, although the minimum core content of Covenant rights aims to set out the baseline of the 'minimum essential levels of each of the rights enunciated in the Covenant',[57] which states have an obligation to provide, it can sometimes be difficult to shield this core from the effects of austerity. The General Comment on the right to health includes in the minimum core content of this right the 'equitable distribution of all health facilities, goods and services'[58], but efforts by the health sector in the UK to preserve service quality and balance budgets have seen community hospitals closed and services transferred to major hospitals where they can be provided with better technical expertise and improved facilities. This has particularly affected rural communities, whose residents may now have to travel much further for specialist care. There is inevitably a tension between providing health services close to communities, and the need to provide high levels of technical expertise and care in specialist areas like cancer care, premature baby care, and orthopaedics, for example, in a way that takes account of the immense cost involved in delivering a modern health service. This reality can in practice complicate the task of interpreting and complying with even the minimum core content of socio-economic rights.

There are in reality many legitimate claims on the state for the provision of services that satisfy economic, social, and cultural rights. In General Comment No. 6, the Committee recognized that 'the industrialized countries in particular, are faced with the task of adapting their social and economic policies to the ageing of their populations'[59] but it is difficult to identify broad areas of state budgets that could be cut without any impact on or link to the rights protected under international law and the principles that have been set out to interpret the state obligations attached to those rights. So far, international law has failed to provide any guideposts on how this could be done.

5. Austerity and Sustainable Human Rights

No matter how strong the support for international human rights law, very difficult choices now have to be made in order to put state finances on a sustainable long-term footing. The reality we are faced with is simply that the provision of public services which fulfil the broad range of socio-economic (and other) human rights have been extended way beyond the capacity of advanced states to afford them in the long run. This is because they have been partially funded over several decades by relying on deficit financing and recourse to the sovereign bond markets,

[57] Committee on Economic, Social and Cultural Rights, General Comment No. 3, *supra* note 22, para. 10.

[58] Committee on Economic, Social and Cultural Rights, General Comment No. 14, *supra* note 48, para. 43(e).

[59] Committee on Economic, Social and Cultural Rights, General Comment No. 6, *supra* note 56, para. 3.

which has built a large stock of debt that needs to be paid back, and because the future costs of ageing populations mean that even to maintain the current level of services, state spending as a proportion of GDP will have to rise substantially over the next few decades. Cleary, the situation that the advanced economies find themselves in requires more than just temporary measures. There is also a growing sense of antipathy towards the welfare state among segments of the electorate, which increases political pressure to tackle abuses in the system and can complicate the task of complying with international human rights law.[60]

This is arguably a central reason why socio-economic rights have not gained traction in debates on the European fiscal and sovereign bond crisis, and why bodies charged with defending these rights have little authority in national or EU-wide policy debates. Where important financial, budgetary, and economic policy decisions have to be made, human rights are not resorted to as key policy tools to guide analysis despite the legal commitments that may have been entered into; in fact they are largely discarded as irrelevant, or a nuisance. The Programme Director for Human Rights at the UK's Equality and Human Rights Commission remarked in a speech on austerity and human rights: '[h]uman rights play only a marginal role in policy discourse in Britain', and 'it does not help our case for human rights to be seen always as an obstacle'. He went on to add that the challenge is to make human rights an essential part of the 'toolkit in starting to build a fair and inclusive recovery'.[61] Without some sense of how broad legal principles translate into a concrete, costed economic agenda, these commitments have little real bearing or functional utility given current fiscal challenges. The fact that the legal expression of socio-economic rights still has not been imbued with any broad economic contextuality despite the fact that the Covenant has now been in force for over 30 years continues to hamper the visibility and effectiveness of Covenant rights.

There are also challenging legal issues under Article 2(1), ICESCR to consider. Although it is normally assumed that states drag their feet on using the 'maximum available resources' to realize socio-economic rights, and that this is in fact an easy 'get-out' clause for them, in the current context it is possible to make the opposite argument: in persistently using the sovereign bond markets to fund growing public sector spending on services linked to the rights guaranteed by the ICESCR and extending future claims without an adequate plan for funding them, states parties have potentially breached Article 2(1) by going beyond the 'maximum available resources'. In doing so they have effectively mortgaged the rights of future generations to enjoy their socio-economic rights in order to satisfy the socio-economic rights of the current generation, as the debt will have to be repaid by future taxpayers. They have potentially breached the 'contract between the generations' and

[60] A. Park et al. (eds.), *British Social Attitudes: the 29th Report* (London: NatCen Social Research, 2012), available at <http://www.bsa-29.natcen.ac.uk> (last accessed 18 November 2013).

[61] N. Crowther, 'Is austerity compatible with the UK's human rights obligations and what tools of analysis are required to find out?', Equality and Human Rights Commission speech, 16 March 2011, available at <http://www.equalityhumanrights.com/human-rights/our-human-rights-work/articles-and-speeches/speech-is-austerity-compatible-with-the-uks-human-rights-obligations> (last accessed 18 November 2013).

directly imperilled the sustainability of rights implementation. The sustainability of a socio-economic human rights regime is not a topic that receives much attention as it is generally assumed that human rights are, by definition, sustainable. From a macroeconomic and budgetary perspective this is not the case and this is an issue that could benefit from further investigation. As Niall Ferguson explained in his 2012 Reith Lecture:

> The heart of the matter is the way public debt allows the current generation of voters to live at the expense of those as yet too young to vote or as yet unborn. In this regard, the statistics commonly cited as government debt are themselves deeply misleading, for they encompass only the sums owed by governments in the form of bonds. The rapidly rising quantity of these bonds certainly implies a growing charge on those in employment, now and in the future, since—even if the current low rates of interest enjoyed by the biggest sovereign borrowers persist—the amount of money needed to service the debt must inexorably rise. But the official debts in the form of bonds do not include the often far larger unfunded liabilities of welfare schemes like—to give the biggest American programs—Medicare, Medicaid and Social Security.
>
> [...]
>
> [The] mind-boggling numbers represent nothing less than a vast claim by the generation currently retired or about to retire on their children and grandchildren, who are obligated by current law to find the money in the future, by submitting either to substantial increases in taxation or to drastic cuts in other forms of public expenditure.[62]

A study of the US situation by the IMF estimated that in order to address this generational gap and put long-term state finances on a sustainable footing, all taxes would need to rise and all transfers would need to be cut immediately by 35 per cent. Delaying this adjustment and pushing the problem out into the future would only make the eventual cost bigger.[63] The study by Kotlikoff (cited) estimated that addressing the generational gap in the US accounts would require an 'immediate and permanent doubling of personal and corporate income taxes' or 'an immediate and permanent two-thirds cut in social security and Medicare benefits' or a 143 per cent cut in all discretionary federal spending.[64] This study was completed before the financial crisis and before President Obama's reform to social security and Medicare, at a time when US debt was half of its present level. The scale of these changes indicate that it is highly unlikely given the scale of the problem that state finances could be put on a stable footing by relying on one course of action alone (that is, tax rises or spending cuts).

In terms of human rights law, it is also interesting to consider whether states have breached the minimum core content of the right to social security. In its General Comment No. 19 on the right to social security, the Committee included in the core content of this right an obligation to 'respect existing social security

[62] N. Ferguson, 'The Human Hive', *The Reith Lectures 2012*, 19 June 2012, available at <http://www.bbc.co.uk/programmes/b01jmx0p/features/transcript> (last accessed 18 November 2013).

[63] N. Batini, G. Callegari, and J. Guerreiro, *An Analysis of U.S. Fiscal and Generational Imbalances: Who Will Pay and How?* (Washington DC: IMF, 2011) IMF Working Paper: WP/11/72, April 2011, at 24.

[64] Kotlikoff, *supra* note 24, at 239.

schemes and protect them from unreasonable interference'. This is cross-referenced to a previous paragraph that specifies that states should refrain 'from engaging in any practice or activity that, for example, denies or limits equal access to adequate social security'.[65] Insofar as the steady accumulation of debt by advanced states is now undermining equal access to social security, it is possible that this has breached these provisions, which could be interpreted as raising a presumption that social security schemes should be sustainably funded.

As this author has pointed out, two of the key principles which should be read as underlying Article 2(1), and indeed the sustainable funding of the whole Covenant are:

a) Objectives set must be affordable given existing economic means; and
b) Objectives set must not be such as to impact detrimentally the future ability of the state to implement the Covenant.[66]

Looking at the current debt and deficit statistics across the advanced economies, coupled with their gross spending figures on areas like healthcare, education, and social services, it is difficult to see how they have lived within the spirit of these two principles. Using human rights law to ossify current levels of entitlements and to demand they be continued as a matter of 'human rights law' would therefore be counterproductive and not in keeping with the broader objectives of this law, which aims to protect future generations as much as the current one. Current levels of provision are plainly unaffordable and unsustainable on a long-term basis given the reality of ageing populations, and human rights risk being seen as an 'obstacle' to the resolution of today's budgetary problems rather than an essential tool for their resolution if this disconnect is not addressed. It also threatens to undermine the viability and respect for human rights law among policymakers and the general population if human rights are only used to counter any efforts to make state spending sustainable. Hopefully, this will drive home to human rights lawyers the importance of developing a comprehensive macroeconomic and fiscal understanding of the issues involved in realizing socio-economic rights, which offers them a chance to be more effective in political discourse in the future.

6. The Role of the Financial Sector in the Debt Crisis

Despite the scale of the challenge in reforming state finances, it is also important to consider both the responsibilities of financial institutions and the role of the financial markets in the current situation. Financial markets and financial institutions are a symbiotic part of the current debt dynamic, as the holders of

[65] Committee on Economic, Social and Cultural Rights, General Comment No. 19: The right to social security (Art. 9), 4 February 2008, UN Doc. E/C.12/GC/19, paras. 59(c) and 44.

[66] M. Dowell-Jones, *Contextualising the International Covenant on Economic, Social and Cultural Rights*, *supra* note 47, at 55.

huge amounts of government debt, as the beneficiaries of bailouts that brought a simmering fiscal crisis to a head, and as the key intermediaries in the web of networks that links sovereign bonds in the advanced economies to broader world economic, financial, and human rights conditions. In considering the human rights implications of the current situation, it is therefore also necessary to look at the crisis from the perspective of the UN Guiding Principles on Business and Human Rights.[67] These set out the human rights responsibilities of private financial institutions. It should be stressed that there is not yet much analysis available of how the Guiding Principles' core responsibility to respect human rights applies across the operations of modern financial institutions. Issues around bonds, derivatives and financial crisis in particular remain murky and largely unaddressed.[68] The following is of necessity a very cursory review of what is a difficult and far-reaching problem, which it will consider from two different angles: the bailouts of the financial sector in 2008–9; and the role of financial markets in funding sovereign borrowing. It will seek to highlight some of the complexities of applying the corporate responsibility to respect human rights to the current debt crisis.

A. Bailouts and sovereign debts

The simmering crisis of sovereign borrowing has been brought to a head by the events of 2007–9 when governments in the advanced economies had to marshal unprecedented amounts of public funds to bail out bankrupt financial institutions and stabilize international financial markets. States had to step in to socialize hundreds of billions of dollars' worth of losses incurred through years of reckless, leveraged risk taking at many of the world's largest financial institutions. Although very few individuals have been held to account criminally for the crisis, it is difficult to read accounts of the financial sector practices that led to it without a certain sense of horror at the shameful lack of ethics in the sector.[69] This has been further cemented by the onslaught of scandals that have steadily leaked out in the years since: LIBOR-rigging, payment protection insurance mis-selling, mis-selling interest rate derivatives to small businesses, insider trading, rogue trading, money laundering, claims over mortgage foreclosure improprieties, and abuses linked to mortgage-backed credit derivatives. These have occurred in tandem with the broad adoption of the ethos of sustainability and corporate social responsibility across the financial sector,

[67] See O. De Schutter, 'Corporations and Economic, Social, and Cultural Rights', ch. 7 in this book.

[68] See M. Dowell-Jones and D. Kinley, 'Minding the Gap: Finance and Human Rights', 25 *Ethics & International Affairs* (2011), 183–210; and Dowell-Jones, 'Financial Institutions and Human Rights', *supra* note 8.

[69] For accounts of the crisis and the financial sector policies that led to it see: S. Das, *Extreme Money: The Masters of the Universe & The Cult of Risk* (London: Pearson, 2011); L. MacDonald, *A Colossal Failure of Common Sense: The Incredible Inside Story of the Collapse of Lehman Brothers* (London: Ebury Press, 2009); and F. Partnoy, *Infectious Greed: How Deceit and Risk Corrupted the Financial Markets* (London: Profile Books, 2010).

and an endorsement of the UN Guiding Principles. The Guiding Principles make it clear that they:

should be understood as a coherent whole and should be read [...] in terms of their objective of enhancing standards and practices with regard to business and human rights so as to achieve tangible results for affected individuals and communities, and thereby also contributing to a socially sustainable globalization.[70]

Businesses are enjoined to 'avoid infringing on the human rights of others and [...] [to] address adverse human rights impacts with which they are involved' (Principle 11). This involves 'taking adequate measures for their prevention, mitigation and, where appropriate, remediation' (Principle 11, Commentary). They should also make sure that they do 'not undermine States' abilities to meet their own human rights obligations' (Principle 11, Commentary). Where they are involved in adverse human rights impacts, either directly or through their business relationships (Principle 13), they are required to provide access to a remedy (Principles 25–31) the aim of which is 'to counteract or make good any human rights harms that have occurred' (Principle 25, Commentary).

In the context of the austerity crisis, it is also interesting to consider the United Nations Environment Programme 'Statement of Commitment by Financial Institutions on Sustainable Development'. In it, member financial institutions recognize that:

[E]conomic development needs to be compatible with human welfare and a healthy environment. To ignore this is to risk increasing social, environmental and financial costs. We further recognize that sustainable development is the collective responsibility of governments, businesses and individuals. We are committed to working collectively toward common sustainability goals.[71]

Over 200 financial institutions, including major banks, insurers, and investors, are now signatories to this statement.

Although it is difficult to calculate exactly how much the bailouts cost the taxpayer, the Bank for International Settlements has estimated that the various support programmes for the financial sector cost governments in the advanced economies roughly US$6.5 trillion, which is equivalent to 18.8 per cent of GDP in the countries surveyed.[72] In countries with large financial sectors the costs were significantly higher—in the UK the costs and guarantees were equivalent to 44.1 per cent of GDP.[73] In most cases a large part of the money needed to finance the rescues was raised through the emergency issue of sovereign debt, leading in some countries to the most rapid rise in

[70] *Guiding Principles on Business and Human Rights,.supra* note 7, at 6.

[71] UNEP FI, *UNEP Statement of Commitment by Financial Institutions (FI) on Sustainable Development*, available at <http://www.unepfi.org/statements/statement/index.html> (last accessed 18 November 2013).

[72] F. Panetta et al, *An assessment of financial sector rescue programmes* (Basel: Bank for International Settlements, 2009), BIS Working Paper No. 48, July 2009, at 1. As some of the guarantees will not be called upon, it is difficult to calculate exactly how much the crisis did cost the taxpayer, although if the economic cost is factored in it is significant.

[73] F. Panetta et al, *An assessment of financial sector rescue programmes* (Basel: Bank for International Settlements, 2009), BIS Working Paper No. 48, July 2009, at 1.

government debt levels since the Second World War. The combined fiscal deficits of the OECD countries exploded from US$478 billion in 2007 to US$2,856 billion in 2009 and US$2,946 billion in 2010, as states absorbed the combined costs of bailing out financial institutions, various support measures for the financial sector, economic stimulus packages, and increased claims on social welfare systems at a time of rising unemployment and declining tax revenue due to the weakening economy.[74] The sharp jump in government debt levels among countries most affected by the financial crisis is revealing (see Table 2.1):

Table 2.1 Total government debt as a percentage of GDP

Country	2006	2010	Change
France	52%	67%	+15%
Greece	107%	147%	+40%
Iceland	24%	81%	+57%
Ireland	20%	60%	+40%
Luxemburg	1%	12%	+11%
Netherlands	39%	51%	+12%
Norway	12%	26%	+14%
Portugal	67%	87%	+20%
Spain	32%	51%	+19%
UK	43%	85%	+42%
USA	36%	61%	+25%

Source: OECD Statistical Database

This rapid jump in debt precipitated the austerity and sovereign debt crisis we are now enduring, although, as has been described, the underlying problems in state finances would have had to have been addressed at some point in the future in any case. However, these figures and the events of 2007–9 and since create a strong presumption that financial institutions have been involved in adverse human rights impacts which they should seek to mitigate or remedy (Principle 11). It is also difficult to ignore the presumption that they have undermined the ability of affected states to meet their own human rights obligations (Principle 11, Commentary). The attribution of specific responsibility to individual financial institutions is however complicated by the fact that regulatory failings, monetary policy failings, government policy failings, and the failure of supervisors to identify problems in the financial sector before the event all contributed markedly to the denouement.[75] It is clear with hindsight that the human rights impacts of the crisis

[74] H. Blommestein and A. Gok, 'The Surge in Borrowing Needs of OECD Governments: Revised Estimates for 2009 and 2010 Outlook', 2 *OECD Journal: Financial Market Trends* (2009), 1–15, see Figure 1 'Fiscal deficits in G–7 countries and the OECD area', at 2.

[75] See, for example, Financial Crisis Inquiry Commission, *The Financial Crisis Inquiry Report: Final Report of the National Commission on the Causes of the Financial and Economic Crisis in the United States*

were as much a consequence of systemic malfunction that spanned state and private actors as the results of malfeasance within particular institutions. Nonetheless the Guiding Principles are clear that corporations should seek to mitigate any adverse human rights impacts with which they are linked through their business relationships (Principle 13(b)) and that the 'responsibility of business enterprises to respect human rights is distinct from issues of legal liability and enforcement, which remain defined largely by national law provisions in relevant jurisdictions' (Principle 12, Commentary). The responsibility of corporations to respect human rights would therefore seem prima facie to apply where a national legal framework such as financial law and regulation fails to protect them and adverse human rights consequences result through corporate activity which is nonetheless largely compliant with the law.

The issue of how banks and other financial institutions involved in the crisis could mitigate the adverse human rights impacts that have ensued is a difficult one. Seeking a remedy at the level of an individual financial institution would arguably require some type of calculation of how much their actions contributed to the crisis and its economic/austerity consequences. This would be in order to ensure proportionality between impact and remedy, and it is not an exercise that has so far been attempted. It is perhaps one which human rights lawyers would not be equipped to undertake given the complexity of the products and chains of causation involved.[76] Implementing such an approach to mitigation/remedy is also complicated by the fact that where there were the largest jumps in sovereign debt as a consequence of the crisis, (Ireland, Iceland, Greece, UK) the banking sector was extremely strained and demands for restitution would have further weakened these already fragile institutions, potentially making the situation worse. In Ireland's case, the cost of recapitalizing its failing banks was €62 billion, almost half of which was attributable to one bank, Anglo Irish Bank.[77] The Irish banking crisis (and similarly the Spanish banking crisis) was 'almost entirely related to property speculation and the unchecked domestic housing bubble of the preceding ten years'[78] —which the governments did little to check—and in light of the collapse of Ireland's property market, there is little immediate scope for the banks to offer meaningful remedies to the afflicted Irish taxpayers for the sharp cuts in public services and economic slump that they have suffered as a result. It may

(New York: Public Affairs, 2011); UK Financial Services Authority, *The Turner Review: A Regulatory Response to the Global Banking Crisis* (London: FSA, 2011); P. Booth (ed.), *Verdict on the Crash: Causes and Policy Implications* (London: Institute of Economic Affairs, 2009); A. Kling, *Not What They Had in Mind: A History of Policies that Produced the Financial Crisis of 2008* (Arlington: Mercatus Center, George Mason University, September 2009).

[76] Dowell-Jones and Kinley, 'The Monster Under the Bed', *supra* note 8, provides an analysis of the financial crisis from the perspective of the Guiding Principles.

[77] B. Clarke, *Crisis in the Irish Banking System* (Dublin: University College Dublin, 2012), UCD Geary Institute Discussion Paper Series WP2012/03, at 2, available at <http://www.ucd.ie/geary/static/publications/workingpapers/gearywp201203.pdf> (last accessed 18 November 2013).

[78] B. Clarke, *Crisis in the Irish Banking System* (Dublin: University College Dublin, 2012), UCD Geary Institute Discussion Paper Series WP2012/03, at 1, available at <http://www.ucd.ie/geary/static/publications/workingpapers/gearywp201203.pdf> (last accessed 18 November 2013).

also be very difficult to tie a calculation of losses on a bank's portfolio or state support received, to the actual economic/human rights costs of the banking crisis due to the 'multiplier effect', that is, the losses at banks triggered further declines in asset values which directly affected economic confidence and growth which in turn impacted both tax receipts and state capacity to fund human rights, and also employment and individual enjoyment of international human rights. The model of human rights due diligence and provision of an appropriate remedy for human rights harm set out in pillar three of the Guiding Principles appears to assume a direct causal relationship between corporate actor and human rights harm which is difficult to apply to the type of causation evidenced by financial crises.

Where it is feasible, however, one of the most immediate ways for financial institutions to provide a remedy is to repay the bailout money they received from their governments.[79] In some cases this has already happened;[80] in other cases it may take many years (for example with the UK government's stakes in RBS and Lloyds), but in other cases it may be impossible, as with the Icelandic banks that became insolvent, leaving the government to pick up a large bill for restructuring the financial system.[81] This approach only addresses the direct cost of bailouts and asset guarantees, and does not account for the wider socio-economic damage done by the banking crisis and the increased cost to the state of unemployment and economic recession.

Another approach would be to assume collective responsibility of the financial sector broadly for the bailouts and costs incurred by states in saving them from collapse. Collective responsibility on the scale of the financial system as a whole is difficult to dovetail into the type of corporate human rights impacts which the Guiding Principles seemed to have in mind[82] (for example, where a corporation impacts rights in a reasonably direct way through its own culpability and malfeasance) as the understanding of what the 'responsibility to respect' human rights means in practice for universal banking organizations in particular is still largely unclear. It has so far been approached from the basis that it is through funding the activities of front-line companies in other sectors, rather than through their own financial market operations, that banks and investors are implicated in adverse human rights impacts.[83] There is still no real understanding among human rights

[79] In some cases it may be difficult to work out the true cost of asset guarantees, and in other cases financial institutions have benefited indirectly through the effect of government action in stabilizing markets and saving counterparties from insolvency.

[80] The United States government has recouped the money it paid directly to many financial institutions. See: US Government Accountability Office Report to Congressional Committees, *Capital Purchase Program: Revenues Have Exceeded Investments, but Concerns about Outstanding Investments Remain* (Washington DC: Government Accountability Office, March 2012), GAO Report GAO-12-301.

[81] IMF, 'Iceland's Recovery: Can the Lessons Be Applied Elsewhere?', *IMF Survey Magazine*, 24 October 2011, available at <http://www.imf.org/external/pubs/ft/survey/so/2011/SurveyartF.htm> (last accessed 18 November 2013).

[82] Dowell-Jones and Kinley, 'The Monster Under the Bed', *supra* note 8.

[83] Dowell-Jones, 'Financial Institutions and Human Rights', *supra* note 8. The following report provides a good example of this approach to human rights and financial institutions: F. Manta and R. Roca, *Values Added: The Challenge of Integrating Human Rights into the Financial Sector* (Copenhagen: The Danish Institute for Human Rights, 2010).

lawyers of how the operations of financial markets per se influence human rights enjoyment, and what this implies for the human rights responsibilities of the financial sector. Nevertheless, the socialization of financial sector losses and the damage done by the crisis to the economy/socio-economic rights should fall squarely within the provisions of Principle 11, and the Guiding Principles are also clear that 'the closer a business enterprise is to the State, or the more it relies on statutory authority or taxpayer support, the stronger the State's policy rationale becomes for ensuring that the enterprise respects human rights' (Principle 4, Commentary). A key question, then, is what type of remedy would be appropriate at the collective level of the financial sector for their contribution to the austerity problems that have flowed from the crisis.

One way for a remedy to be obtained at a collective level would be in the form of a levy or a financial transaction tax. Both are a type of supplemental tax (over and above corporation tax and other taxes to which financial institutions are generally liable) which is in part used to raise revenue for the government and which can thereby be seen as a (forced) contribution by banks/investors to the cause of deficit reduction and paying off some of the debt that was incurred during the bailouts. The UK government introduced such a levy in 2011 in response to the crisis as a revenue raising measure, although it is set at a miniscule amount.[84] This has raised £1.6 billion from the banking sector in 2012–13 and the rate of the levy will be increased in 2014.[85] Many other European Union countries and the USA have also introduced such levies.[86] A financial transaction tax is a similar way of achieving the same result—imposing a small charge on every financial transaction in order to raise revenue for austerity-hit states. The transaction tax is a controversial idea that was proposed by John Maynard Keynes in the 1930s and by James Tobin in the 1970s as a way to limit volatility in the financial markets,[87] and it is currently one that is being pursued by 11 members of the European Union.[88] The plan is to impose a tax of 0.01 per cent on derivatives trades (over-the-counter and exchange traded) and 0.1 per cent on other financial instruments such as stocks and bonds, with the stated aim of generating revenue for the participating states.[89] The proposal clarifies that:

> The financial sector has played a major role in causing the economic crisis whilst governments and European citizens at large have born the costs. [...] the financial sector at large

[84] HM Revenue & Customs, *Bank Levy*, Tax Information and Impact Note, 23 March 2011, available at <http://www.hmrc.gov.uk/budget2011/tiin6123.pdf> (last accessed 18 November 2013). As of 1 January 2013, the rate is set at 0.0525 per cent for chargeable equity and long-term liabilities, and 0.105 per cent for short-term liabilities, with the aim of raising £2.5 billion per year for the Treasury.

[85] A. Seely, *Taxation of Banking* (London: House of Commons Library, 27 March 2013), UK Parliament Briefing Standard Note SN5251, available at <http://www.parliament.uk/briefing-papers/sn05251.pdf> (last accessed 18 November 2013).

[86] KPMG, *Bank Levies—comparison of certain jurisdictions* (London: KPMG, June 2012).

[87] J. Tobin, 'A Proposal for International Monetary Reform', 4 *Eastern Economic Journal* (1978), 153–159; R. Buckley, 'A Financial Transactions Tax: The One Essential Reform', 47 *Intereconomics: Review of European Economic Policy* (March/April 2012), 99–103.

[88] The participating countries are: Austria, Belgium, Estonia, France, Germany, Greece, Italy, Portugal, Spain, Slovenia, and Slovakia.

[89] European Commission, *Proposal for a Council Directive Implementing Enhanced Cooperation in the Area of Financial Transaction Tax*, European Commission Doc. COM/2013/71, 14 February 2013.

has experienced high profitability over the last two decades which could be partially the result of an (implicit or explicit) safety net provided by governments.[90]

The proposal estimates that the tax could raise €30–35 billion per year in revenue for the participating countries.[91]

The proposal is highly controversial, and is already the subject of a legal challenge by the UK because of its extraterritorial dimension.[92] It has also been the subject of intense lobbying and doom-laden scenarios painted by the financial sector. One study has estimated that the tax would add £3.95 billion a year to the cost of issuing UK sovereign debt.[93] The International Banking Federation has warned that:

> Since capital is highly mobile, we expect financial instruments issued in FTT jurisdictions, including government debt securities, to be quickly and negatively impacted as the tax gets factored in to the purchase decision. Governments which already find it difficult to sell their debt will find it even more difficult in future.[94]

The ordinary citizens of Europe, it is warned, will ultimately bear the cost of the tax. In the face of such pressure, including a warning from the Governor of the French central bank that the tax may 'destroy' the French banking industry and damage public finances, the proposals are now being watered down.[95] The tax on derivatives may be excluded entirely, and the tax on bond transactions may not be introduced until 2016. Given the current debt situation of many European countries, it seems likely that many governments are understandably nervous that the tax may increase their cost of borrowing or make it more difficult for them to borrow from the financial markets at all, and the fact that they are prepared to backtrack on this is testament to the lobbying power of the financial sector, and the vulnerability which the sovereign debt situation exposes governments to. The tax may therefore only raise a fraction of the initial estimate and may only cover a fraction of daily financial transactions.

The fact that the tax and bank levy have been set at such miniscule amounts is in itself somewhat surprising given the damage done by the crisis, but it is testament to the intense lobbying power of financial institutions and the central place of financial markets in our economic structures. Financial markets not only provide

[90] European Commission, *Proposal for a Council Directive Implementing Enhanced Cooperation in the Area of Financial Transaction Tax*, European Commission Doc. COM/2013/71, 14 February 2013, 4.

[91] European Commission, *Proposal for a Council Directive Implementing Enhanced Cooperation in the Area of Financial Transaction Tax*, European Commission Doc. COM/2013/71, 14 February 2013, 14.

[92] 'Financial transactions tax: UK launches legal challenge', *BBC*, 20 April 2013, available at <http://www.bbc.co.uk/news/business-22227019> (last accessed 18 November 2013).

[93] London Economics, *The Impact of a Financial Transaction Tax on Corporate and Sovereign Debt* (London: City of London, April 2013), at 15.

[94] Letter from Mrs Sally J. Scutt, Managing Director, International Banking Federation to Mr. Michael Noonan, President of the ECOFIN Council, 23 April 2013, available at <http://www.ibfed.org/news/ibfed-comments-on-the-ecs-proposal-for-a-cd-implementing-enhanced-cooperati> (last accessed 18 November 2013).

[95] P. Aldrick, 'Europe rows bank on FTT plans', *Daily Telegraph* (London, 30 May 2013).

large amounts of funding to states by buying their sovereign bonds, they are also major employers and contributors of direct taxes to the public purse and supporters of business activity through lending. States are therefore very cautious about threats from financial institutions to take their business to more favourable jurisdictions, even despite the wreckage of the financial crisis. The power differential between financial markets and the human rights regime is staggering, and given debates around the financial transaction tax it would seem difficult to believe that this is going to change in the near future despite the widespread endorsement of the Guiding Principles by the financial sector.

From a purely human rights point of view, however, it may appear that such levies and taxes are self-evidently a good thing as they provide a straightforward way of obtaining some type of remedy from the financial sector for the harm done by the financial crisis, bailouts, and ensuing austerity crisis. Although the initial proposals were strongly supported by leading economists,[96] there are perhaps two key points that are worth noting here in relation to human rights and the austerity/sovereign debt crisis. First, the revenue estimates are rather small when compared to the scale of the crisis in public finances. An extra £1.6 billion in the UK or €30 billion spread across 11 countries is in no way a panacea to Europe's debt problems and it does not come close to meeting the funding needs of these governments. Although it is undoubtedly desirable that the financial sector contributes towards remedying the social damage done by the crisis, taxing the financial sector does not provide an easy answer to the underlying problem of the affordability of Europe's welfare states. This is the fundamental problem that needs to be addressed. It is also possible (indeed, likely) that the financial sector will find a way to pass on the cost of the tax to consumers and/or bank shareholders, many of whom are pension funds.

Second, there has to be a very real concern that the tax will serve to further magnify, complicate, and obfuscate risk in the financial markets as new instruments and trading strategies are implemented to avoid it. It could also potentially push more financial activity into unregulated jurisdictions beyond the reach of the tax. When James Tobin first proposed his tax on currency transactions, world markets were very different and his overriding concern was volatility in newly liberalized currency markets after the collapse of the gold standard. Trading was done over the phone and used reasonably straightforward financial instruments. Volumes of trading were also tiny by today's standards. Today's financial markets are a world away from this and thanks to the massive growth of both derivatives markets and computerized trading, it is commonplace for trading strategies to be devised specifically to exploit regulatory loopholes or to avoid rules. Indeed, the financial sector has a solid history of regulatory avoidance and in particular of using

[96] In 2011, 1,000 leading economists including Jeffrey Sachs wrote to the G20 calling for such a tax in order to reduce speculation and raise revenue to help the world's poor. See 'Robin Hood tax: 1,000 economist urge G20 to accept Tobin tax', *The Guardian*, 13 April 2011, available at <http://www.theguardian.com/business/2011/apr/13/robin-hood-tax-economists-letter> (last accessed 18 November 2013).

complex derivatives-based trading strategies to avoid regulatory or legal rules. This was not only a feature of the subprime crisis but dates back to the late 1980s when derivatives were in their infancy and it was one of the key incentives for the adoption of derivatives-based trading strategies by major dealers and corporations.[97] In today's financial markets, the transaction tax will create an incentive for market participants to find ways to gain exposure to financial instruments that are subject to the tax without becoming liable for it. What this will mean is that new or existing forms of derivatives will be the most likely way of doing this, particularly if derivatives trades are excluded from the tax, which will complicate further the task of monitoring and controlling risk in the financial markets. The UK has imposed a tax ('stamp duty') on shares traded on the London Stock Exchange for some years now, and while it does not appear to have curtailed trading volume, it has led to the creation and use of a range of derivatives which avoid the tax (for example, covered warrants and contracts for difference). Imposing a tax on European shares or bonds may well result in more trading in derivatives linked to these instruments. More derivatives in the world (a likely outcome of the tax) or new forms of derivatives where the risks are even more uncertain can surely not be considered to be a good thing in light of the financial crisis, and it has important consequences for human rights. The excessive trading of derivatives, particularly that which is 'over-the-counter' (that is, negotiated privately between financial institutions) and so difficult to monitor, increases the level of risk in financial markets. Increased systemic risk is a particular concern because market integration means that financial disruption is now inevitably global, with enormous human rights consequences which are extremely difficult to contain. The immediate benefits to human rights of the extra revenue may well be overshadowed in the long run by the enhanced risks of global market meltdown from the new trading strategies that will evolve.

In practice, then, how to uphold the principle of the responsibility to respect human rights and to obtain a remedy from the financial sector for their part in the genesis of the current austerity crisis is not straightforward and more work in required on this. As the Euro area crisis has made clear, a weakened banking sector means a weakened economy and therefore further claims on the state. Requiring banks then to make large payments to the state to compensate past failings may prove counterproductive as it may weaken them further. It may also create unanticipated risks for human rights, by for example exacerbating systemic risk.

B. Financial markets and the debt crisis

Private financial institutions such as banks also have a key role to play in the current austerity crisis as major holders and traders of government debt. The fact that the industrialized states have such large ongoing funding requirements (that is, they are relying on demand from private investors for their bonds for them to be

[97] See Partnoy, *Infectious Greed, supra* note 69, for an account.

able to continue funding the existing level of public services) means that financial institutions now have an important role in funding the public sector. This dependency means that states and human rights enjoyment are heavily exposed to the risks of disruption in the bond markets and financial contagion—as we have clearly seen in the Euro area. This can heavily influence economic policy decisions and political priorities, as well as possibilities for rights protection because states have to take account of potential financial market reactions. If financial institutions decide that policy is heading the wrong way, they can desert the market for that country's debt and/or short it which can precipitate problems. The meltdowns in Greece, Spain, Portugal, and Ireland highlight what happens to heavily indebted states and the rights of their citizens when investors reassess their willingness to purchase their bonds and demand higher interest rates for doing so because of increased risk or a chance of default. The fact that the austerity crisis in France, Japan, the UK, and the USA has not so far been worse is largely because these states can continue to sell bonds to investors at low interest rates, although arguably, given how severe the debt problems of these countries now are, it would be beneficial in the long run if they were forced to face up to their looming insolvency.

This dependency of states on the financial markets opens them up to a range of significant risks, including the risk of a currency collapse[98] and/or a bond market crisis, a sharp rise in the interest rates they need to pay to entice investors to buy their bonds, as well as the risk of another broad-based global financial crisis on the scale of 2008–9 (or all of these at the same time).[99] In the short term they are vulnerable to 'funding risk' and 'roll-over risk'—basically the continued functioning of public services depends on the willingness and ability of international investors to purchase each new issue of sovereign bonds. Without this there is a risk that a country could fail to pay its bills. As the US Treasury commented on the constitutional debt ceiling in 2011:

> If Congress fails to increase the debt limit [to allow the US Government to continue to borrow], the government would default on its legal obligations—an event unprecedented in American history. This would cause investors here and around the world to doubt, for the first time, whether the United States will meet its commitments. That would precipitate a self-inflicted financial crisis potentially more severe than the one from which we are now recovering.[100]

Unravelling the implications of this symbiotic dependency of states and the human rights they provide, and the human rights responsibilities of financial

[98] A currency devaluation sparked by the issuance of huge amounts of government debt can have significant human rights consequences, including rising inflation and an increasing cost of imported goods like food and fuel. It can also affect human rights in trading partner countries—for example if factory workers are laid off because the devalued currency has increased the cost of their products and thereby reduced demand for them.

[99] Bain Capital Macro Trends Group, *A World Awash in Money: Capital Trends Through 2020* (Boston: Bain & Company, 2012), available at <http://www.bain.com/Images/BAIN_REPORT_A_world_awash_in_money.pdf> (last accessed 18 November 2013).

[100] US Department of the Treasury, *Debt Limit: Myth v Fact* (Washington DC: Dept. of Treasury, May 2011) at 1, available at <http://www.treasury.gov/initiatives/Documents/Debt%20Limit%20Myth%20v%20Fact%20FINAL.pdf> (last accessed 18 November 2013).

market participants who purchase these bonds, is no easy task. It is unrealistic to expect that financial institutions should buy sovereign bonds or avoid selling them on human rights grounds in order to assist a sovereign that is coming under severe pressure. Such an approach would run the risk that it could generate solvency problems in the banking sector, as sovereign and financial sector solvency become intertwined. This in itself would have far-reaching negative consequences for human rights. As George Soros has explained in relation to the Euro crisis:

> Only at the end of 2009, when the extent of the Greek deficit was revealed, did the financial markets realize that a member country [of the Euro] could actually default. But then the markets raised the risk premiums on the weaker countries with a vengeance. This rendered commercial banks whose balance sheets were loaded with those bonds potentially insolvent and that created both a sovereign debt and a banking crisis. The two are linked together like Siamese twins.[101]

The current austerity crisis in Europe already co-exists with a weakened banking sector that continues to be hampered by distressed assets such as commercial and residential property loans, equity, and bond holdings relating to the weakened Euro area economy. This is at a time when financial regulations enacted in response to the crisis are mandating that they raise more capital in order to make them safer and, hopefully, prevent a repeat of 2007–9. This creates a symbiotic dynamic between the state, the economy and the banking sector which can magnify the state's funding problems. This makes it difficult to interpret the responsibility to respect human rights pragmatically for financial institutions:

> [I]f domestic financial institutions such as banks hold a significant share of outstanding sovereign debt, restructuring this debt would substantially impair the capital base of the domestic banking system. In many cases, this would necessitate a public recapitalization of domestic banks, raising sovereign debt levels. Furthermore, the economy could be weakened by the banking system coming under distress. The total economic cost could thus far exceed the benefit of a reduction of [the] nominal value of debt.[102]

A banking crisis thus became a sovereign debt crisis, which in turn has fed through to another simmering banking crisis.

In the context of the Euro area it is worth considering that the banking sectors of France, Germany, the UK, and the Netherlands are heavily exposed to the sovereign debt of the crisis-hit southern European countries. At the end of 2011 these exposures stood at:

- France—US$541 billion (equivalent to 19.5 per cent of its GDP)
- Germany—US$419 billion (equivalent to 11.7 per cent of its GDP)
- UK—US$301 billion (equivalent to12.5 per cent of its GDP)

[101] G. Soros, 'How to Save the European Union from the Euro Crisis', Remarks delivered at the Center for Financial Studies, Goethe University, Germany, 9 April 2013, available at <http://www.georgesoros.com/interviews-speeches/entry/how_to_save_the_european_union_from_the_euro_crisis> (last accessed 18 November 2013).

[102] H. Tran, 'The Role of Markets in Sovereign Debt Crisis Detection, Prevention and Resolution', *supra* note 21, at 7–8.

- The Netherlands—US$124 billion (equivalent to 14.7 per cent of its GDP)[103]

Underlying the bailouts of the southern European countries, therefore, was a quiet banking crisis in the countries contributing to the rescue programmes, in particular France and Germany.

Where or how human rights can be upheld in this situation is a tricky question as it is important fiscally and for human rights to bring state deficits and debts under control because they cannot be funded indefinitely from the financial markets. This is particularly the case where the banking sector is already weakened as this creates a vicious circle between the solvency of financial institutions and states. Understanding what the Guiding Principles require of banks in this situation is unclear: potentially banks could refuse to buy the bonds of a distressed country as it would weaken their own solvency and so undermine their capacity to fulfil their human rights responsibilities. Equally where banks already hold the bonds of a distressed country this could also impair their solvency but if they refused to sell them for fear of destabilizing the country further and contributing to adverse human rights impacts, it could end up having a detrimental impact on their savers/investors or customers (many financial assets are held by pension funds, ordinary investors, and insurers). This would also weaken their asset base and so undermine their ability to engage in further financial activity so weakening the economy and also reducing liquidity in the market (which can create further risks). Where this strategy is pursued collectively as a means of respecting human rights, it could ultimately lead to the risks of financial crisis and market contagion, which can have devastating consequences for global human rights enjoyment. Despite the enormous impacts that the Euro area crisis has demonstrably had on peoples' rights, it is difficult to see immediately what financial institutions should have done in order to honour their responsibility to respect human rights and this is certainly an area that merits dedicated research.

7. Reconciling Rights and Austerity

So what scope, if any, is there for international human rights law to play a greater, more visible role in this austerity crisis? As this chapter has outlined, the current crisis is multifaceted and the long-term crisis of funding the public sector is not going to be resolved in the near future. Whether or how human rights law could be implemented in the context of austerity and sovereign debt crises raises important theoretical and practical issues in the protection of economic, social, and cultural rights.

[103] Swedbank, *The Euro Area Crisis: 99 Q&A* (Stockholm: Swedbank, 29 June 2012), at 17, available at <http://www.swedbank.lv/files/analitiskie_materiali/The_Euro_Area_%20Crises_99_Q&A_29.06.2012.pdf> (last accessed 18 November 2013). The figures relate to exposures to the sovereign debt of Greece, Ireland, Italy, Portugal, and Spain.

A longstanding principle of the ICESCR is the expectation that states will take extra steps to protect these rights at times of crisis:

> [I]t is in periods of extreme hardship, whether of an economic or political nature, that human rights guarantees assume their greatest relevance. It is precisely at a time when governments and their experts are ready to jettison [...] concern for individual well-being in the interest of an abstraction such as 'the war against inflation' or 'increased productivity' or 'improved terms of trade' that the economic rights recognized in the Covenant assume their real importance.[104]

This principle of international law, which was affirmed by the Committee on Economic, Social and Cultural Rights in its General Comment No. 3,[105] does not appear to have been visibly used to guide policy during the financial crisis of 2007–9 and the ensuing sovereign debt crisis. Whatever objectives policymakers are pursuing, one of the key difficulties of implementing this principle in the context of recession and austerity is that human rights law cannot act as a reference point for policy without a fuller development of how rights can be interpreted in the context of very difficult economic conditions and multiple claims upon the state for support. To reconcile rights and austerity, further research is needed which examines the priorities for rights protection in the context of the crisis of the modern welfare state and the ageing of the population.

Nevertheless, the concept that a certain basic minimum level of social and economic rights enjoyment should be guaranteed at times of crisis is in practice a sound principle of economic and social policy, and it could be used as a starting point for integrating human rights law into economic policy debate. As the European Parliament has written in relation to the impact of the crisis on the young:

> Unemployment, underemployment, socio-economic inequalities, poverty and exclusion disproportionally affect the young generation, whose autonomy, dignity, well-being and access to rights are rapidly eroding. As a result, Europe risks not only producing a 'lost generation' of disillusioned young people, but also undermining its political stability and social cohesion, justice and peace, as well as its long-term competitiveness and development prospects in the global context.[106]

Human rights guarantees can provide certainty to people that a certain basic level of income and services will be observed, which psychologically helps to underpin economic activity. Confidence is an important factor in economic activity, since when people have a basic level of security they will feel able to spend disposable income and plan for the future, which helps underpin economic activity. People require a certain platform of essential goods and services in order to be able to participate

[104] P. Alston and G. Quinn, 'The Nature and Scope of States Parties Obligations under the International Covenant on Economic, Social and Cultural Rights', 9 *Human Rights Quarterly* (1987), 156–229, 164.

[105] Committee on Economic, Social and Cultural Rights, General Comment No. 3, *supra* note 22, para. 12.

[106] European Parliament Committee on Social Affairs, Health and Sustainable Development, *The young generation sacrificed: social, economic and political implications of the financial crisis*, E.P. Doc. 12951, 8 June 2012, available at <http://assembly.coe.int/ASP/Doc/XrefViewHTML.asp?FileId=18739&Language=EN> (last accessed 18 November 2013).

in economic life. This includes those rights that are enshrined in the International Covenant on Economic, Social and Cultural Rights: the right to work, to just and fair conditions of labour, to social security, to food, shelter, to healthcare and education, and to an adequate standard of living. Austerity policies that deprive citizens of even basic levels of these rights can be counterproductive even from an economic perspective because they rob the economy of the floor of dynamism it needs to function. Consumer demand can contract sharply when austerity bites and people are extremely fearful for the future and expect further cuts in services or income guarantees. This can lead to a negative spiral which drags the economy and state finances down even further. This concept is well understood in economics and is generally discussed under the rubric of 'automatic stabilizers', which recognizes the important role that income guarantees play in stabilizing crisis-hit economies.[107] Although this approach conceptually overlaps with the notion of the minimum core content of Covenant rights, the challenge of using the minimum core content as a reference point is the fact that this concept lacks quantitative and contextual specificity. Human rights, if properly framed in the lexicon of economics, could provide a vital part of the toolkit of economic analysis and decision-making in navigating the challenge of austerity. Key to this, however, will be the clarification of practical, quantified boundaries on what parts of current services fall within human rights law and the minimum core content, and what falls outside.

The Greek debt situation provides an illustration of this dynamic. Under the second Greek debt deal of February/March 2012, a debt exchange was agreed whereby bondholders would swap outstanding bonds for new ones with longer maturities (giving Greece much longer to repay) and would also accept a 53.5 per cent reduction in the value of the debt. This equated to a €107 billion write-off (or 'haircut' in financial jargon) in the amount of debt that Greece owed. As part of the deal, Greece agreed to implement a programme of structural reforms which was intended to boost economic growth, which it was assumed would help Greece raise the revenue it needed to meet its debt repayments. In the event, the government failed to implement in full the agreed reforms in the face of mass social protests in Greece at the austerity measures that the deal mandated, and the second tranche of bailout funds was delayed by official creditors. The Greek economy then collapsed even further, with its debt-to-GDP ratio actually increasing to 160 per cent. This ratio was deemed by official creditors to be unsustainable—that is, that it was too high for Greece to be able to generate the revenue needed to meet the repayments on the debt.[108] A significant problem with the bailout conditions was that the sharp cuts to government services, pensions, employment, and spending had a markedly negative impact on standards of living, and also created a realistic expectation of further sharp declines in incomes and state services. This resulted in spending contracting sharply, which

[107] M. Dolls, C. Fuest, and A. Peichl, *Automatic Stabilizers and Economic Crisis: US v Europe*, National Bureau of Economic Research, Working Paper 16275 (August 2010).

[108] Tran, 'The Role of Markets', *supra* note 21, at 6.

significantly undermined economic activity.[109] The conditions of the bailout were largely set by economists, central bankers, and financiers who were largely guided by economic statistics rather than an understanding of human beings as the basic actors in any economic drama.

One way to address this situation would have been for human rights negotiators to have been involved in the debt rescheduling talks and a baseline of human rights protections agreed with all creditors and with Greece—that is, 'these are the essential services/public goods that have to be protected under international human rights law'. Any official assistance and/or debt rescheduling would then have had to commit to ring-fencing this spending before any other concessions or austerity measures contingent upon debt forgiveness were agreed. This would have to be done by reference to the fiscal and economic situation in Greece and so be a realistic interpolation of human rights standards into a complicated and vulnerable economic and financial situation. However, if properly implemented it could help protect rights, give a basic level of assurance to the Greek people, and put a stable floor of demand under the Greek economy, which could potentially have contributed enormously to stabilizing the situation. It would thus have worked to the advantage of human rights protection but also have been in the interests of creditors and the countries and institutions financing the bailout. Given that the member countries of the EU are all party to a number of human rights instruments, it is surprising that human rights standards played no part in the bailout package. Human rights, if applied creatively, could have been a positive force in the attempts to resolve the Greek crisis.

The Council of Europe's Committee on Social Affairs, Health and Sustainable Development has recognized the human cost of austerity:

> The worst employment situation in decades has caused a real social and economic trauma that threatens society's long-term development. The financial and economic crisis is turning into a social crisis. The boom of temporary contract workers, for example, is creating a generation of young people in precarious employment with few social guarantees [...] the rise of precariousness leads to persistent under-employment, social and financial insecurity as well as a more alienated social framework.[110]

There is now active debate among economists on these points as there is increasing recognition that austerity can be counterproductive because it leads to economic stagnation.[111] In order for human rights to contribute actively to these debates,

[109] See the details of the financial assistance programme to Greece and review reports available at the European Union website, <http://ec.europa.eu/economy_finance/assistance_eu_ms/greek_loan_facility> (last accessed 18 November 2013).

[110] Council of Europe Committee on Social Affairs, Health and Sustainable Development, *The Young Generation Sacrificed, supra* note 106, at para. 11.

[111] The debate centred on calculations in a paper by Carmen Reinhart and Kenneth Rogoff which estimated the negative effect on economic growth of high debt levels. The accuracy of the calculations was challenged, which has led to a wide discussion on whether austerity is really the best policy for tackling high growth rates. See C. Reinhart and K. Rogoff, *Growth in a Time of Debt*, NBER Working Paper no. 15639, January 2010. For an overview of the debate see J. Cassidy, 'The Reinhart and Rogoff Controversy: A Summing Up', *The New Yorker* (New York, 29 April 2013), available at <http://www.newyorker.com/online/blogs/johncassidy/2013/04/the-rogoff-and-reinhart-controversy-a-summing-up.html> (last accessed 18 November 2013).

human rights lawyers need to demonstrate an understanding of the seriousness of the current fiscal challenges that advanced economies face, and be able to make a reasoned argument within those constraints as to why rights should be supported and how this can contribute to stabilizing the debt situation. This needs to be a quantitative and costed agenda in the context of today's crisis, rather than appeals to broad principle. There also needs to be far greater clarity as to what socio-economic rights are entitlements to and whose rights should take priority in a crisis which links broadly phrased normative principles to economic reality. There is little point in arguing generally for the guarantee of existing levels of public services on the basis of international human rights law when these services are fiscally unsustainable. In order to help states navigate austerity there needs to be clarity as to what services it is essential to protect from a human rights point of view.

In evaluating the sustainability of a particular level of rights provision, it is also important to understand the broader economic context of rights enjoyment. States do not provide rights in isolation, and the market/private economic actors who play a supporting role in fulfilling the state's human rights obligations can have a key influence on whether policy decisions turn out to be sustainable. Financial institutions and financial markets in particular are important non-state actors in the austerity crisis. They are now subject to a responsibility to respect human rights, and to seek to mitigate or remedy any adverse human rights relationships that they are involved in through their business relationships. So far the question as to whether or how this applies to their activities in the sovereign bond markets has barely been asked, but it is certainly an issue that requires dedicated scrutiny.

8. Conclusion

The current sovereign debt crisis and wave of austerity measures in the Euro area and the advanced economies has to be seen in its longer-term perspective. It is not simply a crisis that has come about as a direct consequence of the financial crisis of 2007–9 and that would not have happened otherwise. Rather it is a crisis that stems from the steady expansion of the state into public services that can be linked to human rights such as education, healthcare, and social welfare, coupled with the demands of an ageing population and the failure to fund existing services on a fully sustainable basis. The financial crisis of 2007–9 has brought this simmering crisis of advanced welfare states to a head and is forcing states to face up to the reality that they cannot indefinitely fund ever-growing claims on the state through the bond markets.

The challenge that this situation raises for human rights is twofold. On the one hand, the battle for austerity across the industrialized countries raises key conceptual issues around the boundaries of internationally protected human rights, which are still unclear despite over 30 years of dedicated scholarship. On the other hand, the symbiotic role of private financial institutions and financial markets in funding public finances through bond purchases raises the question of what human rights responsibilities this entails for them under the reasonably new UN Guiding Principles on Business and Human Rights. There are no clear answers to these questions; indeed, so far the questions themselves have not been fully defined because human rights have only been applied to a very narrow range of activities within financial institutions. Issues related to bond trading, derivatives trading linked to the global bond markets, and financial stability/financial crisis issues are still largely unexplored.

The issues that are central to Europe's crisis of austerity, and the potential reach of the crisis beyond the borders of the Euro area should financial markets succumb to panic and contagion, can easily be cast in human rights terms as issues of the availability of work, standard of living, state provision of services like education, training, healthcare, and social security, and the protection of the rights of groups like the young and elderly who have seen their quality of living markedly impacted by the ongoing crisis. It is therefore disappointing how notably absent human rights bodies have been in the unfolding crisis, but it is difficult to sustain the argument that states are cutting services purely for ideological reasons, as some human rights lawyers have suggested.[112] The aspirations of human rights need to be firmly matched to fiscal reality in order for human rights law to make a meaningful contribution to resolving these budgetary challenges. It is easy to talk in the abstract about human rights at the level of theory or legal principle, but this does not help governments navigate today's fiscal challenges in a way that is conducive to the fulfilment of their international human rights obligations and in compliance with international law. After all, as the Universal Declaration points out, all human beings are entitled to an international order in which their human rights can be fully realized.[113] An international economy where leading economic states are severely indebted creates long-range risks not only for the citizens of those countries (including those as yet unborn), but for people around the world who are all now interlinked, thanks to globalization.

[112] P. O'Connell, 'Let Them Eat Cake: Socio-Economic Rights in an Age of Austerity', in A. Nolan, R. O'Connell, and C. Harvey (eds.), *Human Rights and Public Finance: Budgets and the Promotion of Economic and Social Rights* (Oxford: Hart Publishing, 2013), 3.

[113] Universal Declaration of Human Rights, GA Res. 217A(III) of 10 December 1948, art. 28.

3

Economic and Social Rights in the 'Great Recession'

Towards a Human Rights-Centred Economic Policy in Times of Crisis

Sally-Anne Way, Nicholas Lusiani, and Ignacio Saiz

1. Introduction

The enduring global economic crisis, the deepest since the Great Depression, is arguably one of the greatest contemporary challenges facing the realization and implementation of economic and social rights worldwide. What first erupted as a credit crisis in the global financial system in 2007 quickly spread through the arteries of the global economy. While different countries and regions have been affected in different ways, the successive waves of the Great Recession, and the austerity policies that have been implemented across many countries in its wake has led to a 'Great Regression' in human rights, particularly in relation to economic and social rights. Across the world, persistent mass unemployment, rising levels of hunger and homelessness, deprivations in access to adequate healthcare and education, greater income inequality, and significant cuts in social protection have posed a major setback to the fulfilment of economic and social rights, while the obligation of states to safeguard these rights in responding to the crisis has been largely ignored by policymakers.

This chapter argues that human rights provide a normative framework that should guide economic policy in times of crisis, and it explores how this framework can be more effectively brought to bear in the current context. First, we examine the evidence of the impacts on economic and social rights of the successive waves of financial and economic crisis. Second, we examine the key human rights principles and standards most relevant for guiding economic policymaking in this context. We then explore how these standards and principles can be made operational as governments design their crisis mitigation and economic recovery policies. This is followed by a discussion on some of the challenges of embedding human rights in policy responses to the crisis, as well as in economic policy more broadly. We conclude the chapter by reflecting on the crisis as a historic opportunity to re-envision the role of the state in the economy, not simply to facilitate economic growth, but to guarantee economic and social rights for all. This chapter aims to contribute to the emerging and rich scholarship on the human rights implications of the economic crisis and on the application of human rights standards to the design, implementation, monitoring, and review of economic policy more generally.[1]

2. The Global Economic Crisis as an Economic and Social Rights Crisis

The impacts of the global economic crisis on human rights came in two successive waves: first, from the generalized deterioration in the global economy; and second, through the austerity measures imposed in many countries in the aftermath of the crisis, including deep cuts in social spending.[2]

The first wave of impacts from 2008–10 put directly at risk a number of rights enshrined in the International Covenant on Economic, Social and Cultural Rights (ICESCR), as well as other core international human rights treaties. Mass unemployment and underemployment has jeopardized the right to work. Twenty-seven million jobs were estimated to have been officially lost due to the crisis by 2012,[3] with disproportionate effects on women, migrants, minorities, people with disabilities, and youth.[4] Rights at work have also been undermined. Global wage growth shrunk by at least half and many countries have experienced an increase in casual, non-formal, and more precarious forms of employment. Fifty million more people have entered the ranks of the 'working poor' and workers in vulnerable employment, especially women, have become more prone to labour rights abuses.[5] The economic crisis—in

[1] See for example R. Balakrishnan and D. Elson (eds.), *Economic Policy and Human Rights* (New York: Zed Books, 2012); I. Saiz 'Rights in Recession? Challenges for Economic and Social Rights Enforcement in Times of Crisis', 1 *Journal of Human Rights Practice* (2009), 277–293; International Council on Human Rights Policy and Realizing Rights, 'Human Rights in the Global Economy: Report from a Colloquium' (2010), available at <http://www.ichrp.org/files/documents/185/210_human_rights_global_economy_colloquium_report.pdf> (last accessed 11 November 2013). Report of the United Nations High Commissioner for Human Rights on the impact of austerity measures on economic, social, and cultural rights (7 May 2013), UN Doc. E/2013/51.

[2] For the purposes of this chapter, the global economic crisis refers to the prolonged downturn in much of the global economy which followed the near-collapse of the global financial system in 2007 and 2008, and which resulted in enduring recession, if not depression, and a rapid decrease in levels of employment, trade, investment, consumption, and/or other key economic indicators. See I. Ortiz and M. Cummins, 'Age of Austerity: A Review of Public Expenditures and Adjustment Measures in 181 Countries', Initiative for Policy Dialogue and the South Centre, Working Paper (May 2013).

[3] International Labour Organization (ILO), *Global Employment Trends 2012: Preventing a deeper job crisis* (Geneva: ILO, 2012), 31.

[4] International Labour Organization (ILO), *Global Employment Trends 2012. Preventing a deeper job crisis* (Geneva: ILO, 2012), 36. The global youth unemployment rate on the aggregate rose from 11.8 per cent in 2007 to 12.7 per cent in 2009, the largest increase on record, with at least 1.7 million fewer youth in the labour market than expected pre-crisis. This trend is on evidence in low-income, middle-income, but especially higher-income countries.

[5] International Labour Organization (ILO), *Global Employment Trends 2012. Preventing a deeper job crisis* (Geneva: ILO, 2012), 41–44.

concert with the food and fuel crises—has had severe impacts on the right to an adequate standard of living, forcing at least 64 million people into extreme poverty by 2009, with incomes insufficient to feed their families and to access basic services.[6] The right to housing has been compromised by wide-scale home repossessions and increased homelessness.[7] The right to education has also been affected—with a particular impact on girls in developing countries, where it has been estimated that at least 350,000 children, most of them girls, would drop out of school or fail to complete their basic primary education as a result of the initial global economic downturn.[8] Food price rises, stemming partly from financial speculation in commodity markets, has affected enjoyment of the right to food—particularly in low- and middle-income countries where people spend much larger proportions of their income on food.[9] The number of people suffering from hunger and undernourishment around the world rose to over a billion in 2009, the highest on record.[10] By 2010, up to 1.2 million more children were expected to die before reaching the age of five as a direct result of the economic crisis.[11] Serious food riots broke out in 2008 in countries including Mexico, Haiti, Bangladesh, Indonesia, Senegal, Egypt, and Cameroon.[12] This and other forms of social unrest in response to the crisis have been repressed in many countries putting intense pressure on civil and political rights.[13] Xenophobia and discrimination against migrants and other marginalized groups have also been widely reported in this context, fuelled by perceived competition over jobs and access to public services, and manipulated by politicians eager to find convenient scapegoats on which to deflect public outrage.[14]

The second wave of human rights impacts between 2010 and 2012 stem from deliberate policy responses to the crisis. Initial government responses were unprecedented in terms of the scale of public intervention in markets. Government authorities, especially in the countries where the credit crisis struck hardest, mounted a massive and globally coordinated effort to prevent systemic financial meltdown, injecting trillions of dollars into the banking system. Simultaneously,

[6] World Bank, *The MDGs After the Crisis: Global Monitoring Report 2010* (Washington: World Bank, 2010).

[7] Report of the UN Special Rapporteur on the Right to Adequate Housing, Raquel Rolnik, UN Doc. A/HRC/10/7 (4 February 2009).

[8] World Bank, *MDGs After the Crisis, supra* note 6.

[9] See C. Golay, 'The Food Crisis and Food Security: Towards a New World Food Order?', 1 *International Development Policy* (2010), 215–232.

[10] See Food and Agriculture Organization (FAO), *The State of Food Insecurity in the World 2009: Economic crises: impacts and lessons learned* (Rome: FAO, 2009). See also FAO, *The State of Food Insecurity in the World 2011: How does international price volatility affect domestic economies and food security?* (Rome: FAO, 2011), which analyses why rural workers and peasant farmers around the world rarely benefit from higher food prices but are instead especially vulnerable to price hikes.

[11] World Bank, *MDGs After the Crisis, supra* note 6.

[12] Amnesty International (AI), *Amnesty International Annual Report 2009: The State of the World's Human Rights* (London: AI, 2009).

[13] AI, 'Briefing Note: Human Rights and the Economic Crisis' (January 2012), available at <http://www.amnesty.org/en/library/info/POL30/001/2012/en> (last accessed 11 November 2013).

[14] Council of Europe Human Rights Commissioner, Report on Visit to Greece (16 April 2013), 'Europe must combat racist extremism and uphold human rights', Human Rights Comment, 13 May 2013.

many governments engaged in expansive, counter-cyclical fiscal and monetary stimulus measures to mitigate the social consequences of the crisis and to spur demand and economic growth so as to prevent a full-blown global depression. These stimulus measures were largest in developed countries, but many developing countries also adopted significant counter-cyclical fiscal measures in this period.[15] However, the massive resources devoted to saving the financial sector far exceeded the resources devoted to fiscal stimulus or social protection programmes. Worldwide, the financial sector in 2010 reportedly received about US$20 trillion (30 per cent of global GDP) in public support, while public funding for stimulus packages totalled only US$2.6 trillion (4.3 per cent of global GDP).[16] In addition, just as these steps began to result in a muted economic recovery, albeit largely jobless and wageless,[17] by 2009 and 2010, many governments shifted away from fiscal stimulus measures towards implementing fiscal austerity policies to cut down the government debt incurred from lost tax revenue and from injecting liquidity into the financial system.[18]

These austerity measures have typically consisted of severe cut backs in public social expenditures, reductions in social protection programs including pension schemes, labour reforms restricting workers' rights protections in the name of boosting competitiveness, and selective tax increases as well as the privatization of public services as a primary means of increased revenue generation.[19]

Such policies began to be implemented in 2010 in a swathe of European countries at the heart of the regional sovereign debt crisis, usually at the behest of the European Union, International Monetary Fund, and European Central Bank. Ireland, for example, has made drastic cuts in social expenditures in health, education, and housing in order to plug the deficit created largely by the public rescue of three major Irish banks from collapse.[20] The government also chose to reduce unemployment support just when it was needed most, with a disproportionately harsh

[15] UN Department of Economic and Social Affairs (DESA), *Global Social Crisis:* Report *on the World Social Situation 2011*, UN Doc. ST/ESA/334 (November 2011).

[16] See UN, *World Economic Situation and Prospects 2010* (New York: UN, 2010).

[17] According to the ILO, while financial markets rebounded and economic indicators such as GDP, trade and investment started to recover, largely as a result of government stimulus measures, economic growth since 2009 was remarkable for being on the whole jobless and wageless—with long-lasting costs for individuals and societies. ILO, *Global Employment Trends 2012: Preventing a deeper job crisis* (Geneva: ILO, 2012).

[18] See IMF, 'A New Globalization for a New World,' Opening Address to the 2010 Annual Meetings of the Boards of Governors of the World Bank Group and the IMF (8 October 2008), available at <http://www.imf.org/external/np/speeches/2010/100810.htm> (last accessed 11 November 2013): 'Make no mistake: this increase of 35 percentage points [in the public debt of the high-income countries] is mostly due to low growth, to expenditure linked to the rescue of the financial sector, to lack of revenue because of the economic downturn. Only about one-tenth comes directly from the stimulus. So the lesson is clear: the biggest threat to fiscal sustainability is low growth'.

[19] M. Blyth, *Austerity: The History of a Dangerous Idea* (New York: Oxford University Press, 2013). I. Ortiz and M. Cummins (eds.), *A Recovery for All: Rethinking Socio-Economic Policies for Children and Poor Households* (New York: UNICEF, 2012).

[20] For a detailed human rights analysis of the causes and consequences of Ireland's economic crisis, and the State's responses to it, see CESR, 'Mauled by the Celtic Tiger: Human Rights in Ireland's Economic Meltdown', Rights in Crisis Briefing Paper (Madrid: CESR, 2012).

impact on the most vulnerable and resulting in rising levels of income inequality.[21] Successive Spanish governments since 2009 have also undertaken severe and regressive budget cuts, targeting spending on social and labour protections, work programmes, housing, education, and international development cooperation, despite the fact that per capita social expenditure in the country was comparatively low prior to the economic crisis.[22] The UN Committee on Economic, Social and Cultural Rights has pointed out that Spain's measures to mitigate the negative impacts of the crisis on the most vulnerable have been inadequate,[23] and called on all state parties to guarantee that any restrictive austerity measures be temporary, proportional, strictly necessary, non-discriminatory, and protective of the minimum core obligations of economic and social rights.[24]

However, the trend towards fiscal austerity is global, as a majority of low- and middle-income countries have also introduced austerity measures. In 2013, 5.8 billion people, or 80 per cent of the global population, are estimated to be facing public budget contractions. If trends continue, this could increase to 6.3 billion or 90 per cent of persons worldwide by 2015.[25] A UNICEF study of 128 countries, found that most 'cost-saving measures' enacted commonly involved: a) public sector wage bill cuts (especially primary school teachers and nurses), b) reducing subsidies to basic food items, c) cutting social protection schemes, pensions, and social safety nets, d) regressive taxation measures, with discriminatory effects on the most vulnerable, and e) weakening labour protections.[26] The most vulnerable sectors of the population, especially women, pensioners, people with disabilities[27] and youth,[28] have tended to be the most adversely affected.

[21] CESR, 'Mauled by the Celtic Tiger: Human Rights in Ireland's Economic Meltdown', Rights in Crisis Briefing Paper (Madrid: CESR, 2012).

[22] See CESR, Observatorio de Derechos Económicos, Sociales y Culturales (Observatori DESC), et al. 'Joint Submission to the Committee on Economic, Social and Cultural Rights On the occasion of the review of Spain's 5th Periodic Report at the 48th Session' (May 2012), and CESR, 'Visualizing Rights: Spain: Fact Sheet No. 12', May 2012.

[23] CESCR, 'Concluding Observations: Spain', UN Doc. E/C.12/ESP/CO/5 (June 2012).

[24] CESCR Open Letter to All States Parties to the ICESCR of 16 May 2012. See UN Doc. CESCR/48th/SP/MAB/SW, available at <http://www2.ohchr.org/english/bodies/cescr/docs/LetterCESCRtoSP16.05.12.pdf> (last accessed 29 November 2013).

[25] See I. Ortiz and M. Cummins, 'Age of Austerity; A Review of Public Expenditures and Adjustment Measures in 181 Countries,' Initiative for Policy Dialogue and the South Centre, Working Paper (May 2013).

[26] See I. Ortiz, J. Chai, and M. Cummins, 'Austerity Measures Threaten Children and Poor Households,' Working Paper (September 2011), available at <http://www.unicef.org/socialpolicy/files/Austerity_Measures_Threaten_Children.pdf> (last accessed 11 November 2013); See also Report of the UN Independent Expert on Extreme Poverty and Human Rights, M. Sepúlveda Carmona, UN Doc. A/HRC/17/34 (17 March 2011).

[27] See for example, UK Joint Parliamentary Committee inquiry on impacts of austerity measures on people with disabilities, 'Human Rights Joint Committee: Twenty-Third Report Implementation of the Right of Disabled People to Independent Living' (6 February 2012), available at <http://www.publications.parliament.uk/pa/jt201012/jtselect/jtrights/257/25702.htm> (last accessed 11 November 2013).

[28] See Report of the UN Independent Expert on Extreme Poverty and Human Rights, M. Sepúlveda Carmona, UN Doc. A/HRC/17/34 (17 March 2011).

Many economists, including Nobel Laureate Amartya Sen, have warned that such austerity measures were liable to become a 'spiraling catastrophe',[29] as, when enacted during times of economic crisis, austerity measures often result in exactly what they are designed to prevent, including deeper and longer recessions, deteriorating unemployment levels, reduced government revenues, and thus increased government deficits.[30] Many expert bodies, such as the Commission of Experts appointed by the UN General Assembly on Reforms of the International Monetary and Financial System, chaired by Nobel Laureate economist Joseph Stiglitz, have pointed to the need to replace austerity measures with counter-cyclical policies during economic recessions. [31]

3. Human Rights Law as a Normative Framework to Guide Economic Policy in Times of Crisis

This section explores the relevant normative standards and principles of human rights law most useful for guiding government's economic policy in times of crisis. International human rights law sets out the legal obligations of governments with respect to all aspects of public policy, including political, military, or security affairs, but also economic and social matters. Although international human rights law does not prescribe a specific economic model,[32] and allows for a significant margin of discretion to governments to choose the means which best fit their circumstances, it does nonetheless set out certain normative limits and principles that circumscribe economic and social policymaking.[33]

International human rights law requires state parties to respect, protect, and fulfil economic, social, and cultural rights,[34] duties which entail both positive and negative obligations, and obligations of both conduct and result.[35] A state's duties are primarily to those within their territorial jurisdiction in most cases, but a growing body of literature and expert opinion also attests to the 'extraterritorial'

[29] Financial Times, 'Nobel economist blasts Europe's austerity plans' (London: 14 December 2011).

[30] See J. Guajardo, D. Leigh, and A. Pescatori, 'Expansionary Austerity: New International Evidence,' IMF Working Paper WP/11/158 (Washington: IMF, 2011).

[31] UN, *Report of the Commission of Experts of the President of the United Nations General Assembly on Reforms of the International Monetary and Financial System* (New York: UN, 2009), 10, available at <http://www.un.org/ga/econcrisissummit/docs/FinalReport_CoE.pdf> (last accessed 11 November 2013).

[32] See para. 8 of the CESCR General Comment No. 3, The Nature of States Parties Obligations (Art. 2, par.1), 14 December 1990, ('General Comment No. 3'), para. 8 12/14/1990.

[33] On applying human rights principles to economic policy more broadly, see R. Balakrishnan and D. Elson, 'Auditing Economic Policy in the Light of Obligations on Economic and Social Rights', *Essex Human Rights Review* vol. 5, no. 1 (July 2008); See also, R. Balakrishnan and D. Elson (eds.), *Economic Policy and Human Rights* (New York: Zed Books, 2012); See also, I. Saiz 'Rights in Recession? Challenges for Economic and Social Rights Enforcement in Times of Crisis', 1 *Journal of Human Rights Practice* (2009), 277–293.

[34] See 'Maastricht Guidelines on Violations of Economic, Social and Cultural Rights' (2 October 2000), UN Doc. E/C.12/2000/13.

[35] See CESCR, General Comment No. 3.

application of states' economic, social, and cultural obligations,[36] stemming from the UN Charter,[37] various human rights treaties,[38] and authoritative interpretations of international standards.[39]

The duties to respect, protect, and fulfil human rights are relevant to economic policies in a number of different ways. The obligation to *respect* implies that states must refrain from interfering with the enjoyment of human rights of their citizens (and others in their jurisdiction), but also to 'do no harm' *directly* or *indirectly* across international borders to people living in other countries, including by inhibiting the ability of another state to comply with its own human rights obligations (for example, by implementing policies that negatively affect citizens of other countries, or insisting on international trade, finance, or debt-related commitments which will affect the capacity of another state to realize rights).[40] The obligation to *protect* compels states to take all necessary measures to prevent and protect against human rights abuses by third parties, such as businesses or private financial institutions. The scope of this obligation means that the state must regulate the private actors over which it has jurisdiction, whether the abuse originates on its territory, the actor is a national of, or is registered in, the territorial state, or where there is a reasonable connection between the territorial state and the conduct it seeks to regulate.[41] The UN Guiding Principles on Business and Human Rights clarify that in upholding the duty to protect,

> States should enforce laws that are aimed at, or have the effect of, requiring business enterprises to respect human rights, and periodically to assess the adequacy of such laws and address any gap [and] provide effective guidance to business enterprises on how to respect human rights throughout their operations.[42]

[36] By extraterritorial obligations, we refer to conduct of a State with effects on the enjoyment of human rights in another territory, or obligations of a global character under the UN Charter and other treaties. See 'Maastricht principles on Extraterritorial Obligations of States in the area of Economic, Social and Cultural Rights, with commentary', 34 *Human Rights Quarterly* (2012), 1084–1169.

[37] See art. 56: 'All Members pledge themselves to take joint and separate action in co-operation with the Organization for the achievement of the purposes set forth in Article 55,' which includes 'universal respect for, and observance of, human rights and fundamental freedoms for all without distinction [. . . and] higher standards of living, full employment, and conditions of economic and social progress and development'.

[38] ICESCR art. 2.1; CRC art. 4; UN Charter art. 56; UDHR art. 22; CPRD art. 2; and the Declaration on the Right to Development art. 3.3

[39] On the legally binding obligation to provide international cooperation and assistance, see ICESCR, arts. 2(1), 11, 22, 23, and General Comments Nos. 2, 3, 12, 14, 15, and 19; See also A. Khalfan, 'Development Cooperation and Extraterritorial Obligations' (6 August 2011), available at <http://papers.ssrn.com/sol3/papers.cfm?abstract_id=1929968> (last accessed 11 November 2013); See also, M. Langford and A. Russell (eds.), *The Right to Water Theory, Practice And Prospects* (Cambridge: Cambridge University Press, 2012).

[40] 'Maastricht principles on Extraterritorial Obligations of States in the area of Economic, Social and Cultural Rights,' (September 2011), paras. 19–21.

[41] On the extraterritorial scope of the duty to protect, see CESCR General Comment No. 12, No. 14, para. 39, and No. 15, para. 31. See also Maastricht Principles paras. 23–27.

[42] See Report of the Special Representative of the Secretary General on the issue of human rights and transnational corporations and other business enterprises, John Ruggie, UN Doc 'A/HRC/17/31 (21 March 2011), A, art. 3.

This duty to protect therefore implies that governments must regulate the market to prevent direct forms of exploitation and abuse (for example, in financial and housing markets), as well as regulate private market actors where their activities may foreseeably have profound systemic consequences on economic and social rights (for example, where they provoke a systemic financial crisis that would have widespread effects on livelihoods).

The obligation to *fulfil* requires states to take all appropriate legislative, administrative, fiscal, judicial, monetary, and other measures to create conditions for the full realization of rights without discrimination.[43] The primary state responsibility to fulfil is towards people under its jurisdiction, but there are also international duties on all states to support an international enabling environment, commensurate with their capacity to cooperate internationally, to mobilize resources for the universal fulfilment of rights.[44]

States are not required to fully realize all economic and social rights overnight, but they must take steps to move as swiftly as possible towards this goal, in line with the norm of *progressive realization*.[45] The logical corollary to the duty towards progress is that governments must avoid *retrogression* in the realization of economic and social rights, even in times of severe resource constraints such as economic recessions.[46] The duty of progressive realization and non-retrogression implies that a government's actions or omissions which are likely to result in normative or *de facto* retrogression on rights-fulfilment (for example, through legislative setbacks in protection of rights, or through budget cuts which affect people's enjoyment of social rights) can only be justifiable 'after the most careful consideration of all alternatives and that they are duly justified by reference to the totality of the rights provided for in the Covenant in the context of the full use of the state party's *maximum available resources*'.[47]

The margin of discretion that is built into the duty to fulfil is thus limited, and a state can be found in breach of the Covenant if a deterioration in rights enjoyment cannot be justified (for example, it is the result of unjustified budget cuts which could have been reasonably averted if the state could have found other resources available for realizing human rights). In this sense, the obligation to use the maximum available resources relates not only to the existing resources of the state, but also resources that could reasonably and equitably be mobilized in the future. Knee-jerk assumptions about resource scarcity, irreversible expansion of sovereign debt, and thus the unaffordability of the welfare state, in other words,

[43] CESCR, General Comment No. 3.

[44] Maastricht Principles paras. 28–35.

[45] See ICESCR art. 2.

[46] See CESCR, General Comments No. 4, para. 10, No. 5, para. 13, and No. 11, para. 11 (authors' emphasis); See also Report of the Independent Expert on the question of human rights and extreme poverty, M. Sepúlveda Carmona, UN Doc. A/HRC/17/34 (17 March 2011), para. 12: 'States cannot use the economic damage caused by the crises to justify actions or omissions that amount to violations of basic human rights obligations'.

[47] General Comments No. 14, at para. 32. General Comments No. 3, para. 9, No. 13, para. 45, No. 15, para. 19, No. 17, para. 27, No. 18, para. 34, No. 19, para. 42, and No. 21, para. 65. See also CESCR, Statement: An Evaluation of the Obligation to take steps to the 'Maximum of Available Resources' under an Optional Protocol to the Covenant, UN Doc. E/C.12/2007/1 (10 May 2007).

are thus highly questionable in lieu of a more comprehensive assessment of all financing alternatives. Further resources for ESC rights can be found through (a) reallocations of existing resources, but also through (b) resource generation via fiscal and tax policy (including battling tax evasion), (c) monetary policy and financial regulation, (d) deficit financing, debt restructuring, and (e) development assistance.[48] While the scope for expanding the fiscal space in these five areas is contested between heterodox and orthodox economists,[49] recent evidence from UNICEF concludes that fiscal retrenchment and austerity are rarely the only policy options and far from inevitable. A plethora of financing alternatives today exist to expand expenditure options (or 'fiscal space'), even in the poorest countries.[50]

Jurisprudence around the world is already emerging that challenges budget cuts when these negatively impact on the realization of economic and social rights. For example, the principle of non-retrogression has been invoked in various jurisdictions, to challenge successfully social spending cuts, such as the 2008 ruling by the Colombian Constitutional Court that national health insurance budget reductions amounted to unlawful retrogression, as they would affect the poorest disproportionately.[51] The Constitutional Tribunal of Portugal recently held that pension reforms which undermined the minimum essential levels required for a life of dignity were unconstitutional, while also warning that any regressive tax reforms would also be counter to the constitutionally protected principle of fiscal justice.[52] Even before the global economic crisis, the ESCR Committee stated,[53] in concurrence with other treaty bodies,[54] and UN Special Procedures,[55] that the

[48] See R. Balakrishnan, et al., 'Maximum Available Resources & Human Rights: Analytical Report', Center for Women's Global Leadership, Rutgers University (2011); See also Background paper submitted by Special Rapporteur on the right to education, UN Doc. E/C.12/1998/18 (November 1998).

[49] For a perspective somewhat limited to sovereign debt, see M. Dowell-Jones, 'The Sovereign Bond Markets and Socio-Economic Rights: Understanding the Challenge of Austerity,' ch. 2.

[50] See I. Ortiz, J. Chai, and M. Cummins, 'Identifying Fiscal Space: Options for Social and Economic Development for Children and Poor Households in 184 Countries,' UNICEF (December 2011), available at <http://www.unicef.org/socialpolicy/files/Fiscal_Space_-_REVISED_Dec_2011.pdf> (last accessed 11 November 2013).

[51] See, Corte Constitucional de Colombia, Sala Segunda de Revisión, Sentencia C-1165/2000). Magistrado Ponente: Manuel José Cepeda.

[52] Portugal Constitutional Court (*Tribunal Constitucional*), Lisbon, Portugal (5 April 2013); examination of constitutionality of the Appropriation Bill for the fiscal year 2013 (Rule number 66-B/2012, 31 December 2012).

[53] See CESCR Concluding Observations on China: Hong Kong UN Doc. E/C.12/1/ADD.58 (CESCR, 2001), para. 14: 'The economic policies of HKSAR (Hong Kong), based essentially on the philosophy of "positive non-interventionism", i.e. keeping taxes low and limiting government expenditure to the provision of essential services, in accordance with article 5 of the Basic Law, which guarantees a free trade, free enterprise and low tax regime for at least 50 years, have had a negative impact on the realization and enjoyment of the economic, social and cultural rights of Hong Kong's inhabitants'.

[54] Similar conclusions stem from the Committee on the Rights of the Child, in particular in its review of the government of Guatemala, UN Doc. CRC/C/GTM/CO/3-4 (CRC, 2010)CRC/C/GTM/CO/3-4 (1 October 2010), paras. 25 and 26.

[55] See, in particular, Report of the Independent Expert on the question of human rights and extreme poverty, M. Sepúlveda Carmona on the human rights-based approach to recovery from the global economic and financial crises, with a focus on those living in poverty', UN Doc. A/HRC/17/34 (2011): 'States have an unambiguous responsibility to take steps towards the full achievement of

mode of revenue generation is important, and that low and regressive tax collection can have negative impacts on the realization and enjoyment of economic, social, and cultural rights. In the face of widespread and deepening austerity measures in numerous countries, in May 2012 the ESCR Committee also took a significant step to clarify the content and meaning of the non-retrogression standard,[56] and laid out a set of criteria by which to judge the lawfulness of fiscal readjustments under the Covenant. The Committee emphasized that any proposed policy change or fiscal adjustment must meet the following requirements:

1. the policy is a *temporary* measure covering only the period of the crisis;
2. the policy is *necessary* and *proportionate*, in the sense that the adoption of any other policy, or a failure to act, would be more detrimental to economic, social, and cultural rights;
3. the policy is *not discriminatory* and comprises *all possible measures,* including *tax measures*, to support social transfers and mitigate inequalities that can grow in times of crisis and to ensure that the rights of disadvantaged and marginalized individuals and groups are not disproportionately affected;
4. the policy identifies the *minimum core content of rights, or a social protection floor*, as developed by the International Labor Organization, and ensures the protection of this core content at all times.[57]

Although the obligation to fulfil economic and social rights is a duty which must be progressively realized, this does not mean that all aspects of the rights are to be implemented progressively—at least two obligations are of immediate effect: non-discrimination and 'minimum core obligations'.[58] The fundamental principle of *non-discrimination and equality* is considered an 'immediate and cross-cutting obligation' under the Covenant,[59] requiring states to end *de jure* or

economic, social and cultural rights by using the maximum amount of resources available [...] Low levels of domestic taxation revenue, in particular, could be a major obstacle to a State's ability to meet obligations to realize economic, social and cultural rights'; Daniel Turk, The realization of economic, social and cultural rights, Special Rapporteur on Economic and Social Rights, UN Doc. E/CN.4/Sub.2/1992/16; O. De Schutter, Report of the Special Rapporteur on the right to food, Mission to Brazil, UN Doc. A/HRC/13/33/Add.6 (19 February 2009), para. 36; M. Sepúlveda Carmona, *The Nature of Obligations under the International Covenant on Economic Social and Cultural Rights* (Leiden: Intersentia, 2003).

[56] See also CESCR, 'Statement: An Evaluation of the Obligation to take steps to the 'Maximum of Available Resources' under an Optional Protocol to the Covenant,' UN Doc. E/C.12/2007/1 (10 May 2007).

[57] Committee on Economic, Social and Cultural Rights, 'Open Letter to States Parties regarding the protection of rights in the context of economic crisis' (May 2012), available at <http://www2.ohchr.org/english/bodies/cescr/docs/LetterCESCRtoSP16.05.12.pdf> (last accessed 11 November 2013).

[58] CESCR, General Comment No. 3 'The nature of States parties obligations' (14 December 1990), contained in UN doc. E/1991/23, at para. 5.

[59] See CESCR, General Comment No. 20, Non-discrimination in economic, social and cultural rights, UN Doc. E/C.12/GC/20 (2 July 2009), at para. 7. Arts. 2(2) and 3 of the Covenant call for state parties to guarantee that the rights enumerated within it be 'exercised without discrimination of any kind as to race, color, sex, language, religion, political or other opinion, national or social origin, property, birth or other status' and require that states 'undertake to ensure the equal rights of men and women to the enjoyment of all economic, social and cultural rights set forth' respectively. See also

de facto discrimination resulting from particular government conduct, but also to 'take concrete, deliberate and targeted measures' to eliminate discrimination.[60] In other words, states must concern themselves with who benefits from particular policies, and actively seek to modify existing patterns of discrimination by taking positive steps to ensure substantive equality in the enjoyment of rights. Alongside other traditional grounds such as ethnicity, gender, and nationality, socio-economic status is increasingly recognized as an impermissible ground of discrimination,[61] especially important considering that economic crises affect low- and middle-income populations disproportionately.

Regardless of their level of economic development or resource base, states also have an immediate duty 'to ensure the satisfaction of, at the very least, minimum essential levels' of economic and social rights universally.[62] The failure by the state to meet these minimum levels is assumed to be a prima facie violation unless the state can demonstrate that 'every effort has been made to use all resources that are at its disposition in an effort to satisfy, as a matter of priority, those minimum obligations'.[63] Applied to the context of economic crisis, governments have immediate obligations to prioritize—in revenue raising as well as in expenditures—the achievement of these minimum levels of rights enjoyment essential to survival and a life of dignity.[64] Thus, even in times of economic crisis and economic recession, deliberate and well-targeted measures must be taken to ensure that the most vulnerable sectors of the population can enjoy at least these minimum levels of rights enjoyment.[65]

A human rights-based approach to public policies also requires the respect of key human rights principles, such as participation, transparency, accountability, and access to remedies. In relation to the design, implementation, and monitoring

'Limburg Principles on the Implementation of the International Covenant on Economic, Social and Cultural Rights.' UN Doc. E/CN.4/1987/17 (8 January 1987), at paras. 37–38, which affirm that these obligations include the elimination of both *de jure* and *de facto* discrimination.

60 General Comment No. 20, *supra* note 59, at para. 36.

61 See General Comment No. 21. See also G. MacNaughton, G. 'Untangling equality and non-discrimination to promote the right to health care for all', 11 *Journal of Health and Human Rights* (2009), 47–63, suggesting that the drafters of the UDHR understood the principles of non-discrimination and equality to have broadly egalitarian purposes.

62 General Comment No. 3, at para. 10.

63 General Comment No. 3, at para. 10.

64 The Committee has adopted a number of General Comments that further define the minimum core of the Covenant's rights regarding food, water, health, housing, and education. See e.g. CESCR, General Comment No. 12 'The Right to Adequate Food' (12 May 1999), UN Doc. E/C.12/1999/5; CESCR, General Comment No. 13 'The Right to Education' (8 December 1999), UN Doc. E/C.12/1999/10; CESCR, General Comment No. 14 'The right to the highest attainable standard of health' (11 August 2000), UN Doc. E/C.12/2000/4. Although its general comments on the right to housing (Comments Nos. 4 and 7) do not define a minimum core, this has been elaborated elsewhere. While the notion of enforceable minimum core obligations has been rejected by the South African Constitutional Court, it has been enforced in other jurisdictions including in jurisprudence by the Constitutional Court of Colombia on the right to health. See *Corte Constitucional de Colombia, Sala Segunda de Revisión, Sentencia* T-760 (31 July 2008). For more on the different interpretations of the content of minimum core obligations, see K.G. Young, 'The Minimum Core of Economic and Social Rights: A Concept in Search of Content', 33 *Yale Journal of International Law* (2008), 113–175.

65 See CESCR General Comments No. 3, para. 12, No. 12, para. 28, and No. 14, para. 18; Statement on allocation of resources, UN Doc. E/C.12/2007/1, paras. 4 and 6

of crisis-response policies, the principle of *public participation* would suggest that states must actively involve all those affected by fiscal and economic policy in meaningful channels of participation.[66] *Transparency* is required at all points in the policy cycle, so that people are able to exercise their right to accessible, relevant, and timely information about policies which will affect their lives.[67] States are also obliged to guarantee *effective remedy* for human rights abuses,[68] including when necessary judicial remedies.[69] To be effective, remedies must lead to an end to any ongoing violations; be capable of leading to a prompt, thorough, and impartial investigation; be open to appeal; and ensure adequate reparation, including, as necessary, restitution, compensation, satisfaction, rehabilitation, and guarantees of non-repetition.[70] The right to remedy under international law implies an obligation on governments to provide accessible and effective mechanisms (via courts, political institutions, administrative bodies, or other quasi- and non-judicial mechanisms) to enable rights-holders to enforce their rights and to seek corrective action.[71] Ensuring accountability not only provides effective remedy for harms done, it can also serve to deter future abuse by guaranteeing that public and private agents assume their responsibilities, rather than evading them.[72] Accountability can also promote participation, and clarify procedures to make remedies more accessible in the future. Remedies could include the revocation of legislation or the enactment of remedial legislation or compensation, but should address both individual and systemic injustice. In relation to the economic and financial crisis, non-repetition and reparation might best be guaranteed by meaningful regulation of the financial sector and making fiscal policy more progressive and focused on guaranteeing economic and social rights, even in the midst of crisis.

[66] See CESCR General Comments. See ICCPR, art. 25. See also Limburg principles: 'Popular participation is required at all stages, including formulation, application and review of national policies'. Nothing in this language differentiates economic from social policy as a locus for popular participation. See also Report of the Independent Expert on the question of human rights and extreme poverty, M. Sepúlveda Carmona, UN Doc. A/HRC/17/34 (17 March 2011), para. 26.

[67] As enshrined in ICCPR, art. 19.

[68] See ICCPR art. 2(3). See also General Comment No. 9, The domestic application of the Covenant, para. 2; and UN Basic Principles and Guidelines on the Right to a Remedy and Reparation for Victims of Gross Violations of International Human Rights Law and Serious Violations of International Humanitarian Law, which in Parts I and II states that the obligation pertains to all violations, not just gross violations. See also UDHR, art. 8; CRC, art. 39; and regional charters. International Law Commission, 'Draft articles on Responsibility of States for Internationally Wrongful Acts, with commentaries' (2001).

[69] See ICCPR art. 14 (on the right to a fair trial and compensation). See General Comment No. 9, The domestic application of the Covenant, para. 9.

[70] See Basic Principles and Guidelines on the Right to a Remedy and Reparation for Victims of Gross Violations of International Human Rights Law and Serious Violations of International Humanitarian Law, arts. 18–23; UN Basic Principles and Guidelines on the Right to a Remedy and Reparation for Victims of Gross Violations of International Human Rights Law and Serious Violations of International Humanitarian Law.

[71] See ICCPR art. 2(3). See also General Comment No. 9, The domestic application of the Covenant.

[72] For an economic, instrumentalist reasoning on the fundamental need to ensure accountability for the 2008 financial crisis, see N. Taleb, 'Why did the Crisis of 2008 Happen?' (stand-alone essay, 26 August 2010), available at <http://dx.doi.org/10.2139/ssrn.1666042> (last accessed 11 November 2013).

4. Operationalizing Human Rights Law in Economic Policy in Times of Crisis

The human rights normative framework thus sets out a series of principles and standards that can and should guide governments in setting economic policy. Yet, operationalizing these standards remains a challenge. The UN Committee on Economic, Social and Cultural Rights has taken the lead within the international human rights protection regime in providing some preliminary guidance to policymakers on how best to operationalize and embed the human rights normative framework into economic policies in times of crisis.[73] The persistent lack of understanding or willingness among legislators and policymakers, however, has led many to ignore the practical applicability of human rights to complex and urgent economic dilemmas. This section aims to contribute to the debate by highlighting the relevance of the normative human rights framework and drawing out the practical implications of operationalizing a human rights-centred approach to economic policies in times of economic crisis.

In relation to *fiscal policy* (that is, the generation and expenditure of government resources), operationalizing human rights standards would point to the need to adopt a progressive and expansive fiscal policy that safeguards the realization of economic and social rights, rather than cutting back on human rights protections, especially during economic crises. The use of public revenues to ensure liquidity in the financial sector, while cutting resources for the most vulnerable, raises significant questions of equity and justice. Embedding human rights in fiscal policy would require non-discriminatory, participatory, transparent, accountable, and just tax and budgetary policies,[74] and would also suggest that these should be counter-cyclical in nature (that is, increase government expenditures in times of crisis, recession and unemployment, and stabilize spending in times of economic growth) to ensure the fulfilment of the minimum essential levels of rights in times of crisis, to guard against non-retrogression, and to protect against disproportionate impacts on already disadvantaged groups. Human rights standards also imply the need to ring-fence public budgets to protect social protection programmes and ensure that goods and services essential to minimum essential levels of rights fulfilment are universally available and accessible—as this is even more important in times of crisis when families and individuals are dependent on public programmes. A social protection floor, affordable even for the lowest income countries and promoted by several special procedures and inter-governmental bodies, can be thought of as the

[73] See UN CESCR, E/C.12/ESP/CO/5 (May 2012).

[74] See AWID, CoC, CESR, CWGL, ESCR-Net (2010), 'Bringing Human Rights to Bear in Times of Crisis: A human rights analysis of government responses to the economic crisis', Submission to the High level segment of the 13th session of the UN Human Rights Council on the global and financial crises, available at <http://www.escr-net.org/usr_doc/HRResponsestoEconCrisis_Final.pdf> (last accessed 11 November 2013).

embodiment of a human rights focus on the most vulnerable as it seeks to protect a minimum core level of rights enjoyment.[75]

Given current levels of sovereign debt stemming from the fallout of the economic crisis, more expansive fiscal policies would in many cases require the mobilization of additional revenue to avoid deepening public debt and deficits. Evidence suggests that there are a range of possibilities open to expand the resource base of many countries,[76] and thus more expansive fiscal policies are feasible. Progressive tax reform and the recovery of tax revenue lost to illegal tax evasion and developing new sources of financing, are viable alternatives. Financial transaction taxes, likewise, have been proposed as a way of promoting greater financial sector accountability as well as recuperating some of the public costs incurred as a result of the global financial and economic crises.[77] These kinds of more expansive, progressive fiscal policies would ameliorate the immediate negative impacts of the crisis, but would also work to reduce inequality, stabilize, or even counteract wage and employment vulnerabilities, and thereby help to prevent financial volatility and the emergence of future crises.

In relation to *monetary policy* (that is, central bank control of the money supply to influence inter alia the stability, growth, and employment levels of the economy), operationalizing human rights standards would point to the need for central banks to proactively uphold the human rights principles of transparency, participation, and accountability. While many central banks, including the US Federal Reserve, have improved their efforts to communicate to the public, and expanded access to their records, research, and decision-making processes, there were widespread concerns about the confidentiality rather than the transparency that surrounded emergency bank lending and the rescue operations during the recent financial crisis.[78] Furthermore, while public and legislative participation in monetary decision-making is legally prohibited to ensure independence from political interference in the US, this has not prevented large financial sector actors, including those most responsible for the crisis, for exerting a significant influence that has been institutionalized with formal seats on the regional Boards

[75] See Report of the independent expert on the question of human rights and extreme poverty, M. Sepúlveda Carmona, UN Doc. A/HRC/11/9 (27 March 2009); see also Report of the independent expert on the question of human rights and extreme poverty, M. Sepúlveda Carmona, UN Doc. A/HRC/14/31 (31 March 2010); See also, Report of the independent expert on the question of human rights and extreme poverty, UN Doc. A/64/279 (11 August 2009); See also, Human rights and extreme poverty, Note by the Secretary General, UN Doc. A/65/259 (9 August 2010); See also United Nations, Social Protection Floor for a Fair and Inclusive Globalization, 2011.

[76] See I. Ortiz, J. Chai, and M. Cummins, 'Identifying Fiscal Space: Options for Social and Economic Development for Children and Poor Households in 184 Countries', UNICEF, 2011, available at <http://www.unicef.org/socialpolicy/files/Fiscal_Space_-_REVISED_Dec_2011.pdf> (last accessed 11 November 2013).

[77] See for example B. Gates, 'Innovation with Impact: financing 21st Century Development'. A report to G20 leaders, Cannes Summit (November 2011), available at <http://www.thegatesnotes.com/Topics/Development/G20-Report-Innovation-with-Impact> (last accessed 11 November 2013).

[78] Of interest, the US Supreme Court in the aftermath of the bailouts forced the Federal Reserve, for example, to break a confidentiality policy dating back to 1913 by publishing many of the details of its emergency bank lending operations during the 2008 financial crisis on the grounds of the public's right to information. See B, Appelbaum, 'Supreme Court Denies a Move to Bar the Details of the Fed Bailout', *New York Times* (New York, 21 March 2011).

of the Federal Reserve, for example. This raises questions over the extent to which the Federal Reserve, like many other central banks, are influenced by lobbying of the same financial sector they are supposed to be shaping and regulating, further exposing the myth of effective independence of many central banks.

From the perspective of operationalizing human rights, monetary authorities—as well as the government officials charged with setting their mandate—would also need to consider state obligations in relation to the right to work, given the extent to which their key mandate to control inflation might have negative impacts on objectives related to economic growth and the generation of employment opportunities. In the aftermath of the 1930s Great Depression, many central banks had mandates to address unemployment as well as inflation (an approach which is still formally reflected in the mandate of the US Federal Reserve which has responsibility for the twin objectives of inflation and employment). From the 1970s onwards, however, the mandates of many central banks dropped the focus on unemployment under the shift from the Keynesian to monetarist economic orthodoxy.[79] The focus on managing inflation (price stability) is important, especially during periods of rapid economic growth and rapid price rises, but it can be less appropriate during periods of recession, deflation, and mass unemployment.[80] Managing inflation remains important for realizing human rights—for example, to moderate the prices of essential goods and services, including food, where price volatility hurts poor households disproportionately. Yet, curbing inflation according to some theories can negatively affect the level of employment, which is why balancing the mandate with an objective to address unemployment levels is essential during periods of recession when the right to work is at threat, and inflation is under control. Statements from US Federal Reserve officials have confirmed that America's dual mandate has ensured that central bank authorities give the proper weight to unemployment when determining policy, rather than the spectre of inflation alone, and it has been suggested that the US growth and employment levels have recovered faster than those of other countries due to this dual mandate.[81] In the absence of complementary fiscal measures, monetary policy can at some point become ineffective or even counterproductive to delivering sustainable employment by merely re-inflating rather than preventing unstable housing, stock market, and other asset bubbles, and contributing to excessive leverage rather than setting the conditions for shared and equitable economic growth over the medium and long term.[82] In sum, monetary policy can be a vital tool governments have in fulfilling their obligations towards economic and social rights and the duty to protect and fulfil these

[79] See, for example, J. Stiglitz 'Big Lies about Central Banking', Project Syndicate (5 June 2003), available at <http://www.project-syndicate.org/commentary/big-lies-about-central-banking> (last accessed 11 November 2013).

[80] O. Blanchard, 'Monetary Policy in the wake of the crisis' in O. Jean Blanchard and D. Romer (eds.), *In the Wake of the Crisis: Leading Economists Reassess Economic Policy* (Boston: MIT Press, 2012).

[81] E. Rosengren, 'Should Full Employment Be a Mandate for Central Banks?' *The Federal Reserve Bank of Boston's 57th Economic Conference: 'Fulfilling the Full Employment Mandate—Monetary Policy & The Labor Market'* (12 April 2013), at <http://www.bos.frb.org/news/speeches/rosengren/2013/041213> (last accessed 11 November 2013).

[82] Blanchard and Romer, *supra* note 80.

rights suggests that central banks will need to carefully balance the monetary policy triangle of (a) price stability/exchange rate policy, (b) maximum employment, and (c) macro-prudential and micro-level financial regulation.

Finally, addressing the causes of the crisis requires a focus on the obligation of governments to *protect* their citizens against financial sector abuses by putting in place effective *financial regulation policies*. As the Commission of Experts on Reforms of the International Monetary and Financial System argued, the crisis was neither unforeseeable nor inevitable, but instead 'the result of mistakes by the private sector and misguided and failed policies of the public'.[83] These mistaken public policies included, in the Commission's view, the failure to effectively regulate the banking system.[84] It considered particularly damaging the repeal in 1999 of US legislation serving to protect against financial abuse and prevent systemic collapse, including the 1933 Glass-Steagall Act.[85] The UN General Assembly has concurred that the crisis was caused by 'regulatory failures, compounded by over-reliance on market self-regulation, overall lack of transparency, financial integrity, and responsible behaviour'.[86] By 2011, the UN's 'Global Social Crisis Report' also suggested that still 'many fundamental causes of the crisis have not been addressed, such as insufficient financial sector regulation, unrealistically high executive compensation (salaries and bonuses), stagnating real wages, and consequently rising inequality and debt-financed consumption'.

While financial regulation is a complex and necessarily context-dependent exercise, a human rights approach would refocus attention on the indispensable regulatory roles and responsibilities of the state and question (de-)regulatory laws or policies which tend to favour private over public interests. The UN Special Rapporteur on Extreme Poverty and Human Rights has argued that states 'should ensure adequate means of redress for those adversely affected by the actions taken by financial sector institutions, and adopt regulations that discourage harmful practices by providing for accountability mechanisms that penalize risky behaviours and prosecute perpetrators'.[87] In this way, the human rights normative framework would require a more effective risk management system with associated individual accountability for failures as a safeguard against the recurrence of future crises.

[83] UN Report of the Commission of Experts, *supra* note 31.

[84] See for example, Report by the Commission on the Measurement of Economic Performance and Social Progress (the Stiglitz Commission report), 48, available at <http://www.stiglitz-sen-fitoussi.fr/documents/rapport_anglais.pdf> (last accessed 11 November 2013): 'There is now a consensus that inadequate regulations and regulatory institutions, some of which failed even to implement effectively those regulations that existed, contributed to this crisis. While "blame" should rest on the financial sector, government failed to protect the market from itself and to protect society from the kinds of excesses that have repeatedly imposed high costs on taxpayers, workers, homeowners, and retirees'.

[85] C. Crawford, 'The Repeal Of The Glass-Steagall Act And The Current Financial Crisis', *Journal of Business & Economics Research (JBER)* 9, no. 1 (1 July 2011).

[86] UN General Assembly (2009) Resolution 63/303, 'Outcome of the Conference on the World Financial and Economic Crisis and its Impact on Development' (13 July 2009), A/RES/63/303, para. 7.

[87] See Report of the Independent Expert on the question of human rights and extreme poverty, M. Sepúlveda Carmona, UN Doc. A/HRC/17/34 (17 March 2011), para. 84.

Along with inadequate regulation, rising inequality and falling or stagnating wages are argued by many as one major factor contributing to the crisis. As families increased their consumption and increasing numbers of people struggled to survive on falling real wages, they took on unsustainable levels of debt while income gains among the richest skyrocketed, leaving a top-heavy financial sector increasingly vulnerable to systemic risk.[88] As an IMF paper has pointed out, *redistributive policies* are one way to avoid this: 'because crises are costly, redistribution policies that prevent excessive household indebtedness and reduce crisis-risk ex-ante can be more desirable from a macroeconomic stabilization point of view than ex-post policies such as bailouts or debt restructurings'.[89] While addressing wage inequalities alone through redistributive and pre-distributive policies (for example, strengthening workers' leverage, strengthening the minimum wage, making more progressive the tax regime) is certainly not a silver bullet for debt reduction, it would have an impressive result in driving economic growth, increasing tax revenues, and thus lowering deficits, which over time would quickly make national debts sustainable. Improving regulation and reducing wage and income inequalities, in other words, through a regulatory and redistributive role of the state in the economy, can help to prevent future financial crises as well as mitigate the negative human rights impacts of the crises.

5. Challenges to Implementing Human Rights in Economic Policy

Despite the significant contributions the human rights normative framework can make to guide economic policy in times of crisis, there remain significant challenges to making these human rights standards operational in practice. These include (1) obstacles to public oversight and judicial review in times of crisis, (2) the appropriation of human rights protections by private economic interests, (3) the transnational dimension of gaps in human rights protection and accountability, and (4) the competition between different legal regimes, particularly around sovereign debt.

A. Obstacles to judicial review in times of crisis

In many countries, civil society organizations have expressed indignation at the inequities in crisis responses, and have called for greater public oversight and accountability of political and economic decision-makers for their decisions in relation to economic policymaking. A number of significant legal initiatives have

[88] UN, Report of the Commission of Experts of the President of the United Nations General Assembly on Reforms of the International Monetary and Financial System (2009), 10. 4 oc. on ies to the Covenant'.

[89] M. Kumhof and R. Ranciere, 'Inequality, Leverage and Crises', IMF Working Paper, WP10268 (Washington: IMF, 2011), 3.

challenged fiscal austerity measures on human rights grounds, not without facing significant obstacles however.

In Latvia, for example, pensioners challenged the constitutionality of a state pension law which cut pension payments below constitutionally acceptable levels. The government cited its liabilities to international creditors as justification for changing the pension law, but the Constitutional Court deemed the act unconstitutional. The Court cited the fundamental right to social security and asserted that the state had the obligation to guarantee the minimum essential levels of the right, irrespective of resources. The Court also pointed to the fact that the government had not considered other less restrictive measures nor designed an effective remedy for reduced pensions. Furthermore, the Court refused to consider the conditions set out by international creditors as trumping constitutional guarantees to the right to social security.[90] A similar pension-related case was heard in the Constitutional Court of Romania,[91] with the Court requiring the government to find alternative ways of reducing public debt which would not affect fundamental rights.[92] Several cases before the Hungarian Constitutional Court have also challenged government post-crisis fiscal policies, so much so that the legislature voted by large margins to amend the Constitution to strip the Court of its power to annul tax-related laws except in cases dealing with certain constitutional rights, such as freedom of thought, conscience, and religion, the right to life, and the right to protect personal data.[93] In the US, too, courts in New Jersey and California have received challenges to crisis-induced spending cuts in education[94] and healthcare[95] respectively, holding that budget considerations do not trump human rights protections.

In the UK, claims have also been brought before the courts to challenge retrogression in economic and social rights. One case—eventually rejected—sought judicial review of austerity measures for failing to undertake impact assessments to consider the disproportionate impacts on women and people with disabilities of increased VAT taxes, caps on housing benefits, and child benefit freezes.[96] In a

90 See 'Case No. 2009-43-01 (On Compliance of the First Part of Section 3 of State Pensions and State Allowance Disbursement in 2009–2012) insofar as it Applies to State Old-Age Pension with Art. 1, Art. 91, Art. 105, and Art. 109 of the Satversme (Constitution) of the Republic of Latvia', available at <http://www.escr-net.org/caselaw/caselaw_show.htm?doc_id=1285934&country=13565>.

91 See BBC, 'Romania Pension Cut Ruled Illegal'. (25 June 2010), available at <http://www.bbc.co.uk/news/10421118> (last accessed 19 Octber 2013).

92 See 'Romania forced to find alternatives to austerity plans', available at <http://www.google.com/hostednews/afp/article/ALeqM5jcfUBQVSP5Ggxw08Npeh4zIR3MdQ> (last accessed 11 November 2013).

93 See Financial Times, 'Hungary curbs constitutional court's powers' (16 November 2010), available at <http://www.ft.com/intl/cms/s/0/9ac8db2a-f1af-11df-bb5a-00144feab49a.html#axzz1mZ3893fG> (last accessed 11 November 2013); see also, D. O'Donovan, 'A Twilight of Sovereignty: Eastern Europe's Constitutional Courts, the IMF and Government Austerity Programmes', available at <http://www.humanrights.ie/index.php/2010/11/25/a-twilight-of-sovereignty-eastern-europes-constitutional-courts-the-imf-and-government-austerity-programmes> (last accessed 11 November 2013).

94 *Abbott v Burke*, No. M-1293-09 (Abbott XXI), New Jersey, available at <http://www.edlawcenter.org/cases/abbott-v-burke/abbott-decisions.html> (last accessed 11 November 2013).

95 *California Hospital Ass'n v. Douglas*, 848 F. Supp. 2d 1117 (CD Cal. 2011).

96 See Fawcett Society, *Fawcett's bid for a judicial review of the 2010 budget* (28 February 2013), available at <http://www.fawcettsociety.org.uk/fawcetts-bid-for-a-judicial-review-of-the-2010-budget> (last accessed 11 November 2013).

recent case, British students also brought a case against the government arguing that a tripling of university tuition fees would thwart equal access to university for ethnic minorities, the poor, and other marginalized groups, and was thus in breach of the right to education and non-discrimination guarantees in the UK Human Rights Act and the European Convention of Human Rights. While judges did not deem it appropriate to annul the UK government's decision to raise fees on the argument that it would create 'administrative chaos', the High Court did hold that the Business Secretary had 'failed fully to carry out his public sector equality duties' and to give 'due regard' to promoting equality of opportunity in education.[97]

However, despite these partial successes, there remains a number of obstacles to pursuing this kind of economic and social rights litigation. In the UK example, the judiciary—even while recognizing that the government had failed to assess the discriminatory effects of its emergency budget law—was concerned to be seen as interfering unduly in areas of economic and social policy deemed to be the prerogative of the legislature.[98] Even in jurisdictions where economic and social rights are justiciable in theory, courts have chosen in many cases to defer to the executive or legislature for economic policymaking. It is difficult, moreover, for courts to annul legislation speedily drawn up and passed in the context of crisis. As theories on crisis governance have suggested,[99] the perceived or real exigencies of the moment and panic about the future during crises often subvert generally accepted legal and democratic constraints.[100] Evidence suggests that courts tend to defer more to the executive in times of crisis, with opposition only reappearing once the perceived imminence of the threat has passed.[101] Courts also often face a fait accompli and are too slow to act to prevent certain emergency measures. In many cases, courts are often perceived to lack political legitimacy to challenge the executive's authority

[97] *Hurley and Moore v Secretary of State for Business, Innovation and Skills*, EWHC 201 (2012). See also, *The Guardian*, 'Tuition Fees Rise Does Not Breach Human Rights, Court Rules' (17 February 2012), available at <http://www.guardian.co.uk/education/2012/feb/17/tuition-fees-rise-human-rights-court> (last accessed 11 November 2013).

[98] See J. Kissane, 'The Government's Approach to the Role of Economic and Social Rights in Relation to Austerity Measures', Presentation seminar: 'Economic and Social Rights in Times of Austerity', Faculty of Law, University of Oxford (1 July 2011), available at <http://www.esrinatimeofausterity.com/presentations.html> (last accessed 11 November 2013).

[99] See E.A. Posner and A. Vermeule, 'Crisis Governance in the Administrative State: 9/11 and the Financial Meltdown of 2008', *U of Chicago Law & Economics, Olin Working Paper No. 442; U of Chicago, Public Law Working Paper No. 248; Harvard Public Law Working Paper No. 08-50; Harvard Law School Program on Risk Regulation Research Paper No. 09-04*, available at SSRN: <http://papers.ssrn.com/sol3/papers.cfm?abstract_id=1301164> (last accessed 11 November 2013).

[100] See A. Posner and A. Vermeule, 'Crisis Governance in the Administrative State: 9/11 and the Financial Meltdown of 2008', *U of Chicago Law & Economics, Olin Working Paper No. 442; U of Chicago, Public Law Working Paper No. 248; Harvard Public Law Working Paper No. 08-50; Harvard Law School Program on Risk Regulation Research Paper No. 09-04*, available at SSRN: <http://papers.ssrn.com/sol3/papers.cfm?abstract_id=1301164> (last accessed 11 November 2013).

[101] Many of these conditions were clearly at play in the rushed moments of the 2008 financial bailouts in the US, UK, and Ireland, for example. For more, see E.A. Posner and Adrian Vermeule (eds.), *Terror In The Balance: Security, Liberty, and the Courts* (Oxford: Oxford University Press, 2007). On the issue of separation of powers in a crisis in UK as contrasted to US, see J. Black, 'Managing the Financial Crisis: The Constitutional Dimension', *LSE Legal Studies Working Paper No. 12/2010* (3 June 2010).

in times of crisis, whether or not an emergency is declared, limiting the possibilities for effective accountability.[102]

B. Appropriation of human rights law by private economic actors

A second challenge relates to the ways in which private businesses—including private bondholders, hedge funds, and credit-rating agencies—have sought to appropriate the language and instruments of human rights to protect their revenues, or to secure their immunity from prosecution in the aftermath of the economic crisis.

In the European Court of Human Rights (ECHR) jurisprudence, legal persons, including private bondholders, are considered subjects of human rights law with equal rights as natural persons.[103] Businesses thus have legal standing in the ECHR and can bring claims against governments on the grounds of infringement of the Convention's provisions on the right to property and/or non-discrimination and equality (on the basis of differentiated treatment of creditors). This has meant that, in situations where a government decides to honour the financing requirements of its social rights protections by seeking ways to restructure its debt, the private sector can sue for whatever losses they face. Bondholders, particularly hedge funds, have threatened both the Greek[104] and the Icelandic[105] governments with lawsuits at the ECHR, with potentially chilling effects on European governments' willingness to prioritize financing social rights when deciding budget strategies to pay off debts in times of crisis.

Credit-rating agencies have also used similar tactics to shield themselves from responsibility for their actions in the lead-up to the crisis and its aftermath. Credit-rating agencies assess the financial stability and future productivity of issuers of debt, be they companies, organizations, or nations. The three dominant agencies (Moody's, Fitch, and Standard and Poor's) are widely considered to have contributed to the financial crisis by failing to give objective ratings on mortgage-backed securities because of serious conflicts of interest with their clients.[106] Several civil society organizations have thus brought cases against

[102] See Posner and Vermeule, *supra* note 100.

[103] See art. 1 of Protocol I to the European Convention for the Protection of Human Rights and Fundamental Freedoms; In *Anheuser-Busch, Inc. v Portugal*, No. 73049/01 (Eur. Ct. HR 11 Jan.2007) (Grand Chamber), the ECHR interpreted Art. 1 of Protocol I of the Convention as protecting the right to property of corporations.

[104] See NY Times, 'Hedge Funds May Sue Greece if it Tries to Force Losses' (18 January 2012), available at <http://www.nytimes.com/2012/01/19/business/global/hedge-funds-may-sue-greece-if-it-tries-to-force-loss.html> (last accessed 11 November 2013).

[105] See EU Business, 'Iceland Court Ruling Paves Way to end of Icesave Dispute' (28 October 2011), available at <http://www.eubusiness.com/news-eu/iceland-britain.d83> (last accessed 11 November 2013). The bondholders were as brazen as to state: 'the legislation granting priority to depositors [preventing the use of taxpayers' money to refund a privately contracted debt] breaches fundamental rights contained in the Icelandic constitution and the European Convention on Human Rights'.

[106] See M.B. Cane et al., 'Below Investment Grade and Above the Law: A Past, Present and Future Look at the Accountability of Credit Rating Agencies', *Fordham Journal of Corporate and Financial Law* (forthcoming); *NSU Shepard Broad Law Center Research Paper No. 11-005* (15 September 2011), available at SSRN: <http://ssrn.com/abstract=1927907> (last accessed 11 November 2013).

credit-rating agencies. For example, in Spain, a criminal complaint before Spain's Audiencia Nacional (National Court) brought by the Observatori DESC and others against Moody's, Fitch, and Standard and Poor's, arguing that the conflict of interest inherent in the risk rating by these agencies breached criminal code provisions against unlawful price manipulation and abuse of confidential information for private benefit.[107] A number of similar legal challenges have been made against credit-rating agencies in various states of the US. Advocates in Illinois, Ohio, Connecticut,[108] and California have accused different credit-rating agencies of acting fraudulently in providing factual evidence about investment ratings they knew to be false. The California Public Employees' Retirement Systems, for example, is plaintiff in a case against two agencies alleging that misconduct and misrepresentations of the companies in their risk assessments resulted in losses of $1 billion to their clients, public employees.[109] Government authorities in Italy meanwhile have opened investigations against the three agencies for having downgraded Italy's sovereign rating based on 'untruthful, tendentious, incoherent and unfair' assessments, causing significant damage to the country and its public debt.[110] Yet, in response, credit-rating agencies have invoked the right to free speech in US courts, claiming their ratings are merely private opinions. These agencies have thus been remarkably effective in evading legal accountability,[111] even though their 'opinions' measurably influenced markets, and are shown to have directly contributed to the subprime housing and financial crisis.[112]

[107] *Observatori* DESC, *Querella criminal* 25 *de febrero de* 2011, p. 50. The Audiencia Nacional subsequently held the complaint inadmissible on grounds that there were insufficient indications of criminal behaviour to warrant investigation. See Diario Jurídico, Se archiva la querella contra las agencias de calificación Moody's, Fitch y Standard and Poor's, 31 May 2012, available at <http://www.diariojuridico.com/actualidad/noticias/se-archiva-la-querella-contra-las-agencias-de-calificacion-moody%C2%B4s-fitch-y-standard-and-poor%C2%B4s.html> (last accessed 11 November 2013).

[108] See Reuters, 'Illinois sues Standard and Poor's over Rating, alleges Fraud'. (25 January 2012), available at <http://www.reuters.com/article/2012/01/25/us-mcgrawhill-sandp- lawsuit-id USTRE80O21Y20120125> (last accessed 19 November 2013).

[109] *California Public Employees' Retirement Systems v. Moody's Corp.*, 09-490241, Superior Court of California, County of San Francisco.

[110] See J. Hooper, 'Police raid Milan offices of Moody's and Standard & Poor's', *The Guardian* (London: 4 August 2011), available at <http://www.guardian.co.uk/world/2011/aug/04/police-raid-milan-moodys-standard-poors> (last accessed 11 November 2013); see also S. Rossi, 'Italy extends Rating Agencies Probe to Fitch', Reuters (24 January 2012), available at <http://www.reuters.com/article/2012/01/24/italy-fitch-idUSL5E8CO2CG20120124> (last accessed 11 November 2013).

[111] See Cane, et al. 'Below Investment Grade and Above the Law: A Past, Present and Future Look at the Accountability of Credit Rating Agencies' (September 15, 2011). *Fordham Journal of Corporate and Financial Law* (forthcoming); *NSU Shepard Broad Law Center Research Paper No. 11-005*, available at SSRN: <http://ssrn.com/abstract=1927907> (last accessed 11 November 2013).

[112] The Financial Crisis Inquiry Commission reported in January 2011 that: 'The three credit rating agencies were key enablers of the financial meltdown. The mortgage-related securities at the heart of the crisis could not have been marketed and sold without their seal of approval. Investors relied on them, often blindly. In some cases, they were obliged to use them, or regulatory capital standards were hinged on them. This crisis could not have happened without the rating agencies. Their ratings helped the market soar and their downgrades through 2007 and 2008 wreaked havoc across markets and firms'. US Financial Crisis Inquiry Commission, 'Final Report of the National Commission on the Causes of the Financial and Economic Crisis in the United States' (January, 2011), available at <http://www.gpo.gov/fdsys/pkg/GPO-FCIC/pdf/GPO-FCIC.pdf> (last accessed 11 November 2013).

The concern here then is not only that these private entities are invoking human rights, but that their rights in effect trump the human rights of ordinary people. One way to address this obstacle would be to rely on a proportionality test to balance private interests with the interests of the general public.[113] In this sense, there may be legitimate public interest reasons to place necessary and proportionate limits on the rights to property or freedom of expression and speech of a small group of wealthy businesses so that governments can prioritize the economic and social rights of marginalized sectors of society facing economic and social deprivations.

C. Transnational dimension of gaps in human rights accountability

A third challenge relates to the increasingly transnational dimensions of economic policy and their implications for accountability. The economic crisis has highlighted the extent to which the sovereignty of individual states over economic policy is increasingly being encroached upon by non-state and supra-state actors which carry significant weight in the design, implementation, and monitoring of national economic policies. Whether influenced by other states, civil society organizations, transnational corporations, or financial entities, or inter-governmental trade and financial institutions like the WTO, IMF, World Bank, and Basel Committee on Banking Supervision, economic policy is increasingly made by an array of governmental, inter-governmental, and non-state actors in practice. But as influence and responsibilities are extended below, above, and beyond the state, corresponding and effective mechanisms of accountability have not been instituted.[114] This diffusion of responsibilities poses a problem for embedding human rights law into economic policy because it is difficult to assess compliance of states with their human rights obligations when so many exogenous actors influence their behaviour.

Delineating the human rights responsibilities and legal obligations of transnational actors remains an enormous challenge, particularly as the normative human rights framework for the most part remains state-centric and focused on the notion of a unitary, sovereign, and independent state as primary duty-bearer for human rights. Significant normative developments have been achieved in recent years to clarify the distinct human rights responsibilities of different economic actors at the state, inter-governmental and non-state levels, particularly in relation to foreign

[113] For some guidance on the proportionality test from treaty bodies, see Human Rights Committee, General Comment No. 31, The Nature of the General Legal Obligation Imposed on States Parties to the Covenant, 29 March 2004, para. 6; ICESCR, General Comment No. 17, paras. 22–24. The American Convention for example states clearly, 'the right to property shall be guaranteed. It may only be encroached upon in the interest of public need or in the general interest of the community'.

[114] See, for example, M. Salomon, A. Tostensen, and W. Vanderhoule, *Casting the Net Wider, Human Rights, Development and New Duty-Bearers* (Leiden: Intersentia, 2007), and U. Beck, *Power in the Global Age: A New Global Political Economy* (London: Polity, 2006).

debt,[115] business sector operations,[116] and states' extraterritorial obligations.[117] Nevertheless, the framing of accountability for economic policy in both national and global terms and the development of effective enforcement mechanisms for the responsibilities to respect, protect, and fulfil economic and social rights remains a potent challenge.

D. Competing legal obligations: debt or human rights?

A final challenge relates to the competing legal obligations of governments. States have obligations under international human rights law, but they also have obligations to their creditors under international economic law and domestic law. Government attention has tended to focus on governments' legal commitments to their creditors—be they public (for example, international financial institutions, other governments, the European Central Bank) or private. Many governments including Greece, the US, the UK, Ireland, and Spain have insisted that paying down public debt must take precedence over social protection programmes.

For example, a leaked German government proposal on Greece's debt restructuring clearly set out these priorities:

> Greece has to legally commit itself to giving absolute priority to future debt service. This commitment has to be legally enshrined by the Greek Parliament [...] preferably through constitutional amendment [...] State revenues are to be *used first and foremost for debt service, only any remaining revenue may be used to finance primary expenditure.*[118]

While this language did not make it into the final text of the Memorandum of Understanding setting out the country's credit arrangement, the message was clear—international obligations to creditors and the EU to limit public deficits must be of immediate and absolute priority, even over fundamental human rights duties under international law.

The recent EU Treaty on Stability, Coordination and Governance (Fiscal Compact)[119] also codifies a hierarchy of norms by imposing permanent, preferably constitutional, legal obligations on members to balance their budgets and to keep their fiscal deficits below a certain limit, enabling the European Court of Justice to fine erring countries. While this treaty allows for deficit limits to be waived for 'exceptional circumstances,' it is unclear whether a repeat economic crisis would qualify. Nor is there any provision for exceptions to be made in order to honour

[115] See UN Special Rapporteur on Foreign Debt and Human Rights, Guiding principles on foreign debt and human rights, UN Doc. A/HRC/20/23 (10 April 2011).

[116] UN Special Representative on Business and Human Rights, Guiding principles on business and human rights, UN Doc. A/HRC/17/31 (21 March 2011).

[117] Maastricht Principles on Extraterritorial Obligations of States in the area of Economic, Social and Cultural Rights (Sept. 2011).

[118] See 'Assurance of Compliance in the Second GRC Program', available at <http://www.scribd.com/doc/79835252/German-proposals-for-a-Greek-budget-commissioner> (last accessed 11 November 2013). Emphasis added.

[119] See *EU Treaty on Stability, Coordination and Governance*, available at <http://european-council.europa.eu/media/639235/st00tscg26_en12.pdf> (last accessed 11 November 2013).

obligations to human rights treaties.[120] While addressing fiscal deficits is important, constitutionalizing fiscal deficit limits may restrict governments' ability to engage in counter-cyclical fiscal policies necessary to address economic crises and mitigate the human rights impacts of crises.

This raises a number of serious questions as to whether a government's legal obligations to its national and international creditors enjoy primacy, in practice, over its human rights obligations.[121] From a legal perspective, sovereign debt is usually governed by domestic law which could strictly speaking be superseded by domestic constitutional law. In Greece, Ireland, Spain, Portugal, and Belgium, for example, domestic law governs over 90 per cent of sovereign debt obligations.[122] So, courts could, at least in theory, choose to grant precedence of constitutional commitments to human rights over sovereign debt obligations. A small proportion of sovereign debt may be governed by international treaty law, raising the issue of hierarchy and conflict of laws, although the UN Charter (and its commitments to 'higher standards of living, full employment, and conditions of economic and social progress and development')[123] might be argued to set out the normative supremacy of its provisions over all other legal commitments.[124] While outside the scope of this article, a number of other international legal doctrines might also be invoked to ensure the primacy of human rights obligations, such as *jus cogens, force majeure*, and *rebus sic stantibus, mutual error*, and *state of necessity.* For example, on invoking a *state of necessity,* the International Law Commission (ILC) has commented that:

> A State cannot be expected to close its schools and universities and its courts, to disband its police force and to neglect its public services to such an extent as to expose its community to chaos and anarchy merely to provide the money wherewith to meet its moneylenders, foreign or national. There are limits to what may be reasonably expected of a State in the same manner as with an individual.[125]

More specific soft law also now exists, such as the UN Guiding Principles on Foreign Debt and Human Rights, which provides guidance to lenders and borrowers on how to balance a debtor state's contractual obligations arising from its external indebtedness with its international legal obligations to respect, protect, and fulfil all human rights.[126] In practice, it is often argued that the economic or

[120] See EU Treaty on Stability, Coordination and Governance in the Economic and Monetary Union, available at <http://european-council.europa.eu/media/639235/st00tscg26_en12.pdf> (last accessed 11 November 2013).

[121] See, for example, S. Michalowski, 'Sovereign Debt and Social Rights: Legal Reflections on a Difficult Relationship', 8 *Human Rights Law Review* (2008), 35–68, at 38.

[122] See L. Thomas, 'Given Greek Deal Investors May Consider Sovereign Debt', available at <http://www.nytimes.com/2012/02/25/business/global/as-greek-restructuring-looms-bondholders-think-twice-about-other-sovereign-debt.html> (last accessed 11 November 2013).

[123] See art. 55 of the UN Charter.

[124] See art. 103 of the UN Charter. See also A. Mcbeth, 'Human Rights in Economic Globalization', in S. Joseph and A. McBeth (eds.), *Research Handbook on International Human Rights Law* (Cheltenham: Edward Elgar, 2010), 139–166, at 144–145.

[125] Yearbook of the International Law Commission 1980, Vol. II, Part II, 42–43.

[126] See Report of the Independent Expert on the effects of foreign debt and other related international financial obligations of States on the full enjoyment of all human rights, particularly economic,

financial costs of sovereign debt default or restructuring will be higher than the costs of failing to fulfil rights in the short term, and thus governments must err on the side of caution.[127] But this analysis has been challenged by recent empirical evidence on sovereign default. In the case of Argentina's 2001 default, for example, while the immediate impacts of this crisis were devastating for many Argentines, private capital inflows returned to pre-crisis levels in just two years, while basic economic and social rights programmes were in general protected. Although legal action by a minority of private creditors is still ongoing 10 years later, Argentina's economic recovery was not impaired by its default, nor were its foreign relations significantly affected.[128]

The challenge, however, remains that there are competing international legal regimes that may produce conflicting obligations for governments. The international legal framework shaping economic policy (for example, trade, tax, finance, and taxation) still works largely to protect private interests in contradistinction to the human rights framework. The weaker enforcement mechanisms of international human rights law often mean that, in practice, human rights obligations are not given precedence as governments are more incentivized by stronger enforcement mechanisms of international economic law, costly lawsuits by private actors or political penalties for displeasing creditors.[129] While states might be legally justified in such actions in theory, the dilemma is that in practice private financial markets would likely penalize them by raising the cost of borrowing and the continued ability of states to rely on private finance to fund public services.

6. Conclusion: The Elusive Promise of a Human Rights-Centred Economic Policy in Times of Crisis

This chapter argued that the human rights legal framework does and should provide a key normative framework to guide economic policy in times of crisis. While the global economic and financial crisis presents one of the greatest contemporary challenges facing the realization and implementation of economic and social rights worldwide, it is also an unprecedented opportunity for revitalizing the struggle to make these rights operational in national and global economic policymaking and policy monitoring. In calling into question orthodox assumptions about the roles of the state and the market in the economy, the economic crisis offers an historic opportunity to bolster the resourcing, regulatory, and redistributive role of the state, so that the ultimate aim of any economic recovery policies is not merely to facilitate economic growth, but to guarantee economic and social rights for all.

social and cultural rights, Cephas Lumina See Cephas Lumina. Guiding principles on foreign debt and human rights, UN Doc. A/HRC/20/23 (10 April 2011).

127 See U. Panizza, F. Sturzenegger, and J. Zettelmeyer, 47(3) *Journal of Economic Literature* (2009), 651–698.

128 See U. Panizza, F. Sturzenegger, and J. Zettelmeyer, 47(3) *Journal of Economic Literature* (2009), 651–698.

129 See S. Michalowski, *supra* note 121.

4

Realizing Economic, Social, and Cultural Rights for All

Sandra Ratjen and Manav Satija

1. Introduction

The struggle for non-discrimination and substantive equality in the enjoyment of economic, social, and cultural rights (ESC rights) is fundamentally entangled with the broader cause of fostering greater recognition and acceptance of the universality of human rights, and the position of ESC rights within the human rights framework. The volatile socio-economic climate of recent years has catalysed increased attention on matters of socio-economic equality. Such attention is undoubtedly warranted, as equal and non-discriminatory enjoyment of ESC rights is essential to the broader promotion and fulfilment of ESC rights.

Discrimination remains a blatant negation of the equal value, humanity, and dignity of individuals and groups. In practice, the existence of a perceived inferiority is used to justify all manner of oppressive attitudes, abuses, and violations of rights, from overt and shocking violence to the more insidious paternalism.[1] As the global community has evolved however, so has its intolerance of discrimination based on claimed inferiorities. Non-discrimination is usually among the first principles cited in core human rights instruments,[2] and is thus considered a fundamental standard common to all human rights systems.[3] Since the principle of non-discrimination was first formalized in Article 1 of the United Nations (UN) Charter, it has been continuously

[1] A. Artucio, 'The Role of the NGOs in the Battle Against Discrimination', 53 *International Commission of Jurists Review* (1994), 35–50, at 35. See also the report of the UN Special Rapporteur on the human right to safe drinking water and sanitation, on stigma and the realization of the human rights to water and sanitation, UN Doc. A/HRC/21/42 (2012).

[2] United Nations Charter, Arts. 1(3), 13(1)(b), 55(c), and 76(c); Universal Declaration of Human Rights (UDHR), UN Doc. A/810, Art. 2(1); International Covenant on Civil and Political Rights (ICCPR), UN Doc. A/6316 (1996) (999 UNTS 171), Arts. 2(1) and 26; International Convention on Economic, Social and Cultural Rights (ICESCR), UN Doc. A/6316 (1966) (993 UNTS 3), Art. 2(2).

[3] Such is the prominence of the principle within human rights vernacular, that the Inter-American Court of Human Rights has classified the principle as a peremptory norm: '[t]his Court considers that the principle of equality before the law and non-discrimination belongs to *jus cogens*, because the whole legal structure of national and international public order rests on it and it is a fundamental principle that permeates all laws'. See Inter-American Court of Human Rights, *Juridical Condition*

developed, modified, and clarified in UN treaties and instruments, and by the bodies and mechanisms responsible for monitoring compliance with treaty obligations in response to the shifting needs and perceptions of an evolving global community.

While there is still a long way to go before discriminatory practices stop affecting historically marginalized and excluded groups such as women and ethnic groups, the legal and rhetorical consensus to combat these practices is relatively well established. While it is reasonably well accepted that one should not treat someone differently because of the colour of his or her skin, it is still beyond most states and many societies—or at least sectors of the population within them—to recognize the same unacceptable character of discrimination against people who have been forced to live on the street or work in insecure workplaces. In a time where the scarcity of resources is used to justify all manner of policies, states have been quick to cut public spending and social expenditure, rather than concentrating resources on the protection of those most at risk.[4] The role of ESC rights in shaping the development and proliferation of an equitable socio-economic paradigm is of crucial importance in present times, yet the debate on the status and justiciability of ESC rights remains vivid especially in domestic contexts, and one of the key challenges, still, is securing acceptance of the intrinsic value of ESC rights.[5]

A number of developments in the 1990s and early 2000s suggests important progress in the development of a more holistic understanding of human rights, which encompasses greater acceptance of the importance of ESC rights and the need to ensure their equal protection. This positive momentum unfortunately stalled in the wake of the Global Financial Crisis (GFC) of 2008, and in the years that followed a socio-economic environment has re-emerged, which has been less conducive to the realization of human rights, and in particular, to the fulfilment of ESC rights. In many countries, societal models based on solidarity have been challenged and disrupted by discriminatory patterns of societal interaction and fundamental fears for the social 'acquis'.[6] Simultaneously, the ability of citizens to scrutinize the human rights compatibility of measures taken by governments to

and Rights of the Undocumented Migrants, Advisory Opinion OC-18/03, 17 September 2003 (Ser. A) No. 18 (2003), paras. 100–101.

4 See chs. 2 and 3 in this book.

5 The UN charter recognizes the foundational nature of the respect for human rights for all. As expressed in one of the UN Secretary-General reports: 'The protection and promotion of the universal values of the rule of law, human rights and democracy are ends in themselves'. UN General Assembly, In larger freedom: towards development, security and human rights for all: report of the Secretary-General, 21 March 2005, UN Doc. A/59/2005, at para. 128. See chs. 15 and 16 in this book.

6 One illustration of that trend is the growing attention paid to 'social fraud', and in particular to unduly perceived social benefits. It is interesting to note that in many Western European countries as well as in the US and Canada, the space given to social fraud in the public debate, the resources invested in control and penalization systems are quite important. Critics often compare these efforts to the ones made for the control and sanction of tax evasion for high incomes and corporations. This comparison is all the more pertinent since the two different sets of measures do not have the same impact on social justice and on the available national resources and budgets. See generally, Centre for Economic and Social Rights, 'Mauled by the Celtic Tiger: Human rights in Ireland's economic meltdown, Rights in Crisis Briefing Paper' (2012), available at <http://www.cesr.org/downloads/cesr.ireland.briefing.12.02.2012.pdf> (last accessed 9 November 2013).

alleviate the effects of socio-economic crises has consistently disintegrated, amid growing phobias relating to the perceived scarcity of resources and threats to the established order.[7]

Questions regarding the role and potential of claims against discrimination and inequality in the enjoyment of ESC rights are of particular importance in the current context, as are questions regarding the effectiveness of adjudicative standards used to determine such claims. Importantly, while issues of socio-economic equality and non-discrimination are fundamental to the realization of ESC rights, the efforts needed to ensure full and effective realization of ESC rights must go beyond the elimination of discrimination and inequality alone.

Thus, faced with the socio-economic upheavals and growing inequalities that have been characteristic of recent years, this chapter proposes to reflect on the contribution to the normative advances in the area of ESC rights made by the struggle for non-discrimination and substantive equality, while exploring the challenges and real or perceived limitations of a non-discrimination and equality approach to the general exercise of ESC rights. In particular, the adequacy of the judicial standards of review related to discrimination for the legal enforcement of ESC rights will be discussed. Last, this chapter will examine the possible tensions between the universality of human rights and their individual nature on the one hand, and the defence of specific groups' rights and aspirations for socio-economic equality and justice on the other.

2. The Virtual Circle: Non-Discrimination, Equality, and the Advancement of Economic, Social, and Cultural Rights

A. General Comment No. 20 and beyond: formulating an extensive interpretation of discrimination under ICESCR

The principle of non-discrimination has always retained a significant place within the ESC rights landscape. The prohibition on discrimination is expressed in Article 2(2) of ICESCR as an overarching principle applying to all convention rights, and in Article 3 as a buffer against socio-economic inequality between men and women. The principle is also tailored to meet the demands of specific rights in several other articles.[8] Issues concerning non-discrimination and socio-economic equality have also drawn significant attention from the Committee on Economic, Social and Cultural Rights (CESCR). In General Comment No. 20: Non-discrimination

[7] On the impact of the crisis on specific groups and on ESC rights in general see, Centre for Economic and Social Rights, 'Human Rights and the Global Economic Crisis: Consequences, Causes and Responses' (2009), available at <http://cesr.org/downloads/CESR-Human%20Rights%20and%20the%20Global%20Economic%20Crisis.pdf> (last accessed 9 November 2013).

[8] For example, Art. 7 clarifies the application of non-discrimination to equal remuneration and work progression rights; Art. 10(3) requires states to fulfil their obligations to adopt special measures in relation to children and young persons without discrimination; and, Art. 13 allows for the equal enjoyment of compulsory and free primary education.

in economic, social, and cultural rights (Article 2, para. 2),[9] the Committee endeavoured to clarify the scope of Article 2(2) and the specific obligations of states arising as a result of that provision,[10] while in other general comments the Committee has clarified the application of the principles of equality and non-discrimination as required by specific convention rights.[11] The emphasis on discrimination issues has also carried into the Committee's periodic review of states. Many of its deliberations on the subject have been delivered in concluding observations where it has had the ability to define different situations of discriminatory treatment based on concrete cases.[12]

The focus on discrimination and the impetus for drafting General Comment No. 20 stems in part from the recognition by the Committee, human rights organizations, and civil society actors involved in the consultation process that particular operational aspects of Article 2(2) required clarification. The substance of the Committee's work thus reflects a correlation between an increased attention to discrimination and equality, and an increasingly systematic definition of specific groups requiring particular attention. These groups may be particularly at risk of suffering ESC rights violations, or may have particular needs regarding the specific right at hand, or the specific issue at stake. The increased attention on particular groups at risk may also signify the relative success of human rights organizations representing marginalized and disadvantaged people in bringing discrimination issues to the forefront of the Committee's agenda. The preference to focus on issues of socio-economic equality and non-discrimination also to some extent reflects acceptance of the notion that state compliance with treaty obligations is more easily

[9] UN Doc. E/C.12/GC/20 (42nd session, 2009).

[10] Art. 2(2) states: 'The States Parties to the present Covenant undertake to guarantee that the rights enunciated in the present Covenant will be exercised without discrimination of any kind as to race, colour, sex, language, religion, political or other opinion, national or social origin, property, birth or other status'.

[11] Discrimination relating to the enjoyment of the right to the highest attainable standard of health has, for instance, been defined as including discrimination in accessing both healthcare and its underlying determinants, and the means and entitlements for their procurement (CESCR, General Comment No. 14: The right to the highest attainable standard of health (Art. 12), UN Doc. E/C.12/2000/4 (22nd session, 2000), at 18), while the grounds of prohibited discrimination in relation to the right to work have been expanded beyond the grounds listed in Art. 2(2) to include physical or mental disability, health status (including HIV/AIDS), sexual orientation, and civil, political, social, or other status (CESCR, General Comment No. 18: The right to work (Art. 6), UN Doc. E/C.12/GC/18 (35th session, 2005), at 12). Beyond these examples the Committee has in fact addressed the issue of discrimination in relation to most of the rights contained within the Covenant. See for instance, CESCR, General Comment No. 5: Persons with disabilities, UN Doc. E/1995/22 (11th session, 1994), at 15; General Comment No. 12: The right to adequate food (Art. 11), UN Doc. E/C.12/1999/5 (20th session, 1999), at [18]; General Comment No. 15: The right to water (Arts. 11 and 12), UN Doc. E/C.12/2002/11 (29th session, 2002), at 13; General Comment No 17: The right of everyone to benefit from the protection of the moral and material interests resulting from any scientific, literary or artistic production of which he or she is the author (Art. 15(1)(c)), UN Doc. E/C.12/GC/17 (35th session, 2005), at 19.

[12] See generally, A. Chapman and B. Carbonetti, 'Human Rights Protections for Disadvantaged and Vulnerable Groups: The Contributions of the UN Committee on Economic, Social and Cultural Rights' (2011), 33 *Human Rights Quarterly* 682–732, at 685.

measurable with reference to the obligation imposed by Article 2(2), than to other obligations imposed by the Covenant.

Such notions are fed by the perception that the obligations imposed by Article 2(2) are somehow 'stronger' than obligations imposed by other provisions in ICESCR. One obvious ground for differentiation is the apparent difference in immediacy of obligations imposed by the different provisions. While Article 2(2) has been described as an 'immediate effect' duty,[13] Article 2(1) on the face of it, espouses a 'progressive realization' standard:

> Each State Party to the present Covenant undertakes to take steps, individually and through international assistance and co-operation, especially economic and technical, to the maximum of its available resources, with a view to achieving progressively the full realization of the rights recognized in the present Covenant by all appropriate means, including particularly the adoption of legislative measures.

Within Article 2(1) exists both immediate effect and progressive realization duties. Recognizing the extent of positive measures required to enable full realization of ESC rights, and the financial burden potentially associated with implementing such measures, Article 2(1) recognizes that states generally will only be able to ensure 'full realization' of ESC rights progressively. So as not to authorize inaction or ineffective action by states, the progressive realization duty under Article 2(1) has been qualified with the proviso that states immediately take steps and expend the maximum available resources available to them in working towards the goal of full realization of ESC rights.[14] The steps required of states must be 'deliberate, concrete and targeted as clearly as possible towards meeting the obligations recognized in the Covenant'.[15] This has been clarified as including 'all appropriate means, including particularly the adoption of legislative measures'.[16] 'Appropriate means' for the purposes of Article 2(1) have been defined to include the provision of judicial or other remedies, where appropriate, as well as 'administrative, financial, educational, and social measures'.[17]

While Article 2(2) is often described as an 'immediate effect' obligation, the provision seems to reflect tensions between what should be done immediately and what can only be achieved progressively in a manner similar to Article 2(1). These tensions warrant consideration when defining the scope of obligations under Article 2(2) and assessing compliance. States are obliged under Article 2(2) to eliminate both formal and substantive discrimination in the enjoyment of ESC rights.[18] The former requires states to amend their constitutions, laws, and policy

[13] CESCR, General Comment No. 20, *supra* note 9, at 7.

[14] CESCR, General Comment No. 3: The nature of State parties obligations (Art. 2, para. 1 of the Covenant), UN Doc. E/1991/23 (5th session, 1990), at paras. 2 and 9.

[15] CESCR, General Comment No. 3: The nature of State parties obligations (Art. 2, para. 1 of the Covenant), UN Doc. E/1991/23 (5th session, 1990). at para. 2.

[16] CESCR, General Comment No. 3: The nature of State parties obligations (Art. 2, para. 1 of the Covenant), UN Doc. E/1991/23 (5th session, 1990), at para. 7.

[17] CESCR, General Comment No. 9: The domestic application of the Covenant, UN Doc E/1998/24 (19th session, 1998), at paras. 3–5 and 7.

[18] CESCR, General Comment No. 20, *supra* note 9, at para. 8.

documents so as to remove *de jure* discrimination. The latter is based on the recognition that equality before the law does not always translate to equality in the enjoyment of ESC rights, and states may be required to adopt temporary special measures targeted at specific groups that have traditionally been subject to discrimination, both to negate enduring effects of the past, and to attenuate or suppress conditions which perpetuate discrimination.[19]

A state may be able to eliminate formal discrimination immediately by implementing necessary constitutional, legislative, and policy amendments. However substantive equality will usually require the investment of significantly more time and resources, and therefore full realization of substantive equality may only be achieved progressively. General Comment No. 20 provides that states are obliged to 'immediately adopt the necessary measures to prevent, diminish and eliminate the conditions and attitudes which cause or perpetuate substantive or *de facto* discrimination',[20] and that steps taken by states should be 'concrete, deliberate and targeted'.[21] While a nexus between the measures taken by states and the end-goal of substantive equality is implied here, it is unclear whether these steps would be subject to scrutiny against the appropriateness standard mandated in Article 2(1) or against another standard of review.

An extensive interpretation of non-discrimination must thus provide direction on both the form and function of positive measures required of states to allow for the realization of substantive equality of ESC rights, and the methodologies for monitoring progressive realization of substantive equality. It is equally important to find the appropriate standard of review to serve this extensive interpretation in particular, and to assess adequately the compliance with obligations requiring positive measures in general. This need became particularly evident in the drafting process relating to the Optional Protocol to the International Covenant on Economic, Social and Cultural Rights (OP-ICESCR), an instrument that 'affirms in no uncertain terms that rights claims related to positive measures described in Article 2(1) of the Covenant are to be adjudicated rather than being dismissed as being beyond the proper scope of adjudication'.[22] The adequacy of such positive measures cannot be determined purely by reference to the availability of resources of a state for a number of reasons; one being that levels of protection would drop dramatically in times of crises. Recognizing this risk, the Committee initially took a relatively strict view on the issue of availability of resources in the Working Group sessions leading the formulation of OP-ICESCR:

> The 'availability of resources', although an important qualifier to the obligation to take steps, does not alter the immediacy of the obligation, nor can resource constraints alone justify inaction. Where the available resources are demonstrably inadequate, the obligation remains for a State party to ensure the widest possible enjoyment of economic, social and

[19] CESCR, General Comment No. 20, *supra* note 9, at para. 9.

[20] CESCR, General Comment No. 20, *supra* note 9, at para. 8.

[21] CESCR, General Comment No. 20, *supra* note 9, at para. 36.

[22] B. Porter, 'The Reasonableness of art. 8(4): Adjudicating Claims form the Margins', 27 *Nordic Journal of Human Rights* (2009), 39–53, at 42.

cultural rights under the prevailing circumstances. The Committee has already emphasized that, even in times of severe resource constraints, States parties must protect the most disadvantaged and marginalized members or groups of society by adopting relatively low-cost targeted programmes.[23]

The second part to this chapter will consider, among other things, whether the standard of review that eventually made it into the OP-ICESCR adequately retains the firmness of this approach.

Beyond academic considerations however, the Committee's focus on issues relating to discrimination also correlates with the types of issues brought before it by National Human Rights Institutions, NGOs, and other ESC rights advocates. Analysis of the advocacy work of many human rights organizations reveals a tendency to engage with the Committee on issues of discrimination within particular states, rather than on the effectiveness of general domestic policies and budgetary allocations in ensuring the realization of ESC rights for those within the state's jurisdiction. Faced with a sometimes daunting monitoring methodology based on qualitative and quantitative indicators, and macro fiscal and budgetary analysis,[24] it is perhaps unsurprising that ESC rights advocates have preferred to focus on instances of discrimination. The acquisition, filtering, and analysis of statistical data may be commonplace for social scientists and development professionals, however this know-how has typically been absent from the human rights organization's toolkit.[25]

By comparison, a 'violations approach' to measuring compliance with ESC rights, generally presents fewer problems for advocates. Audrey Chapman identifies three categories of violations that may be targeted: violations resulting from actions and policies on the part of governments; violations related to patterns of discrimination; and violations due to a state's failure to meet minimum core obligations.[26] Of these three categories, violations relating to patterns of discrimination are perhaps the most straightforward to assess because the nature of violation, violator, and remedy are comparatively self-evident, at least in theory.[27] Discrimination claims relating to ESC rights also benefit from the fact that the principle is a cross-cutting duty,[28] common to all human rights instruments and mechanisms. For example, in response to a series of complaints bought before the Human Rights Committee,[29] it was finally settled that

[23] Open-ended Working Group on an Optional Protocol to the International Covenant on Economic, Social and Cultural Rights, Elements for an optional protocol to the International Covenant on Economic, Social and Cultural Rights: Analytical paper by the Chairperson-Rapporteur, Catarina de Albuquerque, UN Doc. E/CN.4/2006/WG.23/2 (3rd session, 2006), at 4.

[24] See A. Nolan, ch. 13 in this book.

[25] E. Felner, 'A New Frontier in Economic and Social Rights Advocacy? Turning Quantitative Data into a Tool for Human Rights Accountability', 9 *Sur International Journal on Human Rights* (2008), 109–146, at 110.

[26] A. Chapman, 'A "Violations Approach" for Monitoring the International Covenant on Economic, Social and Cultural Rights', 18 *Human Rights Quarterly* (1996), 23–66, at 36–46.

[27] K. Roth, 'Defending Economic, Social and Cultural Rights: Practical Issues Faced by an International Human Rights Organization', 28 *Human Rights Quarterly* (2004), 63–73, at 69.

[28] CESCR, General Comment No. 20, *supra* note 9, at para. 7.

[29] In *Zwaan de Vries v The Netherlands,* Communication No. 182/1984, UN Doc. CCPR/C/OP/2 (1990) and *Broeks v The Netherlands* (Communication No. 172/1984, UN Doc. CCPR/C/OP/2) (1990), the Committee found a violation of Art. 26. These cases related to Dutch legislation under

the prohibition of discrimination mandated by Article 26 of the ICCPR extended beyond the ICCPR contained within that instrument to also cover ESC rights.[30] Thus, even outside OP-ICESCR, discrimination claims relating to ESC rights are justiciable under various other individual complaints mechanisms attached to other international treaties.[31] Similarly on the domestic front, the partial or complete absence of ESC rights in the catalogue of rights guaranteed in many domestic Constitutions means that often the only avenue available to victims of ESC rights violations seeking judicial review of their case is via equality legislation and mechanisms.

Another factor catalysing increased receptivity to issues of non-discrimination and equality is the mainstreaming of human rights language and principles in the area of development cooperation and assistance. A human rights-based approach to development programming, as conceived both by UN agencies and other major actors in the development cooperation and assistance field, necessitates a substantial focus on marginalized and excluded groups.[32] The danger of course in focusing exclusively on issues of discrimination is that such a focus could divert attention from other aspects of ESCR, thus inhibiting their normative development. During the working sessions of the Open-ended Working Group on an Optional Protocol to ICESCR, for example, various states including Switzerland, the United Kingdom, and India, advocated for the limitation of adjudication under OP-ICESCR to matters of discrimination when faced with substantial opposition to a broad mandate for the Optional Protocol.[33]

which married women were denied certain unemployment benefits that were granted to unmarried women and to all men, regardless of their marital status. This distinction was implemented through the application of legal presumption according to which a married woman was assumed not to be the 'breadwinner' of her family. Only by submitting evidence proving her to be the breadwinner of her family could a married woman be eligible for the same unemployment benefits granted to male counterparts.

[30] Art. 2(2) of ICESCR, by comparison, has been restricted in application only to the rights contained within the Covenant: see CESCR, General Comment No. 20, *supra* note 9, at 7. While Art. 2(2) is not a free-standing right, it should not be understood however, to lack autonomy—Art. 2(2) is autonomous in the sense that even if there is no violation of a right guaranteed by the Covenant, there may have been discrimination in the exercise of an ESCR without sufficient justification: see B. Wilson, 'The Principle of Non-Discrimination in the International Covenant on Economic, Social and Cultural Rights', in W. Kälin, et. al. (eds.), *International Law, Conflict and Development* (Leiden: Martinus Nijhof, 2010), at 223.

[31] In addition to the possibility of lodging communications relating to an alleged violation of Art. 26 of the ICCPR under the Optional Protocol to the International Covenant on Civil and Political Rights, UN Doc. A/6316 (999 UNTS 171) (entered into force 23 March 1976), individual communications relating to ESCR could potentially be lodged under Art. 14 of the International Convention on the Elimination of All Forms of Racial Discrimination (CERD), UN Doc. A/6014 (1966) (660 UNTS 195); the Optional Protocol to the Convention on the Elimination of All Forms of Discrimination against Women, UN Doc. A/54/49 (2131 UNTS 83) (entered into force 22 December 2000); the Optional Protocol to the Convention on the Rights of Persons with Disabilities, UN Doc. A/61/49 (entered into force 3 May 2008); and, the Optional Protocol to the Convention on the Rights of the Child on a communications procedure (opened for signature 28 February 2012).

[32] See for instance, the UN Statement of Common Understanding on Human Rights-Based Approach to development cooperation and programming, available at <http://www.undg.org/index.cfm?P=221#s2> (last accessed 9 November 2013).

[33] See generally, Open-ended Working Group on an Optional Protocol to the International Covenant on Economic, Social and Cultural Rights, *supra* note 23.

B. The impact of specific actors on the work of the Committee on Economic, Social and Cultural Rights

The receptivity of states to discrimination issues has encouraged the CESCR to frame a significant component of its concluding observations in terms of equality and non-discrimination issues. While this strategy is undoubtedly formulated to allow the Committee to engage with state parties within their comfort zone, as noted earlier, it also reflects the success of organized groups in engaging with and influencing the Committee.

A significant number of civil society actors including NGOs have engaged with the CESCR in an increasingly systematic manner, with the aim of providing specific groups most at risk of suffering ESC rights violations with practical and tailored protection of ESC rights. Beyond the examples given in this section, this is the case of organizations representing indigenous people, rural communities, or people with different sexual orientation or gender identity. Such engagement must be longstanding in order to have a significant impact on the concluding observations of the Committee, and beyond, to influence its interpretive work.

One example of such engagement is the work of the International Disability Alliance (IDA), an alliance of organizations dedicated to promoting the effective and full implementation of the Convention on the Rights of Persons with Disabilities (CRPD) worldwide. IDA 'represents the estimated one billion people worldwide living with a disability. This is the world's largest—and most frequently overlooked—minority group'.[34] IDA has actively engaged with the CESCR over the past decade, consistently making submissions for the Committee's pre-sessional working groups and sessional periodic review of states, and by providing input into the elaboration of general comments.

In its submission to the CESCR on Cameroon, for instance, the IDA drew the Committee's attention to issues relating to discrimination in access to employment, equal remuneration, and working conditions for persons with disabilities. Attention was also drawn to the heightened risk faced by women and children with disabilities of becoming victims of domestic violence and abuse, including the practice of female genital mutilation on girls with disabilities. The IDA also highlighted the absence of education, information, healthcare, and services relating to sexual and reproductive health, HIV and sexually transmitted infections (STIs), and the disturbing prevalence of non-consensual administration of contraception, or fertility treatments for girls and women with disabilities.[35] In its concluding observations the Committee paid special attention to most of the issues raised by the IDA, recommending, for example, the inclusion of disabled persons in education and the labour market, and urging the state to ensure that the denial of reasonable accommodation is regarded as a form of discrimination under the law

[34] See International Disability Alliance, available at <http://www.internationaldisabilityalliance.org/en/about-us> (last accessed 9 November 2013).

[35] IDA, *CESCR 47th Session: recommendations for Concluding Observations*, available at <http://www.internationaldisabilityalliance.org/en/47th-session-november-2011> (last accessed 9 November 2013), at 1–5.

and as a matter of policy. The Committee also made a number of recommendations in relation to sexual and reproductive health, access to healthcare, education, and services for women and girls with disabilities.[36]

In its submission on Israel, the IDA reflected on the absence of adequate data on children and adults with disabilities, issues relating to access to employment and equal remuneration for persons with disabilities, access to appropriate healthcare for persons with disabilities, including in relation to sexual and reproductive healthcare services for women and girls with disabilities, and access to adequate education for disabled persons in the Occupied Palestinian Territories (OPT).[37] In its concluding observations, the Committee requested that Israel acquire and use disaggregated data and results of studies to develop policies and programmes to promote equal opportunities for disabled persons in society, and made specific recommendations along the lines suggested in the IDA shadow report with respect to the right to work and equal remuneration of disabled persons, access to education for children with disabilities, and poverty, social exclusion, and enjoyment of the right to an adequate standard of living with respect to disabled persons in the Israeli-Arab population, and particularly in the OPT.[38]

Another example of civil society actors representing marginalized groups and influencing the work of the Committee is that of the European Roma Rights Centre (ERRC). Since 1996, the ERRC has combated anti-Romani racism, endeavouring to ensure *de jure* and substantive equality for Romani peoples.[39] In its submission to the CESCR on Hungary, the ERRC emphasized the causal connection between limited access to quality, mainstream education for Romani children and the disproportionately high rates of unemployment experienced among the Roma population. The ERRC also highlighted that the situation was compounded by discriminatory practices in the field of employment by potential employers, and noted the worrying continuation of the practice of segregated schooling that prevailed in Hungary, which had a far-reaching impact on generations of Romani children.[40] Many of the Committee's concluding observations on Hungary subsequently focused on the extremely high unemployment rate among the Roma in Hungary and the discriminatory practices and attitudes of private and public employers against the Roma, as well as the practice of segregated schooling. The Committee also expressed deep concern that a fifth of the Roma people in

[36] CESCR, Concluding Observations: Cameroon, UN Doc. E/C.12/CMR/CO/2-3 (47th Session, 2011), at paras. 11, 20, and 30.

[37] IDA, *CESCR 47th Session: recommendations for Concluding Observations*, available at <http://www.internationaldisabilityalliance.org/en/47th-session-november-2011> (last accessed 9 November 2013), at 17–24.

[38] CESCR, Concluding Observations: Israel, UN Doc. E/C.12/ISR/CO/3 (47th session, 2011), at paras. 10, 15, and 34.

[39] See European Roma Rights Centre, available at <http://www.errc.org/about-us-overview> (last accessed 9 November 2013).

[40] ERRC, *Written Comments of the European Roma Rights Centre Concerning Hungary for Consideration by the United Nations Committee on Economic, Social and Cultural Rights at its 38th Session*, available at <http://www.errc.org/article/errc-submission-to-un-cescr-on-hungary-september-2007/3742> (last accessed 9 November 2013).

Hungary were living in slum settlements, often without access to running water, adequate sewerage, or were located close to municipal dumpsites, and that Roma were frequently denied access to social housing.[41]

In its submission on Ukraine, the ERRC noted that a major section of Romani communities in Ukraine lived in extreme poverty, experienced extraordinarily high levels of unemployment and discrimination in the workplace, and faced substantial impediments in accessing adequate housing, health services, and education. Compounding matters further, Romani in Ukraine often faced difficulties in obtaining the official personal documentation necessary for accessing health services, housing services, and the school system.[42] In response to the ERRC's submissions, the Committee made a number of recommendations to Ukraine with regard to the situation of the Roma, including the removal of administrative processing fees and bureaucratic requirements, so as to allow the provision of personal documents to all Roma with a view to enabling access to employment, healthcare, and education, as well as other economic, social, and cultural rights. The Committee also recommended that concrete steps be taken to combat discrimination against Roma in the workplace and to reduce Roma unemployment through specifically targeted measures, such as vocational training, job training and placement, financial incentives for employers, and assistance for Roma opening their own businesses. The Committee further recommended steps be taken to secure access to adequate and affordable housing, increase school attendance by Roma children, combat discrimination against Roma pupils, and promote their admission to mainstream schools and classes.[43]

While the IDA, ERRC, and other organizations representing disadvantaged and marginalized groups have undoubtedly played a role in awareness raising and the realization of equality for these groups, their efforts also inform the normative development of convention rights, and in particular in the monitoring and interpretive work of the Committee. There are several pertinent lessons advocates can take from the stories of organizations such as the IDA and ERRC. One lesson regards how best to engage on multiple fronts to achieve outcomes for the group being represented. Overcoming substantive inequalities in the enjoyment of socio-economic rights usually requires positive action on multiple fronts, as the rights themselves are interrelated and interdependent. As the causal factors protracting socio-economic inequalities are multidimensional and multifaceted, so must be the methodologies aimed at combating these inequalities. The need for multifaceted approaches for combating socio-economic inequality is amplified by the changing socio-economic landscape, where complex forms of

[41] CESCR, Concluding Observations: Hungary, UN Doc. E/C.12/HUN/CO/3 (38th Session, 2007), at paras. 22, 25, 27, 34, 50, and 51.

[42] ERRC, *Written Comments of the European Roma Rights Centre Concerning Ukraine for Consideration by the United Nations Committee on Economic, Social and Cultural Rights at its 39th Session*, available at <http://www.errc.org/article/errc-submission-to-un-cescr-on-ukraine-september-2007/3741> (last accessed 9 November 2013).

[43] CESCR, Concluding Observations: Ukraine, UN Doc. E/C.12/UKR/CO/5 (39th Session, 2007), paras. 34, 37, and 48.

discrimination are being compounded and new groups are becoming marginalized and disadvantaged.

C. Complex forms of discrimination in a complex socio-economic environment

While the CESCR has invested substantial effort in explaining the relationship between non-discrimination and other principles, it has not as yet provided a coherent rationale or framework for conceptualizing vulnerability, nor has it provided criteria for identifying which individuals or groups may be considered disadvantaged or vulnerable in general or in specific contexts.[44] The Committee has, when the opportunity has arisen, added new grounds for prohibited discrimination such as disabilities,[45] age,[46] nationality,[47] marital and family status,[48] sexual orientation and gender identity,[49] health status,[50] place of residence,[51] and economic and social situation.[52] Further, it has left open the question of which grounds of discrimination may be proscribed by emphasizing 'other status' as one of the proscribed grounds for discrimination and reiterating that the list of prohibited grounds was never intended to be exhaustive.[53] The rationale provided for retaining this measure of flexibility in the provision is that '[t]he nature of discrimination varies according to context and evolves over time'.[54]

Not only does the concept of discrimination evolve over time, the aspirations of those subject to discrimination and seeking substantive equality evolve also. An example of this is provided by the CRPD,[55] which recognizes the inherent differences between those with disabilities and those without, and so seeks only to ensure that persons with disabilities not be subject to undue discrimination on the basis of their condition, and that the state provide 'reasonable accommodation' including 'necessary and appropriate adjustments where needed in a particular case to ensure to persons with disabilities the enjoyment or exercise on an equal basis with others of all human rights and fundamental freedoms'.[56] The emphasis of the CRPD is better understood if we recall the distinction between non-discrimination and equality:

> Whilst the principle of non-discrimination prohibits treating a person in a pejorative way on the basis of the various criteria mentioned, the principle of equality prohibits treating

[44] A. Chapman and B. Carbonetti, *supra* note 12, at 692.

[45] General Comment No. 5, *supra* note 11, para. 5; General Comment No. 20, *supra* note 10, at para. 28.

[46] General Comment No. 20, *supra* note 9, at para. 29.

[47] General Comment No. 20, *supra* note 9, at para. 30.

[48] General Comment No. 20, *supra* note 9, at para. 31.

[49] General Comment No. 20, *supra* note 9, at para. 32.

[50] General Comment No. 20, *supra* note 9, at para. 33.

[51] General Comment No. 20, *supra* note 9, at para. 34.

[52] General Comment No. 20, *supra* note 9, at para. 35.

[53] General Comment No. 20, *supra* note 9, at para. 27.

[54] General Comment No. 20, *supra* note 9, at para. 27.

[55] UN Doc. A/61/49 (2006) (2515 UNTS 3).

[56] UN Doc. A/61/49 (2006) (2515 UNTS 3), Art. 2.

two situations differently when their similarity demands that they be treated the same way or treating two situations in the same way when their dissimilarity requires that they be treated differently.[57]

The CRPD requires this type of 'fine-grained' perspective as it is not a Convention designed to eliminate disability or fight against it but rather is designed to ensure that the specific needs of people with disabilities are accommodated within society so as to allow them to enjoy universal human rights. The CRPD thus highlights the need to retain a measure of flexibility in the definition and standard of reviewing non-discrimination claims in respect to ESC rights.

Flexibility is essential as human rights and anti-discrimination advocates develop a more evolved understanding of how inequalities may manifest in modern societies. The development and increasingly systematic use of intersectionality approaches, for example, helps reveal discrimination that occurs on the intersection of different traits which together form a person's being, rather than on one individual trait considered in isolation to other traits. These approaches thus aim to reveal multiple identities and expose the different types of discrimination and disadvantage that occur as a consequence of the combination of different identities. Another approach to complex discrimination is identity performance, which recognizes that individuals may experience discrimination because of stereotypes about behaviours associated with their identity group rather than on the basis of the identify group itself. An example may be where a member of a particular racial group seeking employment is subject to discrimination not on the basis of their racial status, but rather on a preconceived stereotype of the work ethic of employees from that racial group. These phenomena are compounded by 'structural discrimination'; that is, structural dynamics of an environment that effectuate, and often obscure, discriminatory intent.[58]

Beyond providing insight into the complexity of human beings as both individuals and relational beings, such approaches indicate that the realization of substantive equality in the enjoyment of rights will require broad, multifaceted methodologies. CESCR has thus far demonstrated at least some degree of recognition of this need and of the complex forms of discrimination to which persons or groups of persons may become subject. The Committee has noted that:

individuals or groups of individuals face discrimination on more than one of the prohibited grounds... [S]uch cumulative discrimination has a unique and specific impact on individuals and merits particular consideration and remedying and that other grounds of discrimination for the purposes of article 2(2) may include '... the intersection of two prohibited grounds of discrimination'.[59]

[57] B. Wilson, 'The Principle of Non-Discrimination in the International Covenant on Economic, Social and Cultural Rights', in W. Kälin, et. al. (eds.), *International Law, Conflict and Development* (Leiden: Martinus Nijhof, 2010), at 216.

[58] S. Goldberg, 'Discrimination by Comparison', 120 *Yale Law Review* (2011), 728–812, at 737. The phenomenon of structural discrimination has been described by the Committee as 'systemic discrimination': see General Comment No. 20, *supra* note 9, at para. 12.

[59] General Comment No. 20, *supra* note 9, at 17.

The task of monitoring such forms of complex discrimination can, however, be particularly difficult in a fragile socio-economic climate, where new categories and new groups of individuals often find themselves disadvantaged, marginalized, and subject to discrimination.

D. New categories, new groups, and the reflection of a chronic denial of socio-economic rights

The work of the IDA and ERRC, as noted, relates to groups with 'fixed' membership who are relatively well-organized and benefit from a recognition of the discrimination they have suffered historically, including by way of specific human rights conventions and declarations guaranteeing their rights.[60] While these groups continue to be subject to discrimination and inequality, new groups are increasingly being pushed to articulate their interests and rights and advocate against the lack of realization of their socio-economic rights. The struggle of groups to be recognized as precisely that—a group of individuals sharing the same need for recognition and enjoyment of their universal rights—corresponds with a sense of being the victims of targeted and shared social injustice. This is the case of people living in poverty.

If poverty may be considered as 'a human condition characterized by sustained or chronic deprivation of the resources, capabilities, choices, security and power necessary for the enjoyment of an adequate standard of living and other civil, cultural, economic, political and social rights',[61] then poverty, and particularly extreme poverty, becomes both a cause and a consequence of systemic violations of a range of human rights, and in particular, violations of ESC rights. A strong correlation exists between discrimination and poverty through the mechanics of exclusion and marginalization.[62] The cycle is exacerbated by the intergenerational dimension of poverty that allows stigmatization and exclusion to be perpetuated beyond an individual's life cycle.

Despite the shared experience of exclusion, marginalization, and stigmatization, the interests of people living in poverty remain diffuse and under-represented in public policymaking.[63] Such diffusion of interests obviously poses organizational and political challenges for the mobilization of groups of individuals with a heterogeneous composition, potentially narrowly defined interests, and specific

[60] Chapman and Carbonetti, *supra* note 12, at 706.

[61] CESCR, Poverty and the International Covenant on Economic, Social and Cultural Rights, Statement of the Committee to the Third United Nations Conference on the Least Developed Countries, UN Doc. E/C.12/2001/10 (25th session, 2001), at para. 3.

[62] The Social Policy and Development Division of the UN ECOSOC Department of Economic and Social Affairs describes poverty as entailing: 'more than the lack of income and productive resources to ensure sustainable livelihoods. Its manifestations include hunger and malnutrition, limited access to education and other basic services, social discrimination and exclusion, as well as the lack of participation in decision-making. Various social groups bear disproportionate burden of poverty'. See UN Department of Economic and Social Affairs, 'Poverty', available at <http://social.un.org/index/Poverty.aspx> (last accessed 9 November 2013).

[63] M. Olson, *The Logic of Collective Action: Public Goods and the Theory of Groups* (Cambridge: Harvard University Press, 1965).

legal and policy priorities.[64] Beyond the difficulties to mobilize forces among groups consisting of individuals who are dispersed throughout in society, the addition of their interests may not add up to a collective, indivisible, and widely trans-individual whole.[65]

Ongoing debate over the past decade on issues of discrimination and poverty in Canada has often broadened in scope to account for this diffusion of interests. This has resulted in increased support for the explicit recognition of 'social condition' as a prohibited ground of discrimination, and further, for this new ground to be incorporated into the Canadian Charter of Rights and Freedoms.[66] For anti-poverty groups in different Canadian provinces, the inclusion of such a provision may enhance the protection of the most marginalized groups who are currently not sufficiently protected by Section 15 of the Charter, which ensures equal benefits of the law for all. These anti-poverty groups assume that such an altered provision would help improve the protection and enjoyment of ESC rights, a category of rights not guaranteed by the Charter.

Social conditions have, in fact, been recognized and invoked before Canadian courts as grounds for discrimination. The impetus for explicit Charter protection is the advancement of substantive equality and social justice. The problems faced by groups who face historical and structural discrimination, such as single parents and social assistance beneficiaries, would undoubtedly become more visible to the rest of society, and especially to policymakers, if such a change were instituted. At the international level, however, efforts to advocate for the recognition of poverty as a prohibited ground of discrimination, or even for the 'poor' to be recognized as a new category or 'vulnerable' group, faces substantial resistance.[67]

The Human Rights Council's unanimous adoption of the UN Guiding Principles on extreme poverty and human rights in 2012,[68] marks a positive step towards the recognition of the specific challenges and needs of people living in extreme poverty to realize their human rights, and towards the guarantee of a better enjoyment of their rights. However, even if the rights of diffuse groups and subgroups may benefit from formal recognition, the process of exercising such rights presents its own challenges.

[64] A. Constain, 'The Struggle for a National Women's Lobby: Organizing a Diffuse Interest', 33 *The Western Political Quarterly* (1980), 476–491.

[65] For a comparative analysis of class action litigation (or collective actions) in different countries and legal systems, and their advantages and gaps for the protection of diffuse and transindividual rights and interests, see A. Gidi, 'The class action code: A model for civil law countries', in *Public Law and Legal Theory Series* (Houston: University of Houston, 2006).

[66] M. Jackman, 'Constitutional Contact with the Disparities in the World: Poverty as a Prohibited Ground of Discrimination under the Canadian Charter and Human Rights Law', 2 *Review of Constitutional Studies* (1994), 76–122. See also, Federated anti-poverty groups of British Columbia and the British Columbia Public Interest Advocacy Centre, Submission to the Canadian Human Rights Act Review Panel (1999), available online at <http://www.povnet.org/node/1122> (last accessed 9 November 2013).

[67] For records of the position of Morocco and the Philippines, see UN HRC, Analytical compilation of the submissions received in writing and made at the consultation on the progress report on the draft guiding principles on extreme poverty and human rights, UN Doc.A/HRC/19/32, 2011.

[68] UN HRC, Resolution A/HRC/RES/21/11, 2012.

3. Exercising Rights: Harmonizing the Individual and Collective Dimensions of ESC Rights

The struggle for non-discrimination and substantive equality has significantly informed individual and shared understandings of ESC rights and corresponding state obligations under international law. While ingrained prejudices and resistance to ESC rights as justiciable rights remain, anti-discrimination arguments are of continuing strategic advantage for those advocating for more extensive protection of those rights. The extensive use of anti-discrimination and equality provisions to improve recognition of the ESC rights may also, however, be problematic at times, as has been highlighted. It is also worth looking at how these limits and potential tensions are reflected in the adjudication of ESC rights, and particularly, whether the standards of review used in adjudication are capable of overcoming these limits and tensions in actual cases of discrimination or inequality.

A. Formulating a standard of review for equality lawsuits: a comparative perspective

An obvious starting point for assessing standards of review is domestic jurisdictions with a tradition of litigating discrimination claims.

In *Public Service Alliance of Canada v Canada Post Corporation and Canadian Human Rights Commission*,[69] the Canadian Supreme Court reviewed a decision of the Canadian Human Rights Tribunal (CHRT) regarding a claim by the Public Service Alliance of Canada (PSAC) that employees in the male-dominated Postal Operations Group were paid more than employees in the female-dominated Clerical and Regulatory Group for work of equal value, contrary to Section 11 of the Canadian Human Rights Act. Using job evaluations to determine the comparability of the work of the two groups of employees, the CHRT had determined that there was sufficient evidence of wage discrimination between 1982 and 2002. Canada Post commenced judicial review proceedings in the Federal Court, where the CHRT's decision was overturned. On appeal to the Federal Court of Appeal,[70] the majority agreed with Canada Post that the CHRT decision was unreasonable, as the use of job evaluations did not meet the requisite standard of proof to support a finding that wage discrimination had taken place.[71] The dissenting judge, Evans JA, agreed with the CHRT and would have restored its findings. First, he found it reasonable for the CHRT to use the Postal Operators group as the male-dominated comparator, even though this group included a large number of highly paid women.[72] Second, Evans JA supported the CHRT's reliance on the job

[69] (2011) SCC 57 (Sup. Ct. of Canada).

[70] *Canada Post Corp. v Public Service Alliance of Canada* [2010] FCA 56, [2011] 2 RCF 221.

[71] *Canada Post Corp. v Public Service Alliance of Canada* [2010] FCA 56, [2011] 2 RCF 221, at paras. 142–146.

[72] *Canada Post Corp. v Public Service Alliance of Canada* [2010] FCA 56, [2011] 2 RCF 221, at paras. 174–195.

evaluations and its application of the 'balance of probabilities' standard of proof in finding that a wage gap existed between the two groups.[73] The PSA appealed to the Supreme Court of Canada, which in an oral judgment delivered immediately following the parties' submissions, allowed the appeal and endorsed the dissenting reasons of Evans JA. The decision of the CHRT was subsequently restored, requiring Canada Post to compensate for 50 per cent of the wage gap between the two groups over the 20 year period.

The comparator methodology used in this case—looking at the treatment of those who are, for all intents and purposes, alike to the discrimination claimant but for the protected characteristic—represents the classical standard of review used in discrimination lawsuits. While comparators may be useful at times as heuristic tools for identifying discriminatory conduct in certain contexts, these contexts are limited to situations where an appropriate comparator can be found in relation to a specific form of discrimination, and thus such a methodology is largely ineffective in reviewing conduct which relates to more complex forms of discrimination. Importantly, the use of a comparator methodology, in and of itself, does not contemplate lawful differential treatment. The Committee recognizes that there may be situations where differentiation on a particular trait is reasonable and objective.[74] It follows that a standard of review must go beyond identifying only whether differentiation occurred, to consider whether that differentiation is justifiable, reasonable, or proportional to some legitimate objective.

In *Khosa v Minister of Social Development; Mahlaule v Minister for Social Development*,[75] the Constitutional Court of South Africa considered the case of destitute permanent residents in South Africa who were excluded from various social grants payable to citizens under the Social Assistance Act (59 of 1992), including disability grants, grants to the aged, and child support grants. The Court in this instance applied a twin methodology, first examining the claim through the lens of equality rights by assessing whether the exclusion of permanent residents amounted to unfair discrimination, prohibited under Section 9(3) of the Constitution.[76] Through this lens, the Court considered the impact of the exclusion on the permanent residents, noting that non-citizens were a vulnerable group in society,[77] on whom the exclusion had a stigmatizing effect.[78] The second step was to consider whether the discriminatory exclusion of non-citizens contravened the right of access to social assistance under Section 27(1) of the Constitution, or whether the exclusion was reasonable when directed towards a legitimate aim. In response

[73] *Canada Post Corp. v Public Service Alliance of Canada* [2010] FCA 56, [2011] 2 RCF 221, at paras. 196–236.

[74] *General Comment No. 20, supra* note 9, at para. 13.

[75] (2004) 6 BCLR 569 (CC).

[76] Section 9 prohibits direct or indirect unfair discrimination on a range of listed grounds such as race, sex, gender, sexual orientation, age and disability. While this list is not meant to be exhaustive and other unlisted grounds may be recognized as grounds for discrimination if they 'have an adverse effect on the dignity of the individual, or some comparable effect' (see *Harksen v Lane NO and Others* [1997] 11 BCLR 1489 (CC), at para. [46]), the burden of proving that discrimination on a non-listed ground is unfair, falls on the applicant.

[77] *Khosa*, para. 71.

[78] *Khosa*, para. 74.

to arguments by the state that the extension of social grants to non-citizens would impose 'an impermissibly high financial burden on the State',[79] the Court considered whether financial considerations could be a valid ground for limiting access of benefits to citizens only.[80] The state had provided estimates showing that the projected cost of including non-citizens in the welfare scheme would range between 243 million and 672 million South African Rand. Noting that this estimate represented an increase of 2 per cent of the total cost of the welfare programme, the Court found that it was unreasonable to exclude non-citizens on this basis alone.[81] The Court then considered the reasonableness of the exclusion on the basis that it furthered a legitimate aim of the state's immigration policy, that is, to exclude persons who may become a burden on the state and also to promote self-sufficiency among foreign nationals. In this respect, the Court accepted that limiting the cost of social welfare was a legitimate concern of the state, and that the policy of excluding people who may later become a burden on the state from gaining permanent residency was a permissible modus operandi for limiting costs. The Court nevertheless found the exclusion of those who were already permanent citizens, but had become a burden on the state after gaining permanent residency was unconstitutional.[82] Finding a breach of Sections 9(3) and 27(1), the Court provided a 'reading-in' remedy, reading the category of permanent residents into the provisions of the Social Assistance Act.[83]

The methodology utilized by the Court in *Khosa* for identifying discriminatory conduct certainly allows for a more refined assessment than that offered by the comparator methodology used in *Public Service Alliance*. Examining the impact of exclusion on an individual or group, rather than focusing on the comparability of an individual's situation with others, potentially allows for easier identification of discrimination based on complex factors, such as intersectionality and identity performance. However, despite the Court's increased capacity for identifying disadvantage experienced by a person subject to discrimination, the requirement that the individual display some recognizable vulnerability may be problematic unless a sophisticated test for determining vulnerability is established.

These cases demonstrate the need for a flexible standard of review to account for the specific needs of groups subject to socio-economic discrimination. In fact, this is a need that was also reflected in the drafting process of OP-ICESCR. The drafting working group was faced with the challenge of formulating a standard of review that incorporated the temporal dimension of fulfilment and interrelationship with available resources mandated by Article 2(1), without compromising the right to adjudication and rights to remedies of violations of human rights.[84] One contentious issue in the drafting was whether the standard of 'unreasonableness' or the standard of 'reasonableness' should be employed in the standard of review. Observing the tensions created by imposing a standard of unreasonableness, but wary of reducing the vision of adjudication based on fulfilment of ESC rights,[85]

[79] *Khosa*, para. 60.
[80] *Khosa*, paras. 45, and 53–57.
[81] *Khosa*, paras. 61–62.
[82] *Khosa*, para. 116.
[83] *Khosa*, paras. 86–98.
[84] B. Porter, *supra* note 23, at 43.
[85] B. Porter, *supra* note 23, at 45.

the negotiators of the OP-ICESCR finally settled on a standard of reasonableness largely inspired by the South African Constitutional Court's formula in the *Grootboom* case.[86] In its statement of 2007, the CESCR has specified particular factors that could be considered in assessing the reasonableness of the steps taken by states, including:

a) the extent to which the measures taken were deliberate, concrete, and targeted towards the fulfilment of ESC rights;
b) whether the state party exercised its discretion in a non-discriminatory and non-arbitrary manner;
c) whether the State party's decision (not) to allocate available resources is in accordance with international human rights standards;
d) where several policy options were available to the state, whether it adopted the option that least restricted Covenant rights;
e) the time frame in which the steps were taken; and
f) whether the steps had taken into account the precarious situation of disadvantaged and marginalized individuals or groups and, whether they prioritized grave situations or situations of risk.[87]

This 'reasonableness' standard of review, now encapsulated in Article 8(4) of OP-ICESCR, retains a substantial measure of flexibility and addresses several important considerations. In the drafting of OP-ICESCR many states were advocating for the standard for review to import the European 'margin of appreciation' doctrine in order to enable them to implement their preferred policy options in respect to ESC rights according to their domestic context. An alternate doctrine of 'margin of discretion' was later proposed when the contentiousness of the issue stalled progress. While both doctrines were eventually omitted from the final wording of Article 8(4), the second step in CESCR's above formula nonetheless makes it clear that while states will be afforded some degree of discretion, this cannot be used to justify discriminatory practices. The final step outlined by the Committee furthers the protection of disadvantaged and marginalized persons by clearly delineating the link between the positive measures taken by states and those most in need or most at risk.

The effectiveness of Article 8(4) and the criteria underpinning the reasonableness test will ultimately depend, however, on how the CESCR applies the provision in individual complaint procedures, rather than how the provision itself is worded. The experience of litigants in domestic jurisdictions provides illustrations of this challenge, while indicating how courts have dealt with competing interests and resource implications.

[86] *Government of the Republic of South Africa and Others v Grootboom and Others* (2000) 11 BCLR 169 (CC).

[87] CESCR, An evaluation of the obligation to take steps to the 'maximum of available resources' under an optional protocol to the Covenant, Statement, UN Doc. E/C.12/2007/1 (38th session, 2007), at para. 8.

B. The tensions around competing interests, public interest, and the use of (limited) resources

In the 'Blue Moonlight' case, a case with considerable budgetary implications, the South African Constitutional Court considered the reasonableness of state measures in relation to public housing.[88] The Court ultimately sanctioned the discriminatory housing policies of the respondent municipalities, and ordered the broadening of temporary and emergency accommodation schemes to cover evictees from both public and private properties. Beyond this, *Blue Moonlight* is of utmost importance for ESC rights advocates given the manner in which the Court dealt with 'scarcity of resource' arguments advanced by the respondent public authority.

The case involved several families living in old and deteriorated industrial buildings who had unsuccessfully attempted to compel successive owners of the property (Blue Moonlight Properties from 2004 onwards) to remedy the unacceptable safety and sanitary situation of the concerned buildings. In June 2005 and January 2006, Blue Moonlight posted notices to vacate the property and to cancel all existing leases. The occupiers refused to vacate the property as no alternative accommodation had been made available to them, and they would therefore become homeless. This would violate their right to housing guaranteed under Section 26 of the South African Constitution—it was on this basis this provision that the City of Johannesburg joined the proceedings. It is interesting to note that both parties to the case—Blue Moonlight Properties and the Occupiers—also invoked Section 9 of the Constitution, which guarantees equality before the law and equal protection. The Constitutional Court finally settled the proceedings in December 2011 and upheld the earlier decisions of the High Court and Supreme Court of Appeal. The Court confirmed the unconstitutionality of the City's housing policy on the grounds that it discriminated against people in desperate need of emergency and temporary accommodation because they were evicted by private owners and not by the City itself. It did so despite the claim by the municipality that the resource implications of such a decision would be severe and affect its budget, and would thus be to the detriment of the broader public.

The broader question of how 'public interest' and 'general welfare' are used and interpreted in matters concerning ESC rights is particularly important in contexts of high economic and financial uncertainty, where the tension between competing interests and the allocation of resources is often more evident. While the concept of public interest can be used effectively in litigation to advance the rights of minorities and disadvantaged groups, it is also used to justify limitations on socio-economic rights, especially when resources are deemed to be scarce. Such limitations unfortunately impact more on at-risk and already disadvantaged individuals and groups, causing even further regression in their socio-economic rights.

[88] *City of Johannesburg Metropolitan Municipality v Blue Moonlight Properties 39 PTY LTD and Occupiers of Saratoga Avenue*, Case CCT 37/11, [2011] ZACC 33.

Article 4 of the ICESCR stipulates that 'State Parties [...] may subject such rights only to such limitations as are determined by law only insofar as this may be compatible with the nature of these rights and solely for the purpose of promoting the general welfare in a democratic society'.[89] While previous parts of this chapter have alluded to the necessity of balancing interests and rights in particular contexts, the promotion of 'common good' poses key challenges to the universal realization of socio-economic rights. While public interest litigation has often catalysed groundbreaking remedies for ESC rights violations and inspired a more holistic understanding of rights and responsibilities, the exercise of determining what is indeed in the 'public interest', is itself a challenging one. Importantly, the potential broadness of the notion of 'public interest' often provides the justification needed to further limit the socio-economic rights of disadvantaged or marginalized groups (whether they are a 'minority' or simply a large and growing group, often representing the majority of the population).

In recent cases before the European Committee on Social Rights, for example, Greece justified cuts in pensions and social protections offered to pensioners in the face of the urgent measures taken to address the financial and debt situation of the country on the basis of public interest considerations.[90] In its decision, the European Committee found a violation of Article 12 which guarantees the right to social security in the 1961 Social Charter, noting that as the Greek Government had taken measures which seriously reduced the means of subsistence of a part of the population without adequate consideration of their vulnerability it had failed to 'maintain a sufficient level of protection for the benefit of the most vulnerable members of society, even though the effects of the adopted measures risk bringing about a large scale pauperisation of a significant segment of the population'.[91] Furthermore, the European Committee reiterated the 'need to reconcile general interest with individual rights, including any legitimate expectations that individuals may have in respect of the stability of the rules applicable to social security benefits'.[92]

4. Conclusion: Drawing Some Lessons

The promotion and elaboration of non-discrimination standards and obligations have played a seminal role in giving flesh to economic, social, and cultural rights and overcoming the complete or partial lack of judicial remedies for their contravention at national, regional, and international levels. Specific groups and

[89] ICESCR, *supra* note 2, Art. 4.

[90] European Committee of Social Rights, *Panhellenic Federation of Pensioners of the Public Electricity Corporation v Greece* (2012), Complaint No. 79/2012, para. 10.

[91] European Committee of Social Rights, *Panhellenic Federation of pensioners of the Public Electricity Corporation v. Greece* (2012), Complaint No. 79/2012, paras. 77–78.

[92] European Committee of Social Rights, *Panhellenic Federation of pensioners of the Public Electricity Corporation v. Greece* (2012), Complaint No. 79/2012, para. 78.

their representatives have been instrumental in these developments, in particular through their increasingly systematic interaction with the CESCR. This interaction has stimulated further progress towards an extensive interpretation of what constitutes discrimination and what is necessary for substantive equality. Such developments also significantly contribute to the increasing receptivity of states to the legal enforcement and the justiciability of ESC rights, or at the least, with regard to specific dimensions of them. They have helped to illustrate and address injustice, inequalities, and structural, historical, and systemic violations of ESC rights. In addition to the strategic imperatives for employing equality standards and mechanisms for promoting and protecting these rights, the struggle of groups for greater socio-economic equality has catalysed further mobilization and empowerment of specific groups in relation to their interests and rights, the development of greater expertise and a more holistic perspective by specialized bodies such as gender equality commissions.[93] Above and beyond this, their experiences, struggles, victories, and losses are of exemplary value for others.[94]

There is still reason to assess potential limits and risks of a further expansion of the non-discrimination approach, and increasing banding of new 'groups' seeking to assert their socio-economic rights. Any such risks are unfortunately magnified and exacerbated by continuing gaps in ESC rights frameworks generally. For example, while the Optional Protocol to the ICESCR, which entered into force on 5 May 2013, finally closed the 'justiciability' gap at the international level, the general recognition of socio-economic rights as legal and justiciable rights still remains problematic in numerous national frameworks.

The first two parts of this chapter examined particular tensions of the non-discrimination approach, and highlighted the need for flexibility when framing claims related to the socio-economic rights of specific 'groups'. The manner in which individuals may be identified as members of a specific group or in which groups may self-identify as groups, is an unsettled issue that raises many questions, only some of which have been considered in the present chapter. Another dimension to the question of self-identification relates entirely to the strategic implications of such classification—there may well be legitimate and logical reasons for individuals not to claim belonging to specific groups, be it an ethnic or religious minority for reasons of security,[95] or be it because of the stigmatization linked to a certain status, such as being 'poor'. Critics of the 'group' approach would

[93] See R. Carver, 'One NHRI or Many? How Many Institutions Does It Take to Protect Human Rights? Lessons from the European Experience', 3 *Journal of Human Rights Practice* (2011), 1–24.

[94] See R. Carver, 'One NHRI or Many? How Many Institutions Does It Take to Protect Human Rights? Lessons from the European Experience', 3 *Journal of Human Rights Practice* (2011), 1–24.

See, for instance, the experience of same-sex couples in Brazil who achieved greater legal protection of their rights through jurisprudential developments and equality of treatment before the law. This experience opened the path for other groups to claim their rights within the equality and non-discrimination frameworks. A. Moreira, 'Brazilian Courts and Social Inclusiveness', 3 *ReVista: Harvard Review of Latin America* (2007), 46–48.

[95] B. de Gaay Fortman, 'Minority Rights: A Major Misconception', 33 *Human Rights Quarterly* (2011), 265–303, at 277.

argue that some portions of the population would inevitably be excluded by this approach if the particular group in question has a weak organizational capacity, is unable to mobilize, or otherwise lacks the capacity to claim their rights and defend their interests. From this perspective, the increasing use of non-discrimination frameworks and methodologies may in fact promote a surge of new forms of 'communitarianism'.[96]

Such a qualification of the approach is indicative of its inherent challenges and limitations. ESC rights should not be fundamentally confounded with collective rights, even if some rights or some elements of them can be exercised in a collective manner and even if they, like any other human rights, are universal rights that should be enjoyed equally by all. It is imperative to cease from further stigmatizing of these rights by focusing on what differentiates them from, rather than what they share in common with, other categories of rights. This imperative is particularly acute given the continuing resistance and reluctance of various actors, especially states, against the legal enforcement of ESC rights and the use by victims of judicial remedies for obtaining redress. Reiterating the inherent value of ESC rights beyond the legitimate struggles of specific groups is essential to ensure the agency of individuals, and the promise of ESC rights to ensure the greater freedom of choice and dignity that are at their core.

While collective efforts to claim rights can often be of greater impact than individual claims, particularly when the individuals composing the group are marginalized and excluded, the interest of a group is not automatically the sum of individual interests. Individuals will need to retain the potential to claim against what they consider abuses and violations of their individual ESC rights. Finally, the maintenance of the potential to claim ESC rights for individual cases will also be vital for certain 'groups' who are, by virtue of the identity of their members, or by the very nature of the group itself, not as easily organized and mobilized. The struggle of specific groups for greater protection and realization of their economic, social, and cultural rights will thus be served by greater recognition of the intrinsic value all human rights including ESC rights, as legal rights with judicial and legal remedies accessible to victims. Such realization will only be achievable in a robust rule of law regime, in which ESC rights can play their due role towards social justice, and which can ensure the adequate balancing of interests and the acceptance of majority decisions by minorities, even if the latter hold significant powers.[97]

[96] Professor Lucie Lamarche in an intervention at the Collège de France in Paris (May 2011). See L. Lamarche, 'Le droit social et les droits sociaux: des outils dissonants pour la régulation du social dans le contexte du néolibéralisme', in D. Roman (ed.), *La Justiciabilité des droits sociaux: vecteurs et resistances,* Actes du colloque tenu au Collège de France, Paris 25 et 26 mai 2011 (Paris: Editions A. Pedone, 2012), 119–134, at 134.

[97] B. de Gaay Fortman, *supra* note 97, at 269.

5

Gender and Economic, Social, and Cultural Rights

Christine Chinkin

1. Introduction: Human Rights, Sex, and Gender

At the time of adoption of the International Covenant of Economic, Social and Cultural Rights (ICESCR) in 1966, the concept of gender had not entered the international arena. Relations between women and men in the allocation and enjoyment of rights were addressed through the concept of non-discrimination, inter alia on the basis of sex.[1] The term 'gender' began to enter the international agenda in the 1980s, first through the global conferences on women.[2] The World Conference on Human Rights at Vienna in 1993 continued this trend, referring to gender-based violence, gender bias, and gender-disaggregated statistics. It also called for 'the human rights of women [to] be integrated into the mainstream of United Nations system-wide activity'.[3] Two years later, the Fourth World Conference on Women made a commitment to gender equality, as well as to non-discrimination on the basis of sex.[4] Following the Beijing Conference, 'gender mainstreaming' rapidly became the dominant international institutional strategy and tool to respond to women's inequality.[5] 'Gender mainstreaming' was defined by the United Nations (UN) Economic and Social Council in 1997:

Mainstreaming a gender perspective is the process of assessing the implications for women and men of any planned action, including legislation, policies or programmes, in all areas and at all levels. It is a strategy for making women's as well as men's concerns and experiences an

[1] ICESCR, art. 2(2), echoing the 1948 Universal Declaration on Human Rights, art. 2.

[2] The Third World Conference on Women referred to 'gender-based discrimination' and sought changed attitudes towards gender roles; Forward-Looking Strategies for the Advancement of Women, UN Doc. A/CONF.116/12, Nairobi, 1985, especially paras. 6, 121, 138, 167, 257, and 347.

[3] Vienna Declaration and Programme of Action, UN Doc. A/CONF.157/23, 12 July 1993, II, para. 37.

[4] Fourth World Conference on Women, Declaration, UN Doc. A/CONF/177/20, Beijing, 15 September 1995, para. 24.

[5] For a critique of gender mainstreaming see H. Charlesworth, 'Not Waving but Drowning: Gender Mainstreaming and Human Rights in the United Nations', 18 *Harvard Human Rights Journal* (2005), 1–18.

integral dimension of the design, implementation, monitoring and evaluation of policies and programmes in all political, economic and societal spheres so that women and men benefit equally and inequality is not perpetuated. The ultimate goal is to achieve gender equality.[6]

A number of comments can be made about these developments. First, 'gender' per se was not defined. Second, as components of the UN 'system-wide activity' with respect to human rights, it was evident that the human rights treaty bodies should adopt the tool of gender mainstreaming to progress equality between women and men. Third, although the statements referred to 'women and men', there was a slippage between 'gender' and 'women'; that is, an assumption that gender analysis is only relevant to address issues relating to women, rather than to appraise relations between women and men.

The UN human rights treaty bodies have used their general recommendations and comments to develop an understanding of gender.[7] While such documents have no formal legal status and are not binding, they constitute important interpretations of the relevant treaty by the bodies designated by states to monitor their application. The authority of such statements is enhanced by their apparent acceptance by state parties. In 2004, the Committee on the Elimination of Discrimination against Women (CEDAW Committee)[8] led the way by noting the following definition of gender:

as the social meanings given to biological sex differences. It is an ideological and cultural construct, but is also reproduced within the realm of material practices; in turn it influences the outcomes of such practices. It affects the distribution of resources, wealth, work, decision-making and political power, and enjoyment of rights and entitlements within the family as well as public life. Despite variations across cultures and over time, gender relations throughout the world entail asymmetry of power between men and women as a pervasive trait. Thus, gender is a social stratifier, and in this sense it is similar to other stratifiers such as race, class, ethnicity, sexuality, and age. It helps us understand the social construction of gender identities and the unequal structure of power that underlies the relationship between the sexes.[9]

The following year the Committee on Economic, Social and Cultural Rights (CESCR) also recognized gender as socially constructed,[10] as inhibiting equal enjoyment of rights, and as referring to 'cultural expectations and assumptions about the behaviour, attitudes, personality traits, and physical and intellectual capacities of men and women, based solely on their identity as men or women'.[11] In 2009, it

[6] UN, *Platform for Action, ECOSOC Agreed Conclusions* 1997/2 (1997), available at <http://www.un.org/womenwatch/osagi/pdf/ECOSOCAC1997.2.PDF> (last accessed 20 October 2013).

[7] The first definition of gender in an international treaty was that in the 1998 Rome Statute of the International Criminal Court, art. 7(3): 'the term "gender" refers to the two sexes, male and female, within the context of society'.

[8] Established by the Convention on Elimination of All Forms of Discrimination against Women, 1979 (Women's Convention), art. 17.

[9] 1999 World Survey on the Role of Women in Development (UN New York, 1999) ix, cited in CEDAW Committee General Recommendation No. 25, on temporary special measures, 2004, note 2.

[10] Established by ECOSOC Res. 1985/17, 28 May 1985.

[11] CESCR, General Comment No. 16, The equal right of men and women to the enjoyment of all economic, social and cultural rights, UN Doc. E/C.12/2005/4, 11 August 2005, para. 14.

explained how 'the notion of the prohibited ground "sex" has evolved considerably to cover not only physiological characteristics but also the social construction of gender stereotypes, prejudices and expected roles, which have created obstacles to the equal fulfillment of economic, social and cultural rights'.[12]

The CESCR has considered the concept of gender primarily as a means for understanding relations between women and men, and has recognized how gender-based assumptions have served in many instances 'to place women at a disadvantage with respect to substantive enjoyment of rights, such as freedom to act and to be recognized as autonomous, fully capable adults'.[13] In 2010, the CEDAW Committee confirmed that the Women's Convention covers gender-based discrimination against women, as well as sex-based discrimination.[14] It also emphasized that the construction that society imposes on biological difference between women and men results in a hierarchy that 'in the distribution of power and rights favour[s] men and disadvantage[es] women'.[15] While it is not denied that that men can also experience gender-based disadvantage (for example, in a refusal to grant paternity leave or unequal parental leave),[16] much of the focus of the human rights bodies has been on the obstacles women face in seeking equality in enjoyment of their rights, which explains to some extent the slippage between 'women' and 'gender'. A wider reading of gender encompasses sexual orientation and gender identity, including persons who are transgender, transsexual, or intersex.[17] Such persons often face discrimination and serious human rights violations, including violence and harassment in public places, such as schools and the workplace, thereby impacting adversely on their enjoyment of economic and social rights.[18] Nevertheless, while gender mainstreaming has become accepted policy within UN institutions as a tool to further women's advancement, this broader understanding remains controversial.

[12] CESCR, General Comment No. 20, Non-discrimination in economic, social and cultural rights (art. 2, para. 2), UN Doc. E/C.12/GC 20, 2 July 2009, para. 20,

[13] CESCR, General Comment No. 16, *supra* note 11, para. 14.

[14] CEDAW Committee General Recommendation No. 28, on the Core Obligations of States Parties under Article 2 of the Convention on the Elimination of All Forms of Discrimination against Women, UN Doc. CEDAW/C/2010/47/GC, 19 October 2010, para. 5.

[15] CEDAW Committee General Recommendation No. 28, on the Core Obligations of States Parties under Article 2 of the Convention on the Elimination of All Forms of Discrimination against Women, UN Doc. CEDAW/C/2010/47/GC, 19 October 2010, para. 5.

[16] CESCR, General Comment No. 16, *supra* note 11, at para. 26; *Konstantin Markin v Russia*, ECtHR GC, Appln. No. 30078/06, 22 March 2012, para. 151 ('exclusion of servicemen from the entitlement to parental leave, while servicewomen are entitled to such leave, [...] amounted to discrimination on grounds of sex'.)

[17] CESCR, General Comment No. 20, *supra* note 12, at para. 32. See also 'Report of the Special Rapporteur on the promotion and protection of human rights and fundamental freedoms while countering terrorism', UN Doc. A/64/211, 3 August 2009, para. 20; 'Report of the United Nations High Commissioner for Human Rights, Discriminatory laws and practices and acts of violence against individuals based on their sexual orientation and gender identity', UN Doc. A/HRC/19/41, 17 November 2011 (examining discriminatory laws and practices with respect to employment, healthcare, and education).

[18] CESCR, General Comment No. 20, *supra* note 12, at para. 32.

2. Legal Framework

'A notion of equality runs through the heart of the Covenant'.[19] Article 2, paragraph 2 prohibits discrimination in the guarantee of Covenant rights and in the context of relations between women and men is supplemented by the positive obligation of equality spelled out in Article 3: states parties undertake to ensure 'the equal right of men and women' to the enjoyment of all Covenant rights. Despite possible overlap between the two provisions, Article 3 was included because of the many prejudices that prevent women's enjoyment of their rights and the need therefore to recognize expressly the same rights for women and men.[20] Article 2, paragraph 2, and Article 3 are replicated in the International Covenant on Civil and Political Rights and are 'integrally related and mutually reinforcing'.[21] The mandatory obligation of non-discrimination is one of immediate effect, not subject to the constraint of progressive realization.[22] The following substantive articles of the ICESCR require '[s]tate welfare institutions and social safety nets' as social mechanisms of redistribution.[23]

Following the 1948 Universal Declaration on Human Rights (UDHR),[24] the ICESCR is mostly written in gender-neutral language, asserting the applicability of its substantive provisions to 'everyone' and specific goods to be 'accessible to all'.[25] Gender neutrality is, however, undermined by the use of the masculine pronoun throughout, which has the effect of 'directly gendering the universal subject as male'.[26] Formal commitment to universal application may be undermined by differences in women's and men's lived experiences. The apparent inclusiveness of gender-neutral language often renders women invisible and conceals the incidence of human rights abuses that occur to a man or a woman, because of their sex, or social constructions of gender roles.[27]

[19] M. Craven, *The International Covenant on Economic, Social and Cultural Rights: A Perspective on its Development* (Oxford: Clarendon Press, 1995), 157.

[20] CESCR, General Comment No. 16, *supra* note 11, at para. 2.

[21] CESCR, General Comment No. 16, *supra* note 11, at para. 3.

[22] CESCR, General Comment No. 3, The nature of states parties obligations, 14 December 1990, para. 1; CESCR, General Comment No. 16, *supra* note 11, at para. 16.

[23] M. Craven, *supra* note 19, at 158.

[24] Women delegates to the UN Commission on Human Rights resisted the argument that 'all men' would be read generically to include all persons: A. Fraser, 'Becoming Human: The Origins and Development of Women's Human Rights', 21 *Human Rights Quarterly* (1999), 853–906, 888.

[25] ICESCR, art. 13(2)(c).

[26] D. Otto, '"Gender Comment": Why Does the UN Committee on Economic, Social and Cultural Rights Need a General Comment on Women?' 14 *Can J Women and Law* (2002) 1–33, 19. In the context of ICESCR, art. 11(1) the CESCR has commented that '[w]hile the reference to "himself and his family" reflects assumptions as to gender roles and economic activity patterns commonly accepted in 1966 when the Covenant was adopted, the phrase cannot be read today as implying any limitations upon the applicability of the right to individuals or to female-headed households or other such groups'. CESCR, General Comment No. 4, The right to adequate housing, 13 December 1991, para. 6.

[27] E.g. the assumption of men as the family breadwinners; see *Vos v The Netherlands*, CCPR Communication No. 218/1986.

The need to take account of sex-based difference is to some extent provided for in the ICESCR where the context demands gender specificity. Thus, in an echo of Article 3, Article 7(a)(i) refers 'in particular' to women requiring that they be guaranteed working conditions 'not inferior to those of men, with equal pay for equal work'.[28] Article 10, paragraph 2 provides for 'special protection' for mothers before and after childbirth and for working mothers to be accorded either paid leave or adequate social security at that time.[29] Article 12, paragraph 2(a) is indirectly sex-specific in that it provides steps to be taken to reduce rates of stillbirths and infant mortality, measures which are also likely to lower maternal mortality.[30] However, such woman-specific language is solely in the situation of child-bearing and motherhood, thereby reducing women to their reproductive and caring roles and discounting other circumstances in which the denial of economic, social, and cultural rights occurs exclusively or disproportionately to women. Article 10, paragraph 2 casts maleness as the universal norm and women as weak in that they are in need of 'special' protection, presumably from male employers. [31] This is reinforced by the reiteration of 'special measures of protection' in Article 10, paragraph 3 with respect to children, thereby associating women with children. In the case of women, however, the obligation does not extend to protection from 'economic and social exploitation'.

The ICESCR also explicitly includes the concept of 'equality of opportunity'.[32] Nevertheless, despite the commitment to promotion of equality of rights of men and women in the two 1966 Covenants, the reality remained that 'extensive discrimination against women continues to exist'.[33] This motivated the adoption of the women-specific Convention on the Elimination of All Forms of Discrimination against Women (CEDAW) in 1979. The Convention recognizes that civil and political rights can only be secured in the economic, social, and cultural setting within which women find themselves. Inequality in the provision of economic and social resources impacts on women's personal development and economic independence as well as on their enjoyment of a range of human rights, including access to education, paid employment, political participation, family rights,[34] and equality before

[28] CESCR, General Comment No. 16, *supra*, note 11, at para. 24, spells out states parties' obligations under art. 7(a). See also ILO Convention 100, Equal Remuneration Convention, 1951.

[29] Some ILO Conventions are also gender-specific, e.g. ILO Convention 183, Maternity Protection Convention, 2000.

[30] CESCR, General Comment No. 14, The Right to the highest attainable standard of health, UN Doc. E/C.12/2000/4, 11 August 2000, para. 44, confirms as obligations of comparable priority: '(a) To ensure reproductive, maternal (pre-natal as well as post-natal) and child health care'.

[31] Natalie Hevener identifies the 'protective' stance of many treaties directed specifically at women: 'International Law and the Status of Women: An Analysis of International Legal Instruments Related to the Treatment of Women', 1 *Harv. Women's LJ* (1978), 133–157.

[32] ICESCR, art. 10(c) (in the context of employment). See also CEDAW, art. 4(1). The CEDAW Committee has explained that a formal legal programme to achieve equality is inadequate and that the CEDAW Committee requires women to be 'given an equal start and [...] be empowered by an enabling environment to achieve equality of results'. CEDAW, General Recommendation No. 25, *supra* note 9, at para. 8.

[33] CEDAW, 1979, preamble.

[34] The CEDAW Committee has noted how a complainant's illiteracy and illegal migrant status made her vulnerable to disadvantageous terms on divorce in order to obtain custody of her daughter;

the law. Accordingly, CEDAW departs from the separation of rights epitomized in the two UN Covenants by requiring states parties to take appropriate measures in all fields, 'in particular in the political, social, economic and cultural fields [...] to ensure the full development and advancement of women'.[35] In specific articles the Convention requires the elimination of discrimination in education (Article 10), employment (Article 11), access to healthcare (Article 12) and social security, credit, and bank loans, and sporting and cultural activities (Article 13).[36] Article 14 is directed at the problems faced by women in the rural sector and identifies a range of economic and social issues.

Giving effect to the legal obligation of equality in economic, social, and cultural rights requires 'promoting gender-inclusive interpretations of treaty norms, gender-sensitive implementation practices, and gender-responsive remedies'.[37] This involves understanding how the economic and social disempowerment faced by women impacts upon their experience of human rights. The UN human rights treaty bodies have played an important role in seeking an appreciation of economic, social, and cultural rights that takes account of women's as well as men's lives.[38] In particular, the CEDAW Committee has considered the application of economic, social, and cultural rights specifically to women,[39] while the CESCR has, over time, acted in accordance with the Vienna Conference's exhortation that the human rights of women be 'integrated into the mainstream of United Nations system-wide activity'. In addition to General Comments 16 and 20, the CESCR has included gender-specific analysis in other general comments on particular aspects of the Covenant and in its concluding observations on state party reports.[40] The Committee on the Rights

Jallow v Bulgaria, Communication No. 32/2011, UN Doc. CEDAW/C/52/D/32/2011, 28 August 2012, para. 8.2.

[35] CEDAW, art. 3. The CEDAW Committee has clarified that states parties are required to 'promote the equal rights of girls'. General Recommendation No. 28, *supra* note 14, at para. 21.

[36] Unlike the ICESCR, CEDAW, art. 1 defines discrimination. This definition has been read into the ICESCR by CESCR, General Comment No. 16, *supra* note 11, at para. 11; and General Comment No. 20, *supra* note 12, at para. 7.

[37] Otto, *supra* note 26, at 3.

[38] Thematic special rapporteurs mandated by the UN Human Rights Council have also contributed to a gendered understanding of economic, social, and cultural rights: e.g. 'Report of the Special Rapporteur on adequate housing as a component of the right to an adequate standard of living, and on the right to non-discrimination in this context', UN Doc. A/HRC/7/16, 13 February 2008; 'Special Rapporteur on the right to education, Girls' right to education', UN Doc. E/CN.4/2006/45, 8 February 2006; 'Report submitted by the Special Rapporteur on the right to food, Women's rights and the right to food', UN Doc. A/HRC/22/50, 24 December 2012. The Special Rapporteur on violence against women has considered economic, social, and cultural rights on many occasions: see *15 years of the United Nations Special Rapporteur on Violence against Women, its Causes and Consequences (1994-2009): A Critical Review* (Geneva: UN, 2009).

[39] On the CEDAW Committee's application of economic, social, and cultural rights within the Women's Convention see M. Freeman, C. Chinkin, and B. Rudolf, *The UN Convention on the Elimination of All Forms of Discrimination against Women: A Commentary* (Oxford: Oxford University Press, 2012).

[40] 'In previous General Comments, the Committee has considered the application of the principle of non-discrimination to specific Covenant rights relating to housing, food, education, health, water, author's rights, work, and social security'. CESCR, General Comment No. 20, *supra* note 12, at para. 6.

of the Child has recognized a 'gender component' in its analysis of the applicability to girls of some of the economic, social, and cultural rights included in, or flowing from, the Convention on the Rights of the Child.[41]

3. Equal Enjoyment of Economic, Social, and Cultural Rights

A. The obligations to respect, protect, and fulfil

The European Committee on Social Rights has explained that indirect discrimination includes 'failing to take due and positive account of all relevant differences or by failing to take adequate steps to ensure that the rights and collective advantages that are open to all are genuinely accessible by and to all'.[42] The last words are crucial—determining whether rights are 'genuinely accessible by and to all' requires identifying deeply embedded structural obstacles to their enjoyment that confront one sector of the population. While individuals' situations differ according to such factors as location, class, ethnicity, disability, sexuality, and age, in many instances women face different and additional barriers to those faced by similarly placed men that stem from legal, social, cultural, and practical matters grounded in gender. For example, in its General Comment on the economic, social, and cultural rights of older persons, the CESCR explained that the ICESCR, Article 3 required it to consider the particular condition of many older women.[43] Family and caring responsibilities that fall most heavily on women mean that such women have not undertaken waged employment giving rise to adequate, or even any, pension entitlements, and may not receive even a widow's pension. They are often in 'critical situations'. Governments must take account of this reality and should 'institute non-contributory old-age benefits or other assistance for all persons, regardless of their sex, who find themselves without resources on attaining an age specified in national legislation'.

The CESCR has developed a model of multilayered state obligations, the obligations to respect, protect, and fulfil rights,[44] to assist states in identifying circumstances of gender disparity and obstacles to the enjoyment of economic, social, and cultural rights by either women or men, in order to take them into account in setting polices, adopting legislation, and providing for remedies.[45] For example,

[41] E.g. CROC, General Comment No. 4, adolescent health and development in the context of the Convention on the Rights of the Child, UN Doc. CRC/GC/2003/4, 1 July 2003; General Comment No. 13, The right of the child to freedom from all forms of violence, UN Doc. CRC/C/GC/13, 18 April 2011.

[42] *Autisme-Europe v France*, Complaint No. 13/2002, 7 November 2003, para. 52.

[43] CESCR, General Comment No. 6, on the economic, social and cultural rights of older persons, 8 December 1995, paras. 20–21; cf., CEDAW Committee General Recommendation No. 27, on older women and their protection of human rights, UN Doc. CEDAW/C/GC/27, 16 December 2010.

[44] CESCR General Comment No. 16, *supra* note 11 para. 17. See also CEDAW Committee, General Recommendation No. 28, *supra* note 14, at para. 16.

[45] E.g. CESCR, Concluding Observations, Afghanistan, UN Doc. E/C.12/AG/CO/2-4, 7 June 2010, para. 18 (pervasive social, political, and economic discrimination against women, stereotypes, and customary practices that marginalize women, and 'discrepancy between the legal framework and the inequality in practice in sectors such as work, public life, education and health').

the goal of gender equality in education 'implies that girls and boys have the same opportunities to go to school and receive education of a high quality [...] equality of outcomes [...] and, more broadly, equal job opportunities and earnings for similar qualifications and experience'.[46]

The obligation to respect means that states must ensure that their policies do not have unseen or unintended adverse consequences for either sex.[47] This requires a gender audit to determine the differential impact of policies and practices on women and men, and steps to redress disparity through ensuring substantive and not merely formal equality. This may require examination of the impact of cultural or traditional practices, stereotypes or attitudes,[48] and attempts to counter them, for example, through public policy incentives, such as introducing parental and paternity leave, which seek to change gender stereotypes that operate within the family.[49] Continuing the example of the 'right of everyone to education',[50] increasing school fees or imposing the obligation upon pupils to buy textbooks or writing implements—apparently gender-neutral provisions—might result in fewer girls being able to attend schools where poor families select to direct their resources towards educating their sons, perceiving it as a waste of money to educate girls, especially where there is an assumption that a girl will move to her husband's household on marriage.

The obligation to protect would require states to protect girls and women from being denied access to education by third parties, such as parents, community, or religious groups who deny girls freedom of movement in public places. It also necessitates ensuring a safe environment for girls in educational establishments,[51] including sanitary protection, separate toilets, appropriate lighting, and security from harassment by other pupils, teaching staff, or support staff.

The obligation to fulfil requires structural change aimed at transforming gender relations at all levels of education involving such positive measures as ensuring the availability of schooling for girls, the design of curricula, and provision of textbooks that do not perpetuate gender stereotypes,[52] public awareness campaigns to

[46] S. Pimentel, 'Education and Legal Literacy', in H. Schöpp-Schilling and C. Flinterman (eds.), *The Circle of Empowerment* (New York: The Feminist Press at CUNY, 2007), 90 and 93.

[47] 'It is incumbent upon States parties to take into account the effect of apparently gender-neutral laws, policies and programmes and to consider whether they could result in a negative impact on the ability of men and women to enjoy their human rights on a basis of equality'. CESCR, General Comment No. 16, *supra* note 11, at para. 18.

[48] CEDAW, art. 5 requires states parties to take appropriate measures to modify social and cultural patterns of conduct with a view to eliminating prejudice and practices that are based on the inferiority of one sex. See R. Cook and S. Cusack, *Gender Stereotyping Transnational Legal Perspectives* (Philadelphia: University of Pennsylvania Press, 2010).

[49] E.g. CESCR, Concluding Observations, Republic of Korea, UN Doc. E/C.12/KOR/CO/3, 17 December 2009, para. 13(c); CESCR Concluding Observations, Mauritius, UN Doc. E/C.12/MUS/CO/4, 8 June 2010, para. 21; CESCR, Concluding Observations, United Kingdom of Great Britain and Northern Ireland, the Crown Dependencies, and the Overseas Dependent Territories, UN Doc. E/C.12/GBR/CO/5, 12 June 2009, para. 19.

[50] ICESCR, art. 13(1).

[51] E.g. CEDAW Committee, Concluding Observations, Burkino Faso, UN Doc. CEDAW/C/BFA/CO/6, 5 November 2010, para. 31.

[52] E.g. CESCR, Concluding Observations, Kazakhstan, UN Doc. E/C.12/KAZ/CO/1, 7 June 2010, para. 15.

change attitudes towards gender roles, and available procedures and institutions for challenging discriminatory practices and remedies.[53] Accordingly, where boys face a disadvantage in education, this too must be identified and the root causes, including 'societal stereotypes about, and expectations from, boys and girls',[54] addressed.

As is evident from these examples, state obligations with respect to one right, such as equal rights in the field of education, cannot be looked at in isolation but must be understood in their wider social, economic, and cultural context. For example, early marriage or pregnancy may create a significant obstacle to girls continuing in education. This requires both legislative action with respect to the minimum age for marriage,[55] and action directed at changing attitudes with respect to women's and girls' position in the family and society.[56] It also necessitates joined-up thinking with respect to equal access to education and to healthcare services, including providing confidential and reliable sex education for girls and boys,[57] appropriate gender-sensitive training for healthcare personnel, and ensuring 'the removal of all barriers to women's access to health services, education, and information'.[58]

The individual communication to the CEDAW Committee in the case of *AS v Hungary* illustrates these linkages and the importance of interpreting economic and social rights in a way that takes account of the realities of women's lives.[59] Ms AS, a Hungarian Roma woman and mother of three children, was subjected to coerced sterilization at a Hungarian hospital. This had a profound impact on her life, leaving her in need of medical treatment for depression. Hungary argued that Ms AS had consented to the intervention after receiving correct and appropriate information that she was able to understand. The CEDAW Committee concluded that Hungary had violated CEDAW Article 10(h), which provides a right

[53] E.g. CESCR, Concluding Observations, Bulgaria, UN Doc. E/C.12/BGR/CO/4-5, 11 December 2012, para. 8 (recommends that Bulgaria 'intensify its efforts to eliminate the societal gender role stereotypes and prejudices, including through awareness-raising campaigns'); CESCR, General Comment No. 16, *supra* note 11, at para. 15 (correction of discriminatory language and images in textbooks and the media).

[54] CESCR, Concluding Observations, The Kingdom of the Netherlands, UN Doc. E/C.12/NDL/CO/4-5, 19 November 2010, para. 23 (discrimination against boys in the former Netherlands Antilles, which affects their education).

[55] ICESCR, art. 10(1) (free consent to marriage); CEDAW, art. 16(b). See, e.g. CESCR Concluding Observations, Uruguay, UN Doc. E/C.12/URY/CO/3-4, 1 December 2010, para. 17 (concern that different minimum ages for marriage (12 years for girls and 14 years for boys) are discriminatory and inconsistent with the ICESCR, art. 10(1)); CESCR Concluding Observations, Sri Lanka, UN Doc. E/C.12/LKA/CO/2-4, 9 December 2010, para. 15.

[56] The CEDAW Committee has noted that 'family structures, gendered labour division within the family and family laws affect women's economic well-being no less than labour market structures and labour laws'. It has made a number of recommendations with respect to economic equality during and on the dissolution of marriage. CEDAW Committee, General Recommendation No. 29, Economic consequences of marriage, family relations and their dissolution, UN Doc. CEDAW/C/GC/29, 26 February 2013, para. 1.

[57] E.g. CESCR Concluding Observations, Uruguay, *supra* note 55, para. 24; CESCR Concluding Observations, Kazakhstan, *supra* note 52, at para. 33.

[58] CEDAW Committee, General Recommendation No. 24, Women and Health, 1999, para. 31(b).

[59] CEDAW Committee, Communication No. 4/2004, UN Doc. CEDAW/C/36/D/4/2004, 29 August 2006.

to specific educational information, including on family planning. The Committee took account of Ms AS's condition when she signed her consent to the operation. There were 17 minutes between her arrival at the hospital and her undergoing two medical procedures (the sterilization and a caesarean section to remove her foetus, which was known to be dead). She was distressed, bleeding, and in a state of shock. The Committee found it implausible that in such circumstances and so little time the hospital staff had given her sufficient counselling and relevant information for her to 'make a well-considered and voluntary decision to be sterilized'.[60] In accordance with its women-specific mandate, the CEDAW Committee's analysis centred on the violation of Ms AS's rights. A gendered approach would also have considered the impact of the forcible sterilization on her husband who, like Ms AS, 'live[d] in accordance with traditional Roma customs—where having children is said to be a central element of the value system of Roma families'.[61]

The case also highlights the vulnerabilities of some sections of society to deprivation of rights through multiple and intersecting discrimination: coercive sterilization was carried out on Ms AS because she was a woman and because she was a member of a marginalized group of society—the Roma. The Committee on the Elimination of Racial Discrimination has suggested a fourfold inquiry for understanding the intersection of race and gender discrimination.[62] This requires identifying the form or nature of the violation, the circumstances or context of the violation, the consequences of violation, and the availability and accessibility of remedies. Applying this methodology to the case at hand, the nature and context of the violation was denial of adequate information within a hospital setting, which consequently had a profound impact on Ms AS's life and for which she was denied any remedy by the courts. Indeed, the consequences for her were largely discounted by the appellate court, which reasoned that she had suffered no lasting handicap as the process could be reversed, or she might seek artificial insemination. The CEDAW Committee made no mention of her position as a member of a minority group, although in 2002 the government representative had indicated that the Roma faced problems in Hungary,[63] and the Committee had asked for further information at the next reporting session.[64] Its recommendations were directed solely to the denial of rights

[60] CEDAW Committee, Communication No. 4/2004, UN Doc. CEDAW/C/36/D/4/2004, 29 August 2006, para. 11.3.

[61] CEDAW Committee, Communication No. 4/2004, UN Doc. CEDAW/C/36/D/4/2004, 29 August 2006, para. 2.4.

[62] CERD, General Recommendation No. 25, Gender related dimensions of racial discrimination, 20 March 2000.

[63] CEDAW Committee, Concluding Observations, Hungary, UN Doc. A/57/38 (Supp.) Exceptional Session 2002, paras. 307, 331, 332. On discrimination against Roma children in education see *Horváth and Kiss v Hungary*, ECtHR, Appln. No. 11146/11, 29 January 2013.

[64] In 2007, the CEDAW Committee noted that Roma women 'remain in a vulnerable and marginalized situation and subject to discrimination, including with regard to education, health, housing, employment and participation in political, public and economic life'. It recommended 'a holistic approach to eliminating the multiple and intersecting forms of discrimination that Roma women face'. CEDAW Committee, Concluding Observations, Hungary, UN Doc. CEDAW/C/HUN/CO/6, 10 August 2007, paras. 30 and 31; in 2013 the Committee again noted 'with concern' that prejudices significantly affected the enjoyment of Convention rights by Roma women; and that Roma women

as a woman, not as a woman member of a minority group. A holistic response would have addressed the intersection of policies directed towards controlling the reproduction of particular groups and targeting of the most vulnerable within the group, the women. Conversely, '[w]here systems of race, gender and class domination converge [...] intervention strategies based solely on the experiences of women who do not share the same class or race backgrounds will be of limited help to women who because of race and class face different obstacles'.[65]

B. Gender-based violence

A particular obstacle to women's enjoyment of economic, social, and cultural rights is gender-based violence. Neither the ICESCR nor CEDAW makes any explicit mention of violence, although the omission was rectified by the adoption by the CEDAW Committee of its General Recommendation No. 19.[66] Gender-based violence is a form of discrimination which impedes women's enjoyment of economic and social rights on a basis of equality,[67] including to education, employment, and cultural activities. It puts women's lives and their health at risk. In turn denial of economic and social rights creates dependency, vulnerability to violence, and to being trafficked. As clarified by the UN Special Rapporteur on violence against women:

> Violence is not only a human rights violation but also a key factor in obstructing the realisation of women's and girls' rights to security, adequate housing, health, food, education, and participation. Millions of women find themselves locked in cycles of poverty and violence, cycles that fuel and perpetuate one another.[68]

The Committee on Migrant Workers has noted that women make up the 'overwhelming majority' of migrant workers engaged in domestic work.[69] Migrant workers face multiple violations of their human rights relating to their conditions of work, access to social security protection, and adequate standards of living conditions. Women 'face additional risks related to their gender, including gender-based violence',[70] and perceptions of domestic work as 'tasks associated with unpaid work in the home performed by women and girls'.[71]

suffer 'multiple discrimination and exclusion'; CEDAW Committee, Concluding Observations, Hungary, UN Doc. CEDAW/C/HUN/CO/7-8, 26 March 2013, paras. 18, 19, 36, and 37.

[65] K. Crenshaw, 'Mapping the Margins: Intersectionality, Identity Politics and Violence against Women of Color', 43 *Stanford Law Review* (1991), 1241–1299.

[66] CEDAW Committee General Recommendation No. 19, Violence against women, 11th session, 1992.

[67] CESCR, General Comment No. 16, *supra* note 11, at para. 27.

[68] Report of the Special Rapporteur on violence against women, its causes and consequences: Political economy of women's human rights, UN Doc. A/HRC/11/6, 18 May 2009, para. 14 (citing Irene Khan, Amnesty International Executive Director, 25 November 2008).

[69] Committee on the Protection of the Rights of all Migrant Workers and Members of Their Families, General Comment No. 1 on migrant domestic workers, UN Doc. CMW/C/GC/1, 23 February 2011, para. 1.

[70] Committee on the Protection of the Rights of all Migrant Workers and Members of Their Families, General Comment No. 1 on migrant domestic workers, UN Doc. CMW/C/GC/1, 23 February 2011, at para. 7.

[71] Committee on the Protection of the Rights of all Migrant Workers and Members of Their Families, General Comment No. 1 on migrant domestic workers, UN Doc. CMW/C/GC/1, 23

The obligation upon state parties to act with 'due diligence to prevent, investigate, mediate, punish and redress acts of violence [...] by private actors'[72] is important to secure economic, social, and cultural rights for women as well as men. The CESCR has explained that ICESCR, Article 3 requires states:

> to provide victims of domestic violence [...] with access to safe housing, remedies and redress for physical, mental and emotional damage; to ensure that men and women have an equal right to choose if, whom and when to marry—in particular, the legal age of marriage for men and women should be the same, and boys and girls should be protected equally from practices that promote child marriage, marriage by proxy, or coercion; and to ensure that women have equal rights to marital property and inheritance upon their husband's death.[73]

Legal provisions for equality between women and men (for example, with respect to age for marriage) must be supplemented by addressing the social and cultural practices that undermine formal equality. Article 20 of the 2011 Council of Europe Convention on preventing and combating violence against women and domestic violence requires states parties to take the necessary steps 'to ensure that victims have access to services facilitating their recovery from violence'. Such services include basic economic and social rights, including healthcare services, housing, education, and training and assistance in finding employment.[74] Nevertheless, in formulating policies for addressing violence against women, governments rarely include socio-economic issues, focusing instead on juridical and legal structures.[75] During its review of states parties' reports, the CESCR routinely expresses concern about widespread violence against women and seeks information from states about what they have done to address it. Alongside measures relating to access to justice, it recommends measures such as adequate shelter, medical care and counselling, and social support.[76] It does not, however, refer to the gender-specific social and economic needs of male victims of violence.[77]

February 2011, at para. 19; cf. ILO Convention 189, Domestic Workers Convention, 2011, preamble: 'Considering that domestic work continues to be undervalued and invisible and is mainly carried out by women and girls'. The Convention entered into force on 5 September 2013.

[72] CESCR, General Comment No. 16, *supra* note 11, at para. 27.

[73] CESCR, General Comment No. 16, *supra* note 11, at para. 27. Feminist campaigns have long focused on women's right to ownership of and access to property, to occupations and professions of their choice; D. Barak-Erez, 'Social Rights as Women's Rights', in D. Barak-Erez and A. Gross (eds.), *Exploring Social Rights Between Theory and Practice* (Oxford: Hart, 2007), 397.

[74] CETS No. 210, signed at Istanbul, 11 May 2011.

[75] Report of the Special Rapporteur on violence against women, Political economy of women's human rights, *supra* note 68, at paras. 38–39.

[76] E.g. CESCR, Concluding Observations, Republic of Moldova, UN Doc. E/C.12/MDA/CO/2, 20 May 2011, para. 14; CESCR, Concluding Observations, Madagascar, UN Doc. E/C.12/MDG/CO/2, 16 December 2009, para. 23.

[77] The Council of Europe Convention recognizes that although domestic violence affects women disproportionately, men may also be victims and art. 2 encourages states parties to apply the Convention to all such victims.

C. Gender and economic inequalities

The Beijing Platform for Action adopted by the Fourth World Conference on Women in 1995 pointed to the feminization of poverty as a critical area of concern.[78] Statistics continue to show that women are more likely to be poor than men and that this is directly caused by the 'systematic discrimination they face in education, healthcare, employment and control of assets'.[79] Low economic status reinforces women's subordination, constrains their enjoyment of rights,[80] reduces their choices, and creates vulnerability to exploitation and violence, including being trafficked.[81] In order to attain an adequate standard of living for themselves and their families and to be free from hunger,[82] women and girls may turn to prostitution.[83]

In its General Comment No. 16, the CESCR highlights 'economic, social and cultural inequalities' but does not challenge the prevailing climate of neo-liberalism and economic globalization. In 2004, a group of non-state actors had adopted the Montreal Principles on Women's Economic, Social and Cultural Rights,[84] to guide the 'interpretation and implementation of guarantees of non-discrimination and equal exercise and enjoyment of economic, social, and cultural rights, in order to ensure that women can enjoy these rights fully and equally'. The Montreal Principles include 'the gender-differentiated effects of economic globalization' among the impediments it identifies to women's equal enjoyment of economic, social, and cultural rights.[85]

The UN Special Rapporteur on violence against women has gone further in examining how the current international economic order has contributed to gender inequality in the enjoyment of these rights. She identifies three 'key structural elements highlighted by the political economy approach' that contribute to the unequal delivery of economic and social rights, and hence to violence against women: the sexual division of labour, the 'global, macroeconomic environment', and the gender dimensions of armed conflict.[86]

[78] UN Doc. A/CONF.177/20, 15 September 1995, Critical Area of Concern A, Women and Poverty.

[79] UN Women, 'Women, Poverty & Economics', available at <http://www.unifem.org/gender_issues/women_poverty_economics> (last accessed 12 September 2013).

[80] Montréal Principles on Women's Economic, Social and Cultural Rights, 26 *Human Rights Quarterly* (2004), 760–780.

[81] CEDAW Committee, Concluding Observations, Burkino Faso, UN Doc. CEDAW/C/BFA/CO/6, 5 November 2010, para. 28 (recommending measures to improve the economic situation of girls and women, access to land, and gainful employment to eliminate vulnerability to traffickers).

[82] ICESCR, arts. 11(1) and (2).

[83] E.g. CEDAW Committee, Concluding Observations, Kenya, UN Doc. CEDAW/C/KEN/CO/7, 2 February 2011, para. 27 (also expressing concern that the law only criminalizes prostitutes without sanctioning demand).

[84] Montréal Principles on Women's Economic, Social and Cultural Rights, *supra* note 80, at para. 12.

[85] Montréal Principles on Women's Economic, Social and Cultural Rights, *supra* note 80, at para. 12.

[86] Report of the Special Rapporteur on violence against women, Political economy of women's human rights, *supra* note 68, at paras. 28–34.

The distinction between unpaid 'care' work in the home and waged work in the public sphere is gendered, with women performing the bulk of the former. Protective labour regulation and workplace structures all too often adopt the basic assumption of men as the primary wage earners.[87] Where women are in the paid labour market, the sexual division of labour fences many women into low-paid, unskilled, and undervalued work, often in the private sphere and with a high risk of abuse, including denial of employment and other rights. The CESCR has noted the high numbers of women working in part-time work[88] and the unregulated informal economy,[89] both of which impact negatively on eligibility for social security benefits.[90] It has also commented on how women's over-representation in the caring services sees them migrate for work as domestic servants, which often involves their enduring slavery-like conditions, for example, expressing its concern to Sri Lanka that the state had not 'studied the impact of such massive labour migration on Sri Lankan families, nor provided women with alternative employment opportunities'.[91] It has noted the case of *Siliadin v France* before the European Court of Human Rights, which illustrates the nature of the situation in which women can find themselves trapped.[92] A 15-year-old girl came to France from Togo to work in domestic service on the understanding that her employer would help her to attend school. In reality she became an unpaid housemaid. She was then 'lent' to another couple where she worked all week without a day off, except when she was exceptionally allowed to attend mass on Sundays. Her working day began at 7.30 a.m. and continued until she went to bed at about 10.30 p.m. Her tasks included preparing meals, looking after the children, housework, and doing the laundry. She slept on a mattress in the baby's room where she had to look after him if he woke. She lacked any employment or social rights and was denied freedom of movement, including access to education and healthcare.[93] The European Court of Human Rights found that the conditions she endured amounted to forced labour and servitude and that France was in violation of its positive obligations under Article 4 of the European Convention on Human Rights. Some violations of economic and social rights are suffered disproportionately by male migrant workers,[94] for instance working conditions in construction sites or mines—but the particular conditions suffered

[87] G. Mundlak, 'The Right to Work: The Value of Work', in D. Barak-Erez and A. Gross (eds.), *supra* notes 73, 341, and 351–352.

[88] E.g. CESCR, Concluding Observations, Switzerland, UN Doc. E/C.12/CHE/CO/2-3, 26 November 2010, para. 8.

[89] E.g. CESCR, Concluding Observations, Kazakhstan, *supra* note 52, para. 19; CESCR, Concluding Observations, Republic of Korea, *supra* note 49, at para. 13 (women's low rate of labour market participation 'despite high female enrolment in tertiary education').

[90] E.g. CEDAW Committee, Concluding Observations, Vietnam, UN Doc. CEDAW/C/VNM/CO/6, 2 February 2007, para. 22.

[91] CESCR, Concluding Observations, Sri Lanka, *supra* note 55, at para. 21.

[92] *Siliadin v France*, ECtHR, Appln. No. 73316/01, 26 July 2005; see also *C.N. v The United Kingdom*, ECtHR, Appln. No. 4239/08, 13 November 2012.

[93] Such conditions for women migrant workers in domestic work are described in CEDAW Committee, General Recommendation No. 26, on women migrant workers, UN Doc. CEDAW/C/2009/WP.1/R, 5 December 2008, para. 15; see also Committee on the Protection of the Rights of all Migrant Workers and Members of Their Families, General Comment No. 1, *supra* note 69.

[94] *Juridical Condition and Rights of the Undocumented Migrants* (Adv. Op.) OC-18/03, 17 September 2003, IACtHR (Ser. A), No. 18 (2003).

by Ms Siliadin were based on 'gender inequality, traditional female roles, a gendered labour market, the universal prevalence of gender-based violence and the worldwide feminization of poverty and labour migration'.[95]

The global, macro-economic environment, characterized by markets, movements of capital, and the desire to enhance conditions for foreign investment, have weakened the state's effective decision- and policy-making power, notably in economic and labour policies. Consequences such as social exclusion, unemployment, or low-paid employment, and weakening of trade union organization all have gendered dimensions. In the words of the Special Rapporteur on violence against women: 'Economic systems which value profits often do so at the expense of female labour'.[96] Women are seen, and hence favoured, as a passive, compliant, temporary workforce that will accept low wages without demanding labour and human rights. Privatization and structural adjustment programmes have impacted adversely upon the enjoyment of economic and social rights,[97] with gendered impact. Globalization may have dire consequences for human rights generally, and women's human rights particularly, by eroding civil, political, economic, social, and cultural rights in the name of development and macro-level economic restructuring and stability. In the countries of the South, structural adjustment programmes have led to increased impoverishment—particularly among women—displacement and internal strife resulting from the political instabilities caused by devaluing national currencies, increasing debt, and dependence on foreign direct investment.[98]

The CEDAW Committee has expressed concern about the unequal impact on women of structural adjustment programmes,[99] privatizations,[100] trade liberalization,[101] and the unequal benefit of development programmes.[102] The Montreal Principles call for states to be bound by the obligation to exercise due diligence 'to assess, foresee, and prevent any adverse consequences of trade agreements, structural

[95] CEDAW Committee, General Recommendation No. 26, *supra* note 93, at para. 5.

[96] Special Rapporteur on violence against women, its causes and consequences, preliminary report, UN Doc. E/CN.4/1995/42, para. 55.

[97] Effects of structural adjustment policies on the full enjoyment of human rights, report by the independent expert, UN Doc. E/CN.4/1999/50, 24 February 1999.

[98] Special Rapporteur on violence against women, its causes and consequences, on trafficking in women, migration, and violence against women, UN Doc. E/CN.4/2000/68, 29 February 2000, para. 59.

[99] E.g. CEDAW Committee Concluding Observations, Trinidad and Tobago, A/57/38 (Supp), 26th session (2002), para. 156.

[100] E.g. CEDAW Committee, Concluding Observations, Albania, UN Doc. CEDAW/C/ALB/CO/3, 16 September 2010, para. 32 (concern about 'the social insurance situation of a high number of women who were laid off following the economic reforms and privatizations undertaken during the transitional period in the 1990s'); CEDAW Committee, Concluding Observations, Hungary, UN Doc. CEDAW/C/HUN/CO/7-8, 26 March 2013, para. 9 (Hungary urged to ensure that 'the policy of the privatization of health, education and other services does not deprive women of continuous access to good quality basic services in the field of economic, social and cultural rights'); see also CESCR, General Comment No. 16, *supra* note 11, at para. 20.

[101] E.g. CEDAW Committee, Concluding Observations, the Philippines, UN Doc. CEDAW/C/PHI/CO/6, 25 August 2006, para. 25.

[102] E.g. CEDAW Committee, Concluding Observations, China, UN Doc. CEDAW/C/CHN/CO/6 (2006), paras. 15 and 16 (states parties should ensure that all poverty alleviation programmes fully benefit women).

adjustment programs, development and humanitarian assistance, and other economic and social policies on women's economic, social, and cultural rights'.[103] The CEDAW Committee has been alert to the foreseeable consequences of global economic crisis on women's human rights, notably through rising unemployment, an increase in their responsibilities at work and at home, coupled with a decrease in income and a 'potential increase in societal and domestic violence'.[104] It has been suggested that such consequences may be more a result of pre-existing inequalities (including under-representation of women in economic decision-making and over-representation in informal, vulnerable, and casual employment) than of gender inequalities arising directly from the crisis.[105] However, consequences of crisis may be unpredictable and differ according to local factors. What follows is that in any such situation '[g]ender perspectives should be taken into account in relation to the impacts of the crisis on both a long- and short-term basis, including in relation to education, health, security and livelihoods'.[106]

D. Economic, social, and cultural rights, and armed conflict

The Special Rapporteur on violence against women also identified the gendered dimensions of armed conflict and the political economy of conflict as contributing to unequal enjoyment of economic and social rights.[107] In conflict and military occupation the basic needs of civilian populations are protected by international humanitarian law[108] as well as human rights law.[109] Nevertheless during conflict and its aftermath, access to humanitarian aid, including food and medical provisions, may be restricted and internally displaced persons may lack basic shelter, access to sanitation, clean water, and livelihood opportunities.[110] The former

[103] Montréal Principles on Women's Economic, Social and Cultural Rights, *supra* note 80, at para. 20.

[104] Decision 43/II, Statement by the CEDAW Committee on the international financial crisis and its consequences for the human rights of women and girls, UN Doc. A/64/38 (Supp.), 43rd session, 2009, Annex I.

[105] R. King and C. Sweetman, 'Gender Perspectives on the Global Economic Crisis', Oxfam International Discussion Paper (February 2010).

[106] Decision 43/II, *supra* note 104; see also CEDAW Committee Concluding Observations, Greece, UN Doc. CEDAW/C/GRC/CO/7, 1 March 2013, para. 6 ('even in times of fiscal constraints and economic crisis, special efforts must be made to respect human rights, sustain and expand social investment and social protection and to employ a gender sensitive approach, giving priority to women in vulnerable situations').

[107] On the relationship between ESC rights and international humanitarian law, see G. Giacca, ch. 11 in this book.

[108] Convention Relative to the Protection of Civilian Persons in Time of War, August 12, 1949 (Geneva IV), art. 55; Protocol Additional to the Geneva Conventions of 12 August 1949, and relating to the Protection of Victims of International Armed Conflicts (Protocol I), 8 June 1977, art. 69.

[109] *Legal Consequences of the Construction of a Wall in the Occupied Palestinian Territory*, 2004 ICJ Rep. 136, paras. 102–113.

[110] CESCR, Concluding Observations, Sri Lanka, *supra* note 55, at paras. 28 and 29. The CEDAW Committee made explicit reference to the need for the state to provide 'adequate infrastructure for women IDPs and returnees especially housing and health facilities, water and sanitation' and more generally to include economic and social rights in post-conflict reconstruction'; CEDAW Committee Concluding Observations, Sri Lanka, UN Doc. CEDAW/C/LKA/CO/7, 4 February 2011, paras. 40 and 41.

High Commissioner for Human Rights has drawn attention to how the denial of economic and social rights during conflict may be an intentional war tactic. She details as an illustration the situation in Darfur where 'the systematic burning of houses and villages, the forced displacement of the population, and the starvation caused by restrictions on delivery of humanitarian assistance, and the destruction of food crops are deliberately used alongside other gross human rights violations—such as murder and rape—as instruments of war'.[111] These violations have gendered dimensions. Conflict-related sexual violence is accompanied by the loss of livelihood and the destruction of social support structures.[112] Property devastation and spoiling of food sources impose burdens on women who, as the primary carers within their family and community, are responsible for finding food and shelter. Women's security is put further at risk as they have to venture out to seek such essentials. The Special Rapporteur on Sexual Violence in Armed Conflict has highlighted the lack of emergency health services for women who are raped and the conditions of extreme poverty often endured by mothers of children who have been born following rape. The children, too, suffer psychological and socio-economic consequences.[113] Without discounting the abuses suffered by men in conflict,[114] the disadvantaged position of women in society make them especially vulnerable to gross violations of socio-economic rights when conflict erupts.[115]

This continues in the aftermath of conflict. The CESCR has expressed its alarm at the situation in the Democratic Republic of the Congo where men accused of rape may be accorded bail or otherwise released 'while survivors of sexual violence end up rejected by their families, without healthcare, socio-economic reintegration, support and compensation being provided to them by the state party'.[116] The CEDAW Committee has urged, for example in the context of communal violence in Gujarat in Western India where women were targeted by violence, the state to provide 'a clean water supply, electricity, roads and sanitation facilities and [...] a plan [...] for guaranteeing the right to education, health and employment for women and children in all colonies'.[117]

Some 10 years after the end of the armed conflict in Bosnia–Herzegovina the CEDAW Committee expressed concern at the disadvantage experienced by female heads of household and internally displaced persons who had been victims

[111] L. Arbour, 'Economic and Social Justice for Societies in Transition', 40 *NYU J Int'l Law and Politics* (2007), 1–27, 9.

[112] Concept Note, General Discussion on the protection of women's human rights in conflict and post-conflict contexts (CEDAW Committee, 18 July 2011), available at <http://www2.ohchr.org/english/bodies/cedaw/discussion2011.htm> (last accessed 12 September 2013).

[113] Report of the Secretary General on Sexual Violence in Conflict, UN Doc. A/67/792–S/2013/149, 14 March 2013, para. 12.

[114] Including sexual violence; S Sivakumaran,'Sexual Violence against Men in Armed Conflict', 18 EJIL (2007), 253.

[115] Concept Note, *supra* note 111.

[116] CESCR, Concluding Observations, Democratic Republic of the Congo, UN Doc. E/C.12/COD/CO/4, 20 November 2009, para. 25.

[117] CEDAW Committee, Concluding Observations, India, UN Doc. CEDAW/C/IND/CO/SP.1, 3 November 2010, para. 35.

of wartime sexual violence. Such persons are often not sufficiently recognized in post-conflict legal frameworks. The Committee urged the state to protect these women through legislation and allocation of financial resources for adequate social provision, including health insurance and housing, at a level comparable to that applicable to the (mostly male) military victims of war.[118] Such services should be recognized as having been provided in accordance with the state's obligations under the ICESCR, and not as discretionary benefits that can be withdrawn when economically expedient to do so. The UN Fact Finding Mission to Gaza reported that:

> the blockade and the military operations had aggravated poverty, which particularly affected women, who must find food and other essentials for their families. Women were often the sole breadwinners [...] but jobs were hard to come by. [...] [W]omen bore a greater social burden, having to deal with daily life made harsher by the crisis and, at the same time, provide security and care for injured family members and children, their own and others who have lost their parents.[119]

The simultaneous continuance of women's traditional tasks (as carers) and their shifting responsibilities (as sole breadwinners) point to the contingent nature of gender roles and the need for contextual determination.

There is growing institutional recognition of the importance of the guarantee of economic and social rights of women in conditions of conflict and post-conflict. The former High Commissioner for Human Rights has urged that the prevailing neglect of economic and social rights in transitional justice programmes be redressed.[120] Although the CEDAW Committee has asserted that the obligations contained in the Women's Convention continue to apply during armed conflict,[121] it is currently in the process of elaborating a general recommendation on women in conflict and post-conflict situations. During discussion on the proposed general recommendation, Lakshmi Puri, from UN Women, suggested that the general recommendation engage the full range of human rights protections: civil, political, economic, and social rights.[122] And the UN Security Council has affirmed that 'women's political, social and economic empowerment, gender equality [...] are central to long-term efforts to prevent sexual violence in armed conflict and post-conflict situations'. The Security Council also recognized the need to engage men and boys in this enterprise.[123] To this end, women's participation in decision-making and policy-making

[118] CEDAW Committee, Concluding Observations, Bosnia-Herzegovina, UN Doc. CEDAW/C/BIH/CO/3 (2006), paras. 37–38; see also Issues and Questions, Mozambique, UN Doc. CEDAW/C/MOZ/Q/2 (2007), para. 13; and Concluding Observations, Guatemala, UN Doc. A/57/38 (Supp.) exceptional session (2002), para. 205.

[119] 'Report of the United Nations Fact-Finding Mission on the Gaza Conflict', UN Doc. A/HRC/12/48, 25 September 2009, paras. 1275–1279.

[120] L. Arbour, 'Economic and Social Justice for Societies in Transition', *supra* note 110.

[121] CEDAW Committee, General Recommendation No. 28, *supra* note 14, para. 11; the Council of Europe Convention on preventing and combating violence against women, applies in peace and armed conflict; *supra* note 74, art. 2(3).

[122] CEDAW Committee, Day of General Discussion, 'Women in conflict and post-conflict situations', New York, 18 July 2011.

[123] UN Security Council Res. 2106, 24 June 2013.

with respect to peace processes and institutions for post-conflict reconstruction, as envisaged by Security Council resolution 1325,[124] is critical; unfortunately, to-date, women remain largely excluded from such developments.[125]

Other situations of crisis, such as natural disasters, have similar gendered impact. The CEDAW Committee has noted that following a natural disaster women's caring roles mean they incur greater responsibilities with respect, inter alia, to children, the elderly, and the injured. It has urged all those engaged in humanitarian relief to apply a gender perspective in their work, including 'diverse and innovative' food distribution strategies, to pay attention to women-headed households, and to make certain of security from the sexual violence that threatens in times of heightened stress.[126] The Montreal Principles also urge states to ensure that in such situations of scarcity 'the basic needs of women are satisfied, especially in regard to healthcare, access to potable water, sanitation services, housing, education, energy, and social protection'.[127] It is, however, important that women are not seen solely as victims in such situations: their resilience and strength should be supported as 'the role of women in early recovery is critical to effective implementation and long-term sustainability'[128] in societal reconstruction after disaster or conflict.[129]

The first inquiry carried out by the CEDAW Committee under Article 8 of the CEDAW Optional Protocol, into the multiple deaths and disappearances of women in Ciudad Juárez, Mexico, illustrates the complex linkages between the three structural elements identified by the Special Rapporteur on violence against women.[130] The scale of the killings, and the torture and rapes endured by the victims before their deaths, make an analogy to a war zone appropriate. Ciudad Juárez in many ways represents a paradigm of labour conditions in a globalized economy. Industry has been located to the peripheries of the country, in the border area between Mexico and Texas. It is a place of transit for Mexican and foreign migrants where the 'maquila' industry (export-processing industry, manufacturing, and/or assembly plants) has flourished.[131] The maquila was started up in 1965 and expanded as a consequence of the North American Free Trade Agreement in 1993.[132]

[124] UN Security Council Res. 1325, women, peace, and security, 31 October 2000; UN Security Council Res. 1889, 5 October 2009

[125] C. Bell and C. O'Rourke, 'Peace Agreements or Pieces of Paper? The Impact of UNSC Resolution 1325 on Peace Processes and their Agreements', 59 *Int'l & Comp. L.Q.* (2010), 941–980.

[126] Decision 45/III. 'Statement of the Committee on the Elimination of Discrimination against Women on the Situation on Haiti', UN Doc. A/65/38 (Supp.) 45th session, 2010, para. 4.

[127] Montreal Principles, *supra* note 79, at para. 21.

[128] Decision 45/III, *supra* note 125, at para. 8.

[129] UN Security Council Res. 1325; UN Security Council Res. 1889, *supra* note 123.

[130] Report on Mexico produced by the Committee on the Elimination of Discrimination against Women under Article 8 of the Optional Protocol to the Convention, and reply from the Government of Mexico, UN Doc. CEDAW/C/2005/OP8/Mexico, 27 January 2005 (CEDAW, Mexico Inquiry).

[131] *González* et al. *('Cotton Field') v Mexico*, Inter-American Court of Human Rights, 16 November 2009 (Preliminary Objection, Merits, Reparations, and Costs), para. 113.

[132] The CESCR has expressed its desire to receive information on the impact of Free Trade Agreements on the fulfilment of Covenant rights, especially on vulnerable persons but without express reference to gender difference; e.g. CESCR, Concluding Observations, Dominican Republic, UN Doc. E/C.12/DOM/CO/3, 26 November 2010, para. 8.

Hiring policies in the maquilas give preference to women,[133] reflecting practice in other export-processing zones, which hire young migrant workers 'to take advantage of their "cheap" and "more flexible" labour, constructed as such by prevailing gender, class and racial ideologies'.[134] Social inequalities and organized crime (including drug, arms, and human trafficking) have increased levels of insecurity and extreme violence for all in the area.

Women's entry into paid employment (however lacking in basic labour rights) constituted a shift in gender relations within families as 'traditional roles began to change, with women becoming the household provider'. But modified social roles did not denote any change in 'traditionally patriarchal attitudes and mentalities' or stereotypes of men's and women's social roles.[135] Although the reasons for the killings of women remain unknown, the CEDAW Committee noted that women in Ciudad Juárez are subject to 'systematic violations of women's rights, founded in a culture of violence and discrimination that is based on women's alleged inferiority'.[136] They also lacked basic needs—work, education, healthcare, housing, sanitation infrastructure, and lighting—indicating a failure by the state in its obligation to protect economic, social, and cultural rights.[137] Among its many other recommendations, the CEDAW Committee sought compliance with CEDAW, which includes such rights.[138] The tragedy in Ciudad Juárez shows how gender impacts upon the consequences of denial of employment and other economic and social rights to create a situation of extreme vulnerability.

The CEDAW Committee and the Inter American Court of Human Rights paid attention to the role played by gender in constructing an environment where women's deaths became commonplace and committed with impunity. Such analysis should be routinely undertaken. For example, the case before the African Commission of Human Rights involving actions taken by the Nigerian government against the Ogoni people is an important landmark in the judicialization of economic, social, and cultural rights.[139] However, the Commission treated the Ogoni people as a homogenous group and drew no distinctions such as regarding age or gender, thereby assuming all its findings and recommendations to be equally applicable to women and men. It can be informative to consider the omissions of

[133] Another form of gender-based discrimination in employment is the demand by employers in the *maquiladora* for women to undergo pregnancy tests; CESCR, Concluding Observations, Mexico, UN Doc. E/C.12/MEX/CO/4, 9 June 2006, para. 15; and CCPR, Concluding Observations, Mexico, UN Doc. CCPR/C/MEX/CO/5, 17 May 2010, para. 7.

[134] Report of the Special Rapporteur on violence against women, Political economy of women's human rights, *supra* note 68, at para. 21.

[135] *Cotton Field, supra* note 130, para. 129.

[136] CEDAW Committee, Mexico Inquiry, para. 261. The Inter-American Court of Human Rights also noted the 'culture of gender-based discrimination'; *Cotton Field, supra* note 130, para. 129.

[137] Mexico Inquiry, para. 289.

[138] Mexico Inquiry, at para. 290. In 2012 the CEDAW Committee again expressed its deep concern about feminicide and forced disappearances of women in Ciudad Juárez and elsewhere in Mexico and recommended further measures; UN Doc. CEDAW/C/MEX/CO/7-8, 7 August 2012, paras. 11–12 and 15–16.

[139] *Social and Economic Rights Action Center for Economic and Social Rights v Nigeria*, African Commission on Human Rights Communication 155/96 (2001).

such a gender-blind approach and what information the Commission might have sought in order to take gender into account, in addition to the many other dimensions of the case.

The complaints were of environmental harm through contamination and disposal of toxic waste in the process of oil production that caused ill health and increased risk of cancers; repressive action by the state security forces that killed civilians and attacked and burned villages, houses, and animals; and the creation of malnutrition and hunger among Ogoni people caused by the destruction of farming land, rivers, crops, and animals. In finding violations of the complainants' rights under the African Charter on Human and Peoples' Rights,[140] the Commission adopted the typology of state obligations that requires the state to respect, protect, promote, and fulfil all human rights. In its examination of the state's actions it failed to consider the gendered dimensions of housing, health, and food. It recognized that destruction of shelter adversely affects family life and health. However it did not consider the disproportionate impact of homelessness on women; for example, how it heightens their vulnerability to violence and sexual abuse.[141] The CEDAW Committee has expressed concern at the 'discriminatory practices with regard to land ownership, administration of property and inheritance [which] limit women's access to economic resources, as well as credit and loan facilities' in Nigeria.[142] Such discrimination is likely to have further adverse consequences for women where there is widespread forced homelessness. The destruction of food sources by the Nigerian government and its failure to prevent private companies from doing the same impacts upon the health, education, work and political participation of all Ogoni people. However, food shortages have major implications for women where they overlap with gender discrimination, including higher rates of malnutrition[143] whenever there is unequal distribution of food, and the additional hardships on women responsible for preparation of food when food sources are destroyed. In the words of the FAO:

> Considering the role women have in the household, with regard to food production, food preparation and child care, gender inequality in access to and control of resources may well result in misallocation of scarce resources, increased health care costs, lowered productivity, and poor human development trends.[144]

[140] The Commission found violations of the rights to life (art. 4), to property (art. 14), to health (art. 16), to housing (read into art. 18(1) as a constituent of the duty to protect the family), and the right to food (read into arts. 4, 16, and 22).

[141] CESCR, General Comment No. 7, The right to adequate housing (Art.11.1): forced evictions, 20 May 1997, para. 10; Report of the Special Rapporteur on adequate housing as a component of the right to an adequate standard of living, and on the right to non-discrimination in this context, UN Doc. A/HRC/16/42, 20 December 2010, para. 16 (impact of displacement most acutely felt by those vulnerable to discrimination, including women).

[142] CEDAW Committee, Concluding Observations, Nigeria, CEDAW/C/NGA/CO/6, 8 July 2008, para. 338.

[143] E.g. CESCR, Concluding Observations, Sri Lanka, *supra* note 55, para. 33 (concern that malnutrition affects nearly one-third of children and one-quarter of women).

[144] I. Rae, *Women and the Right to Food, International Law and State Practice* (Rome: Food and Agriculture Organization, 2008), 8, available at <http://www.actuar-acd.org/uploads/5/6/8/7/5687387/ fao_women_and_the_rtf.pdf> (last accessed 12 September 2013).

Women's security is threatened when environmental contamination entails their having to seek water or fuel away from their accustomed areas of supply.[145] Health concerns include increased risks of cancers and reproductive problems, but there is no gender-disaggregated data with respect to the victims of cancer, or of the types of cancer suffered. Concern has been expressed by the CEDAW Committee at the high rate of maternal mortality in Nigeria (the second highest in the world)[146] and the 'precarious situation of women's health, the insufficient and inadequate health-care facilities'. It has urged greater spending on women-specific health-care services.[147] Gender analysis is required to identify who are the victims of any increased rates of cancer and the need for appropriate and affordable gender-specific healthcare (for women and men) as the need may arise.[148] Attention also needs to be paid to the potential for miscarriages and birth deformities arising from environmental degradation and pollution.

There is no gender breakdown of the consequences of the violence by the Nigerian forces, including through the use of sophisticated weapons. Were there killings and, if so, of whom? Was there harassment by security guards? What are the consequences for women whose male relatives were killed in a country where there are entrenched harmful traditional and cultural norms and practices, including widowhood rites and practices?[149] Did the violence include sexual violence? And did the displacement and terror impact upon rates of domestic violence?[150] Asking and seeking answers to these questions would have provided a richer understanding of the situation of all the Ogoni people. Recommendations for remedies could also have been worded to ensure their accessibility, acceptability, availability, and appropriateness for all sectors of the society.[151]

[145] CESCR, General Comment No. 15, The right to water, UN Doc. E/C.12/2002/11, 20 January 2003, para. 16(a) (States should ensure that 'the disproportionate burden women bear in the collection of water should be alleviated'); para. 37(d) asserts that a core obligation is to ensure that 'personal security is not threatened when having to physically access to water' but does not mention the gender elements of this.

[146] CEDAW Committee, Concluding Observations, Nigeria, UN Doc. CEDAW/C/NGA/CO/6, 8 July 2008, para. 336.

[147] CEDAW Committee, Concluding Observations, Nigeria, UN Doc. CEDAW/C/NGA/CO/5, 2004, para. 307.

[148] CEDAW Committee General Recommendation No. 24, *supra* note 58, at paras. 10 (States to report on hazardous conditions that impact on health in different ways between women and men) and 16 (provide trauma treatment and counselling for women in 'especially difficult circumstances').

[149] CEDAW Committee, Concluding Observations, Nigeria, UN Doc. CEDAW/C/NGA/CO/6, 8 July 2008, para. 322.

[150] The CEDAW Committee has expressed concern at the 'continuing prevalence of violence against women, including domestic violence'. CEDAW Committee, Concluding Observations, Nigeria, UN Doc. CEDAW/C/NGA/CO/6, 8 July 2008, para. 326; see also CEDAW, Concluding Observations, Nigeria, UN Doc. CEDAW/C/NGA/CO/5, 2004, para. 298.

[151] For example, CESCR, General Comment No. 4, The Right to adequate housing, *supra* note 26. See also the Preliminary report of the Special Rapporteur on the right to education, UN Doc. E/CN.4/1999/49, 13 January 1999, and subsequent reports.

4. Temporary Special Measures

Gender analysis exposes inequalities in the effective enjoyment of economic, social, and cultural rights. States may determine affirmative action to accelerate the achievement of substantive equality. Temporary special measures are provided for under a number of international human rights treaties for the purpose of redressing historic disadvantage and subordination. For example, CEDAW, Article 4, allows for the adoption of temporary special measures that are 'aimed at accelerating *de facto* equality between men and women'.[152] In 1988, the CEDAW Committee had recommended that states 'make more use of temporary special measures such as positive action, preferential treatment or quota systems to advance women's integration into education, the economy, politics and employment'.[153] The Committee returned to temporary special measures in 2004, emphasizing the importance of continuous monitoring of laws, policies, and programmes to ensure their equal application to women and men, in terms of result.[154] The CEDAW Committee has noted that attention must be given to the difference between temporary special measures, designed to accelerate the achievement of women's equality and general policies adopted to improve the situation of women. It draws specific attention to this distinction in the context of healthcare.[155]

The CESCR has also turned to temporary special measures as a tool or strategy towards a concrete goal of achieving substantive equality between women and men in the guarantee of economic, social, and cultural rights. Although the ICESCR does not expressly provide for such measures, their adoption does not constitute discrimination. The CESCR has explained that:

> The principles of equality and non-discrimination, by themselves, are not always sufficient to guarantee true equality. Temporary special measures may sometimes be needed in order to bring disadvantaged or marginalized persons or groups of persons to the same substantive level as others. Temporary special measures aim at realizing not only de jure or formal equality, but also de facto or substantive equality for men and women. However, the application of the principle of equality will sometimes require that states parties take measures in favour of women in order to attenuate or suppress conditions that perpetuate discrimination. As long as these measures are necessary to redress de facto discrimination and are terminated when de facto equality is achieved, such differentiation is legitimate.[156]

Temporary special measures are often considered in the context of political participation, but also in that of paid employment—for example to enhance women's

[152] See also the International Convention on the Elimination of Racial Discrimination, 1965, art. 1(4) and the Convention on the Rights of Persons with Disabilities, 2006, art. 5.

[153] CEDAW Committee General Recommendation No. 5 on temporary special measures, 1988. See also CEDAW General Recommendation No. 8, 1988 and CEDAW General Recommendation No. 23, political and public life, 1997, para. 15.

[154] CEDAW Committee, General Recommendation No. 25, on temporary special measures, *supra* note 9.

[155] CEDAW Committee, General Recommendation No. 25, on temporary special measures, *supra* note 9, para. 37.

[156] CESCR General Comment No 16, *supra* note 11, at para. 15.

decision-making,[157] redress occupational segregation, the unemployment gap, and unequal pay.[158] Education is another sector where temporary special measures may be needed. They may be adopted by government but may also be negotiated in the private employment sector, or be applied 'on a voluntary basis by public or private enterprises, organizations, institutions and political parties'.[159] Their content should be determined by reference to the particular context to determine what is most needed to remedy the particular problem identified. This may require adoption of temporary special measures targeted at specific categories of persons; for example, victims of sexual violence in the aftermath of conflict, or victims of trafficking. Needs may be immediate such as access to basic economic and social rights including adequate, accessible and appropriate shelter, social security, immediate and very specific healthcare needs, and food.[160] More long-term permanent legislative changes may be needed in other areas; for example, to enable access to property, to make changes to the law of inheritance, or to allow access to courts.

5. Implementation of Economic, Social, and Cultural Rights

In order to assist states to comply with their obligations to deliver economic, social, and cultural rights the CESCR has indicated that in all cases services must be made available, accessible, affordable, and appropriate. These standards should also be made subject to gender analysis. Using the right to education as an example, states might consider the following practical measures to deliver gender equality:

- A national gender plan;
- National plans for education at all levels;
- 'A gender perspective in schools including legal aspects, public policies, ministerial responsibilities, the functioning of educational centres, research and the role of parents';[161]
- Requiring enrolment in schools of a specific number of each sex;
- Requiring training and recruitment of women teachers, at all educational levels;
- Non-discrimination in expenditure on educational services for girls and boys and gender budgeting within relevant economic units;
- Non-discrimination in facilities for girls and boys, including access to and use of computers and other technical aids, and sporting facilities;

[157] CESCR Concluding Observations, Sri Lanka, *supra* note 55, at para. 18.

[158] CESCR, Concluding Observations Kazakhstan, *supra* note 52, at para. 19(c); CESCR, Concluding Observations Mauritius, *supra* note 49, at para. 17.

[159] CEDAW Committee, General Recommendation No. 25, *supra* note 9, at para. 32.

[160] C. Chinkin, 'The Protection of Economic, Social and Cultural Rights in Post- Conflict', available at <http://www2.ohchr.org/english/issues/women> (last accessed 12 September 2013).

[161] Girls' right to education, Report submitted by the Special Rapporteur on the right to education, Mr. V. Muñoz Villalobos, 8 February 2006 (citing a proposal from the Council of Europe).

- Non-discrimination in time spent in schools for girls and boys;
- Non-discrimination in time spent on girls and boys; for example in the classroom where it is currently estimated that girls have eight times less contact with teachers than boys;[162]
- Non-discrimination in subjects made available to girls and boys; for example providing science and technology only to boys; cookery and domestic subjects only to girls; and non-discrimination in access to vocational training;
- Ensuring adequate security and transport, especially for girls when going to school, within school and returning home;
- Providing economic incentives to send girls to school;
- Adapting school hours to fit family seasonal schedules;
- Ensuring the curriculum does not reinforce stereotypes or traditional gender roles, including social expectations (and those of girls themselves) that girls' future lies in marriage and motherhood;
- Ensuring the curriculum depicts positive images of women and girls, as well as men and boys in non-traditional roles;
- Avoiding and sanctioning the use of sexist language in teaching and materials;
- Ensuring that girls receive as much encouragement and support as boys; for example publicizing prizes and other achievements won by girls, giving positive feedback to girls and boys;
- Revising texts and materials to ensure they do not reproduce stereotypes;
- Ensuring that it is made clear to all pupils and people within all educational establishments that harassment and bullying is unacceptable and sanctioning such behaviour;
- Providing appropriate sex education for girls and boys;
- Integrating gender sensitisation and human rights education at all levels of curricula, including teacher training; and
- Developing and applying qualitative and quantitative human rights indicators that facilitate identification of the causes of exclusion and discrimination.[163]

6. Conclusion and the Way Forward

Women's equal enjoyment of economic, social, and cultural rights with men is core to their relationships with the state, their community, private employers, and within their family. It has been suggested that there are four different approaches

[162] Report submitted by the Special Rapporteur on the right to education, Mr. V. Muñoz Villalobos, 8 February 2006, para. 104.

[163] Report submitted by the Special Rapporteur on the right to education, Mr. V. Muñoz Villalobos, 8 February 2006, paras. 104 and 135.

to a gender-sensitive analysis of human rights: a focus on non-discrimination and equality; a focus on human rights of particular importance to women [or men]; on human rights specific to women, such as protective rights relating to pregnancy; and on gender-sensitive interpretations and applications of human rights.[164] The CESCR as the monitoring body for the implementation of the ICESCR has adopted at least three of these. It has focused on equality and non-discrimination through its General Comments Nos. 16 and 20, to which it now routinely draws attention in its concluding observations to states parties, as well as indicating the potential of temporary special measures as a tool for accelerating such equality. It also seeks better information in the form of disaggregated data on a range of issues. It has recognized the particular importance to women of economic, social, and cultural rights, such as older women's need for social security rights, and the 'extent of statutory and other forms of discrimination which often apply in relation to property rights (including home ownership) or rights of access to property or accommodation, and [women's] particular vulnerability to acts of violence and sexual abuse when they are rendered homeless'.[165] The importance of gender-specific rights has also been recognized; for example, protection of maternity and the right to paternity leave.

However, where there has been less progress has been in integrating gender interpretation and application into all the work of the CESCR (as well as that of other human rights bodies), not just in those situations which obviously impact upon women, such as pregnancy and maternal mortality. Thus gender-specific concerns are frequently expressed in the contexts of employment, education, domestic violence, abortion, and maternal mortality, but this attention is not consistent in that reference may be made to such issues as the impact of single parenthood on enjoyment of economic, social, and cultural rights, or to the situation of prisoners, or those with HIV/AIDS, or domestic workers without any consideration of gender perspectives. A comprehensive approach to gender analysis is sought with a view to transformation of prevailing social structures—the workplace, the family, the global economy. It would also counter the tendency to equate women and gender. Some such analysis is undertaken and the need for modification of gender stereotypes and hierarchies emphasized but traditional stances remain in many instances largely intact. The adoption of the Optional Protocol to the ICESCR may offer the CESCR new opportunities for consideration of structural impediments to gender equality,[166] although the limited use made of the Optional Protocol to CEDAW since its coming into force suggests that these may not be widespread.[167] Much will depend on whether non-governmental organizations

[164] K. Frostell and M. Scheinin, 'Women', in A. Eide, C. Krause, and A. Rosas (eds.), *Economic, Social and Cultural Rights* 2nd rev. edn. (Leiden: Martinus Nijhoff, 2001), 331 and 332.

[165] CESCR, General Comment No. 7, *supra* note 140, at para. 10.

[166] Adopted by UN General Assembly Res. 63/117, 10 December 2008, in force 5 May 2013. ((official citation to be used))

[167] See Ministry of Justice, *The Optional Protocol to the United Nations Convention for the Elimination of all forms of Discrimination Against Women (CEDAW): The Experience of the United Kingdom*, October 2008, available at <http://webarchive.nationalarchives.gov.uk/20110322191207/http:/www.justice.gov.uk/publications/docs/un-optional-protocol-women.pdf> (last accessed 12 September 2013).

develop strategies around appropriate cases to bring before the Committee. The possibility of seeking interim measures 'as may be necessary in exceptional circumstances to avoid possible irreparable damage to the victim' also allows for some innovative thinking with respect to economic and social rights.[168] Could, for example, interim measures be sought against the introduction of measures on the basis that they would have regressive impact on the equal delivery of economic, social, and cultural rights? In the United Kingdom, the Fawcett Society unsuccessfully attempted a legal challenge against the government's budget on the basis that there had been no gender audit and that women would be the most adversely affected by the economic cuts.[169] Could the Optional Protocol be used in such a case and interim measures ordered to delay the adoption of the budget until such a gender audit is carried out? In seeking real change, the treaty bodies should also take account of the emerging programme of the recently established UN Entity for Gender Equality and the Empowerment of Women, (UN Women),[170] which was established in part as a response to the UN Secretary-General's expressed concern that gender equality be better and more fully addressed by the United Nations.[171]

As Di Otto has observed, 'achievement of women's substantive equality is an ongoing and dynamic process [...] which requires continual monitoring by states parties as well as the direct participation of women in policy development and implementation design'.[172] The process has begun, but remains far from complete.

[168] ICESCR, Optional Protocol, art. 5.

[169] L. Phillips, 'Fawcett Society Loses Budget Discrimination Challenge,' *Public Finance*, 7 December 2010, available at <http://www.publicfinance.co.uk/news/2010/12/fawcett-society-loses-budget-discrimination-challenge> (last accessed 12 September 2013).

[170] UN General Assembly Res. 64/289, 2 July 2010, 'System-Wide Coherence'.

[171] Kofi Annan included this as part of the mandate of the High-Level Panel on System-wide Coherence in the areas of development, humanitarian assistance and the environment. The Panels' Report, 'Delivering as One' UN Doc. A/61/583, 9 November 2006 proposed reform of the UN's gender architecture, as carried out through the creation of UN Women.

[172] Otto, *supra* note 26, at 52.

III

INTERNATIONAL DIMENSION OF ESC RIGHTS OBLIGATIONS

6

The Nature and Meaning of 'International Assistance and Cooperation' under the International Covenant on Economic, Social and Cultural Rights

Takhmina Karimova

1. Introduction

This contribution enquires into the concept and meaning of international assistance and cooperation. The notion, as encapsulated in the UN Charter and Article 2(1) of the Covenant on Economic, Social and Cultural Rights (ICESCR), is among the principal legal bases to argue for the existence of the international dimension of human rights.[1] International assistance and cooperation is assigned a particularly vital importance in the development discourse, for it has always been thought of as the key principle of the right to development and its extensive use in that context has rendered the content and implications of the notion problematic.

Recent attempts to give more visibility to economic, social, and cultural rights in human rights debates, as well as the drafting of the Optional Protocol to ICESCR, have renewed the interest in the Covenant's provision on international assistance and cooperation and its potential. The concept has gradually acquired autonomy from the right to development in the debates and serves as a self-standing legal justification for a variety of claims relevant to 'external context' of the ESC rights, be it social or distributive justice at international level, obligations to address systemic causes of human rights violations, or, importantly, the evolving idea of extraterritorial human rights obligations of states.[2]

[1] Arts. 55–56 of the UN Charter; Art. 2(1) of the International Covenant on Economic, Social and Cultural Rights.

[2] M. Salomon, *Global Responsibility for Human Rights: World Poverty and the Development of International Law* (New York: Oxford University Press, 2007); International Council on Human Rights Policy, *Duties sans frontières: Human Rights and Global Social Justice* (Geneva: International Council on Human Rights Policy, 2003); M. Sepúlveda Carmona, 'Obligations of "international assistance and cooperation" in an Optional Protocol to the International Covenant on Economic, Social

While many significant arguments have been constructed around the notion of international assistance and cooperation in recent years, the aim here is to address its legal nature and more specifically the existence of an obligation to cooperate and assist particularly in the area of development (cooperation). We shall first enquire about the controversies surrounding the notion of international assistance and cooperation and the basic questions underpinning the debates (Section 2). The next endeavour is to provide an analysis of the ICESCR's provision on international assistance and cooperation including obligation to cooperate for development, as well as its various problem dimensions that have to be seen in conjunction (Sections 3 and 4). It is suggested that such an analysis can benefit from the current international and individual states' practice but also from comparable debates in other areas of international law, such as international humanitarian law and the emerging rules on the protection of persons in the event of disasters (Sections 5 and 6).

2. Controversies concerning the Legal Status and Meaning of International Assistance and Cooperation

International cooperation appears in Articles 2(1), 11(1), 11(2), 15(4), 22, and 23 within the International Covenant on Economic, Social and Cultural Rights.[3] An 'umbrella' provision of the Covenant in Article 2(1) on states parties' obligations reads as follows:

> Each State Party to the present Covenant undertakes to take steps, *individually and through international assistance and co-operation*, especially economic and technical, to the maximum of its available resources with a view to achieving progressively the full realization of the rights recognized in the presented Covenant.[4]

The basic elements of 'international assistance and cooperation' were raised in the process of drafting the International Covenant on Economic Social and Cultural Rights, but remained unanswered in the final text, as adopted: what is the import of 'international assistance and cooperation' given the fact that it is placed in the main 'covering provision' stipulating states parties' obligations?[5] What is the legal nature of 'international assistance and cooperation'? Does it imply a duty to provide

and Cultural Rights', 24 *Netherlands Quarterly of Human Rights* (2006) 86–109; W. Vandenhole, 'Economic, Social and Cultural Rights in the CRC: Is There a Legal Obligation to Cooperate Internationally for Development?', 17 *International Journal of Children's Rights* (2009), 23–63.

[3] Provision on international cooperation and assistance is included in: art. 4 of Convention on the Rights of the Child; arts. 4 and 32 of Convention on the Rights of Persons with Disabilities; art. 26 of the American Convention on Human Rights and in art. 1 of the Additional Protocol to the American Convention on Human Rights in the Area of Economic, Social and Cultural Rights (Protocol of San Salvador);

[4] Emphasis added.

[5] The Committee on Economic, Social and Cultural Rights describes the role of this provision as having a dynamic relationship with all of the other provisions of the CESCR. This provision read together with each and every provision, defines the scope and nature of obligations. See CESCR, General Comment No. 3, The Nature of States Parties' Obligations, UN Doc. E/1991/23, 14 December 1990, para. 1.

international assistance and cooperation? What are the specific means to implement such a duty? If there is an obligation, what are the consequences for its violation? Does this automatically translate into the right of individuals to receive assistance? And, if so, what would be the means for enforcing such a right? It is difficult to address all these questions and identify the content of provisions in light of the ordinary meaning of Articles 2(1), or 11(1), 11(2), 15(4), 22, 23,[6] and the Covenant's context and its object and purpose, as the Vienna Convention on the Law of Treaties (VCLT) would require.[7]

The Committee on ESC Rights (CESCR) has provided useful guidance but has not yet clarified these aspects comprehensively or systematically so that they can be applied in a uniform manner in any given situation. It had, however, clarified that:

> [I]n accordance with Articles 55 and 56 of the Charter of the United Nations, with well-established principles of international law, and with the provisions of the Covenant itself, international cooperation for development and thus for the realization of economic, social and cultural rights is an obligation of all States. It is particularly incumbent upon those States which are in a position to assist others in this regard. The Committee notes in particular the importance of the Declaration on the Right to Development adopted by the General Assembly in its resolution 41/128 of 4 December 1986 and the need for States parties to take full account of all of the principles recognized therein. It emphasizes that, in the absence of an active programme of international assistance and cooperation on the part of all those States that are in a position to undertake one, the full realization of economic, social and cultural rights will remain an unfulfilled aspiration in many countries.[8]

Yet, the requirement of realizing ESC rights *through* international assistance and cooperation has different shades of meaning for '[s]tates in a position to provide assistance' on the one hand, and those who are in need of it on the other.[9] The debates surrounding the issue in the negotiation of the Optional Protocol to the ICESCR affirm that developed states considered that international cooperation was a moral obligation.[10] However, the fact that references to 'international assistance and cooperation' invoked debates on the existence of an obligation for

[6] Art. 11(1) on the right to food, reaffirms the necessity of international cooperation and in para. 2, stipulates that States 'shall take, individually and through international cooperation, measures', and art. 15(4) on cultural rights, makes use of the term 'cooperation'.

[7] Art. 31(1), Vienna Convention on the Law of the Treaties.

[8] CESCR, General Comment No. 3, The Nature of States Parties' Obligations, UN Doc. E/1991/23, 14 December 1990, para. 14.

[9] Report of the Open-ended Working Group to Consider Options Regarding the Elaboration of an Optional Protocol to the International Covenant on Economic, Social and Cultural Rights on its Third Session, 2006, UN Doc.E/CN.4/2006/47. While the developing states held the view that the obligation of international assistance and cooperation was a legally binding duty, developed states doubted this position and some even deemed it merely a moral obligation.

[10] Report of the Open-ended Working Group to Consider Options Regarding the Elaboration of an Optional Protocol to the International Covenant on Economic, Social and Cultural Rights on its Second Session, UN Doc. E/CN.4/2005/52, para. 76, according to which 'In relation to article 2 (1), the discussions focused on the reference to international assistance and cooperation. The representatives of the United Kingdom, the Czech Republic, Canada, France, and Portugal believed that international cooperation and assistance was an important moral obligation but not a legal entitlement, and did not interpret the Covenant to impose a legal obligation to provide development assistance or give a legal title to receive such aid'.

resource transfers indicates that states see the provision as requiring mainly positive duties, or even a narrow 'resource-based' action. For this reason, it is not clear whether international cooperation and assistance is controversial in its entirety (particularly adopted in broad terms) or only regarding one of its components, that is, development assistance.[11]

During the *travaux préparatoires* of the International Covenant on Economic, Social and Cultural Rights, international assistance and cooperation as a mandatory obligation was not supported in the debates, since it was held that the legal duty would serve as an excuse for countries to evade any obligation on the basis of inadequacy of international assistance.[12] The legislative history shows that discussions took place to identify the meaning of 'international assistance and cooperation', and more specifically whether it was confined to technical assistance only.[13]

Reference can also be made to the provisions of other treaties on socio-economic rights that contain similar elements on international assistance and cooperation (Article 4 of the Convention on the Rights of a Child,[14] and Article 4(2) of the Convention on the Rights of Persons with Disabilities). Article 4 of the Convention on the Rights of the Child (CRC) does not make reference to 'assistance', adopting rather a broader term 'international cooperation'.[15] In Articles 4, 23(4), 24(4),

[11] On general issues related to the international cooperation in the field of human rights see the Report of the Human Rights Council's Advisory Committee, Report on Enhancement of International Cooperation in the Field of Human Rights.The version as submitted to the HRC is under A/HRC/19/74, 29 February 2012.

[12] P. Alston and G. Quinn, 'The Nature and Scope of States Parties' Obligations under the International Covenant on Economic, Social and Cultural Rights', *9 Human Rights Quarterly* (1987), 156–229 and 189. For a detailed discussion on the drafting history see S. Skogly, *Beyond National Borders: States' Human Rights Obligations in International Cooperation* (Antwerp: Intersentia, 2006).

[13] In fact, the earlier draft of the provision referred only to 'cooperation', therefore it can be interpreted that assistance was inserted to underline its importance as a form of cooperation. The 1952 draft of art. 2(1) reads 'Each State Party hereto undertakes to take steps, individually and through international cooperation, to the maximum of available resources, with a view to achieving progressively the full realisation of the rights recognised in this Covenant by legislative as well as other means'. Commission on Human Rights, Report, 8th session (14 April to 14 June 1952), ECOSOC Official Records, 14th session, Supp. No.4, Annex I. The same wording was contained in the draft which the Human Rights Commission handed over to the General Assembly in 1954, and which was then further discussed in the Third Committee of the General Assembly between December 1954 and December 1966.

[14] The wording of the CRC on international obligations differs. Art. 4 of the Convention on the Rights of a Child stipulates: 'States Parties shall undertake all appropriate legislative, administrative, and other measures for the implementation of the rights recognized in the present Convention. With regard to economic, social and cultural rights, States Parties shall undertake such measures to the maximum extent of their available resources and, where needed, within the framework of international cooperation'. According to the commentaries they are not as explicit as ICESCR. See M. Rishmawi, *A Commentary on the United Nations Convention on the Rights of the Child, Article 4: The Nature of States Parties' Obligations* (Leiden: Martinus Nijhoff Publishers, 2006), 7. The comparison with the Child's Rights Covenant shows, that 'full realisation' of the ESC rights of children unlike in CESCR is not made explicit.

[15] CRC, General Comment No. 5 (2003), General Measures of Implementation of the Convention on the Rights of the Child (Arts. 4, 42 And 44, para. 6), UN Doc. CRC/GC/2003/5, 27 November 2003, also see CRC, 7th Session, Overview of the Reporting Procedures, UN Doc. CRC/C/33, 24 October 1994, See also S. Detrick, *Commentary on the United Nations Convention on the Rights of the Child* (Leiden: Kluwer International, 1999), 109.

and 28(3) international cooperation is explicitly linked to the 'needs of developing countries'.[16] The importance of international cooperation was stressed in the adoption of the Optional Protocol to the Convention on the Rights of the Child on the Involvement of Children in Armed Conflict.[17] In its General Comment on the Implementation of the Convention, the Committee on the Rights of the Child pointed out that: '[w]hen States ratify the Convention, they take upon themselves obligations not only to implement it within their jurisdiction, but also to contribute, through international cooperation, to global implementation'.[18] Implementation of the Convention, is 'a cooperative exercise for the States of the world', the CRC stated.[19] On another occasion, the Committee, in light of the divergent views on the meaning of references to international cooperation, stated that it 'believes that children's rights are a shared responsibility between the developed and the developing countries'.[20]

Similar to the CESCR, the Committee on the Rights of the Child closely links the provision on international assistance and cooperation to the issues of cooperation for development.[21] First, it advised states parties to approach the Convention

[16] Art. 4 of the CRC: 'States Parties shall undertake all appropriate legislative, administrative, and other measures for the implementation of the rights recognized in the present Convention. With regard to economic, social and cultural rights, States Parties shall undertake such measures to the maximum extent of their available resources and, where needed, *within the framework of international cooperation*' [emphasis added]. Art. 23(4) of the CRC speaks of 'the spirit of international cooperation' while arts. 24 and 28(3), concerning the right to health and education respectively, employ the notion of obligation to 'promote' and 'encourage' international cooperation.

[17] International assistance and cooperation was included as one of the nine main areas and in fact as voiced by the representative of the Indian delegation, 'it did raise standards in a real and substantive manner over the existing norms in its various provisions including those on international cooperation' in its Report of the working group on a draft optional protocol to the Convention on the Rights of the Child on involvement of children in armed conflicts on its 6th session, UN Doc. E/CN.4/2000/74, para. 145. Discussions that took place in the drafting process of the Optional Protocol indicate the importance attached to international cooperation, moreover it was articulated by the United States that '[s]tates can and should assist in bringing an end to this tragedy through international cooperation and assistance' See Report of the working group on a draft optional protocol to the Convention on the Rights of the Child on involvement of children in armed conflicts on its 6th session GE.00-12043 (E), UN Doc. E/CN.4/2000/74, para. 145. Inter-sessional open-ended working group on a draft optional protocol to the Convention on the Rights of the Child on involvement of children in armed conflicts Comments on the Report of the Working Group, UN Doc. E/CN.4/2000/WG.13/2/Add.1, paras. 18–20. The position of the US was interpreted as acceptance of the human rights obligation to cooperate for the rehabilitation and integration of child soldiers. Vandenhole, *supra* note 2, at 39.

[18] CRC, General Comment No. 5 (2003), General measures of implementation of the Convention on the Rights of the Child (arts. 4, 42, and 44, para. 6), para. 7.

[19] CRC, General Comment No. 5 (2003), General measures of implementation of the Convention on the Rights of the Child (arts. 4, 42, and 44, para. 6), para. 60.

[20] The Committee also stressed that: 'State parties must respect and protect economic, social and cultural rights of children in all countries with no exceptions, and take all possible measures to fulfil these rights—whenever they are in a position to do so—through development cooperation' in CRC, General Discussion on 'Resources for the Rights of the Child-Responsibility of States', 46th session, 21 September 2007, paras. 50–51.

[21] In this context, it recalls the UN Charter's provisions and pledges of states in economic and social cooperation as well as the UN Millennium Declaration, where states have 'pledged themselves, in particular, to international cooperation to eliminate poverty' in CRC, General Comment No. 5 (2003), General measures of implementation of the Convention on the Rights of the Child (arts. 4, 42, and 44, para. 6), para. 60.

on the Rights of the Child as a framework for international development assistance, that is, as a legal basis of cooperation.[22] Second, the Committee stressed that development programmes and policies should be rights-based.[23] Third, the Committee reminds donors to meet the target for international development assistance. Fourth, it was of the view that the UN and UN-related agencies should be guided by the Convention and mainstream children's rights in their activities. Additionally,

> [t]hey should seek to ensure within their influence that international cooperation is targeted at supporting States to fulfil their obligations under the Convention. Similarly the World Bank Group, the International Monetary Fund and World Trade Organization should ensure that their activities related to international cooperation and economic development give primary consideration to the best interests of children and promote full implementation of the Convention.[24]

References to international cooperation in the framework of the Convention on the Rights of Persons with Disabilities are contained in the preamble, Article 4(2) on state obligations, [25] and in Article 32 specifically dealing with international cooperation where 'the importance' of cooperation is recognized.[26] Although importance was attached to the necessity of cooperation, it remained a difficult

[22] It 'urges States to meet internationally agreed targets, including the United Nations target for international development assistance of 0.7 per cent of gross domestic product'. See CRC, General Comment No. 5 (2003), General measures of implementation of the Convention on the Rights of the Child (arts. 4, 42, and 44, para. 6), para. 60. In para. 64, the CRC stated that states parties recipients of international aid are asked to apportion 'substantive part of that aid' to children.

[23] The CRC, in particular urges that PRSP and sector-wide approaches to development (SWAps) should reflect children's rights principles, in CRC, General Comment No. 5 (2003), General measures of implementation of the Convention on the Rights of the Child (arts. 4, 42, and 44, para. 6), para. 62.

[24] CRC, General Comment No. 5 (2003), General measures of implementation of the Convention on the Rights of the Child (arts. 4, 42, and 44, para. 6), para. 64.

[25] Art 4 (2): With regard to economic, social, and cultural rights, each State Party undertakes to take measures to the maximum of its available resources and, where needed, within the framework of international cooperation, with a view to achieving progressively the full realization of these rights, without prejudice to those obligations contained in the present Convention that are immediately applicable according to international law.

[26] Art 32 of the CRPD reads as follows:

1. States Parties recognize the importance of international cooperation and its promotion, in support of national efforts for the realization of the purpose and objectives of the present Convention, and will undertake appropriate and effective measures in this regard, between and among States and, as appropriate, in partnership with relevant international and regional organizations and civil society, in particular organizations of persons with disabilities. Such measures could include, inter alia:
   a. Ensuring that international cooperation, including international development programmes, is inclusive of and accessible to persons with disabilities;
   b. Facilitating and supporting capacity-building, including through the exchange and sharing of information, experiences, training programmes and best practices;
   c. Facilitating cooperation in research and access to scientific and technical knowledge;
   d. Providing, as appropriate, technical and economic assistance, including by facilitating access to and sharing of accessible and assistive technologies, and through the transfer of technologies.
2. The provisions of this article are without prejudice to the obligations of each State Party to fulfil its obligations under the present Convention.

subject matter on which to reach consensus.[27] Summaries of debates on the issue state the following:

Some members expressed particular concern about creating international obligations with regard to international cooperation, development aid or assistance in the context of a binding instrument, although they actively engaged in international cooperation. Other members considered that the issue should not be interpreted as imposing obligations beyond any other existing model of international cooperation.[28]

Objections to the insertion of a specific article on international cooperation were grounded on the fact, that the Disability Convention as a human rights treaty involved rights of individuals as opposed to international cooperation, which was not a 'specific' human right. Furthermore, the EU stated that inclusion of an international cooperation provision would make the Convention deal with states' obligations towards other states.[29] In negotiations at a later stage, it was the general framework for cooperation that was supported rather than international cooperation (understood as development assistance).[30]

3. International Assistance and Cooperation: Towards a Minimalist or Maximalist Approach?

Neither the Committee on ESC Rights nor doctrine seems to have consistently theorized the concrete implications of the requirement of 'international assistance and cooperation'.[31] Very frequently, scholarly writings focus on states' extraterritorial obligations under the ICESCR, building on Article 2(1) of the Covenant's prescription on 'international assistance and cooperation'.[32] Applying

[27] The discussions in the drafting process underscored that implementation of the Convention will be primarily a national responsibility and that compliance with the Convention should not be conditional on receiving international development aid or assistance. While another view held that international cooperation was an important means to support national efforts for the realization of goals and objectives of the Convention and even though it was agreed that primary responsibility for implementation will rest upon states domestically, there was a shared responsibility, and international cooperation is to complement national efforts. As seen from the records of the discussions, the issue of shared responsibility was later seen with regard to the allocated resources (once development assistance is provided by donor-state to recipient-state), e.g. how they are used.

[28] Annex II, Summary of the discussions held regarding the issue of international cooperation to be considered by the Ad Hoc Committee, UN Doc. A/AC.265/2004/WG/1, paras. 2, 3, and 5.

[29] Daily summary of discussion at the 6th session 1 August 2005, vol. 7, No. 1 of 1 August 2005, available at <http://www.un.org/esa/socdev/enable/rights/ahc6sum1Aug.htm> (last accessed 20 October 2013.

[30] W. Vandenhole, *supra* note 2, at 23–63 and 59.

[31] For a critique of the CESCR's treatment on the issue, see K. Mechlem, 'Treaty Bodies and the Interpretation of Human Rights', 42 *Vanderbilt Journal of Transnational Law* (2009), 907–947, 34, who opined in this regard that '[w]ith every new General Comment the scope of such obligations seems either to expand or to shrink again'.

[32] F. Coomans and M.T. Kamminga, *Extraterritorial Application of Human Rights Treaties* (Antwerp, Intersentia: 2004); M. Gibney, K. Tomasevski, and J. Vedsted-Hansen, 'Transnational State Responsibility for Violations of Human Rights', 12 *Harvard International Law Journal* (1999), 267–295; M.T. Kamminga, *Inter-state Accountability for Violations of Human Rights* (Philadelphia: University

the tripartite typology to analyse state obligations under various rights to 'international assistance and cooperation',[33] the texts on ESC rights allude to the existence of three distinct obligations to respect, protect, and fulfil ESC rights with an international dimension (that is, with respect to individuals in other states).[34] Accordingly, '[s]tates parties [are] to avoid measures that hinder or prevent the enjoyment of the Covenant's rights in another State', 'to take measures to prevent that non-State entities under their jurisdiction interfere with the enjoyment of the Covenant's rights abroad', and to provide assistance for 'satisfaction of rights' of individuals in other states.[35]

More theorists find that from among these obligations only those of a negative nature (obligations not to do) are well established at the international level, and arrive at a conclusion that positive duties (such as duty to fulfil) are the least set.[36] It is striking to note that current thinking seems to have transformed to a large degree previous debate on the issue, which generally understood the concept of international assistance and cooperation as primarily (but not exclusively) linked to the positive obligations as specified broadly by the notion of a right to development and the related New International Economic Order (NIEO), and more narrowly construed as official development assistance (ODA).

There is, however, a non-negligible counterweight to this approach in the doctrine. According to one view, international assistance and cooperation is not a self-standing, independent obligation that is incumbent upon the states parties at

of Pennsylvania Press, 1992); S. Narula, 'The Right to Food: Holding Global Actors Accountable Under International Law', 44 *Columbia Journal of Transnational Law* (2006), 691–800; M. Sepulveda Carmona, 'Obligations of 'International Assistance and Cooperation' in an Optional Protocol to the International Covenant on Economic, Social and Cultural Rights,' 24 *Netherlands Quarterly of Human Rights* (2006), 271–303; S.I. Skogly, *Beyond National Borders: States' Human Rights Obligations in International Cooperation* (Antwerp, Intersentia: 2006); J.B. de Mesquita, *International Covenant on Economic, Social and Cultural Rights: Obligations of International Assistance and Cooperation* (Human Rights Centre, University of Essex: 2002); M. Gibney and S. Skogly (eds.), *Universal Human Rights and Extraterritorial Obligations* (Philadelphia, University of Pennsylvania Press: 2010).

33 The levels of obligations have been elaborated on the basis of works of Shue. H. Shue, *Basic Rights: Subsistence, Affluence, and U.S. Foreign Policy*, 2nd edn. (Princeton: Princeton University Press, 1996); and A. Eide, The Right to Adequate Food as a Human Right, UN Commission on Human Rights, Report on the Right to Adequate Food by A. Eide, Special Rapporteur, UN.doc. E/CN.4/Sub.2/1987/23, 7 July 1987. See Maastricht Guidelines (No. 6) for the description of the obligations.

34 Craven earlier suggested that: 'The precise nature of the obligations in this field may be usefully analysed by reference to the tripartite typology. [...] It may be seen that the obligations to respect, protect, and ensure operate at the international level just as they do at the national level. Thus States could be said to have an initial duty to restrain themselves from any action that might impede the realization of economic, social and cultural rights in other countries' in M. Craven, *The International Covenant on Economic, Social and Cultural Rights: A Perspective on Its Development* (Oxford: Oxford University Press, 1995), 147; For examples of analysis of international assistance and cooperation by reference to the tripartite obligations: Sepúlveda Carmona, *supra* note 2; and J. Tobin, *The Right to Health in International Law* (New York: Oxford University Press: 2012), 325–370.

35 Sepúlveda Carmona, *supra* note 2, at 280–289.

36 International Council on Human Rights Policy, *Duties sans frontières: Human Rights and Global Social Justice* (Geneva: International Council on Human Rights Policy, 2003); Sepúlveda Carmona, *supra* note 2; and W. Vandenhole, *supra* note 2, at 23–63.

all times and in all circumstances.[37] Article 2(1) does not envisage international assistance and cooperation as a separate obligation but only as one of the possible means to achieve realization of the rights guaranteed by the ICESCR.[38] More specifically, attention is drawn to the fact that the provision speaks of international assistance and cooperation, especially *economic and technical*.[39]

Indeed, the argument that international cooperation as such is not a self-standing and autonomous obligation can be even further reinforced by the wording of Article 4 of the Convention on the Rights of the Child (CRC) which provides that states for the fulfilment of rights enshrined in the Convention are to 'undertake such measures to the maximum extent of their available resources and, *where needed*, within the framework of international cooperation'. The Convention on the Rights of Persons with Disabilities (CRPD) similarly circumscribes the international cooperation to situations where it is *needed*. One has to ask, therefore, whether states have over time actually transformed their understanding of the notion of 'cooperation' to a more complex, all-encompassing one, as currently proposed by the scholarship. The nature of the notion of the international assistance and cooperation as a *measure* rather than an independent obligation can be further brought into sharp relief by reference to regional instruments.[40]

In light of these arguments, it is possible to state that the requirement of Article 2(1) on assistance and cooperation is not a substantive legal provision requiring states parties to abstain from or perform certain actions. It does not set out what states parties are to do or not do in relation to a specific matter; rather it creates a legal obligation on *how* all the specific obligations contained in substantive provisions of the Covenant are to be performed. Put in these terms, an obligation of assistance and cooperation can only be a rule of secondary nature, specifying means by which obligations under specific rights are to be achieved.[41] If such an interpretation is accepted, it will be difficult to extrapolate on the basis of international assistance and cooperation (Article 2(1)) *only*, specific obligations that potentially cover all possible acts and omissions that may have an impact on the ESC rights of persons in third states.

Relevant to this is the question of whether international assistance and cooperation is to be reduced to resources, that is, development aid stricto sensu, or rather

[37] R. Pisillo Mazzeschi, Responsabilité de l'état pour violation des obligations positives relatives aux droits de l'homme, 333 *Recueil des Cours* (2008), 456.

[38] R. Pisillo Mazzeschi, Responsabilité de l'état pour violation des obligations positives relatives aux droits de l'homme, 333 *Recueil des Cours* (2008), 457.

[39] As Craven notes, 'it is not clear whether the terms 'assistance' and 'cooperation' have discrete meanings. Neither is it obvious whether the terms 'economic and technical' refer to both forms of international action or merely to 'cooperation', in Craven, *supra* note 34, at 147.

[40] Art. 1, Additional Protocol to the American Convention on Human Rights in the Area of Economic, Social and Cultural Rights. See also for a discussion on the meaning of international cooperation in the context of the OAS Charter, D.M. Negro, 'Article 17 and Chapter VII of the Revised OAS Charter and Relevant Experience of OAS Institutions', in S.P. Marks (ed.), *Implementing the Right to Development: the Role of International Law* (Friedrich Ebert Stiftung: Geneva, 2008), 64–72.

[41] The formulation of this para. is inspired by the analysis of art. 1 of Geneva Conventions of 1949 by A. Cassese (ed.), in A. Cassese, *International Law* 2nd edn (New York: Oxford University Press, 2005), 18.

denotes a comprehensive concept. The normative content of international assistance and cooperation as reflected in Article 2(1) as well as its different manifestations in other articles of the Covenant point towards a notion going beyond the issue of assistance. This is mainly because the text of the Covenant itself seems to be in favour of an expansive approach to the notion. The aforementioned Article 11 of the Covenant, in paragraph 2 dealing with the fundamental right of everyone to be free from hunger, requires states 'individually and through international cooperation' to take measures 'to ensure an equitable distribution of world food supplies in relation to need' taking into account 'the problems of both food-importing and food-exporting countries'.[42]

Indeed, to reduce international assistance to mere ODA will be an unduly restrictive approach to the framework of rights that are premised on international action and the enjoyment of which is dramatically influenced by external socio-economic processes. This scholarly consensus to visualize international assistance and cooperation expansively can be attributed to the changes of perception in relation to ESC rights generally. For a long time, ESC rights were conceived as being based on a different logic. In particular, the obligation of states parties to the Covenant when 'examined' through notions of 'maximum available resources' has given an impression that 'compliance is not an important concern: states wish to comply and will do so if they have the necessary resources'.[43] This longstanding perception has been gradually reversed. The Committee on Economic, Social and Cultural Rights, in a number of general comments, has clarified that certain ESC rights are of immediate effect. The obligation to respect ESC rights, similar to civil and political rights, obliges states not to deprive someone from a right he or she already enjoys.[44]

[42] For Alston the meaning of the provision implies a duty to avoid depriving and duties to protect from deprivation. The obligation to avoid depriving may imply: '1. The duty to avoid international policies and practices which deprive other states of their means of subsistence or which promote an inequitable distribution of world food supplies. 2. The duty to mitigate national policies which have the effect of promoting an inequitable distribution of world food supplies. 3. The duty not to use food as an international sanction', in P. Alston, 'International Law and the Human Rights to Food', in P. Alston and K. Tomasevski (eds.), *The Right to Food: Towards a System for Supervising States' Compliance with the Right to Food* (Leiden: Martinus Nijhoff Publishers, 1984), 44.

[43] As a result, the focus at international level has also been on generating resources (financial transfers, investment, etc.) rather than on developing rules to ensure that the process of development is not harmful to individual rights. L. Henkin, 'International Law: Politics, Values and Functions', 216 *Recueil des Cours* (1989). 270 (available at <http://nijhoffonline.nl/book?id=er216_er216_009-416> (last accessed 21 November 2013)).

[44] The contents of ESC rights and their corresponding obligations have been established in various general comments, supplemented by documents produced by experts defining the nature and scope of obligations arising from the ESC rights at national and international levels. See also the 1986 Limburg Principles on the Implementation of the International Covenant on Economic, Social and Cultural Rights, contained in UN Commission on Human Rights, *Note verbale dated 86/12/05 from the Permanent Mission of the Netherlands to the United Nations Office at Geneva addressed to the Centre for Human Rights ('Limburg Principles')*, 8 January 1987, UN Doc. E/CN.4/1987/17; International Commission of Jurists (ICJ), *Maastricht Guidelines on Violations of Economic, Social and Cultural Rights*, 26 January 1997; International Commission of Jurists, *The Bangalore Declaration and Plan of Action*, Bangalore, India, 23–25 October 1995; *Quito Declaration on the Enforcement and Realization of Economic, Social, and Cultural Rights in Latin America and the Caribbean*, 24 July 1998; 'Maastricht

These efforts to define the international dimension of obligations are significant in that they attempt to respond to exogenous causes of systematic denials of basic subsistence rights to a large majority of individuals and deterioration of standards of living due to crises of an external nature.[45] In fact, proponents of the broad reading of 'international assistance and cooperation' find ample assistance in the views of the CESCR to support their arguments.[46] Admittedly, the Committee on ESC rights has not been entirely clear on what is meant by referring to international assistance and cooperation and which purpose such a reference is meant to serve.

Sometimes the Committee construes a purely resource-based notion of international assistance and cooperation.[47] But on a closer look, it becomes apparent that the Committee, in expressing its views on the obligations of states at the international level, does not rely exclusively on the concept of 'international assistance and cooperation' as a basis to clarify the substantive obligations of states parties.[48] The Committee has relied upon the UN Charter and relevant commitments expressed in the policy statements, framing them as 'international obligations' which 'all reinforce the obligation of States parties in relation to the provision of international assistance and cooperation'.[49] Furthermore, the Committee defines the obligations to respect and to prevent third parties from violating the ESC rights in third countries, by reference to the UN Charter and *applicable international law*.

Two meanings of international assistance and cooperation therefore can be deduced from the practice of the Committee. One is international assistance and cooperation stricto sensu, meaning primarily technical and financial, what can be referred to 'as means of implementation', that is, assistance. The second meaning,

Principles on Extraterritorial Obligations of States in the area of Economic, Social and Cultural Rights, and the Commentary' by O. De Schutter, A. Eide, A. Khalfan, M. Orellana, M. Salomon, and I. Seiderman, available at <http://www.lse.ac.uk/humanRights/articlesAndTranscripts/2012/HRQMaastricht.pdf> (last accessed 21 November 2013).

45 International welfare inducing law 'can also be used as a means of obtaining international aid, despite the fact that the sharp rise in poverty and famine over recent years has actually been due to negligence, blind collectivism, terror, or civil war' in E. Jouannet, 'What is the Use of International Law? International Law as a 21st Century Guardian of Welfare', 28 *Michigan Journal of Law* (2007), 815–862, and 853.

46 See, e.g. Sepúlveda Carmona, *supra* note 32, at 278, who supports her approach to develop states' obligations at international level by reference to the Committee who 'itself applies the 'tripartite typology' to analyse international obligations'.

47 CESCR, General Comment No. 14, The Right to the Highest Attainable Standard of Health, UN Doc. E/C.12/2000/4, 11 August 2000, para. 45. CESCR, General Comment No. 3, The Nature of States Parties' Obligations, UN Doc. E/1991/23, 14 December 1990, para. 14. CESCR, General Comment No. 4, The Right to Adequate Housing, contained in UN Doc. E/1992/23, 13 December 1991, para. 10; CESCR, General Comment No. 5, Persons with Disabilities, contained in UN Doc. E/1995/22, 12 September 1994, para. 13. CESCR, General Comment No. 6, The Economic, Social and Cultural Rights of Older Persons, contained in UN Doc. E/1996/22, 12 August 1995, para. 18.

48 For example, in certain instances, the Committee reads international assistance and cooperation in conjunction with 'the spirit' of art. 56 of the Charter of the United Nations, the specific provisions contained in arts. 11 and 23 of the Covenant, and sometimes global policy statements, such as for example the Rome Declaration of the World Food Summit.

49 See, for example, CESCR, General Comment No. 12, The Right to Adequate Food, UN Doc. E/CN.12/1999/5, 12 May 1999, para. 36; and General Comment No. 13, The Right to Education, UN Doc. E/C.12/1999/10, 8 December 1999, para. 56.

which tends to be identified under the umbrella concept of 'cooperation', is interpreted broadly in light of the obligations of states under UN Charter. On one occasion, the Committee clearly makes this distinction between the two, when it states: 'International cooperation requires States parties to refrain from actions that interfere, directly or indirectly, with the enjoyment of the right to water in other countries'.[50]

The assumption here is that, distinct from the approach of many authors, obligations to respect and protect socio-economic rights in other states are more complex. The Committee itself, on numerous occasions, had referred to a number of legal sources such as the UN Charter, and albeit in a much more ambiguous manner to '*applicable international law*' to construe an argument that states are to abstain from interfering directly or indirectly with ESC rights of individuals in other countries. Consequently, a more complex analysis in search of this 'applicable law' is required.[51]

4. The Question of Cooperation for Development and the ICESCR

As suggested earlier, the ICESCR, perhaps in line with its genuine direction, absorbs the notion of cooperation for development, in toto or in part, by designating it as one of the means for the purpose of realization of socio-economic rights. However, by doing so, it incorporates a highly contentious element of inter-state economic relations, namely development assistance.[52] The question is whether, considering the consistent flows of development assistance to developing states,[53] it can be defined in terms of rights and obligations. The answer to this question did not change for the last few decades since the Secretary General report on NIEO principles. In this report, the Secretary General conceded that despite the existence of the 'regularity of flows of assistance' between developed and developing countries for an extended period of time, it is 'difficult to maintain that they have given place to a concrete normative proposition, specific as to their content (level) or individualized as to their destination (or beneficiaries)'.[54]

To make this general principle of the obligation to provide assistance operational, 'not only does its content need to be specified, but so do also the parties to the legal

[50] CESCR, General Comment No. 15, The Right to Water, UN Doc. E/C.12/2002/11, 20 January 2003, para. 31.

[51] See T. Karimova, *Human Rights Legal Framework in Development Cooperation*, (Graduate Institute of International Studies and Development, Doctoral Dissertation, Geneva, 2013).

[52] Official Development Assistance (ODA) is not always automatically linked with compliance with the ICESCR obligations, but rather is channelled for the purposes of development.

[53] Development assistance is a permanent item of the budgets of both developed and developing countries and one of the main features of international organizations.

[54] Report of the Secretary General, Progressive Development of the Principles and Norms of International Law Relating to the New International Economic Order, UN Doc. A/39/504/Add.1, 23 October 1984, para. 179.

relations deriving therefrom and the institutional arrangements which relate them to each other'.[55] While this assessment is made in relation to the issue of development assistance generally as a feature of inter-state economic relations under international law, it remains valid for the implications of international assistance and cooperation under the ICESCR, to the extent that the legal import of Article 2(1) is questioned.

If, however, one considers 'international cooperation' under Article 2(1) providing this legal link between developing and developed members to assist each other in terms of financial and technical resources, then, in order for 'assistance and cooperation' to become an operational legal principle, it may well require an institutional framework of implementation.[56] Such a shift would move development assistance towards a more objective regime, and make it possible to assert development assistance as a legal obligation or entitlement towards the states parties to the Covenant. There is, of course, no shortage of multilateral frameworks for this purpose, the problem being that states still prefer to provide assistance bilaterally.[57]

The readiness of the states to accept a concrete as well as 'compelled' cooperation in the framework of ESC rights can be assessed by looking at the drafting history of the Optional Protocol to the ICESCR. The Optional Protocol contains Article 14 on international assistance and cooperation, which provides for, inter alia, the establishment of a trust fund.[58] The provision caused much debate in the drafting of the Protocol, but in the end was accepted as it is based solely on voluntary contributions.[59] Similarly, commitments as formulated in the various global pledges remain voluntary.[60]

[55] Report of the Secretary General, Progressive Development of the Principles and Norms of International Law Relating to the New International Economic Order, UN Doc. A/39/504/Add.1, 23 October 1984, para. 180.

[56] Report of the Secretary General, Progressive Development of the Principles and Norms of International Law Relating to the New International Economic Order, UN Doc. A/39/504/Add.1, 23 October 1984, para. 31.

[57] Currently only 29 per cent of development assistance is channelled through multilateral institutions, a share of which is earmarked, thus undermining freedom of programming by multilateral institutions and ownership by programme countries. See Report of Secretary General on Trends and Progress in International Development Cooperation, UN Doc. E/2010/93, 10 June 2010, para. 52.

[58] The purpose of a trust fund is to 'enhance implementation of the rights' contained in the ICESCR and to help build national capacities of states in the area of ESC rights.

[59] E. Riedel, 'New Bearings in Social Rights? The Communications Procedure Under the ICESCR', in U, Fastenrath et al., *From Bilateralism to Community Interest: Essays in Honour of Bruno Simma* (New York: Oxford University Press, 2011), 575–589 and 587.

[60] Some transient contractual proposals have been designed since the 1990s. The logic of these approaches is a shared responsibility. These proposals did not generate much success, since no serious follow-up ensued to such undertakings. These include the Copenhagen Declaration and Programme of Action 1995, Report of the World Summit for Social Development (Copenhagen, 6–12 March 1995), UN Doc. A/CONF.166/9, para. 88; The Beijing Declaration and Platform for Action 1995, Report of the Fourth World Conference on Women, UN Doc. A/CONF.177/20, 17 October 1995, paras. 353 and 358 requiring allocation of 20 per cent of ODA and 20 per cent of national budgets, respectively, for basic social programmes. Art. 24 of the 2005 World Summit Outcome Document endorsed GA Resolution 57/265 on Establishment of the World Solidarity Fund, UN Doc. A/RES/57/265, 28 February 2003.

The Covenant has defined only the objective of obligation to cooperate and assist, in general, for the full realization of human rights. It would seem logical to suggest that the first responsibility of states parties to ICESCR is *to define* the obligations incumbent upon them in accordance with Article 2(1) on international assistance and cooperation.[61] In the absence of this definition agreed by states parties, the Committees on Economic Social and Cultural Rights, and on the Rights of the Child, have (rightly or wrongly) on occasion and where appropriate, referred to state pledges for development cooperation in outcome documents of UN summits.[62] The CESCR has consistently requested states to report on their efforts on the ODA target of 0.7 per cent, the volume of aid defined as a standard of achievement (as opposed to a legal obligation) in the area of development. In any event, the primary obligation rests with the domestic state.[63] States have an obligation to seek assistance and cooperation.[64] Hence, international assistance depending on the circumstances may either be subsidiary (the most common case) or concurrent.[65] On one occasion, the CESCR clarified that when a state is *clearly lacking* in financial or technical resources, 'the international community has a clear obligation to assist'.[66]

One understanding of the international assistance and cooperation provision by the treaty monitoring bodies of both ICESCR and CRC comes very close to the meaning of the right to development; that is, when it links the provision with cooperation for development. It is useful to iterate the view of the CESCR in this regard: 'international cooperation *for development and thus for* the realization

[61] Similarly, the Report of the Secretary General on Progressive Development of the Principles and Norms of International Law Relating to the New International Economic Order suggested that the normative prescription of the duty to cooperate 'can at most, in addition to defining the objective in general, create a duty or an obligation to negotiate with a view to defining more precisely the targets to be reached and the ways and means of reaching them'. However, as the Report admits, 'such a normative prescription is not sufficient by itself to constitute a normative proposition. In other words, the purely normative approach reaches its limits in the context of the international law of cooperation, which, by modulating the legal regulation closely to its subject-matter, is rich in specific applications that do not, or not yet, lead themselves to normative generalizations', in UN Doc. A/39/504/Add.1, 23 October 1984, paras. 134–135.

[62] The CESCR has made references to the agreements reached in the 1996 Declaration of the World Food Summit, the Alma-Ata Declaration on Primary Health Care, and CRC has made references to the Millennium Development Goals.

[63] See CESCR, General Comment No. 3, para. 11. Similarly '[w]hile development facilitates the enjoyment of all human rights, the lack of development may not be invoked to justify the abridgement of internationally recognized human rights' in UNGA, Vienna Declaration and Programme of Action, UN Doc. A/CONF.157/23, 12 July 1993, para. 10.

[64] See, e.g. CESCR, Statement: An evaluation of the obligation to take steps to the 'Maximum of available resources' under an optional protocol to the Covenant, UN Doc. E/C.12/2007/1, 10 May 2007, para. 10.

[65] For instance, in the context of the right to food, the CESCR clarified that states 'have a joint and individual responsibility, in accordance with the Charter of the United Nations, to cooperate in providing disaster relief and humanitarian assistance in times of emergency, including assistance to refugees and internally displaced persons'. CESCR, General Comment No. 12, The Right to Adequate Food, UN Doc. E/CN.12/1999/5, 12 May 1999, para. 38.

[66] CESCR, General Comment No. 11, Plans of action for primary education, UN Doc. E/C.12/1999/4, 10 May 1999, para. 9.

of economic, social, and cultural rights is an obligation for all States'.[67] Perhaps a somewhat far-fetched, but nonetheless theoretically conceivable, argument for the existence of an obligation to cooperate for development *via* human rights can be developed on the basis of the UN Charter and interpretations given to the provisions of the Covenant on Economic, Social and Cultural Rights and the Convention on the Rights of the Child.[68] This understanding however is to be construed as only one element of a greater and more expansive conception 'taking steps [...] through international assistance and cooperation [...] to achieving [...] the full realization of [...] rights', as discussed in section 4.

In what follows, an attempt will be made to verify these broad assumptions, that is, explore the nature of legal obligations, and where possible the meaning of international assistance and cooperation, by recourse to the interpretative scheme devised by Article 31 of the Vienna Convention on the Law of the Treaties. First, it will allow constructing a more complex investigation of the subject. Second, the rule of interpretation helps us to identify a number of so-far neglected avenues where answers can be sought. But more importantly, the rule of interpretation helps us identify the type of 'material' that may be relevant as an interpretative guide. Finally, the proposed approach will take the discussion beyond a narrow confine of socio-economic rights and development debate, but cast the notion of assistance and cooperation broadly to reach other areas of international law on similar issues.

5. Subsequent Practice

To begin with, no agreement has been reached between the parties to the ICESCR in connection with the conclusion of the Covenant[69] nor any subsequent agreement regarding the interpretation or the application of its provisions.[70] The successive step suggested by the rule of interpretation is looking at practice, namely it is important to ascertain whether the words of the Covenant are given meaning by states' deeds.[71] According to the International Law Commission the importance of practice, 'as an element of interpretation, is obvious; for it constitutes objective evidence of the understanding of the parties as to the meaning of the treaty'.[72]

Recourse to practice can indeed shed light on some of the questions, given that international cooperation is a permanent function of all donor and recipient

[67] Emphasis added. The Committee repeated its position regarding an obligation to cooperate for development in General comment No. 17, The right of everyone to benefit from the protection of the moral and material interests resulting from any scientific, literary, or artistic production of which he or she is the author (art. 15), UN Doc. E/C.12/GC/17, 12 January 2006, para. 37.

[68] Louis Henkin suggests that 'The Covenant serves as justification for demands for international economic change [...] and for assistance from international institutions and from other States'. Henkin, *supra* note 43, 270.

[69] Art. 31(2)(a), VCLT.

[70] Art. 31(3)(a), VCLT.

[71] This formulation is taken from a similar quote 'words are given meaning by deeds' from R. Gardiner, *Treaty Interpretation* (New York: Oxford University Press, 2008), 225.

[72] Yearbook of International Law Commission, vol. II, 1966, 221, para. 15.

countries and is one of the main objectives of the United Nations.[73] The difficulty here is obviously that establishing a required practice expressing an agreement is complex. If Article 2(1) of the ICESCR itself did not render a precise result, one has to admit that resultant practice is also difficult to reconcile. Assessment of conduct,[74] possibly meeting the requirement of subsequent practice, has also to satisfy two criteria: first, that the practice is 'in application of the treaty', and second that it 'establishes the agreement of the parties regarding its interpretation'.[75]

A. States acting individually

Earlier, references were made to the opinion of states. To the extent that the discussion of opinions and reactions of states on the issue is relevant 'practice', a few observations need to be made. The position of developed states expressed in the negotiation of the Optional Protocol to the ICESCR has sometimes been considered as reflecting the position taken on the interpretation of international assistance and cooperation. It is suggested here that it would be a misinterpretation to consider the opinion of donor states as *the* interpretation of the provision rather than *one* of its possible interpretations. This is particularly so, first, given that the position of developed states is contradicted by others.[76] One has to consider that the ICESCR is a multilateral treaty, and donor states represent only some of the states parties, therefore making their position insufficient to be regarded as *the* interpretation of Article 2(1) of the ICESCR. Of course, the wording of Article 31(3)(b) of the VCLT does not require that the practice be performed by all the parties; what it requires is that the agreement be that of all parties.[77] Therefore, the

[73] Art. 31(3)(b) of VCLT stipulates 'any subsequent practice in the application of the treaty which establishes the agreement of the parties regarding its interpretation'. For subsequent practice for the purposes of the interpretation of 'international assistance and cooperation' imply answers to questions such as type of conduct, who 'must engage in the conduct for it to count', which parties need to participate in the practice and what it is that constitutes an interpretative agreement in J. Arato, 'Subsequent Practice and Evolutive Interpretation: Techniques of Treaty Interpretation over Time and their Diverse Consequences', 9 *The Law and Practice of International Courts and Tribunals* (2010), 443–494 and 459.

[74] See the list of material sources often referred to as evidence of international custom as provided by Brownlie: 'diplomatic correspondence, policy statements, press releases, the opinions of legal advisers, official manuals on legal questions, e.g. manuals of military law, executive decisions and practices, orders to naval forces etc., comments by governments produced by International Law Commission, State legislation, international and national judicial decisions, recitals in treaties and other international instruments, a pattern of treaties in the same form, the practice of international organs, and resolutions relating to legal questions in the United Nations General Assembly' in I. Brownlie, *Principles of Public International Law* 6th edn (New York: Oxford University Press, 2003), 6.

[75] See also ICJ, *Kasikili/Sedudu Island (Botswana/Namibia)*, Judgment 13 December 1999, ICJ Reports 1999, 1094, para. 74, where the Court, in the assessment of the meaning of 'subsequent practice', clarified that two criteria have to be met: first, that the conduct 'was linked to a belief' on the part of the authors of the conduct as reflecting the interpretation of the treaty and, second, that the other party to the treaty 'were fully aware of and accepted this as a confirmation of the Treaty boundary'.

[76] China, Egypt, and Congo attributed legal title to the obligation of assistance and cooperation. See Report of the open-ended working group to consider options regarding the elaboration of an Optional Protocol to the International Covenant on Economic, Social and Cultural Rights on its 2nd session, UN Doc. E/CN.4/2005/52, para. 77.

[77] Gardiner, *supra* note 71, at 235.

equally important counterweight position of developing countries will have to be factored in.

But even the position of donor states themselves is not conclusive. As far as the obligation of cooperation and assistance contained in Article 2(1) is concerned, the overall impression is rather mixed. Analysis of the consideration of state reports by the CESCR from 2004 to 2012 indicates that the Committee has systematically raised the issue of compliance with Article 2(1) in its dialogue with states parties. It required, among others, reporting on three points: (a) provision of development assistance; (b) on the way the development policies of a state concerned contributed to realization of ESC rights in developing countries; and (c) measures states take as members of international financial institutions to ensure their policies are in compliance with the Covenant. The majority of states in their response reported with varying degree of detail on measures they undertake, including their current and planned volumes of ODA, contributions to development and poverty reduction, etc.[78] This raises an important question on whether the positive response and absence of refutation in the context of monitoring compliance with international obligations amounts to endorsement of the existence of an obligation to cooperate and provide assistance. The plausibility of such an interpretation is further highlighted by the fact that only one state so far clarified that its development cooperation efforts 'stem from a strong and solid political commitment, *rather than from its obligations under the Covenant*'.[79]

Other relevant material could be the practice of individual donor states. The general caveat in this regard is that relevant government policy statements are very ambiguous. It is not possible to discern a straightforward and explicit answer to the question of whether 'international assistance and cooperation' is understood as legally binding (or not). The language of obligation is generally carefully avoided in donors' policy statements. Some examples, however, are suggestive and come close to the type of material that could be relevant for the purpose of identifying 'subsequent practice'. Consider, for instance, the following development policy on human rights:

> Germany and the majority of its development partners have ratified the international human rights conventions and have thus recognised the implementation of these conventions as a legally binding obligation. This also provides the binding frame of reference for Germany's development cooperation with partner countries.

Furthermore, defining the MDG 8 (Global partnership for development), the same policy document contains:

> This MDG relates to the establishment of a global partnership for development. Besides the UN Charter (Articles 1, 55 and 56), the human rights treaties (including Article 2(1) ICESCR,

[78] Italy (UN Doc. HR/CESCR/NONE/2004/3), Finland (UN Doc. E/C.12/FIN/Q/5/Add.1), Netherlands (UN Doc. E/C.12/NLD/Q/3/Add.1), Belgium (UN Doc. E/C.12/BEL/Q/3/Add.1), Sweden (UN Doc. E/C.12/SWE/Q/5/Add.1), UK (UN Doc. E/C.12/GBR/Q/5/Add.1), Australia (UN Doc. E/C.12/AUS/Q/4/Add.1), Switzerland (UN Doc. E/C.12/CHE/Q/2-3/Add.1), New Zealand (UN Doc. E/C.12/NZL/Q/3/Add.1), Spain (UN Doc. E/C.12/ESP/Q/5/Add.1).

[79] See the response of Sweden to the list of issues, UN Doc. E/C.12/SWE/Q/5/Add.1, para. 48, [emphasis added].

Article 4 of the Convention on the Rights of the Child, and Article 32 of the Convention on the Rights of Persons with Disabilities) contain binding provisions for international cooperation that is aimed at the realisation of human rights. For example, developing countries are required to use the maximum of their available resources, including funds from international cooperation, for the implementation of human rights obligations and hence, inter alia, for the attainment of the MDGs. The targets defined for MDG 8 give rise to human rights-related obligations for the donor countries as well. These include, for example, their participation in further developing an open, rule-based, predictable, non-discriminatory trading and financial system and providing access to affordable essential drugs in developing countries.[80]

This statement contains at least three elements: (a) the legal sources cited are legally binding; (b) indirect reference to the international assistance as part of resources devoted to the fulfilment of human rights (that is, linking cooperation for development with human rights); and (c) some indicia interpreting possible action flowing from the legal obligation to cooperate, such as measures to create an enabling environment. All of these questions have been raised in the examination of the nature and scope of 'international assistance and cooperation'. Yet other examples of state practice are less informative on these issues. The Canadian Official Development Assistance Accountability Act provides that all Canadian official development assistance is provided 'with a central focus on poverty reduction and in a manner that is consistent with [...] democracy promotion and that promotes international human rights standards'.[81]

Iceland's legislation on development cooperation stipulates that 'Iceland's international development cooperation shall be based on the Charter of the United Nations and other international conventions on development cooperation that the Icelandic Government has undertaken to comply with'.[82] Or, in another example, Luxembourg's strategy titled 'Gouvernance pour le développement', stipulates that: '[e]n tant que signataire, le Luxembourg s'engage à respecter et à faire respecter les droits fondamentaux contenus dans ce document. En outre le Luxembourg a *pris des engagements internationaux* en ratifiant les textes relatifs à la gouvernance suivants', and lists among others the ICCPR and ICESCR.[83]

From the these excerpts it is not clear whether donor states themselves are beginning to recognize or accept that they are under a human rights' obligation to provide development cooperation (for example, contribute to the 'fulfil' aspect of ESC rights obligations), or whether they need to ensure that the manner in which they provide development cooperation is consistent with their human

[80] BMZ of Germany, *Human Rights in German Development Policy*, BMZ Strategy Paper 4, BMZ: 2011e., 12.

[81] Art 2(1), Official Development Assistance Accountability Act S.C. 2008, c. 17, Canada, available at <http://laws-lois.justice.gc.ca/eng/acts/O-2.8/page-1.html> (last accessed 21 November 2013).

[82] Act No. 121/2008 on Iceland's International Development Cooperation amended with Act No. 126/2008, available at <http://www.iceida.is/english/iceida/iceida-act> (last accessed 21 November 2013).

[83] *Gouvernance pour le développement*, Ministère des Affaires étrangères, Direction de la coopération au développement, 5, available at <http://www.mae.lu> (last accessed 21 November 2013), [emphasis added]. See also art. 1 of the Spanish Law on International Cooperation, i.e. Ley 23/1998, de 7 de julio, de Cooperación Internacional para el Desarrollo, available at <http://www.boe.es/aeboe/consultas/bases_datos/act.php?id=BOE-A-1998-16303> (last accessed 21 November 2013).

rights obligations (that is to say, those which focus on the respect aspects of ESC rights). All in all, these statements confirm a lack of convergence in the practice of states at the moment. At the same time, these examples, in comparison with multilateral frameworks (as will be seen), illustrate the type of material that may be close to meet evidentiary standards as required by the 'subsequent practice' doctrine, and in particular they may have more resonance to what one can term as a belief reflecting relevant authorities' position '*in application of the treaty*'.[84] In any event, such a practice is not sufficiently developed and more importantly does not yet represent the agreement of the parties (that is, all parties) regarding *the* interpretation of the Covenant.[85]

B. Practice of states at the multilateral level

What can be made of the wealth of practice in the area of socio-economic development taking place in the multilateral fora and day-to-day workings of international institutions? Can they provide clues to construct an interpretation? Are they legally relevant for the purposes of interpretation in the first place? Whether the legal regimes of the development institutions (that is, the World Bank, the European Commission, and bilateral donors; or recent international declarations dealing with development cooperation, such as the UN Millennium Declaration (2000), the Monterrey Consensus of the International Conference on Financing Development (2002), Paris Declaration on Aid Effectiveness (2005), and its subsequent Accra Agenda For Action and the recent Busan Partnership for Effective Development Cooperation) qualify as reflecting state practice is a judgement to be made on the basis of a number of factors.

As far as the practice of international organizations are concerned, first, the VCLT refers to the practice of states and not international organizations, although it allows its application to a treaty that is a constituent instrument of an international organization.[86] Second, there is a difference between the practice of international organizations in relation to the treaty establishing them and the practice of international organizations in relation to a treaty other than their constituent instrument, hence a more cautious approach should be taken in choosing what would count relevant for 'subsequent practice'.[87]

[84] This is not however limited to a conduct referable to a particular treaty, but applies to the treaty as a whole in Gardiner, *supra* note 71, at 232.

[85] This is not however limited to a conduct referable to a particular treaty, but applies to the treaty as a whole in Gardiner, *supra* note 71, 236.

[86] Art. 5, Vienna Convention on the Law of the Treaties.

[87] In the latter case, subsequent practice will derive primary from international courts and tribunals, which in the present subject is almost non-existent. In the former case, where States 'by treaty entrust performance of activities to an organization, how these activities are conducted can constitute practice under the treaty', although whether such practice establishes agreement of the parties regarding the treaty's interpretation requires consideration of the powers of the organ acting on the issues, the way in which states parties to the treaty participate in the activities of the organization, etc. in Gardiner, *supra* note 71, at 246.

Relevant practice of UN organs deals with international cooperation for the respect and observance of human rights as provided for by Article 55(c) in conjunction with Article 56 of the UN Charter. Assessment of the record of the practice of UN organs reveals that development cooperation and financing for development as subject areas are dealt with entirely in relation to Article 55(a) and (b) of the Charter.[88] More precisely, the vast body of practice of the UN's principal bodies, such as ECOSOC and the General Assembly, relating to development cooperation is barely addressed with respect to or within the purview of Article 55(c), despite the convergence of subject matter. A large proportion of UN practice dealing with the matters under Article 55(a) and (b) falls squarely within the domain of economic, social, and cultural rights, where the relevance of the ICESCR is most 'immediate and direct'. It will not be a mistake to state that the views and concerns expressed by General Comment No. 2 on Article 22 of the ICESCR on the state of ESC rights in development cooperation within the UN system remain largely valid to-date. [89]

With regard to the international declarations as enumerated, as we noted earlier, the important characteristics of subsequent practice are that it be '*in the application of the treaty*', whereas none of these instruments were adopted in application of the ICESCR, nor does any use the language of the ESC rights treaty.[90] Despite significant progress in past decades, ESC rights have been largely neglected in the UN-sponsored social, economic, or sustainable development conferences at the global level.[91] The Committee on Economic, Social and Cultural Rights has repeatedly called for inclusion of references to ESC rights in those fora that were, in the opinion of the Committee, contexts which 'could give content and effect to those norms', and that '[u]pholding and invoking relevant international human rights instruments in general, and the Covenant in particular, will provide a solid legal basis for international cooperation and a sense of duty to demonstrate the seriousness of the efforts'.[92] In the words of the Committee itself, ESC rights are 'systematically downgraded to be covered by terms which have no specific normative content, such as "basic needs", "human

[88] See Repertory of Practice of the United Nations Organs, available at <http://www.un.org/law/repertory> (last accessed 21 November 2013).

[89] CESCR, General Comment No. 2, International Technical Assistance Measures, UN Doc. E/1990/23, 2 February 1990.

[90] Conversely, the human rights treaty and charter bodies have integrated the aforementioned development frameworks extensively in their work.

[91] See e.g. Statements of the Committee on Economic, Social and Cultural Rights: Statement of the Committee to the Commission on Sustainable Development acting as the Preparatory Committee for the World Summit for Sustainable Development, Bali, Indonesia, 27 May to 7 June 2002, 28th session, UN Doc. E/2003/22-E/C.12/2002/13, annex VI; The World Summit for Social Development and the International Covenant on Economic, Social and Cultural Rights: Statement of the Committee, 10th session, UN Doc. E/1995/22-E/C.12/1994/20 and Corr.1, annex V; Economic, social and cultural rights in the context of the World Summit for Social Development: Statement of the Committee, 11th session, UN Doc. E/1995/22-E/C.12/1994/20 and Corr.1, annex VI.

[92] Statement of the Committee to the Commission on Sustainable Development acting as the Preparatory Committee for the World Summit for Sustainable Development, Bali, Indonesia, 27 May to 7 June 2002, 28th session, UN Doc. E/2003/22-E/C.12/2002/13, annex VI, para. 4.

needs", "equal opportunity", "the eradication of poverty" [. . .] etc.', and 'it would appear that these open ended terms are used primarily because they do not recall any legal obligations for States' arising out of human rights treaties affirming obligations on ESC rights.[93]

These accounts are relevant to current negotiations, practice, and behaviour of states in the context of socio-economic development. Deriving elements relevant for the purpose of establishing practice is difficult in the absence of any link with the treaty on ESC rights or any ESC rights' legal standards under other treaties. In fact, the current Millennium Development Goals, which represent a blueprint for the international community's development cooperation efforts, lack references to human rights' commitments and put into doubt whether they have any implications for the content and effect of ESC rights norms, and in particular translating 'international assistance and cooperation' for the fulfilment of ESC rights in practice.[94] Recent developments, however, may forge a more optimistic view about future direction of the obligation to assist and cooperate. The example of this is the Food Assistance Convention adopted in 25 April 2012, which is perhaps the only legally binding treaty on food aid at the international level. [95]

To conclude this cursory review, evidentiary standards for establishing subsequent practice are not always straightforward. What is settled, however, is that subsequent practice should at least be 'consisting of non-isolated actions, committed consistently in application of the treaty, reflecting a position on interpretation, and engaged in or legitimately acquiesced by all of the parties'.[96] That being said, there is clearly a need for more reputable studies to be undertaken to see whether the emerging practice of individual states can meet the test of Article 31(3)(b) as often the failure of development cooperation to comply with human rights obligations is well documented, while positive achievements are rarely recorded or analysed. Self-assessments by the donors themselves could also contribute to such an undertaking, if only they were carried out from the perspective of human rights legal standards.

[93] Economic, social and cultural rights in the context of the World Summit for Social Development: Statement of the Committee, 11th session, UN Doc. E/1995/22-E/C.12/1994/20 and Corr.1, annex VI, paras. 2 and 3.

[94] The Office of the High Commissioner for Human Rights, however, closely relates the MDGs with human rights.

[95] Food Assistance Convention, adopted on 25 April 2012, in London, UK. The text of the treaty is available at <http://treaties.un.org/doc/source/signature/2012/CTC_XIX-48.pdf> (last accessed 21 November 2013). The Convention is expected to enter into force 1 January 2013 if by 30 November 2012 five signatories have deposited instruments of ratification, acceptance, or approval. As of today, there are 12 signatories with four countries having accepted the treaty.

[96] J. Arato, *supra* note 73, at 461.

6. Completing the Legal Picture with 'Any Relevant Rules of International Law'

Progressing from the assessment of the Covenant on Economic, Social and Cultural Rights' text, through its context to subsequent practice, Article 31 of VCLT suggests recourse to the relevant rules of international law.[97] The importance of the last element stipulated by paragraph 3 of the Article is clear as 'an international instrument has to be interpreted and applied within the framework of the entire legal system prevailing at the time of the interpretation'.[98] Consistent with this principle of *systemic integration*, inquiry into the concept of international assistance and cooperation can be usefully inspired by principles of cooperation and assistance in parallel treaty provisions and as understood in other areas of international law.[99]

In this context, international humanitarian law and the ongoing work of the International Law Commission on legal aspects of the protection of persons in the event of disasters can be deemed relevant, given that these fields of international law are also based on the notions of obligations of international cooperation, human dignity, and solidarity. Parallels found in these two bodies of law can provide 'a rich source of comparative understanding on generic issues' such as assistance and cooperation.[100]

A. International humanitarian law

International humanitarian law is directly relevant to the subject of our inquiry not only in terms of regulation of issues concerning assistance but also because its normative content overlaps with provisions of ESC rights, in particular those that govern basic needs essential to the survival of civilians.[101] These humanitarian law rules prescribe humanitarian assistance as an unconditional obligation to ensure protection of survival rights,[102] which 'shall, to the fullest extent of the means available', be provided.[103] The provisions of IHL leave open the question of who is to

[97] Art. 31(3)(c) of the VCLT stipulates that together with the context 'any relevant rules of international law applicable in the relations between the parties' shall be taken into account.

[98] ICJ, *Legal Consequences for States of the continued presence of South Africa in Namibia (South West Africa), notwithstanding Security Council Resolution 276 (1970)*, Advisory Opinion, ICJ Reports 16, 1971, para. 53.

[99] Gardiner, *supra* note 71, at 260.

[100] C. McLachlan, 'The Principle of Systemic Integration and art. 31(3)(c) of the Vienna Convention', 54 *International and Comparative Law Quarterly* (2005), 279–320, 286.

[101] The rules govern the scope of 'basic needs' including food and medical supplies, clothing, bedding, means of shelter, other supplies essential to the survival of the civilian population and objects necessary for religious worship. See e.g. art. 55, Geneva Convention IV, and art. 69 of the Additional Protocol I.

[102] Commentary to Geneva Convention IV, 1958, 320.

[103] It is argued that in the context of humanitarian assistance, 'it is rather the rights to emergency medical and health care and life-sustaining services that are at stake, as opposed to the more long-term aims of an adequate standard of living' comprising a group of so called 'survival rights' which can be related also to the minimum core of the ESC rights in M. Sandvik-Nylund, *Caught in*

provide relief to civilians; that is, national or international relief providers. In most cases the text of the provisions applicable to both international and domestic armed conflict stipulate that relief actions 'shall be undertaken' when a civilian population 'is not adequately provided'[104] with the supplies essential for its survival, subject to the consent of the party concerned in the relief action.[105] (in the case of international armed conflicts), or 'is suffering undue hardship' (in the context of internal armed conflicts).

The language employed (that is, 'shall be undertaken') seems to refer to both internal and external humanitarian assistance, when the preconditions set out above exist.[106] Humanitarian law explicitly conceives the duty to ensure that civilians have access to humanitarian assistance as resting with the party controlling the area. In this sense, both humanitarian law and human rights law coincide in designating the external assistance functioning as a subsidiary duty.

There is a widely supported proposition that obligations relating to humanitarian assistance should be read in conjunction with Article 1 of the Geneva Conventions that provides a system of collective responsibility,[107] requiring all states parties 'to respect and to ensure respect' for the Conventions and the Protocol I 'in all circumstances'. Article 1 reflects the principle that each state 'contracts obligations vis-à-vis itself and at the same time vis-à-vis the others'.[108] The ICJ in the *Nicaragua* case confirmed that the obligation to respect and ensure respect derived from general principles of international humanitarian law,[109] and in relation to humanitarian assistance it would imply the duty of all parties to

conflicts: civilian victims, humanitarian assistance and international law 2nd edn (Abo: Abo Academy University, Institute for Human Rights, 2003) VIII, 54.

[104] Art. 70, Additional Protocol I, and art. 18, Additional Protocol II to the 1949 Geneva Conventions.

[105] It is said that the rules found in the Geneva Conventions and Protocol I reflect to a greater degree the rules of customary international law. See Rule 55: 'The parties to the conflict must allow and facilitate rapid and unimpeded passage of humanitarian relief for civilians in need, which is impartial in character and conducted without any adverse distinction, subject to their right of control' in J.-M. Henkaerts and L. Doswald-Beck, *Customary Rules of International Humanitarian Law*, ICRC Study (vol. I and II) (New York: Cambridge University Press, 2005), 193–200.

[106] Sandvik-Nylund, *supra* note 103, at 31.

[107] L. Boisson de Chazournes and L. Condorelli, 'Common Article 1 of the Geneva Conventions revisited: Protecting Collective interests', 887 *The International Review of the Red Cross*, 67–87; L. Boisson de Chazournes and L. Condorelli, 'Quelles perspectives pour la responsabilité de protéger?' in A. Auer, A. Flückiger, and M. Hottelier (eds.), *Les droits de l'homme et la constitution: études en l'honneur du Professeur Giorgio Malinverni* (Genève: Schulthess, 2007). ICTY stated that these normes 'do not pose synallagmatic obligations, i.e. obligations of a State vis-à-vis another State. Rather [...] they lay down obligations towards the international community as a whole, with the consequence that each and every member of the international community has a "legal interest" in their observance and consequently a legal entitlement to demand respect for such obligations'. *Prosecutor v Zoran Kupreskic and others*, ICTY Trial Chamber, Judgment, The Hague, 14 January 2000, Case No. IT-95-16-T, para. 519.

[108] See J.S. Pictet, *The Geneva Conventions of 12 August 1949*, Commentary, Fourth Geneva Convention Relative to the Treatment of Civilian Persons in Time of War (Geneva: ICRC, 1958), 26.

[109] ICJ, *Military and Puramilitary Activities in and against Nicaragua (Nicaragua v United States of America)*, Judgment, ICJ Reports 1986, para. 220.

respect and ensure respect for guaranteeing supplies essential for the survival of civilians.[110]

IHL does not, however, specify what measures should be undertaken to implement the obligation to ensure respect,[111] in particular when it comes to providing assistance to civilians. In precise terms, what does it say in relation to duties of third states;[112] for example, states not party to the conflict? There is no settled view in the doctrine on this dynamic interpretation of the obligation to ensure respect, and the extent it imposes individual obligations on third states.[113] Ensuring respect requires positive actions and it was questioned 'what kind of positive actions resulting from this obligation, may be expected from individual States, apart from diplomatic demarches'.[114] In the same way, the ICRC study of customary IHL did not deal with the scope of obligations of third states.[115]

B. Legal aspects of the protection of persons in the event of disasters

The current work of the ILC on the draft articles on legal aspects of the protection of persons in the event of disasters, although still a work in progress, provides contemporary thinking on efforts to articulate norms on the role of assistance and cooperation and the scope of rights and duties of the affected state and other relevant actors in disaster situations.[116] It has been suggested that

[110] In the *Wall* opinion, ICJ held that 'Article 1 of the Fourth Geneva Convention, a provision common to the four Geneva Conventions, provides that 'The High Contracting Parties undertake to respect and to ensure respect for the present Convention in all circumstances'. It follows from that provision that every state party to that Convention, whether or not it is a party to a specific conflict, is under an obligation to ensure that the requirements of the instruments in question are complied with' in ICJ, *Legal Consequences of the Construction of a Wall in the Occupied Palestinian Territory*, Advisory Opinion, ICJ Reports, 199–200, para. 158. It is also argued that the notion of erga omnes is expressed in art. 1 of the Geneva Conventions and Additional Protocol I and since humanitarian assistance is based on the principles and rules concerning the basic rights of human persons as pronounced in the dictum of ICJ in the *Barcelona Traction*, obligations related to assistance are *erga omnes* obligations.

[111] References to possible measures include art. 7 and art. 89 Additional Protocol I, e.g. meetings of the High Contracting Parties and cooperation with the United Nations in situations of severe violations respectively. This can include means such as diplomacy, on-site missions, specific counter-measures, deployment of UN peace operations, including the role of judicial mechanisms such as the ICC in repression of crimes.

[112] Third states in this context is used to connote states not parties to the conflict.

[113] ICJ, *Legal Consequences of the Construction of a Wall in the Occupied Palestinian Territory*, Advisory Opinion, ICJ Reports, 199–200, Separate Opinion of Judge Higgins, para. 39.

[114] ICJ, *Legal Consequences of the Construction of a Wall in the Occupied Palestinian Territory*, Advisory Opinion, ICJ Reports, 199–200, Separate Opinion of Judge Kooijmans, para. 50.

[115] Dieter Fleck, notes that ICRC study 'takes a rather cautious approach, in relating this obligation of a State only to 'its armed forces and other persons or groups acting in fact on its instructions, or under its direction or control'. With this approach, methods and means of influencing the conduct of other States, groups or individuals remain unexplored. It would be worthwhile to go beyond the practice of parties to an armed conflict and explore the practice of third States and legal doctrine in this context'. See D. Fleck, 'International Accountability for Violations of the *Ius in Bello*: The Impact of the ICRC Study on Customary International Humanitarian Law', 11 *Journal of Conflict & Security Law* (2006) 179–199, 182. See also J.-M. Henckaerts and L. Doswald-Beck, *Customary International Humanitarian Law* (ICRC Vol. I, Rules) (New York: Cambridge University Press, 2006), Rule 144.

[116] See UNGA 46/182, Strengthening of the coordination of humanitarian emergency assistance of the United Nations, UN Doc. A/RES/46/182, 19 December 1991, where linkages are established among relief, rehabilitation, and development.

dealing with these aspects could help 'to elucidate the content of obligations *erga omnes*'.[117] While taking the rights of individuals as an overall approach in dealing with the issues of protection of persons,[118] the Commission adopted a dual-axis analysis, by which it decided to examine rights and obligations of states vis-à-vis each other first,[119] and only thereafter, the rights and obligations of states towards individuals. The latter, referred to as a 'rights-based' approach, was deemed troublesome. More specifically, the Commission needed to assess 'carefully whether in fact a rights-based approach would be the most propitious approach'. This is because individual rights would invoke fundamental questions about consequences that 'would flow from a rights-based approach, in particular whether such an approach would also require addressing questions on how such rights would be enforced'.[120]

Furthermore, the work of the Commission recognized the difficulties inherent in the topic, in particular as far as determining 'the rights and obligations of the assisting actor and those of the State affected by a disaster' are involved. Therefore, it decided not to invoke concepts such as the 'responsibility to protect' in the study, since it would have involved possible complex questions as to the extent of these obligations for third parties, their content, the circumstances to trigger those obligations, and whether they will be singular or collective.[121]

From a state-to-state perspective, a draft article on a 'duty to cooperate' was formulated providing that states 'shall cooperate among themselves' and when appropriate with the UN, etc. The draft article received a wide support in the Sixth Committee of the General Assembly, with states noting 'that cooperation was a central principle of international law'.[122] There was no dispute on the status of a 'duty to cooperate' for the respect and observance of human dignity. This well-established principle of international law should not, however, 'be interpreted as diminishing the prerogatives of a sovereign State within the limits of international law'[123] as '[c]ooperation complements the primary duty of States'. The principles of sovereignty and non-intervention[124]

[117] International Law Commission, Report on the work of its 60th session (5 May to 6 June and 7 July to 8 August 2008), GAOR 63rd Session Supp. No. 10, UN Doc. A/63/10, para. 231.

[118] China expressed doubts about viability of rights based approach, as it would imply 'that individuals were in a position to appeal for international disaster relief', UNGA, Sixth Committee, Summary record of the 20th meeting, UN Doc. A/C.6/64/SR.20, para. 21.

[119] See International Law Commission, Second report on the protection of persons in the event of disasters, by Mr. Eduardo Valencia-Ospina, Special Rapporteur, UN Doc. A/CN.4/615, paras. 20 and 21.

[120] International Law Commission, Report on the work of its 60th session (5 May to 6 June and 7 July to 8 August 2008), GAOR 63rd Session Supp. No. 10, UN Doc. A/63/10, para. 229.

[121] International Law Commission, Preliminary report on the protection of persons in the event of disasters, by Mr. Eduardo Valencia-Ospina, Special Rapporteur, UN Doc. A/CN.4/598, para. 55.

[122] International Law Commission, Third report on the protection of persons in the event of disasters, by Mr. Eduardo Valencia-Ospina, Special Rapporteur, UN Doc. A/CN.4/629, para. 12.

[123] It was however recalled that 'the principles of sovereignty and non-intervention were a point of departure and not a point of conclusion, and implied both rights and obligations'. See A/65/10, para. 307.

[124] International Law Commission, Second report on the protection of persons in the event of disasters, by Mr. Eduardo Valencia-Ospina, Special Rapporteur, UN Doc. A/CN.4/615, paras. 63 and 65. See also UNGA Resolution 46/182, Annexed Guiding Principles, Principle 3.

would interpret the scope of duty to cooperate.[125] Since the draft article on the duty to cooperate at this level of abstraction remained unclear,[126] an article clarifying the primary responsibility of the affected state was drafted.[127]

To balance the interest of international community in the protection of persons in the event of disasters with the sovereignty of the affected state, a special provision complementary to the provision on the primary responsibility of the concerned state has been formulated stipulating the right to 'offer' assistance.[128] Draft Article 5 establishing a duty to cooperate and Article 12 on the right to offer assistance operating together would put states and other actors under some pressure to offer assistance.[129] However, the role of the international community in offering assistance should not be considered in terms of 'assertion of rights' but rather be based on the principles of cooperation and solidarity. Further, the precise relationship between the duty to cooperate and the principles of sovereignty and non-intervention, as well as possible derogations therefrom, remains to be defined.[130]

In view of the very delicate nature of the questions at stake, the Commission decided to raise the issue of interrelationship between the legal duties established under Articles 5 (duty to cooperate) and 10 (duty of the affected state to seek assistance).[131] The Commission put a blunt question to states:

> The Commission has taken the view that States have a duty to cooperate with the affected State in disaster relief matters. Does this duty to cooperate include a duty on States to provide assistance when requested by the affected State?[132]

States did not provide written replies but expressed their views in negative terms in response to the question. There was no such basis under existing international law, customary law, or practice.[133] One view was that the duty to cooperate in effect

[125] This would include elements such as imposition of obligation on the part of disaster-affected states to accept relief or on the part of states providing relief to satisfy requests for assistance, since that depended on their capacity.

[126] Austria, UNGA, Sixth Committee, Summary record of the 20th meeting, UN Doc. A/C.6/64/SR.20, para. 17; See International Law Commission, 3rd report on the protection of persons in the event of disasters, by Eduardo Valencia-Ospina, Special Rapporteur, UN Doc. A/CN.4/629, para. 12.

[127] Draft art. 8 on Primary Responsibility of Affected State reads as follows:

1. The affected State has the primary responsibility for the protection of persons and provision of humanitarian assistance on its territory. The State retains the right, under its national law, to direct, control, coordinate and supervise such assistance within its territory.
2. External assistance may be provided only with the consent of the affected State.

[128] Draft art. 12 of the Draft Rules on the Protection of Persons in the Event of Disasters.

[129] International Law Commission, 5th Report on the Protection of Persons in the Event of Disasters, by Special Rapporteur E. Valencia-Ospina, UN Doc. A/CN.4/652, 9 April 2012, para. 44.

[130] International Law Commission, Fifth Report on the Protection of Persons in the Event of Disasters, by Special Rapporteur E. Valencia-Ospina, UN Doc. A/CN.4/652, 9 April 2012, para. 37.

[131] International Law Commission, Fifth Report on the Protection of Persons in the Event of Disasters, by Special Rapporteur E. Valencia-Ospina, UN Doc. A/CN.4/652, 9 April 2012, paras. 55 and 56.

[132] International Law Commission, Report on the work of its 63rd session (26 April to 3 June and 4 July to 12 August 2011), GAOR 66th Session, Supp. No. 10, UN Doc. A/66/10 and Add.1.

[133] Mexico (A/C.6/66/SR.18, para. 55, and A/C.6/66/SR.22, para. 21), Slovenia (A/C.6/66/SR.20, para. 12), Singapore (A/C.6/66/SR.21, para. 76), Italy (A/C.6/66/SR.21, para. 91), Colombia (A/C.6/66/SR.22, para. 28), Austria (A/C.6/66/SR.23, para. 23), Germany (A/C.6/66/SR.23,

expressed the duty to 'consider' requests for assistance.[134] Another view in contrast felt 'sympathetic' to the idea of duty to provide assistance, however, it suggested formulating the duty to provide assistance rather as 'a strong recommendation or as an example, using wording that took into account the capacities of the States to which requests were made'.[135] All these discussions demonstrate the adagio of the subsidiarity principle of international efforts to protect persons and the primary role of the affected state.[136]

C. Is there a right to humanitarian assistance?

To the initial question as to whether international assistance and cooperation under the ICESCR automatically translates into the right of individuals to receive assistance, discussions within humanitarian law and rules on disaster response provide proof that such a right is very controversial.[137] Humanitarian law lays down a strong legal construct guaranteeing assistance to civilians, but does not automatically confer rights upon private individuals or private actors to receive assistance, nor does it provide the recipient state with any corresponding rights to receive such assistance from other High Contracting Parties. In the context of disaster relief, the ILC confirmed no specific instrument supporting the existence of such a right and that it could only be implicit in international human rights law.[138]

The resolution adopted by the Institut de Droit International states that 'leaving the victims of disaster without humanitarian assistance constitutes a threat to human life and an offence to human dignity and therefore a violation of fundamental human rights. The victims of disaster are entitled to request and receive humanitarian assistance'.[139] It is true that the nature of such a right is unclear and would raise a number of questions: '[w]ould it be a human right or just a

para. 28), United Kingdom (A/C.6/66/SR.23, para. 45), Netherlands (A/C.6/66/SR.23, para. 48), Spain (A/C.6/66/SR.23, para. 50), Hungary (A/C.6/66/SR.24, para. 59), Malaysia (A/C.6/66/SR.24, para. 120), Republic of Korea (A/C.6/66/SR.24, paras. 120 and 121), Ireland (A/C.6/66/SR.25, para. 21).

134 Mexico (A/C.6/66/SR.18, para. 55).

135 Hungary (A/C.6/66/SR.24, para. 59).

136 International Law Commission, Report on the work of its 60th session (5 May to 6 June and 7 July to 8 August 2008), GAOR 63rd Session Supp. No. 10, UN Doc. A/63/10, para. 228.

137 International Law Commission, Report on the work of its 60th session (5 May to 6 June and 7 July to 8 August 2008), GAOR 63rd Session Supp. No. 10, UN Doc. A/63/10, paras. 241–246.

138 For Nigel Rodley it is clear that 'there is no right to humanitarian assistance or that, even if there ought to be one and if there were in fact one, it would not be a human right', further arguing that 'human rights have already been flouted when a person is in this situation. And it hardly seems useful…to suggest that another human right has been violated, namely, the right to receive assistance' in '*Le droit à l'assistance humanitaire: actes du Colloque international organisé par l'Unesco*', UNESCO, SHS-95/CONF.805/3, 146. See also ILC, Protection of persons in the event of disasters: Memorandum by the Secretariat, UN Doc. A/CN.4/590, para. 244. Compare also with the Preamble of the European Union's Council Regulation No. 1257/96 concerning humanitarian aid, which stated: 'people in distress, victims of natural disasters, wars and outbreaks of fighting, or other comparable exceptional circumstances have a right to international humanitarian assistance where their own authorities prove unable to provide effective relief' in Council Regulation (EC) No. 1257/96 of 20 June 1996, concerning Humanitarian Aid.

139 Institut de Droit International Resolution of 2003 on Humanitarian Assistance, Bruge Session, Sect. II, paras. 1 and 2.

right of those affected by a disaster [*or armed conflict or even poverty*], or [w]ould it be an individual right or a collective right? Against whom, if at all, would it be enforceable?'[140] Importantly, all these questions preoccupying the legal minds recall uncertainties surrounding the ICESCR provision on the same subject. For the time being, the ILC has suggested:

> instead of considering the right to humanitarian assistance as 'a right to impose assistance', it was more appropriate to envisage it as a 'right to provide assistance'; such an approach would be in line with the reasoning of the International Court of Justice in the *Nicaragua* case. The point was also made that if an affected State cannot discharge its obligation to provide timely relief to its people in distress it must have an obligation to seek outside assistance.[141]

D. Drawing a common basis for 'international assistance and cooperation' in international law

International humanitarian law, rules on protection of persons in the event of disasters, and the ICESCR identify a common general norm—the obligation to assist and cooperate and its different levels and cases of application, that is, in armed conflict, disasters, and in the area of development. Importantly, the scope of all these rules essentially converges with the core content of socio-economic rights, although the ICESCR sets a higher standard of achievement for international cooperation of states, namely the 'full realization of ESC rights'. None of the rules examined provides unconditional support for a conclusion that there is a duty incumbent upon the international community to offer for the protection of persons whether in the context of armed conflict or disaster events.[142] Explicit positive obligations to provide assistance would have to be in the form of separate agreements. Examples of such a practice include the aforementioned Food Assistance Convention (2012), whereby donor states pledge to provide specified minimum amounts of food aid to those developing nations with the greatest needs. Hence, there is a consensus that there is a duty for a state to protect and take care of persons in its territory and where needed to *seek assistance*.[143] Such a right to seek assistance is affirmed especially if directed towards the international community.

[140] International Law Commission, Preliminary report of the Special Rapporteur, Mr. Eduardo Valencia-Ospina, UN Doc. A/CN.4/598, para. 54.

[141] International Law Commission, Report on the work of its 60th session (5 May to 6 June and 7 July to 8 August 2008), GAOR 63rd Session Supp. No. 10, UN Doc. A/63/10, para. 243.

[142] In the framework of disaster response, Memorandum of Secretariat concluded that 'while most agreements and instruments deal explicitly with requests, few provide guidance on offers' in Protection of Persons in the Event of Disasters, Memorandum prepared by the Secretariat, Doc. A/CN.4/590, 11 December 2007, para. 60.

[143] Institut de Droit International, Resolution of 2003 on Humanitarian Assistance, Bruge Session, Sect. II, paras., Section III (3). At the same time, states at the 64th session of the International Law Commission (7 May to 1 June and 2 July to 3 August 2012) commenting on the Draft Article of the obligation to seek assistance in the event of disasters, stated that such a duty will be contrary to sovereignty and it had no legal basis in current international law. It was hence proposed to change 'duty to

The CESCR takes the same position with regard to the primary obligation of the state,[144] although this is somewhat different from the accepted view in humanitarian law and the disaster relief framework. The Committee is of the opinion that '[s]tates have a joint and individual responsibility, to cooperate in providing disaster relief and humanitarian assistance in times of emergency'.[145] In contrast to the language of duties, states have a *right to offer* assistance which is predicated upon the inability or unwillingness of the primary duty bearer.[146] As a corollary to the right to offer assistance is the duty of the state not to reject the offer arbitrarily. The latter element is clearly elucidated both in IHL and in the current project of draft articles. In relation to disaster response it has been said that a 'more definitive obligation' to provide assistance has been ascribed to international organizations, which is mainly due to their mandate to provide assistance and cooperation.[147] It is suggested that the same approach can and should be adopted in the context of ESC rights in relation to organizations in the UN system entrusted with a mandate that covers a wide spectrum of socio-economic rights.

Further, IHL and international disaster-response rules provide certain ideas that might usefully inspire understanding of cooperation and assistance in ESC rights. These include the principles of humanity, neutrality, impartiality, and independence that guide humanitarian and disaster-response assistance, with the aim of ensuring that persons in need receive the right aid, at the right time, and delivered in the right way. While these principles are strongly embedded in these areas of laws, they did not yet find their definite expression in the field of development cooperation.[148]

To sum up, there is a great degree of convergence between three sets of rules in terms of their logic, in particular the subsidiary nature of obligations incumbent upon third states. All have common elements, thus the difference is the question of emphasis rather than the content of the norms. The rights that these rules generate for the 'affected' state or state in need of assistance are imperfect.

seek assistance' with a hortatory wording 'should' seek assistance. See UN Doc. A/CN.4/652, para. 28 and UN Doc. A/C.6/66/SR.23 and A/C.6/66/SR.24 for the separate opinions of the opposing states.

[144] CESCR, General Comment No. 3: 'The Committee wishes to emphasize, however, that even where the available resources are demonstrably inadequate, the obligation remains for a State party to strive to ensure the widest possible enjoyment of the relevant rights under the prevailing circumstances'.

[145] CESCR, General Comment No. 12, The Right to Adequate Food, UN Doc. E/CN.12/1999/5, 12 May 1999 and General Comment No. 14, The Right to the Highest Attainable Standard of Health, UN Doc. E/C.12/2000/4, 11 August 2000, specifically refer to the general framework of 'obligation to cooperate' and make it explicit that States should cooperate in providing disaster relief and humanitarian assistance for the rights in question.

[146] Institut de Droit International, Resolution of 2003 on Humanitarian Assistance, Bruge Session, Section IV (1).

[147] Institut de Droit International, Resolution of 2003 on Humanitarian Assistance, Bruge Session, Section V (2).

[148] The reader may recall the description in section C. 'Is there a right to humanitarian assistance?' on the attempts within the UN to push forward the principles of non-selectivity, impartiality, and objectivity, and the political context in which these issues were involved.

The difference between the rules on humanitarian assistance in IHL and disaster relief, and the rules of international assistance and cooperation in the ESC rights context, thus appear narrower than the prima facie impression one might gain. Therefore, there is no tangible reason why the nature of the obligation of assistance and cooperation as envisaged by the ICESCR would be any different. The Covenant can be said to envisage a similar form of 'collective responsibility' for states parties in attaining the fulfilment of rights enshrined in it. Notably, all these areas share identical constraints—neither is sufficiently precise to address the question of regarding the moment the subsidiary obligations (for example, the obligations of third states) are activated and what the extent of these positive obligations incumbent upon third states is. Irrespective of this, these constraints derive from the fact that they require a great degree of cohesion within the international community and as a minimum institutionalized identification of positive obligations and their enforcement.

7. Conclusion

The obligation to cooperate for human rights can be traced from the UN Charter through declarations to specific human rights treaties such as the ICESCR, whereby international cooperation for ensuring human rights constitutes an essential component of the obligations of states. There is an acceptance at the general level of the existence of such an obligation. The CESCR has progressively identified some units of obligation to assist and cooperate that seem to transform the normative content of Article 2(1) that originally was interpreted as mainly referring to *cooperation for development*. In line with the genuine direction of the Covenant, the Committee is moving towards defining the obligations in specific terms. It has interpreted the requirement of cooperation in light of the UN Charter and with reference to the notion of 'applicable international law' structuring them together as international obligations flowing from the Covenant.

However, not all elements of the obligation to cooperate enjoy the same degree of recognition. The drafting history, negotiations, and current debates of the present day all underline the resistance to any implication of a legally binding duty in terms of transfer of resources—the resources that can be essential for ensuring food, water, access to essential healthcare, education, and a decent and secure place to live for the prevalent majority of the world.

By phrasing the *problématique* broader, we find that international law in general as yet does not provide answers to some of the important questions raised in the context of international cooperation and assistance. Even in cases of severe distress, be it armed conflict, disaster situations, or extreme poverty, if there is a right to assert or to receive assistance (for states, on behalf of individuals) it has to be directed towards the international community, and not towards any individual state.

7

Corporations and Economic, Social, and Cultural Rights

Olivier De Schutter

1. Introduction

The view that corporations have duties towards society, and not simply towards their shareholders, emerged in the 1930s from the findings of a handful of corporate lawyers and economists linked to the Progressive movement in the United States. In *The Modern Corporation and Private Property*, which they published in 1932, Adolf A. Berle and Gardiner C. Means famously argued that there existed a huge gap between the world of business as described in classic treatises on economics, and the reality they documented.[1] They noted that American business was dominated by a handful of firms: half of the total US corporate assets were in the hands of 200 top companies, out of several million companies in total. Borrowing from Veblen's famous thesis presented in his 1923 book *Absentee Ownership and Business Enterprise*,[2] they also remarked that in these giant enterprises, control had passed from the owners, the shareholders, to their agents, the senior managers of the companies, although the latter may have different objectives and priorities than their principals. Berle and others, particularly E. Merrick Dodd, immediately drew the following conclusions: since power was exercised in fact not for the exclusive interest of the property owners of companies, who were often not in a position to effectively control the decisions made by corporate executives in their name, the acts of the corporation should be better controlled, and its social service functions—its contributions to the public good—should be openly acknowledged as coexisting with its profit-making function.[3]

[1] A.A. Berle and G.C. Means, *The Modern Corporation and Private Property* (originally published in 1932 by Harcourt, Brace & World; reprinted: New York: Transaction Publishers, 1991), esp. ch. VI.

[2] T. Veblen, *Absentee Ownership and Business Enterprise in Recent Times: the case of America* (New York: Transaction Publishers, 1923).

[3] See A.A. Berle, 'Corporate Powers as Powers in Trust', 44 *Harvard Law Review* (1931), 1049–1074 (arguing that the management of the corporation should be controlled in order to ensure that they act for the benefit of the shareholders, rather than in their own interest); and E. Merrick Dodd, 'For Whom are Corporate Managers Trustees?', 45 *Harvard Law Review* (1932), 1145–1163 (arguing

The views of these scholars exerted a powerful influence on the F.D. Roosevelt administration's approach to business during the New Deal. But their message was broader, and it is one still worth listening to today. Berle and Means were describing a new world, strikingly different from the world described by Marshallian economics. They were making two claims about the modern corporation. First, they argued that large corporations were concentrating such power that the antitrust legislation—the pressure from competition—would be unable, in and by itself, to control them effectively: their power was compared to that of the medieval church, or even to the political power in the nation state. Second, they noted that the decisions of the corporation, made by largely unaccountable executives (unaccountable even to the owners of stock), had impacts on a wide range of interests, both within and outside the corporation itself. Those were descriptive claims, but the normative implications were evident: they were that, since corporations had gained such an ability to affect the communities in which they operated, responsibilities commensurate with this ability should be imposed on them; as their impacts reached the whole of society, so too could they be asked to contribute to the realization of society-wide goals.

Yet today there is still resistance to the idea that economic and social rights may be invoked against corporate actors and that companies have duties towards these rights. This chapter seeks to identify the origins of such resistance, and to provide answers to the sceptics. It builds on the considerable progress that was achieved in recent years in clarifying the human rights responsibilities of companies. In June 2011, the Human Rights Council endorsed a set of Guiding Principles on Business and Human Rights that are now seen as the most authoritative statement of the human rights responsibilities of corporations and corresponding state duties adopted at the UN level.[4] These Guiding Principles go beyond the plethora of voluntary initiatives, often sector-specific, that existed hitherto. They have been widely endorsed, by business organizations and in intergovernmental settings—including, notably, by the Organisation for Economic Cooperation and Development (OECD) when it revised its Guidelines on Multinational Enterprises in 2011.[5] They have also been invoked, albeit at times grudgingly, by civil society. And they are now subject to a follow-up mechanism within the United Nations system, through the Working Group on business and human rights and an annual forum to be held on this issue.[6] But the questions that are listed below remain, some of them taboo, many of them unanswered—or, if answered at all—still controversial.

that the corporation is now seen as having, aside from its profit-making function, a social service function).

[4] Human Rights Council Res. 17/4 (16 June 2011). See also M. Dowell-Jones, 'The Sovereign Bond Markets and Socio-Economic Rights: Understanding the Challenge of Austerity', ch. 2 in this book.

[5] The new version of the OECD Guidelines on Multinational Enterprises include a chapter IV on human rights, that is based on the 'Protect, Respect and Remedy' framework.

[6] The Working Group on the issue of human rights and transnational corporations and other business enterprises was established by Resolution 17/4 of the Human Rights Council, at the same time that the Council endorsed the proposed Guiding Principles on Business and Human Rights.

Four questions are examined. This chapter first explores whether international human rights law applies to corporations. It then asks whether imposing positive duties on corporations poses specific problems, and how these can be addressed. It moves, next, to how such positive duties can be identified and defined. Finally, it discusses the role of courts in enforcing such duties.

2. Does International Human Rights Law Apply to Corporate Actors?

A first source of confusion concerns the status of international human rights vis-à-vis corporations. The hesitations expressed by the federal courts of the United States are illustrative in this regard. Since it was revived in 1980, the Alien Tort Statute (ATS) allows federal courts in the United States to have jurisdiction over tort actions filed by non-US citizens for violations of international law.[7] In *Kiobel*,[8] residents of Nigeria claimed that Dutch, British, and Nigerian corporations that were engaged in oil exploration and production aided and abetted the Nigerian government in committing serious violations of human rights law. The United States Court of Appeal for the Second Circuit was asked whether the ATS could be invoked to seek damages from corporations.[9] Relying on the notion that 'to attain the status of a rule of customary international law, a norm must be "specific, universal, and obligatory"', as stated by the United States Supreme Court in the only case where it interpreted the ATS,[10] the Second Circuit Court took the view that 'there is no historical evidence of an existing or even nascent norm of customary international law imposing liability on corporations for violations of human rights'. The Court explained that, while individuals could in some cases be held responsible for violations of international law,

> the principle of individual liability for violations of international law has been limited to natural persons—not 'juridical' persons such as corporations—because the moral

[7] The ATS provides that: 'The district courts shall have original jurisdiction of any civil action by an alien for a tort only, committed in violation of the law of nations or a treaty of the United States' (28 USC § 1350). Passed by the first Congress in 1789 as part of the First Judiciary Act, the ATS remained largely dormant until, in 1980, it was revived in a decision adopted by the Court of Appeal for the Second Circuit relied on this provision to assert that federal courts had jurisdiction over (1) tort actions, (2) brought by aliens (only), and (3) for violations of the law of nations (*Filartiga v Pena-Irala*, 630 F.2d 876, 890 (2d Cir. 1980)).

[8] *Esther Kiobel*, et al. *v Royal Dutch Petroleum Co.*, et al., 621 F.3d 111 (2d Cir. 2010), *reh'g en banc denied*, No. 06-4800-cv, 2011 WL 338048 (2d Cir., 4 Feb. 2011).

[9] Since its revival in 1980, the ATS was used in a number of cases against corporate defendants, but these cases were either still pending when Kiobel came to be decided by the Court of Appeal or had been settled. See, inter alia, *Doe v Unocal Corp.*, 963 F. Supp. 880 (C.D. Cal. 1997), aff'd in part and rev'd in part, 395 F.3d 932 (9th Cir. 2002); *Wiwa v Royal Dutch Petroleum Co.*, 226 F.3d 88 (2d Cir. 2000); *Bigio v Coca-Cola Co.*, 239 F.3d 440 (2d Cir. 2000); Flores, 414 F.3d 233; *Khulumani v Barclay Nat'l Bank Ltd.*, 504 F.3d 254 (2d Cir. 2007); *Viet. Assoc. for Victims of Agent Orange v Dow Chem. Co.*, 517 F.3d 104 (2d Cir. 2008); *Abdullahi v Pfizer, Inc.*, 562 F.3d 163 (2d Cir. 2009); *Presbyterian Church of Sudan v Talisman Energy, Inc.*, 582 F.3d 244 (2d Cir. 2009).

[10] *Sosa v Alvarez-Machain*, 542 US 692, 732 (2004).

responsibility for a crime so heinous and unbounded as to rise to the level of an 'international crime' has rested solely with the individual men and women who have perpetrated it.

Quite apart from the outcome of that case and from the future use of ATS in human rights litigation,[11] the approach of the Court of Appeal betrays a misconception that is as common as it is easily identifiable. International law is addressed primarily to states and other subjects of international law. In addition, in some cases international law has developed mechanisms to hold individuals directly accountable for violation of certain rules, particularly those defining international crimes. No such mechanism exists, either at universal or at regional level, to hold corporations accountable for violation of rules set out in international law.[12] However, that is *not* to say that rules of international law cannot be applied directly to corporations if, consistent with their obligation to protect human rights,[13] this is how states choose to discharge their duties under international law to control the behaviour of private persons under their jurisdiction. Indeed, it is common for states to opt for the direct applicability of international human rights law before their domestic courts, as a means of complying with their international obligations. This leads domestic courts to impose on private actors obligations that have their source in international law, although the enforcement mechanisms are defined in national law: in *Kiobel*, the error of the Court of Appeal was that it failed to make this elementary distinction between the primary rules (regulating conduct) and the secondary rules (allocating responsibilities for the enforcement of primary rules). Where international law rules pertaining to human rights are implemented, primary and secondary rules are combined with one another in order to ensure that conduct complies

[11] The US Supreme Court took the view in June 2013 that there is nothing in the ATS that allows to rebut the presumption against the extraterritoriality of US law, and that therefore, being residents of Nigeria seeking reparation for damages inflicted outside the US territory, the claims should be dismissed: *Kiobel*, et al. *v Royal Dutch Petroleum Co.*, et al., 569 US __ (2013). The Supreme Court did not pronounce itself on the question of the applicability of international norms to private actors.

[12] In this contribution, the expressions 'corporations', 'companies', or 'corporate actors' are used interchangeably and in a generic sense, to refer to the economic reality of entities that are set up for profit-seeking motives, generally by owners whose liability is limited to the assets that they invest in the company. A distinction shall be made, however, between those economic entities and the separate legal entities of which they are composed, linked within the corporate group by an investment nexus. I return to that distinction later.

[13] The Committee on Economic, Social and Cultural Rights has repeatedly stated that their obligation to comply with internationally recognized human rights imposes on states three levels of duties: to respect, protect, and fulfil human rights. The duty to protect imposes on the state to control private actors to ensure that they do not violate the rights of individuals, that the state is prohibited from violation directly, by the activities of its own organs: see, e.g. Committee on Economic, Social and Cultural Rights, Report on the 20th and 21st sessions (1999), UN Doc. E/2000/22, E/C.12/1999/11, para. 53 and annex IX; Committee on Economic, Social and Cultural Rights, General Comment No. 12 (1999): The Right to Adequate Food (Art. 11), UN Doc. E/C.12/1999/5, paras. 14–20; Committee on Economic, Social and Cultural Rights, General Comment No. 13 (1999): The Right to Education (Art. 13), UN Doc. E/C.12/1999/10, paras. 46–48; Office of the High Commissioner for Human Rights, Principles and Guidelines for a Human Rights Approach to Poverty Reduction Strategies (2005), paras. 47–48; African Commission on Human and Peoples' Rights, *The Social and Economic Rights Action Centre and the Centre for Economic and Social Rights v Nigeria*, Communication No. 155/96 (2001) AHRLR 60 (15th Annual Activity Report), paras. 44–48.

with their requirements: while international law does not contain mechanisms to enforce its prescriptions vis-à-vis corporations, it relies on enforcement mechanisms established at the domestic level to ensure that corporations shall not violate these prescriptions.

States obviously have a duty to protect economic and social rights, by the adoption of measures that regulate private actors, including corporations, in order to ensure that these actors shall not adopt conduct that violates these rights. This is an obligation of means, rather than of result. It consists in an obligation to take all measures that can reasonably be adopted to ensure that human rights shall not be violated as a result of the conduct of private actors.[14] There is a wealth of cases where the duty of the state to protect human rights extended to economic and social rights, requiring from the state to adequately regulate the conduct of non-state actors.[15] Indeed, among the most famous examples is the finding of the African Commission on Human and Peoples' Rights, based on the same pattern of facts as that presented in *Kiobel*, that Nigeria had failed to protect the rights of the Ogoni people in the Niger delta. These rights were violated by the activities of oil companies exploiting the oilfields of the region: the Commission concluded that

> despite its obligation to protect persons against interferences in the enjoyment of their rights, the Government of Nigeria facilitated the destruction of the Ogoniland. Contrary to its [obligations under the African Charter on Human and Peoples' Rights] and despite such internationally established principles, the Nigerian Government has given the green light to private actors, and the oil Companies in particular, to devastatingly affect the well-being of the Ogonis.[16]

Among the rights affected were the right to housing and the right to food.[17]

If that were the only channel through which obligations can be imposed on corporations in the area of economic and social rights, we would be bound to conclude that corporations are not concerned by international human rights law, which is only relevant to them *indirectly*, when states have adopted measures by

[14] See, for a detailed discussion of the content of this obligation to protect, O. De Schutter, *International Human Rights Law* (New York: Cambridge University Press, 2010), ch. 4. Ssenyonjo writes: 'The obligation to protect [...] generally entails the creation and maintenance of an atmosphere or framework by an effective interplay of laws, regulations and other measures so that individuals and groups will be able freely to realise their rights and freedoms. This demands that the state has to protect against harmful activities carried out by [non-state actors] and to prevent violations by [non-state actors] through creating and implementing the necessary policy, legislative, regulatory, judicial, inspection and enforcement frameworks' (M. Ssenyonjo, 'The Applicability of International Human Rights Law to Non-State Actors: What Relevance to Economic, Social and Cultural Rights?', 12 *The International Journal of Human Rights* (2008), 725–760, at 729).

[15] See Ssenyonjo, *supra* note 14; and A. Nolan, 'Addressing Economic and Social Rights Violations by Non-State Actors through the Role of the State: A Comparison of Regional Approaches to the 'Obligation to Protect', 9 *Human Rights Law Review* (2009), 225–255.

[16] Communication 155/96, *The Social and Economic Rights Action Center and the Center for Economic and Social Rights v Nigeria*, Annex to the 15th Annual Activity Report of the African Commission on Human and Peoples' Rights, 8 July 2002, AHG/Dec.171 (XXXVIII), at para. 58; 10 IHRR 282 (2003).

[17] See Communication 155/96, *The Social and Economic Rights Action Center and the Center for Economic and Social Rights v Nigeria*, Annex to the 15th Annual Activity Report of the African Commission on Human and Peoples' Rights, 8 July 2002, AHG/Dec.171 (XXXVIII), paras. 63–66.

which they discharge their obligation to protect, by clarifying the obligations of corporations in areas such as environmental or labour law, land planning, or food safety. However, states may also wish to discharge their obligations towards economic and social rights by imposing on corporations to comply with these rights *directly*, that is, even in the absence of domestic legislation ensuring the implementation of international human rights norms into the national legal order. While such direct application of human rights norms is encouraged by the Committee on Economic, Social and Cultural Rights,[18] the question arises whether economic and social rights as stipulated in international human rights law can fittingly be applied to corporations: are rules set out for states in international human rights law too vague and indeterminate, or simply unsuitable for application to corporate actors, or is such a transposition possible?

3. May Positive Duties be Imposed upon Corporations with regard to Economic and Social Rights?

There is no shortage of authoritative statements according to which corporations may have responsibilities towards the fulfilment of economic and social rights. The Committee on Economic, Social and Cultural Rights, for instance, has noted:

> While only States are parties to the Covenant and thus ultimately accountable for compliance with it, all members of society—individuals, including health professionals, families, local communities, intergovernmental and non-governmental organizations, civil society organizations, as well as the private business sector—have responsibilities regarding the realization of the right to health. State parties should therefore provide an environment which facilitates the discharge of these responsibilities.[19]

The key difficulty in addressing the human rights obligations of corporations, however, is that there are important differences between these actors and states. States have a territory over which they exercise sovereignty. They also may exercise

[18] See, e.g. Committee on Economic, Social and Cultural Rights, General Comment No. 15: The right to water (arts. 11 and 12 of the Covenant), UN Doc. E/C.12/2002/11 (2002), para. 57 ('The incorporation in the domestic legal order of international instruments recognizing the right to water can significantly enhance the scope and effectiveness of remedial measures and should be encouraged in all cases. Incorporation enables courts to adjudicate violations of the right to water, or at least the core obligations, by direct reference to the Covenant'); for an identical statement, Committee on Economic, Social and Cultural Rights, General Comment No. 14: The right to the highest attainable standard of health, UN Doc. E/C.12/2000/4 (11 August 2000), para. 60. The use of the term 'incorporation' to refer to the status of the Covenant in the domestic legal order is ambiguous: in its General Comment No. 9: The domestic application of the Covenant (UN Doc. E/C.12/1998/24, 3 December 1998), the term is used in para. 6 to designate either the process of copying the provisions of the Covenant into domestic law, while leaving the wording intact, so as to allow the Covenant's rules to be invoked before national authorities, or the direct application of the Covenant, which the Committee recommends (see para. 4: 'In general, legally binding international human rights standards should operate directly and immediately within the domestic legal system of each State party, thereby enabling individuals to seek enforcement of their rights before national courts and tribunals').

[19] Committee on Economic, Social and Cultural Rights, General Comment No. 14: The right to the highest attainable standard of health, UN Doc. E/C.12/2000/4 (11 August 2000), para. 42.

jurisdiction over persons and assets, either because those persons or assets are present on their territory, or because of some other jurisdictional link. States also have a power to tax and spend, and thus to provide public services to their population. In all these respects, states do occupy a specific position. And since human rights law has been designed and developed with states in mind, transposing the doctrines that have shaped this body of law to the acts of corporations may present delicate problems of transposition.[20]

As long as corporations have imposed on them only 'negative' duties—to abstain from adopting measures that would result in violations of human rights—such a transposition is not particularly problematic: indeed, it has been common for domestic legal systems to impose such prohibitions on corporate actors, in particular by allowing victims to file civil claims against the corporation where its 'fault' or 'negligence' has caused an injury, the 'fault' or 'negligence' consisting in a failure to respect human rights. Such 'indirect' application is an alternative to the 'direct' application of internationally recognized human rights to inter-individual relationships: it consists in courts interpreting notions of domestic law (such as the notions of 'fault' or 'negligence' in civil liability cases, 'good faith' in contracts, 'abuse of rights', or 'public policy') in order to ensure that these notions embody the requirements of international human rights.[21]

This is the classic obligation to 'respect' human rights, and it may apply to economic and social rights just as it may apply to civil and political rights:[22] corporations, for instance, may be found liable for violating the right to housing or the right to food by encroaching on people's land,[23] or for violating their right to water

[20] For attempts along these lines, see S.R. Ratner, 'Corporations and Human Rights: A Theory of Legal Responsibility', 111 *Yale Law Journal* (2001), 443–545; J.J. Paust, 'Human Rights Responsibilities of Private Corporations', 3 *Vanderbilt Journal of Transnational Law* (2002), 801–825; O. De Schutter, 'Human Rights in Employment Relationships: Contracts as Power', 1 *European Journal of Human Rights/Journal européen des droits de l'Homme* (2013), 21–56.

[21] This is a technique sometimes referred to as '*mittelbare Drittwirkung*', in reference to the practice inaugurated with the 1958 *Lüth* decision of the German Federal Constitutional Court (7 BverfGE (1958)): see, e.g. A. Barak, 'Constitutional human rights and private law', in D. Friedmann and D. Barak-Erez (eds.), *Human rights in private law*, Oxford-Portland-Oregon, Hart Publishing, 2001, p. 13, at 21–24; S. Gardbaum, 'The 'horizontal effect' of constitutional rights', *Michigan Law Review*, vol. 102 (2003), 401 and ff. For a well-known example, see the position of the South African Constitutional Court in *Du Plessis v De Klerk*, decided under the South African interim Constitution of 1993 ([1996](3) SA 850 (CC)).

[22] As was noted by J. Ruggie, in his official capacity as the UN Secretary-General's Special Representative on the issue of transnational corporations and other business enterprises and human rights, 'there are few if any internationally recognized rights business cannot impact—or be perceived to impact—in some manner' (Protect, Respect and Remedy: A Framework for Business and Human Rights, Report of the Special Representative of the Secretary-General on the issue of transnational corporations and other business enterprises and human rights, UN Doc. A/HRC/8/5 (7 April 2008) (hereafter 'Protect, Respect and Remedy'), para. 51).

[23] See, for instance, the phenomenon referred to in Brazil as 'grilagem', i.e. the fraudulent appropriation of untitled lands by private persons: according to official estimates, this concerned some 100 million hectares in total in 2009, or roughly 12 per cent of the national territory, and it is particularly rampant in the Amazon region, 45 per cent of the surface of which has not been officially titled, and where low population density invites informal occupation (see for details Report of the Special Rapporteur on the right to food, Olivier De Schutter: Mission to Brazil (12–18 October 2009), UN Doc. A/HRC/13/33/Add.6 (March 2010), para. 31).

by extracting water from ground reserves in ways that are considered unsustainable or by polluting groundwater reserves.[24] In 2013, the High Court of Uganda at Kampala ordered that compensation be paid to 2,041 individuals who had been evicted from their land in August 2001, when the government of Uganda gave the land to a German company to establish what is now the Kaweri-Coffee-Plantation. The Court stated that the investors

> had a duty to ensure that our indigenous people were not exploited. They should have respected the human rights and values of people and as honorable businessman [*sic*] and investors they should have not moved into the lands unless they had satisfied themselves that the tenants were properly compensated, relocated and adequate notice was given to them.[25]

This illustrates how courts are in a position to impose on companies that, consistent with their responsibility to respect human rights, they have in place a 'human rights due diligence process to identify, prevent, mitigate and account for how they address their impacts on human rights', as stipulated in the Guiding Principles on Business and Human Rights.[26]

But 'positive' duties fulfilling human rights are more contested. States discharge their positive duties to protect and to fulfil human rights by using their regulatory powers or by providing public services to the population, relying on the tool of taxation and following a ranking of the priorities—education, health, public utilities, national defence, and so forth—that is settled through democratic debate. Because such tools are not at the disposal of corporations, it may legitimately be asked whether positive duties may be imposed at all on corporations, and if so, how the scope of such obligations is to be defined. Indeed, it is because he believed a negative answer should be given to this question that John Ruggie, as the UN Secretary-General's Special Representative on the issue of transnational corporations and other business enterprises and human rights between 2005 and 2011, concluded that while corporations should respect human rights, they could not have imposed on them an obligation (analogous to that imposed on states) to protect human rights, even though they might be in a position to influence certain situations. 'While corporations may be considered "organs of society" ', he noted, 'they are specialized economic organs, not democratic public interest institutions. As such, their responsibilities cannot and should not simply mirror the duties of States'.[27]

[24] See, for instance, the protracted legal battle fought against the presence of Coca-Cola in the State of Kerala in India, as described on the website of the Special Rapporteur on the right to water and sanitation, available at <http://www.righttowater.info/ways-to-influence/legal-approaches/case-against-coca-cola-kerala-state-india/> (last accessed 17 November 2013). The litigation is based in part on the recognition by the Indian Supreme Court in *M C Mehta v Union of India* (2004(12) SCC118), that 'groundwater is a social asset' and that 'citizens have the right to the use of air, water and earth as protected under Article 21 of the Constitution (the protection of life and personal liberty)'.

[25] *Baleke and Others v Attorney General of Uganda and Others*, Civil Suit 179 of 2002.

[26] A/HRC/17/31, paras. 6 and 17–21.

[27] Protect, Respect and Remedy, para. 53.

However, while corporations have neither regulatory powers nor the power to tax and spend, their influence over the past half-century has increased significantly (as measured by their ability to affect the lives of individuals with whom they interact), both as a result of economic globalization and the accompanying deregulation of economic activities, and because of the privatization of a range of public services.[28] Corporations do not legislate. They do not exercise coercive power in the sense that they cannot impose sanctions on individuals unless these individuals have expressed, at some point, a consent to be thus made dependent on the will on the corporation. Yet, while corporations may not imprison or execute, they do set policies in the areas of recruitment and wage-setting, they decide at which price and under what conditions to buy from their suppliers, and to sell to their clients; and they choose which goods and services to provide and how to produce them.

There is more than the reality of corporate power alone. Once we acknowledge that, in exercising their activities, corporations must take into account human rights, tracing a line between the 'negative' duty to respect human rights and the 'positive' duties to protect and to fulfil them becomes quite contestable, because of the intrinsic continuity between these various dimensions. For instance, in deciding on remuneration, the corporation may not ignore 'fair remuneration' as defined in the International Covenant on Economic, Social and Cultural Rights, as one that enables workers and their families to enjoy an adequate standard of living, in which the Covenant includes 'adequate food, clothing and housing', and to the 'continuous improvement of living conditions'.[29] In setting prices as commodity buyers or in defining standards, agrifood corporations may have to take into account the specific needs of smallholders, and ensure that whichever conditions are set do not result in depriving these producers from their ability to achieve a level of income that allows them to achieve a decent standard of living.[30] In providing water services to the population, companies may have to ensure that they do not compromise equal, affordable, and physical access to sufficient, safe and acceptable water to all.[31] In all these examples, the frontier dissolves between

[28] See, *inter alia*, K. De Feyter and F. Gomez Isa (eds.), *Privatisation and Human Rights in the Age of Globalisation* (Antwerp: Intersentia, 2005).

[29] See International Covenant on Economic, Social and Cultural Rights (adopted on 16 December 1966, G.A. Res. 2200(XXII), UN GAOR, 21st sess., Supp. No. 16, US Doc. A/6316 (1966), 993 UNTS 3) (Arts. 7 (a) (ii) and 11) and Committee on Economic, Social and Cultural Rights, General Comment No. 18: The right to work (Art. 6 of the Covenant) (adopted on 24 November 2005), UN Doc. E/C.12/GC/18 (6 Feb. 2006), para. 44. See also Christian Courtis, 'The Right to Food as a Justiciable Right: Challenges and Strategies', 11 *Max Planck Yearbook of United Nations Law* (2007), 317–337, at 326 (n. 6) and, on the need to define a methodology for the definition of a 'living wage' corresponding to the requirements of Art. 6 of the Covenant, see Agribusiness and the right to food. Report of the Special Rapporteur on the right to food, Olivier De Schutter, UN Doc. A/HRC/13/33 (22 Dec. 2009), paras. 14–17.

[30] Agribusiness and the right to food. Report of the Special Rapporteur on the right to food, Olivier De Schutter, UN Doc. A/HRC/13/33 (22 Dec. 2009), paras. 37–45.

[31] This of course paraphrases what the Committee on Economic, Social and Cultural Rights says about the duty of the states parties to the Covenant to protect the right to water: see Committee on Economic, Social and Cultural Rights, General Comment No. 15: The right to water (arts. 11 and 12 of the Covenant), UN Doc. E/C.12/2002/11 (2002), para. 23 ('Where water services (such as

a (negative) duty to abstain from measures that impact on economic and social rights and a (positive) duty to contribute to the full realization of these rights. What matters is *how the company goes about doing things*, not whether it refrains from acting or takes action: it is the overall conduct of the company that may have to take into account the requirements of human rights, whether that conduct takes the form of actions or of omissions.

Indeed, the contributions of the Special Representative of the Secretary-General on the issue of business and human rights at least implicitly recognize this, where they note for instance that the obligation to respect (or to 'do no harm') 'is not merely a passive responsibility for firms but may entail positive steps—for example, a workplace anti-discrimination policy might require the company to adopt specific recruitment and training programmes',[32] or where they define the 'sphere of influence' of companies as defined by 'the company's web of activities and relationships'.[33] These contributions also insist that a company

> cannot be held responsible for the human rights impacts of every entity over which they may have some influence, because this would include cases in which they were not a causal agent, direct or indirect, of the harm in question. Nor is it desirable to have companies act whenever they have influence, particularly over governments. Asking companies to support human rights voluntarily where they have influence is one thing; but attributing responsibility to them on that basis alone is quite another.[34]

This would seem to exclude extending the responsibilities of companies towards human rights to situations which companies could contribute to improving but which they have had no role in causing. However, this apparent simplicity is put into question by what is said in the same reports about the due diligence requirement that is included in the responsibility of companies to respect human rights. That requirement, it is stated, imposes on a company the obligation to examine 'what human rights impacts their own activities may have within that context—for example, in their capacity as producers, service providers, employers, and neighbours', as well as 'whether they might contribute to abuse through the relationships connected to their activities, such as with business partners, suppliers, state agencies, and other non-state actors'.[35] Due diligence thus described clearly goes beyond merely 'negative' duties to abstain from certain types of behaviour that could have an impact on the enjoyment of human rights: it in fact imposes on companies to ensure that, as market participants, they contribute to positive human rights outcomes.

These conceptual hesitations illustrate the difficulty of tracing a clear-cut distinction between such 'negative' duties as described and 'positive' duties to contribute to human rights by exercising one's influence wherever possible. However valid it may be in theory, such a distinction is untenable in practice. And especially, it creates the wrong incentive: it encourages a company faced with certain delicate

piped water networks, water tankers, access to rivers and wells) are operated or controlled by third parties, states parties must prevent them from compromising equal, affordable, and physical access to sufficient, safe and acceptable water').

[32] Protect, Respect and Remedy, para. 55.

[33] Protect, Respect and Remedy, para. 71.

[34] Protect, Respect and Remedy, para. 69.

[35] Protect, Respect and Remedy, para. 57.

situations where human rights are at risk to adopt a 'hands-off' approach, in order to escape the accusation of bearing part of the responsibility in the alleged violation of human rights, when what we would need is for the company to be encouraged to exercise its influence for the benefit of human rights. We therefore need something else: a definition of the human rights obligations that should be imposed on corporations, commensurate with their ability to influence certain actors with whom they interact or certain situations over which they make decisions, that recognizes the important role they can play in the fulfilment of human rights.

4. How to Define the Scope of Positive Duties Imposed on Corporations?

It is the difficulty to provide such a definition that has been the main obstacle to the recent attempts to impose human rights obligations on companies. At the international level, the attempt to revive the debate on this issue began with the presentation by the UN Sub-Commission for the Promotion and Protection of Human Rights—made up of independent experts appointed by the Commission on Human Rights to provide expert advice in support of its work—of a set of 'Norms on the Human Rights Responsibilities of Transnational Corporations and Other Business Enterprises', which they approved in August 2003.[36] The draft Norms presented themselves as a restatement of the human rights obligations imposed on companies under international law. They were based on the idea that 'even though States have the primary responsibility to promote, secure the fulfillment of, respect, ensure respect of and protect human rights, transnational corporations and other business enterprises, as organs of society, are also responsible for promoting and securing the human rights set forth in the Universal Declaration of Human Rights', and therefore 'transnational corporations and other business enterprises, their officers, and persons working for them are also obliged to respect generally recognized responsibilities and norms contained in United Nations treaties and other international instruments'.[37]

However, the Norms met with strong opposition both from the business community and from a number of governments.[38] Among the concerns that were

[36] UN Doc. E/CN.4/Sub.2/2003/12/Rev.2 (2003); and for the Commentary, which the Preamble of the draft Norms states is 'a useful interpretation and elaboration of the standards contained in the Norms', UN Doc. E/CN.4/Sub.2/2003/38/Rev.2 (2003). On the drafting process of these draft Norms and a comparison with previous attempts of a similar nature, see D. Weissbrodt and M. Kruger, 'Current Developments: Norms on the Responsibilities of Transnational Corporations and Other Business Enterprises with Regard to Human Rights', 97 *American Journal of International Law* (2003), 901–922; D. Weissbrodt and M. Kruger, 'Human Rights Responsibilities of Businesses as Non-State Actors', in P. Alston (ed.), *Non-State Actors and Human Rights* (Oxford: Oxford University Press, 2005), 315–350.

[37] Preamble, 3d and 4th Recital.

[38] *Report of the United Nations High Commissioner on Human Rights on the responsibilities of transnational corporations and related business enterprises with regard to human rights*, 15 February 2005, UN Doc. E/CN.4/2005/91.

raised was the vagueness with which the positive duties of corporations were outlined. While acknowledging the primary responsibility of states in the fulfilment of human rights, Principle 1 of the draft Norms stated that:

> Within their respective spheres of activity and influence, transnational corporations and other business enterprises have the obligation to promote, secure the fulfillment of, respect, ensure respect of and protect human rights recognized in international as well as national law, including the rights and interests of indigenous peoples and other vulnerable groups.

The notion of 'sphere of influence' was therefore key in defining the scope of the positive duties the Norms intended to impose on corporations to support the realization of human rights. The notion had not in fact originated with the Norms: it had been put forward a few years earlier in the 'Global Compact', the flagship initiative of the United Nations in promoting corporate social responsibility, initially proposed by the United Nations Secretary-General Kofi Annan at the 1999 Davos World Economic Forum. Yet, though not entirely unknown, the notion of 'sphere of influence' still appeared to be a relatively vague notion. It is best understood as a compromise between two ideas: on the one hand, companies are not to be equated to the states in which they operate, which are primarily responsible for the provision of public services such as health or education, and for the maintenance of law and order; on the other hand, the more powerful companies become, the more it will be justified to impose on them to exercise leverage on their business partners or on the host government to ensure that they, too, comply with the set of internationally recognized human rights. Still, the notion was not sufficiently well delineated in the Norms. To many, it appeared as a potential source of legal insecurity and, if the Norms were to develop into a hard instrument, of endless litigation.

It may be argued, however, that the notion of 'sphere of influence' simply seeks to align the human rights responsibilities of companies with the effective power that they exercise. Three examples may serve as an illustration. What these examples have in common is that they show the need to move beyond legal fictions, or an idealized view of a market composed of a multitude of economic actors competing against one another, towards a realistic assessment of the power yielded by large corporate actors, who have the capacity to shape the markets in which they operate,[39] and whose influence often extends even beyond national territories.

A. Corporations as service providers

Consider first the situation where companies are in such a dominant role that they occupy the same monopolistic position as governments providing public services. The case of *Verein gegen Tierfabriken v Switzerland* provides an illustration. Verein gegen Tierfabriken (VgT), a Swiss association dedicated to the protection of animals, had been seeking to react to various television commercials of the meat

[39] As noted, memorably enough, by John Kenneth Galbraith in his 1967 book, *The New Industrial State* (Boston: Houghton Mifflin, 1967).

industry. It prepared to that effect a 35-second-long television commercial aiming to convince the viewers to eat less meat 'for the sake of your health, the animals and the environment', as stated in the slogan closing their clip. As VgT wished its film to be broadcast in the programmes of the Swiss Radio and Television Company, it sent the film to the then Commercial Television Company (AG für das Werbefernsehen, renamed Publisuisse after the facts) responsible for television advertising. That company however refused to air the clip, arguing that it had a 'clearly political character' and that section 18(5) of the Federal Radio and Television Act prohibited political advertising. The Swiss courts to which VgT applied agreed with the company that, in matters of advertising, the company acted as a private entity and did not fulfil a duty of public law when it broadcast commercials. VgT turned to the European Court of Human Rights, alleging a violation of its freedom of expression guaranteed under Article 10 of the European Convention on Human Rights.

The Court recognized that, in principle, a state party to the Convention may legitimately aim to prevent financially powerful groups from obtaining a competitive political advantage by advertising political commercials. However, it responded to the argument of the Swiss government according to which the association has 'various other possibilities to broadcast the information at issue', that VgT,

> aiming at reaching the entire Swiss public, had no other means than the national television programmes of the Swiss Radio and Television Company at its disposal, since these programmes were the only ones broadcast throughout Switzerland. The Commercial Television Company was the sole instance responsible for the broadcasting of commercials within these national programmes. Private regional television channels and foreign television stations cannot be received throughout Switzerland.[40]

The lesson is this: because the private corporation to which all responsibilities in the area of advertising had been delegated had in effect a monopoly, it was duty-bound to protect the freedom of expression of the applicant association by allowing it to air its commercial.[41] A similar conclusion can be drawn from the case of *Appleby and Others v the United Kingdom*, decided two years later by the European Court of Human Rights, where the owner of a privately owned town centre denied the applicants the authorization to collect signatures for a petition, arguing that the owner wished to remain neutral: although concluding in the circumstances that freedom of expression of the petitioners had not been violated, the Court did note that where

> the bar on access to property has the effect of preventing any effective exercise of freedom of expression or it can be said that the essence of the right has been destroyed, the Court

[40] Eur. Ct. HR (2nd sect.), *VgT Verein gegen Tierfabriken v Switzerland* judgment of 28 June 2001 (final on 28 September 2001) (Appl. No. 24699/94), para. 77.

[41] The European Court of Human Rights later found a fresh violation of Article 10 of the European Convention on Human Rights to result from the failure of Switzerland to faithfully execute the 2001 judgment: see Eur. Ct. HR (GC), *Case of VgT Verein gegen Tierfabriken v Switzerland*, judgment of 30 June 2009 (Appl. No. 32772/02).

would not exclude that a positive obligation could arise for the State to protect the enjoyment of the Convention rights by regulating property rights.[42]

Nor is the European Court of Human Rights isolated in this regard. It was inspired, in fact, by the United States Supreme Court's case law in the area of free speech. In the well-known case of *Marsh v Alabama*,[43] a Jehovah's Witness was convicted of trespassing after she refused to stop distributing religious literature on the sidewalk near a post office in the town of Chickasaw, a town wholly owned and run by the Gulf Shipbuilding Corporation: although she was on private property, the majority of the Court reasoned, her First Amendment rights trumped the private property of the company owning the town. The Court compared the position of the company to that of a municipality, asking: '[c]an those people who live in or come to Chickasaw be denied freedom of press and religion simply because a single company has legal title to all the town?'[44] Framing the question thus—explicitly making an analogy of the company, because of the position it occupied, with the state—could lead the Court to no other answer.

In American constitutional law, the fact that the Bill of Rights appended to the Federal Constitution in principle cannot be invoked against private persons as it only applies to 'state action' has sometimes led to confusion in the case law.[45] But in the later case of *Pruneyard Shopping Center v Robbins*,[46] the Court did not object to a provision in the Californian Constitution that protected 'speech and petitioning, reasonably exercised, in shopping centers even when the shopping centers are privately owned'.[47] In the eyes of the Court, an obligation imposed on a private shopping centre owner to accept the exercise of free speech on their premises does not violate his property rights under the Fifth and Fourteenth Amendments or his free speech rights under the First and Fourteenth Amendments. In rejecting the argument by the Pruneyard Shopping Center that such an obligation—confirmed by the Californian Supreme Court[48] —amounted to a prohibited taking of property, the United States Supreme Court again reasoned by comparing the situation of the shopping centre to that of a municipality. Just like a municipality would be allowed to impose certain time, place, and manner restrictions on speech, so a shopping centre could impose such restrictions for the sake of preserving its commercial functions: beyond that, states are free to extend the protection of free speech, and may even have to do so.[49]

[42] Eur. Ct. HR (4th sect.), *Appleby and Others v the United Kingdom* judgment of 6 May 2003 (final on 24 September 2003) (Appl. No. 44306/98), para. 47.

[43] 326 US 501 (1946).

[44] 326 US 501, 504.

[45] See, inter alia, *Hudgens v NLRB*, 424 US 507 (1976); see also *Lloyd Corp. v Tanner*, 47 US 551, 92 S.Ct. 2219, 33 L.Ed. 2d 131 (1972) (where a stict 'no handbilling policy' could be imposed by a private shopping centre because the petitioners had alternative means of communicating their message to the public and because, in contrast to other cases (*Amalgamated Food Employees Union Local 590 v Logan Valley Plaza, Inc.*, 391 US 308 (1972)), the handbilling was unrelated to any activity within the centre).

[46] 447 US 74 (1980).

[47] Art. 1, 2 of the California Constitution.

[48] 23 Cal. 3d 899, 910, 592 P.2d 341, 347 (1979).

[49] See 447 US 74, 83: 'There is nothing to suggest that preventing appellants from prohibiting this sort of activity will unreasonably impair the value or use of their property as a shopping center. The

Company-owned towns are an extreme situation and there is a world of difference, of course, between the private shopping centre asked to tolerate people distributing handbills on its premises and the company asked to protect access to health, education, or housing for the benefit of the communities in which they operate. The point of the comparison, however, is this: what truly matters as we seek to identify the duty-bearers of any particular right of the individual, should not be the private or the public nature of the actor concerned, as it is in the classic state action doctrine in United States constitutional law. The focus should be rather on the degree of dependency of the right-holder vis-à-vis the actor concerned, or the degree of control over any particular good or resource that the actor possesses. In domestic legal systems that attach a great weight to the private/public distinction in determining when and against whom human rights can be invoked, as the US system does, that distinction is premised on the idea that market relationships are chosen 'freely', whereas the individual cannot freely choose whether or not to submit to the authority of the state. But the fragility of that presumption has been demonstrated since the realist turn in legal thought.[50] It is one that clearly falls where companies take over public functions or have a monopoly in the delivery of certain services, holding individuals in subordination just as states may do by the monopoly over-enforcement powers. Indeed, it is precisely because the market is not devoid of coercion and of power imbalances that international human rights law imposes on states a duty to protect, which amounts to nullifying the private/public distinction as it is used in the context of state international responsibility:[51] if market relationships were always truly free—if individuals only entered into legal relationships based on their free consent, and on the choice they make between different alternatives—the protection by the state would be superfluous except in the most extreme of cases.

If, then, we agree to define the human rights obligations that should be imposed on corporations as a function of their ability to influence certain actors with whom they interact or certain situations over which they make decisions, it is evident that where one private actor monopolizes the delivery of education, housing, healthcare services, or food it must be imposed to deliver those goods and services that are essential to a decent life, in order to ensure that they are adequate and available and accessible to all: a state not imposing such an obligation on that private actor

PruneYard is a large commercial complex that covers several city blocks, contains numerous separate business establishments, and is open to the public at large. The decision of the California Supreme Court makes it clear that the PruneYard may restrict expressive activity by adopting time, place, and manner regulations that will minimize any interference with its commercial functions'.

[50] Robert Lee Hale was one of the most insightful writers on this apparent paradox. See generally R.L. Hale, 'Coercion and Distribution in a Supposedly Non-Coercive State', 38 *Political Science Quarterly* (1923), 470–494. For an excellent comment from an institutionalist economist's perspective, see W.J. Samuels, 'The Economy as a System of Power and its Legal Bases: The Legal Economics of Robert Lee Hale', 27 University of Miami Law Review (1973), 261–371.

[51] On the private/public distinction in the international law on state responsibility and the duty to protect in human rights law, see O. De Schutter, 'The responsibility of states', ch. 2 in S. Chesterman and A. Fisher (eds.), *Public Security, Private Order: The Outsourcing of public services and its limits* (New York: Cambridge University Press, 2009), 17–37.

would be in violation of its own human rights obligations. We reach the same conclusion where such a monopoly is exercised by a number of private actors, conspiring together rather than competing against one another: antitrust law, in this regard, is a key instrument in ensuring the protection of human rights, since it helps to equalize the relationships in the sphere of the market and in principle should be a check against the abuse by one actor of the dominant position it has acquired.[52]

B. Corporations as groups of companies

Delicate questions concerning the 'sphere of influence' within which corporations have imposed on them human rights responsibilities also arise as a result of corporations developing as networks of companies, related to one another through investment or contractual links. Corporate groups today comprise distinct legal entities, each with their own juridical personalities, usually including one parent (controlling) corporation on the one hand, and its (controlled) subsidiaries on the other. This too raises the issue of the scope of the human rights duties of the actors involved. The doctrine of limited liability holds that the shareholders in a corporation may not be held liable for the debts of that corporation beyond the level of their investment.[53]

The doctrine may also play a role in international law, where states' duties to control corporations are invoked. In the *Barcelona Traction* case, the International Court of Justice followed the classical approach to corporate entity law and appeared to accept its consequence—that the piercing of the corporate veil should remain limited to exceptional cases.[54] As regards the determination of nationality

[52] See, for instance, United Nations Special Rapporteur on the right to food, 'Addressing Concentration in Food Supply Chains: The Role of Competition Law in Tackling the Abuse of Buyer Power', Briefing Note 3 (1 December 2010); and A.R. Ganesh, 'The Right to Food and Buyer Power', 11 *German Law Journal* (2010), 1190–1244.

[53] *Anderson v Abbott*, 321 US 349, 362 (1944) ('Normally the corporation is an insulator from liability on claims of creditors. The fact that incorporation was desired in order to obtain limited liability does not defeat that purpose. Limited liability is the rule, not the exception' (citations omitted)); *Burnet v Clark*, 287 US 410, 415 (1932) ('A corporation and its stockholders are generally to be treated as separate entities').

[54] Case concerning *The Barcelona Traction, Light and Power Co. (Belgium v Spain)*, [1970] ICJ Rep. 3. Following the adjudication in bankruptcy in Spain of Barcelona Traction, a company incorporated in Canada but having its head office in Spain, Belgium sought reparation for damage alleged to have been sustained by Belgian nationals, both natural and legal persons, shareholders in the company, as a result of acts said to be contrary to international law committed towards the company by organs of the Spanish State. One of the preliminary objections of the Spanish Government was to the effect that the Belgian Government lacked capacity to submit any claim in respect of wrongs done to a Canadian company even if the shareholders were Belgian. This objection was joined to the merits and, by fifteen votes to one, the Court agreed with this contention of the Spanish government. The Court found that Belgium lacked jus standi to exercise diplomatic protection of shareholders in a Canadian company with respect to measures taken against that company in Spain. The Court reasoned that since, in municipal law, a distinction is made between the rights of the company and those of the shareholders, when an act is committed against a foreign company, in alleged violation of international law, it is for the national state of that company alone to file a claim to diplomatic protection (in this case, Canada); the shareholder's national state (Belgium) has no right to do so.

for the purposes of the exercise by a state of its right to diplomatic protection, it noted that a distinction should be made between the legal situation of the corporation and that of its shareholders: '[s]eparated from the company by numerous barriers', the Court said, 'the shareholder cannot be identified with it. The concept and structure of the company are founded on and determined by a firm distinction between the separate entity of the company and that of the shareholders, each with a distinct set of rights'.[55] It is highly doubtful whether this position should be considered as determinative beyond the narrow field of diplomatic protection.[56] Indeed, warning against the abuse of the corporate form, the International Court of Justice explicitly acknowledged already in its judgment of 5 February 1970 that, as a matter of international law, the separate status of an incorporated entity may be disregarded in certain exceptional circumstances:

> Forms of incorporation and their legal personality have sometimes not been employed for the sole purposes they were originally intended to serve; sometimes the corporate entity has been unable to protect the rights of those who entrusted their financial resources to it; thus inevitably there have arisen dangers of abuse, as in the case of many other institutions of law. Here, then, as elsewhere, the law, confronted with economic realities, has had to provide protective measures and remedies in the interests of those within the corporate entity as well as of those outside who have dealings with it: the law has recognized that the independent existence of the legal entity cannot be treated as an absolute. It is in this context that the process of 'lifting the corporate veil' or 'disregarding the legal entity' has been found justified and equitable in certain circumstances or for certain purposes. The wealth of practice already accumulated on the subject in municipal law indicates that the veil is lifted, for instance, to prevent the misuse of the privileges of legal personality, as in certain cases of fraud or malfeasance, to protect third persons such as a creditor or purchaser, or to prevent the evasion of legal requirements or of obligations [...] In accordance with the principle expounded above, the process of lifting the veil, being an exceptional one admitted by municipal law in respect of an institution of its own making, is equally admissible to play a similar role in international law.[57]

But the principle of limited liability, and lifting the corporate veil having to remain exceptional, remains the dominant one. Consistent with this doctrine, the liability of the parent company may not be engaged solely on the basis of the fact of the control it exercises on the subsidiary, where the latter commits human rights violations or contributes to such violations. This may make it difficult for victims of the conduct of the subsidiary to seek reparation by filing a claim against the parent company. How can this obstacle be overcome?

[55] Case concerning *The Barcelona Traction, Light and Power Co. (Belgium v Spain)* (second phase: merits), 5 February 1970, [1970] ICJ Rep. 3, 184.

[56] On the relevance of the *Barcelona Traction* case beyond the exercise of diplomatic protection, see already the doubts expressed by S.D. Metzger, 'Nationality of Corporate Investment Under Investment Guaranty Schemes: The Relevance of Barcelona Traction', 65 *American Journal of International Law* (1971), 532–543.

[57] Case concerning *The Barcelona Traction, Light and Power Co. (Belgium v Spain)* (second phase: merits), 5 February 1970, [1970] ICJ Rep. 3, at 38–39.

A first approach, classically described as the 'piercing the corporate veil' approach, requires one to examine the factual relationship between the parent and the subsidiary in order to identify whether the nature of that relationship is not more akin to the relationship between a principal (the parent) and an agent (the subsidiary), or whether, for other motives, there are reasons to suspect that the separation of corporate personalities does not correspond to economic reality. This approach is the one alluded to by the International Court of Justice in the *Barcelona Traction* case, where it cautions against the risk of abuse. It is the technique mostly relied upon, for instance, in South Africa[58] or in the United States. Thus, the US courts will allow claimants to establish that the parent company exercises such a degree of control on the operations of the subsidiary that the latter cannot be said to have any will or existence of its own,[59] and that treating the two entities as separate (and thus allowing the parent to shield itself behind its subsidiary) would sanction fraud or lead to an inequitable result.[60] In such cases, the corporate veil will be lifted: the subsidiary, in such circumstances, is a mere instrument in the hands of the parent company,[61] so that the parent and the subsidiary are 'alter egos'.[62] Alternatively, it may be shown that the subsidiary was acting in a particular case as the agent of the parent company.[63] This will be allowed, again in exceptional cases, where the parent company controls the subsidiary and where both parties agree that the subsidiary is acting for the agent: in such a case, 'the acts of a subsidiary acting as an agent are, from the legal point of view, the acts of its parent corporation, and it is the parent that is liable'.[64] An example is the reasoning followed in the case of *Bowoto v Chevron Texaco*, where Judge Illston concluded that CNL, the subsidiary of Chevron in Nigeria, which allegedly had acted in concert with the Nigerian military in order to suppress,

[58] International Commission of Jurists, *Human Rights Abuses Involving Corporations: South Africa*. Geneva, 2009, 10 and ff.

[59] Taken alone, neither majority or even complete stock control, nor common identity of the parent's and the subsidiary's officiers and directors, are sufficient to establish the degree of control required. What is required is 'control (…) of policy and business practice in respect to the transaction attacked so that the corporate entity as to this transaction has at the time no separate mind, will or existence of its own' (*Lowenthal v Baltimore & Ohio R.R. Co.*, 287 NYS 62, 76 (N.Y. App. Div.), aff'd, 6 N.E.2d 56 (1936), cited by Ph.I. Blumberg, 'Accountability of Multinational Corporations: The Barriers Presented by Concepts of the Corporate Juridical Entity', 24 *Hastings International & Comparative Law Review* (2001), 297–330, at 304).

[60] See *Taylor v Standard Gas Co.*, 306 US 307, 322 (1939) ('the doctrine of corporate entity, recognized generally and for most purposes, will not be regarded when to do so would work fraud or injustice').

[61] *Chicago, M. & St. P. Ry. Co. v Minneapolis Civic and Commerce Assn.*, 247 US 490, 501 (1918) (principles of corporate separateness 'have been plainly and repeatedly held not applicable where stock ownership has been resorted to, not for the purpose of participating in the affairs of a corporation in the normal and usual manner, but for the purpose (…) of controlling a subsidiary company so that it may be used as a mere agency or instrumentality of the owning company').

[62] See, e.g. *United States v Betterfoods*, 524 US 51 (1998).

[63] As Justice (then Judge) Cardozo summarized in *Berkey v Third Avenue Ry. Co.*, 244 NY 84, 95, 155 NE 58, 61: 'Dominion may be so complete, interference so obtrusive, that by the general rules of agency the parent will be a principal and the subsidiary an agent'.

[64] P.I. Blumberg, 'Accountability of Multinational Corporations: The Barriers Presented by Concepts of the Corporate Juridical Entity', 24 *Hastings International and Comparative Law Review* (2001), 297–330, at 307.

sometimes violently, protests against Chevron's activities in the region, could be considered as the agent of Chevron, in view in particular of the volume, content, and timing of communications between Chevron and CNL, notably on the day of a protest when 'an oil platform was taken over by local people'.[65] These and other indicia showed that Chevron 'exercised more than the usual degree of direction and control which a parent exercises over its subsidiary'.

In order to establish either that the corporate form has been abused—by a parent artificially seeking to shield itself from liability by establishing a subsidiary which has in fact no existence of its own—or that the subsidiary has been acting in fact as the agent of the parent corporation, claimants will have to establish that the separation of legal personalities is a mere legal fiction to which the economic reality does not correspond and which should not be admitted, as this might sanction fraud.[66] This approach thus may constitute a source of legal insecurity, since the criteria allowing the 'piercing of the veil' are many, without either the list of admissible criteria or their hierarchization having been authoritatively identified. It also imposes a heavy burden on plaintiffs seeking to invoke the indirect liability of the parent corporation for the acts of its subsidiary. This results in a situation where, in fact, very few such attempts to 'pierce the veil' end up succeeding.[67]

Because of the limitations of this first approach, it has been suggested, as an alternative, that corporate groups are formed of entities, legally separate perhaps, but whose interconnectedness is such that a presumption should be allowed according to which any act committed by one subsidiary of the group should be treated as if it were adopted by the parent. In this perspective, the corporate group is seen as 'a conglomeration of units of a single entity, each unit performing a specific function, the function of the parent company being to provide expertise, technology, supervision and finance. Insofar as injuries result from negligence in respect of any of the parent company functions, then the parent should be liable'.[68]

This technique has been used in the United States not only in New Deal legislation and by courts and agencies seeking to ensure that legislation protecting employees would not be outplayed by the abuse of the corporate form, but also in order to define the conditions under which certain legislations protecting employees from discrimination could extend to the operations of subsidiaries of American undertakings operating

[65] *Bowoto v Chevron Texaco*, No. C 99-2506 SI, 2004 US Dis LEXIS 4603 (ND, Cal 2004).

[66] See, e.g. *Labor Board v Deena Artware*, 361 US 398, 402 (1960).

[67] For this reason, courts may be tempted to set aside the classical tests for allowing the piercing of the corporate veil in order to ensure that the legislative policy will not be defeated by the choice of corporate forms. See, e.g. *Anderson v Abbott*, 321 US 349, 362–363 (1944) ('It has often been held that the interposition of a corporation will not be allowed to defeat a legislative policy, whether that was the aim or only the result of the arrangement'); *Bangor Punta Operations, Inc. v Bangor & Aroostook R. Co.*, 417 US 703, 713 (1974) ('the corporate form may be disregarded in the interests of justice where it is used to defeat an overriding public policy'); *First National City Bank v Banco Para El Comercio Exterior de Cuba*, 462 US 611, 630 (1983) ('the Court has consistently refused to give effect to the corporate form where it is interposed to defeat legislative policies').

[68] R. Meeran, 'The Unveiling of Transnational Corporations', in M. Addo (ed.), *Human Rights Standards and the Responsibility of Transnational Corporations* (The Hague: Kluwer Law International, 1999), 170.

overseas:[69] the 1990 American with Disabilities Act[70] or Title VII of the Civil Rights Act of 1964 provide examples.[71] The District Court of Illinois also took this approach in the *Amoco Cadiz Oil Spill* case, even absent a clear legislative mandate, in order to conclude that the parent corporation should be held liable for environmental damage caused by an oil spill from a tanker off the coast of France: the close degree of control of the parent corporation over its subsidiaries allowed the Court to overcome the separation of legal personalities.[72] It has also been proposed in legal doctrine to adopt a similar approach in the Alien Tort Statute, where, it has been argued, the fact that the subsidiary has allegedly violated the law of nations should be sufficient to allow for piercing the veil, and impose a liability on the parent (controlling) company unless it is proven by the latter that 'no reasonable effort would have discovered evidence from documents of any applicable government, non-governmental organizational documents and reports, employee information, or anecdotal information in the state that would have moved a reasonable person to inquire further'.[73]

Finally, a third avenue consists in abandoning the idea of linking the behaviour of the subsidiaries to that of the parent altogether, and to focus instead on the *direct* liability of the parent company arising from the failure to exercise due diligence in controlling the acts of the subsidiaries it may exercise control upon. The OECD Guidelines on Multinational Enterprises appear to follow this approach, where they state that they 'extend to enterprise groups, although boards of subsidiary enterprises might have obligations under the law of their jurisdiction of incorporation. Compliance and control systems should extend where possible to these subsidiaries'.[74] This formulation amounts to imposing on a parent company a duty to monitor the activities of the subsidiary, consistent with the emerging notion that corporations have a due diligence obligation to ensure that human rights are complied with within their sphere of influence.

This approach creates an incentive for the parent company to ensure that the subsidiaries which it can influence comply with human rights. In contrast, a doctrine requiring that claimants bring forward elements justifying the lifting of the corporate veil (as in the first of the three approaches discussed here) creates an incentive for the parent company to remain at arm's length from the activities

[69] Blumberg, *supra* note 59, at 313–315.

[70] Pub. L. 101–336, title I, § 102, July 26, 1990, 104 Stat. 331; amended by Pub. L. 102–166, title I, § 109(b)(2), Nov. 21, 1991, 105 Stat. 1077; codified as 42 USC § 12112 (c)(2)(A) (1994).

[71] Pub. L. 88–352 (Title VII), 42 USC § 2000e and ff., as amended by the Civil Rights Act of 1991 (Pub. L. 102–166).

[72] See *Amoco Cadiz Oil Spill*, 1984 AMC 2123, 2 Lloyd's Rep 304 (ND Ill. 1984): 'As an integrated multinational corporation which is engaged through a system of subsidiaries in the exploration, production, refining, transportation and sale of petroleum products throughout the world, standard [the American parent corporation] is responsible for the tortious acts of its wholly owned subsidiaries and instrumentalies AIC and Transport'.

[73] S. Coye-Huhn, 'No More Hiding behind Forms, Factors and Flying Hats: A Proposal for a per se Piercing of the Corporate Veil for Corporations that Violate the Law of Nations under the Alien Tort Claims Statute', 72 *University of Cincinatti Law Review* (2003), 743–770, at 758. In contrast with this proposal, however, the presumption established under statutes such as the Civil Rights Act or the American With Disabilities Act is non-rebuttable.

[74] OECD Guidelines on Multinational Enterprises (as revised on 25 May 2011), II. General Policies, Commentaries, para. 9.

of its subsidiary, in order not to be held liable for its behaviour.[75] A comparison between the cases of *Connelly v RTZ Corporation plc and Others* and *Lubbe and 4 Others v Cape plc*, which both concerned violations of the right to health of workers employed in the extractive industry, provides an illustration.

In *Connelly*,[76] the claimant was a former employee for Rössing Uranium Ltd. (RUL), a Namibian subsidiary of the defendant corporation (RTZ Corporation plc, incorporated in the United Kingdom). He had been employed by RUL in a uranium mine, following which it was discovered, three years after his return, that he was suffering from cancer of the larynx, apparently due to exposure to radioactive material in the mine. According to the description by the House of Lords, the claim was based on the allegation that 'R.T.Z. had devised R.U.L.'s policy on health, safety and the environment, or alternatively had advised R.U.L. as to the contents of the policy', and that 'an employee or employees of R.T.Z., referred to as R.T.Z. supervisors, implemented the policy and supervised health, safety and/or environmental protection at the mine'. The argument was therefore not (as in classical piercing-the-veil analysis) that separation between the parent and the subsidiary should be treated as a mere fiction, a fraudulent means of limiting the liability of the parent corporation, without any correspondence in economic reality: it was that RTZ had itself contributed, by its acts, in causing the damage for which the victim sought compensation. Such an argument would have had no chance of succeeding if, instead of being involved in defining the policy of its subsidiary on health and safety or environmental issues, RTZ had simply ignored any risks associated with the mining of uranium, and had acted merely as a shareholder, monitoring the financial performances of its subsidiary, but without seeking to be informed about, let alone participating in, its daily operations in such areas.

The direct liability of the parent corporation in *Connelly* was asserted on the basis of the *actions* it had taken in defining the policies of its subsidiary. By contrast, the *omissions* of the parent corporation were at stake in *Lubbe and 4 Others v Cape plc*, which the House of Lords was presented with again only three years later.[77] Over 3,000 plaintiffs claimed damages for personal injuries (and in some cases death) allegedly suffered as the result of exposure to asbestos in South Africa,

[75] As noted by Sarah Joseph, where direct liability attaches to parent companies only in cases of actions rather than omissions 'parents will be discouraged from intervening in their subsidiary's operations, even though they may have superior knowledge and technical expertise. Alternatively, parent companies might maintain 'strategic control' but avoid responsibility by delegating operational matters, which are more likely to give rise to tortious consequences' (S. Joseph, *Corporations and Transnational Human Rights Litigation* (Oxford–Portland: Hart Publishing, 2004)), 134 (citing A.J. Natale, 'Expansion of Parent Corporate Shareholder Liability through the Good Samaritan Doctrine: A Parent Corporation's Duty to Provide a Safe Workplace for Employees of its Subsidiary', 57 *University of Cincinnati Law Review* (1988), 717–750, at 736; and J. Cassels, 'Outlaws: Multinational Corporations and Catastrophic Law', 31 *Cumberland Law Review* (2000), 311–335, at 326).

[76] *Connelly v RTZ Corporation plc and Others* [1997] UKHL 30; [1998] AC 854; [1997] 4 All ER 335; [1997] 3 WLR 373 (24 July 1997).

[77] On 14 December 1998, the House of Lords had already refused to allow leave to the defendants for filing a further appeal against an initial decision by the Court of Appeal. Following this, over 3,000 new plaintiffs emerged, fundamentally transforming the nature of the litigation presented before the United Kingdom courts.

either upon working in mines owned by the defendant (until 1948) or by a fully owned South African subsidiary of the defendant, or as a result of living in an area contaminated by the mining activities of the defendant or its subsidiaries. As noted in the leading opinion of Lord Bingham of Cornhill,

> the claim is made against the defendant as a parent company which, knowing (so it is said) that exposure to asbestos was gravely injurious to health, *failed to take proper steps to ensure that proper working practices were followed and proper safety precautions observed throughout the group*. In this way, it is alleged, the defendant breached a duty of care which it owed to those working for its subsidiaries or living in the area of their operations (with the result that the plaintiffs thereby suffered personal injury and loss).[78]

Central to the *Cape plc* case was, therefore, the question

> whether a parent company which is proved to exercise de facto control over the operations of a (foreign) subsidiary and which knows, through its directors, that those operations involve risks to the health of workers employed by the subsidiary and/or persons in the vicinity of its factory or other business premises, owes a duty of care to those workers and/or other persons in relation to the control which it exercises over and the advice which it gives to the subsidiary company.[79]

This approach, the third in our typology, may be relied upon in all legal systems that impose a 'duty of care' on companies, understood as a duty to exercise due diligence, obliging parent companies to monitor the subsidiaries. In German law for instance, obligations derived from the duty of care (*Verkehrspflichten*) would include a duty of the parent company to control the subsidiary whose behaviour it can influence, and where that subsidiary adopts conduct that leads to human rights violations, the parent company would only escape liability by showing that it put in place all the monitoring systems that could be reasonably expected, and that would have had an effective chance of preventing the realization of the risk of violation.[80]

To summarize, there are three ways of dealing with the complexities resulting from the distinction between the economic reality of the corporate group and its organization into separate legal entities bound through an investment nexus. The first approach, based on 'derivative liability' of the parent corporation, creates a disincentive on the parent company to exercise a strict control over the activities of the subsidiary, even in situations where it could exercise such control in fact. Indeed, to the extent that the relationships between the parent and the subsidiary remain fully consistent with the norms of corporate behaviour, that is, do not lead to the suspicion that the parent-subsidiary separation has been misused in order to artificially insulate the parent from liability for the behaviour of the subsidiary, the corporate veil will not be pierced: only where it has been established that the

[78] Emphasis added.

[79] As indicated by the opinion of Lord Bingham of Cornhill, this is the issue as reformulated during the first Court of Appeal hearing in the case.

[80] G. Wagner, § 823. In: Münchener Kommentar zum BGB, vol. 4. München, Beck, 2009, para. 99; V. Emmerich, and M. Habersack (2010): Aktien- und GmbH-Konzernrecht. Kommentar, § 311: para. 13.

control by the parent company is such that the subsidiary has no existence of its own (has no 'separate mind'), will the separation of legal personalities be overcome. Thus, insofar as this serves to limit its potential legal liability, it will be in the interest of the parent company, not to monitor closely the everyday operations of the subsidiary, but on the contrary to abandon broad discretion to the subsidiary as to how to implement the general policies set for the multinational group. By contrast, if—under the 'integrated enterprise' approach—we establish a presumption that the parent is liable for all the acts adopted by the subsidiaries within the multinational group, or if we seek to engage the 'direct liability' of the company for failing to exercise due diligence in controlling the activities of its subsidiary, close monitoring of the subsidiary will be in the interest of the parent: instead of making it vulnerable to attempts to pierce the corporate veil, it may be seen as a way to avoid liability or as an insurance against the risk of being accused of being negligent in exercising oversight over the subsidiary's activities.

C. Corporations as networks of business partners

Supply chain management is the third area where the ghost of the 'sphere of influence' continues to haunt discussions on the human rights duties of corporations. Here too, a due diligence obligation is emerging, that largely responds to the same concerns that the notion of 'sphere of influence' initially sought to address, and replicates its solutions. Principle 17 of the Guiding Principles on Business and Human Rights provides that human rights due diligence should cover 'adverse human rights impacts that the business enterprise may cause or contribute to through its own activities, or which may be directly linked to its operations, products or services by its business relationships'. Similarly, the OECD Guidelines on Multinational Enterprises, as revised in 2011, provide that business enterprises domiciled in OECD should 'seek ways to prevent or mitigate adverse human rights impacts that are directly linked to their business operations, products or services by a business relationship, even if they do not contribute to those impacts'. The Commentary to these Guidelines explains that meeting this expectation:

> would entail an enterprise, acting alone or in co-operation with other entities, as appropriate, to use its leverage to influence the entity causing the adverse human rights impact to prevent or mitigate that impact. 'Business relationships' include relationships with business partners, entities in its supply chain, and any other non-state or state entity directly linked to its business operations, products or services. Among the factors that will enter into the determination of the appropriate action in such situations are the enterprise's leverage over the entity concerned, how crucial the relationship is to the enterprise, the severity of the impact, and whether terminating the relationship with the entity itself would have adverse human rights impacts.[81]

[81] OECD Guidelines on Multinational Enterprises (as revised on 25 May 2011), Commentary, para. 43.

The OECD Guidelines on Multinational Enterprises also provide that:

> In addition to addressing adverse impacts in relation to matters covered by the *Guidelines*, [multinational enterprises should] encourage, where practicable, business partners, including suppliers and sub-contractors, to apply principles of responsible business conduct compatible with the *Guidelines*.[82]

Business enterprises increasingly operate as part of large networks of suppliers, subcontractors, and clients, and it may be difficult for the enterprise to systematically monitor the activities of all its business partners. However, due diligence may be exercised in two ways. First, a reference to human rights, including the core labour rights and economic and social rights such as the right to health or the right to food—all of which can be directly affected by corporate behaviour—could be inserted systematically in any contract that establishes a long-term, ongoing relationship between an enterprise and its business partner.[83] Secondly,

> where due diligence on every individual relationship is impossible, business enterprises should identify general areas where the risk of adverse human rights impacts is most significant, whether due to certain suppliers' or clients' operating context, the particular operations, products or services involved, or other relevant considerations, and prioritize these for human rights due diligence. This would include, for example, agricultural products sourced from suppliers in an area known for child labour; security services provided by contractors or forces in areas of conflict or weak governance and rule of law; and drug trials conducted through partners in areas of low education, literacy and legal safeguards.[84]

The leverage a business enterprise may exercise on its business partners is usually referred to as an element to be taken into consideration in order to assess whether it has acted with the required due diligence as regards that partner's impacts on human rights. In scenarios where the business partner is not in fact dependent, such influence may be difficult or indeed impossible to exercise. This may be the case, for instance, of a supplier with a large number of clients, or one on whom the buyer depends for an essential supply for which they are few or no other sellers on the market. However, the option of cutting off relationships must always be considered, even if the business partner cannot be influenced, at least where the partnership is not essential to a core activity of the business enterprise concerned. In addition, there are a number of tools business enterprises could use in order to ensure that they manage the supply chain responsibly, taking into account their human rights due diligence responsibilities. The OECD Guidelines on Multinational Enterprises refer for instance to influencing suppliers 'through contractual arrangements such as management contracts, pre-qualification

[82] OECD Guidelines on Multinational Enterprises (as revised on 25 May 2011), II. General Policies, para. 13.

[83] On the rise of this tendency, see L.C. Backer, 'Economic Globalization and the Rise of Efficient Systems of Global Private Lawmaking: Wal-Mart as Global Legislator', 39 *University of Connecticut Law Review* (2007), 1739–1784.

[84] The Corporate Responsibility to Respect Human Rights: An Interpretive Guide, Office of the High Commissioner for Human Rights, advance unedited version (November 2011), para. 7.8 (internal quotation marks omitted).

requirements for potential suppliers, voting trusts, and licence or franchise agreements',[85] adding:

22. Appropriate responses with regard to the business relationship may include continuation of the relationship with a supplier throughout the course of risk mitigation efforts; temporary suspension of the relationship while pursuing ongoing risk mitigation; or, as a last resort, disengagement with the supplier either after failed attempts at mitigation, or where the enterprise deems mitigation not feasible, or because of the severity of the adverse impact. The enterprise should also take into account potential social and economic adverse impacts related to the decision to disengage.

23. Enterprises may also engage with suppliers and other entities in the supply chain to improve their performance, in co-operation with other stakeholders, including through personnel training and other forms of capacity building, and to support the integration of principles of responsible business conduct compatible with the *Guidelines* into their business practices. Where suppliers have multiple customers and are potentially exposed to conflicting requirements imposed by different buyers, enterprises are encouraged, with due regard to anti-competitive concerns, to participate in industry-wide collaborative efforts with other enterprises with which they share common suppliers to coordinate supply chain policies and risk management strategies, including through information-sharing.[86]

Imposing on corporations certain obligations in the area of economic and social rights is thus justified theoretically, where they exercise a command over goods or resources that are essential to the enjoyment of those rights (whether as a result of the position they acquired in the market or whether by decree). It has also come to be accepted that corporations have a duty to control the economic actors over which they can exercise an influence, due to investment links within the corporate group or through supply chain management. Although the notion of 'sphere of influence' has fallen into disrepute, what it aimed at effecting is now achieved, to a large extent, by the notion of 'due diligence', which has become its functional substitute.

Courts have nevertheless been reluctant to impose on corporations duties on the basis of economic and social rights such as the right to health, to education, or to food. The next section discusses two motives that could explain this reluctance. One is that corporations should be left free to pursue the objectives they see fit for them, and that they should not be imposed to contribute to broader aims related to social justice. Another is that freedom of contract, which companies exercise when they hire, when they buy, or when they sell, should be respected as fundamental. Both of these ideas betray a common misunderstanding: they equate the corporate body with a natural person, elevating a profit-making device to the dignity of the individual human being.

[85] OECD Guidelines on Multinational Enterprises (as revised on 25 May 2011), II. General Policies, Commentaries, para. 21.

[86] OECD Guidelines on Multinational Enterprises (as revised on 25 May 2011), II. General Policies, Commentaries, paras. 21–23.

5. May Courts Enforce Economic and Social Rights Against Corporate Actors?

Courts have routinely imposed on corporations certain duties that correspond to economic and social rights. They have done so, for instance, by enforcing minimum wage legislation, or by imposing levels of compensation in cases of unfair dismissal that take into account the cost of living and the rate of inflation.[87] The direct application of human rights law in private litigation—the so-called 'horizontal' application of human rights law—has been developing in recent years, and it has extended to labour rights and to economic and social rights.[88]

Yet, this development has not gone unchallenged. Courts may fear that the application to 'horizontal' private relationships of norms designed to regulate the 'vertical' relationships between the state and the individuals under its jurisdiction, will draw them into political controversy, and oblige them to make difficult choices between the application of private law doctrines and the requirements of human rights law. For instance, when it was proposed in South Africa to make certain of the provisions of the Interim Bill of Rights applicable to bodies and persons other than state organs 'where just and equitable', thus leaving it to the courts to decide when such horizontal application of constitutional rights was justified,[89] the judiciary expressed its scepticism. It stated:

> This clause will create great uncertainty and confusion. The reference to the application of the Bill to 'other bodies and persons' implies the horizontal application of the Bill. This entails the application of the Bill to, inter alia, the actions of companies and corporations (whether public or private), partnerships, societies and clubs, and all individuals. In consequence, all private relationships will be governed by the Bill of Rights. The phrase quoted above can, and notionally will, be interpreted to mean that the provisions of the Bill override the common law.[90]

[87] See Argentine Supreme Court, *Jáuregui, Manuela Yolanda c. Unión Obreros y Empleados del Plástico*, of 7 August 1984, cited by Courtis, 331, note 23. Courtis cites a range of cases decided by the Argentine Supreme Court that impose on the state to define the minimum wage, the level of state pension, or social security allocations, taking into account these requirements; these determinations as a matter of course reflect on the duties of the employer towards the employees.

[88] J.A. Hessbruegge, 'Human Rights Violations Arising from Conduct of Non-State Actors', 11 *Buffalo Human Rights Law Review* (2005), 21–88; D. Oliver and J. Fedtke (eds.), *Human Rights and the Private Sphere: A Comparative Study* (New York: Routledge Cavendish, 2007) (providing a comparison of the role of human rights in inter-individual litigation in a range of jurisdictions).

[89] 7th Report of the Technical Committee on Fundamental Rights (29 July 1993).

[90] M. Corbett, Memorandum submitted on behalf of the Judiciary of South Africa on the Draft Interim Bill of Rights (3 September 1993), at 3 (cited by Jörg Fedtke, 'From Indirect to Direct Effect in South Africa: A System in Transition', ch. 11 in Oliver and Jörg Fedtke (eds.), *Human Rights and the Private Sphere*, cited supra, at 369). The controversy was put to rest even before the adoption of the Final Constitution in 1996, by the insertion into the 1993 Interim Constitution (Constitution of the Republic of South Africa Act 200 of 1993) of Section 35(3), providing that '[I]n the interpretation of any law and the application and development of the common law and customary law, a court shall have due regard to the spirit, purport and objects' of the Bill of Rights.

Taking into account these concerns, in part at least, the 1996 Final Constitution now uses a formula that is more cautious as regards the direct applicability of the Bill of Rights to private relationships.[91] But it remains important to inquire about the reasons for the scepticism that was expressed then. Two reasons, we may suppose, explain these doubts. First, in contrast to states, corporate actors are not supposed to act in pursuance of the public interest: imposing on them the requirement that they contribute to the fulfilment of economic and social rights therefore leads to a conflict with their primary purpose, which is to make profit, and this is a conflict which the courts may find difficult to arbitrate. Second, most cases in which they are asked to take human rights into account, are cases where corporations in fact have entered into contracts with other parties, on the basis of mutual consent. Although such contractual arrangements may lead to restrictions to the human rights of those concerned, whether the underpaid employee, the small farmer supplying raw materials to the processing company, or the client to which water is being delivered, should this element of consent not suffice to remove all doubts as to the acceptability of the restriction?

A. Corporate actors and the public interest

It is of course the duty of the state to act in the public interest, and it is the duty of courts to ensure that, in imposing restrictions on human rights, it remains faithful to what the public interest requires. In contrast, private persons pursue a variety of aims, and it would violate an elementary principle of moral pluralism to impose on all individuals that they only act in accordance with some predefined notion of what serves the common good.

But the situation of corporations is different. With the exception of organizations whose ethos is based on religion or conviction or which are set up for political aims—what the German doctrine calls *Tendenzbetriebe*[92] —corporations in general

[91] See Constitution of South Africa, section 8: '(1) The Bill of Rights applies to all law, and binds the legislature, the executive, the judiciary and all organs of state. (2) A provision of the Bill of Rights binds a natural or a juristic person if, and to the extent that, it is applicable, taking into account the nature of the right and the nature of any duty imposed by the right'. For a discussion, see Johan van der Walt, 'Progressive Indirect Application of the Bill of Rights: Towards a Co-operative Relation Between Common-Law and Constitutional Jurisprudence', *South African Journal of Human Rights*, vol. 17 (2001), 341–363.

[92] Courts have recognized that legal persons may in certain circumstances invoke a right to 'expressive freedom of association'. This benefits not only churches, but also (non-religious) organizations who wish to convey certain messages or values. It may for instance justify them in choosing whom to employ on the basis of criteria that may otherwise be suspect, or in choosing who can join as a member (for US federal courts, see in particular *Roberts v United States Jaycees*, 468 US 609, 622 (1984); *Boy Scouts of America and Monmouth Council*, et al. *v Dale*, 530 US 640 (2000); in the case law of the (now abolished) European Commission on Human Rights, see *Van der Heijden v the Netherlands* (Appl. No. 11002/84, dec. of 8 March 1985, *D.R.*, 41, p. 264; and see Eur. Ct. HR (4th sect.), *Case of Associated Society of Locomotive Engineers & Firemen (ASLEF) v the United Kingdom* (Appl. No. 11002/05), judgment of 27 February 2007, para. 39 ('Where associations are formed by people, who, espousing particular values or ideals, intend to pursue common goals, it would run counter to the very effectiveness of the freedom at stake if they had no control over their membership. By way of example, it is uncontroversial that religious bodies and political parties can generally regulate their membership to include only those who share their beliefs and ideals')). This is not the place for exploring the specific

are established for one main purpose, which is to create wealth for their owners. Unlike individuals, they have neither a life plan, nor a conscience. The directors of the corporation in principle should act according to their fiduciary duty to the shareholders, and they should aim therefore at maximizing profits. Therefore—and this was the central message of jurists like Adolf Berle or E. Merrick Dodd, writing in the 1930s—it is entirely legitimate to impose on corporations the requirement that they also pursue other aims, serving the public purpose, and contributing, in particular, to the fulfilment of economic and social rights which they may help realize. There is no freedom of conscience issue at stake here, nor is there any right to privacy to be opposed: by imposing on corporations the requirement that they comply with certain requirements related to the human rights of those whom they interact with, the state simply does indirectly, through them, what it otherwise would do directly, through the acts of public authorities.

The way courts assess restrictions to the rights of workers provides a good illustration of this. Such restrictions, in principle, should only be allowed based not on the 'tastes' of the employer or any view the employer holds about the 'good life', but based only on 'business necessity'; that is, the constraints of a competitive market environment. The market itself may be seen to occupy an intermediate position, between the public sphere (in which the state seeks to fulfil the public interest) and the private sphere (in which individuals are free to make choices that correspond to their beliefs and convictions, whether or not these are aligned with those of the majority): in the market sphere, economic actors are expected to behave according to certain norms that can be objectively ascertained, and in which their subjective preferences should in principle be irrelevant, or play at best a marginal role.

This may not always be easy to apply. For instance, the conduct of an employer based exclusively on what is objectively in the interest of the business enterprise may lead to deference to the 'tastes' of the public, which may be tainted by social norms and discriminatory attitudes.[93] But the point made here is normative, not factual: it is that it would not be acceptable for an employer, or for any other market actor, to adopt decisions on the basis of such illegitimate motives, for instance by refusing to recruit an employee who would be in contact with the clientele from which hostile reactions are feared, or who may not be welcome by his or her colleagues.[94]

case of such organizations, although it cannot be excluded that, in some cases, this will justify exempting them from duties they would otherwise be imposed to contribute to a certain economic or social right: the case of catholic hospitals which may refuse to perform abortions or to provide euthanasia, or that of catholic schools refusing to teach other religions make this clear.

[93] See, e.g. C. Sunstein, 'Why Markets Won't Stop Discrimination', *Social Philosophy and Policy*, vol. 8 (1992), 21 (reproduced in *Free Markets and Social Justice* (Oxford: Oxford University Press, 1997)).

[94] See for instance before the European Court of Justice, Case C-54/07, *Centrum voor gelijkheid van kansen en voor racismebestrijding v Firma Feryn NV*, [2008] ECR I-5187, and especially the opinion of AG Poiares Maduro (citing the work of Cass Sunstein referred to previously, and noting that it would not be acceptable for an employer to justify discrimination on grounds of ethnicity by referring to the preferences expressed by its clients).

Once it is acknowledged that corporations are legal constructs, without a 'will' of their own, and that they are established from the start as a means to fulfil certain social ends—in particular, to encourage risk-taking and the growth of competitive markets—it follows naturally that such ends can be redefined and expanded in the name of human rights. Consider for instance the consequences that follow from the recognition of the right to work in international human rights law. Such a right has been variously decribed as imposing on states a duty to formulate and implement an employment policy with a view to 'stimulating economic growth and development, raising levels of living, meeting manpower requirements, and overcoming unemployment and underemployment',[95] or to adopt 'effective measures to increase the resources allocated to reducing the unemployment rate, in particular among women, the disadvantaged and marginalized'.[96] But a core obligation of states in this regard—one that states must comply with even if they face important resource constraints—is also to ensure non-discrimination and equal protection in employment, and thus in particular to ensure 'the right of access to employment, especially for disadvantaged and marginalized individuals and groups, permitting them to live a life of dignity'.[97] It follows again that 'business necessity' alone is not sufficient, if that leads to take as given certain routine ways of organizing the workplace, of recruiting the workforce, or of defining the tasks of the individual workers, that result in excluding certain categories of workers (or potential workers) and prohibiting them from acceding to employment or from realizing their full potential within the organization. In short, there is nothing sacrosanct about the market as an institution, and certainly nothing that compares to the recognized freedom of individuals in choosing their life plans.

D. Freedom of contract

In *Carna Foods Ltd v Eagle Star Insurance Co Ltd (Ireland) Ltd*,[98] where the issue arose whether an insurance company could without providing a justification refuse to renew an insurance contract when the prospective client had no other insurance company to turn to, McCracken J expressed concern as to the effect of imposing constitutional rights directly in the context of purely commercial relationships between private parties, describing it as a 'serious interference in the contractual position of parties in a commercial contract'. This, we may suspect, is a second

[95] ILO Convention (No. 122) concerning Employment Policy, 1964 (entered into force on 15 July 1966), article 1, para. 1.

[96] Committee on Economic, Social and Cultural Rights, General Comment No. 18: The Right to Work (Article 6 of the International Covenant on Economic, Social and Cultural Rights) (2005), UN Doc. E/C.12/GC/18 (6 February 2006), para. 26.

[97] Committee on Economic, Social and Cultural Rights, General Comment No. 18: The Right to Work (Article 6 of the International Covenant on Economic, Social and Cultural Rights) (2005), UN Doc. E/C.12/GC/18 (6 February 2006), para. 31.

[98] [1995] 1 IR 526 (HC); [1997] 2 ILRM 499 (SC). For a discussion, see S. Mullally, 'Equality Guarantees in Irish Constitutional Law: The Myth of Constitutionalism and the Neutral State', in T. Murphy and P. Twomey (eds.), *Ireland's Evolving Constitution, 1937–97: Collected Essays* (Oxford: Hart Publishing, 1998), 147–162.

reason why courts have sometimes been reluctant to impose on corporate actors that they contribute to economic and social rights. As noted by Heilbroner, any power such actors may exert, although it may be considerable in fact, remains qualitatively distinct from that of the state:

> Even if we imagined that all capital was directed by a single capitalist, the sentence of starvation that could be passed by his refusal to sell his commodities or to buy labor power differs from the sentence of the king who casts his opponents into a dungeon to starve, because the capitalist has no legal right to forbid his victims from moving elsewhere, or from appealing to the state or other authorities against himself. Thus, the domination of the merchant, for instance, resides in his legal right not to sell to those who will not meet his price—a right that can involve great social deprivation, as in the case of a famine, but that is nonetheless entirely free of direct personal coercion: the merchant cannot require a potential buyer to become an actual one [...] However harsh the domination of capital may be, it therefore always operates at a remove, and with a degree of voluntary submission implicit in the potential refusal of the other party to accept the capitalist's terms, an option generally absent from precapitalist modes of domination.[99]

This, however, should not imply that freedom of contract, even where it has been exercised, should always trump the requirements of human rights. As recognized by Heilbroner, although it may be of a different kind, private compulsion may exercise an equally powerful constraint on the free will of the individual right-holder. In situations where the right-holder is in a situation of need and where he or she faces few alternatives (or none at all, as in situations of monopoly or monopsony), in particular, the possibility for the private actor with whom the right-holder interacts to withhold certain goods or services (such as food, life-saving medical treatment, or a waged employment) may in fact lead to a form of coercion equivalent in practice to that at the disposal of the state.[100] Particularly since the rise of large-scale private organizations in the early 20th century, it is understood that the liberty of the individual whether or not to submit to certain conditions which another actor seeks to impose on him is not always more present in inter-individual (or 'horizontal') relationships, particularly in market relationships, than in the ('vertical') relationships between the state and the individual.[101]

It is therefore fitting that human rights courts have generally considered with suspicion the argument that the state should be allowed not to intervene in private contractual relationships, out of respect for the 'free will' embodied in such contracts. On the contrary, they have generally adopted the view that, while the

[99] R.L. Heilbroner, *The Nature and Logic of Capitalism* (New York: W.W. Norton & Co., 1985), 40.

[100] In addition, even in situations where 'coercion' is not present and where the right-holder seems to have consented 'freely' to certain restrictions, the State would be justified in seeking to remove certain obstacles to the individual making fully rational choices, for instance because of phenomena of addiction of myopia (i.e. the individual placing his short-term desires above his long-term interests): see R. Thaler and C. Sunstein, *Nudge: Improving Decisions About Health, Wealth, and Happiness* (New Haven: Yale University Press, 2008) (reviewing how individual choices may be guided—not forced—by reshaping the context in which they are made).

[101] See, in particular, R.L. Hale, 'Force and the State: A Comparison of Political and Economic Compulsion', 35 *Columbia Law Review* 149–201; R.L. Hale, 'Our Equivocal Constitutional Guarantees', 39 *Columbia Law Review* (1939), 563–594.

consent of the individual may be *necessary* to justify certain restrictions to his/her rights, such a consent, as expressed in contractual clauses, should never be considered, as such, a *sufficient* justification.[102] They have also recognized the dangers of allowing powerful private actors, such as large employers, to use their financial might to induce individuals to make certain choices, for instance as regards membership in a union: because of the strong imbalances of power in private relationships, it is the duty of the state to intervene and to impose compliance with human rights where such rights could be threatened as a result of such imbalances.[103]

6. Conclusion

In 1933, Justice Brandeis, then in his 15th year as a Justice on the United States Supreme Court, was the first magistrate to draw the full consequences of the findings of Berle and Means. Only months after the publication of their book, he noted:

Able, discerning scholars have pictured for us the economic and social results of [...] removing all limitations upon the size and activities of business corporations and of vesting in their managers vast powers once exercised by stockholders—results not designed by the states and long unsuspected. They show that size alone gives to giant corporations a social significance not attached ordinarily to smaller units of private enterprise. Through size, corporations, once merely an efficient tool employed by individuals in the conduct of private business, have become an institution—an institution which has brought such concentration of economic power that so-called private corporations are sometimes able to dominate the state. The typical business corporation of the last century, owned by a small group of individuals, managed by their owners, and limited in size by their personal wealth, is being supplanted by huge concerns in which the lives of tens or hundreds of thousands of employees and the property of tens or hundreds of thousands of investors are subjected, through the corporate mechanism, to the control of a few men. Ownership has been separated from control, and this separation has removed many of the checks which formerly operated to curb the misuse of wealth and power. And, as ownership of the shares is becoming continually more dispersed, the power which formerly accompanied ownership is becoming increasingly concentrated in the hands of a few. The changes thereby wrought in the lives of the workers, of the owners, and of the general public are so fundamental and far-reaching as to lead these scholars to compare the evolving 'corporate system' with the feudal system, and to lead other men of insight

[102] Eur. Ct. HR (1st sect.), dec. of 7 November 2002, *Madsen v Denmark*, Appl. no. 58341/00 (inadmissibility); and Eur. Ct. HR (4th sect.), dec. of 9 March 2004, *Wretlund v Sweden*, Appl. no. 46210/99 (inadmissibility).

[103] See, e.g. Eur. Ct. HR (2nd sect.), *Wilson, National Union of Journalists and Others v the United Kingdom* (Appl. nos. 30668/96, 30671/96 and 30678/96), judgment of 2 July 2002, § 47 (finding that the United Kingdom had failed to protect freedom of association, as guaranteed under Article 11 of the European Convention on Human Rights, because 'domestic law did not prohibit the employer from offering an inducement to employees who relinquished the right to union representation', thus substantially reducing the ability for unions to gain the support of workers).

and experience to assert that this 'master institution of civilized life' is committing it to the rule of a plutocracy.[104]

Brandeis intended the reference to Berle and Means—he also quoted Veblen—to support his view that the constitutionality of restrictions imposed on the operations of business should be based on facts, not ideology—on an appreciation of the real power that companies yield, rather than on an idealized representation of the marketplace. Then still unorthodox, this view now enjoys such a currency that it may be difficult to imagine how the opposite view ever could have prevailed. Yet three generations later we are still to reap the full consequences of the concerns that he expressed.

[104] *Louis K. Liggett Co. v Lee*, 288 US 517, 564–565 (1933) (Brandeis, J., partially diss.).

IV

THE RELATIONSHIP BETWEEN ESC RIGHTS AND OTHER LEGAL REGIMES

8

Trade and Investment Agreements

What Role for Economic, Social, and Cultural Rights in International Economic Law?

Hans Morten Haugen

1. Introduction

Are economic, social, and cultural rights actually taken into account when arbitration or adjudicating bodies (panels or tribunals) seek to solve disputes arising under international economic law (IEL)? The term 'human rights' is seldom applied in the substantive provisions of trade or investment agreements, but the exception provisions in these agreements are becoming more encompassing, covering subject matter that is also covered by human rights treaties. Recent academic contributions in the realm of international investment law differ on whether human rights obligations are actually taken into account.[1] In general, IEL jurisprudence is influenced by principles and rules of public international law. The distinction between principles and rules is explained by Robert Alexy by stating that '[r]ules are norms that, given the satisfaction of specific conditions, definitively command, forbid, permit, or empower. Thus they can be characterized as "definitive commands"',

[1] A full issue of *Transnational Dispute Management*, no. 1–2013, available at <http://www.transnational-dispute-management.com/journal-browse-issues-toc.asp?key=46> (last accessed 14 November 2013), is devoted to the theme 'Aligning Human Rights and Investment Protection'; see particularly U. Kriebaum, 'Foreign Investments & Human Rights: The Actors and Their Different Roles', and S.B. Leinhardt, 'Some Thoughts on Foreign Investors' Responsibilities to Respect Human Rights'; see also D.A. Desierto and B. Simma, 'Bridging the Public Interest Divide: Committee Assistance for Investor-host State Compliance with the ICESCR' exploring human rights procedures that can be applied in order to ensure that human rights are taken into account. Other recent contributions include A. Tanzi, 'Recent Trends in International Investment Arbitration and the Protection of Human Rights in the Public Sector', in N. Boschiero (ed.), *International Courts and the Development of International Law: Essays in Honour of Tullio Treves* (Heidelberg: Springer 2013), 587–598, finding that investment law and human rights are gradually being harmonized by the application of the due diligence requirement; for arguments that human rights are ignored by investment tribunals, see European Centre for Constitutional and Human Rights, *Human Rights inapplicable in International Investment Arbitration? A commentary on the non-admission of ECCHR and Indigenous Communities as Amici Curiae before the ICSID tribunal* (Berlin: ECCHR 2012), criticizing the two cases against Zimbabwe; see *infra* note 3.

while principles 'are norms commanding that something must be realized to the highest degree that is actually and legally possible'.[2] However, the degree of this influence differs between the various fields of IEL and the actual jurisdiction of the bodies and tribunals. Many investment agreements, including the 2012 US Model Treaty, explicitly state that 'tribunals shall decide the issue in dispute in accordance with [...] applicable rules of international law'.[3]

This chapter also explores how home states (where the head management is located) and host states (where the economic activity takes place) are themselves under an obligation to assess the impacts of the IEL treaties that they have ratified or are about to ratify. For the home state, this is essentially about how to supervise, advise, or withhold incentives to its economic actors in order to ensure that it does not contribute to human rights violations in other states. For the host state, this is essentially about ensuring that the economic activities it seeks to facilitate by entering into the agreements do not negatively impact on its human rights obligations. A guide to human rights impact assessment of trade and investment agreements has been formulated by the UN Special Rapporteur on the right to food.[4] IEL treaties tend to have effective enforcement mechanisms with robust sanctions in the form of compensation or suspension of concessions, in cases where breaches of treaties have been found or there is a non-compliance with a court, tribunal, or judicial body ruling.[5] The fear of being subject to threats of, or actually having been brought before, costly tribunal proceedings provides disincentives for undertaking measures that would be in line with their human rights obligations. The phrase 'regulatory chill' describes this effect of IEL treaties on states.

While IEL covers a wide range of fields,[6] this chapter will place emphasis on trade and investment. Intellectual property rights (IPR) will also be addressed. Both IPR and international investment law recognize and regulate rights for both natural and legal persons.

[2] R. Alexy, 'Legal Reasoning and Rational Discourse', 5 *Ratio Juris* (1992), 143–152, at 145.

[3] 2012 US Model Bilateral Investment Treaty, Art. 30.1 (extracts); see also ICSID Convention Art. 42 and NAFTA Art. 1131. This approach is broader than the jurisdiction and applicable law as specified in the WTO's Dispute Settlement Understanding Articles 3.2 and 19. A recent ICSID panel, however, stated that the term applicable international law 'does not incorporate the universe of international law', see *Pezold v Zimbabwe, ARB/10/15* and *Border Timbers Ltd. v Zimbabwe, ARB/10/25, Procedural Order No. 2*, 26 June 2012, para. 57.

[4] Special Rapporteur on the right to food, Appendix: Guiding Principles on human rights impact assessments of trade and investment agreements, UN Doc. A/HRC/19/59/Add.5, (2011). While not endorsing the Guiding Principles as such, the Human Rights Council, in resolution 19/7, *The right to food* (2012), para. 42 took note 'with appreciation of the report of the Special Rapporteur'.

[5] Art. 22 of WTO's Dispute Settlement Understanding lists both suspension of concessions and compensation, in cases of non-implementation of the panels' or Appellate Body's rulings. So far, compensation has been decided in four cases: *EC—Bananas (WT/DS27), EC—Hormones (WT/DS26 & WT/DS48), US—Tax treatment for 'foreign sales corporations' (WT/DS108)* and *Canada—Export of aircrafts (WT/DS70 & WT/DS71).*

[6] Finance, taxation, and competition legislation are among the fields that will not be covered in this chapter.

Trade is regulated by the World Trade Organization (WTO), regional trade agreement (RTAs),[7] and free trade agreements (FTAs). Increasingly, these agreements include chapters on investment. In addition, approximately 3,200 agreements have been agreed between two or more states specifically to regulate rights for investors.[8] There have been failed attempts, both in the WTO[9] and in the OECD,[10] at having a multilateral investment agreement. While the WTO manages a system for dispute settlement between states, the investor–state arbitration under investment agreements is built on the model of commercial arbitration. The main difference between the two is that investor–state arbitration is done under international law, and hence should take into account states' obligations under international law.

Human rights enter the trade and foreign direct investment (FDI) realm in various ways; first, by giving legitimacy to arguments relating to investors' property rights—that is to say, by framing these as human rights issues. Second, it establishes human rights as defences against further trade and investment liberalization, as the impact on affected communities from certain economic activities might be negative, even if there are overall positive impacts for the economy as a whole. Third, it establishes minimum requirements on the conduct of public policies and economic activities, unlike the more instrumental justifications and objectives

[7] According to the WTO, 297 RTA are in force, and another 192 have been notified to the WTO; see the list available at <http://www.wto.org/english/tratop_e/region_e/region_e.htm> (last accessed 14 September 2013). Many contain IPR provisions which go beyond what is required under TRIPS, and are therefore referred to as 'TRIPS+'; see L. Liberti, *Intellectual Property Rights in International Investment Agreements An Overview*, OECD Working Papers on International Investment 2010/01 (Paris: OECD, 2010).

[8] According to UNCTAD, there are 2,857 bilateral investment agreements (BITs) and 339 other international investment agreements (IIAs); see UNCTAD, *World Investment Report 2013: Global Value Chains: Investment and Trade for Development* (New York and Geneva: UNCTAD, 2013), 100. The number of new BITs and IIAs was particularly high in 1994–1998 and 2001, with more than 170 BITs and other IIAs agreed each of these years; see *International Investment Agreements: Trends and Emerging Issues* (New York and Geneva: UNCTAD, 2006), 6. Also 2009 saw a considerable increase from previous years, see UNCTAD, *World Investment Report 2013: Global Value Chains: Investment and Trade for Development* (New York and Geneva: UNCTAD, 2013), 102. Some BITs include IPR provisions; see UNCTAD, *Intellectual Property Protection in International Investment Arrangements, IAA Monitor No. 1 (2007).*

[9] The Singapore Declaration (WT/MIN(96)/DEC), adopted at the first WTO Ministerial Conference, reads in para. 20 on investment and competition (extract): 'the work undertaken shall not prejudge whether negotiations will be initiated in the future'; hence investment was subsequently referred to among the 'Singapore issues'. In 2001, the attempt of having investments as a part of the Doha Development Agenda, resulted in the postponement of the decision to the subsequent Ministerial conference, to be taken 'by explicit consensus'; see Doha Ministerial Declaration (WT/MIN(01)/DEC), para. 20. In 2003, the draft declaration presented before the start of the Conference included a para. with two alternatives, differing on whether negotiations were to commence in order to 'establish an agreement to secure transparent, stable and predictable conditions' for foreign direct investments; see Draft Cancún Ministerial Text, para. 13 and Annex D, para. 1; available at <http://www.wto.org/english/thewto_e/minist_e/min03_e/draft_decl_e.htm> (last accessed 22 April 2013). The pressure by the EU to discuss investments *before* EU had been forthcoming on agriculture, explains the breakdown of the negotiations.

[10] Documents from the 1995–1998 negotiations on the proposed Multilateral Agreement in Investments are available at <http://www.oecd.org/daf/mai/> (last accessed 14 November 2013).

behind trade and investment promotion. This chapter will primarily address the second approach and, to some extent, the third.

An introduction of the legal and policy environment for addressing issues relating to IEL and human rights will be given, followed by an analysis of specific provisions of WTO, FTA, and BIT treaties. How human rights can be introduced by international tribunals when seeking to resolve disputes will then be analysed. This will be followed by an analysis of some of the prominent cases from international investment disputes in light of interpretative principles, including how to justify measures by their relationship to legitimate policy objectives, the essence of the proportionality test, and what is legitimately included in the fair and equitable treatment standard under international investment law. Finally, the chapter will identify whether states have a duty to give more weight to their human rights obligations when agreements under IEL are negotiated, implemented, and enforced.

This chapter will not assess the procedural aspects of disputes, including issues of enhanced transparency, the possibility to submit amicus curiae briefs, and the institutionalization of an appeals system for investment disputes similar to what is found in the WTO. Awards from arbitration tribunals can be annulled by subsequent decisions by a new tribunal. On amicus curiae briefs, it must be acknowledged that the International Centre on the Settlement of Investment Disputes (ICSID), the United Nations Commission on International Trade Law (UNCITRAL), and the North American Free Trade Association (NAFTA) allow for third party participation.[11]

[11] ICSID Arbitration Rules (2006), Art. 37(2); UNCITRAL Arbitration Rules (2010), Art. 17(5); North American Free Trade Commission Statement of on Non-Disputing Party Participation (7 October 2003), para. A.1; on amicus curiae, see in general C. Reiner and C. Schreuer, 'Human Rights and International Investment Arbitration', in P-M Dupuy, F. Francioni, and E.-U. Petersmann (eds.), *Human Rights in International Investment Law and Arbitration* (Oxford & New York: Oxford University Press, 2009), 82–96, at 90–93; J. Harrison, 'Human Rights Arguments in Amicus Curiae Submissions: Promoting Social Justice?', in Dupuy et al. (eds.), *Human Rights in International Investment Law and Arbitration* (Oxford & New York: Oxford University Press, 2009), 396–421. For a case where the tribunal accepted amicus curiae submissions from no less than three parties, one raising explicit human rights concern under the International Covenant on Civil and Political Rights (ICCPR) Art. 27 but said that it 'does not reach the particular issues addressed by these submissions', see *Glamis Gold v USA, UNCITRAL, Award*, 8 June 2009, para. 8, see also paras. 267–286. For a case where the tribunal rejected amicus curiae submissions, because the submissions were allegedly 'unrelated to the matters before the Arbitral Tribunals'; see *Pezold et al. v Zimbabwe, supra* note 3, at para. 57; see also ECCHR, *supra* note 1; S. Schadendorf, 'Human Rights Arguments in Amicus Curiae Submissions: Analysis of ICSID and NAFTA Investor-State Arbitrations', *Transnational Dispute Management*, supra note 1, at 10–15; and Eric de Brabandere, 'Human Rights Considerations in International Investment Arbitration', in M. Fitzmaurice and P. Merkouris (eds.), *The Interpretation and Application of the European Convention of Human Rights: Legal and Practical Implications* (Leiden & Boston: Martinus Nijhoff Publishing, 2012), 183–215; both concluding that investment arbitration panels are reluctant to accept amicus curiae submissions, but that where they have been accepted, the panels tend to side with the arguments put forward in the submissions.

2. Human Rights and IEL

Why did human rights bodies at the end of the 1990s become more involved with IEL actors, and is this higher involvement reflected in the actual wording of the relevant human rights treaties to which their mandates relate? The emphasis in this context will be on the International Covenant on Economic, Social and Cultural Rights (ICESCR) and the Committee on Economic, Social and Cultural Rights (CESCR). Turning to soft law, there will be a review of what is said about both trade and investment and human rights in the Millennium Summit documents, adopted in 2000, 2005, and 2010. Finally, relevant documents from the former Special Representative of the Secretary-General on the Issue of Human Rights and Transnational Corporations and other Business Enterprises (Special Representative) will be analysed. The Human Rights Council endorsed his Guiding Principles on Business and Human Rights in 2011.[12]

A. Human rights treaties

While human rights have been a part of the UN's mandate from its inception,[13] only since the late 1990s has attention been paid to how international human rights treaties can provide some guidance in the realm of trade and investments negotiations.[14] Five issues on which attention grew in the 1990s explain this awakening, all of which can be negatively impacted by the implementation of IEL agreements: first, the issue of access to medicines in the context of IPR; second, the expansion of patent rights and plant breeders rights, whose broad scope might encompass plants developed and used by local communities—being neither recognized nor compensated; third, the privatization of public services, to be provided by corporations based on user payments; fourth, the increased emphasis on enhancing food and other exports—in order to gain hard currency to service debts—while people were suffering from hunger; and fifth, serious health consequences resulting from contamination of air, soil, and water. More recently,

[12] Resolution 17/4, *Human rights and transnational corporations and other business enterprises* (2011), para. 1. The Guiding Principles are outlined in Human Rights Council, Guiding Principles on Business and Human Rights: Implementing the United Nations 'Protect, Respect and Remedy' Framework, UN Doc. A/HRC/17/31, (2011).

[13] Responsibilities in relation to human rights were established in the UN Charter, both for states (Art. 56) and specialized agencies (Art. 59); see also the Vienna Declaration of 1993, UN Doc. A/CONF.157/23, para. 1, saying that human rights promotion and protection 'is the first responsibility of Governments'.

[14] The 1998 Statement on globalization by the Committee on Economic, Social and Cultural Rights (CESCR) calls for 'more systematic consideration of the impact upon human rights of particular trade and investment policies'. All statements by the CESCR are available at <http://www2.ohchr.org/english/bodies/cescr/statements.htm> (last accessed 14 November 2013). For diverse contributions analysing how international economic law can work in favour of the world's poor, see K. Nadakavukaren Schefer (ed.), *Poverty and the International Economic Legal System: Duties to the World's Poor* (New York: Cambridge University Press, 2013).

the transfer (or long-term lease) agreements of land to investors, the largest deals signed with foreign investors, became a grave concern.

All these issues are regulated by human rights provisions. The ICESCR states in Article 12(2)(c) that states 'shall take steps necessary for [...] [t]he prevention, treatment and control of epidemic and endemic [...] diseases'. This must include access to effective and affordable medicines. On plants and varieties, Article 15(1)(c) recognizes the right to benefit from the moral and material interests arising from one's innovative contributions, and the CESCR has confirmed that this provision also applies to the collective authorship of indigenous peoples.[15] In addition, Article 1(2) states that 'all peoples shall dispose of their natural wealth and resources [...] and shall in no case be deprived of its own means of subsistence'. The term 'peoples' applies to indigenous peoples.[16] On the privatization of public services, there is no substantive provision of the ICESCR regulating the conduct of corporate actors,[17] but Article 2(2) includes property status as one of the prohibited grounds for discrimination. Hence, persons who do have not their property regulated and included in property registers shall not on account of their property status be subject to subordinate public services or inadequate regulation or monitoring if others provide the services, such as water provision. Also concerns relating to affordability, which have been emphasized in the general comments on food, health, and water, are highly relevant in the context of the privatization of public services. On food trade, Article 11(2)(b) recognizes the 'problems of both food-importing and food-exporting countries', stating that states shall take measures to 'ensure an equitable distribution of world food supplies in relation to need'. This implies that food needs must influence food trade decisions.[18] On health impacts of industrial emissions, Article 12(2)(b) requires states to take steps necessary for

[15] General Comment No. 17, The right of everyone to benefit from the protection of the moral and material interests resulting from any scientific, literary or artistic production of which he or she is the author (Art. 15, paragraph 1 (c), of the Covenant), UN Doc. E/C.12/GC/17, para. 32. A position saying that Art. 15.1(c) 'does not cover anyone who can directly or indirectly benefit from existing intellectual property rights' (P. Cullet, 'Human Rights and Intellectual Property Protection in the TRIPS Era', 29 *Human Rights Quarterly* (2007), 403–430, at 425) has been refuted by the present author; see H.M. Haugen, *Technology and Human Rights: Friends or Foes? Highlighting Innovations Applying to Natural Resources and Medicine* (Dordrecht: Republic of Letters Publishing, 2011), ch. 3.

[16] As confirmed in the non-binding, but influential United Nations Declaration on the Rights of Indigenous Peoples (General Assembly resolution 61/295) Art. 3; see also Arts. 26, 28, and 31.

[17] Interestingly, General Comment No. 3, The nature of States parties obligations (Art. 2, para. 1) (1990) states in para. 8 that 'in terms of political and economic systems the Covenant is neutral'. Three subsequent General Comments—which are non-binding but nevertheless influences how states understand the respective rights—address under which circumstances a state may be in violation of the ICESCR, namely through 'failure to regulate activities of individuals or groups', General Comment No. 12, The right to adequate food (Art.11), E/C.12/1999/5), para. 19; or corporations, General Comment No. 14, The Right to the Highest Attainable Standard of Health (Art. 12), UN Doc. E/C.12/2000/4, para. 51; or water service providers, General Comment No. 15, The right to water (Arts. 11 and 12), UN Doc. E/C.12/2002/11, para. 44(b)(ii).

[18] For an analysis of ICESCR Art. 11.2(b), see H.M. Haugen, 'Food sovereignty: an appropriate approach to ensure the right to food?', 78 *Nordic Journal of International Law* (2009), 263–292, at 271–273.

'the improvement of all aspects of environmental and industrial hygiene'.[19] Finally, both Article 1(2) on peoples' rights over their natural wealth and resources and Article 11(2)(a) on an adequate standard of living are relevant human rights obligations that must be observed in land transfer agreements.

Article 1(2) is rather specific, by applying the phrase 'in no case'. While little interpretive material has been developed on the content of Article 1(2),[20] this wording must be understood as a prohibition against deprivation of any peoples' means of subsistence.[21] On the other hand, the relatively vague wording of Articles 11(2)(b) and 12(2)(c) should be noted. As 'shall' is the verb applied in the context of the taking of measures in both Article 11(2) and 12(2), this gives overall direction to states to take measures, but does not specify the exact content of these measures. The provisions do not, however, instruct the states exactly which measures to take, as long as these measures are contributing to 'achieving progressively the full realization of the rights recognized in the present Covenant', as stated by ICESCR Article 2(1).

Finally, on the general standing of these provisions in the wider context of international law, three of the provisions quoted do have a solid standing. Article 1(2), in the form of permanent sovereignty of peoples over their natural resources, has been recognized in a declaration that has been found by the International Court of Justice to represent customary international law.[22] The non-discrimination provision of Article 2(2) also has such status, and access to medicine, as is implicitly recognized in Article 12(2)(c) has been confirmed in several resolutions and in national jurisprudence.[23] Article 12(2)(b) on the improvement of all aspects of environmental and industrial hygiene has later been rephrased to a human right to a satisfactory or clean environment, which is increasingly recognized.[24]

[19] Moreover, the Additional Protocol to the American Convention on Human Rights in the Area of Economic, Social and Cultural Rights, recognizes in Art. 11 *everyone's* human right to a healthy environment, and the African Charter on Human and Peoples' Rights recognizes in Art. 24 *peoples'* human right to a satisfactory environment favourable to their development.

[20] For a comprehensive assessment of rights and obligations relating to peoples' free disposal of natural resources, see N. Schrijver, *Sovereignty Over Natural Resources: Balancing Rights and Duties* (New York: Cambridge University Press, 1997), particularly chs. 9 and 10.

[21] The International Law Commission has referred to the last sentence of Art. 1(2) in the context of obligations not affected by countermeasures (Art. 50 of the Draft Articles on State Responsibility); see ILC, Report on the work of its 53rd session, UN Doc A/56/10 (2001), 336.

[22] In *Case Concerning Armed Activities on the Territory of the Congo (DR Congo v Uganda)* Judgment, ICJ Reports 2005, p. 168, finds at p. 251, para. 244, that 'the principle of permanent sovereignty over natural resources [...] is a principle of customary international law', referring to A/RES/1803 (XVII) of 1962, and A/RES/3201 (S.VI) and A/RES/3281 (XXIX), both of 1974.

[23] The first resolution was resolution 2001/33 of the Commission on Human Rights, *Access to medication in the context of pandemics such as HIV/AIDS* (1 abstention), and the first time the General Assembly addressed the issue—with an identical title—was in 2003 with its resolution 58/179. Similar resolutions have been adopted, and the Human Rights Council resolution 12/24 (2009) was adopted without a vote; moreover, its resolution 15/22, *Right of everyone to the enjoyment of the highest attainable standard of physical and mental health* (adopted without a vote) addresses in para. 4(p) access to medicines in the context of IPR; see also UNAIDS and Canadian HIV/AIDS Legal Network, *Courting Rights: Case Studies in Litigating the Human Rights of People Living with HIV* (Geneva: UNAIDS, 2006).

[24] There are very few references to ICESCR Art. 12(2)(b); for one example, see Concluding observations of the Committee on Economic, Social and Cultural Rights: Argentina, UN Doc. E/1995/22, para. 241. There are, however, 140 constitutions that include explicit references to environmental

Conversely, neither Article 11(2)(b) on a fair food trade regime,[25] nor Article 11(2)(a) on an adequate standard of living, nor Article 15(1)(c) on recognition of individual and collective authorship as a human right,[26] have strong standing in international law.

B. Millennium Declaration and Millennium Development Goals (MDGs)

Fulfilling the MDGs, as approved at the Millennium Summit in 2000,[27] will considerably strengthen the realization of social rights, although the MDGs are not embedded in human rights language. As observed by Alston, 'the content of the MDG norms is much more limited than that of economic and social rights'.[28] It is relevant to remember the fact that MDG 8 addresses trade. Unlike the other MDGs, it does not contain any quantifications, but simply reads: 'Develop a global partnership for development'. Trade is referred to in the first target, and the last, sixth, target reads: 'In cooperation with the private sector, make available the benefits of new technologies, especially information and communications'.[29] This

rights in one form or another; see UN High Commissioner for Human Rights, Analytical study on the relationship between human rights and the environment, UN Doc. A/HRC/19/34 (2011) para. 30. For a review of international court cases finding that pollution has violated the human rights to life, health, food, and water, see International Network for Social, Economic and Cultural Rights, *Collective Report on Business and Human Rights, Submission to the 8th Session of the United Nations Human Rights Council* (New York, ESCR-Net, 2008), 9–12; see also J. Cassel, 'Enforcing Environmental Human Rights: Selected Strategies of US NGOs', 6 *Northwestern Journal of International Human Rights* (2007), 104–127; for an ongoing case affecting the Mayas in Guatemala, see Inter-American Court of Human Rights' precautionary measures (PM 260-07) relating to the dispute over GoldCorp's Marlin I mine in Guatemala, adopted 20 May 2010, available at <http://www.cidh.oas.org/medidas/2010.eng.htm> (last accessed 14 November 2013).

[25] Food trade concerns are, however, addressed in resolutions on *the right to food*; see General Assembly resolution 667158 (2012) [adopted 19 December 2011]—adopted without a vote), para. 21, and General Assembly resolution 22/9 (2013—adopted without a vote), para. 25, both calling upon states to (extract): 'ensure that their international policies of a political and economic nature, including international trade agreements, do not have a negative impact on the right to food in other countries'. In the WTO context, the disagreements between India and USA on the Special Safeguard Mechanism (SSM), allowing developing countries to increase their tariffs when faced with import surge, were the primary reason for the breakdown of the negotiations during the so-called 'July 2008 package' WTO meeting on ministerial level in 2008; for more background, see Haugen, *supra* note 18, at 263–264.

[26] The World Intellectual Property Organization's (WIPO) Intergovernmental Committee on Intellectual Property and Genetic Resources, Traditional Knowledge and Folklore, has developed three draft instruments (see *WIPO/GRTKF/IC/25/7, WIPO/GRTKF/IC/25/6*, and *WIPO/GRTKF/IC/25/7*, respectively) without any explicit references to human rights, but as explained in *WIPO/GRTKF/IC/16/4, The Protection of Traditional Cultural Expressions/Expressions of Folklore: Revised Objectives and Principles, Annex* (2010), 8 and 10, the general Guiding Principles (c) and (g) on respect for international agreements and respect for rights of indigenous peoples are implicitly referring to international human rights.

[27] , United Nations Millennium Declaration, UN Doc. A/RES/55/2, para. 19.

[28] P. Alston, *A Human Rights Perspective on the Millennium Development Goals: Paper prepared as a contribution to the work of the Millennium Project Task Force on Poverty and Economic Development* (undated), at 21, available at <http://www.hurilink.org/tools/HRsPerspectives_on_the_MDGs—Alston.pdf> (last accessed 21 October 2013).

[29] The indicators for target 8.6 are the only ones that apply numbers, applying to telephone lines, cellular subscribers, and internet users.

target is the only one that explicitly refers to the private sector, even if there can be no doubt that the involvement of the private sector is crucial for the achievement of other MDGs, particularly MDG 6.[30]

Turning to the outcome documents of the three summits addressing the MDGs, identifying how they address the issues of human rights, trade, and investments, the most comprehensive approach is taken in the 2005 declaration, calling for 'further mainstreaming of human rights throughout the United Nations system'.[31] This is an implicit affirmation of the responsibilities outlined in Article 59 of the UN Charter and Article 22 of the ICESCR—both referring to specialized agencies, but they must be read as to apply also to UN funds and programmes. These provisions, which are not adequately observed by most UN bodies,[32] were not included in the declaration emanating from the 2010 summit.[33]

What is most interesting in the three millennium declarations for the purpose here is the shift in assessing foreign investments in the 2005 and 2010 declarations. The 2005 declaration says that states should support developing countries' efforts in:

> attracting investments through, inter alia, achieving a transparent, stable and predictable investment climate with proper contract enforcement and respect for property rights and the rule of law and pursuing appropriate policy and regulatory frameworks that encourage business formation.[34]

Particularly, the phrase 'stable and predictable investment climate with proper contract enforcement' must be read as to establish high requirements for the host state. The term 'stable' implicitly refers to stabilization clauses which are found in several BITs, with the purpose of guarding against legislative changes,[35] and the term 'predictable' refers to fair and equitable treatment (FET) clauses, seeking to protecting the legitimate expectations of the investor.[36] In the ICSID *Tecmed* arbitral award, this is elaborated as follows: 'The foreign investor expects the host State to act in a consistent manner, free from ambiguity and totally transparently

[30] The Millennium Declaration, *supra* note 27, at para. 20 refers both to the pharmaceutical industry and the private sector.

[31] 2005 World Summit Outcome, UN Doc. A/RES/60/1, para. 126.

[32] For an analysis of the various UN specialized agencies, funds and programmes, see G. Oberleitner, 'A Decade of Mainstreaming Human Rights in the UN: Achievements, Failures, Challenges', 26 *Netherlands Quarterly of Human Rights* (2008), 359–390.

[33] While General Assembly resolution on *Keeping the promise: united to achieve the Millennium Development Goals*, UN Doc. A/65/RES/1, (2010) contains explicit references to human rights when outlining the contents of MDG 2, 3 and 6, see paras. 71(a), 72(g), and 76(b), respectively, and while human rights feature prominently throughout the document, the emphasis on mainstreaming human rights throughout the UN system is not repeated.

[34] 2005 World Summit Outcome, *supra* note 31, para. 25(a) (extract).

[35] M. Hirsch, 'Investment Tribunals and Human Rights', in Dupuy et al., *supra* note 11, 97–117, at 108.

[36] M. Hirsch, 'Investment Tribunals and Human Rights', in Dupuy et al., *supra* note 11, 97–117, at 109. For a detailed analysis of how the FET standard currently covers more situations than previously, see S.A. Spears, 'The Quest for Policy Space in a New Generation of International Investment Agreements, 13 *Journal of International Economic Law* (2010), 1037–1075, at 1052–1057.

in its relations with the foreign investor, so that it may know beforehand any and all rules and regulations that will govern its investments'.[37]

A totally different approach was taken in the 2010 summit declaration:

the emergence of rules-based regimes for international economic relations have meant that the space for national economic policy, that is, the scope for domestic policies, especially in the areas of trade, investment and international development, is now often framed by international disciplines, commitments and global market considerations. It is for each Government to evaluate the trade-off between the benefits of accepting international rules and commitments and the constraints posed by the loss of policy space.[38]

This must be understood as justifying a position that states should consider staying out of international trade and investment agreements, at least those that are too demanding and limiting of the domestic policy space. Other paragraphs in the 2010 summit declaration address FDI, one referring to FDI as 'vital'.[39]

None of the 18 'Thematic Think Pieces' written in the UN-wide process leading up to the adoption of the post-2015 development goals address trade and investments, while culture, disasters and migration are among the new topics on the post-2015 agenda. However, in the Report of the High-Level Panel of Eminent Persons on the Post-2015 Develoment Agenda, both trade and long-term investments are included in their proposed goal number 12, together with climate, foreign aid, tax evasion, and access to technology.[40]

C. Investment policies in light of the UN Guiding Principles and other non-binding documents

The main emphasis of this section will be on the UN Guiding Principles on Business and Human Rights, which were endorsed by the Human Rights Council in 2011.[41] The Working Group on the issue of human rights and transnational corporations and other business enterprises has been entrusted with a mandate to promote the Guiding Principles, including capacity-building and development of domestic legislation.[42]

The OECD Guidelines for Multinational Enterprises were updated in 2011 to include a separate section on human rights,[43] and these Guidelines reflect

[37] *Medioambientales Tecmed, SA v United Mexican States, ICSID Case No. ARB (AF)/00/2, Award, 29 May 2003*, para. 154; cases are available at <http://italaw.com/alphabetical_list_content.htm> (last accessed 14 September 2014); see also I. Knoll-Tudor, 'The Fair and Equitable Treatment Standard and Human Rights Norms', in Dupuy et al., *supra* note 11, 310–343.

[38] 2010 summit declaration, *supra* note 32, at para. 37 (extract).

[39] 2010 summit declaration, *supra* note 32, at para. 39.

[40] High-Level Panel of Eminent Persons on the Post-2015 Development Agenda, *A New Global Partnership: Eradicate Poverty and Transform Economies Through Sustainable Development* (New York: United Nations 2013), 31.

[41] Human Rights Council resolution 17/4, *supra* note 12, at para. 1. The Guidelines are contained in UN Doc. A/HRC/17/31.

[42] Human Rights Council resolution 17/4, *supra* note 12, at para. 6(c).

[43] OECD, *Guidelines for Multinational Enterprises, C(2011)59* (2011), 16 (section IV), with six paragraphs, which in substance address similar duties as do the UN Guiding Principles (prevent or

the content of the UN Guiding Principles. Moreover, Section I of the OECD Guidelines outlines general principles which, inter alia, specify that '[g]overnments have the right to prescribe the conditions under which multinational enterprises operate within their jurisdictions, subject to international law' and 'treat enterprises equitably and in accordance with international law and with their contractual obligations'.[44] The UN Guiding Principles are more detailed, and will therefore be emphasized.

Two other non-binding documents will be included. First, the Principles for Responsible Agricultural Investment (RAI) that Respects Rights, Livelihoods and Resources, adopted by the World Bank, FAO, UNCTAD, and IFAD in January 2010 ('RAI Principles'). Second, the Voluntary Guidelines on the Responsible Governance of Tenure of Land, Fisheries and Forests in the Context of National Food Security adopted in 2012 ('FAO Guidelines'), where the main disagreement between the states has been over investments.

We see that the terms 'guidelines' and 'principles' are applied. As noted,[45] principles are by their very nature less specific than rules. While the term 'general principles of law' is considered to be a source of law in accordance with Article 38.1(c) of the Statutes of the International Court of Justice, serving to 'fill gaps or weaknesses in the law',[46] the term 'principle' is defined by Black's Law Dictionary as a basic rule, law, or doctrine. Moreover, principles are understood as being derived from international law, and in order to be effective, they should operate in conjunction with substantive rules, for instance human rights.

1. UN Guiding Principles

The end of the mandate of the Special Representative simultaneously marked the adoption of the UN Guiding Principles on Business and Human Rights. The Guiding Principles are catalogued under three pillars: the state responsibility to protect human rights,[47] the business enterprises' responsibility to respect human

mitigate adverse human rights impacts that are directly linked to their business operations, even if they do not contribute to those impacts; have a policy commitment to respect human rights; carry out human rights due diligence; and provide for remediation of adverse human rights impacts).

[44] OECD, *Guidelines for Multinational Enterprises, C(2011)59* (2011), 13 (section I.8 and I.9—extracts).

[45] Alexy, *supra* note 2.

[46] R. Jennings and A. Watts, *Oppenheim's International Law* 9th edn (London and New York: Longman, 1992) 38; see also A. Cassese, *International Criminal Law* (Oxford and New York: Oxford University Press, 2003) 28. As noted by A. van Aaken, 'Defragmentation of Public International Law Through Interpretation: A Methodological Proposal', 16 *Indiana Journal of Global Legal Studies* (2009), 483–512, at 499: 'the theoretical character of Article 38 [para. 1(c) of the Statute of the International Court of Justice] is similar to the principles as understood in legal theoretical terms'.

[47] The standard typology for state obligations says that states are to respect (not interfere), protect (prevent others' interference) and fulfil human rights, where the latter includes facilitation and if necessary provision. The fact that only state obligations relating to protect are specified in the UN Guidelines on business and human rights cannot be understood as an attempt to question the fact that state obligations also apply to respect and fulfil.

rights,[48] as well as an effective access to remedies. The emphasis in this section will be on the state obligation to protect human rights, which constitute Principles 1 to 10, with a particular emphasis on Principles 3, 5, and 9.

Reviewing those three Guiding Principles that are most relevant in the context of investment treaties and investment contracts, Principle 3(b) states that

> States should [e]nsure that other laws and policies governing the creation and ongoing operation of business enterprises, such as corporate law, do not constrain but enable business respect for human rights.

The term 'other laws and policies' must be read in light of the previous subparagraph on 'laws that are aimed at, or have the effect of, requiring business enterprises to respect human rights'. Principle 3(b) therefore addresses all those laws and policies that are *not* primarily aimed at requiring business enterprises to respect human rights. Laws and policies relating to investments fall within the scope of Guiding Principle 3(b). By requiring that business enterprises shall enable the respect of human rights, the relevant treaties and contracts must as a minimum ensure that public non-discriminatory regulations with the purpose of ensuring compliance with human rights obligations cannot be understood as constituting indirect expropriations.[49]

Principle 5 reads: 'States should promote respect for human rights by business enterprises with which they conduct commercial transactions'. Even if only commercial transactions are explicitly referred to, this must be understood to encompass any investment contracts, including for public service delivery. The wording of these contracts is crucial, so as to make sure that no specific commitments are formulated in manners which might give rise to unjustified expectations. As the holder of the human rights obligations, it is the state that must ensure that relevant human rights concerns are adequately addressed in the treaty, including in the context of potential regulatory measures that the state will adopt.

Finally, Principle 9 reads:

> States should maintain adequate domestic policy space to meet their human rights obligations when pursuing business-related policy objectives with other States or business enterprises, for instance through investment treaties or contracts.

In order to ensure an adequate policy space, the state has the responsibility to prevent wide-ranging stabilization clauses from being included in its BITs or

[48] What is encompassed by the duty to respect implies an active approach, implying that businesses 'should have in place policies and processes' (Principle 15), and—in the context of the due diligence requirement—assess 'actual and potential human rights impacts, integrating and acting upon the findings, tracking responses, and communicating how impacts are addressed' (Principle 17).

[49] On indirect expropriation and compensation, see *Compañia del Desarrollo de Santa Elena v Costa Rica, ICSID Case No. ARB(AF)/96/1, Award, 17 February 2000*, para. 71 (extract): 'While an expropriation or taking for environmental reasons may be classified as a taking for a public purpose, and thus be legitimate, the fact that the Property was taken for this purpose does not affect either the nature or the measure of the compensation'; see also *Metalclad v Mexico, ICSID Case No. ARB(AF)/97/1, Award, 30 August 2000*, para. 103. See also C. Golay and I. Cismas, *Legal Opinion: The Right to Property from a Human Rights Perspective* (Montreal: Rights and Democracy, 2010).

investment Chapters in FTAs.[50] Moreover, the fair and equitable treatment standard has been interpreted to encompass not only the requirement of stability and predictability, but also the requirement of total transparency, and to fulfil the legitimate expectations of the investor.[51] These requirements imply that states limit their policy space, making it more difficult to adopt legislation for the protection of human rights without risking proceedings before international tribunals by corporate actors. The UN Guiding Principles warn that 'international investment agreements may constrain states from fully implementing new human rights legislation, or put them at risk of binding international arbitration'.[52]

2. *Principles relating to land investments*

Investments on land have seen a rapid increase, in particular since 2008.[53] Such investments have not yet been subject to arbitration processes, but a study commissioned by the World Bank found that 'actual farming has so far only started on 21 percent of the announced deals',[54] hence there are several of these land acquisition processes which seem to be speculative and not productive. These concerns add to the obvious concerns about the impact on those peoples that are currently depending on the land, when they no longer have access to this land.

The use of principles to guide policies and practices has been weak in the context of human rights protection, especially in comparison with their use in the context of the protection of the environment.[55] One of the first attempts was to identify human rights principles is the CESCR's General Comment 12 on the right to food, listing the following in various paragraphs: dignity, non-discrimination, accountability, transparency, people's participation, decentralization, legislative

[50] See A. Shemberg, *Stabilization Clauses and Human Rights: A research project conducted for IFC and the United Nations Special Representative to the Secretary-General on Business and Human Rights* (2009), available at <http://tinyurl.com/poy9efx> (last accessed 14 November 2013); see also H. Mann, *International Investment Agreements, Business and Human Rights: Key Issues and Opportunities* (2008), available at <http://www.iisd.org/pdf/2008/iia_business_human_rights.pdf> (last accessed 14 November 2013). Stabilization clauses refer to a wide range of provisions seeking to protect the interests of the investor, and encompass freezing clauses, consistency clauses or economic equilibrium clauses; see L. Cotula, *Regulatory Takings, Stabilization Clauses and Sustainable Development, Paper prepared for the OECD Global Forum on International Investment VII* (2008), available at <http://www.oecd.org/dataoecd/45/8/40311122.pdf> (last accessed 14 November 2013).

[51] J.R. Picherack, 'The Expanding Scope of the Fair and Equitable Treatment Standard: Have Recent Tribunals Gone too Far?', 9 *Journal of World Investment and Trade* (2008), 255–291; A. Wythes, 'Investor-State Arbitrations: Can the "Fair and Equitable Treatment" Clause Consider International Human Rights Obligations?', 23 *Leiden Journal of International Law* (2010), 241–256.

[52] UN, *supra* note 12, 12 (commentaries to Principle 9).

[53] The shift can also be witnessed by UNCTAD's World Investment Report 2009, with the title *Transnational Corporations, Agricultural Production and Development* (New York and Geneva: UNCTAD, 2009).

[54] K. Deininger and D. Byerlee, *Rising Global Interest in Farmland. Can It Yield Sustainable and Equitable Benefits?* (World Bank: Washington DC, 2010), xiv.

[55] H.M. Haugen, 'Human Rights Principles: Can they be Applied to Improve the Realization of Social Human Rights?', *Max Planck Yearbook of United Nations Law* (vol. 15, Leiden: Martinus Nijhoff, 2011).

capacity, and the independence of the judiciary.[56] A more consistent catalogue of principles has subsequently been adopted by the FAO, namely, participation, accountability, non-discrimination, transparency, human dignity, empowerment, and the rule of law.[57] These are derived from human rights provisions and apply to all forms of conduct. Hence, the requirement for being considered a human rights principle is that it has an explicit legal content and that it specifies a minimum standard of conduct.[58]

The RAI Principles, initially adopted in 2010,[59] outline seven principles but do not refer explicitly to human rights. These seven principles are: respecting land and resource rights; ensuring food security; ensuring transparency, good governance, and a proper enabling environment; consultation and participation; responsible agro-enterprise investing; social sustainability; and environmental sustainability. FAO, UNCTAD, and IFAD have responsibilities to promote human rights in accordance with Article 59 of the UN Charter, and as large-scale transfers of land are deemed to have several substantial human rights impacts, particularly on the most vulnerable, it is noteworthy that human rights are absent. Moreover, the process has been criticized for having a top-down approach rather than an inclusive approach.[60]

The RAI Principles have been acknowledged by De Schutter as reflecting a realistic understanding of risks relating to investments in agriculture.[61] The same author finds, however, that the RAI Principles fail to understand what the real issue at stake is; namely, how to best use land that is available.[62] Based on the requirement specified, saying that human rights principles will only be effective if they operate in conjunction with substantive human rights, the RAI Principles as they currently stand are not adequate from a human rights point of view.

[56] CESCR, General Comment No. 12, The right to adequate food (Art. 11), UN Doc. E/C.12/1999/5: paras. 4, 21, 23, and 26.

[57] FAO, *Right to Food and Indigenous Peoples* (2007), available at <http://www.fao.org/docrep/016/a1603e/a1603e.pdf> (last accessed 14 November 2013); the same principles are reiterated in FAO, *A right to food based approach to enhance the contribution of non-wood forest products to food security and nutrition. Background paper 3 for the International Conference on Forests for Food Security and Nutrition* (2013), 3–5. See also C. Golay and M. Büschi, *The right to food and global strategic frameworks: The Global Strategic Framework for Food Security and Nutrition (GSF) and the UN Comprehensive Framework for Action (CFA)* (Roma: FAO, 2012).

[58] Therefore, the catalogue made in 2003 in the context of 'The Human Rights Based Approach to Development Cooperation: Towards a Common Understanding among UN Agencies', available at <http://tinyurl.com/bngy63r> (last accessed 14 November 2013)—emphasizing, inter alia, universality and inalienability, indivisibility, and interdependence and inter-relatedness—describes the nature of human rights, hence operating on a meta level, not the conduct level.

[59] In accordance with a FAO decision, see FAO's Committee on World Food Security, *39th Session, Final report* (2012), 9 and Annex D, FAO is now in a process to 'develop' the RAI Principles for possible adoption at its 2014 Session.

[60] O. De Schutter and P. Rosenblum, 'Large-Scale Investments in Farmland: The Regulatory Challenge', in K.P. Sauvant (ed.), *The Yearbook on International Investment Law and Policy 2010/2011* (New York: Oxford University Press, 2011), 563–610, at 576.

[61] O. De Schutter and P. Rosenblum, 'Large-Scale Investments in Farmland: The Regulatory Challenge', in K.P. Sauvant (ed.), *The Yearbook on International Investment Law and Policy 2010/2011* (New York: Oxford University Press, 2011), 563–610, at 576.

[62] O. De Schutter, 'The Green Rush: The Global Race for Farmland and the Rights of Land Users', *Harvard International Law Journal* (2011), 503–559, at 521.

The FAO Guidelines is a lengthy document, where the two first parts integrate many human rights concerns,[63] but human rights are not integrated equally throughout the Guidelines.

In the context of foreign investment in land, Guideline 22.1 is the most relevant, reading: 'In States where transboundary matters related to tenure rights arise, parties should work together to protect such tenure rights, livelihoods and food security of the migrating populations while on their respective territories'. This must be understood to apply to any purchase or lease agreements that affect the traditional use and tenure rights. The wording on states working together is, however, very vague.

While the length of the FAO Guidelines can imply that they will not easily be read,[64] the adoption of these Guidelines implies that all relevant actors are provided with a non-binding tool in order to assess and make adequate decisions regarding any investment relating to land and resources.

3. *Interim conclusion*

Several recently adopted non-binding documents apply to the human rights responsibility of companies and the human rights obligations of states in the context of corporate conduct abroad. While they address pertinent issues, they do not adequately address the deeper problem of inadequate regulation and supervision capacities in many states, nor these states' various attempts of lowering standards in order to attract foreign investments. The emphasis should be placed on adequate laws and institutions, as well as adequate professional capacity when negotiating treaties and contracts.

Whether or not states are under an international legal obligation to regulate by law or regulation, the conduct of their registered companies when these undertake investments abroad is answered in the following manner in the UN Guiding Principles:

> At present States are not generally required under international human rights law to regulate the extraterritorial activities of businesses domiciled in their territory and/or jurisdiction. Nor are they generally prohibited from doing so [...] There are strong policy reasons for home States to set out clearly the expectation that businesses respect human rights abroad.[65]

This assertion implies that it is possible to foresee a future development where regulation of companies is not only a duty for the host state, but also for the home state. A document by international human rights law experts takes a different approach, by stating: 'All States must take necessary measures to ensure that non-State actors

[63] Note that Principle 3B specifies no less than 10 'principles of implementation', but these are arguably less clear than the human rights principles that FAO has introduced earlier; see FAO, *supra* note 57 and accompanying text. In the latter parts, Principles 9, 12, 16, 22, and 26 refer to human rights.

[64] The Special Rapporteur on the right to food has identified 11 such minimum principles in his report on Large-scale land acquisitions and leases: A set of minimum principles and measures to address the human rights challenge, UN Doc. A/HRC/13/33/Add.2. The Human Rights Council, in its resolution 3/4, *The right to food* (2010), para. 35 took note with appreciation of this report.

[65] UN, *supra* note 12, at 7 (commentary to Principle 2).

which they are in a position to regulate […] do not nullify or impair the enjoyment of economic, social and cultural rights'.[66] UNCTAD expresses a similar position: 'Home-country governments also have a duty to protect against human rights abuses committed abroad by their nationals and TNCs'.[67]

It must also be noted that the UN Guiding Principle 7, on conduct in conflict-affected areas requires states to '[e]nsuring that their current policies, legislation, regulations and enforcement measures are effective'.[68] The subsequent commentary specifies that in conflicts over territories or resources, the human rights regime cannot be expected to function as intended.[69]

3. WTO, FTAs, and BITs: Are Human Rights Explicitly Recognized?

The wording of the Agreement establishing the World Trade Organization (WTO Agreement) and its annexed agreements, NAFTA, as well as some examples of Model BIT agreements will now be examined to assess the degree to which human rights are explicitly or implicitly recognized.

A. WTO Agreement and Annexes

1. How are investment-related issues covered by WTO agreements?

Despite the fact that negotiations on a substantive investment agreement under the auspices of the WTO have failed,[70] three WTO agreements address investment issues. First, the General Agreement on Trade in Services (GATS) Article 1.2(c) defines 'commercial presence in the territory of any other Member' as one of the modes of service delivery. Also mode (d), namely 'presence of natural persons' in another territory, can be subject to GATS-incompatible practice—provided that the service sector is included in the schedules of specific commitments. Moreover, transparency is recognized in Article III, as one of the general obligations under GATS. Domestic law restrictions on foreigners' possibility to possess land have not become an issue in the context of the WTO.

Second, the Trade-Related Investment Measures (TRIMS) Agreement states that the national treatment requirement applies also to investments, so that it is

[66] The Maastricht Principles on Extraterritorial Obligations of States in the area of Economic, Social and Cultural Rights (2012), para. 24 (extracts).

[67] UNCTAD, *World Investment Report 2007. Transnational Corporations, Extractive Industries and Development* (New York and Geneva: UNCTAD 2007), 178, referring to the report by the UN Special Representative on business and human rights, *A/HRC/4/35* (2007), para. 16.

[68] UN, *supra* note 12, Principle 7(d).

[69] UN, *supra* note 11 (commentary to Principle 7). See also the ILC's draft articles on the effects of armed conflicts on treaties, in ILC, Report on the work of its 63rd session, UN Doc. A/66/10 (2010), 175–178.

[70] *Supra* note 9 and accompanying text.

neither permitted to require an enterprise to purchase products of domestic origin, nor to restrict the exportation or importation of products to this enterprise.[71]

Third, while not being an investment agreement per se, the Trade-Related Aspects of Intellectual Property Rights (TRIPS) applies, inter alia, to investor-relevant patent rights and trademarks. On patents, TRIPS Article 27.1 states that 'patents shall be available and patent rights enjoyable without discrimination as to the place of invention, the field of technology and whether products are imported or locally produced'. Any legislation seeking to restrict the enjoyment of these rights beyond what is provided for in the exclusion or limited exceptions provisions (which will be reviewed) can be subject to a WTO dispute. Moreover, patent litigation before domestic courts is common and represents additional costs for developing countries.

Hence, we see that the overall scope of the WTO also applies to investments. Unlike investor–state disputes, the disputes in the context of the WTO take place between states and relate to domestic laws or regulations, not to specific cases of alleged misconduct. The WTO disputes can emerge, however, because of initiatives taken by business associations in certain states, believing that another state does not comply with its WTO obligations.

2. *Implicit recognition of human rights in WTO treaties?*

Although there is no explicit reference to human rights in any of the WTO Agreements, an analysis to assess the extent to which central provisions are formulated in a manner which encompasses human rights follows.

The first paragraph of the preamble to the WTO Agreement emphasizes that the relations between states shall be conducted with a view to 'raising standards of living, ensuring full employment [...] and effective demand'. These are formulations which relate to the subject matter of ICESCR Article 11 on the right to an adequate standard of living and ICESCR Article 6 on the right to work.[72]

Remaining within GATT Article XX, there can be no doubt that Article XX(e) relating to the products of prison labour addresses human rights concerns. The relevant provision of the International Covenant on Civil and Political Rights (ICCPR), however, allows exemptions from the general prohibition of 'forced or compulsory labour' in Article 8.3(a) for those states where 'imprisonment with hard labour may be imposed as a punishment for a crime'.[73] Therefore, while some states might allow compulsory labour as part of the imprisonment in accordance with the ICCPR, other states can restrict importation of the resulting products

[71] TRIMS, Annex, arts. 1(a), 2(b), and 2(c).

[72] This is acknowledged in *A/55/342, Globalization and its impact on the full enjoyment of all human rights. Preliminary report of the Secretary-General,* noting in para. 16: 'The goals and principles of the WTO agreements and those of human rights law do [...] share much in common'. See also A. McBeth, *International Economic Actors and Human Rights* (Oxford: Routledge, 2010), 86–88.

[73] ICCPR, Art. 8(3)(b); see also Art. 8(3)(c)(i).

from such labour in accordance with GATT—provided that the requirements of the GATT Article XX chapeau are met.[74]

GATT Article XX(b) allows trade-restricting measures necessary to protect human life or health. This wording must also be understood to refer to human rights, as the right to life is recognized in ICCPR Article 6(1) and the right to the highest attainable standard of health is recognized in ICESCR Article 12(1). In a case where India challenged an EC Council regulation seeking to combat drug production and trafficking by giving tariff preferences to certain states,[75] the panel said that it 'finds nothing linking the preferences to the protection of human life or health in the European Communities'.[76] Hence, the panel never challenged the objective of protecting life and health, but simply found that the way the relevant regulation was formulated and the lack of a factual relationship between the scope of the regulation and the scope of GATT Article XX(b) did not qualify for the GATT exception to be applicable. In general, the necessity requirement, found in GATT Article XX(b), is much more demanding than the 'relating to' requirement of GATT Article XX(e) (prison labour) and Article XX(g) (exhaustible natural resources).

GATT Article XX(a) permits trade-restricting measures necessary to protect public morals. There are no cases from the WTO's dispute settlement system that have sought to clarify the scope of this provision. Hence, as Article XIV(a) of GATS has a similar wording, which has been clarified in the dispute settlement system, we will rather address the scope of this provision, which permits measures necessary to protect public morals or maintain public order.[77]

In a case where USA wanted to restrict its citizens' access to gambling and betting services, and was challenged by Antigua, the Appellate Body has found that the necessity test of GATS Article XIV(a) has been met,[78] but not the chapeau of GATS Article XIV.[79] As the relevant US statutes reviewed were found to protect 'very important societal interests', as 'strict controls may be needed to protect [such] interests' and as the relevant US statutes 'contribute to the realization of the

[74] These requirements are that measures are not applied in a manner which would constitute a means of arbitrary or unjustifiable discrimination, and that the measures do not represent disguised restriction on international trade.

[75] *Council Regulation (EC) No. 2501/2001 of 10 December 2001 applying a scheme of generalised tariff preferences for the period from 1 January 2002 to 31 December 2004.*

[76] *EC—Tariff preferences, panel report, WT/DS246/R*, para. 7.202. In para. 7.207, it continued by stating that it found 'no evidence presented before the Panel to suggest that providing improved market access is aimed at protecting human life or health in drug importing countries'.

[77] A footnote explaining 'public order' reads: 'The public order exception may be invoked only where a genuine and sufficiently serious threat is posed to one of the fundamental interests of society'.

[78] *US—Gambling and Betting Services, Appellate Body Report, WT/DS285/AB/*R, paras. 322–326, approving in para. 323 the panel's review of the US measures in light of the necessity test developed in Korea—Beef (*WT/DS161/AB/R*, para. 157). On the human rights aspect of GATT Art. XX(a) (and GATS Art. XIV(a)), see N. Wenzel, 'Article XX(a)', in R. Wolfrum, P.-T. Stoll, and A. Seibert-Fohr (eds.), *WTO: Technical Barriers and SPS Measures* (Leiden & Boston: Brill, 2007), 80–95, at 89–95.

[79] N. Wenzel, 'Article XX(a)', in R. Wolfrum, P.-T. Stoll, and A. Seibert-Fohr (eds.), *WTO: Technical Barriers and SPS Measures* (Leiden & Boston: Brill, 2007), para. 373(D)(vi)(a), 126.

ends they pursue',[80] the scope of GATS Article XIV(a) was broad enough to also encompass human rights.

While we see that public order is the term applied in GATS Article XIV(a), *ordre public* is applied in the provision of TRIPS providing for the exclusion of certain inventions. The requirement is that this is necessary to protect *ordre public* or morality, including to protect human, animal, or plant life or health, or to avoid serious prejudice to the environment, provided that such exclusion is not made merely because the exploitation is prohibited by their law'.[81] According to a detailed analysis of TRIPS, *ordre public* was deliberately chosen instead of public order as the former is a narrower term, setting a high threshold for excluding inventions from patentability.[82] In any case, human rights can fall within the scope of Article 27.2, but the requirement ('exclusion is not made merely because the exploitation is prohibited by their law') implies that it is demanding to comply with this provision.

Two other TRIPS provisions are relevant. First, Article 8.1 ('Principles') permits states to take 'measures necessary to protect public health and nutrition [...] provided that such measures are consistent with the provisions of this Agreement'. This is a weak provision,[83] but the Doha Declaration on TRIPS and Public Health says that all TRIPS provisions 'shall be read in the light of the object and purpose of the Agreement as expressed, in particular, in its objectives and principles'.[84] Hence, public health and nutrition concerns must be addressed when the scope of the substantive provisions are clarified.

Finally, TRIPS Article 30 ('Limited exceptions'), which has been clarified by the dispute settlement panel,[85] but not by the Appellate Body, and the narrow focus

[80] N. Wenzel, 'Article XX(a)', in R. Wolfrum, P.-T. Stoll, and A. Seibert-Fohr (eds.), *WTO: Technical Barriers and SPS Measures* (Leiden & Boston: Brill, 2007), para. 323, the Appellate Body quoting the panel.

[81] TRIPS Art. 27.2. For a detailed analysis of both TRIPS Art. 27.2 and other relevant provisions, see H.M. Haugen, 'Human Rights and TRIPS Exclusion and Exception Provisions', 11 *Journal of World Intellectual Property* (2008), 345–374.

[82] D. Gervais, *The TRIPS Agreement: Drafting History and Analysis* 2nd edn (London: Sweet & Maxwell, 2003), 222. United Nations High Commissioner for Human Rights (UNHCHR) says that *ordre public* refers to the 'basic and fundamental values of a domestic legal system'; see UNHCHR, *Human Rights and World Trade Agreements: Using General Exception Clauses to Protect Human Rights* (2005), 10. TRIPS Art. 27.2 sets a lower threshold than the similar provision of the European Patent Convention (EPC), on which TRIPS builds. Art. 53(a) of the EPC reads: 'European patents shall not be granted in respect of [...] inventions the publication or exploitation of which would be contrary to "ordre public" or morality, provided that the exploitation shall not be deemed to be so contrary merely because it is prohibited by law or regulation in some or all of the Contracting States'. In no cases which have been brought before various bodies of the European Patent Office have the requirements of Art. 53(a) been found to have been met. Haugen, *supra* note 81, at 347–351, has analysed the difference between EPC Art. 53(a) and TRIPS Art. 27(2), finding that life and health, and environment constitute independent basis for exclusion, drawing upon the jurisprudence of EPO bodies.

[83] H. Grosse Ruse-Khan, 'Assessing the need for a general public interest exception in the TRIPS Agreement', in A. Kur (ed.), *Intellectual Property Rights in a Fair Trade System. Proposals for Reform of TRIPS* (Cheltenham: Edward Elgar, 2011), 167–207, 183 says that 'TRIPS [...] does not allow for anything close to the policy space allowed in Art. XX GATT or Art. XIV GATS'.

[84] *WT/MIN(01)/DEC/W/2*, Art. 5(a).

[85] *WT/DS114/R, Canada—Pharmaceuticals.*

taken by the panel has been criticized.[86] It must also be noted that the last words of Article 30, reading 'taking account of the legitimate interests of third parties' were deliberately not addressed by the panel. Hence, Article 30 provides a basis upon which patent legislation seeking to protect the legitimate interests of third parties can be justified, provided that the exception is limited.

As we see, there is a certain basis to state that human rights concerns can be understood to be encompassed by the scope of several WTO provisions. As shown by Hestermeyer in another chapter of this book,[87] human rights are, however, rarely introduced in the dispute settlement system. The dispute settlement bodies seem to acknowledge 'very important societal interests' irrespective of whether these interests are sought to be protected by legislation without an explicit human rights basis, or through human rights legislation and arguments highlighting the state's international human rights obligations.

3. *Implicit recognition of human rights in investment treaties?*

Arbitration panels must solve any disputes based on the wording of the investment treaty, *some* of which contain language encompassing human rights obligations. This section will review the few investment agreements which contain provisions that relate to economic, social, and cultural rights. It must be recalled that the potential for human rights in international investment law extends beyond these treaties, as the requirements of the ICSID Convention and NAFTA imply that the disputes shall be decided in accordance with applicable rules of international law. This can imply that human rights can be applied by the investment tribunal, if the state party to the dispute presents their arguments based on its human rights obligations, if an amicus curiae submission identifies human rights obligations in a convincing manner, or if the arbitration panel itself resorts to human rights treaties or jurisprudence in order to clarify and decide on the case before it.

First, when reviewing investment chapters in FTA, the most comprehensive acknowledgement of non-trade concerns is found in NAFTA, whose investment regulation is found in Chapter 11. The preamble to Chapter 11 mimics the preamble to the WTO Agreement ('working conditions and living standards'). The NAFTA Chapter 11 preamble goes further, by explicitly recognizing the flexibility to safeguard the public welfare and the protection of workers' rights.

Another provision of Chapter 11 which addresses subject matter that is also encompassed by human rights provisions is Article 1101.4, which reads:

> Nothing in this Chapter shall be construed to prevent a Party from providing a service or performing a function such as [...] social security or insurance, social welfare, public

[86] R. Howse, 'The Canadian Generic Medicines Panel: A Dangerous Precedent in Dangerous Times', 3 *Journal of World Intellectual Property* (2000), 493–508; A. Kur, 'Limitations and Exceptions under the three-steps test: how much room to walk the middle ground?', in A. Kur, *supra* note 83, at 208–261.

[87] See H.P. Hestermeyer, 'Economic, Social, and Cultural Rights in the World Trade Organization: Legal Aspects and Practice', ch. 9, in this book.

education, public training, health, and child care, in a manner that is not inconsistent with this Chapter.

The phrase 'not inconsistent with this Chapter' is basically similar to Article 8.1 of TRIPS, which restricts its application.

Turning to the EU, it is acknowledged that 'the EU is obliged under its internal treaties to promote democracy, the rule of law and human rights in its international agreements'.[88] In most of its FTAs, the term 'human rights' is hardly applied, except for a reference in the preamble and in the context of data protection.[89] A more comprehensive acknowledgement of human rights is found in the EU-CARIFORUM Economic Partnership Agreement (EPA) which specifies that the conduct of investors shall be in accordance with core labour standards (Article 72(b)), and that foreign direct investment shall not be encouraged by lowering legislation and standards (Article 73). Both of these exceptions provisions apply the necessity requirement.[90]

Turning to the BITs, the Canadian and US Model BITs stand out by addressing subject matter which is encompassed by human rights. Some of the provisions also have a wording almost identical to WTO exception provisions.[91]

While neither of these Model BITs apply the term 'human rights' explicitly, the US Model BIT stands out as having very explicit provisions on labour rights, as outlined in Article 13(2), referring to 'labor law' as covering the right of association, the right to organize and bargain collectively, prohibition of forced or compulsory labour, labour protections for children, and acceptable conditions of work. These human rights are recognized in a number of human rights treaties, including ICCPR Articles 21(2) and 8(3), and ICESCR, Articles 8(1), 10(3), and 7(b), and even more detailed in ILO treaties.

Specific BITs, such as the US–Argentina BIT, contain exception provisions reading: 'The Treaty shall not preclude the application by either Party of measures necessary for the maintenance of public order or [...] the [p]rotection of its own

[88] EU's acting head of delegation to the WTO, John Clarke, as quoted at the WTO Public Forum 2010, Session 22: Social standards and human rights clauses in trade agreements: Window-dressing, hidden protectionism or furthering the cause?, available at <http://www.wto.org/english/news_e/news10_e/pfor_am_17sept10_e.htm#session22> (last accessed 14 November 2013). According to Claudia Hofmann, in the same session, 31 per cent of regional trade agreements already have a labour clause. For an analysis of the human rights provisions in EU and US FTA, see Emilie Hafner-Burton, *Forced to Be Good: Why Trade Agreements Boost Human Rights* (New York: Cornell University Press, 2009).

[89] EU-CARIFORUM Economic Partnership Agreement (EPA), preambular para. 3, Arts. 107.2 and 197.1(a) (applying the term 'fundamental rights'). The same applies to the EU-South Korea FTA, where human rights is referred to in the fourth preambular paragraph and 'fundamental rights' in Art. 7.43 (privacy protection; see also note 41); the term 'fundamental rights' is also applied in Art. 13.4.3 (labour standards).

[90] These provisions are found in Title II ('Investments, trade in services and e-commerce'). Labour rights are more comprehensively regulated in Title IV ('Trade-related issues'), Arts. 191–196; see also a note to Art. 224.1(a) which specifies that 'measures necessary to combat child labour' fall within the scope of both measures necessary to protect public morals and measures necessary for the protection of health.

[91] See Art. 8.3(c)(2) of the US Model BIT and 10(a) of the Canadian Model BIT, both permitting measures necessary to protect human, animal, or plant life or health.

essential security interests'.[92] This provision has been central in several disputes, and will be included in the analysis that follows.

Moreover, the Canadian Model BIT has three interesting provisions. First, Article 7, which prohibits performance requirements, permits in Article 7(2) any 'measure that requires an investment to use a technology to meet generally applicable health, safety or environmental requirements'. Second, Article 11 reads:

The Parties recognize that it is inappropriate to encourage investment by relaxing domestic health, safety or environmental measures', in other wording similar to Article 73 of the EU—CARIFORUM EPA. In other words, high standards for the protection of public interests are the norm. Third, Annex B.13(1), Article (1)(c), which explains Article 13 on expropriation, says that measures apply non-discriminatorily to 'protect legitimate public welfare objectives, such as health, safety and the environment, do not constitute indirect expropriation.[93]

As this review reveals, some FTAs and BITs are encompassing subject matter that is also covered by human rights provisions. The 'necessity' requirement in most of these provisions implies, however, that the taking of measures that are falling within the investment treaty's exceptions provisions must be justified before the arbitration panel.

4. How Can Human Rights be Included in the Reasoning of an IEL Dispute Settlement Body?

There are five different manners through which human rights may be included in an award from a tribunal addressing a trade or investment dispute, arising under a FTA or BIT: (1) a treaty's specification of what sources of law are to be applied in a dispute; (2) a treaty's specification of the applicable law; (3) a treaty's explicit referral to human rights; (4) a treaty's referral to domestic human rights provisions; and (5) treaty interpretation, in accordance with the Vienna Convention on the Law of Treaties (VCLT), Article 31.3(c), stating that 'any relevant rules of international law applicable in the relations between the parties' are to be taken into account when interpreting the treaty.[94]

[92] USA-Argentina BIT (1992), Art. XI. For BITs, available at <http://tinyurl.com/bvrex8v> (last accessed 14 November 2013).

[93] See also Annex B, para. 4(b) to the 2012 US Model Law. Note that Art. 35 of the Model Law states that Annexes and footnotes shall form an integral part of this Treaty. Moreover, *American Law Institute's Restatement (3rd) of the Foreign Relations Law of the United States* Vol. 1 (1987), section 712, comment g, reading (extracts): 'a State is not responsible for [...] economic disadvantage resulting from *bona fide* [...] regulation'.

[94] See U. Kriebaum, 'Human Rights of the Population of the Host State in International Investment Arbitration', 10 *Journal of World Investment and Trade* (2009), 653–677, at 660–671; see also A. van Aaken, 'Fragmentation of International Law: The Case of International Investment Protection', in *Finnish Yearbook of International Law Vol. 17* (Leiden: Martinus Nijhoff, 2008), 91–130, and M. Jacob, *International Investment Agreements and Human Rights, INEF Research Paper Series Human Rights, Corporate Responsibility and Sustainable Development 03/2010* (2010), 26–31.

We see that the three verbs used are 'refer', 'take into account', and 'apply'. The verb 'apply' is restricted to what the treaty specifies as being applicable law. In the interpretation of the specific treaty, other sources of law will need to be taken into account.[95] Trade and investment law, emerging from treaties between states, constitute an integral part of public international law.[96] The five manners through which human rights may be brought into a tribunal report will now be reviewed.

A. Jurisdictional clause

Different treaties specify which disputes may be brought before the tribunal. The 1991 Agreement between the Czech and Slovak Federal Republics and Norway on the Mutual Promotion and Protection of Investments, and the 1992 Agreement between Norway and Lithuania on the Promotion and Mutual Protection of Investments will be used to illustrate the differences. Under the former, there can only be disputes 'concerning the interpretation and application of this agreement'.[97] Under the latter, 'any dispute [...] in connection with an investment' can be subject to negotiations and subsequent dispute settlement.[98]

Hence, investment disputes beyond those provisions covered in the BIT may be subject to dispute settlement by an investment tribunal; but only if the parties expressly agree so. A tribunal's competence is therefore 'governed by [those] instruments expressing the parties' consent'.[99]

B. Applicable law

The ICSID Convention Article 42.1 reads:

> The Tribunal shall decide a dispute in accordance with such rules of law as may be agreed by the parties. In the absence of such an agreement, the Tribunal shall *apply* the law of the Contracting State party to the dispute (including its rules on the conflict of laws) and such rules of international law as may be applicable.[100]

If the parties agree that human rights are relevant rules to be applied, human rights law will become applicable law in this specific dispute.

[95] As an illustration, the WTO's Dispute Settlement Understanding (DSU) specifies in Art. 3.2 that it applies to the 'covered agreements' and that the provisions shall be clarified 'in accordance with customary rules of interpretation of public international law', which obviously refers to the VCLT, arts. 31–33.

[96] See the 1965 Report of the Executive Directors on the Convention on the Settlement of Investment Disputes between States and Nationals of Other States, reprinted in ICSID, *ICSID Convention, Regulations and Rules* (Washington DC: ICSID, 2006), 35–49, at 47, para. 44, defining international law by referring to the Statute for the ICJ, Art. 38. The fact that the VCLT is not referred to is due to the fact that when the 1965 Report was adopted, the VCLT had not been adopted.

[97] Czech/Slovak Federal Republic and Norway BIT, Art. IX.2.

[98] Norway and Lithuania BIT, Art. IX.1.

[99] *CMS Gas v Argentina, ICSID Case No. ARB/01/8, Annulment Decision*, 25 September 2007, para. 68; *CMS Gas v Argentina, ICSID Case No. ARB/01/8, Decision on Jurisdiction,* 17 July 2003, para. 42.

[100] Emphasis added.

A dispute where the defence was based on constitutional human rights provisions, but where the tribunal noted that the parties had not chosen a particular law to be applied, will be used as an illustration. The tribunal found that domestic law was applicable, but it noted that only some basic treaties on human rights have been recognized by a 1994 Argentinian constitutional amendment as having constitutional standing, and found that Article 27 of the Constitution gives a prominent role to commercial treaties.[101] Hence, the understanding by the tribunal that Argentina had a more explicit recognition of commercial law treaties than of human rights treaties in its Constitution was central. Despite the fact that the Annulment Decision found that 'the Award contained manifest errors of law',[102] the Annulment Decision upheld Argentina's liability to pay compensation.

Moreover, two 2010 decisions analysed the application of the defence of necessity as specified under Article 25 of the 2001 ILC Articles on Responsibility of States for Internationally Wrongful Acts, concluding that Argentina could not use its human rights treaty obligations 'to take actions in disregard of its BIT obligations', emphasizing that 'Argentina could have respected both types of obligations'.[103] Article 25 of the 2001 ILC Article was also central in two annulment decisions in 2010, where the original awards were criticized for not applying the exceptions provision found in Article XI of the US-Argentina BIT.[104]

[101] *CMS Gas v Argentina, ICSID Case No. ARB/01/8, Award,* 12 May 2005, paras. 108–122, particularly paras. 114 and 119. The necessity test was based on the International Law Commission's (ILC) Draft Articles on State Responsibility, Art. 25 and Art. XI of the US-Argentina BIT ('necessary for the maintenance of public order or [...] the protection of the protection of its own essential security interests'). A subsequent Annulment Decision, *supra* note 99, found that the Tribunal had failed to separate these two provisions and had not examined whether the conditions laid down by Art. XI were fulfilled, and then stated in para. 135: 'If the Committee was acting as a court of appeal, it would have to reconsider the Award on this Ground'. Moreover Art. 27 of the ILC's Draft Articles on State Responsibility ('circumstances precluding wrongfulness') were also found not to have been applied correctly by the tribunal; see paras. 146–147.

[102] *CMS Gas v Argentina Annulment Decision, supra* note 99, para. 158.

[103] *Suez, Sociedad General de Aguas de Barcelona SA, and InterAguas Servicios Integrales del Agua SA v Argentina, ICSID Case No. ARB/03/17 Decision on Liability*, 30 July 2010, para. 240; see also *Suez, Sociedad General de Aguas de Barcelona SA, and Vivendi Universal SA v Argentina, ICSID Case No. ARB/03/19 Decision on Liability*, 30 July 2010, para. 262.

[104] US-Argentina BIT Art. XI reads: 'This Treaty shall not preclude the application by either Party of measures necessary for the maintenance of public order, the fulfillment of its obligations with respect to the maintenance or restoration of international peace or security, or the Protection of its own essential security interests'. The first decision found a basis for annulment in accordance with the ICSID convention Art. 52(1)(b) and Art. 52(1)(e), based on the understanding of the 'essential security' provision in Art. XI, read in light of the various provisions of Art. 25 of the 2001 ILC Articles on Responsibility of States for Internationally Wrongful Acts (listed in following parentheses); see *Enron Corp. v Argentina, ICSID Case No. ARB/01/3, Annulment Decision*, 30 July 2010, paras. 377 (25(1)(a)), 384 (25(1)(b)); 393 (25(2)(b)); 395 (25(2)(a)); see also para. 359. The second decision stated that only failure to apply the law—and not misapplication of the law—could result in annulment, in accordance with the ICSID convention Art. 52(1)(b) (para. 206), and that by treating Art. 25 of the ILC's Draft Articles on State responsibility—and not Art. XI of the BIT—as the primary rule, the tribunal 'made a fundamental error in identifying and applying the applicable law' (para. 208), constituting a 'total failure to apply Article XI' (para. 214); see *Sempra Energy Inc. v Argentina, ICSID Case No. ARB/02/16, Annulment Decision*, 29 July 2010.

C. Explicit referrals to international human rights

As stated, while the preamble of US and EU FTA and the Canada and US Model BITs refer in general to human rights, there are few such references in the substantive provisions of these treaties. To the extent that they exist at all, they tend to relate to labour rights and to health, environment, and safety, which can all be encompassed by human rights provisions. As noted by Kriebaum, explicit references to human rights are 'the exception rather than the rule'.[105]

If the preamble or other substantive provisions of the BIT refers to subject matter regulated by a human rights treaty, the author agrees with van Aaken, stating that 'the interpretation of the treaty should take human rights concerns into account'.[106] Human rights could even be part of the applicable law. The question is whether the persons sitting on the tribunal are adequately competent to interpret and apply human rights law.

D. Treaty referral to domestic human rights provisions

The ICSID Convention Article 42.1 is also relevant in this context. As stated, however, the dispute over the US/Argentina BIT found domestic law, including human rights provisions in the Constitution, to be applicable law,[107] also in the absence of an explicit reference in the BIT. Furthermore, as noted by a recent award: '[n]obody would suggest that ICSID protection should be granted to investments made in violation of the most fundamental rules of protection of human rights, like investments made in pursuance of torture or genocide or in support of slavery or trafficking of human organs'.[108] While this award did not actually apply human rights beyond this, it demonstrates that, even in the absence of an explicit reference, human rights must be taken into account, and even be applied by the tribunal.

E. Treaty interpretation by taking into account relevant rules of international law

The actual scope of Article 31(3)(c) of the VCLT is still subject to disagreement. On the one hand, the WTO's dispute settlement panel has found that 'the rules of international law to be taken into account in interpreting the WTO agreements at issue in this dispute are those which are applicable in the relations between the WTO Members'.[109] This could imply that if only one WTO member state is not

[105] Kriebaum, *supra* note 94, at 664.

[106] A. van Aaken, 'Defragmentation of Public International Law Through Interpretation: A Methodological Proposal', 16 *Indiana Journal of Global Legal Studies* (2009), 483–512, 495.

[107] *CMS Gas v Argentina* Award, *supra* note 101, para. 116 ('application of both domestic law and international law if the specific facts of the dispute so justifies'). The claimant alleged that the BIT shall be applied as lex specialis, complemented by customary international law where necessary (para. 109).

[108] *Phoenix Action v Czech Republic, ICSID Case No. ARB/06/5, Award,* 15 April 2009, para. 78.

[109] *EC Biotech, WT/DS291-293/R* (2006), para. 7.68 (note omitted); for support of this position, see M. Samson, 'High Hopes, Scant Resources: A Word of Skepticism about the Anti-Fragmentation Function of Article 31(3)(c) of the Vienna Convention on the Law of Treaties', 24 *Leiden Journal of*

a party to a given treaty, this treaty cannot be taken into account in the interpretation. On the other hand, there are arguments in favour of systemic integration and against clinical isolation in treaty interpretation.[110] Acknowledging that there are disagreements on the general applicability of Article 31(3)(c), the author nevertheless concurs with Simma in finding that human rights norms fulfil the three requirements set up by Article 31(3)(c); that it is a rule, that it is relevant, and that it is applicable.[111]

F. Interim conclusion

This review shows that there are several bases through which the arbitral tribunals may be able to apply human rights law, and there are various ways through which human rights may be considered as being relevant to a dispute. As the emphasis has been on the ICSID Convention, it is relevant to note that other relevant treaties include provisions on interpretation which refer to international law. The Investment Chapter of NAFTA states in Article 1102.2 that all provisions shall be interpreted and applied in accordance with applicable rules of international law. Moreover, the UNCITRAL Arbitration Rules Article 35.1 states that the tribunal 'shall apply the law which it determines to be appropriate'. A tribunal set up by the Stockholm Chamber of Commerce in accordance with these Rules specifies that 'international law generally applies'.[112]

In order to be a relevant rule, the human rights provision must have a particular relationship to the subject matter that is the core of the dispute. As an example, provisions relating to non-discrimination may be relevant to the interpretation of non-discrimination provisions of the BITs, and human rights provisions recognizing the unimpeded access to affordable public services can contribute to clarify legitimate use of public measures which might infringe on investors' property rights in given circumstances.[113]

International Law (2011), 701–714. Note, however, that the panel in para. 7.67 confirmed that rules of international law encompass treaties, international customary law, and general principles of law.

[110] See B. McGrady, 'Fragmentation of International Law or "Systemic Integration" of Treaty Regimes: EC—Biotech Products and the Proper Interpretation of Art. 31(3)(c) of the Vienna Convention on the Law of Treaties', 42 *Journal of World Trade* (2008), 589–618; see also van Aaken, *supra* note 106, at 496–502.

[111] B. Simma, 'Foreign Investment Arbitration: A Place for Human Rights?', 60 *International and Comparative Law Quarterly* (2011), 573–596, at 585; building on B. Simma and T. Kill, 'Harmonizing Investment Protection and International Human Rights: First Steps Towards a Methodology', in C. Binder et al. (eds.), *International Investment Law for the 21st Century: Essays in Honour of Christoph Schreuer* (Oxford: Oxford University Press, 2009), 678–708.

[112] *Eastern Sugar v Czech Republic, SCC Case No. 088/2004, Partial Award*, 27 March 2007, para. 196.

[113] Simma, *supra* note 111, at 586–591.

5. Jurisprudence of Investment Tribunals

As stated initially, human rights may be integrated into the IEL realm in three ways: by giving legitimacy to arguments relating to investors' property rights; by establishing human rights as defences against liberalization; and by establishing minimum standards of conduct for public and corporate policy. Hence, human rights can both serve to strengthen and to weaken appropriationist justifications.[114] This section will identify trends in investment tribunals' jurisprudence, in the context of a lack of any appellate body under investment law,[115] and the diverse approaches taken by various tribunals' call for more clarity. As observed by UNCTAD: '[s]ome awards increased the inconsistency and lack of coherence'.[116] Others use stronger terms, saying that the BITs themselves and the BITs arbitration face a legitimacy crisis due to inconsistent decisions.[117]

The analysis will take place under three subheadings: the requirements of relating public measures to legitimate policy objectives; the requirements of the proportionality test; and the requirements of the fair and equitable treatment standard. Under these principles, it is possible to review the role that human rights obligations have actually played in investment disputes.

A. Relating public measures to legitimate policy objectives

There are still different understandings regarding what constitutes indirect expropriations.[118] On the one hand, as expressed by UNCTAD, 'non-discriminatory regulatory actions by a party aimed at protecting legitimate public welfare objectives, such as public health, safety and the environment, do not constitute indirect expropriations',[119] which is in line with the US and Canadian Model Laws.[120] Hence, by

[114] See M. Langford, 'Cosmopolitan competition. The case of international investment', in C.M. Bailliet and K. Franko Aas (eds.), *Cosmopolitan Justice and its Discontents* (Oxford: Routledge, 2011), 178–204, at 181 criticizing D. Fry's article 'International Human Rights Law in Investment Arbitration: Evidence of International Law's Unity', 18 *Duke Journal of International and Comparative Law* (2007), 77–149, for not understanding the critique of appropriationism.

[115] Arts. 50, 51 and 52 of the ICSID Convention provide for any of the parties to request interpretation, revision and annulment, respectively, of the award; annulment being possible if the tribunal has manifestly exceeded its power (Art. 52(1)(b)), or failed to state reasons on which the award is based (Art. 52(1)(e)).

[116] UNCTAD, *World Investment Report 2010: Investing in a Low-Carbon Economy* (New York and Geneva: UNCTAD, 2010), 83.

[117] S.D. Franck, 'The Legitimacy Crisis in Investment Treaty Arbitration: Privatizing Public International Law Through Inconsistent Decisions', 73 *Fordham Law Review* (2005), 1521–1625; A. Al Faruque, 'Mapping the Relationship between Investment Protection and Human Rights', 11 *Journal of World Investment and Trade* (2010), 539–560, at 542.

[118] Earlier tribunals' broad understanding of what constitutes indirect expropriations were quoted earlier. Metalclad and Santa Elena, both *supra* note 49.

[119] UNCTAD, *Investor-State Dispute Settlement and Impact on Investment Rulemaking* (Geneva and New York: UNCTAD, 2007), 77.

[120] *Supra* note 94 and accompanying text.

this understanding, the purpose is decisive in determining whether or not the alleged expropriation is justified.

On the other hand, in an ICSID tribunal report finding a breach of the US–Argentina BIT, the purpose of the expropriation is only relevant 'for determining whether the expropriation is in accordance with the terms of the Treaty and not for determining whether an expropriation has occurred'.[121] Hence, under this reasoning, if a measure is undertaken for the purposes of bona fide regulations, in line with legitimate policy objectives, this can nevertheless be considered an expropriation under the terms of a BIT. The understanding expressed by the tribunal limits the possibility for the tribunal to assess whether an expropriation can be found to be justified under the BIT. In the words of Kriebaum, we 'are left with an all or nothing solution',[122] unlike the way human rights courts identify damages and compensation.

Finally, while words 'relating to' are applied in the title of this subsection, most provisions permitting the taking of measures use the words 'necessary for', and it has already been found that this sets a higher threshold for such measures to be found as being in compliance with the BIT. This leads us to the next relevant principle.

B. The proportionality test

While proportionality allegedly is not an established principle or standard in international investment law,[123] it is nonetheless a general principle of international law and is increasingly applied in IEL. One arbitral award which has been recognized for its balancing is Tecmed.[124] The proportionality principle consists of three elements: suitability, necessity, and proportionality stricto sensu.[125] In other words, the measure should be appropriate to achieve the objectives, there should be no

[121] *Siemens v Argentina, ICSID Case No. ARB/02/8, Award*, 6 February 2007, para. 270.

[122] U. Kriebaum, 'Privatizing Human Rights. The Interface between International Investment Protection and Human Rights', in A. Reinisch and U. Kriebaum (eds.), *The Law of International Relations. Lieber Amicorum Hanspeter Neuhold* (Utrecht: Eleven International Publishing, 2007), 165–189, at 182. According to the Tribunal in *Noble Ventures v Romania, ICSID Case No. ARB/01/11 Award*, 12 October 2005, para. 52, 'it is not permissible, as is too often done regarding BITs, to interpret clauses exclusively in favour of investors' (italics in original deleted). While this might well be correct, the *World Investment Report 2011 (Overview)*, 12; shows that states have won 78 and lost 59 of all closed investor–state dispute settlement cases.

[123] In A. Reinisch (ed.), *Standards of Investment Protection* (Oxford and New York: Oxford University Press, 2008), proportionality is addressed in two chapters: K. Yannaca-Small, 'Fair and Equitable Treatment Standard', 111–130, at 126–129; and A.K. Hoffmann, 'Indirect Expropriation', 151–170, at 163–164. For a criticism of how international arbitration tribunals are applying the proportionality test, recommending a more deferential approach, see C. Henkels, 'Indirect Expropriation and the Right to Regulate: Revisiting Proportionality Analysis and the Standard of Review in Investor-State Arbitration', 15 *Journal of International Economic Law* (2012), 223–255.

[124] Tecmed, *supra* note 37, at para. 122, containing references to three cases from the European Court of Human Rights; Kriebaum, *supra* note 122, 181, noting that the award 'included human rights considerations in balancing the various interests at stake', and finding at 183 that this represents an 'intermediate approach'.

[125] P. van den Bossche, 'Looking for Proportionality in WTO Law', 35 *Legal Issues of Economic Integration* (2008), 283–294, at 285; M. Andenæs and S. Zleptnig, 'Proportionality: WTO Law in Comparative Perspective', 42 *Texas International Law Review* (2007), 371–427, at 388–392.

other measures available that are less restrictive and that are equally effective in achieving the objective, and the effects of the measure should not be disproportionate or excessive in relation to the interests involved. Investment tribunals have hardly applied the proportionality principle, and, as stated, neither have the purposes of the measure(s) in relation to the stated objective been adequately reviewed. The application of the proportionality principle in the Tecmed case resulted in a conclusion that Mexico had to provide full compensation.

In *Saluka Investments v the Czech Republic*, the latter was found to be in breach of the 'fair and equitable treatment' obligation.[126] One line of reasoning in the award is most interesting, however, and the most relevant part is quoted:

> the principle that a State does not commit an expropriation and is thus not liable to pay compensation to a dispossessed alien investor when it adopts general regulations that are 'commonly accepted as within the police powers of States' forms part of customary international law today.[127]

Hence, states are given wide margins to introduce new regulations and should not be subject to any forms of compensation. This reasoning has been criticized, as allegedly the 'regulatory capacity of host States to introduce new measures to promote and protect human rights will be unlimited in the long run'.[128]

The present author agrees that an investment tribunal—whose members are to have 'recognized competence in the fields of law, commerce, industry or finance', as specified in Article 14(1) of the ICSID Convention—should be careful to claim that a norm represents international customary law. Moreover, the absence of qualifying factors in the quoted paragraph, including that the regulation must be undertaken in a non-discriminatory and non-arbitrary manner, does open things up for criticism. The author does not, however, agree with Kriebaum's criticism of states' legitimate and legal obligations to take measures for the protection and promotion of human rights. Moreover, the award did consider the interests of the investor versus the interests of the state, both when clarifying the term 'legitimate expectations' as an element of the fair and equitable treatment standard,[129] and when clarifying the 'full protection and security' standard,[130] but it did not apply the proportionality principle in a systematic manner.

[126] *Saluka Investments BV (The Netherlands) v The Czech Republic, UNCITRAL Partial Award*, 17 March 2006, para. 497.

[127] *Saluka Investments BV (The Netherlands) v The Czech Republic, UNCITRAL Partial Award*, 17 March 2006, para. 262; followed by a note referring to five investment tribunal awards, one being Tecmed, *supra* note 37, para. 119, which applies the term 'undisputable' about States' exercise of the police power.

[128] Kriebaum, *supra* note 122, at 182.

[129] Saluka, *supra* note 126, at paras. 302–306.

[130] Saluka, *supra* note 126, at paras. 483–484; see also para. 505. In para. 484, 'full security and protection' is said to protect 'the physical integrity of an investment against interference by use of force'. Hence, the award specifies that 'use of force' must be involved, and Moss notes that whether the 'full security and protection' has an application beyond physical safety 'remains rather controversial' (G.C. Moss, 'Full Security and Protection', in A. Reinisch, *supra* note 123, at 131–150, especially 142).

C. The fair and equitable treatment standard

Among the central principles for the protection of investments—in addition to protection against unjustified and arbitrary expropriation[131]—is the 'fair and equitable treatment'. This principle has evolved under BIT treaties from the original 'minimum standards for treatment of aliens'.[132] This standard has been interpreted as containing several elements: fulfilling the legitimate expectations; providing stability and predictability; and promoting total transparency.[133]

In Tecmed, the tribunal found that the fair and equitable treatment standard requires the state to provide 'treatment that does not affect the basic expectations that were taken into account by the foreign investor to make the investment'.[134] This reliance on investors' expectations has been criticized, as the state obligations must 'derive from the terms of the applicable investment treaty and not from any set of expectations', implying that a tribunal that sought to generate rights on the basis of these expectations risks to 'exceed its powers'.[135]

On stability and predictability, we saw above that the Award in Tecmed stated that the legal framework shall be constructed so that any foreign investor 'may know beforehand any and all rules and regulations that will govern its investments'.[136] This has been stated even more explicitly in other awards: 'there is certainly an obligation not to alter the legal and business environment in which the investment has been made'.[137] These two positions cannot be considered to be representative, however: 'No investor may reasonably expect that the circumstances prevailing at the time the investment was made remain totally unchanged'.[138]

Turning to the requirement of total transparency, the Tecmed Award provides an example, as the tribunal found that the requirement on the state is to provide 'total transparency'.[139] In another award, the tribunal found that 'the absence of a clear rule [...] as well as the absence of any established practice or procedure as to the manner of handling applications [...] amounts to a failure on the part of Mexico to ensure the transparency required by NAFTA'.[140] The basis for this was NAFTA Article 1105.1 on 'treatment in accordance with international law, including fair and equitable treatment and full protection and security'. The transparency requirement was interpreted as falling within the scope of Article 1105,

[131] To these can also be added the principles of 'denial of justice' and 'full protection and security', T.G. Nelson, 'Human Rights and BIT Protection: Areas of Convergence', 12 *Journal of World Investment and Trade* (2011), 27–47, at 40–43; see also Reinisch, *supra* note 123.

[132] T.G. Nelson 'Human Rights and BIT Protection: Areas of Convergence', 12 *Journal of World Investment and Trade* (2011), 27–47, at 38.

[133] See also Picherack, *supra* note 51, at 272–285.

[134] Tecmed, *supra* note 37, at para. 154.

[135] *MTD Equity Sdn. Bhd. & MTD Chile SA v Chile, ICSID Case No. ARB/01/7, Decision on Annulment*, 21 March 2007, para. 67. As specified in note 115, ICSID Convention Art. 52(1)(b) says that annulment can be based on a tribunal having 'manifestly exceeded its power'.

[136] Tecmed, *supra* note 37, at para. 154.

[137] *Occidental Exploration and Production Company [OPEC] v Ecuador, LCIA Case No. UN3467, Award*, 1 July 2004, para. 191.

[138] Saluka, *supra* note 125, at para. 305; see also *EDF v Romania, ICSID Case no. ARB/05/13, Award*, 8 October 2009, para. 217.

[139] Tecmed, *supra* note 37, at para. 154.

[140] *Metalclad v Mexico, supra* note 48, at para. 88.

as transparency is not mentioned explicitly in the provisions. Hence, by this understanding, states' conduct in relation to foreign investors is expected to be most forthcoming.

In addition to these very broad interpretations of the fair and equitable treatment standard, which basically strengthen investors' property protection, another problem with such legal reasoning is the tendency in some of the most controversial decisions to refer to certain norms as being 'not different to' or 'equated with' the international customary law on minimum treatment of foreigners, without referring to opinio juris or state practice.[141]

D. Interim conclusion

Two main trends in the jurisprudence of investment tribunals can be discerned. First, standards and principles under international investment law have been subject to more expansionist interpretation, especially the stabilization clauses as elements of a fair and equitable treatment standard. Second, tribunals include a broader range of applicable law, including human rights law, in order to justify regulatory measures as not being in violation of state obligations under BITs. This trend is also reflected by the US 2012 Model Law.

Inadequate conduct by the state, such as the absence of clear rules or procedures to which the investor can relate, might result in the conclusion that the state has violated its obligations. Human rights law specifics obligations of conduct,[142] for instance in relation to non-discrimination, participation, transparency, and accountability. By complying with these obligations of conduct, public policy is improved. The requirements on states' conduct under international investment law seem, however, to be much more demanding—and with harsher monetary consequences if the state is found in violation of the BIT.

6. Conclusion

Foreign direct investments and trade might promote technology and knowledge transfers and enhance the overall capacity for service provision. Some of these investments might, however, also represent a risk for peoples' safe and affordable access to natural resources, and such access is crucial for poor and vulnerable persons and communities. Examples of investments which might seriously affect the

[141] *CMS v Argentina*, Award, *supra* note, 101, para. 284; *OPEC v Ecuador, supra* note 136, at para. 190. Note that the 2012 US Model, BIT specifies in Art. 5(2) that the 'customary international law minimum standard of treatment of aliens [i]s the minimum standard of treatment', and specifies in Art. 5(2)(a) that '"fair and equitable treatment" includes the obligation not to deny justice [...] in accordance with the principle of due process'. On stabilization clauses in BITs, see UN Special Representative on business and human rights, Principles for responsible contracts: integrating the management of human rights risks into State-investor contract negotiations: guidance for negotiators, UN Doc. A/HRC/17/31/Add.3 (2011), 12–14.

[142] Committee on Economic, Social and Cultural Rights, General Comment No. 3, The nature of States parties' obligations (Art. 2, para. 1 of the Covenant) (1991), para. 1.

enjoyment of human rights, as already identified, include water provision contracts, resulting in excessive prices to consumers;[143] land sales or leases, restricting peoples' access to their traditional lands and resources;[144] and mining activities, leading to dangerous contamination of water and soil.[145]

International investment law, allowing companies to initiate proceedings against states without exhausting domestic remedies, is characterized by overprotection and underregulation of the foreign investors.[146] Examples of underregulation include the lack of price ceilings in water provision contracts or the lack of requirements that production activities are undertaken within a given time frame in land transfer contracts. Moreover, the prohibition against performance requirements specified in the Annex to the TRIMS agreement under the WTO is also found in some BIT agreements.[147] Many BITs reflect the fact that they were negotiated before the increased awareness of corporate social responsibility, and are therefore silent on companies' responsibilities in the realm of human rights and the environment.

Provisions on applicable law in BITs imply that investment tribunals have in principle a jurisdiction which extends to apply human rights law. Moreover, even in the absence of explicit human rights provisions in the BITs, some tribunals have taken states' human rights obligations into account when clarifying provisions on necessary measures.[148] To some extent, human rights have been applied as a defence, but human rights arguments have also been used to strengthen the investor's rights, as property protection is encompassed by human rights.[149] To the extent that tribunals assess the impact on the affected communities or the population, they emphasize the accessibility of services, not their affordability or quality.[150] It is therefore reasonable to state that the understanding of human rights obligations is inadequate. Moreover, no awards have been found where the investment tribunals search for the basic purposes of human rights protection such as human dignity.[151]

[143] Section 1.A; See *Suez v Argentina, supra* note 103. For a critical review of this and some other arbitration reports, see J. Perez, M. Gistelinck, and D. Karbala, *Sleeping lions. International investment treaties, state-investor disputes and access to food, land and water*, Oxfam Discussion Papers (2011), available at <http://www.oxfam.org/sites/www.oxfam.org/files/dp-sleeping-lions-260511-en.pdf> (last accessed 14 November 2013).

[144] See *Pezold v Zimbabwe* and *Border Timbers Ltd. v Zimbabwe, supra* note 3.

[145] See *Pac Rim Cayman LLC. v El Salvador, ICSID case no. ARB/09/12, Decision on the respondent's jurisdictional objections*, 1 June 2012 (no decision taken on merits).

[146] See C. Häberli, 'God, the WTO—and hunger' in Nadakavukaren Schefer (ed.), *supra* note 14, 79–106, at 96; see also Dimsey, 'Foreign Direct Investment and the Alleviation of poverty', in Nadakavukaren Schefer (ed.), *supra* note 14, 159–176.

[147] See UNCTAD, *Foreign Direct Investment and Performance Requirements: New Evidence from Selected Countries* (New York and Geneva: UNCTAD 2003), with examples of agreements prohibiting such requirements, at 4–5.

[148] *Suez v Argentina, supra* note 103, at para. 240.

[149] *CMS v Argentina*, Award, *supra* note 101, at para. 121.

[150] *CMS v Argentina*, Award, *supra* note 101, at para. 121.

[151] *Society for Unaided Private Schools of Rajasthan v India, Supreme Court of India*, challenging the Right to Education Act mandating the private schools to reserve 25 per cent of their seats for the students coming from socially disadvantaged sections of society, where the Supreme Court held that this requirement entitled children from disadvantaged sections to live a life with dignity; (waiting for the final verdict) available at <http://www.sify.com/news/compulsory-education-gives-poor-right-to-dignity-court-news-national-lcrv4edjfba.html> (last accessed 14 November 2013).

Regarding the WTO, human rights concerns are included in treaties on trade liberalization, which is the discipline under IEL where developing countries have an offensive interest. In those areas where developed countries have offensive interests, such as services and investments liberalization, and stronger IPR protection, it has been much harder to have human rights explicitly or implicitly recognized. WTO's Director-General Pascal Lamy acknowledges both that the WTO is bound to respect human rights and that its members states are 'bound to fulfil the [human rights] obligations incumbent on them at international level'.[152]

While this chapter has confirmed that both treaties and disputes are only to a limited extent integrating international human rights, the number of treaties which incorporate human rights in the preamble and the substantive provisions—not only the exceptions provisions—is increasing. Moreover, the June 2010 annulment decisions on two awards against Argentina confirm that there is a policy space to take appropriate measures, provided that the necessity requirement is fulfilled.[153]

In accordance with the 2011 UN Guiding Principles 3(b), 5, and 9, relating to the commercial transactions or contracts with business enterprises, states should ensure that when negotiating treaties and contracts, provisions relating to respecting, protecting, and fulfilling human rights should be included, preferably based on a human rights impact assessment[154] or human rights audits.[155] As tribunals acknowledge the importance of domestic legal systems,[156] the phrasing of legal and constitutional provisions is important, and the more explicitly relevant provisions are formulated in human rights terms, the less they can be ignored by tribunals. Moreover, even if the relevant treaty that the dispute is based upon does not contain explicit human rights language, human rights can be applicable law, and the states themselves can contribute to make human rights obligations relevant in the dispute by basing their arguments on human rights obligations.[157] Hence, as states have a right and a duty to regulate ensuring an effective human rights protection of its inhabitants, this includes a duty to give more weight to human rights obligations when agreements under IEL are negotiated, implemented, and enforced.

[152] P. Lamy, *Globalization and trade opening can promote human rights* (2009), available at <http://www.wto.org/english/news_e/sppl_e/sppl128_e.htm> (last accessed 14 November 2013).

[153] *Supra* note 104. See S. Walker 'Human Rights Impact Assessments: Emerging Practice and Challenges', ch. 14 in this book.

[154] See the Guiding Principles on human rights impact assessments of trade and investment agreements, *supra* note 4; see also Report of the High Commissioner for Human Rights, Human rights, trade and investment, UN Doc. E/CN.4/Sub.2/2003/9, para. 31(c) and para. 38, and Jacob, *supra* note 94, at 44–45 for more general recommendations.

[155] Simma, *supra* note 111, at 594–596.

[156] *CMS Gas v Argentina*, Award, *supra* note 101, at paras. 114, 119–122.

[157] For additional advice, see *UNCTAD, IIA Issues Note No. 3. Interpretation of IIAs: What States can do* (2011).

9

Economic, Social, and Cultural Rights in the World Trade Organization

Legal Aspects and Practice

Holger P. Hestermeyer

1. Introduction

To the uninitiated, international law presents a number of perplexities, not least of which is its fragmented character. The bulk of international law stems from bilateral or multilateral treaties between states covering a vast variety of fields. A hierarchy between these norms, that could create some consistency, is largely absent.[1] So is a centralized court system applying international norms: quite to the contrary, each treaty can provide for its own enforcement system. Such systems are commonly endowed with jurisdiction only over the system they have been set up to enforce and at times are only allowed to apply the rules of that system.[2] This limitation compounds the differentiation of international law into separate fields.[3]

The International Covenant on Economic, Social and Cultural Rights (ICESCR)[4] and the World Trade Organization (WTO) Agreements[5] are instances of this

[1] The limited instances of hierarchy in international law are Art. 103 of the Charter of the United Nations and the doctrine of *ius cogens*. See ILC, *Fragmentation of International Law*, UN Doc. A/CN.4/L.682 of 13 April 2006. Despite the evolution of international law towards a more complex, constitutional order protecting community interests, the bulk of international law continues to consist of non-hierarchical rules created in a decentralized manner. See, e.g. A. Paulus, *Die internationale Gemeinschaft im Völkerrecht* (München: Beck, 2001); B. Simma, 'From Bilateralism to Community Interest in International Law', 250 *Recueil des Cours* (1994), 217–384, 221; C. Tomuschat, 'Obligations Arising for States Without or Against Their Will', 241 *RdC* (1993), 195–374, 199. The author wishes to thank Gabrielle Marceau, Lorand Bartels, and Hans Morten Haugen for helpful comments, and Tim Kuhn for research assistance. All remaining errors are mine.

[2] For two different views on the proliferation of international tribunals see N. Matz-Lück, 'Promoting the Unity of International Law', in D. König et al. (eds.), *International Law Today*, 99 (Heidelberg: Springer 2008); and H. Hestermeyer, 'Where Unity Is at Risk', *International Law Today*, 123.

[3] This structural observation also belies the concept of a constitutionalization of international law. See C. Walter, 'Constitutionalizing (Inter)national Governance: Possibilities for and Limits to the Development of an International Constitutional Law', 44 *GYIL* (2001) 170, 189.

[4] 993 UNTS 3; GA Res. 2200 (XXI) 1966, entry into force 3 January 1976.

[5] WTO, *The Legal Texts: The Results of the Uruguay Round of Multilateral Trade Negotiations* (Cambridge: Cambridge University Press, 1999).

fragmented system. The former, a treaty with currently 161 state parties,[6] relies for its enforcement on a system of naming and shaming violators.[7] The WTO, an international organization with its roots in the 1947 General Agreement on Tariffs and Trade (GATT) and with 159 members as of March 2013,[8] boasts a highly ambitious and successful dispute-settlement mechanism for states, with proceedings that can ultimately allow trade retaliation for violations of the WTO Agreements.[9] As pointed out by Hans Morten Haugen in chapter 8, the WTO Agreements do not contain explicit references to human rights, nor does the ICESCR make references to international trade law. The two regimes thus seemingly live entirely separate lives.[10] Accordingly, for much of their history the two regimes existed in blissful ignorance of each other and experts of one rarely became involved in the other.

The fact that the norms of the two regimes do not refer to each other does not imply, however, that in any given situation only one of the two regimes applies. Reality simply cannot be compartmentalized in the way that normative regimes are.[11] States in that situation, too, must comply with all of their obligations under international law—from both regimes. The WTO covers such diverse fields as trade in goods and services, agriculture, sanitary standards, technical regulations, and intellectual property, imposing, for example, non-discrimination obligations on members.[12] Such a broad regime on economic affairs necessarily affects many other legal regimes.[13] The human rights regime is one of them.[14] Examples of factual

[6] Ratification data for the ICESCR and its Optional Protocol is available at <http://treaties.un.org> (last accessed 22 October 2013.

[7] The Optional Protocol providing for communications to the Committee on Economic, Social and Cultural Rights has entered into force on 5 May 2013. However, the protocol does not provide for legally binding views on such communications by the Committee, see its Art. 9.

[8] Current membership data is available at <http://www.wto.org/english/thewto_e/whatis_e/tif_e/org6_e.htm> (last accessed 4 November 2013.

[9] Doctrinal works extolling the virtues of WTO dispute settlement abound. See only J. Bacchus, '"Woulda, Coulda, Shoulda": The Consolations of WTO Dispute Settlement', in J. Bacchus, *Trade and Freedom* (Nottingham: CMP Publishing, 2004), 361, 368; J. Jackson, 'International Economic Law: Jurisprudence and Contours', 93 *ASIL Proceedings* (1999), 98, 102.

[10] Despite the impact of the UN system on both, see Art. 55 of the UN Charter.

[11] Martti Koskenniemi once stated that 'international law comes to us in separate boxes such as 'trade law' and 'environmental law' that may have different principles and objectives that do not apply across the boundaries between such boxes'. In reality though, as Frank Garcia wrote, '[t]here is no such thing as a pure trade issue'. M. Koskenniemi, 'International Law: Between Fragmentation and Constitutionalism' (Canberra, 27 November 2006), available at <http://www.helsinki.fi/eci/Publications/Koskenniemi/MCanberra-06c.pdf> (last accessed 4 August 2013). F.J. Garcia, *Trade, Inequality and Justice* (Ardsley: Transnational Publishers, 2003), 212.

[12] See Arts. I and III of the GATT. In detail, see G. Sacerdoti and K. Castren, 'Article I', and H. Hestermeyer, 'Article III', in R. Wolfrum et al. (eds.), *WTO: Trade in Goods* (Leiden: Martinus Nijhoff, 2011), 53 and 116 respectively.

[13] J. Neumann, *Die Koordination des WTO-Rechts mit anderen völkerrechtlichen Ordnungen* (Berlin: Duncker & Humblot, 2002); J. Pauwelyn, *Conflict of Norms in Public International Law* (Cambridge: Cambridge University Press, 2003).

[14] Until fairly recently drafters of broad economic agreements commonly did not think that such agreements could interact with human rights. The EU's slow path towards human rights protection stands as an example of how such awareness develops. See, e.g. P. Alston (ed.), *The EU and Human Rights* (Oxford: Oxford University Press, 1999); D. Ehlers (ed.), *Europäische Grundrechte und Grundfreiheiten* 3rd edn (Berlin: De Gruyter, 2009).

situations in which both regimes apply abound: Robert Howse and Ruti Teitel in their study on the WTO and the ICESCR cite, by way of example, impacts of WTO rules on the rights to work, health, and food.[15] Where both the ICESCR and WTO law apply to a factual situation, state parties to both systems must take measures that comply with both systems.

Scholars and practitioners discovered the relationship of the WTO and human rights in the second half of the 1990s. The initial impulse came from the human rights community,[16] which did not always hold the WTO in high esteem. Thus, a preliminary report for the Sub-Commission on the Promotion and Protection of Human Rights declared the WTO to be a 'veritable nightmare' for certain sectors of humanity, particularly the developing countries of the South.[17] Some scholars charged the WTO with putting markets ahead of human rights.[18] By now, however, a rich and much more nuanced body of literature has developed,[19] throwing light on the relationship between the WTO and human rights from such diverse perspectives as international law, economics, philosophy, political science, and sociology.[20] It attests to a complex relationship between the two regimes, in which WTO rules at times further human rights interests, and at other times conflict with them. In the latter case, WTO provisions such as Article XX(a) of the GATT or Article 2.2 of the Agreement on Technical Barriers to Trade (TBT)[21] can and often do provide states with the possibility to protect human rights interests without running afoul of WTO obligations.[22] WTO Members may also waive WTO

[15] R. Howse and R.G. Teitel, 'Beyond the Divide: the International Covenant on Economic, Social and Political (*sic*) Rights and the World Trade Organization', in S. Joseph et al. (eds.), *The World Trade Organization and Human Rights* (Cheltenham: Edward Elgar, 2009), 39 and 50.

[16] R. Howse and R.G. Teitel, 'Beyond the Divide: the International Covenant on Economic, Social and Political (*sic*) Rights and the World Trade Organization', in S. Joseph et al. (eds.), *The World Trade Organization and Human Rights* (Cheltenham: Edward Elgar, 2009), 40.

[17] J. Oloka-Anyango and D. Udagama, *The Realization of Economic, Social and Cultural Rights: Globalization and its Impact on the Full Enjoyment of Human Rights*, UN Doc. E/CN.4/Sub.2/2000/13, of 15 June 2000, para. 15.

[18] See, e.g. M. Cohn, 'The World Trade Organisation: Elevating Property Interests above Human Rights', 29 *Georgia Journal of International & Comparative Law* (2001), 427–440.

[19] L. Bartels, 'Trade and Human Rights', in D. Bethlehem et al. (eds.), *International Trade Law* (Oxford: Oxford University Press, 2009), 571; J. Harrison, *The Human Rights Impact of the World Trade Organisation* (Oxford: Hart, 2007); H. Hestermeyer, *Human Rights and the WTO* (Oxford: Oxford University Press, 2007); T. Cottier et al. (eds.), *Human Rights and International Trade* (Oxford: Oxford University Press, 2005). Few authors tackled the topic before the 1990s. See, e.g. P. Alston, 'Linking Trade and Human Rights', 23 *German Yearbook of International Law* (1980), 126–158.

[20] J. Waincymer, 'The trade and human rights debate: Introduction to an Interdisciplinary Analysis', in S. Joseph et al., *The World Trade Organization and Human Rights* (Cheltenham: Edward Elgar, 2009), 1, 4.

[21] Art. 2.2 of the TBT Agreement permits technical regulations that are not more trade-restrictive than necessary to 'fulfil a legitimate objective'. The protection of human rights is such a 'legitimate objective'. In 2012, three Appellate Body reports provided some urgently needed clarification in the application of the TBT Agreement. See *US—Tuna II*, WT/DS381/AB/R; *US—COOL*, WT/DS 384, 386/AB/R; *US—Clove Cigarettes*, WT/DS406/AB/R, as well as G. Marceau, 'Trade and Labour', in D. Bethlehem et al. (eds.), *International Trade Law* (Oxford: Oxford University Press, 2009), 554–557; H. Nottage and A. Sánchez, 'Navigating Uncharted Waters: A Review of US—Tuna II', 7 *Global Trade and Customs Journal* (2012), 59–65.

[22] H.M. Haugen discusses some of these possibilities in more depth in his ch. 8 in this book.

obligations under Article IX:3 of the WTO Agreement to allow for more flexibility, as in the case of pharmaceutical patents,[23] where a waiver allows countries without manufacturing capacity to benefit from compulsory licenses—even though it is arguable to what extent that waiver is actually effective in practice.[24]

The normative relationship between the WTO Agreements and the ICESCR, complex though it is, constitutes only part of the story of the interplay of the two international regimes. The WTO is also an international organization with both numerous organs and a highly effective dispute settlement system that can, unlike the enforcement system of the ICESCR, authorize trade retaliation.[25] The strength of the WTO regime raises a haunting spectre for human rights: a country choosing which obligation to follow may, irrespective of the normative relationship between the two regimes, choose to follow WTO law, because a failure to implement WTO obligations entails more severe consequences than a failure to properly implement the ICESCR. I have referred to this phenomenon elsewhere as a 'factual hierarchy' of regimes.[26]

This phenomenon shifts the focus of our analysis from the normative question of how the ICESCR relates to the WTO Agreements under general international law to the question of what role the ICESCR plays *within* the WTO as an international organization. Is the WTO bound by the ICESCR? Can the Covenant be applied in WTO dispute settlement, allowing states to justify violations of WTO law with their quest to implement obligations under the Covenant? Both of these questions have been much discussed in legal scholarship, and they will serve as background for the issue covered in this chapter, namely the extent to which human rights arguments are actually made within the WTO's organs. This empirical question, of obvious importance for describing the reality of the relationship between the two regimes, has been neglected so far. The WTO's documents database, however, provides scholars with ample material to gauge the real impact of the ICESCR on WTO bodies. The chapter concludes with an analysis of the findings.

2. Analysing Human Rights Obligations of the WTO

Two normative questions need to be answered to understand the legal background for analysing the empirical impact of the ICESCR within debates in the WTO. The first of these is whether the WTO as an international organization is bound by the Covenant.

[23] For an in-depth study, see I. Feichtner, *The Law and Politics of WTO Waivers: Stability and Flexibility in Public International Law* (Cambridge: Cambridge University Press, 2011).

[24] See H.P. Hestermeyer, 'Canadian-made Drugs for Rwanda: The First Application of the WTO Waiver on Patents and Medicines', in 11 *American Society of International Law: Insights* 28 (2007).

[25] Joel Trachtman identified a certain jealousy of the strength of WTO dispute settlement on the part of proponents of other regimes and irreverently referred to it as 'penance envy'. J.P. Trachtman, 'Transcending 'Trade and…An Institutional Perspective', *SSRN Working Paper Series* (2001), available at <http://papers.ssrn.com/sol3/papers.cfm?abstract_id=271171> (last accessed 4 November 2013.

[26] Hestermeyer, *supra* note 19, at 193–197.

At first sight the question might appear odd: 133 of the Members of the WTO—84 per cent of the membership—have ratified the ICESCR, 4 more have signed it but not ratified.[27] It would be detrimental to international law if states could escape their human rights obligations simply by setting up an international organization and conducting their business through the organization. Article 61 of the International Law Commission (ILC)'s Draft Articles on the Responsibility of International Organizations reflects this consideration.[28]

A. Obligations of states in the WTO

Hence it comes as no surprise that under international law states remain bound by their obligations when founding an international organization, delegating powers to that organization, or acting within it.[29] To what extent they are also responsible for measures undertaken to implement obligations imposed by the organization has been the subject of much discussion. Legal rules and practice allow for diverging arguments. The measures could be attributed to the organization to the exclusion of the state, an approach taken (erroneously as to the standards of attribution) in the *Behrami* case of the European Court of Human Rights (ECtHR)[30] involving acts of states undertaken under KFOR and UNMIK missions.[31] Even in that case member states of the organization can still be responsible for the measures under Articles 58–62 of the ILC's Draft Articles on the Responsibility of International Organizations. Responsibility would, for example, arise under Article 61(1) if the state circumvented its obligations by causing the organization to take the measures in question, taking advantage of the fact that the organization has competence in relation to the subject matter.

[27] Conversely, 83 per cent of the state parties to the ICESCR are WTO Members and 13 per cent have observer status. Note that some WTO Members, such as Hong Kong, cannot ratify the ICESCR as they are not states.

[28] Yearbook of the ILC, 2011, vol. II, Part Two. Art. 61(1) of the ILC Articles reads: 'A State member of an international organization incurs international responsibility if, by taking advantage of the fact that the organization has competence in relation to the subject-matter of one of the State's international obligations, it circumvents that obligation by causing the organization to commit an act that, if committed by the State, would have constituted a breach of the obligation.'

[29] See, e.g. S. Hörmann, 'WTO und Menschenrechte', in M. Hilf and S. Oeter (eds.), *WTO-Recht* (Nomos: Baden-Baden 2005), 652. See also *Statement of the Committee on Economic, Social and Cultural Rights to the Third Ministerial Conference of the World Trade Organization*, in UN Doc. E/2000/22, Annex VII, para. 8.

[30] ECtHR, *Behrami and Behrami v France and Ruzhdi Saramati v France, Germany and Norway* (App. Nos. 71412/01 and 78166/01) of 2 May 2007, para. 151. For criticism see M. Milanović and T. Papić, 'As Bad as it Gets', 58 *International and Comparative Law Quarterly* (2009), 267–296; A. Breitegger, 'Sacrificing the Effectiveness of the European Convention on Human Rights on the Altar of the Effective Functioning of Peace Support Operations', 11 *International Community Law Review* (2009), 155–183. For further ECtHR case law see ECtHR, *Waite and Kennedy v Germany* (App. No. 26083/94) of 18 February 1999, para. 67; ECtHR, *Matthews v the United Kingdom* (App. No. 24833/94) of 18 February 1999, para. 32; ECtHR, *Bosphorus Hava Yollari Turizm ve Ticaret Anonim Şirketi v Ireland* (App. No. 45036/98) of 30 June 2005; ECtHR, *Rambus v Germany* (App. No. 40382/04) of 16 June 2009 (with further references).

[31] Arts. 6–9 of the ILC's Draft Articles on the Responsibility of International Organizations govern attribution to an international organization. However, they do not answer the question whether this attribution is exclusive. According to the ILC's commentary on the Draft Articles, the question of the

In many cases, however, the measures will also be attributable to the state,[32] which is bound by and has to comply with both the obligations imposed by the international organization it founded and its other obligations under international law.[33] Since full scrutiny of state action under its international obligations, even where that state action is taken to comply with obligations imposed by an international organization, can complicate international cooperation, the ECtHR allows states to justify acts taken in compliance with obligations stemming from the international organization if that organization offers an equivalent substantive and procedural protection of human rights to the one granted in the European Convention on Human Rights. In the *Bosphorus* case, the ECtHR held:

> The Convention does not, on the one hand, prohibit Contracting Parties from transferring sovereign power to an international (including a supranational) organization in order to pursue cooperation in certain fields of activity. [...] On the other hand, it has also been accepted that a Contracting Party is responsible under Article 1 of the Convention for all acts and omissions of its organs regardless of whether the act or omission in question was a consequence of domestic law or of the necessity to comply with international legal obligations. [...] In reconciling both these positions and thereby establishing the extent to which a State's action can be justified by its compliance with obligations flowing from its membership of an international organization to which it has transferred part of its sovereignty, the Court has recognized that absolving Contracting States completely from their Convention responsibility in the areas covered by such a transfer would be incompatible with the purpose and object of the Convention [...] In the Court's view, State action taken in compliance with such legal obligations is justified as long as the relevant organization is considered to protect fundamental rights, as regards both the substantive guarantees offered and the mechanisms controlling their observance, in a manner which can be considered at least equivalent to that for which the Convention provides.[34]

Following these principles and transposing them to the ICESCR, actions taken by state parties of the ICESCR to implement WTO obligations do not benefit from the presumption established by the ECtHR in *Bosphorus*. Any attempt to justify a breach of the ICESCR with obligations under the WTO Agreements would have to fail, because the WTO does not possess any mechanism to protect rights flowing from the ICESCR.

attribution to states remains subject to the ILC Articles on the Responsibility of States. *Draft Articles on the Responsibility of International Organizations, with Commentaries*, Yearbook of the ILC, 2011, vol. II, Part Two, Part Five, para. 2.

[32] The standards of attribution are contained in Arts. 4–11 of the ILC *Articles on Responsibility of States for Internationally Wrongful Acts*, Yearbook of the ILC, 2001, vol. II, Part Two.

[33] The ECtHR had to deal with this issue in several cases. See L. Bartels, *WTO Member Responsibility for Acts Implementing Obligations of Organizations Established by Regional Trade Agreements*, BIICL presentation of 20 May 2010 (on file with the author).

[34] ECtHR, *Bosphorus Hava Yollari Turizm ve Ticaret Anonim Şirketi v Ireland* (App. No. 45036/98) of 30 June 2005, paras. 152–155 (internal references deleted); see also ECtHR, *MSS v Belgium and Greece* (App. No. 30696/09) of 21 January 2011, para. 338.

B. Obligations of the WTO itself

The fact that state parties to the ICESCR remain bound by the Covenant when acting within the WTO does not imply, however, that the WTO is *itself* bound by the Covenant. It has been argued that when states bound by a treaty set up an international organization, the treaty also binds the organization. Logically this result is supposed to flow either from the principle *nemo plus iuris transferre potest quam ipse habet*; that is, states have limited their legal competences by ratifying a treaty and when they transfer competences they can only do so within those limits,[35] or from an analogy to state succession.[36] The argument can claim some support in the case law of the European Union (EU), which applies the so-called 'doctrine of functional succession' to treaties concluded by all member states prior to the establishment of the European Communities/EU,[37] most prominently the GATT and the UN Charter.[38]

However, this position fails to take into account the fact that international organizations themselves are subjects of international law with their own rights and obligations and their own capacity to enter into treaties,[39] at least for the area of law in which they possess competences according to their founding documents.[40] States have a duty to set up international organizations so that these do not violate states' obligations.[41] However, the organizations are not automatically bound by all obligations incumbent on the states that set them up, but by their own obligations, namely—according to the ICJ—'any obligations incumbent upon them under general rules of international law, under their constitutions or under international agreements to which they are parties'.[42] The separate legal personality and obligations

[35] H.G. Schermers, 'The Legal Bases of International Organization Action', in R.-J. Dupuy (ed.), *A Handbook on International Organizations* 2nd edn (Cambridge: Kluwer, 1998), 401 and 403.

[36] H.G. Schermers and N.M. Blokker, *International Institutional Law* 5th edn (Leiden: Martinus Nijhoff, 2011), 996 (also arguing with the weakness of legal systems of international organizations, the reluctance to accept international organizations as parties to treaties, and the fact that international organizations have no reason to claim a right to abstain from treaties).

[37] A. von Bogdandy and M. Smrkolj, 'European Community and Union Law and International Law', in R. Wolfrum (ed.), *Max Planck Encyclopedia of Public International Law* (Oxford: Oxford University Press, 2009), para. 17.

[38] ECJ, Joined Cases 21 to 24/72, *International Fruit Company v Produktschap voor Groenten en Fruit*, ECR 1972, 1227, para. 18; CFI, T-315/01, *Kadi v Council and Commission*, paras. 192–204; see also ECJ, Joined Cases C-402/05 and C-415/05, *Kadi v Council and Commission*, paras. 291 and 293.

[39] See also Art. 6 of the Vienna Convention on the Law of Treaties between States and International Organizations or between International Organizations (not in force); in-depth: ILC, *First report on the question of treaties concluded between States and international organizations or between two or more international organizations by Mr Paul Reuter*, Special Rapporteur, Yearbook ILC 1972, vol. II, 171, 178–182.

[40] ICJ, Reparation for Injuries Suffered in the Service of the United Nations, Advisory Opinion, ICJ Rep. 1949, 174, 178 et seq. of 11 April 1949; see also I. Brownlie, *Principles of Public International Law* (6th edn, Oxford: Oxford University Press, 2003), 648–650; Schermers and Blokker, *supra* note 36, at 1123.

[41] The EU case law can be read as an approach to fulfil this obligation. Treaties can also explicitly provide for solutions to possible conflicts, see Art. XXI (c) of the GATT.

[42] ICJ, Interpretation of the Agreement of 25 March 1951 between the WHO and Egypt, Advisory Opinion of 20 December 1980, ICJ Rep. 1980, 73, 89–90; cited also by ILC, *Draft articles on the responsibility of international organizations, with commentaries*, 14 (2011).

of international organizations raise numerous complex issues, such as the applicability of international humanitarian law to UN peacekeeping missions,[43] or of human rights law to UN sanctions.[44] That is, however, the natural consequence of endowing international organizations with their own personality. This, too, has been acknowledged by the ECtHR that held that even an international organization that was granted sovereign powers by contracting parties of the European Convention on Human Rights is not responsible for a violation of the Convention as long as it is not a contracting party itself.[45] The WTO is thus not bound by the ICESCR, as it is not a contracting party of the Covenant.

C. Obligations under general international law

The fact that the WTO is not bound by the ICESCR does not imply that it can ignore the document in its entirety. As subjects of international law, international organizations are bound by general international law.[46] To the extent that ICESCR obligations constitute general principles or customary international law, they thus also bind the WTO. The WTO Secretariat has acknowledged the WTO's human rights obligations under customary international law.[47]

This statement comes with a caveat, however: most international law is dispositive and states are free to contract out of it.[48] The exceptions to this rule are norms *iuris cogentis*.[49] States could thus, by ratifying the WTO Agreements, have implicitly contracted out of any human rights standard under general international law that contradicts WTO law to the extent that the human rights standard is not *iuris cogentis*.

[43] Secretary-General's Bulletin, *Observance by United Nations Forces of International Humanitarian Law*, UN Doc. ST/SGB/1999/13 of 6 August 1999; U. Palwankar, 'Applicability of International Humanitarian Law to United Nations Peacekeeping Forces', 294 *International Review of the Red Cross* (1993), 227–240.

[44] E. de Wet, 'Human Rights Limitations to Economic Enforcement Measures under Article 41 of the United Nations Charter and the Iraqi Sanctions Regime', 14 *Leiden Journal of International Law* (2001), 277–300.

[45] ECtHR, *Bosphorus Hava Yollari Turizm ve Ticaret Anonim Şirketi v Ireland* (App. No. 45036/98) of 30 June 2005, para. 152; see also European Commission on Human Rights, *Confédération Française Démocratique du Travail v the European Communities* (App. No. 8030/77) of 10 July 1978, para. 3.

[46] H.G. Schermers, 'The Legal Bases of International Organization Action', in R.-J. Dupuy (ed.), *A Handbook on International Organizations* 2nd edn (Cambridge: Kluwer, 1998), 401–402; M. Bedjaoui, 'Du Contrôle de Légalité des Actes du Conseil de Sécurité', in *Nouveaux Itinéraires en Droit*, 69, 82 et seq. (Bruxelles: Bruylant, 1993); contrast with A. Bleckmann, 'Zur Verbindlichkeit des allgemeinen Völkerrechts für international Organisationen', 37 *Zeitschrift für ausländisches öffentliches Recht und Völkerrecht/Heidelberg Journal of International Law* (1977), 107–121.

[47] UN Doc. E/CN.4/Sub.2/2001/SR.13 of 18 March 2002, para. 40, UN Doc. E/CN.4/Sub.2/2001/SR.12 of 14 August 2001, para. 24. See also A. Clapham, *Human Rights Obligations of Non-State Actors* (Oxford: Oxford University Press, 2006), 164.

[48] ILC, *Fragmentation of International Law*, UN Doc. A/CN.4/L.682 of 13 April 2006; Pauwelyn, *supra* note 13, at 200 ff.

[49] Art. 53 of the Vienna Convention on the Law of Treaties of 23 May 1969, UNTS 1155, 331.

D. Conclusion

The analysis shows that while the state parties to the ICESCR are bound by the Covenant, also when acting within the ambit of the WTO, the WTO itself is not. The WTO, however, is subject to norms *iuris cogentis* and to general international law to the extent that members have not contracted out of it.

3. The ICESCR in WTO Dispute Settlement

The second normative question that awaits an answer is to what extent the WTO dispute settlement system is empowered to apply the ICESCR? Logically this question divides into two parts: jurisdiction and applicable law. Jurisdiction refers to the types of claims that a tribunal can entertain; applicable law to the law the tribunal may apply.[50]

A. Jurisdiction

The WTO dispute settlement system has been set up, according to Article 1.1 of the Dispute Settlement Understanding (DSU), to rule on 'disputes brought pursuant to the consultation and dispute settlement provisions of the agreements listed in Appendix 1 to this Understanding'. Appendix 1 lists the so-called 'covered agreements', namely the WTO Agreements except for the Trade Policy Review Mechanism and the plurilateral agreements unless otherwise notified to the Dispute Settlement Body.[51] The consultation and dispute settlement provisions of those agreements primarily provide for complaints relating to violations of the covered agreements.[52] The so-called 'non-violation complaints' also mentioned in the provisions, granting the possibility to use dispute settlement procedures if benefits accruing under the agreements are nullified or impaired even without a violation, were barely used during the days of the GATT 1947 and are even more rarely invoked (let alone successfully) these days.[53] Even if that were not case, it is highly unlikely that a violation of the ICESCR could be argued as a non-violation

[50] Note that not all authors use the terminology in an identical manner.

[51] See G. Marceau, 'WTO Dispute Settlement and Human Rights', 13 *European Journal of International Law* (2002), 753–814, 762–763.

[52] See Arts. XXII and XXIII of the GATT, referred to (at times with variations) in Art. 19 of the Agreement on Agriculture, Art. 11 of the SPS Agreement, Art. 14 of the TBT Agreement, Art. 8 of the TRIMs Agreement, Arts. 7 and 8 of the Agreement on Preshipment Inspection, Arts. 7 and 8 of the Agreement on Rules of Origin, Art. 7 of the Agreement on Import Licensing Procedures, Art. 30 of the Agreement on Subsidies and Countervailing Measures, Art. 14 of the Agreement on Safeguards, Art. 64 of the TRIPS Agreement, Art. 8.8 of the Agreement on Trade in Civil Aircraft, as well as Art. 17.1 of the Anti-Dumping Agreement, Art. 19.1 of the Customs Valuation Agreement, Arts. XXII and XXIII of the GATS, and Art. XXII of the Agreement on Government Procurement.

[53] The Panel in *Japan—Film* identified eight cases in WTO/GATT dispute settlement. Markus Böckenförde counts four cases since the establishment of the WTO, none of them successful. *Japan—Film*, WT/DS44/R, para. 10.36. M. Böckenförde, 'Article 26 DSU', in R. Wolfrum et al., *WTO—Institutions and Dispute Settlement* (Leiden: Martinus Nijhoff 2006), para. 8.

claim.[54] WTO Dispute Settlement thus can only rule on claims of violations of WTO Agreements,[55] not of violations of the ICESCR.

Joost Pauwelyn has argued, however, that the scope of jurisdiction of WTO dispute settlement can be enlarged ad hoc to include violations of non-WTO law if the parties to a case so agree.[56] This seems erroneous, for Article 1 of the DSU does not allow for jurisdictional exceptions.[57] Such exceptions are also politically undesirable; the WTO is a specialized dispute settlement procedure with expertise in a particular regime of international law, and so it would be inappropriate to use the procedure outside that expertise.

The latter argument also disfavours an enlargement of the scope of WTO dispute settlement *de lege ferenda*. The appeal of such an enlargement is obvious: enforcing the ICESCR via the strong WTO dispute settlement procedure could give a boost to compliance with human rights law. However, such a change is both practically unlikely and conceptually undesirable. Countries did not agree to a court enforcing the ICESCR with binding rulings and the possibility of sanctions. There is no reason to assume that they would look upon the enforcement of the Covenant in WTO dispute settlement in a different light.[58] Conceptually, the international trade culture is a culture of trade-offs, anathema to human rights law.

B. Applicable law

The limitation of jurisdiction to WTO law does not imply, however, that WTO dispute settlement organs cannot *apply* non-WTO law. Parties are free to limit the law that a tribunal may apply, with the exception of *ius cogens* that remains applicable under any circumstances. The question of the law a tribunal can apply is distinct from that of its jurisdiction[59] and has to be tackled only if the latter has been answered in the affirmative.[60]

[54] Marceau, *supra* note 51, at 768.

[55] This includes non-WTO provisions incorporated by the covered agreements.

[56] Allegedly this can be done by agreeing on non-standard terms of reference under Art. 7.3 of the DSU. J. Pauwelyn, 'The Role of Public International Law in the WTO: How Far Can We Go?', 95 *American Journal of International Law* (2001), 535–578, 554. See also *Canada/European Communities—Article XXVIII Rights*, DS12/R, which was decided before the entry into force of the DSU.

[57] M. Böckenförde, 'Zwischen Sein und Wollen', 63 *ZaöRV* (2003), 971, 981, footnote 39.

[58] P. Alston, 'Resisting the Merger and Acquisition of Human Rights by Trade Law', 13 *EJIL* (2002), 815–844, 833–834. Developing countries in particular would regard human rights arguments as a justification of denying developing countries market access. E.-U. Petersmann, 'Human Rights and the Law of the World Trade Organization', 37 *Journal of World Trade* (2003), 241–281, 280.

[59] It can also be the subject of a different provision. See, e.g. Arts. 36 and 38 of the ICJ Statute, with commentaries by C. Tomuschat and A. Pellet in A. Zimmermann et al. (eds.), *The Statute of the International Court of Justice* (Oxford: Oxford University Press, 2006); Art. 34.1 of the Protocolo de Olivos para la Solución de Controversias en el MERCOSUR, but see also *Laudo No 1/2005*, para. 9.

[60] For a discussion on the interplay of jurisdiction and applicable law clauses see L. Bartels, 'Jurisdiction and Applicable Law Clauses', in T. Broude and Y. Shany (eds.), *Multi-Sourced Equivalent Norms in International Law* (Oxford: Hart 2011), 115.

The notion of 'applying' a norm also needs to be distinguished from using a norm for purposes of interpreting a provision of WTO law. If a norm is part of the applicable law, a state can rely on it to defend the measures it takes. Whether the defence is successful is a matter of resolving the conflict between the provision allegedly breached and the norm relied on in defence. Relevant rules for resolving such conflicts are, for example, contained in Article 30 of the Vienna Convention on the Law of Treaties or such rules as *lex superior, lex posterior*, or *lex specialis*.[61] If a norm can only be used to interpret WTO law, a state would always have to find a WTO provision to defend its measures and could then rely on the norm to interpret the WTO provision in its favour.

The DSU does not contain a clause explicitly entitled 'applicable law'. It does, however, contain a rule on the 'terms of reference' for dispute settlement panels. Article 7 of the DSU offers two options in this regard: standard and special terms of reference. Under the standard terms of reference, panels examine cases 'in the light of the relevant provisions in (name of the covered agreement(s) cited by the parties to the dispute)'.[62] Non-standard terms of reference, on the other hand, have not gained practical relevance, as they have been used only once.[63]

It is the subject of some dispute what exactly the language in Article 7 of the DSU implies. For some authors it does not settle the question of applicable law. Petros Mavroidis states that 'the question whether a WTO Panel can consult sources of law other than the covered agreements [...] is not prejudged in a categorical manner by the DSU'.[64] Lorand Bartels and Pauwelyn would agree.[65]

However, it is difficult to see the function Article 7 of the DSU serves if it is not to limit the law that panels can apply. The wording clearly indicates that the provision regulates the applicable law.[66] This is in line with the obligation of panels under Article 11 of the DSU to make an objective assessment of 'the applicability of and conformity with the relevant covered agreements' and the prohibition

[61] None of these rules are particularly appropriate for resolving inter-systemic conflicts, as pointed out by R. Michaels and J. Pauwelyn, 'Conflict of Norms or Conflict of Laws?: Different Techniques in the Fragmentation of International Law', in Broude and Shany, *supra* note 60, at 19, 33–39.

[62] Art. 7.1 DSU.

[63] *Brazil—Desiccated Coconut*, WT/DS22/R. See P. Mavroidis, 'Article 7 DSU', in R. Wolfrum et al., *WTO—Institutions and Dispute Settlement* (Leiden: Martinus Nijhoff, 2006), paras. 1 and 9. The WTO Analytical Index, updated on an on-going basis, still only cites this one example. Available at <http://www.wto.org/english/res_e/booksp_e/analytic_index_e/analytic_index_e.htm> (last accessed 4 November 2013).

[64] P. Mavroidis, 'Article 7 DSU', in R. Wolfrum et al., *WTO—Institutions and Dispute Settlement* (Leiden: Martinus Nijhoff, 2006), para. 2.

[65] L. Bartels, 'Applicable Law in WTO Dispute Settlement Proceedings', 35 *JWT* (2001) 499–515, 505; Pauwelyn, *supra* note 56, at 560–562. Note, however, that both authors now apparently give preference to WTO law in cases of conflict within the WTO system. R. Michaels and J. Pauwelyn, 'Conflict of Norms or Conflict of Laws?: Different Techniques in the Fragmentation of International Law', in T. Broude and Y. Shany (eds.), *Multi-Sourced Equivalent Norms in International Law* (Oxford: Hart, 2011), 19 and 36.

[66] Böckenförde, *supra* note 57, at 979; J. Trachtman, 'The Domain of WTO Dispute Resolution', in 40 *Harvard International Law Journal* (1999), 333–377, 342; G. Marceau, 'A Call for Coherence in International Law' 33 *JWT* (1999), 87–152, 110; Hestermeyer, *supra* note 19, at 216–218.

of 'add[ind] and diminish[ing] the rights and obligations provided in the covered agreements' in Articles 3(2) and 19(2) of the DSU.[67] Accordingly, states cannot successfully invoke an obligation under the ICESCR as a defence against a claim of a violation of WTO obligations in WTO dispute settlement.[68]

What about those rules of the ICESCR, however, that are part of customary international law? Article 3.2 of the DSU states that the dispute settlement system of the WTO serves to clarify the provisions of WTO law 'in accordance with customary rules of interpretation of public international law'. It is more than doubtful whether this means that all of customary international law applies. According to one study, not one of over 200 WTO-era and 120 GATT-era reports found any custom other than good faith to be applicable.[69] Even if one were to concede that customary international law applies in WTO dispute settlement as a source of law in addition to WTO law, such law would only apply 'to the extent that the WTO treaty agreements do not "contract out" from it', in the words of a panel report from 2000.[70] An argument based on the customary status of an ICESCR norm thus could not prevail as a defence against a claim of violation of WTO law. A claim based on general principles would fare equally.[71] Even though studies found WTO dispute settlement to apply general principles extensively, their use is largely limited to interpretation or procedural matters.[72] The best way to conceptualize such use is to regard it as part of the inherent jurisdiction of WTO tribunals.[73] The only exceptions are norms *iuris cogentis*—those cannot be contracted out of and hence must be applied.

C. Use of the ICESCR for interpretation

As stated, under Article 3.2 of the DSU, WTO dispute settlement clarifies the provisions of the WTO Agreements 'in accordance with customary rules of interpretation of public international law'. Thus, while the applicable law in WTO dispute settlement is limited to WTO law, that law cannot be read 'in clinical isolation from public international law',[74] but has to be interpreted according to the customary

[67] G. Marceau, 'WTO Dispute Settlement and Human Rights', 13 *EJIL* (2002), 753–814, 762–764.

[68] Several of the authors considering non-WTO law to be applicable concur with this result, because of a different conception of applicable law. See, e.g. P. Mavroidis, 'Article 7 DSU', in R. Wolfrum et al., *WTO—Institutions and Dispute Settlement* (Leiden: Martinus Nijhoff, 2006), para. 6.

[69] P. Mavroidis, 'No Outsourcing of Law? WTO Law as Practiced by WTO Courts', 102 *AJIL* (2008), 421–474, 439.

[70] *Korea—Measures Affecting Government Procurement*, WT/DS163/R, para. 7.96.

[71] For an account of human rights as general principles see B. Simma and P. Alston, 'The Source of Human Rights Law', 12 *Australian Yearbook of International Law* (1992), 82–108. For an argument relating to the right to health see H. Hestermeyer, 'Access to Medication as a Human Right', 8 *Max Planck UNYB* (2004), 101–180, 176–178.

[72] Mavroidis, *supra* note 69, at 443; Hestermeyer, *supra* note 19, at 227.

[73] A. Mitchell and D. Heaton, 'The Inherent Jurisdiction of WTO Tribunals', 31 *Michigan Journal of International Law* (2010), 561–621. Thomas Schoenbaum speaks of 'implied powers' in an arguably much broader sense, see T. Schoenbaum, 'WTO Dispute Settlement', 47 *ICLQ* (1998), 647–658, 653.

[74] Appellate Body, *US—Gasoline*, WT/DS2/AB/R, para. 17.

rules of interpretation of public international law.[75] The act of interpretation is the act of selecting the pertinent meaning from the plethora of meanings, limited by—as is emphasized in Article 3.2 of the DSU[76]—the scope of possible meanings of the words used.[77] If non-WTO law can be taken into account in this process, the meaning most palatable to that law can be chosen and conflicts between legal regimes largely avoided, all the more so because determining the limit of the scope of meanings of the words used is far from being a scientific process.

Non-WTO law and thus the ICESCR can seep into the interpretative process through several argumentative means: through the application of a customary 'presumption against conflict';[78] the principle of harmonious interpretation;[79] or via the application of Article 31 of the Vienna Convention on the Law of Treaties (VCLT), acknowledged to contain customary rules of interpretation of public international law.[80] The latter route for inserting non-WTO law is both the one WTO dispute settlement organs have preferred and the one that internationalists have pinned their hopes on in order to combat the tendency of international law to fragment.[81] It is Article 31(3)(c) of the VCLT in particular that enables an interpreter to glance at the wider realm of international law. Thus, it can serve the purpose of systemic integration and contribute to an international legal order that is more consistent in that it takes the normative environment of rules into account.[82] The provision provides that a 'treaty shall be interpreted in good faith in accordance with the ordinary meaning to be given to the terms of the treaty in their context and in the light of its object and purpose',[83] and, furthermore, that '[t]here shall be taken into account, together with the context: [...] (c) any relevant rules of international law applicable in the relations between the parties'. As the ILC points out, such rules 'may include other treaties, customary rules or general principles of law'.[84] It should be noted that recourse to these documents in interpretation is compulsory, not optional.[85]

[75] See also E. Canal-Forgues, 'Sur l'Interprétation dans le droit de l'OMC', RGDIP 5, 7 et seq. (2001).

[76] The provision continues '[r]ecommendations and rulings of the D[ispute]S[ettlement]B[ody] cannot add to or diminish the rights and obligations provided in the covered agreements'.

[77] See also the definition in B.A. Garner (ed.), *Black's Law Dictionary* 7th edn (St. Paul: West, 2000).

[78] *Indonesia—Certain Measures Affecting the Automobile Industry*, WT/DS54, 55, 59, 64/R, para. 14.28; *India—Measures Affecting the Automotive Sector*, WT/DS146, 175/R, para. 7.58, footnote 332; *Canada—Term of Patent Protection*, WT/DS170/R, para. 6.45.

[79] I. van Damme, *Treaty Interpretation by the WTO Appellate Body* (Oxford: Oxford University Press, 2009), 357–360 (regarding Art. 31(3)(c) of the Vienna Convention on the Law of Treaties as a partial codification of the principle).

[80] See, e.g. *US—Measures Affecting Imports of Certain Passenger Vehicle and Light Truck Tyres from China*, WT/DS399/AB/R, para. 120.

[81] See ILC, *Fragmentation of International Law*, UN Doc. A/CN.4/L.682 of 13 April 2006.

[82] See ILC, *Fragmentation of International Law*, UN Doc. A/CN.4/L.682 of 13 April 2006, paras. 413, 415; C. McLachlan, 'The Principle of Systemic Integration and Article 31(3)(c) of the Vienna Convention', 54 *ICLQ* (2005), 279–319.

[83] Art. 31(1) of the VCLT.

[84] ILC, *Conclusions of the Work of the Study Group on the Fragmentation of International Law*, para. 18 (2006); see also *EC—Biotech*, WT/DS291/R, para. 7.67.

[85] Mavroidis, *supra* note 69, at 448. Note that the Appellate Body regards the elements listed in Art. 31 of the VCLT as being in a hierarchical order. *US—Shrimp*, WT/DS58/AB/R, para. 114.

Article 31(3)(c) of the VCLT imposes conditions on taking a rule of international law into account with the context in treaty interpretation. The rule must be 'applicable in the relations between the parties' and it must be 'relevant'. The latter is the case, according to the Appellate Body, 'if it concerns the subject matter of the provision at issue', which the Appellate Body examined under rather strict standards in *EC and Certain Member States—Large Civil Aircraft*.[86]

Not only is the strict standard for relevance likely to cause grievance among scholars, but the proviso on applicability 'between the parties' is also likely to furrow brows across the legal academy. Some authors argued that the relevant 'parties' are the parties to dispute settlement.[87] However, Article 2(1)(g) of the VCLT defines parties to be states which consented to the treaty (to be interpreted) and for which it is in force. If that means that a rule needs to be in force between all the members of the WTO to be relevant in the interpretation of WTO law—as the panel in *EC–Biotech* argued[88]—other treaties cannot be taken into account in the interpretation of WTO law given that the WTO Agreements, unlike other international agreements, allow separate customs territories to become members.[89] The ILC criticized the panel report accordingly,[90] and even the panel itself seems to have had some doubt in its opinion, as it held slightly later in the very same report that irrespective of Article 31(3)(c) of the VCLT 'a panel may consider other relevant rules of international law when interpreting the terms of WTO agreements if it deems such rules to be informative'.[91]

The fact that the *EC–Biotech* panel seems to distinguish between taking a rule into account together with the context when interpreting a treaty in its context and taking a treaty into account when determining the ordinary meaning exposes a basic misunderstanding about the interpretative process. Treaty terms *have to be* interpreted and a choice between the different meanings that each term offers *has to be* made. Article 31(3)(c) of the VCLT forces interpreters to take account of other international law rules in this process as context.[92] Arguments gained from this exercise may or may not be convincing. They are, however, helpful and certainly as convincing as the alternatives available. Interpreting a treaty term with a view to the ICESCR may seem inappropriate to a non-state party to that Covenant. However, it is difficult to see why using a definition from the Oxford English Dictionary—a common tool in WTO dispute settlement—is necessarily better.

[86] *EC and certain member States—Large Civil Aircraft*, WT/DS316/AB/R, paras. 846–855.

[87] D. Palmeter and P.C. Mavroidis, 'The WTO Legal System: Sources of Law', 92 *AJIL* (1998), 398–413, 411. The EU argued this position in Appellate Body, *EC and certain member States—Large Civil Aircraft*, WT/DS316/AB/R, para. 80.

[88] WT/DS291, 292, 293/R, para. 7.68.

[89] See Art. XII:1 of the WTO Agreement for details.

[90] ILC, *Fragmentation of International Law*, UN Doc. A/CN.4/L.682 of 13 April 2006, para. 450.

[91] *EC—Biotech*, WT/DS291, 292, 293/R, para. 7.93. For an overview of jurisprudence relating to Art. 31(3)(c) of the VCLT see I. van Damme, *Treaty Interpretation by the WTO Appellate Body* (Oxford: Oxford University Press, 2009), 367–376.

[92] This effect of the provision also seems to be misunderstood by the panel in *Argentina—Poultry Anti-Dumping Duties*, WT/DS241/R, para. 7.41.

The Appellate Body of the WTO explicitly revisited the issue of the interpretation of the term 'the parties' in Article 31(3)(c) of the Vienna Convention in its May 2011 report on *EC and Certain Member States—Large Civil Aircraft*, even though it was merely *obiter dictum*. It stated that it had not yet ruled on whether the term refers to all WTO members or just a subset of them and staked out an intermediate position. On the one hand, WTO law should be interpreted to reflect the common intention of all WTO members.[93] On the other, individual WTO member's international obligations and the drive for 'systemic integration' also deserve due consideration.[94] 'The parties' should thus be interpreted to refer to a large number of WTO members.[95] This is in line with the Appellate Body's approach in *US—Shrimp*, in which it interpreted WTO law with reference to such diverse international instruments as UNCLOS, the Convention on Biological Diversity and the Agenda 21.[96] As 84 per cent of the WTO membership is bound by the ICESCR, the Covenant clearly fulfils this requirement.

WTO dispute settlement organs thus do not have jurisdiction over ICESCR claims, nor is the ICESCR part of the applicable law in WTO dispute settlement (with the exception of rules *iuris cogentis*). However, the Covenant can be relied on in the interpretation of WTO law.

D. The ICESCR in dispute settlement: an empirical assessment

Despite the fact that the ICESCR is a legitimate source to turn to when interpreting WTO obligations, there is no dispute settlement practice in this regard. Economic, social, and cultural rights were only brought up as an aside and in passing. Nicaragua referred to the Covenant in a third-party submission in 2001 in a case where the core issue was the question of ownership of the Havana Club trademark taken over by the Cuban government.[97] Cuba, in a discussion of the case in the

[93] In footnote 1916 of the report the Appellate Body curiously cross-references its interpretation relating to Art. 31(3)(b) of the VCLT according to which agreement of all Members as to the interpretation of a treaty taking account of subsequent practice may—according to the circumstances—be deduced from the silence of members. It seems difficult to interpret Art. 31(3)(c) of the VCLT along the same lines, but the reference certainly implies that the Appellate Body is ready to require something less than full adherence of all WTO members to the relevant treaty.

[94] Appellate Body, *EC and Certain Member States—Large Civil Aircraft*, WT/DS316/AB/R, para. 845.

[95] A systematic argument can also be adduced for this position: Art. 31(2)(a) of the VCLT refers to 'all the parties', Art. 31(2)(b) to 'one or more parties', 'the parties' thus implies more than one, but less than all parties. The argument is not as strong as the one made in the text relating to the purpose of Art. 31(3)(c), as the wording of para. 2 of the provision could have been chosen to indicate the contrast between lits. a and b. See Hestermeyer, *supra* note 19, at 219–222.

[96] Appellate Body, *US—Shrimp*, WT/DS58/AB/R. The Appellate Body did not refer to Art. 31(3)(c) of the VCLT to justify its mode of argumentation.

[97] *US—Section 211 Appropriations Act*, WT/DS176/R, paras. 5.5–5.6 (erroneously pointing to the right to participate in the cultural life of a country as recognizing implicitly IP rights and wrongly citing the ICESCR's supposed equivalent provision to Art. 17 of the Universal Declaration on Human Rights). On the background of the case see C. Denny, 'WTO Referees Rum Punch-up', *The Guardian* (London, 18 July 2000), available at <http://www.theguardian.com/business/2000/jul/18/9> (last accessed 7 November 2013).

Dispute Settlement Body in 2009, relied on the right to self-determination to argue the illegality of the Cuba embargo of the United States.[98]

A case involving generic drugs and the Agreement on Trade-Related Aspects of Intellectual Property Rights (TRIPS Agreement) is the first in which the prospect of the proper use of the ICESCR to interpret WTO law was raised. In *EU and a Member State—Seizure of Generic Drugs in Transit*, India argued in its 2010 request for consultations that the TRIPS Agreement provisions cited must be read in the light of the ICESCR's right to health.[99] However, the case is not likely be resolved by dispute settlement.[100]

E. Conclusion

The ICESCR's role in WTO dispute settlement is limited. The WTO only has jurisdiction over claims of violations of WTO law, not of the ICESCR. A defence against the claim of a violation of WTO law cannot be based solely on the ICESCR (unless the relevant rule has become *ius cogens*), as the Covenant is not part of the applicable law in WTO dispute settlement. However, the ICESCR can be used as an argument when interpreting WTO law. In practice, however, this has not happened. Cuba and Nicaragua have both referred to the ICESCR or its rights in the context of dispute settlement, but neither of them for the purposes of a thorough interpretative exercise of WTO law. The situation might change with India's 2010 request for consultations explicitly stating that TRIPS Agreement provisions have to be read in the light of Article 12(1) of the ICESCR, but the dispute will probably be resolved by way of a mutually acceptable solution.

4. The ICESCR in the Discourse of Political Organs of the WTO

This section will consider the use of the ICESCR in the discourse of the WTO's political organs. It is interested in whether, by whom, and how economic, social, and cultural rights are brought up within the WTO. This focus determines the scope of the study. It is interested in *legal* arguments from one regime brought up in another, not in *factual* arguments.[101] By way of example, this means that a WTO member's argument in the WTO's General Council in favour of the Kimberley process certification scheme for rough diamonds based on the suffering caused by

[98] WT/DSB/M/271 of 25 September 2009, para. 7.

[99] WT/DS408/1, 3. Brazil's internal right to health had already been mentioned in the *Brazil—Tyres* dispute, see WT/DS332/R; WT/DS332/19 of 10 March 2009; WT/CTE/M/40 of 2 September 2005.

[100] M. Williams, 'Update 2—India, EU heal drugs seizures dispute with interim agreement', *Reuters* (28 July 2011).

[101] For an excellent study without that legal focus (and hence by necessity selective), see A. Aaronson and J.M. Zimmerman, *Trade Imbalance* (Cambridge: Cambridge University Press, 2008).

civil wars,[102] is outside the scope of this chapter. An argument based on the right to health, however, is within its scope.

The WTO makes available numerous documents, including minutes of meetings, in its official online database.[103] GATT documents are available to a more limited extent.[104] For the purposes of this chapter, the database was searched for pertinent terms such as 'economic, social, and cultural rights', and irrelevant uses of the term (such as in addresses) were disregarded. The selection of search terms and the elimination of 'irrelevant' hits introduce limited elements of subjectivity into the research. Nevertheless, the outcome reveals recognizable and important facts and trends.

A. The GATT years

The GATT database makes only two explicit mentions of economic, social, and cultural rights. Both of them were made in speeches by Latin American representatives (Guatemala and Venezuela). The first occurred at the beginning of the Tokyo Round in 1973, referring to the many statements made in promotion of the 'economic, social, cultural and political rights of the under-developed countries' and emphasizing the importance of the new trade round for developing countries.[105] Similarly, during the waning days of the GATT in the negotiations for the WTO, the minister for foreign affairs of Guatemala pointed out that his country could only succeed in its drive towards consolidating democracy if it guaranteed economic, social, and cultural rights. For this purpose Guatemala requires economic growth and access to world markets and looks to the WTO to achieve this more successfully than GATT.[106]

Additionally, GATT documents mention several of the rights now contained in the ICESCR independent of the Covenant itself, and at times before the Covenant was drafted. Such references to economic, social, and cultural rights are, however, episodic. They occurred, for example, when Article 55 of the UN Charter was invoked,[107] a basis for the negotiations leading up to the GATT, or in an argument to support the principle of one country, one vote.[108] In the 1980s, Latin American countries invoked the right to self-determination in opposition to US trade measures against Nicaragua and Cuba.[109]

Worker's rights, today guaranteed by Articles 6 to 9 and 12(2)(b) of the ICESCR, constitute an exception to the almost complete absence of economic, social, and

[102] G/C/W/432/Rev.1 of 24 February 2003.

[103] Available at <http://docsonline.wto.org> (last accessed) 4 November 2013.

[104] These can be accessed in Stanford's 'GATT Digital Library: 1947–1994', at <http://gatt.stanford.edu/page/home> (last accessed 7 November 2013).

[105] MIN(73)SR/Add.4 of 22 October 1973, 172.

[106] MTN.TNC/MIN(94)/ST/98 of 14 April 1994, 2.

[107] By Lebanon in E/PC/T/PV/3 of 17 October 1946.

[108] Venezuela supported this principle with the right to self-determination in E/CONF.2/C.6/SR.7 of 10 December 1947.

[109] C/M/188 of 28 June 1985; C/M/204 of 19 November 1986; and SR.43/ST/10 of 18 December 1987.

cultural rights in the GATT debates.[110] It was, however, the International Labour Organization (ILO) and its normative work, not the ICESCR, that was commonly referenced.[111] From the negotiation of the GATT/Havana Charter onwards, workers' rights were part of the discussion.[112] In fact, the Havana Charter of the International Trade Organization contained an article on fair labour standards, envisaging a cooperation between the planned International Trade Organization and the ILO.[113] That article was lost with the failure of the Havana Charter. Workers' rights did, however, remain on the agenda and countries continued to propose their inclusion into the trade order, for example, in the Tokyo and Uruguay Rounds.[114] Each of these attempts met with fierce resistance, however, by developing countries that regarded the inclusion of workers' rights as a direct threat to their advantage relating to the cost of labour. With more developing countries joining the GATT, the attempts to include workers' rights in the trade order was thus bound to fail.

To summarize: with the exception of workers' rights, references to economic, social, and cultural rights during the GATT years are sparse. Where such rights (outside workers' rights) were mentioned, they were usually referred to by developing countries rather than the developed world and in the context of negotiations, rather than to defend a legal position *de lege lata*, the exception being the defence against embargoes based on the right to self-determination.

B. The WTO

WTO Members have mentioned economic, social, and cultural rights explicitly by name somewhat more frequently than their GATT counterparts. With roughly 20 explicit references to these rights,[115] almost all of them in this millennium, they are, however, statistically insignificant. Even though more documents mention rights contained in the ICESCR without explicitly referring to the Covenant itself or the notion of economic, social, and cultural rights, this does not change the fact that references to such rights remain highly unusual. A caveat has to be added as to workers' rights: much like during the days of the GATT, these are referred to in a statistically more significant number. This quantitative

[110] The term 'workers' rights' can be found 60 times, the term 'labour standards' or 'labour standards' even 211 times in the Stanford GATT Digital Library. 'Right to work' is mentioned 13 times.

[111] References to the ILO abound. See, e.g. PREP.COM(86)/SR/8 of 13 August 1986; C/M/156 of 7 May 1982; or SR.10/3 of 3 November 1955.

[112] Argentina: E/CONF.2/11/ADD.3 of 1 December 1947; and Mexico: E/CONF.2/11/Add.28 of 2 December 1947. The work of the ILO and the Commission on Human Rights was acknowledged in E/CONF.2/C.1/9.

[113] Art. 7 of the Havana Charter.

[114] For an account of the history of the trade and labour debate, see S. Charnovitz, 'The Influence of International Labour Standards on the World Trading Regime', 126 *International Labour Review* (1987), 565–584.

[115] Not counting several versions of the same document, references of the rights contained in the ICESCR without mentioning the Covenant itself and references in dispute settlement. The quantitative work for this chapter was finalized at the beginning of 2013.

finding should not detract attention from the fact, however, that economic, social, and cultural rights have gained some prominence in the debates on food and health.

Outside these two core discussions, references to economic, social, and cultural rights occurred on varied occasions. The analysis of national law undertaken both during accession negotiations and in trade policy reviews is one of them. Thus, ICESCR membership was mentioned in documents relating to WTO accession by Belarus and Cape Verde,[116] and the right to education under national law was mentioned in Andorra's accession negotiations (in the discussion of the education services regime)[117] and in Ghana's trade policy review (in the context of child labour).[118] The EU's generalized system of preferences, as well as its arrangements with the African, Caribbean, and Pacific (ACP) states imposing human rights conditionalities also relating to the ICESCR, were referenced.[119] Conference reports circulated in the WTO and technical cooperation activities equally mention the Covenant.[120] Much as with GATT, countries attacked embargoes based on economic, social, and cultural rights. Thus, Cuba attacked US trade measures by relying on the right to self-determination,[121] and Burundi criticized trade sanctions imposed against it after a military coup as depriving the people of Burundi of basic rights,[122] such as the right to food, health, education, employment, and so on.[123] Finally, trade negotiations offered a forum for bringing up human rights concerns. Thus, Bolivia and Venezuela expressed their desire that trade negotiations should be conducive to economic social, and cultural rights or that they should even include them as obligations for the WTO in order to prevent a conflict between the two regimes.[124] More concretely, Bolivia commented on a proposal in the Trade Negotiations Committee to address issues relating to the financial crisis by way of the Trade Policy Review Mechanism. It wondered whether other circumstances would be taken into account and gave as an example its own situation, as

[116] WT/ACC/BLR/1 of 16 January 1996 and WT/ACC/CPV/3 of 13 January 2004. Belarus also referred to social and economic rights such as social security in Belarus in response to a question on national treatment of foreigners; see WT/ACC/BLR/7 of 19 December 1997.

[117] WT/ACC/AND/3 of 4 March 1999.

[118] WT/TPR/M/194/Add.1 of 31 March 2008 (also mentioning the right to health and shelter).

[119] WT/TPR/S/214/Rev. 1 of 8 June 2009; WT/COMTD/N/4/Add.4 of 12 March 2009; WT/TPR/S/177/Rev.1 of 15 May 2007; WT/COMTD/N/4/Add. 3 of 29 March 2006; WT/COMTD/57 of 29 March 2006; and G/C/W/187/Add. 3 of 14 April 2000. For a scholarly treatment see L. Bartels, 'The WTO Legality of the EU's GSP+ Arrangement', 10 *Journal of International Economic Law* (2007), 869–886 and L. Bartels, 'The Appellate Body Ruling on EC—Tariff Preferences to Developing Countries and its Implications for Conditionality in GSP Programmes', in T. Cottier et al. (eds.), *Human Rights and International Trade* (Oxford: Oxford University Press, 2005), 463.

[120] IP/C/W/304 of 12 September 2001; WT/COMTD/W/106/Rev.1 of 20 December 2002; G/TBT/W/247 of 3 November 2004; and WT/L/725 of 5 June 2008.

[121] TN/MA/W/71 of 15 May 2006.

[122] 'Africans Vote for Sanctions Against Coup in Burundi', *New York Times* (New York City, 1 August 1996), available at <http://www.nytimes.com/1996/08/01/world/africans-vote-for-sanctions-against-coup-in-burundi.html> (last accessed 7 November 2013).

[123] WT/MIN(98)/ST/78 of 18 May 1998.

[124] TN/C/M/22 of 10 March 2006; WT/GC/M/112 of 4 March 2008.

climatic conditions in 2006–8 forced Bolivia to impose export restrictions to protect its population's right to food and health.[125]

The two most significant debates in which the ICESCR was mentioned concerned agriculture and the TRIPS Agreement. Article 20(c) of the Agreement on Agriculture envisages that negotiations on continuing agricultural reform take non-trade concerns into account. The negotiations started in 2000 and in July a conference was held in Norway to discuss relevant non-trade concerns.[126] Both Mauritius and Norway identified the ICESCR, specifically Article 11, as a relevant non-trade concern.[127] They repeated this position on other occasions, in particular when asked to list agreements they consider relevant for the negotiations on agriculture.[128] Burkina Faso identified the protection of the right to food for its population as one of its objectives in agricultural negotiations and Switzerland noted that the Food and Agriculture Organization Food Summit 'had established the right to food production'.[129] However, agreement on non-trade issues in agricultural negotiations could not be reached.[130]

As to the TRIPS Agreement, the focal point of the debate was the discussion about patents and access to medicines. The Agreement, with appropriate transition periods,[131] obliges WTO members to grant patent protection for pharmaceuticals, resulting in a factual monopoly of the patent-holder, which causes concern for access to pharmaceuticals. Countries had already voiced public health concerns during the negotiations of the TRIPS Agreement, although they had not couched these concerns in human rights language.[132] The WHO had also been working on the topic of patents and accessibility of pharmaceuticals.[133] A broader public took note of the issue for the first time when the pharmaceutical industry filed a lawsuit against South Africa in South African courts in 1998. South Africa had enacted a law enabling its minister of health to limit patent rights to guarantee affordable

[125] WT/GC/M/117 of 23 February 2009 (continuing that Bolivia 'had been unable to stop applying restrictions simply to satisfy the WTO or the markets, while overlooking the most fundamental and basic human rights of the most vulnerable sector of its population'.)

[126] See on this background J.A. McMahon, *The WTO Agreement on Agriculture* (Oxford: Oxford University Press, 2006), 192–193 and 214–219.

[127] G/AG/NG/W/36/Rev.1 of 9 November 2001 (also mentioning the General Comment No. 12 on the right to adequate food adopted by the Committee on ESCR in 1999).

[128] G/AG/NG/S/22 of 23 January 2001; see also G/AG/NG/W/52 of 10 October 2000; G/AG/NG/S/17 of 16 October 2000; G/AG/NG/R/3 of 10 November 2000; G/AG/NG/W/75 of 30 November 2000; G/AG/NG/W/101 of 16 January 2001; and G/AG/NG/R/4 of 24 January 2001.

[129] TN/AG/R/10 of 9 September 2003. We can safely assume that the comment was meant to recognize the importance of the right to food.

[130] Aaronson and Zimmerman, *supra* note 101, at 56–57.

[131] Art. 65 of the TRIPS Agreement provides for a number of different transition periods that have expired by now. However, the least-developed Members still benefit from an extended transition period currently set to expire on 1 July 2013. See IP/C/40 of 30 November 2005. See also WT/L/845 of 19 December 2011.

[132] See, e.g. MTN.GNG/NG11/5 of 14 December 1987; MTN.GNG/NG11/12 of 13 June 1989; MTN.GNG/NG11/14 of 12 September 1989; MTN.GNG/NG11/20 of 24 April 1990; MTN.GNG/NG11/21 of 22 June 1990; and MTN.GNG/NG11/27 of 14 November 1990. See also Art. 8 of the TRIPS Agreement.

[133] See, e.g. C. Correa, *Health Economics: The Uruguay Round and Drugs* (Geneva: WHO, 1997).

medicines.[134] Human rights bodies established a link with the right to health,[135] a link that also can be found in a presentation made at a 1998 seminar of the World Intellectual Property Organization.[136] The topic of patents and medicines was brought up at the TRIPS Council of the WTO in 2001, which decided to hold a special discussion on the issue.[137] During that discussion Venezuela stressed the right of WTO members to take measures pursuant to Articles 2 and 12 of the ICESCR, and the Dominican Republic pointed out that the Committee on Economic, Social and Cultural Rights would condemn the use of trade regulation which impeded access to medicines. Bolivia and Kenya also mentioned concerns for the right to health.[138] Bolivia suggested that human rights considerations prevail over commercial ones, an argument later seconded by Venezuela.[139] Ecuador's new Constitution of 2008[140] explicitly affirms the supremacy of the right to health (among others) over international trade instruments in constitutional law,[141] a position it has communicated to other WTO members.[142] A proposal by the African Group and other countries for a Ministerial Declaration on TRIPS and Public Health suggested mentioning that the decision was taken to discharge obligations under the ICESCR.[143] Argentina and other developing countries also pointed out a possible threat of non-violation complaints to the right to health.[144] The debate about patents and the right to health quietened somewhat after the successful passage of a number of measures in the field by the WTO. The most significant of these were the 2001 Doha Declaration on the TRIPS Agreement and public health, affirming that the agreement 'can and should be interpreted and implemented in a manner supportive of WTO members' right to protect public health',[145] and a 2003 decision establishing a mechanism to help WTO Members with insufficient manufacturing capacities in the pharmaceutical sector make use of compulsory licensing.[146] Ongoing discussions about the implementation and

[134] See Hestermeyer, *supra* note 19.

[135] See only Sub-Commission on the Promotion and Protection of Human Rights, *Intellectual Property Rights and Human Rights*, resolution 2000/7.

[136] *Intellectual Property and Human Rights* with a presentation on *Intellectual Property and the Right to Health* by S. Salazar, available at <http://www.wipo.int/edocs/mdocs/tk/en/wipo_unhchr_ip_pnl_98/wipo_unhchr_ip_pnl_98_3.doc> (last accessed 17 September 2013).

[137] IP/C/M/30 of 1 June 2001.

[138] IP/C/M/31 of 10 July 2001. See also IP/C/W/296 of 29 June 2001.

[139] WT/MIN(03)/ST/48 of 11 September 2003. See also WT/GC/M/82 of 13 November 2003 (Zambia emphasizing the WTO could concentrate on recognizing the overriding right to health and food security before tackling the Singapore issues).

[140] Adopted September 2008. An English translation is available in R. Wolfrum and R. Grote (eds.), *Constitutions of the Countries of the World* (Oxford: Oxford University Press, 2013).

[141] Art. 421.

[142] IP/C/M/59 of 25 May 2009.

[143] IP/C/W/312 of 4 October 2001.

[144] IP/C/W/385 of 30 October 2002.

[145] WT/MIN(01)/DEC/2 of 14 November 2001.

[146] WT/L/540 and Corr. 1 of 1 September 2003 (the decision was transformed into a treaty amendment: WT/L/641 of 8 December 2005). See also IP/C/25 of 1 July 2002; WT/L/478 of 12 July 2002.

effectiveness of these measures, as well as related capacity building, ensure that the right to health continues to be brought up from time to time.[147]

The debate about patents and access to medicines was rekindled when generic drugs exported from India to Brazil and not patented in either country were seized in transit by Dutch customs in 2008 as violating Dutch patent law.[148] In a contribution to debates in the TRIPS Council widely supported by other developing countries, India stated that this was not just a trade but also a right to health issue.[149] As has been described, the dispute resulted in consultations but, likely, will not be the subject of a panel report.

Even in these two core areas of debate, references to economic, social, and cultural rights remain an exception. The only field in which such rights are more commonly mentioned, even though usually based on the work of the ILO rather than on the ICESCR, is the field of labour rights, which are mentioned in a statistically more relevant number each year in the WTO, with two 'spikes' in 1996 and 1999.[150]

As shown, labour rights were included in the stillborn Havana Charter. Proposals to include them in the WTO order came to naught.[151] Only the Preamble to the WTO Agreement refers to 'raising standards of living, ensuring full employment and a large and steadily growing volume of real income'. The topic also proved divisive after the WTO was established: at the Singapore ministerial conference in 1996 some (in particular developed) members demanded negotiations on labour standards over the objection of developing countries,[152] which saw such suggestions as attempts to undermine their advantage in labour costs. Although in the ministerial declaration members 'renewed' their commitment to the observance of internationally recognized core labour standards, they also agreed that the ILO 'is the competent body to set and deal with these standards' and that the use of such standards for protectionist purposes or to defeat the advantage of low-wage developing countries must be rejected.[153] The issue was raised again at the 1999 Seattle

[147] See, e.g. IP/C/M/64 of 17 February 2011 (Brazil mentioning the right to access to medicines and the WHO mentioning its perspective on access in light of the right to health in the WHO Constitution); IP/C/W/549/Add.4 of 25 October 2010 (concerning technical cooperation activities of the WHO); and IP/C/W/516/Add.1 of 15 October 2008 (the WHO stating it would develop a training course assisting developing countries in implementation patent regimes in a manner supportive to the right to health).

[148] See Williams, *supra* note 100.

[149] IP/C/M/61 of 12 February 2010. Note also Egypt's concern about IP enforcement and the right to health in IP/C/M/60 of 28 September 2009.

[150] Searches for the terms 'workers' rights', 'labo(u)r standards' and 'right to work'—representing just some of the possible search terms in the field—resulted in the following number of documents in English: 22 (1995), 122 (1996), 35 (1997), 51 (1998), 110 (1999), 34 (2000), 77 (2001), 38 (2002), 33 (2003), 25 (2004), 28 (2005), 29 (2006), 19 (2007), 24 (2008), 23 (2009), 20 (2010), and 30 (2011).

[151] See, e.g. PREP.COM(86)W/43 of 25 June 1986 for an attempt by the US to introduce the topic into the negotiations.

[152] See, e.g. WT/MIN(96)/ST/5 of 9 December 1996 (the United States), WT/MIN(96)/ST/2 of 9 December 1996 (the EC), WT/MIN(96)/ST/4 of 9 December 1996 (Argentina) favouring using the WTO as a forum for the discussion, and e.g. WT/MIN(96)/ST/8 of 9 December 1996 (Brazil), WT/MIN(96)/ST/16 (Cuba), WT/MIN(96)ST/76 of 11 December 1996 (Botswana) against such a link.

[153] WT/MIN(96)/DEC of 18 December 1996, para. 4.

ministerial conference.[154] No agreement was reached.[155] However, the wording of the Singapore ministerial declaration was reaffirmed in the Doha Declaration.[156]

The mostly developed countries that favour inclusion of labour standards in trade agreements have used other free trade agreements as an outlet to negotiate such standards, achieving their inclusion either within the agreements themselves or in parallel agreements.[157] Within the WTO, however, it remains difficult for members to agree beyond a general commitment to a small set of core labour standards—and the question of international enforcement remains, according to the WTO website, 'a minefield'.[158]

Beyond the substantive invocation of economic, social, and cultural rights, there is some limited inter-institutional cooperation in the field of these rights. The precise extent of such cooperation is difficult to ascertain. The WTO Secretariat has working relations with some 200 organizations.[159] However, these relate to diverse fields and only a few of them are relevant in the area of economic, social, and cultural rights. Moreover, the intensity of the cooperation is unclear. The prominence of the conflict between patents and access to medicines and increasing criticism of the WTO from human rights bodies have led to the invitation of the WTO to act as an observer to sessions of the Committee on Economic, Social and Cultural Rights.[160] The practice continued for some time, but seems to have become more sporadic in recent years.[161] The WTO Secretariat also attends sessions of the ILO Governing Body as an observer and collaborates with the ILO in respect of the ILO's Working Party on the Social Dimension of Globalization, in seminars and some other projects.[162] Neither the Committee nor the ILO has observer status in the WTO,[163] an issue that currently cannot be resolved because Arab states are blocking the granting of observer status to any inter-governmental organization

[154] The United States, EU and Canada submitted proposals in this respect. See Aaronson and Zimmerman, *supra* note 101, at 52.

[155] See *Labour Standards*, available at <http://www.wto.org/english/thewto_e/whatis_e/tif_e/bey5_e.htm> (last accessed 7 November 2013).

[156] WT/MIN(01)/DEC/1 of 20 November 2001, para. 8.

[157] The ILO provides information on such agreements at <http://www.ilo.org/global/standards/information-resources-and-publications/free-trade-agreements-and-labour-rights/lang—en/index.htm> (last accessed 7 November 2013).

[158] Available at <http://www.wto.org/english/thewto_e/whatis_e/tif_e/bey5_e.htm> (last accessed 7 November 2013). For an in-depth treatment of trade and labor see G. Marceau, 'Trade and Labour', in D. Bethlehem et al. (eds.), *International Trade Law* (Oxford: Oxford University Press, 2009), 539.

[159] Available at <http://www.wto.org/english/thewto_e/coher_e/igo_divisions_e.htm> (last accessed 7 November 2013).

[160] Starting with the 21st session at the end of 1999. UN Doc. E/2000/22, Chapter II, para. 5.

[161] UN Doc. E/2001/22, Chapter I para. 8 (22nd–24th session); UN Doc. E/2002/22, Chapter I para. 8 (25th and 27th session); UN Doc. E/2003/22, Chapter I para. 10 (28th–29th session); UN Doc. E/2004/22, Chapter I para. 9 (30th–31st session); UN Doc. E/2005/22, Chapter I para. 6 (32nd–33rd session); UN Doc. E/2007/22, Chapter I para. 8 (37th session); UN Doc. E/2009/22, Chapter I para. 6 (40th–41st session). See also WT/BFA/W/98 of 8 July 2003.

[162] See information available at <http://www.wto.org/english/thewto_e/coher_e/wto_ilo_e.htm> (last accessed 7 November 2013).

[163] See information available at <http://www.wto.org/english/thewto_e/igo_obs_e.htm> (last accessed 7 November 2013).

given the refusal to grant observer status to the Arab League.[164] Cooperation with the ILO has been such a charged topic that the WTO Director-General Pascal Lamy told union leaders that 'the WTO and its secretariat do not have a mandate to work on coherence between what is done in the WTO and what is done in the ILO',[165] and Gabrielle Marceau has written that 'the two organizations have sometimes given the impression that they were turning their back to each other'.[166] Nevertheless the ongoing cooperation mostly at the secretariat level is reason for some hope.

5. Conclusion

Despite WTO members' obligations under the ICESCR and the dispute settlement organs' legal competence to take the Covenant into account for the purposes of interpreting WTO law when deciding cases, a closer examination reveals that references to economic, social, and cultural rights in the WTO outside the area of workers' rights remain sparse.

Where such rights are referred to, it is usually in a political context *de lege ferenda*, such as trade negotiations or to describe a country's national legal system. Only rarely are economic, social, and cultural rights relied on explicitly to defend or oppose specific trade measures. The most prominent case in that respect is the case of patents and access to medicines, in which intense pressure opened a door for using such arguments. It should also be noted that more often than not it is developing countries that refer to such rights, dispelling the myth that human rights arguments are the developed world's domain. Here, too, workers' rights are the exception, as they are heavily favoured by developed countries.

The limited practical relevance of the ICESCR in dispute settlement is easily explained by the limited legal relevance of non-WTO law in such proceedings. As it is WTO bodies that act in this case, it dovetails to some extent with the WTO's lack of treaty-based human rights obligations. Given WTO members' obligations under the ICESCR when acting within the WTO, the almost complete absence of ICESCR-based arguments by those very members in the WTO's political organs deserves some more thought, particularly in light of the more frequent references to workers' rights.

The prevailing myth that the WTO as an organization is to blame for a culture hostile to human rights is certainly wrong; it is the representatives of the states that fail to bring up considerations based on the ICESCR. This is the consequence of Director-General Lamy's often-repeated tenet that the WTO is a 'member-driven

[164] For two opposing points of view on the issue see A. Reich, 'The Threat of Politicization of the WTO', 26 *University of Pennsylvania Journal of International Economic Law* (2005), 779–814, 805–806; B.H. Malkawi, 'The Case of Arab Countries and the World Trade Organization', 19 *International Trade and Finance Association Working Paper* (2006).

[165] Aaronson and Zimmerman, *supra* note 101, at 54.

[166] G. Marceau, 'Trade and Labour', in D. Bethlehem et al. (eds.), *International Trade Law* (Oxford: Oxford University Press, 2009), 539–540.

organization'. If the members bring up economic, social, and cultural rights, they will form part of the debate; if they do not mention the rights, they will simply not become an issue.

The argument that the lack of debate on economic, social, and cultural rights shows that the two regimes do not interfere with each other is equally incorrect. While Dame Rosalyn Higgins rightly states that concerns of the fragmentation of international law are exaggerated,[167] a thorough look at WTO debates shows that obvious arguments based on the ICESCR have not been made. Even on the prominent topic of patents and access to medicines, WTO members are far more likely to refer to Article 8 of the TRIPS Agreement and health concerns than to the right to health.[168] And while a search for Committee on Agriculture documents in English mentioning 'right to food' brings up nine documents, 97 documents mentioned 'food security' in 2001 alone.[169] Members thus seem to raise their arguments as policy arguments rather than legal arguments based on the ICESCR.

This choice is not necessarily harmful to economic, social, and cultural rights. An argument based on human suffering can be just as effective as one based on the right to health. As the human rights movement has taught us, however, an argument based on legal obligations and legal rights can have more strength than one based on policy. States apparently recognize this in the field of workers' rights. What, then, explains the reluctance to resort to arguments based on other economic, social, and cultural rights?

First, economic, social, and cultural rights are relative latecomers in the field of human rights. Until recently, they were commonly regarded as merely 'programmatic' and some legal systems still view them with suspicion. Labour rights, on the other hand, have a long history as justiciable.

Second, country representatives in the WTO are trade experts who are rarely schooled in economic, social, and cultural rights. They move within a different system that has its own rules and language. Labour rights are closer to their mindset, as they have traditionally been part of commercial law. Representatives of countries with small permanent missions in Geneva entrusted with a portfolio encompassing the WTO as well as human rights mechanisms are an exception to this rule and are more likely to establish a connection between the regimes, but they are spread too thinly to bring about change.

Third, and most importantly, national lobbies rarely exercise pressure on their governments to prompt concerns related to economic, social, and cultural rights in the WTO. In contrast, labour rights benefit from the politically influential lobbies of the unions that pressure governments to bring up relevant concerns in WTO debates.

These shortcomings indicate a work plan for the future. The Committee on Economic, Social and Cultural Rights and several national courts have made much

[167] R. Higgins, 'A Babel of Judicial Voices?', 55 *ICLQ* (2006), 791–804, 796.

[168] A search for references to Art. 8 of the TRIPS Agreement and 'health' brings up 149 documents in English.

[169] Admittedly this term encompasses other concerns as well.

headway in clarifying the content of the respective rights, ensuring their recognition as justiciable. The entry into force of the Optional Protocol advances this process. More work, however, is necessary to overcome the second and the third shortcomings mentioned. National actors in the field of international trade law, both state representatives and relevant lobbies, lack knowledge about economic, social, and cultural rights. Raising ICESCR-related concerns over international trade with them and involving them in discussions are vital components to ensuring respect for economic, social, and cultural rights in the WTO.[170] National and international debate could also be enhanced by conducting human rights impact studies of trade agreements.[171] Such an exercise would encourage relevant actors to include human rights considerations in their strategies.

[170] C. Dommen, 'Raising Human Rights Concerns in the World Trade Organization', 24 *HRQ* (2002), 1–50, 50.

[171] The Committee on Economic, Social and Cultural Rights recommended undertaking such an assessment of its foreign trade policy to Switzerland. See UN Doc. E/C.12/CHE/CO/2-3 of 26 November 2010, para. 24.

10

From the Other Shore

Economic, Social, and Cultural Rights from an International Environmental Law Perspective

Stéphanie Chuffart and Jorge E. Viñuales

1. Introduction

The relationship between human rights and international environmental law is usually approached from the perspective of human rights. The question is how can human rights be used to implement international environmental law or, more generally, what is the influence of human rights on international environmental law? The 'dependent variable' is thus international environmental law whereas human rights are the independent or 'explanatory variable'. For a number of legitimate reasons, including the significant contribution made by human rights' adjudicatory and quasi-adjudicatory bodies to environmental protection,[1] this standpoint is still the prevailing one.[2] The present chapter takes the reverse perspective as its starting point, focusing on how international environmental law can help implement human rights obligations. Conceptually, such an approach would look at human rights in general, without distinguishing between, on the one hand, civil and political rights (CP rights) and, on the other, economic, social, and cultural rights (ESC rights). However, given the specific focus of the present volume, we concentrate on how international environmental law influences (or could be used to influence) the implementation of ESC rights, referring to CP rights only incidentally when this appears useful to illustrate our reasoning.

[1] See A. Boyle and M. Anderson (eds.), *Human Rights Approaches to Environmental Protection* (Oxford: Oxford University Press, 1996); A. Boyle, 'Human Rights or Environmental Rights? A Reassessment' (2007), 18 *Fordham Environmental Law Review*, 471–512; F. Francioni, 'International Human Rights in an Environmental Horizon' (2010), 21 *European Journal of International Law*, 41–55.

[2] For instance, the chapter on the relationship between human rights and international environmental law by a distinguished environmental lawyer in a major human rights textbook published in 2010 circumscribes its topic as follows: '[t]he main issue is whether human rights constitute an efficient and practical tool that can be used to combat environmental degradation'. M. Fitzmaurice, 'Environmental Degradation', in D. Moeckli, S. Shah, S. Sivakumaran, and D. Harris (eds.), *International Human Rights Law* (Oxford: Oxford University Press, 2010), 622–643, 622.

The conclusion that we reach is, admittedly, no surprise to an audience specialized in human rights: the impact of international environmental law is, essentially, to broaden the scope of human rights, and particularly of ESC rights, in a variety of ways.[3] Perhaps more interesting is how this broadening takes place. There are three main avenues through which it happens: international environmental law broadens the substantive scope of ESC rights (Section 2); international environmental law broadens the way in which we think about ESC rights (Section 3); and international environmental law broadens the palette of enforcement mechanisms available in connection with ESC rights (Section 4).

2. International Environmental Law Broadens the Substantive Scope of ESC Rights

It seems today widely accepted that certain human rights involve environmental components.[4] This is the reason why the development of a 'human rights approach' to environmental protection has attracted much attention in the last two decades.[5] Already in the early 1990s, efforts towards asserting this approach went beyond the use of existing human rights to protect the environment, stressing the need to recognize substantive environmental rights.[6] In addition, some commentators called for further development of procedural (rather than substantive) environmental rights, in line with Principle 10 of the Rio Declaration on Environment and Development.[7]

[3] The relationship between international environmental law and human rights, even approached from the perspective of international environmental law, is not necessarily synergistic. In some cases, limitations and even violations of human rights may be the consequence of a rigorist application of international environmental law. An obvious example would concern the forced relocation (and prohibition of resettlement) of an indigenous people from a natural preserve. See D. Brockington and J. Igoe, 'Eviction for Conservation: A Global Overview' (2006), 4 *Conservation & Society*, 424–470; J.P. Brosius, 'Indigenous Peoples and Protected Areas at the World Parks Congress' (2004), 18 *Conservation Biology*, 609–612.

[4] Mention of the most relevant case law in this regard follows.

[5] See D. Shelton, 'Human Rights, Environmental Rights and the Right to the Environment' (1991), 28 *Stanford Journal of International Law*, 103–138; A. Boyle, and M. Anderson (eds.), *Human Rights Approaches to Environmental Protection* (Oxford: Oxford University Press, 1996); G. Handl, 'Human Rights and Protection of the Environment', in A. Eide, C. Krause, and A. Rosas (eds.), *Economic, Social and Cultural Rights* (The Hague: Kluwer, 2001), 303–328; A. Kiss and D. Shelton, 'Human Right and the Environment', in *International Environmental Law* 3rd edn (Ardsley, NY: Transnational Publishers, 2004), 661–731; M. Fitzmaurice and J. Marshall, 'The Human Right to a Clean Environment—Phantom or Reality? The European Court of Human Rights and English Courts Perspective on Balancing Rights in Environmental Cases', 76 *Nordic Journal of International Law* (2007), 103–152.

[6] See UN Commission on Human Rights, Sub-Commission on Prevention of Discrimination and Protection of Minorities, Human Rights and the Environment, Final Report of the Special Rapporteur, 6 July 1994, UN Doc. E/CN.4/Sub.2/1994/9 ('Ksentini Report'). See also M. Anderson, 'Human Rights Approaches to Environmental Protection: An Overview', in Boyle and Anderson, *supra* note 1, at 4–10.

[7] Principle 10 of the Rio Declaration reads: '[e]nvironmental issues are best handled with the participation of all concerned citizens, at the relevant level. At the national level, each individual

With the benefit of hindsight, we know that of the main three strategies followed by the human rights approach to environmental protection—that is, (1) broadening existing rights, (2) asserting substantive environmental rights, (3) asserting procedural environmental rights—only the first and third have been used in practice so far.[8] Moreover, the assertion of procedural environmental rights has often been carried out through a broadening of the scope of existing human rights.[9] What could be called, for ease of reference, the 'environmental broadening phenomenon' can be detected in connection with both CP and ESC rights. Illustrations of the first category are provided by the progressive interpretation of provisions such as Article 8 (right to private and family life) of the European Convention on Human Rights (ECHR),[10] or Article 21 (right to property) of the American Convention on Human Rights (ACHR).[11] In the area of ESC rights, relevant examples include the

shall have appropriate access to information concerning the environment that is held by public authorities, including information on hazardous materials and activities in their communities, and the opportunity to participate in decision-making processes. States shall facilitate and encourage public awareness and participation by making information widely available. Effective access to judicial and administrative proceedings, including redress and remedy, shall be provided'. Report of the United Nations Conference on Environment and Development (Rio de Janeiro, 3–14 June 1992), Annex I, Rio Declaration on Environment and Development, UN Doc. A/CONF.151/26 (Vol. I) ('Rio Declaration'). See Boyle 'The Role of International Human Rights Law in the Protection of the Environment', in Boyle and Anderson, *supra* note 1, at 59–63.

[8] A right to a safe environment has been enshrined in some instruments, such as Art. 11 of the Additional Protocol to the American Convention on Human Rights in the area of Economic, Social and Cultural Rights, 17 November 1988, OAS Treaty Series No. 69 ('Protocol of San Salvador') and Art. 24 of the African Charter on Human and Peoples' Rights, 27 June 1981, OAU Doc. CAB/LEG/67/3 rev. 5, 21 I.L.M. 58 (1982) ('African Charter'). But the enforcement of these provisions remains limited. Art. 11 of the San Salvador Protocol cannot ground a claim before the Commission or the Court (Protocol of San Salvador, Art. 19(6) *a contrario*). Art. 21 of the African Charter has been rarely applied by the African Commission. The landmark case in this regard is: The Social and Economic Rights Action Centre and the Centre for Economic and Social Rights/Nigeria, African Commission on Human and Peoples' Rights in its Communication 155/96, done at the 30th Ordinary Session, held in Banjul on 13–27 October 2001 ('Ogoni case').

[9] See G. Triggs 'The Rights of Indigenous Peoples to Participate in Resource Development: An International Legal Perspective', in D.N. Zillman, A.R. Lucas, and G. Pring (eds.), *Human Rights in Natural Resource Development* (Oxford: Oxford University Press, 2002), 123–154.

[10] Convention for the Protection of Human Rights and Fundamental Freedoms, 4 November 1950, Europ.T.S. No. 5, 213 UNTS 221 ('European Convention' or 'ECHR'). The right to private and family life enshrined in Art. 8 of the ECHR has been broadened in several cases, including the following: European Court of Human Rights (ECtHR), *Powell and Rayner v the United Kingdom* (Judgment) (21 February 1990), Application No. 9310/81, para. 40 (noise pollution); ECtHR, *Case of Lopez-Ostra v Spain* (Judgment) (9 December 1994), Application No. 16798/90, para. 51 (pollution from tanneries); ECtHR, *Case of Guerra and Others v Italy* (Judgment) (19 February 1998), Application No. 14967/89, para. 57 (pollution from the operation of a chemical factory); ECtHR, *Case of Hatton et al. v The United Kingdom* (Judgment) (8 July 2003), Application No. 36022/97, paras. 96–104 (noise pollution); ECtHR, *Case of Moreno Gomez v Spain* (Judgment) (16 November 2004), Application No. 4143/02, paras. 53–56 (noise pollution); ECtHR, *Case of Taskin and others v Turkey* (Judgment) (10 November 2004), Application No. 46117/99, paras. 98–100 (granting of permits to exploit a gold mine); ECtHR, *Case of Ivan Atanasov v Bulgaria* (Judgment) (12 December 2010), Application No. 12853/03, paras. 55–57 (pollution from a former copper-ore mine).

[11] American Convention on Human Rights (Pact of San Jose, Costa Rica), 22 November 1969, OAS Treaty Series No. 36 ('American Convention' or 'ACHR'). The right to property (enshrined in articles 21 of the ACHR and XXIII of the American Declaration of Human Rights) has been broadened in several cases, including: Inter-American Court of Human Rights (IACtHR), *Maya Indigenous*

broadening of the right to adequate food, the right to health, or the right to water enshrined in the International Covenant on Economic, Social and Cultural Rights (ICESCR).[12] We shall comment briefly on these latter rights.

Regarding, first, the right to adequate food, as defined by Article 11 of the ICESCR and further interpreted by CESCR in General Comment No. 12,[13] reference to international environmental law is used as a tool for circumscribing the substantive scope of this right. For example, General Comment No. 12 states that:

> [t]he notion of sustainability is intrinsically linked to the notion of adequate food or food security, implying food being accessible for both present and future generations. The precise meaning of 'adequacy' is to a large extent determined by prevailing social, economic, cultural, climatic, ecological and other conditions, while 'sustainability' incorporates the notion of long-term availability and accessibility.[14]

Moreover, according to CESCR, Article 11:

> sets requirements for food safety and for a range of protective measures by both public and private means to prevent contamination of foodstuffs through adulteration and/or through bad environmental hygiene or inappropriate handling at different stages throughout the food chain; care must also be taken to identify and avoid or destroy naturally occurring toxins.[15]

The reference in General Comment No. 12 to the concept of sustainability, which in 1999 was already firmly rooted in international environmental law,[16] plays an important role in expanding the scope of the right to adequate food well beyond

Communities of the Toledo District v Belize, Case No. 12-053 (Merits), Report No. 40/04, 12 October 2004, paras. 27–36 (logging and oil concessions and their impact on the environment); IACtHR, *The Mayagna (Sumo) Awas Tingni Community v Nicaragua* (Judgment) (31 August 2001), Ser. C, No. 79, paras. 139, 149, 153, and 155 (protection of Nicaraguan forests in lands traditionally owned by the Awas Tingni Community); IACtHR, *Saramaka people v Surinam* (Judgment) (28 November 2007), Ser. C, No. 172, paras. 78–158, 214 (property over traditional lands and obligations to respect, ensure and give domestic legal effect to Art. 21).

[12] International Covenant on Economic, Social and Cultural Rights, 16 December 1966, 993 UNTS 3 ('ICESCR').

[13] Committee on Economic, Social and Cultural Rights (CESCR), General Comment No. 12: The Right to Adequate Food (Art. 11), 12 May 1999, UN Doc. E/C.12/1999/5.

[14] Committee on Economic, Social and Cultural Rights (CESCR), General Comment No. 12: The Right to Adequate Food (Art. 11), 12 May 1999, UN Doc. E/C.12/1999/5, para. 7.

[15] CESCR General Comment No. 12: The Right to Adequate Food (Art. 11), 12 May 1999, UN Doc. E/C.12/1999/5, para. 10.

[16] The concept of sustainability was referred to in principles 4, 5, and 8 of the 1992 Rio Declaration, as well as in the judgment of the International Court of Justice (ICJ) in the *Gabčikovo-Nagymaros* case: Gabčikovo-Nagymaros Project (Hungary/Slovakia), Judgment, ICJ Reports 1997, 3, para. 140. It was subsequently taken up in many other international instruments, including the 2002 New Delhi Declaration of the International Law Association (New Delhi Declaration of Principles of International Law relating to Sustainable Development, Resolution 3/2002, points 1, 3, 4, and 7); the 2002 Johannesburg Declaration (A/CONF.199/20 para. 5); the WTO Appellate Body *Shrimp Turtle* case (*United States—Import Prohibition of Certain Shrimp and Shrimp Products* (Shrimp Turtle Case), WTO Appellate Body, 1998, para. 153); and, more recently, the judgment of the ICJ in the *Pulp Mills* case (ICJ, Case concerning Pulp Mills on the River Uruguay (Argentina *v* Uruguay), Judgment, 20 April 2010, paras. 75–77 and 177 especially).

access to certain quantities of food to include environmental quality standards and even the preservation of the needs of future generations.

In a similar vein, the outer limits of the right to health enshrined in Article 12 of the ICESCR, and further interpreted by CESCR in General Comment No. 14,[17] are defined by reference to international environmental law. General Comment No. 14 states, for instance, that

> [t]he Committee interprets the right to health, as defined in article 12.1, as an inclusive right extending not only to timely and appropriate health care but also to the underlying determinants of health, such as access to safe and potable water and adequate sanitation, an adequate supply of safe food, nutrition and housing, healthy occupational and environmental conditions, and access to health-related education and information [....][18]

Referring explicitly to Principle 1 of the 1972 Stockholm Declaration, CESCR adds that:

> [t]he improvement of all aspects of environmental and industrial hygiene (art. 12.2 (b)) comprises, inter alia, preventive measures in respect of occupational accidents and diseases; the requirement to ensure an adequate supply of safe and potable water and basic sanitation; the prevention and reduction of the population's exposure to harmful substances such as radiation and harmful chemicals or other detrimental environmental conditions that directly or indirectly impact upon human health.[19]

Thus, CESCR seeks support from environmental considerations and principles in defining the scope of the right to health. While this is understandable, we must not neglect the fact that environmental standards evolve over time, stretching the outer limits of ESC rights.

The third illustration of the environmental broadening phenomenon is provided by the right to water, derived as an independent right from Articles 11 and 12 of the ICESCR in CESCR's General Comment No. 15.[20] In assessing the scope of the right to water, General Comment No. 15 also refers to principles of international environmental law. Indeed, Paragraph 11 of General Comment No. 15 states that '[t]he manner of the realization of the right to water must [...] be sustainable, ensuring that the right can be realized for present and future generations'.[21] General Comment No. 15 also seeks support from international environmental law in

[17] CESCR, General Comment No. 14: The Right to the Highest Attainable Standard of Health (Art. 12), 11 August 2000, UN Doc. E/C.12/2000/4.

[18] CESCR, General Comment No. 14: The Right to the Highest Attainable Standard of Health (Art. 12), 11 August 2000, UN Doc. E/C.12/2000/4, para. 11. For a reference to 'nutritiously safe food and potable drinking water' see also paras. 36 and 40.

[19] CESCR, General Comment No. 14: The Right to the Highest Attainable Standard of Health (Art. 12), 11 August 2000, UN Doc. E/C.12/2000/4, para. 15.

[20] CESCR, General Comment No. 15: The Right to Water, 20 January 2003, UN Doc. E/C.12/2002/11.

[21] CESCR, General Comment No. 15: The Right to Water, 20 January 2003, UN Doc. E/C.12/2002/11, para. 11 *in fine*. The legal bases of the concept of sustainable development and of the principle of intergenerational equity referred to in the foregoing quotation are identified in a footnote to para. 11 as follows:

> [f]or a definition of sustainability, see the Report of the United Nations Conference on Environment and Development, Rio de Janeiro, 3–14 1992, Declaration on Environment

connection with the management of water resources. Paragraph 28, devoted to this issue, refers to Chapters 5, 7, and 18 of Agenda 21, to the Plan of Implementation adopted at the 2002 World Summit on Sustainable Development, as well as to the 'Convention on Biological Diversity, the Convention to Combat Desertification, the United Nations Framework Convention on Climate Change, and subsequent protocols'.[22] As the right to water includes complex and diverse legal components, answers provided by international environmental law seem of particular relevance in the definition of its scope and boundaries.

As suggested by these remarks, international environmental law supplements ESC rights by pushing and helping define the outer boundaries of the substantive scope of ESC obligations. As we shall see, international environmental law could play an even more significant role in the understanding of ESC rights. Consideration of the interplay between ESC rights and international environmental law may, indeed, lead to a broadening of the way we normally think about ESC rights.

3. International Environmental Law Broadens the Way We Think about ESC Rights

The second mechanism through which international environmental law broadens ESC rights has received less attention, perhaps because the influence of international environmental law on ESC rights at this level seems misleadingly simple. International rules and mechanisms that command the protection of the environment obviously contribute, by this very fact, to the respect and fulfilment of ESC rights. As noted by one commentator:

> [t]he creation of a reliable and effective system of environmental protection would help ensure the well-being of future generations as well as the survival of those persons, often including indigenous or economically marginalized groups, who depend immediately upon natural resources for their livelihoods.[23]

But this assertion does not fully reflect the implications of the impact of international environmental law on the implementation of human rights.[24] To explore how the synergies between international environmental law and ESC rights may lead to a substantial broadening of the way in which we think about ESC rights, it seems useful to take an example, like the right to water.

and Development, principles 1, 8, 9, 10, 12, and 15; and Agenda 21, in particular principles 5.3, 7.27, 7.28, 7.35, 7.39, 7.41, 18.3, 18.8, 18.35, 18.40, 18.48, 18.50, 18.59, and 18.68.

[22] CESCR, General Comment No. 15: The Right to Water, 20 January 2003, UN Doc. E/C.12/2002/11, para. 28.

[23] Anderson, *Human Rights Approaches, supra* note 1, at 3.

[24] A more general statement of this relationship is the one given by the Human Rights Council in the Preamble to its Resolution A/HRC/16/L.7 of 18 March 2011, which states that 'sustainable development and the protection of the environment can contribute to human well-being and to the enjoyment of human rights'.

In discussing the formulation of the right to water introduced by CESCR in its General Comment No. 15, we have seen that international environmental law is referred to in order to provide more solid ground for some of the corollaries of the right to water, such as its implications for the management of freshwater resources. It may, however, be particularly challenging to derive, from a right which is not even explicitly formulated in the ICESCR, general far-reaching obligations, such as the requirements to adopt integrated water resources management or to assess the impacts of 'climate changes, desertification and increased soil salinity, deforestation and loss of biodiversity'.[25] General Comment No. 15 seeks to identify specific norms to provide additional grounding to these 'distant corollaries' of the right to water. In doing so, it raises a theoretical question with important practical implications; namely, what are the outer limits of a given human right and what legal materials mark its boundaries? In other words, what is the 'fabric' of which the legal creature that we call 'the right to water' is made?

The first part of the answer is fairly obvious: it is made of those provisions in human rights and other treaties that provide for a right to water, either explicitly or implicitly.[26] To this first layer of materials we could add a second layer consisting of General Comment No. 15 as well as other documents prepared by CESCR as part of its consideration of reports of states parties.[27] A third layer of materials would include resolutions of an array of international bodies as well as the case law of international and domestic adjudicatory and quasi-adjudicatory bodies relating to the right to water.

But is that all? What about regulations governing the quantity and the quality of water that must be made available, or the ways in which water policy must be organized domestically and coordinated internationally? Some of these more 'distant materials' clearly seem to be part of the fabric of the right to water. A good illustration of this point would be the WHO Guidelines for drinking-water quality, to which General Comment No. 15 explicitly refers.[28] The link with some other distant materials may be less explicit, but that does not mean that it is weaker. As a matter of fact, certain environmental treaties go very far in establishing a system of 'distant corollaries' or obligations that are a logical but distant consequence of respecting, protecting, and fulfilling the right to water. A treaty such as the UNECE Water Convention,[29] with its network of some 150 specific treaties,[30] its Protocol

[25] CESCR, General Comment No. 15: The Right to Water, 20 January 2003, UN Doc. E/C.12/2002/11, para. 28.

[26] The main such provisions are identified in paras. 3 and 4 (and their footnotes) of General Comment No. 15.

[27] CESCR, General Comment No. 15: The Right to Water, 20 January 2003, UN Doc. E/C.12/2002/11, para. 5.

[28] WHO, *Guidelines for drinking-water quality*, 2nd edn, vols. 1–3 (Geneva, 1993), referred to in footnote 15 to para. 12(a) of General Comment No. 15.

[29] Convention on the Protection and Use of Transboundary Watercourses and International Lakes, 18 March 1992, 1936 UNTS 269 ('UNECE Water Convention').

[30] Pursuant to Art. 9(1) of the UNECE Water Convention: 'The Riparian Parties shall on the basis of equality and reciprocity enter into bilateral or multilateral agreements or other arrangements, where these do not yet exist, or adapt existing ones, where necessary to eliminate the contradictions with the basic principles of this Convention, in order to define their mutual relations and conduct regarding

on Water and Health,[31] and the implementing domestic (or community) laws,[32] would offer a firmer foundation for the obligations of management and quality of water than the distant obligation formulated in General Comment No. 15. There is, indeed, a continuum between the provisions formulated in human rights language and other provisions formulated in regulatory language or, in other terms, between the different layers of materials that blend together to form the fabric of the right to water. Our understanding of the right to water as consisting only of certain layers must not prevent us from seeing the normative environmental context of this and other rights. The system of the UNECE Water Convention[33] is an important component of this normative context.[34] Within the framework of this Convention, the Protocol on Water and Health provides an apposite illustration of the type of apparently distant materials with a strong link to the right to water.

The Protocol links sustainable water management with the reduction of water-related disease and, thereby, spells out the connection between environmental

the prevention, control and reduction of transboundary impact. The Riparian Parties shall specify the catchment area, or part(s) thereof, subject to cooperation. These agreements or arrangements shall embrace relevant issues covered by this Convention, as well as any other issues on which the Riparian Parties may deem it necessary to cooperate'. A network of some 150 water treaties, either already existing or concluded afterwards, have come under the umbrella of the UNECE Water Convention. The status of bilateral and multilateral agreements can be followed through the UNECE's website, available at <http://www.unece.org/env/water/partnership/part621.htm> (last accessed 11 November 2013).

[31] Protocol on Water and Health to the 1992 Convention on the Protection and Use of Transboundary Watercourses and International Lakes, 17 June 1999, 2331 UNTS 202 ('Protocol on Water and Health').

[32] For instance, within the European Union, the water management policy has been adjusted in accordance with the Protocol. See in particular: the Water Framework Directive (OJ L 327), the Bathing Water Directive (OJ L 64), the Groundwater Directive (OJ L 372), and the Shellfish Directive (OJ L 376). See also: the Drinking Water Directive (OJ L 330), the Urban Wastewater Treatment Directive (OJ L 135), and the Abstraction Directive (OJ L 194).

[33] The Convention aims at strengthening national measures for the protection of transboundary surface and ground waters (Art. 2). It enjoys a high ratification rate (38 Parties including the European Union), and it was amended in 2003 to allow accession by countries from outside the UNECE region (Art. 25(3)). The Convention takes a comprehensive approach in the regulation of freshwater resources, recognizing their fundamental role in both ecosystems and human societies. It sets compulsory minimum standards for the prevention, control, and reduction of pollution of transboundary watercourses and international lakes (Arts. 3(1)(f) and (2)), as well as providing States Parties with a comprehensive system of assistance, including joint monitoring and assessment programmes, warning and alarms systems, and mutual assistance procedures (Arts. 2(6), 5, 6, and 9 to 15). As already noted, the Convention obliges States Parties to enter into bilateral or multilateral agreements or to adapt existing ones where necessary to eliminate contradictions with the basic principles set out by the Convention (Art. 9(1)). This has led to the development of a network of some 150 water treaties, which evidences the practical relevance of the Convention in the international order. Moreover, in 2000, an International Water Assessment Centre (IWAC) was established in order to offer scientific and technical support to states parties on questions relating to monitoring and assessment.

[34] Other potential components of the normative environmental context of the right to water include the 1997 UN Convention on the Law of Non-Navigational Uses of International Watercourses, 21 May 1997 (General Assembly Resolution (GA Res.) 51/229, annex, GAOR, 51st session, Supp. No. 49, UN Doc. A/51/49 (not yet in force)) or the 2008 International Law Commission (ILC) Draft Articles on the Law of Transboundary Aquifers (Text adopted by the ILC at its 60th session, in 2008, GAOR, 63rd session, Supp. No. 10, UN Doc. A/63/10), as well as a number of water and environmental treaties operating beyond the UNECE system.

protection and the promotion of human health. Pursuant to Article 1, the objective of the Protocol is:

> to promote at all appropriate levels, nationally as well as in transboundary and international contexts, the protection of human health and well-being, both individual and collective, within a framework of sustainable development, through improving water management, including the protection of water ecosystems, and through preventing, controlling and reducing water-related disease.

To this end, Article 4(1) of the Protocol requires states parties to:

> take all appropriate measures to prevent, control and reduce water-related disease within a framework of integrated water-management systems aimed at sustainable use of water resources, ambient water quality which does not endanger human health, and protection of water ecosystems.

It is worth noting that the integrated water resources management approach is couched here as a component of a binding obligation, by contrast with the reference to soft-law instruments (for example, Agenda 21) found in paragraph 28 of General Comment No. 15. This point stresses the idea, as we have discussed, that environmental treaties may be important for the proper expression and grounding of certain obligations arising from ESC rights, such as the right to water. The Protocol on Water and Health offers one of the clearest illustrations of this point. Although it is premised on the need to provide access to water and sanitation 'for everyone',[35] it is not couched in human rights language.[36] Yet, the significance of the Protocol for the implementation of the right to water must not be underestimated. As noted by one distinguished commentator:

> [t]he formulation in the Protocol of access to water in terms of basic human needs [...] could [...] provide a criterion for the review of the legitimacy of state policies which authorize the unsustainable use of water resources in such a way as to deprive affected people of their access to safe drinking and sanitation.[37]

The two core mechanisms through which the Protocol operates, namely surveillance/early warning mechanisms[38] and a system of water quality targets and implementation deadlines,[39] are among the most ambitious international tools for the preservation of the quality of water bodies. In addition, a sophisticated

[35] Other potential components of the normative environmental context of the right to water include the 1997 UN Convention on the Law of Non-Navigational Uses of International Watercourses, 21 May 1997 (GA Res. 51/229, annex, GAOR, 51st session, Supp. No. 49, UN Doc. A/51/49 (not yet in force)) or the 2008 International Law Commission (ILC) Draft Articles on the Law of Transboundary Aquifers (Text adopted by the ILC at its 60th session, in 2008, GAOR, 63rd session, Supp. No. 10, UN Doc. A/63/10, art 6(1)), as well as a number of water and environmental treaties operating beyond the UNECE system.

[36] The text of the Protocol makes only two explicit references to the right to water in Arts. 5(m) and 9(1)(b), respectively.

[37] Francioni, *supra* note 1, at 46.

[38] Protocol on Water and Health, Art. 8.

[39] Protocol on Water and Health, Art 6(2)(a) to (n). To assist Parties in setting targets, a Task Force on Indicators and Reporting was established in 2007, UN Doc. ECE/MP.WH/2/Add.3, EUR/06/5069385/1/Add.3, 3 July 2007.

compliance mechanism, which is open to communications from the public, has been established to monitor the implementation of the obligations of the Protocol.[40] Thus, this system constitutes a detailed binding implementation of some components of the right to water; a system that goes beyond the broad references to water quality and management included in General Comment No. 15 and provides, among others, for an enforcement mechanism of a kind that is lacking in the ESC rights context.[41]

This latter point provides a suitable transition to our third section, namely the broadening of the palette of enforcement mechanisms available for the implementation of ESC rights. Indeed, as we shall see next, a broadening of the scope as well as of the way in which we think about ESC rights could foster the use of a variety of enforcement mechanisms that are sometimes beyond the radar of human rights activists. From a practical perspective, the use of such mechanisms, initially conceived for the implementation of environmental obligations, is perhaps the most important implication of the environmental broadening phenomenon discussed in the previous sections of this chapter.

4. International Environmental Law Broadens the Palette of Enforcement Mechanisms

The third avenue through which international environmental law influences ESC rights is the broadening of the palette of enforcement mechanisms. Until recently, there were few mechanisms available to private parties to bring individual complaints for violation of ESC rights (as opposed to those available for CP rights).[42] The most promising instrument in this connection is now the Optional Protocol to

[40] Protocol on Water and Health, Art. 15.

[41] The first reporting exercise under the Protocol was conducted during autumn 2009 and spring 2010 and flagged that a number of Parties were facing difficulties in implementating the Protocol. To respond to this situation, the Compliance Committee decided at its fifth meeting in June 2010 to enhance its facilitation and assistance functions, and agreed to enter into consultations with a number of Parties. At its sixth meeting in March 2011, the Compliance Committee outlined the main features for a new consultation process geared to help Parties implement their obligations under the Protocol, UN Doc. ECE/MP.WH/C.1/2010/4-EUR/10/56335/16, 21 July 2010, paras. 25–30; UN Doc. ECE/MP.WH/C.1/2011/2-EUR/DHP1003944/4.2/2011/2, 11 April 2011, paras. 9–20.

[42] The main procedures available in this connection focus indeed on the ESC components of CP rights or on rights situated at the juncture between ESC and CP rights: Optional Protocol to the International Covenant on Civil and Political rights, 16 December 1966, 999 UNTS 171; Optional Protocol to the Convention on the Elimination of All Forms of Discrimination against Women, 6 October 1999, 2131 UNTS 83; Optional Protocol to the Convention on the Rights of Persons with Disabilities, 13 December 2006, Doc.A/61/611; and procedure according to Art. 14 of the International Convention on the Protection of the Rights of All Migrant Workers and Members of their Families, 18 December 1990, 2220 UNTS 3. Therefore, until the adoption of the Optional Protocol to the ICESCR there was arguably no specific mechanism for bringing individual complaints for breach of ESC rights. See C. Mahon, 'Progress at the Front: The Draft Optional Protocol to the International Covenant on Economic, Social and Cultural Rights' 8 *Human Rights Law Review* (2008), 617–646.

the ICESCR that entered into force in May 2013.[43] As a supplement to this and other mechanisms, some procedures established by environmental treaties could potentially be used to bring individual complaints for breach of certain ESC rights (or some components of such claims). To the extent that, through the broadening process already discussed, certain ESC rights have acquired environmental content, questions relating to the implementation of measures and policies relating to such rights may potentially fall within the mandate of some compliance bodies established to deal with environmental questions. Such a development could be seen as a sort of 'reverse mirror' of the treatment of environmental questions by adjudicatory and quasi-adjudicatory human rights bodies.

Two types of environmental mechanisms that could be used to enforce ESC rights will be discussed. The first type authorizes individuals or NGOs to file communications complaining about a state's failure to implement the environmental measures required by a given treaty. These mechanisms will be illustrated by reference to institutional arrangements set out in the North American Agreement for Environmental Cooperation (NAAEC) and in the Protocol on Water and Health.[44] The second type of mechanism consists of using certain procedural rights developed in connection with the implementation of environmental measures; for example, access to information, participation in decision-making procedures, and access to justice. This second type of instrument, which we will illustrate by reference to the Aarhus Convention,[45] is significantly more sophisticated than the first in that it is fully geared towards increased transparency, and it also includes a compliance mechanism open to individuals and NGOs. Moreover, the principles of the Aarhus Convention have some influence beyond its member states.

A. Broadening access to environmental compliance procedures

1. Communications under the North American Agreement for Environmental Cooperation

The first example of larger access to compliance mechanisms is given by the system of individual communications established by the NAAEC. A side agreement to the North American Free Trade Agreement,[46] the NAAEC aims at enhancing environmental cooperation[47] and compliance with environmental regulations,[48] as well as promoting transparency and public participation.[49] The governing body of the

[43] Optional Protocol to the International Covenant on Economic, Social and Cultural Rights, 10 December 2008 (in force since 5 May 2013). For the text of the Protocol see GA Res. A/RES/63/117, 5 March 2009.

[44] North American Agreement on Environmental Cooperation, 17 December 1992, 32 ILM 1480 (1993) ('NAAEC').

[45] Convention on Access to Information, Public Participation in Decision-making and Access to Justice in Environmental Matters, 25 June 1998, 2161 UNTS 447 ('Aarhus Convention').

[46] North American Free Trade Agreement, 17 December 1992, 32 ILM 289 (1993) (table of contents, preamble, parts I–III), and 32 ILM 605 (1993) (parts IV–VII, annexes).

[47] NAAEC, Art. 1(b), (c), and (f). [48] NAAEC, Art. 1(g). [49] NAAEC, Art. 1(h).

NAAEC is the Council of Ministers, which consists of the environment ministers of the three states parties.[50] The participation of civil society within the framework created by the NAAEC is ensured through the Joint Public Advisory Committee, an advisory committee consisting of 15 members from civil society,[51] and through the citizen Submissions on Enforcement Matters procedure (SEM procedure).[52] The SEM procedure is open to claims 'asserting that a Party is failing to effectively enforce its environmental law',[53] an expression that could potentially cover claims relating to laws or measures affecting ESC rights.[54]

However, the potential of the system laid out in the NAAEC seems rather limited given that the Joint Public Advisory Committee has only an advisory role and, more significantly, that complaints brought under the SEM procedure are subject to very strict conditions.[55] Moreover, transparency is not guaranteed within the SEM procedure. As we shall see later, compared with the approach followed by the Aarhus Convention, the compliance procedure of the NAAEC seems rather weak in terms of transparency, efficiency, and effective public participation.[56]

2. *The 'non-compliance procedure' of the Protocol on Water and Health*

The second example of an environmental compliance procedure that could potentially be used to bring claims relating to the violation of ESC rights is the mechanism set up by the Protocol on Water and Health. Under Article 15 of the Protocol, the Meeting of the Parties was mandated to establish a mechanism of a 'non-confrontational, non-judicial and consultative nature' for reviewing compliance with the Protocol by States Parties. In January 2007, at the first Meeting of the Parties to the Protocol, a 'Decision on review of compliance' was adopted,[57] setting out a compliance procedure managed by a Compliance Committee. From the perspective of environmental lawyers, this procedure would be more accurately characterized as a 'non-compliance procedure', in that it aims at managing non-compliance[58] rather than operating

[50] NAAEC, Art. 9. [51] NAAEC, Art. 16(1). [52] NAAEC, Arts. 14 and 15.

[53] NAAEC, Art. 14(1).

[54] See, for example, the Final Factual Record regarding the *Tarahumara* Submission (SEM-00-006), Commission for Environmental Cooperation, July 2005, Record released 9 January 2006. The case concerned the alleged failure by Mexico to effectively enforce its environmental law by denying access to environmental justice to Indigenous communities in the Sierra Tarahumara in the State of Chihuahua. Section 10 of the Record asserts numerous failures by Mexico (83–85). Solutions to enhance compliance with Mexico's obligation regarding access to environmental justice are mentioned in Sections 9 (67–83), and 10 of the Record.

[55] NAAEC, Arts. 14(1)–(2).

[56] For a comparative analysis of both compliance procedures see M. Fitzmaurice, 'Environmental justice through international complaint procedures? Comparing the Aarhus Convention and the North-American Agreement on Environmental Cooperation', in J. Ebbesson and P. Okowa (eds.), *Environmental Law and Justice in Context* (Cambridge: Cambridge University Press, 2009), 211–227.

[57] 'Review of Compliance', Decision I/2, 3 July 2007, UN Doc. ECE/MP.WH/2/Add.3, EUR/06/5069385/1/Add.3 ('Decision I/2').

[58] See J.E. Viñuales 'Managing Compliance with Standards for the Protection of the Environment', in A. Cassese (ed.), *Towards a Realistic Utopia* (Oxford: Oxford University Press, 2012), 326–339.

as a quasi-jurisdictional body.[59] The Compliance Committee can nevertheless 'examine compliance issues and make recommendations or take measures if and as appropriate'.[60]

One major feature of the Protocol's non-compliance procedure is that the procedure can be initiated not only by states or by the Secretariat, as is usually the case in most other non-compliance procedures,[61] but also by members of the public. Paragraph 16 of the Annex to Decision I/2 provides that:

> communications may be brought before the Committee by one or more members of the public concerning that Party's compliance with the Protocol, unless that Party has notified the Depositary in writing by the end of the applicable period that it is unable to accept, for a period of not more than four years, the consideration of such communications by the Committee.

Even more interesting is the fact that, as stressed by the Compliance Committee, applicants do not need to be directly affected by a situation of non-compliance to bring a communication,[62] a feature that will most likely facilitate the use of the non-compliance procedure. The 'Guidelines on Communications from the Public', adopted by the Committee at its third meeting, identify the types of non-compliance that a communication may address. The list, which is not exhaustive, mentions inter alia '[s]pecific instances of violation of rights of individuals under the Protocol'.[63] This is noteworthy for at least two reasons. First, as discussed above, the Protocol on Water and Health is not specifically couched in human rights language, although it is clearly based on the need to implement the right to water and sanitation. Second, despite the absence of practice, we cannot exclude that this non-compliance procedure may be used to challenge measures touching upon certain ESC rights, including the rights to water and sanitation, the right to health, the right to an adequate standard of living, the right to food, and even, perhaps, the right to housing. Some of the factual situations that could potentially be covered have already been subject to scrutiny through the lens of Article 8 of the ECHR. For example, a state would be in breach of its obligation under Article 4(1) of the Protocol on Water and Health to 'take all appropriate measures to prevent, control and reduce water-related disease' if it failed to take action to prevent

[59] As noted in para. 3 of the Annex to Decision I/2: 'The compliance procedure shall be conducted bearing in mind the interests of the Party facing difficulties, of the Parties as a whole and of populations potentially or actually adversely affected by non-compliance'.

[60] As noted in para. 12 of the Annex to Decision I/2.

[61] See F. Romanin Jacur, 'Triggering Non-Compliance Procedures', in T. Treves, L. Pineschi, A. Tanzi, C. Pitea, C. Ragni, and F. Romanin Jacur (eds.), *Non-Compliance Procedures and Mechanisms and the Effectiveness of International Environmental Agreements* (The Hague: TMC Asser Press, 2009), 373–387.

[62] See Report of the Third Meeting of the Compliance Committee, 30 April 2009, ECE/MP.WH/C.1/2009/2, EUR/09/5086338/6, 30 April 2009 ('Report of the Third Meeting'), para. 19. This point is mentioned in the Report's discussion of the connection between the work of the Compliance Committee and that of the Office of the UN High Commissioner for Human Rights.

[63] 'Guidelines on communications from the Public', available at <http://www.unece.org/fileadmin/DAM/env/water/meetings/CC/Guidelines_on_communication_revised_cleaned.pdf> (last accessed 11 November 2013), para. 17(d).

pollution of a water source by an industrial facility. Such inaction may, by the same token, amount to a violation of the rights to health, water, and food, depending on the circumstances. The use of such a complaint procedure to challenge some instances of state inaction would in all likelihood strengthen the implementation of ESC rights, which are not well endowed in enforcement mechanisms.

Although the Committee has not yet received any submission, referral, or communication, the potential of the Protocol's non-compliance procedure for the implementation of ESC rights (and of human rights in general) is further highlighted by the express recognition, since the third meeting of the Compliance Committee, of the connection between the work of the Committee and that of the UN Office of the High Commissioner for Human Rights, as well as of the potential synergies between the two.[64] Interestingly, the Compliance Committee has also referred to the potential, in this same connection, of the institutional arrangements established by the Aarhus Convention,[65] to which we now turn.

B. Broadening the scope of 'environmental democracy'

The Aarhus Convention is relevant for our analysis in several ways. First, the Convention obliges states to implement what could be broadly referred to as 'transparency measures' or 'environmental democracy' measures. Thus, states must introduce into their domestic systems three clusters of environmental procedural rights that allow civil society to put pressure on states (and therefore, to some extent, to monitor them) in connection with environmental policies and environment-related activities. Second, where states fail to implement such measures, civil society groups can bring a complaint before a compliance committee specifically established by the Convention for this purpose. In less than 10 years, almost 60 such complaints have been brought against states parties (or against the European Community). Third, as we shall see, the 'environmental democracy' obligations provided in the Aarhus Convention have received additional recognition in the case law of the European Court of Human Rights, even in cases involving a State not party to the Aarhus Convention.

1. Environmental procedural rights

The main purpose of the Aarhus Convention is 'to contribute to the protection of the right of every person of present and future generations to live in an environment adequate to his or her health and wellbeing'.[66] With this aim, the Convention

[64] See Report of the Fourth Meeting of the Compliance Committee, 15 May 2010, ECE/MP.WH/C.1/2010/2, EUR/10/5086338/VIII, paras. 26–31. The Report of the Fifth Meeting does not address the connection between the work of the Compliance Committee and that of the Office of the High Commissioner for Human Rights, but this issue was included in the agenda for the sixth meeting, scheduled for the beginning of March 2011. See 'Annotated Provisional Agenda for the Sixth Meeting', 18 January 2011, ECE/MP.WH/C.1/2011/1, EUR/DHP1003944/4.2/2011/1, point 5. The Report of the Sixth Meeting was not yet available at the time of writing.

[65] See Report of the Third Meeting, para. 21.

[66] Aarhus Convention, Art. 1.

requires states parties to introduce into their domestic legislation three clusters of environmental procedural rights.

The first cluster concerns rights to access environmental information (Articles 4 and 5). The term 'environmental information' is expansively defined in Article 2(3) by reference to three categories of what that information could concern,[67] namely: '[t]he state of elements of the environment' (letter (a)), '[f]actors, such as substances, energy, noise and radiation, and activities or measures' (letter (b)), and, most importantly for our analysis:

> [t]he state of human health and safety, conditions of human life, cultural sites and built structures, inasmuch as they are or may be affected by the state of the elements of the environment or, through these elements, by the factors, activities or measures referred to in subparagraph (b) above (letter (c)).

The link formulated in the latter paragraph between, on the one hand, 'human health and safety' or 'conditions of human life' and, on the other hand, the environment highlights the interest in broadening the scope of human rights to include environmental components. Through such broadening, this link could become increasingly explicit, extending the right to have access to environmental information to measures and policies relating to ESC rights (for example, measures and policies concerning standards of water quality, the use of communal lands by third parties, health-related zoning requirements, etc.). This link is further clarified by the Implementation Guide of the Aarhus Convention, which refers, for instance, to the fact that 'human health may include a wide range of diseases and health conditions that are directly or indirectly attributable to or affected by changes in environmental conditions'.[68] However, the broadening of the concept of 'environmental information' has limits. Although the Implementation Guide states that the three categories circumscribing the term 'environmental information' are non-exhaustive,[69] it would be difficult to argue that measures presenting no discernible link to the environment are covered. Thus, information relating to

[67] Art. 2(3) of the Aarhus Convention states: '"Environmental information" means any information in written, visual, aural, electronic or any other material form on: (a) The state of elements of the environment, such as air and atmosphere, water, soil, land, landscape and natural sites, biological diversity and its components, including genetically modified organisms, and the interaction among these elements; (b) Factors, such as substances, energy, noise and radiation, and activities or measures, including administrative measures, environmental agreements, policies, legislation, plans and programmes, affecting or likely to affect the elements of the environment within the scope of subparagraph (a) above, and cost-benefit and other economic analyses and assumptions used in environmental decision-making; (c) The state of human health and safety, conditions of human life, cultural sites and built structures, inasmuch as they are or may be affected by the state of the elements of the environment or, through these elements, by the factors, activities or measures referred to in subparagraph (b) above.'

[68] The Aarhus Convention: An Implementation Guide, available at <http://www.unece.org/env/pp/implementation%20guide/english/part2.pdf> (last accessed 11 November 2013) ('Implementation Guide'), 38.

[69] The Aarhus Convention: An Implementation Guide, available at <http://www.unece.org/env/pp/implementation%20guide/english/part2.pdf> (last accessed 11 November 2013) ('Implementation Guide'), 35.

measures concerning the right to education or the right to work would not be covered by the term 'environmental information' unless a sufficient link with the 'state of elements of the environment' or with '[f]actors, such as substances, energy, noise and radiation, and activities or measures' can be established.

The second cluster of environmental procedural rights concern public participation in decisions regarding specific activities (Article 6), plans, programmes, and policies relating to the environment (Article 7), as well as public participation during the preparation of executive regulations and/or legally binding instruments of general application (Article 8). These rights can be seen as specific applications of a broader right to participate in public affairs provided, most notably, in Article 25(a) of the ICCPR,[70] which applies also to ESC rights.[71] Of the variety of questions raised by this cluster,[72] a particularly relevant one is the identification of the types of activities that require public participation under the Aarhus Convention. Two basic standards are used in this regard. Articles 6(1) and 8 (chapeau) refer to those activities or generally binding rules that 'may have a significant effect on the environment'. This expression is not defined in the Convention, but the Implementation Guide[73] characterizes it by reference to paragraph I of Appendix III to the Espoo Convention on Environmental Impact Assessment in a Transboundary Context.[74] Among the criteria that must be considered to assess 'significance' (size, location, and effects), the Espoo Convention mentions 'proposed activities in locations where the characteristics of proposed development would be likely to have significant effects on the population'[75] or those 'giving rise to serious effects on humans'.[76] Article 7 uses a slightly lower standard by referring to plans and programmes 'relating to the environment'. According to the Implementation Guide such a connection must be 'determined with reference to the implied definition of 'environment' found in the definition of 'environmental information' (Article 2, paragraph 3)'.[77] Thus, in both cases, there is some room for activities,

[70] International Covenant on Civil and Political Rights, 16 December 1966, 999 UNTS 171 ('ICCPR'), Art. 25(a).

[71] On the scope of Art. 25 of the ICCPR, see Human Rights Committee, General Comment No. 25: The right to participate in public affairs, voting rights and the right of equal access to public service (Art. 25), 12 July 1996, UN Doc. CCPR/C/21/Rev.1/Add.7, paras. 5–8 referring to the application of Art. 25(a).

[72] One important question concerns the scope of public participation. This is discussed in detail in the Implementation Guide (Implementation Guide, 85–122). For our purpose, it will suffice to note that the requirement of public participation does not mean that the public has a veto on activities, measures or plans (See Aarhus Convention, art 6(8), 7, and 8 *in fine*; Implementation Guide, 109–110).

[73] Aarhus Convention, art 6(8), 7, and 8 *in fine*; Implementation Guide, 94.

[74] Convention on Environmental Impact Assessment in a Transboundary Context, 25 February 1991, 1989 UNTS 309 ('Espoo Convention').

[75] Convention on Environmental Impact Assessment in a Transboundary Context, 25 February 1991, 1989 UNTS 309 ('Espoo Convention'), appendix III, para. 1(b) *in fine*.

[76] Convention on Environmental Impact Assessment in a Transboundary Context, 25 February 1991, 1989 UNTS 309 ('Espoo Convention'), appendix III, para. 1(c).

[77] Implementation Guide, 115. According to the guide, this would include 'land-use and regional development strategies, and sectoral planning in transport, tourism, energy, heavy and light industry, water resources, health and sanitation, etc., at all levels of government'.

measures, and regulations affecting the situation of human beings and their ESC rights to be included among those requiring public participation. Indeed, the activities and measures targeted are those with potentially serious consequences for the environment, a category that overlaps, to a significant degree, with those affecting human health (for example, through the safety and quality of water, food production, the safety of the working environment, etc.). Thus, the public participation requirements laid out in the Aarhus Convention could operate as an additional layer of protection based on which measures relating to the implementation of ESC rights could be further scrutinized by the public. This point will be discussed in more detail in the next section.

The third cluster of environmental procedural rights concerns access to justice in connection with access to environmental information and public participation in environmental decision-making (Article 9). Interestingly, this right is extended by Article 9, paragraph 3, to empower members of the public 'to challenge acts and omissions by private persons and public authorities which contravene provisions of its national law relating to the environment'. In the language of ESC rights, this extension would also cover the obligations 'to protect from deprivation' by third parties.

For all three clusters of rights, the public concerned encompasses 'the public affected or likely to be affected by, or having an interest in, the environmental decision-making [...] and meeting any requirements under national law'.[78] Moreover, Article 9(b) expressly states that:

> the interest of any non-governmental organization meeting the requirements referred to in article 2, paragraph 5, shall be deemed sufficient for the purpose of subparagraph (a) above [sufficient interest by members of the public]. Such organizations shall also be deemed to have rights capable of being impaired for the purpose of subparagraph (b) above [maintaining impairment of its own right].

The application of the Aarhus framework is thus facilitated, making the Convention a powerful enforcement tool of states' obligations. In addition, as we shall see, when a state party fails to implement the obligations arising from the Convention within its domestic system, the affected individuals or groups may resort to the non-compliance procedure established by the Convention.

2. *The non-compliance procedure of the Aarhus Convention*

The states parties to the Aarhus Convention have also established a sophisticated non-compliance procedure of some relevance for the enforcement of ESC rights.[79] The non-compliance procedure has a number of particular features that deserve attention. First, it is managed by a Compliance Committee consisting of eight members who serve in their personal capacity.[80] NGOs take part in the

[78] Aarhus Convention, Art. 2(5).

[79] Aarhus Convention, Art. 15, and 'Review of Compliance', Decision I/7, UN Doc. ECE/MP.PP/2/Add.8, 2 April 2004, Addendum, p. 1 ('Decision I/7').

[80] Aarhus Convention, annex, paras. 1 and 2.

procedure for the nomination of candidates.[81] Second, as a rule 'no information held by the Committee shall be kept confidential'[82] and the Committee's reports and recommendations are public.[83] Third, as in the non-compliance procedure of the Protocol on Water and Health, a member of the public (either individuals or NGOs) may bring a complaint before the Compliance Committee of the Aarhus Convention.[84] In such a case, the applicant is entitled to participate in the discussions of the Committee,[85] even though deliberations are conducted in closed-door sessions.[86] Individuals are thus granted a leading role in the procedure. As stated by a distinguished commentator, this procedure 'reflects the procedural human rights-based approach underlying the Aarhus Convention'.[87]

The possibility offered to the public by this procedure has been widely used. In less than eight years, the Committee has already received 83 communications from the public (including some communications against the European Community).[88] This remarkable record proves how serious the involvement of the civil society

[81] Aarhus Convention, annex paras. 2 and 4. [82] Aarhus Convention, annex, para. 26.

[83] Aarhus Convention, annex, paras. 26–31.

[84] Aarhus Convention, annex, paras. 18–24. As in most other non-compliance procedures, the procedure can also be triggered by states parties and by the Secretariat of the Aarhus Convention. See Aarhus Convention, annex, paras. 15–17. For an example of a case referred by a State see Doc. ACCC/C/2004/3 (Ukraine). So far, no case has been referred by the Secretariat.

[85] Aarhus Convention, annex, paras. 32 and 34.

[86] Aarhus Convention, annex, para. 33.

[87] Fitzmaurice, *supra* note 56, at 214.

[88] See ACCC/C/2004/1 (Kazakhstan), ACC/C/2004/2 (Kazakhstan), ACCC/C/2004/3 (Ukraine), ACCC/C/2004/4 (Hungary), ACCC/C/2004/5 (Turkmenistan), ACCC/C/2004/6 (Kazakhstan), ACCC/C/2004/7 (Poland), ACCC/C/2004/8 (Armenia), ACCC/C/2004/9 (Armenia), ACCC/C/2004/10 (Kazakhstan), ACCC/C/2005/11 (Belgium), ACCC/C/2005/12 (Albania), ACCC/C/2005/13 (Hungary), ACCC/C/2005/14 (Poland), ACCC/C/2005/15 (Romania), ACCC/C/2006/16 (Lithuania), ACCC/C/2006/17 (European Community), ACCC/C/2006/18 (Denmark), ACCC/C/2007/19 (United Kingdom), ACCC/C/2007/20 (Kazakhstan), ACCC/C/2007/21 (European Community), ACCC/C/2007/22 (France), ACCC/C/2008/23 (United Kingdom), ACCC/C/2008/24 (Spain), ACCC/C/2008/25 (Albania), ACCC/C/2008/26 (Austria), ACCC/C/2008/27 (United Kingdom), ACCC/C/2008/28 (Denmark), ACCC/C/2008/29 (Polan d), ACCC/C/2008/30 (Republic of Moldova), ACCC/C/2008/31 (Germany), ACCC/C/2008/32 (European Community), ACCC/C/2008/33 (United Kingdom), ACCC/C/2008/34 (Spain), ACCC/C/2008/35 (Georgia), ACCC/C/2009/36 (Spain), ACCC/C/2009/37 (Belarus), ACCC/C/2009/38 (United Kingdom), ACCC/C/2009/39 (Austria), ACCC/C/2009/40 (United Kingdom), ACCC/C/2009/41 (Slovakia), ACCC/C/2009/42 (Hungary), ACCC/C/2009/43 (Armenia), ACCC/C/2009/44 (Belarus), ACCC/C/2010/45 (United Kingdom), ACCC/C/2010/46 (United Kingdom), ACCC/C/2010/47 (United Kingdom), ACCC/C/2010/48 (Austria), ACCC/C/2010/49 (United Kingdom), ACCC/C/2010/50 (Czech Republic), ACCC/C/2010/51 (Romania), and ACCC/C/2010/52 (United Kingdom), ACCC/C/2010/53 (United Kingdom), ACCC/C/2010/54 (European Union), ACCC/C/2010/55 (United Kingdom), ACCC/C/2010/56 (United Kingdom), ACCC/C/2011/57 (Denmark), ACCC/C/2011/58 (Bulgaria), ACCC/C/2011/59 (Kazakhstan), ACCC/C/2011/60 (United Kingdom), ACCC/C/2011/61 (United Kingdom), ACCC/C/2011/62 (Armenia), ACCC/C/2011/63 (Austria), ACCC/C/2011/64 (United Kingdom), ACCC/C/2012/65 (United Kingdom), ACCC/C/2012/66 (Croatia), ACCC/C/2012/67 (Denmark), ACCC/C/201 2/68 (European Union and United Kingdom), ACCC/C/2012/69 (Romania), ACCC/C/2012/70 (Czech Republic), ACCC/C/2012/71 (Czech Republic), ACCC/C/2012/72 (European Union), ACCC/C/2012/73 (United Kingdom), ACCC/C/2012/74 (United Kingdom), ACCC/C/2012/75 (United Kingdom), ACCC/C/2012/76 (Bulgaria), ACCC/C/2012/77 (United Kingdom), ACCC /C/2012/78 (Spain), ACCC/C/2013/79 (Italy), ACCC/C/2013/80 (Croatia), ACCC/C/2013/81 (Sweden), ACCC/C/2013/82 (Norway), ACCC/C/2013/83 (United Kingdom). 24 June 2013. The

is. The practical impact of the non-compliance procedure can be illustrated by reference to one recent case brought against Slovakia.[89] The communication was submitted by an Austrian NGO (in collaboration with other NGOs) and alleged failure by Slovakia to provide for public participation in the decision-making procedure leading to the construction of a nuclear power plant, in violation of Slovakia's obligations under Article 6 of the Aarhus Convention.[90] Under the Convention, nuclear power plants are activities requiring public participation in procedures towards the granting of a permit.[91] Of special interest is the fact that at the time the communication was submitted, an appeal of one of the NGOs involved was still pending before a regional court in Bratislava.[92] Nevertheless, the construction of the nuclear plant was being conducted despite the appeal for judicial review and it was possible that it may be completed before the regional court could render its decision. The Compliance Committee therefore decided that it would examine the communication without waiting for the decision of the local court.[93] The Committee pragmatically reasoned that:

> for a major installation [...] when a permit has been granted and the construction is carried out, there may be considerable pressure on a court not to stop the activity and not to annul the permit decision for lack of public participation. Even if it were to do so, the construction in itself is likely to cause significant environmental effects.[94]

Regarding the substance of the communication, the Compliance Committee considered that it was 'not sufficient to provide for public participation only at the stage of the EIA [environmental impact assessment] procedure, unless it [was] also part of the permitting procedure'.[95] On this basis, the Committee concluded that Slovakia had failed to comply with Articles 6(4) and 6(10) of the Aarhus Convention[96] and recommended that Slovakia 'review its legal framework so as to ensure that early and effective public participation is provided'.[97] Slovakia was furthermore invited to 'submit to the Committee a progress report on 1 December 2011 and an implementation report on 1 December 2012'.[98] As to the effectiveness of the Committee's recommendations, national implementation reports suggest that they play a significant role in the implementation of participatory rights.[99]

Committee's findings are available at <http://www.unece.org/env/pp/pubcom.htm> (last accessed 11 November 2013).

[89] Findings and Recommendations of the Compliance Committee with regard to Communication ACCC/C/2009/41 concerning compliance by Slovakia, 17 December 2010 ('Committee Findings (Slovakia)'), available at <http://www.unece.org/env/pp/pubcom.htm> (last accessed 11 November 2013).

[90] Committee Findings (Slovakia), paras. 1 and 2.

[91] Aarhus Convention, Art. 6(1)(a) and annex I(1).

[92] Committee Findings (Slovakia), para. 45.

[93] Committee Findings (Slovakia), para. 46.

[94] Committee Findings (Slovakia), para. 46.

[95] Committee Findings (Slovakia), para. 64.

[96] Committee Findings (Slovakia), paras. 64 and 68.

[97] Committee Findings (Slovakia), para. 70.

[98] Committee Findings (Slovakia), para. 70.

[99] National Implementation Report, available at <http://www.unece.org/env/pp/reports_implementation_2011.html> (last accessed 10 September 2013). On the impact of the Compliance Committee's evaluations and recommendations see also Fitzmaurice, *supra* note 56, at 217–219.

The institutional features of the Aarhus non-compliance procedure, as well as the progressive stances taken in some cases by the Compliance Committee, highlight the potential of this mechanism as a tool for the enforcement of ESC rights. Indeed, the Compliance Committee has acknowledged a violation of the Aarhus Convention in cases presenting a link to certain ESC rights, including the right to an adequate standard of living or the right to health. To date, ESC rights were directly or indirectly concerned in at least nine cases brought before the Compliance Committee. Among the issues discussed in these cases are the impact on the population of activities such as mining,[100] the modification of nuclear plants and equipment,[101] a hydropower plant project on a river,[102] the storage of cement and coal and the production of cement-based materials in an industrial zone with residences,[103] changes in land use in an agricultural area,[104] the construction of a navigation canal in a river,[105] the construction of high-voltage overhead electric power lines,[106] the import and disposal of radioactive waste,[107] as well as the implementation of the

[100] Findings and recommendations with regard to communication ACCC/C/2009/43 concerning compliance by Armenia, Compliance Committee, 17 December 2010, ECE/MP.PP/C.1/2010/8/Add.2. Case concerning the issuance and renewal of licences to a developer for the exploitation of copper and molybdenum deposits in the Lori region of Armenia; link with the right to health and the right to adequate standard of living.

[101] Findings and recommendations with regard to communication ACCC/C/2009/41 concerning compliance by Slovakia, Compliance Committee, 17 December 2010, ECE/MP.PP/C.1/2010/8/Add.1. Case concerning public participation in three specific instances of decision-making by the Slovak Nuclear Regulatory Authority concerning the Mochovce Nuclear Power Plant; link with the right to health and the right to adequate standard of living.

[102] Findings and recommendations with regard to communication ACCC/C/2009/37 concerning compliance by Belarus, Compliance Committee, 24 September 2010, ECE/MP.PP/C.1/2010/6/Add.4. Case concerning the information available to the public with regard to the hydropower plant project on the Neman River in Belarus; link with the right to health and the right to adequate standard of living.

[103] Findings and recommendations with regard to communication ACCC/C/2004/06 concerning compliance by Kazakhstan, Compliance Committee, 16 June 2006, ECE/MP.PP/C.1/4/Add.1. Case concerning the storage of cement and coal and the production of cement-based materials in an industrial zone with private residences; link with the right to health and the right to adequate standard of living.

[104] Findings and recommendations with regard to communication ACCC/C/2004/08 concerning compliance by Armenia, Compliance Committee, 31 March 2006, ECE/MP.PP/C.1/2006/2/Add.1. Case concerning access to information and public participation in the decision-making on modification of land use designation and zoning as well as on the leasing of certain plots in an agricultural area of Dalma Orchards; link with the right to adequate standard of living and the right to food.

[105] Findings and recommendations with regard to communications ACCC/C/2004/01 and 03 concerning compliance by Ukraine, Compliance Committee, 18 February 2005, ECE/MP.PP/C.1/2005/2/Add.3. Case concerning public participation in the decision-making process regarding the construction of a navigation canal in the Danube Delta passing through an internationally recognized wetland; link with the right to adequate standard of living and the right to water.

[106] Findings and recommendations with regard to communication ACCC/C/2004/02 concerning compliance by Kazakhstan, Compliance Committee, 18 February 2005, ECE/MP.PP/C.1/2005/Add.2. Case concerning the permit procedure for the construction of high-voltage overhead electric power lines in the Gornyi Gigant district in Almaty; link with the right to health and the right to adequate standard of living.

[107] Findings and recommendations with regard to communication ACCC/C/2004/01 concerning compliance by Kazakhstan, Compliance Committee, 18 February 2005, ECE/MP.PP/C.1/2005/2/Add.1. Case concerning access to information related to the proposed draft act on the import and disposal of radioactive waste in Kazakhstan held by the National Atomic Company Kazatomprom; link with the right to health and the right to adequate standard of living.

right to public association.[108] Although the implementation of ESC rights was not the primary object of these complaints, the reasoning of the Committee suggests that there is sufficient room for a more ambitious approach to be explored in connection with the enforcement of ESC rights. Moreover, the type of relief that the Compliance Committee may grant,[109] or the measures that may be adopted by the Meeting of the Parties on the basis of the Committee's recommendations,[110] could be sufficiently specific to provide some measure of redress for violations of ESC rights.[111] In addition, as we shall see, the Aarhus Convention is starting to influence the interpretation of human rights provisions in other systems.

3. *The broader influence of the Aarhus Convention*

In the last several years, the Aarhus Convention has played a significant role in broadening the scope of some human rights provisions, particularly Article 8 of the ECHR. In a number of cases, the European Court on Human Rights has indeed resorted to the principles laid out in the Aarhus Convention to interpret the contents of Article 8.

In *Taşkın et al. v Turkey*, the Court grounded the environmental components of Article 8 of the ECHR by reference, inter alia, to principles enshrined in the Aarhus Convention. The Court, indeed, mentioned the Aarhus Convention as part of the 'relevant international texts on the right to a healthy environment'.[112] The case concerned the granting of permits to exploit a gold mine in the district of Bergama (Turkey). Interestingly, the fact that Turkey was not (and is still not) a state party to the Aarhus Convention did not prevent the Court from referring to this instrument. This could be seen as an indication that the Court considers some provisions of the Aarhus Convention as part of customary international law. This latter view is strengthened by the reasoning of the Court in *Okyay et al. v Turkey*, a case concerning the failure by Turkish authorities to implement an order from a domestic court to shut down three thermal power plants causing pollution in the province of Muğla,[113] as well as in *Demir and Baykara v Turkey*, a case relating to the right of municipal civil servants to form a trade union.[114]

[108] Findings and Recommendations adopted by the Compliance Committee with regard to compliance by Turkmenistan with the obligations under the Aarhus Convention in the case of the Act on Public Associations, Communication ACCC/C/2004/05, Compliance Committee, 18 February 2005, ECE/MP.PP/C.1/2005/2/Add.5: Newly adopted Act of Turkmenistan on Public Associations deteriorating the legal situation of NGOs, link with Art. 25(a) ICCPR (right to participate in public affairs).

[109] Decision I/7, annex, para. 36.

[110] Decision I/7, annex, para. 37.

[111] See, in particular, Decision I/7, annex, para. 37(d), stating that: '[i]n cases of communications from the public, [the Committee may] make recommendations to the Party concerned on specific measures to address the matter raised by the member of the public'.

[112] ECtHR, *Taskin and others v Turkey* (Judgment) (10 November 2004), Application No. 46117/99, paras. 99 and 100. Principle 10 of the Rio Declaration as well as Parliamentary Assembly of the Council of Europe Recommendation 1614 (2003) on environment and human rights were also quoted (paras. 98 and 100). For a discussion of the *Taskin* case, see Boyle, *Human Rights or Environmental Rights?, supra* note 1, at 487–490.

[113] ECtHR, *Okyay and Others v Turkey* (Judgment) (12 July 2005), Application No. 36220/97, paras. 51–52.

[114] ECtHR, *Demir and Baykara v Turkey* (Judgment) (12 November 2008), Application No. 34503/97, para. 83.

More recently, the principles of the Aarhus Convention (more specifically Articles 3, 4, and 9) have also been referred to in connection with the interpretation of Article 8 of the European Convention in *Tătar v Romania*, a case concerning environmental degradation caused by the exploitation of a gold mine, as relevant international law for the interpretation of Article 8 of the ECHR.[115] Similarly, in *Ivan Atanasov v Bulgaria*, the Aarhus Convention was also considered as part of the 'relevant international materials' for the interpretation of Article 8 of the ECHR.[116]

These developments illustrate the impact that the Aarhus Convention is having not only at the domestic level, but also in the interpretation of international human rights and ESC rights provisions.

5. Conclusion

The three avenues through which international environmental law influences ESC rights have the overall effect of broadening ESC rights as well as their means of enforcement. In this chapter, we have endeavoured to spell out the main mechanisms by which the environmental broadening phenomenon takes place.

The exploratory analysis conducted here would need to be extended to several ESC rights (right to housing, right to health, right to food, right to an adequate standard of living, conditions of work and occupational safety, right to water, cultural rights, and perhaps also to the right to education) as well as to a wide variety of environmental treaties and mechanisms potentially useful for their enforcement. In this latter regard, one must take into account that some non-compliance procedures that, technically, cannot be triggered by individuals or NGOs are, in practice, more open than they seem, to the extent that such individuals or NGOs may informally submit information to the secretariat of the relevant convention, which in turn is entitled to launch the procedure. Thus, the room for synergies is wider than our brief survey of mechanisms would suggest.

More fundamentally, the analysis conducted in this chapter also seeks to highlight one important point often neglected in studies of the relationship between human rights and international environmental law; namely, that this relationship must not be limited to the use of human rights approaches to environmental protection. Human rights have, of course, much to offer to international environmental law, but the opposite is also true. This is only natural, as international environmental law is by now a mature branch of international law, with its own approaches and mechanisms. We submit that looking at human rights from the environmental shore provides a number of insights which are potentially useful not only for a broader understanding of human rights and their normative context but also, and more importantly, for the continuing quest for their implementation.

[115] ECtHR, *Tătar c. Romania* (Judgment) (27 January 2009), Application No. 67021/01, para. 69 (in French only). The Court further noted that, at the international level: 'l'accès à l'information, la participation du public au processus décisionnel et l'accès à la justice en matière d'environnement sont consacrés par la Convention d'Aarhus du 25 juin 1998' (para. 118).

[116] ECtHR, *Ivan Atanasov v Bulgaria* (Judgment) (12 December 2010), Application No. 12853/03, paras. 55–57.

11

The Relationship between Economic, Social, and Cultural Rights and International Humanitarian Law

Gilles Giacca

1. Introduction

Under human rights treaties, no reference is made to the types of situations to which the provisions apply, but it is evident from the wording of some of these instruments and their subsequent interpretation that they apply at all times: not only in peacetime but also during internal violence, disturbances, tensions, and public emergencies, as well as in armed conflict.[1] Indeed, the basic premise of human rights law is to confer legal protection on all individuals in all types of situations. This is confirmed by abundant international practice of various United Nations (UN) organs, human rights bodies, and jurisprudence.

As early as 1967, the UN Security Council had emphasized, in its Resolution 237 on the situation in the Middle East, that essential and inalienable human rights should be respected even in times of war.[2] The Final Act of the International Conference on Human Rights, held in Tehran in 1968, declared that humanitarian

[1] Some treaty provisions explicitly confound a traditional argument made by certain states that human rights law would not be applicable in situations of armed conflict. There are, notably, treaties that contain derogation clauses that govern the suspension of rights during states of emergency, which include conflict situations. See International Covenant on Civil and Political Rights (ICCPR), Art. 4, 16 December 1966, 99 United Nations Treaty Series (UNTS) 171; European Convention for the Protection of Human Rights and Fundamental Freedoms (ECHR), Art. 15, 213 UNTS 222, 3 September 1953; and American Convention on Human Rights (ACHR), Art. 27, 1144 UNTS 123, 22 November 1969. See also Convention on the Rights of the Child of 1989, 20 November 1989, 1577 UNTS 3; the 2000 Optional Protocol to the Convention on the Rights of the Child on the involvement of children in armed conflict, 1577 UNTS 3, 20 November 1989, as well as Art. 30(1) European Social Charter 1961, CETS 35 and Art. F(1) Revised European Social Charter 1996, 529 UNTS 89, CETS 163.

[2] UN Security Council Resolution 237, preambular para. 1(b), UN Doc. A/237/1967, 14 June 1967; see also UNGA Res. 2252 (ES-V), UN Doc. A/2252/ESV, 4 July 1967, which refers to this resolution.

principles must prevail during periods of armed conflict.[3] Although the content of these resolutions referred primarily to international humanitarian law (IHL), it can be assumed, unless otherwise stated, that the applicability of human rights was not excluded by the existence of war. General Assembly Resolution XXIII—*Respect for Human Rights in Armed Conflict*, also adopted in 1968, invited the UN Secretary-General to undertake a study of how to enhance the protection of civilians in armed conflict, and endorsed the broad recommendation of the Tehran Conference. Notwithstanding a lack of clarity in the language of the resolution, human rights law and conflict-related issues appeared not to be mutually exclusive.

Ever since, extensive state practice has supported the notion that this body of international law applies at all times, including in armed conflict. A variety of resolutions and reports by various UN Charter-based organs and human rights bodies have 'recognized', 'acknowledged', 'confirmed', 'reaffirmed', or implied its application, whether in international or in domestic armed conflict. A further important development is the vast amount of UN treaty body practice and regional commissions and courts on human rights law interpretation.[4]

This practice has been much commented on over recent years. Extensive examination has addressed issues relating to the regime of limitation to, and derogation from, human rights treaties; extraterritorial application of competing norms; and the relationship between human rights law and international humanitarian law (IHL), among others. In contrast to the literature on the applicability of civil and political rights in armed conflict and other situations of violence, however, internationally recognized economic, social, and cultural rights have been largely ignored in this analysis. The legal guarantees related to work, food, housing, healthcare, social security, or education are not generally seen as a priority amid widespread armed violence, since other affected rights relating to life, liberty, and security typically attract greater attention. However, for individuals living in territories affected by armed violence, conflict, or foreign military occupation, the enjoyment of ESC rights is equally vital.

[3] Final Act of the International Conference on Human Rights, UN Doc. A/Conf.32/41, 1968; see also UNGA Res. 2675 (XXV) on *Basic Principles for the Protection of Civilian Populations in Armed Conflict*, 9 December 1970. The UNGA stated in its first operative paragraph preamble that 'fundamental human rights, as accepted in international law and laid down in international instruments, continue to apply fully in situations of armed conflict'.

[4] See, for instance, F. Hampson, 'The Relationship between International Humanitarian Law and Human Rights Law from the Perspective of a Human Rights Treaty Body' 90 *IRRC* (2008), 549–572; C. Droege, 'Elective Affinities? Human Rights and Humanitarian Law',90 *IRRC* (2008), 501–548.

The main texts in the area either remain silent on ESC rights or they relegate the issue to a few lines, almost *en passant*.[5] Lubell, for example, was quite cautious in his assessment of the extent to which ESC rights apply:

If human rights law applies during armed conflict, then it can be assumed, unless otherwise stated, that this holds true for the whole body of human rights law and does not exclude ESC rights. Nor are they directly excluded in any way.[6]

The earlier absence of scholarly attention can be quite easily explained. Security measures traditionally revolve around questions of arbitrary deprivation of life, or liberty, torture and ill-treatment, as well as other abuses that occur in a national state of emergency. Owing to the human rights law enforcement machinery being much stronger in this area, solid international practice has developed in recent years, which prompted significant scholarly attention.

Another reason could be that ESC rights have remained the 'poor relative' of the human rights law family. For a long time such rights have had to play 'second fiddle' to the primacy of civil and political human rights. Doctrinal and technical objections based on their lower normative status, implementation, and enforcement have contributed to their marginalization. ESC rights are said to require positive state action and allocation of large resources, underlining their aspirational nature, which one cannot expect in a situation of armed conflict. But while there are certain conceptual differences and procedural disparities between the two sets of rights, the claim is not entirely accurate and there is still significant misunderstanding regarding the nature of ESC rights in international law.[7]

The scholarship has not provided a coherent conceptual framework in the way they are to be applied and how to further evaluate their relationship with other bodies of law such as IHL.[8] This marginalization is also perceptible in other fields such as international refugee law,[9] international criminal law,[10] trade law and investment law,[11] as well as environmental law.[12] As discussed in another chapter of this book, this trend is also observed in the transitional justice debate.[13] The relative neglect for ESC rights can be considered, again, an illustration of the state of the law. With increased fragmentation arising from the diversification and expansion of international law and legal disciplines, the protection of ESC rights should be

[5] See, for instance, R.E. Vinuesa, 'Interface, Correspondence and Convergence of Human Rights and International Humanitarian Law', 1 *Yearbook of International Humanitarian Law* (1998), 69–110; N. Prud'homme, 'Lex Specialis: Oversimplifying a more Complex and Multifaceted Relationship?', 40 *Israel Law Review* (2007), 356–395; C. Droege, 'The Interplay between International Humanitarian Law and International Human Rights Law in Situations of Armed Conflict', 40 *Israel Law Review* (2007), 310–355.

[6] N. Lubell, 'Challenges in Applying Human Rights Law to Armed Conflict', 87 *IRRC* (2005), 751. See also from the same author: 'Human Rights Obligations in Military Occupation' 94 *IRRC* (2012), 317–337.

[7] See Ch. 1 of this book.

[8] E. Riedel, 'Economic, Social and Cultural Rights in Armed Conflict', in A. Clapham and P. Gaeta (eds.), *Oxford Handbook of International Law in Armed Conflict* (Oxford: Oxford University Press, 2014).

[9] See M. Foster, *International Refugee Law and Socio-economic Rights: Refuge from Deprivation* (Cambridge: Cambridge University Press, 2007).

[10] See L. van den Herik, Ch. 12; E. Schmid, 'War Crimes Related to Violations of Economic, Social and Cultural Rights', 71 *Heidelberg Journal of International Law* (2011), 523–540.

[11] See Chs. 8 and 9 of this book.

[12] See Ch. 10 of this book.

[13] See Ch. 18 of this book.

examined in a broader sense and on the basis of the different but complementary branches of international law. And there is certainly room to investigate the way ESC rights obligations may lead to a more sophisticated understanding of how human rights law applies in times of armed conflict alongside IHL.

In parallel with the growing legal discourse and practice pertaining to armed conflict, valuable work has nonetheless sought to impart more visibility to ESC rights more generally. As discussed in the general introduction of this book, in recent years, scholars, policy-makers, international organizations such as the UN, NGOs, as well as and national courts have, with increasing resolution, attempted to clarify and reinterpret the legal content and validity of ESC rights, in the absence of any international forum for enforcing ESC rights obligations.[14] In that respect, research has largely focused on the conceptual clarification and judicial application of ESC rights. This growing legal doctrine has sought to proffer an international framework of ESC rights.

However, remarkably, this 'community' has not actively sought to clarify relevant principles or respond to the legal challenges that their application in times of conflict might potentially raise. Why should this be? Does the applicability of ESC rights not pose any particular legal issues compared to the more contentious context of forcible operations involving killings, abductions, or detention? Does their progressive nature render them less relevant (or even inapplicable) in conflict settings? It is one thing to claim that human rights law, and ESC rights in particular, applies at all times, and quite another to examine the legal logic and content by which this conclusion is reached, and its implications in international law.

Despite the rich vein of subject matter and the scholarly attention paid separately to both ESC rights and IHL we are still faced by a relatively underplayed hand when it comes to considering the two regimes together. This chapter thus looks at the importance of this relationship to the main topic and examines whether such a close interaction between human rights law and IHL impacts on their complementary protection when it comes to ESC rights. It seeks to demonstrate that there is no one-size-fits-all answer to questions about the relationship between these legal regimes, or more specifically between some of the apparently conflicting norms within each branch.

The chapter first explores the meaning of 'ESC rights' from the perspective of international humanitarian law. It then examines the general articulation of both human rights law and IHL.[15] It moves, next, to the relevance of ESC rights in the application of IHL. As the UN human rights bodies develop their approach on the application of human rights law in armed conflict, we are likely to see terms and rules of IHL being complemented or interpreted in the light of the developing law in this area. Finally, the role of IHL in the interpretation of ESC rights is examined to understand how the CESCR, as well as other mechanisms, have referred directly or indirectly to IHL rules in practice in order to interpret or define the content of certain rights.

[14] Efforts regarding their judicial enforcement led to the adoption of an Optional Protocol to CEDAW in 1999, and an Optional Protocol to the ICESCR in 2008, which entered into force in May 2013.

[15] It should be noted that questions relating to limitations to and derogation from ESC rights, as well as the extraterritorial applicability of international human rights treaties setting out ESC rights have been left out from the scope of this chapter. See generally, G. Giacca, *Economic, Social and Cultural Rights in Armed Conflict and other Situations of Armed Violence* (Oxford: Oxford University Press, 2014).

2. ESC Rights Embodied in IHL Rules

It is important to understand what the term 'ESC rights' means when dealing with IHL. There are more than 1,000 treaty provisions on IHL and a number of these provisions perforce address certain aspects or components of substantive ESC rights in one form or another with regard to the following matters: health; food and relief assistance; work and employment; the protection of the family, in particular mothers and children; cultural matters; the protection of natural resources; or the protection of the environment.[16] IHL rules were drafted to seek to meet the basic protection and needs of people in some of the most dangerous situations, namely in armed conflicts. More importantly, it can be said that there is a wider dimension of the contribution of IHL: compliance with its rules in conflict situations creates preconditions favourable not only for peace but also the recovery of the country concerned enabling it better to meet its obligations to realize socio-economic rights.

The fact that many IHL rules aim to ensure that civilians are not denied healthcare, food, water, shelter, or access to them, has prompted certain commentators to employ a language of 'rights' when considering those rules.[17] The idea is advanced whereby the rights listed in the ICESCR are 'included in one form or another' under IHL.[18] Reference is made to 'ESC rights embodied in IHL treaty-based rules', 'types of economic and social rights addressed by IHL', 'protection of economic, social and cultural rights', or 'economic social and cultural rights in occupied territory'.[19]

One can question the accuracy of such qualification, not only because rules embodied under IHL speak of duties of contracting parties, rather than articulating rights of individuals, but also because most human rights law of ESC rights obligations are simply not mirrored in IHL rules. Armed conflicts encompass a larger spectrum of situations than those foreseen by IHL. Contemporary armed conflicts are characterized nowadays by a decline of formality at the beginning

[16] See generally, G. Giacca, *Economic, Social and Cultural Rights in Armed Conflict and other Situations of Armed Violence* (Oxford: Oxford University Press, 2014).

[17] L. Doswald-Beck, *Human Rights in Times of Conflict and Terrorism* (Oxford: Oxford University Press, 2011) at 473; Sassòli, Bouvier and Quintin argue, for instance, that in contrast to four specific areas in which human rights law seems to provide more detail (procedural guarantees in case of detention, use of firearms by law enforcement officials, medical ethics, and the definition of torture), IHL provisions are better adapted to armed conflict with respect to: the right to life in the conduct of hostilities; the prohibition of inhuman and degrading treatment; the right to health; the right to food; and the right to individual freedom (in international armed conflicts). M. Sassòli, A. Bouvier, and A. Quintin, *How does law protect in war?* 3rd edn (Geneva: ICRC, 2011), Vol. I, 455–457.

[18] L. Doswald-Beck, *Human Rights in Times of Conflict and Terrorism*, 473.

[19] M. Sassòli, A. Bouvier, and A. Quintin, *How does law protect in war?*, 246. Arai-Takahashi argues that 'IHL contains detailed rules concerning economic, social, and cultural rights specifically tailored to occupation. The parties to an armed conflict must implement such rules *immediately*, rather than *progressively* as in relation to the rights embodied in the ICESCR'. Y. Arai-Takahashi, *The Law of Occupation: Continuity and Change of International Humanitarian Law, and its Interaction with International Human Rights Law* (Leiden: Martinus Nijhoff Publishers, 2009), 355–374 and 413.

and end of conflict, and so to break a situation into discrete categories of before, during and after does not reflect the complexity of the phenomenon, especially for low-intensity armed conflict.[20]

This general comment is warranted for a number of reasons, at least from the point of view of the civilian population. It remains apparent that IHL has not been conceived so as to regulate all the situations in territories that are caught by armed conflict. First, it may sound trite to point out that the content and scope of IHL rules are limited to those situations that have a nexus to an armed conflict, dealing as they do almost exclusively with the humane treatment of persons in the power of a party to the conflict and the conduct of hostilities.[21]

Second, no matter how numerous and detailed most of the treaty rules here mentioned are, they apply almost exclusively to international armed conflict and belligerent occupation compared to the rudimentary framework of minimum standards developed for internal conflicts.[22] The rules regulating the relations between the party to a conflict and the persons and objects in territory under its control have been developed only for belligerent occupation.[23] In this respect, analogous governance-related norms stipulating the duty and power of the occupying power in the law of occupation does not exist in internal armed conflict. There is in fact no 'humanitarian law of occupation for domestic armed conflict'.

Third, under IHL the mechanisms of monitoring, implementation, and enforcement of the applicable 'Geneva' law is relatively weak.[24] In contrast, the applicability of human rights law opens the door to human rights monitoring and bodies and enforcement mechanisms. Thus, human rights law provides procedures for individual complaint that do not exist under the Geneva Conventions. Although IHL rules are not justiciable per se before human rights bodies, violation of ESC rights—whether or not regulated by IHL—of individuals caught in armed conflict and independently from their status under IHL, could fall under the scrutiny of judicial or quasi-judicial human rights bodies.[25] This means that much of the existing practice focuses on applying human rights treaty regimes in

[20] See G. Giacca, *Economic, Social and Cultural Rights in Armed Conflict and other Situations of Armed Violence* (Oxford: Oxford University Press, 2014).

[21] IHL rules are and remain of primary relevance when it comes to humanitarian relief aimed at ensuring that persons or groups not or no longer taking part in hostilities have access to healthcare, food, or shelter.

[22] One may argue of course that customary IHL rules can fill the gap left in internal conflict; however, depending of the context in which they are applied they may lack specificity and articulation to provide sufficient protection for individuals.

[23] See G. Giacca 'Economic, Social and Cultural Rights in Occupied Territories' in A. Clapham, P. Gaeta, and M. Sassòli (eds.), *The 1949 Geneva Conventions: A Commentary* (Oxford: Oxford University Press, 2014) (forthcoming).

[24] E. Riedel, 'Economic, Social and Cultural Rights in Armed Conflict', in A. Clapham and P. Gaeta (eds.), *Oxford Handbook of International Law in Armed Conflict* (Oxford: Oxford University Press, 2014).

[25] On the indirect protection of socio-economic rights through civil and political rights, see G. Giacca, *Economic, Social and Cultural Rights in Armed Conflict and other Situations of Armed Violence* (Oxford: Oxford University Press, 2014).

the light of IHL, rather than the other way around: human rights bodies generally do not have jurisdiction to apply IHL in the light of human rights law.[26]

The application and implementation of international human rights law is relevant to the extent it adds substantive duties to those found in IHL, where it may be silent on a number of questions not only related to ESC rights but also to civil and political rights, such as freedom of opinion, of assembly, or the freedom of the press. For instance, there is virtually nothing under the 1949 Geneva Conventions, at least not in treaty law, on the right to housing, the rights to water and sanitation, or the right to education.[27] These rights, however, may be significantly affected during military operations, for practical and/or legal reasons. The fact that human rights law may provide detailed guidance on the parties to the conflict does not mean that they cannot be lawfully restricted by limitations and derogations under this law or by the application of IHL rules.[28]

The point is that IHL rules applicable in the more prevalent form of conflict today, that is, domestic armed conflict, may seem to bear little relevance to socio-economic entitlements. This is not surprising given the fact that it is presumed that within the state's national territory any acts or omissions of the state have to be assessed in accordance with applicable international human rights law.

Most of the areas pertaining to that relationship remain therefore the exclusive province of human rights law, as it presupposes the capacity of the state to carry out a range of governmental functions, functions which IHL does not regulate outside situations of military occupation. It should be noted, however, that even in occupation the IHL rules are limited. Suffice to mention here that 1949 Geneva Convention IV (GCIV)[29] provides scant protection of the right to work beyond questions relating to compulsory labour, requisitioning services, and labour conditions of protected persons working at the request of the occupier.[30]

This brings us to the issue of armed non-state actors (ANSAs). The IHL framework might be applicable and binding on ANSAs, but it is argued that it is not suitable for dealing with the relationship between these entities and all the persons and objects under their control. The situation goes beyond humane treatment of

[26] As an exception see for instance, Article 38 of the Convention on the Rights of the Child. T. Karimova, G. Giacca, and S. Casey-Maslen, *United Nations Human Rights Mechanisms and the Right to Education in Insecurity and Armed Conflict* (Doha/Geneva: Education Above All, and Geneva Academy of International Humanitarian and Human Rights Law), 2013.

[27] For instance, if children living in a village administered by an armed non-state actor do not attend school for many months due to the damage or destruction of the school, does this mean they are protected under IHL *in concreto* for that specific problem in an internal armed conflict?

[28] See G. Giacca, *Economic, Social and Cultural Rights in Armed Conflict and other Situations of Armed Violence* (Oxford: Oxford University Press, 2014).

[29] Convention (IV) Relative to the Protection of Civilian Persons in Time of War (Geneva Convention IV), adopted 12 August 1949, entered into force 21 October 1951, 75 UNTS 287.

[30] The ICJ appropriately relied on the obligation of the occupier not to interfere with the right to work of the occupied population, where the physical barriers created by the construction of the wall, as well as numerous other restrictions on movement, undermined the ability of the occupied population to earn their livelihood. ICJ, *Legal Consequences of the Construction of a Wall in the Occupied Palestinian Territory*, Advisory Opinion, ICJ Reports 2004, paras. 130, 133, and 134.

those in the hands of a party to the conflict. This may create a protection gap for the civilian population and possible solutions to this deficit could be found in the application of human rights law to ANSAs, an issue that will not be discussed in this chapter.[31] Such conflicts by definition require more obligations on the part of all the actors involved to move beyond the minimum approach, especially when the parties to the conflict exert sufficient and stable control over a territory. In the words of the ICRC,

> Armed conflict causes unspeakable suffering, whatever is done to prevent it and however well international humanitarian law is respected. It is therefore vital to encourage and intensify all efforts to tackle the root causes of conflicts, such as poverty, inequality, illiteracy, racism and the uncontrolled growth of huge cities, the collapse of governmental and social structures, corruption, crime organized on a world-wide scale, drug trafficking and arms dealing. To encourage *compliance* with international humanitarian law is not enough.[32]

Therefore, the reference to ESC rights in this context should be understood in a broad sense referring to rules belonging to both legal regimes.

3. The General Articulation of the Relationship between ESC Rights and IHL

The relationship between human rights law and IHL has been a matter of controversy among scholars and governmental experts.[33] Most attention has concerned civil and political rights regarding primarily question related to arbitrary deprivation of the right to life or arbitrary detention. Different strands of doctrine have claimed that these two legal regimes of law are concurrent, convergent, confluent, complementary, contradictory, or even in conflict. In turn, it is suggested that the rules belonging to both regimes can indeed be applied and interpreted in the light of one another when they provide rules in areas that are common to both. As a matter of cross-interpretation, not only could human rights law be construed in the light of IHL, as observed by the International Court of Justice (ICJ) through the *lex specialis* maxim,[34] but IHL could also be interpreted in light of human rights law. Alternatively, it has been suggested that one legal regime can displace, replace, or curtail the other.

The extent to which an application of the *lex specialis* maxim can articulate the relationship between human rights law and IHL has been discussed extensively by

[31] See See G. Giacca, *Economic, Social and Cultural Rights in Armed Conflict and other Situations of Armed Violence* (Oxford: Oxford University Press, 2014), Chapter 5; A. Bellal, G. Giacca, and S. Casey-Maslen, 'International law and Armed Non-state Actors in Afghanistan', 93 *International Review of the Red Cross* (2011), 47–79.

[32] ICRC, 'Report on the Protection of War Victims', No. 296 *IRRC* (September/October 1993), 404–405.

[33] See S. Sivakumaran, *The Law of Non-International Armed Conflict* (Oxford: Oxford University Press, 2012), 87.

[34] *Legality of the Threat or Use of Nuclear Weapons*, ICJ Rep (1996), at para. 25; the *Legal Consequences of the Construction of a Wall in Occupied Palestinian Territory*, ICJ Rep. (2004), at para. 106.

commentators. However, it does not seem to be a satisfactory basis for conceptualizing this relationship.[35] It is not the place to engage in detailed analysis of this doctrinal debate, suffice it here to make three general remarks.

First, some authors are of the opinion that the ICJ's understanding of the *lex specialis* concept is not entirely clear,[36] and others criticized the Court for failing to provide a clear methodological framework capable of clarifying the interplay between the two legal regimes.[37]

Second, in the context of the Occupied Palestinian Territories and the armed conflict between the Democratic Republic of Congo and Uganda, the ICJ considered the law of occupation and the law of human rights together, and did not suggest that one or other regime or norm should be displaced.[38]

Third, the *lex specialis* maxim should not be considered as applying to the general relationship between the two legal regimes; the principle applies to a particular rule or norm in specific circumstances.[39] In the 1996 Advisory Opinion, the Court referred to IHL as the *lex specialis* with regard to prohibited weapons to determine whether nuclear weapons were outlawed as an arbitrary deprivation of the right to life under human rights law.[40] Reliance on the *lex specialis* approach does not solve all the problems as it can mean different things to different people. It is submitted that the *lex specialis* approach should be abandoned in favour of a contextual approach in order to enable the debate to move forward.[41]

The enduring debate on this relationship and related norm conflict may not be as thorny as it can be suggested, especially when it comes to ESC rights. It is argued here that there is a general presumption of compatibility of the two sets of norms that can operate together. To this effect, the question of complementarity between IHL and human rights, as discussed, can reflect the principle of systemic integration.[42] This technique for conflict avoidance can be useful to delineate coherence within the international law system, in harmony, against its tendency

[35] G. Giacca and L.A. Hill-Cawthorne, *Symmetries: International Humanitarian law and International Human Rights Law*, Report of the Transatlantic Workshop on International Law and Armed Conflict, Oxford University, 2013.

[36] Centre Universitaire de Droit International Humanitaire (CUDIH), *Expert Meeting on the Right to Life in Armed Conflicts and Situations of Occupation*, Geneva, 2005, 19. See also ICRC, *Occupation and other forms of administration of foreign territory: expert meeting*, Geneva, ICRC, 2012, 63–64.

[37] D. Thürer, *International Humanitarian Law: Theory, Practice, Context*, Hague Academy of International Law, The Hague: Martinus Nijhoff, 2011, 137.

[38] In both situations, the occupant was responsible for violations of both human rights law and international humanitarian law. ICJ *Legal Consequences of the Construction of a Wall in Occupied Palestinian Territory* ICJ Rep (2004), at para. 131; *Armed Activities on the Territory of the Congo (Democratic Republic of the Congo v Uganda)* ICJ Rep. (2005), at para. 220.

[39] C. Greenwood, 'Scope of Application of Humanitarian Law', in D. Fleck (ed.), *The Handbook of Humanitarian Law in Armed Conflict*, 2nd edn (Oxford: Oxford University Press, 2007), 45–78, at 75.

[40] International Court of Justice (ICJ), *Legality of the Threat or Use of Nuclear Weapons*, Advisory Opinion, 8 July 1996, para. 25.

[41] G. Giacca and L.A. Hill-Cawthorne, *Symmetries: International Humanitarian law and International Human Rights Law*, Report of the Transatlantic Workshop on International Law and Armed Conflict, Oxford University, 2013.

[42] *Article 31(3)(c), Vienna Convention on the Law of Treaties, adopted 23 May 1969, entered into force 27 January 1980, 1155 UNTS 133.*

towards fragmentation.[43] The main rationale is to contribute to greater coherence in international law and to the avoidance of further fragmentation, making the application of human rights practicable and realistic, having in mind that states have not created two legal regimes which complement each other perfectly.[44]

More specifically, complementarity means that ESC rights and IHL are mutually influencing when they impose certain obligations that overlap. Beyond what has been stated above on the relationship between IHL and human rights, generally the cumulative approach of ESC rights and IHL is possible from a treaty law point of view. The interplay between IHL and ESC rights would favour a rule more protective of individual victims, being derived from one or the other set of rules. This principle can find its legal basis under Article 5(2), ICESCR, which obliges states parties to apply other 'law, conventions, regulations or custom' which may provide better protection than the Covenant.[45]

As a matter of cross-interpretation, not only could human rights law be construed in the light of IHL, as observed by the ICJ, but IHL could also be interpreted in the light of human rights law. On the one hand, as we shall see in the last section of the present chapter, the CESCR for instance, has referred directly or indirectly to IHL rules in its practice in order to interpret or define the content of certain rights. On the other hand, ESC rights can also help to elucidate elements or aspects that are mentioned under IHL when it comes specifically to positive obligations, which remain too vague and ambiguous to provide effective guarantees for individuals, a question to which we now turn.[46]

[43] See generally ILC, Fragmentation of International Law, UN Doc. A/CN.4/L.682 of 13 April 2006.

[44] See Ch. 9, Section 3.C of this book.

[45] This is also recognized under IHL: Article 75(8), API states that 'no provision of this Article may be construed as limiting or infringing any other more favourable provision granting greater protection, under any applicable rules of international law, to persons covered by paragraph 1'. Moreover, Art. 158(5), GCIV emphasizes the applicability of 'the laws of humanity' regardless of the actual obligations under the Geneva Convention. It is difficult today not to conclude that it includes the regime of human rights law as applicable in times of armed conflict. This reinforces the complementarity of the two legal set of obligations. The Geneva Conventions codify a version of the Martens clause in their denunciation clauses: Common Article 63/62/142/158. See generally S.A. Sadat-Akhavi, *Methods of Resolving Conflicts between Treaties* (The Hague: Martinus Nijhoff, 2003), 219.

[46] The 2005 ICRC Study on Customary International Humanitarian Law relies on human rights law in its examination of 'state practice'. The 'state practice' identified in the Study takes generally the form of official declarations rather than actual behaviour, an approach that has given rise to some criticism. This endeavour 'does not purport…to provide an assessment of customary human rights law' but holds that 'human rights law has been included in order to support, strengthen and clarify analogous principles of IHL'. The work of the ICRC taking into account human rights law shows that both legal regimes can no longer be treated as two disconnected fields of international law that develop independently of one another. J.-M. Henckaerts and L. Doswald-Beck, *Customary International Humanitarian Law* Vol. 1 (Cambridge: Cambridge University Press, 2005), p. xxxi.

4. Relevance of ESC Rights in the Application of IHL

The specific legal effect of the applicability of human rights law is that it may impact on assessment of the content of the obligations under IHL as well as provide additional obligations where such rules are silent. In this context, human rights law may broaden the scope of protection beyond basic humanitarian protection.

The protection afforded by the human rights law of ESC rights through its application may affect the assessment of the content of the obligations derived from IHL. In situations of belligerent occupation, the needs and welfare of the inhabitants in an occupied territory can be interpreted in light of the human rights law regime. The rules relative to living conditions of civilians under occupation are derived from the occupant's general duty to take all feasible measures to restore and ensure 'civil life' (*vie public*) as set forth under Article 43, 1907 Hague Regulations.[47] The term 'civil life' has therefore been reinterpreted according to its assumed purpose as referring to the general welfare of the local population as a whole.[48] Relevant substantive ESC rights provisions can be incorporated into the terms such as '*civil life*', 'the *proper working* of all institutions devoted to the care and *education* of children',[49] or the 'duty of ensuring the *food and medical supplies* of the population'.[50] As such, human rights law can provide a normative clarification with its extensive practice (lacking under IHL) in addressing specific guidance for interactions between the occupant's administration and the civilian population in the context of ordinary life.[51]

[47] Art. 43 Hague Regulations: 'The authority of the legitimate power having in fact passed into the hands of the occupant, the latter shall take all the measures in his power to restore, and ensure, as far as possible, public order and safety'. In its authoritative French version, Art. 43 reads: '[L'occupant] prendra toutes les mesures qui dépendent de lui en vue de rétablir et d'assurer, autant qu'il est possible, l'ordre et la vie publics [...]'.This regime aims at fulfilling immediate needs of the civilian population and places the occupant 'under a definite obligation to maintain at a reasonable level the material conditions under which the population of the occupied territory lives'.

[48] The travaux préparatoires of 1874 denote in the expression 'vie publique' 'des fonctions sociales, des transactions ordinaires, qui constituent la vie de tous les jours'. *Actes de la Conférences de Bruxelles de 1874 sur le projet d'un convention internationale concernant la guerre, protocoles des séances plénières, protocoles de la Commission déléguée par la conférence, annexes*, 1874, protocole No. 10, séance du 12 août, p. 23. Such a reading was subsequently endorsed by a tribunal created in the British occupied zone of Germany after WWII in *Grahame v the Director of Prosecutions* which referred to 'the whole social, commercial and economic life of the community'. Germany, British Zone of Control, Control Commission Court of criminal Appeal, *Grahame v the Director of Prosecutions,* 26 July 1947, 14 AC 227, p. 237

[49] Art. 50(1), GCIV.

[50] Art. 55(1), GCIV. It should, 'in particular, bring in the necessary foodstuffs, medical stores and other articles if the resources of the occupied territory are inadequate'. The list of essential supplies was extended with the adoption of Art. 69 of API by adding 'clothing, bedding, means of shelter, other supplies essential to the survival of the civilian population of the occupied territory'.

[51] See G. Giacca 'Economic, Social and Cultural Rights in Occupied Territories' in A. Clapham, P. Gaeta, and M. Sassòli (eds.), *The 1949 Geneva Conventions: A Commentary* (Oxford: Oxford University Press, 2014) (forthcoming).

IHL rules revolve primarily around the ways to achieve *operational effectiveness* with regard to matters such as public health, food, or humanitarian relief supplies.[52] However, this is only one of the many challenges in armed conflict concerning protection of individuals and which cannot be reduced to a 'first-aid' approach. Even though IHL imposes certain obligations with regard to education, health, food, or work, the meaning and content of these obligations are actually far more developed in human rights law. Suffice it here to say that in addition to the fact that human rights law confer rights to individuals, IHL does not seem to contain the required specifics for understanding what these obligations might actually imply.[53] This is valid for both negative and positive obligations.

For instance, the right to health is understood as a right to the enjoyment of a variety of facilities, goods, services, and conditions necessary for the realization of the highest attainable *standard* of health.[54] The meaning of healthcare under IHL has an emergency connotation with a curative approach. For instance, in occupied territories the occupant has the duty of ensuring and maintaining the medical and hospital establishments and certain public health services.[55] This is not different from certain minimum core duties developed under the right to health, but it does not deal with the different levels of healthcare, such as primary, preventive, or tertiary healthcare system, which typically deals with small numbers of minor or serious illnesses requiring specially trained health professionals and doctors and special equipment. In this ambit one would be tempted to say 'qu'il n'y a pas de médecine humanitaire, mais une seule médecine'.[56]

In addition, Article 12(2)(a) of the ICESCR outlines the need to take measures to reduce infant mortality and promote the healthy development of infants and children and a violation of the right to health can occur if the state fails to reduce infant and maternal mortality rates or when it lacks a national strategy to ensure to all the enjoyment of the right to health.[57] In light of the content of the obligation informed by human rights law, it might be difficult to sustain the argument that IHL provides sufficient protection with regard to the right to health outside circumstances dealing with first aid, trauma care, or surgery services, and medical supplies.

[52] IHL contains in fact important norms which protect vital conditions or elements that are essential to the enjoyment of ESC rights.

[53] See generally ch. 1 by E. Riedel, G. Giacca, and C. Golay in this book.

[54] Art. 12, ICESCR and CESCR, General Comment No. 14, The Right to the Highest Attainable Standard of Health, 2000, paras. 9 and 11.

[55] Moreover it is responsible to adopt and apply prophylactic and preventive measures necessary to combat the spread of contagious diseases and epidemics. Arts. 55 and 56, GCIV.

[56] B. Hours, *L'idéologie humanitaire ou le spectacle de l'altérité perdue* (Paris: L'Harmattan, 1998), 48. This author challenges the notion of 'médecine humanitaire': '[q]u'il s'agisse de réhabilitation des structures de santé, de la formation des personnels, de la gestion des épidémies, de la chirurgie, des médicaments, des soins maternels et infantiles, tous ces domaines sont classiques de la santé publique, et il existe des médecins formés qui ne présentent aucune spécificité humanitaire. Il n'y a donc pas de médecine humanitaire distincte de la médecine et de la santé publique telles qu'elles sont enseignées. Ce qui est spécifique, c'est la *justification idéologique de ces interventions*' (emphasis added).

[57] CESCR, General Comment No. 14, The right to the highest attainable standard of health, 2000, para. 52.

This reasoning can well be applied to other ESC rights. For instance, Article 4(3)(a), 1977 Additional Protocol II states that children shall 'receive an education, including religious and moral education, in keeping with the wishes of their parents, or in the absence of parents, of those responsible for their care'.[58] In a rather similar manner, under the law of occupation, the occupant shall, 'with the cooperation of the national and local authorities, facilitate the proper working of all institutions devoted to the care and education of children'.[59] It becomes rather obvious here that there is little guidance concerning the nature and substance of educational provision. As we have seen, armed conflict can interrupt the education of children through destruction of schools, absence of teachers, or deterioration of economic means in the household, which may prevent parents from sending their children to school. Thus, compared with these provisions on education, human rights law is far more detailed and provides a contemporary understanding of the educational needs in a modern society in terms of availability, accessibility, and quality of education.[60]

In most cases, ESC rights cover areas left unregulated by IHL, especially in situations of non-international armed conflict. The co-application can enhance the protection to the individuals in a productive manner[61] and the obstacles coming into play are therefore not of a legal nature, but of a practical nature, related to the effect that the armed conflict can have on state behaviour.

5. The Role of IHL in Interpreting ESC Rights' Obligations in Practice

A. International Court of Justice

It will be recalled that in the *Wall* Advisory Opinion, the construction of the wall destroyed or rendered inaccessible property belonging to the Palestinians as well as

[58] Protocol II Additional to the Geneva Conventions of 12 August 1949, and relating to the Protection of Victims of Non-International Armed Conflicts (Protocol II), 8 June 1977. The ICRC Commentary is rather vague and does seem to have a rudimentary approach of the meaning of education:

> 'It answers the concern to ensure continuity of education so that children retain their cultural identity and a link with their roots. This rule is aimed at removing the risk that children separated from their family by the conflict might be uprooted by being initiated into a culture, religion or moral code which may not correspond with the wishes of their parents, and in addition could in this way become political pawns. Religion and morality are an integral part of education, but as was considered preferable to specify "including religious and moral education" so that the word "education" should be understood in its broadest sense, and not be interpreted restrictively'.

ICRC, Commentary on the Additional Protocols of 8 June 1977 to the Geneva Conventions of 12 August 1949 (Geneva: ICRC/Martinus Nijhoff, 1987), para. 4552.

[59] Art. 50, GCIV.

[60] The right to education under human rights law serves two general purposes. It seeks on the one hand to give individuals an education and it aims to ensure that education is provided in an adequate and appropriate manner on the other. Arts. 13 and 14, ICESCR and Arts. 28 and 29, CRC.

[61] H.J. Heintze, 'On the Relationship between Human Rights Law Protection and International Humanitarian Law', 86 *IRRC* (2004), 856, 789–814.

restricting their freedom of movement.[62] This interfered with a number of rights under the ICESCR (work, health, education, and an adequate standard of living including adequate food, clothing, and housing)[63] and the International Covenant on Civil and Political Rights (ICCPR) (freedom of movement, privacy, family, home, or correspondence).[64] In this context, the Court found that the route chosen for the wall was not justified by military exigencies.[65]

The ICJ considered both human rights law and IHL to assess the legality of the construction of the wall, but opted for a *separate* analysis between relevant IHL rules and limitations clauses under human rights law.

First, the Court assessed the situation through IHL rules observing that such rules contain provisions 'enabling account to be taken of military exigencies in certain circumstances'.[66] The Court did not substantiate its legal reasoning to support its findings that the wall was not justified by military exigencies. In a rather succinct manner, the Court referred to four specific provisions (Article 46, Hague Regulations; Articles 47, 49, and 53, GCIV).[67] It referred to the possibility of deportation of protected persons and destruction of personal property only for 'imperative military reasons' or rendered 'absolutely necessary by military operations'.[68] It observed, however, that it was prohibited to transfer its own population into occupied territory and concluded that the destruction of property (Article 53, GCIV) was not justified by the alleged defence of military exigency.[69] The Court failed to provide the detailed criteria to be satisfied within the meaning of military necessity, especially what proportionality really entails in this context.[70]

[62] The construction of the wall is considered by Israel as a 'security measure'. The government stated that land requisitions were 'proportionate given the number of deaths and injuries sustained by Israeli citizens'. UNGA, Report of the Secretary-General prepared pursuant to General Assembly resolution ES-10/13, A/ES-10/248, 24 November 2003, para. 7.

[63] Arts. 6, 7, 10, 11, 12, 13, and 14, ICESCR. See, ICJ, *Wall* Advisory Opinion, para. 130. Relevant CRC provisions were also referred to, namely Arts. 16, 24, 27, and 28; ICJ, *Wall* Advisory Opinion, para. 131.

[64] Arts. 12(1) and 17, ICCPR. ICJ, *Wall* Advisory Opinion, para. 136.

[65] Arts. 12(1) and 17, ICCPR. ICJ, *Wall* Advisory Opinion, paras. 135 and 137.

[66] Arts. 12(1) and 17, ICCPR. ICJ, *Wall* Advisory Opinion, para. 126. Reference was made to Arts. 43, 46, and 52, Hague Regulations, and Arts. 47, 49, 52, and 53, GCIV.

[67] Arts. 12(1) and 17, ICCPR. ICJ, *Wall* Advisory Opinion, para. 135.

[68] Art. 49, GCIV, prohibits 'individual or mass forcible transfers, as well as deportations of protected persons from occupied territory [...] regardless of their motive'; it also stipulates that 'the Occupying Power may undertake total or partial evacuation of a given area if the security of the population or imperative military reasons so demand'. Finally, Art. 53 GCIV provides that any 'destruction by the Occupying Power of real or personal property belonging individually or collectively to private persons [...] is prohibited, except where such destruction is rendered absolutely necessary by military operations'.

[69] Art. 49, GCIV, para. 135.

[70] This can be explained by the fact that there was an important discrepancy between the material regarding the living conditions of the Palestinian population and the information regarding the security argument advanced by Israel. As Judge Buergenthal noted, 'Lacking is an examination of the facts that might show why the alleged defences of military exigencies, national security or public order are not applicable to the wall as a whole or to the individual segments of its route'. Declaration of Judge Buergenthal, para. 7. In any event, Judge Owada was of the opinion that 'no justification based on the "military exigencies", even if fortified by substantiated facts, could conceivably constitute a valid basis for precluding the wrongfulness of the act on the basis of the stringent conditions of proportionality'. Separate opinion of Judge Owada, para. 24 in the ICJ, *Wall* Advisory Opinion case.

Second, the Court went on to assess the lawfulness of the construction of the wall under Article 4, ICESCR and concluded that the restrictions on ESC rights, resulting from the construction of the wall, 'fail to meet a condition laid down by Article 4', ICESCR; that is to say that their implementation must be 'solely for the purpose of promoting the general welfare in a democratic society'.[71]

The separate analysis of the impact of the wall on the enjoyment of ESC rights means that the rights to work, to health, to education, and to an adequate standard of living cannot be defined by IHL, in the same manner that the Court indicated that the arbitrary deprivation of the right to life could in its 1996 Advisory Opinion on *the Legality on the Threat or Use of Nuclear Weapons.*[72]

Would this mean that IHL may not be taken into account when assessing the ICESCR? The short answer is that it depends on whether both legal regimes deal with the subject matter or not. After all, as regards this interaction, the Court noted that some rights may be exclusively matters of IHL; others may be exclusively matters of human rights law; and others matters of both.[73] The problem is that the Court returned to the law of occupation in its overall conclusion and stated that the wall

> gravely infringe[s] a number of rights of Palestinians residing in the territory occupied by Israel, and the infringements resulting from that route cannot be justified by military exigencies or by the requirements of national security or public order. The construction of such a wall accordingly constitutes breaches by Israel of various of its obligations under the applicable international humanitarian law and human rights instruments.[74]

This can be interpreted in a manner that the Court took into account the violations of IHL (absence of military exigencies) to either determine ESC rights violations or to simply reinforce its final conclusions on human rights law.[75] The general question remains as to whether the test for limiting human rights law (that is, general welfare, national security or public order) should be read in light of the principle of military exigencies.[76] Even though no reasons of military necessity were found, the Court's consideration of, and approach to, this question suggests that it envisaged such justification under IHL.

It is noteworthy that the ICJ relied only on Article 53, GCIV dealing with property confiscation, requisition and destruction of individual properties, which interfered simultaneously with the rights to work and to an adequate standard of living.[77] This is evidence that IHL may not provide adequate legal protection when

[71] ICJ, *Wall Advisory Opinion*, para. 136. On the general limitation clause of the ICESCR, see G. Giacca, *Economic, Social and Cultural Rights in Armed Conflict and other Situations of Armed Violence* (Oxford: Oxford University Press, 2014).

[72] ICJ, *Legality of the Threat or Use of Nuclear Weapons*, para. 25.

[73] ICJ, *Wall* Advisory Opinion, para. 106.

[74] ICJ, *Wall* Advisory Opinion, para. 137.

[75] In any event, in the circumstances of the case, there was a violation of both fields of laws so the situation was rather straightforward. The measures taken by Israel were considered disproportionate in the face of the severe infringements suffered by the Palestinian people.

[76] As referred to Arts. 46 and 52, Hague Regulations, and Art. 53, GCIV.

[77] The wall and its associated regime reduced the availability of certain goods, by seizing and destroying land and property. This includes 'fruit and olive trees, wells, and hothouses upon which

it comes to the physical accessibility to land, workplaces, and markets, as well as access to schools and universities and health facilities in a non-discriminatory manner, that create severe repercussions on the welfare of the Palestinian population. This gap in the protection is thus filled by human rights law. However, a brief reference to Article 43, 1907 Hague Regulations, was made *en passant* by the Court which imposes a duty on the occupant to 'take all the measures in his power to restore, and ensure, as far as possible, public order and safety [*l'ordre et la vie publics*], while respecting, unless absolutely prevented, the laws in force in the country'.[78] As noted, this framework provides a basis to develop a legal construction aiming at protecting access to, and providing, the aforementioned services, as informed by human rights law.

In the *DRC v Uganda* case, the ICJ addressed inter alia, the application of the African Charter on Human and Peoples' Rights, the Convention on the Rights of the Child (CRC) (and its Optional Protocol), which both encompass ESC rights, although as such, no direct violations of these rights were found.[79] However, the ICJ discussed the exploitation of natural resources on the part of high-ranking Ugandan officers and soldiers and the failure of the Ugandan forces to respect of the applicable rules of IHL and human rights law.[80] The Court first relied on Article 47, 1907 Hague Regulations and Article 33, GCIV on prohibition of pillage and reprisals against protected persons and their property, and then on Article 21(1) and (2), ACHPR which reads as follows:

> 1. All peoples shall freely dispose of their wealth and natural resources. This right shall be exercised in the exclusive interest of the people. In no case shall a people be deprived of it.
> 2. In case of spoliation the dispossessed people shall have the right to the lawful recovery of its property as well as to an adequate compensation.[81]

The Court found that the looting, plundering, and exploitation of the DRC's natural resources amounted to concurrent violations of this provision.[82] As in its *Wall*

thousands of Palestinians rely for their survival', Arts. 46 and 52, Hague Regulations, Art. 53, GCIV, ICJ, *Wall* Advisory Opinion, para. 133. See also General Assembly, Report of the Special Committee to Investigate Israeli Practices Affecting the Human Rights of the Palestinian People and Other Arabs of the Occupied Territories, A/58/311, 22 August 2003, para. 26.

[78] ICJ, *Wall* Advisory Opinion, para. 124. The Court departed from the wording of Article 43 and used the term 'to insure public order and life'.

[79] ICJ, *Case concerning armed activities on the territory of the Congo (Democratic Republic of the Congo v Uganda)*, Judgment, 19 December 2005. It should however be noted that the Court failed to include the ICESCR in the list. In spite of the fact that both the DRC and Uganda were parties to the ICESCR and regardless of DRC's invocation of the ICESCR in its memorial as being pertinent to the case before hand, the Court did not rely on the ICESCR. Indeed, the credible documentation referred to by the Court included numerous ESC rights violations and the ICJ does not seem to provide any information motivating this omission. Both DRC and Uganda were parties to the ICESCR. Mémoire de la République Démocratique du Congo, 147, No. 3.58, available at <http://www.icj-cij.org/icjwww/idocket/ico/icoframe.htm> (last accessed 30 November 2013).

[80] ICJ, *Case concerning armed activities on the territory of the Congo (Democratic Republic of the Congo v Uganda)*, Judgment, 19 December 2005, paras. 178–179 and 242.

[81] ICJ, *Case concerning armed activities on the territory of the Congo (Democratic Republic of the Congo v Uganda)*, Judgment, 19 December 2005, para. 245.

[82] ICJ, *Case concerning armed activities on the territory of the Congo (Democratic Republic of the Congo v Uganda)*, Judgment, 19 December 2005, paras. 244–245.

Advisory Opinion, the Court considered both IHL and human rights law separately, finding violations of their respective rules. This shows that both fields of law apply to the same situation and can prohibit the same conduct, without necessarily impacting on each other in the determination of the lawfulness.

B. Practice of the UN Committee on Economic, Social and Cultural Rights

This section discusses the way the CESCR—through its General Comments and Concluding Observations—conceptualizes some of these rights by examining how IHL is treated and whether there are any indications of its co-application with the Covenant. It should be noted from the outset that while the CESCR has underlined that the Covenant does apply in a situation of armed conflict, it has elaborated little on the relationship between ESC rights and IHL. This is rather unsurprising as UN treaty bodies, as their title suggests, have the mandate to monitor the implementation of a specific treaty and in fact the CESCR asserted that the compliance with IHL rules is a matter 'considered to fall outside the sphere of the Committee's responsibility'.[83]

Having said this, it has nonetheless referred or relied directly or indirectly to IHL rules in its General Comments, but also in its Concluding Observations. For instance, in response to the DR Congo's state party report, the Committee expressed its concerns that due to continuous insecurity in the eastern provinces of the state party, IDPs are 'regularly victims of gross human rights and humanitarian law violations committed *by all factions* engaged in the fighting', including the armed forces of the DR Congo. It placed such violations into the protection offered by the Covenant, such as Articles 10, 11, and 12.[84]

In four of its 21 General Comments (housing, food, health, and water) the CESCR has included humanitarian considerations and principles in defining the scope of ESC rights. General Comment No. 7 on the right to housing notes that instances of forced eviction are often associated 'with violence, such as evictions resulting from international armed conflicts, internal strife and communal or ethnic violence'.[85] Such practices of forced relocations or house demolition termed 'as a punitive measure are also inconsistent with the norms of the Covenant'.[86] Reference is then made to IHL obligations, where the Committee 'takes note' of the 1949 Geneva Conventions and 1977 Additional Protocols (APs) 'concerning prohibitions on the displacement of the civilian population and the destruction of

[83] CESCR, Concluding Observations: Israel, Israel, UN Doc. E/C.12/1/Add.90, 26 June 2003, para. 258.

[84] It is interesting to point out that the CESCR appears to consider human rights law to be applicable to non-state actors operating in DRC. CESCR, Concluding Observations: DRC, UN Doc. E/C.12/COD/CO/4, 20 November 2009, para. 25 (emphasis added).

[85] CESCR, General Comment No. 7, The right to adequate housing (Art. 11(1)): forced evictions, 20 May 1997, para. 6.

[86] CESCR, General Comment No. 7, The right to adequate housing (Art. 11(1)): forced evictions, 20 May 1997, para. 12.

private property as these *relate to the practice of forced eviction*'.[87] It is interesting to note here the cross-border application of the right to housing and IHL rules. IHL can be used to give content to the notion of private property and provide guidance on types of unlawful conducts that are not explicitly stipulated under the Covenant. If the Committee 'takes note' of the obligations under the GCIV and the APs in relation to forced eviction, it means that the ICESCR and IHL are interpreted in a way to avoid a conflict of norms.[88]

On Israel, the CESCR took a similar approach with regard to the right to cultural life when recommended the state party to take measures to ensure that Palestinians living in the OPT 'can exercise their right to take part in cultural and religious life, without restrictions other than those that are strictly proportionate to security considerations and are non-discriminatory in their application, in accordance with international humanitarian law'.[89] Interestingly, the Committee unequivocally framed the application of Article 15, ICESCR within the regime of IHL.[90]

In a similar vein, General Comment No. 14 on the right to health submits that the notion of 'the highest attainable standard of health' in Article 12(1) and its related normative content 'takes into account [...] socially related concerns as violence and armed conflict'.[91] In this context, the Committee refers explicitly to fundamental guarantees set out in Common Article 3, Geneva Conventions, Article 75(2)(a), Additional Protocol I (API),[92] and Article 4(2)(a), Additional Protocol I (APII),[93] which would need to be taken into account when interpreting this provision. Furthermore, the CESCR defines the 'right to treatment' as including the creation of a system of urgent medical care for a variety of cases, including humanitarian assistance in emergency situations.[94] In this respect, the states parties have a duty to cooperate and '[p]riority in the provision of international medical

[87] CESCR, General Comment No. 7, The right to adequate housing (Art. 11(1)): forced evictions, 20 May 1997, para. 12 (emphasis added). The CESCR refers also to other human rights norms when it acknowledges that such practices may also result in 'violations of civil and political rights, such as the right to life, the right to security of the person, the right to non-interference with privacy, family and home and the right to the peaceful enjoyment of possessions'. CESCR, General Comment No. 7, The right to adequate housing (Art. 11(1)): forced evictions, 20 May 1997, para. 4.

[88] CESCR, General Comment No. 7, The right to adequate housing (Art. 11(1)): forced evictions, 20 May 1997, para. 11.

[89] CESCR, Concluding Observations: Israel, UN Doc. E/C.12/ISR/CO/3, 16 December 2011, para. 36.

[90] This is in line with a previous Concluding Observation which stated that even in armed conflict 'fundamental human rights must be respected and that basic economic, social and cultural rights as part of the minimum standards of human rights are guaranteed under customary international law and are also prescribed by international humanitarian law'. CESCR, Concluding Observations: Israel, UN Doc. E/C.12/1/Add.90, 26 June 2003, para. 31.

[91] CESCR, General Comment No. 14, The right to the highest attainable standard of health, 2000, para. 10.

[92] Protocol Additional (I) to the Geneva Conventions of 12 August 1949, and relating to the Protection of Victims of International Armed Conflicts (API), adopted 8 June 1977, entered into force 7 December 1978, 1125 UNTS 3.

[93] Protocol Additional (II) to the Geneva Conventions of 12 August 1949, and Relating to the Protection of Victims of Non-International Armed Conflicts (APII), adopted 8 June 1977, entered into force 7 December 1978, 1125 UNTS 609.

[94] CESCR, General Comment No. 14, The right to the highest attainable standard of health, 2000, para. 16.

aid, distribution and management of resources, such as safe and potable water, food and medical supplies, and financial aid should be given to the most vulnerable or marginalized groups of the population'.[95] Even though IHL is not explicitly mentioned, it is evident that these obligations reflect the synergies between IHL and ESC rights.

As the CESCR puts it, violations of the right to food can occur through the direct action of states or other entities insufficiently regulated by states, which include 'denial of access to food to particular individuals or groups', or 'the prevention of access to humanitarian food aid in internal conflicts or other emergency situations'.[96] Rightly, the Committee tied Sri Lanka's failure to grant humanitarian access under IHL to a violation of the right to adequate food. During the last months of the armed conflict in 2009, civilians were in the CESCR's view, 'deliberately deprived of food, medical care and humanitarian assistance which constitute violations of article 11 of the Covenant'.[97] It even qualified the prevention of access to humanitarian food aid as a 'grave violation of international humanitarian law', which 'may amount to a war crime'.[98] This view indicates a complementary interaction of the right to food/health and the customary law prohibition of the use of starvation of the civilian population as a method of warfare, as well as on humanitarian relief to civilians in need.[99]

Reference to analogous rules and principles of IHL in General Comments can be useful in order to support, strengthen, and perhaps clarify the normative contours of certain ESC rights associated with conflict and especially during the conduct of hostilities. In this regard, the CESCR has dealt with the prohibition on the use of certain weapons, although very generally, under the heading 'obligation to respect' of General Comments on the right to health and water. The comments underscore the negative obligation to refrain from interfering directly or indirectly with the enjoyment of the right to health including the prohibition of 'using or testing of nuclear, biological or chemical weapons if such use results in diminishing or polluting water or in the release of substances harmful to human health'.[100] This is in

[95] CESCR, General Comment No. 14, The right to the highest attainable standard of health, 2000, para. 40.

[96] CESCR, General Comment No. 14, The right to the highest attainable standard of health, 2000, para. 19. The CESCR also notes generally, that a 'State claiming that it is unable to carry out its obligation for reasons beyond its control therefore has the burden of proving that this is the case and that it has unsuccessfully sought to obtain international support to ensure the availability and accessibility of the necessary food'. CESCR, General Comment No. 14, The right to the highest attainable standard of health, 2000, para. 17.

[97] CESCR, Concluding Observations: Sri Lanka, UN Doc. E/C.12/LKA/CO/2-4, 9 December 2010, para. 28.

[98] This remains the only instance where the CESCR has relied to an international crime, with specific reference to the prohibition of starvation. CESCR, Concluding Observations: Sri Lanka, UN Doc. E/C.12/LKA/CO/2-4, 9 December 2010, para. 28.

[99] Rules 53 and 55, ICRC Customary Law Study.

[100] CESCR, General Comment No. 14, The right to the highest attainable standard of health, 2000, para. 34 and General Comment No. 15, The right to water, 2002, para. 21.

line with certain international instruments that formally prohibit the use of chemical and biological weapons.[101]

The impact of IHL rules on the operationalization of ESC rights in the context of the conduct of hostilities has led perhaps to a substantial broadening of the way these rights are apprehended, which can be called the humanitarian 'broadening phenomenon'.[102] What can be inferred from this is that a violation IHL may lead to a violation of ESC rights in a number of cases, but this also implies an *a contrario* reasoning that where the military conduct would be justified by military necessity[103] it will preclude a breach of ESC rights norms.

It seems useful to take the example of the right to water through the recent General Comment, which illustrates more explicitly how IHL can broaden the substantive scope of this right. The General Comment on the right to water refers to a wide range of international documents, either as evidence of its recognition or as a basis on which to derive such a right, which is not explicitly set out in the Covenant. Among various treaties, declarations and various standards, the Committee refers to the Geneva Conventions and Additional Protocols in construing some of the corollaries of the right to water. IHL is thus explicitly imported and incorporated in the Covenant to elucidate the existence of this right.[104] This means that the CESCR goes beyond the simple acknowledgment of the concurrent international obligations; it incorporates IHL instruments into its analysis of ESC rights protection.

Under the heading 'obligation to respect' the Committee instructs states parties that the right to water 'embraces' those obligations by which states are bound under IHL. The obligation requires that states parties refrain from limiting access to, or destroying, water services and infrastructure 'as a punitive measure' during armed conflicts in violation of IHL.[105] This language is comparable to that of a resolution adopted at 26th International Conference of the Red Cross and Red Crescent that requires parties to a conflict to 'take all feasible measures to avoid in their military operations, all acts liable to destroy or damage water sources'.[106] Reference to IHL is used as a tool for circumscribing the substantive scope of this

[101] Protocol for the Prohibition of the Use of Asphyxiating, Poisonous or Other Gases, and of Bacteriological Methods of Warfare. Geneva, 17 June 1925; 1972 Biological Weapons Convention (BWC); 1993 Chemical Weapons Convention (CWC) and The Comprehensive Test Ban Treaty (CTBT).

[102] This terminology is borrowed from S. Chuffart and J. E. Viñuales, 'From the Other Shore: Economic, Social and Cultural Rights from an International Environmental Law Perspective', Ch. 10 in this book.

[103] Y. Dinstein, 'Military Necessity' in R Wolfrum (ed.), *The Max Planck Encyclopedia of Public International Law* (Oxford: Oxford University Press, 2008).

[104] Reference is made to Arts. 20, 26, 29, and 46, GCIII; Arts. 85 and 89, GCIV; Arts. 54 and 55, API; Arts. 5 and 14 APII; CESCR, General Comment No. 15, The right to water, 2002, para. 4.

[105] CESCR, General Comment No. 15, The right to water, 2002, para. 21. It should be noted that while the CESCR refers to the prohibition of 'punitive measures' it does not refer to Art. 33 GCIV relating to 'collective punishment' which provides that '[n]o protected person may be punished for an offence he or she has not personally committed. Collective penalties and likewise all measures of intimidation or of terrorism are prohibited'.

[106] 26th International Conference of the Red Cross and Red Crescent, Res. II, 29 February 1996 (adopted by consensus).

right. In protecting access to water during armed conflicts, specific rules of IHL are further cited, in particular:

the protection of objects indispensable for survival of the civilian population, including drinking water installations and supplies and irrigation works, protection of the natural environment against widespread, long-term and severe damage and ensuring that civilians, internees and prisoners have access to adequate water.[107]

This passage substantially refers to Articles 35(3), 54, 55, and 56, API, and Articles 14 and 15, APII, and generally to all relevant rules concerning humane treatment in internment during armed conflict. The major point here is that the CESCR relies on a number of rules and principles relating to the means and method of warfare and as such it defines the outer limits of the right, which become interrelated with IHL rules.[108] On the basis of this 'humanitarian broadening phenomenon', can it be argued that any unlawful damage or destruction of water services and infrastructure under IHL would lead necessarily to a violation of the right to water?[109] Is it a threshold question, that is, the level of damage and/or impact on the civilian population? Conversely, would any lawful attacks under IHL preclude a violation of the obligation to respect the right to water? There is a presumption that destruction of water services and infrastructure can negatively impact on the population, when it comes to potable water installations, but it appears in this case that the obligation to respect the right to water would have to be read in the light of IHL to determine the lawfulness of the attack.

This still raises a question as to whether this 'humanitarian broadening phenomenon' gives rise to a viable methodology to be applied to other rights, such as the right to education? On the protection of school buildings, General Comment No. 13 is not explicit regarding this matter. Mention can be made of the 2011 Concluding Observations on Israel, where the CESCR voiced its concerns that:

Palestinian children living in the Occupied Palestinian Territory are not able to enjoy their right to education, as a consequence of restrictions on their movement, regular harassment by settlers of children and teachers on their way to and from school, attacks on educational facilities, and sub-standard school infrastructure. The Committee also notes with concern

[107] CESCR, General Comment No. 15, The right to water, 2002, para. 22. See also Rule 55, ICRC Customary Law Study.

[108] Similarly, on its Concluding Observations on Israel, the CRC substantively situated the right to an adequate standard of living within the regime of IHL when recommending Israel to fully comply with the rules of distinction (between civilians and combatants) and proportionality (of attacks that cause excessive harm to civilians) and thus refrain from the demolition of civilian infrastructure, including homes, water supplies and other utilities. CRC, Concluding Observations: Israel, UN Doc. CRC/C/15/Add.195, 9 October 2002, para. 51.

[109] The obligation to *respect* requires 'that States parties refrain from interfering directly or indirectly with the enjoyment of the right to water. The obligation includes, inter alia, refraining from engaging in any practice or activity that denies or limits equal access to adequate water; arbitrarily interfering with customary or traditional arrangements for water allocation; unlawfully diminishing or polluting water, for example through waste from State-owned facilities or through use and testing of weapons; and limiting access to, or destroying, water services and infrastructure as a punitive measure, for example, during armed conflicts in violation of international humanitarian law'. CESCR, General Comment No. 15, The right to water, 2002, para. 21.

that there are as many as 10,000 unregistered children in East Jerusalem, out of which around 5,500 are of school age but do not attend school due to their lack of registration. (arts. 13 and 14)[110]

One can see here that it is difficult to single out a specific act; rather, it is a variegated number of interferences with the right to education that may lead to the violation of the right to education.

The Committee on the Rights of the Child (CRC)'s practice appears to be more explicit on this issue.[111] In its general discussion on 'the Right of the Child to Education in Emergency Situations', the Committee held that the right to education in a situation of armed conflict is 'further protected' by GCIV and both APs.[112] In this context, the CRC recommended that states parties ensure that schools are protected from military attacks or seizure and from use as centres for recruitment, and that they criminalize attacks on schools as war crimes in accordance with the International Criminal Court (ICC) Statute.[113] The CRC has further commented on the effects of attacks on schools on the right to education in at least five countries: Burundi, Ethiopia, Israel, Moldova, and Afghanistan.[114]

When considering the report of Afghanistan the CRC Committee expressed its 'extreme' concern about attacks by insurgents on school facilities and their use, in the prevailing conditions of conflict, as polling stations during elections and occupied by international and national military forces.[115] This problem was dealt with under the section 'Education' (Article, 28, CRC) of the Concluding Observations. Thus the CRC recommended that the government '[u]se all means to protect schools, teachers and children from attacks, and include communities, in particular parents and children, in the development of measures to better protect schools against attacks and violence'.[116] In its Concluding Observations for Nepal, the

[110] CESCR, Concluding Observations: Israel, UN Doc. E/C.12/ISR/CO/3, 16 December 2011, para. 35

[111] Under the CRC, children's human rights and humanitarian law protection is considered as interconnected and forming an integral part of the Children's Convention. See Art. 38, CRC.

[112] CRC, Day of General Discussion: 'The rights of all children in the context of international migration', 28 September 2012, para. 3.

[113] Art. 8(2)(b)(ix).

[114] CRC, Concluding Observations, Burundi, UN Doc. CRC/C/15/Add.133, 16 October 2000, paras. 64–65; CRC, Concluding Observations, Ethiopia, UN Doc. CRC/C/ETH/CO/3, 1 November 2006, paras. 27–28; CRC, Concluding Observations, Israel, UN Doc. CRC/C/15/Add.195, 9 October 2002, para. 52: 'The Committee is concerned about the serious deterioration of access to education of children in the occupied Palestinian territories as a result of the measures imposed by the Israeli Defence Forces, including road closures, curfews and mobility restrictions, and the destruction of school infrastructure'; CRC, Concluding Observations Republic of Moldova, UN Doc. CRC/C/MDA/3, 10 July 2008, paras. 423 and 435: 'Under the false pretext that these eight schools were not registered by the local (Transnistrian) administration, the buildings of the high schools Lucian Blaga in Tiraspol and Evrica in Ribnita and the boarding school in Bender were attacked, devastated, and besieged in July 2004 for more than one month by the Transnistrian police. After Lucian Blaga was closed, the Transnistrian authorities, despite the protests from parents, teachers, students, as well as the international community, closed the other schools that were using Moldovan with Latin letters'.

[115] CRC, Concluding Observations: Afghanistan, UN Doc. CRC/C/AFG/CO/1, 8 April 2011, para. 60.

[116] CRC, Concluding Observations: Afghanistan, UN Doc. CRC/C/AFG/CO/1, 8 April 2011, para. 61 (i).

CRC expressed its concern at 'the large-scale bombing, destruction and closing of schools'.[117] While in the absence of a military target and military necessity destruction of education facilities is clearly in breach of IHL, the Committee did not frame such unlawful acts explicitly by reference to IHL, per Article 38 (which incorporates applicable IHL into the Convention). Instead, the CRC determined merely that such acts are 'in violation of the fundamental rights to education of children'.[118]

This leaves open the question as to whether unlawful attacks on schools under IHL would constitute a violation in and of itself of the right to education. Arguably, the CESCR and the CRC tend to link the Covenant to explicit IHL standards. However, the final assessment of whether a violation of the right to education occurs would depend on the specific context.

Despite the fact that the CESCR has no mandate or authority to pronounce on state violations of IHL, it has on numerous occasions incorporated the IHL regime in its analysis. But this practice is far from being consistent, and such analysis provides limited conclusions as to the relationship between the Covenant and IHL. First, this is explained by the simple fact of the Committee's structure and mandate that limit it within the boundary of the Covenant. The state reporting process prevents it from performing fact-specific analysis; therefore the concerns and recommendations remain at a certain level of generality. Second, the Covenant may offer many of the same protections as IHL, because they tend to lead to the same results. Third, lack of coherence in analysis is also contingent on the substantial information the Committee receives from the state party, the OHCHR, and from various NGOs and depends also on the sensitivity and expertise of the country rapporteur entrusted with the task to lead the debate.

The General Comments and the Concluding Observations issued in response to states parties' reports are considered the two functions performed by the CESCR that result in written interpretations of the Covenant.[119] When the Optional Protocol to the ICESCR receives individual communications, it may offer a promising avenue to develop more technical analysis of the application of the Covenant in times of armed conflict and explore the relationship between specific rights and their equivalents in IHL.[120]

[117] CRC, Concluding Observations: Nepal, UN Doc. CRC/C/15/Add.261, para. 10.

[118] CRC, Concluding Observations: Nepal, UN Doc. CRC/C/15/Add.261, para. 10.

[119] Perhaps, there is a need to further develop the application of the ICESCR in armed conflict situations, for example by holding a Day of General Discussion, and adopting a key document in the future, in the form of a general comment, on this topic which should contain concrete guidance for state practice.

[120] Optional Protocol to the International Covenant on Economic, Social and Cultural Rights, A/RES/63/117, 10 December 2008, entry into force: 5 May 2013.

C. Fact-finding Mission and Commission of Inquiry Reports

What follows are concrete illustrations of how ESC rights have been evaluated by commissions of inquiry and fact-finding missions and how IHL has been used to support an ESC rights assessment. In comparison with human rights bodies, it should be noted that generally the mandates of these mechanisms are not limited to international human rights law. As such they do not impede the application of IHL, either as a means of interpreting human rights law or as a direct source of law. In this context, there are no such institutional or procedural constraints and the situation is generally assessed on the basis of 'international law' as it applies to both states and non-state actors, which can also include for that matter international criminal law. The practice of the following selected reports will be examined in turn: the Special Rapporteur on the situation of human rights in Kuwait under Iraqi Occupation 1990–1991,[121] the 2004 Darfur Commission of Inquiry,[122] the 2006 UN Commission of Inquiry on Lebanon,[123] and the 2009 UN Fact Finding Mission on the Gaza Conflict.[124]

1. *The Special Rapporteur on the situation of human rights in Kuwait under Iraqi Occupation 1990–91*

The Special Rapporteur on the situation of human rights in Kuwait under Iraqi Occupation 1990–91 stressed the importance of human rights law during military occupation. During that period the occupying forces committed grave violations of human rights, including systematic destruction and pillaging of the economic infrastructure of Kuwait (banks, transport companies, industrial installations, schools, museums, libraries, religious and cultural institutions, hotels, private housing, etc.), which was considered as having seriously undermined the enjoyment by the Kuwaiti people of their ESC rights.[125]

The healthcare system was seriously debilitated by the departure of a large number of health professionals as a result of intimidation, attacks, the closing, dismantling and pillage of health facilities, and denial of access to hospitals for those who would not comply with the order to exchange Kuwaiti identity documents for Iraqi documents.[126] For instance, when looking at the destruction of the Kuwaiti

[121] Report on the situation of human rights in Kuwait under Iraqi occupation, prepared by Mr. Walter Kälin, Special Rapporteur of the Commission on Human Rights, in accordance with Commission resolution 1991/67, UN Doc. E/CN.4/1992/26, 16 January 1992.

[122] Report of the International Commission of Inquiry on Darfur to the UN Secretary-General pursuant to Security Council Resolution 1564 of 18 September 2004, 25 January 2005.

[123] Report of the Commission of Inquiry on Lebanon pursuant to Human Rights Council Resolution S-2/1, Implementation of General Assembly Resolution 60/251 of 15 March 2006, UN doc. A/HRC/3/2, 23 November 2006.

[124] Report of the United Nations Fact Finding Mission on the Gaza Conflict, Human Rights in Palestine and Other Occupied Arab Territories, UN Doc. A/HRC/12/48, 25 September 2009.

[125] W. Kälin, *Human rights in Times of Occupation: The Case of Kuwait* (Berne: LBE, 1994), 1.

[126] Report on the situation of human rights in Kuwait under Iraqi occupation, prepared by Mr. Walter Kälin, Special Rapporteur of the Commission on Human Rights, in accordance with Commission resolution 1991/67, UN doc. E/CN.4/1992/26, 16 January 1992, paras. 189–194.

health system by Iraqi occupying forces, the reference to the detailed and rather *operational* obligations of Articles 55 and 56, GCIV did not allow, according to Kälin, a true assessment of the gravity and seriousness of this situation: 'The true significance of these events was only elucidated by recourse to the concept of the right to health as guaranteed by the [ICESCR]'.[127]

There was substantial and large-scale environmental damage related to oil spills polluting water and coastline and the burning of oil wells generating smoke emissions.[128] The attacks on the oil wells by the retreating Iraqi forces were considered to be deliberate and systematic.[129] Interestingly, the Rapporteur assessed the situation on the basis of their 'effects on human rights' exclusively, because the relevant provisions on the protection of the environment under API, (to which Iraq was not a party), had not reached the status of customary law.[130] The Rapporteur then concluded that although warfare may have inevitable detrimental effect to the environment:

> the deliberate causing of large-scale environmental damage which severely affects the health of a considerable portion of the population concerned, or creates risks for the health of future generations, amounts to a serious violation of the right to the enjoyment of the highest attainable standard of health as embodied in article 12 of the [ICESCR].[131]

However, in the circumstances of the case, the Rapporteur noted that it was 'too early' to assess whether it would amount to a violation of this right, 'because of the limited short-term consequences for the health of the civilian population and of the difficulties in determining the long-term impact on the health situation'.[132]

The Special Rapporteur also observed evidence of a 'systematic dismantling and destruction of the major educational, scientific and cultural institutions' by Iraqi forces, including on the one hand several primary and secondary schools and archives containing material for doctoral dissertations, research and laboratory findings on the other.[133] The Rapporteur noted for instance that the dismantling

[127] W. Kälin, *Human rights in Times of Occupation: The Case of Kuwait*, p. 28.

[128] On the protection of the environment see M. Bothe, C. Bruch, J. Diamond, and D. Jensen, 'International Law Protecting the Environment during Armed Conflict: Gaps and Opportunities', 879 *IRRC* (2010), 569–592.

[129] Report on the situation of human rights in Kuwait under Iraqi occupation, prepared by Mr. Walter Kälin, Special Rapporteur of the Commission on Human Rights, in accordance with Commission resolution 1991/67, UN doc. E/CN.4/1992/26, 16 January 1992, paras. 203–204.

[130] Commission resolution 1991/67, UN doc. E/CN.4/1992/26, 16 January 1992, para. 205. The Rapporteur nevertheless concluded that the damage breached the very general duty to 'maintain public health' under Article 56, GCIV; Commission resolution 1991/67, UN doc. E/CN.4/1992/26, 16 January 1992, para. 208. See Arts. 35(3) and, 55 API as well as Rules 43–45, ICRC Customary Law Study.

[131] Commission resolution 1991/67, UN doc. E/CN.4/1992/26, 16 January 1992, para. 208. Even though the right to a clean environment has yet to become part of international treaty or customary law, the Rapporteur relied on Principle 1 of 1972 Stockholm Declaration and General Assembly resolution 45/94 (14 December 1990) to substantiate its claim; Commission resolution 1991/67, UN doc. E/CN.4/1992/26, 16 January 1992, para. 206.

[132] Commission resolution 1991/67, UN doc. E/CN.4/1992/26, 16 January 1992, para. 208.

[133] Commission resolution 1991/67, UN doc. E/CN.4/1992/26, 16 January 1992, paras. 212–216.

and destruction of the Kuwait Institute for Scientific Research had a serious impact because no 'applied research will allegedly be possible for a number of years'.[134]

Moreover, scientific production constituting a significant body of intellectual property was stolen and taken to Iraq.[135] In this regard, Article 15(2), on the right to enjoy scientific progress, specifically requires steps to be taken that 'include those necessary for the conservation, the development and the diffusion of science and culture'. The Rapporteur concluded the pillaging and dismantling of educational institutions was intentional and systematic in violation of the right to enjoy scientific progress and the right to education as well as Article 50 of the Fourth Geneva Convention, which requires that the occupant facilitates the proper working of all institutions 'devoted to the care and education of children'.[136] On the other hand, it is interesting to note that the Rapporteur assessed the destruction, dismantling, and pillaging of public infrastructure and private property under the section devoted to ESC rights exclusively in IHL terms.[137] The report states that the *confiscation or damage could have been in certain cases justified* under IHL, since they may have been necessitated by military considerations.[138] However, it noted that the large amount of damage and destruction was 'deliberate, premeditated, systematic and large scale, in clear violation with international law'.[139]

2. *International Commission of Inquiry on Darfur*

The International Commission of Inquiry on Darfur, which was required to investigate violations of international human rights and IHL by all parties to the conflict, was less explicit on this interrelationship.[140] Although the Commission explicitly referred to the right to adequate food, clothing, and housing (Article 11 ICESCR), it remains unclear what role IHL and criminal law played in the assessment of this

[134] Commission resolution 1991/67, UN doc. E/CN.4/1992/26, 16 January 1992, para. 213.

[135] Commission resolution 1991/67, UN doc. E/CN.4/1992/26, 16 January 1992, para. 217.

[136] Art. 15(1), ICESCR that establishes the right of everyone 'to take part in cultural life', 'to enjoy the benefits of scientific progress and its applications', as well as 'to benefit from the protection of the moral and material interests resulting from any scientific, literary or artistic production of which he is the author. Art. 15(1), paras. 211 and 218.

[137] Art. 15(1) and Arts. 16, 33 and 53, GCIV. Reference could have been made concurrently to the right to an adequate standard of living (including adequate housing).

[138] For instance, reference was made to the confiscation and transformation of private properties for military use. Art. 15(1), para. 234.

[139] Art. 15(1), para. 235. The Security Council established Iraq's legal responsibility for such losses in its resolution 687 of 3 April 1991: 'Iraq…is liable under international law for any direct loss, damage, including environmental damage and the depletion of natural resources, or injury to foreign Governments, nationals, and corporations, as a result of Iraq's unlawful invasion and occupation of Kuwait'. For the War Reparations Claims, see generally The United Nations Compensation Commission, available at <http://www.uncc.ch/> (last accessed 24 November 2013).

[140] The Commission was set up by the UN Secretary-General further to UN Security Council resolution 1564 which required the Commission to investigate 'reports of violations of international human rights and humanitarian law by all parties'. Report of the International Commission of Inquiry on Darfur to the United Nations Secretary General pursuant to Security Council resolution 1564 of 18 September 2004, 25 January 2005, paras. 1–2.

right, which was merely said to be relevant in this context.[141] For instance, the assessment concerning the deliberate and large-scale destruction of entire villages was based on IHL and criminal law. It was reported that some rebels might have been present in the villages, but the devastation was considered not to be justified by military necessity.[142] In addition to constituting a war crime, the Commission held that the attacks may have amounted to the crime of persecution as a crime against humanity if carried out on discriminatory grounds. In the case the acts had a 'detrimental effect on the liberty and livelihood of those people in that area'.[143]

3. UN Commission of Inquiry on Lebanon

Regarding the hostilities between Israel and Hezbollah, the Commission of Inquiry on Lebanon dealt with destruction or damage of civilian infrastructure, including bridges, roads, power plants, housing, medical facilities, water facilities, schools, historical, archaeological and cultural sites, mosques and churches, and TV and radio transmission stations.[144] The Commission generally noted that the attacks conducted by Israeli forces were characterized by 'a significant *pattern* of excessive, indiscriminate, and disproportionate use of force against Lebanese civilians and civilian objects, failing to distinguish civilians from combatants and civilian objects from military targets'.[145]

Accordingly, it repeatedly found concurrent violations of IHL and human rights law without further elaboration. For instance, the attack on the oil tanks resulting in massive pollution of the Lebanese coast was a violation of IHL based on the failure to take the necessary precautionary measures as well as 'human rights obligations to protect the natural environment and the right to health'.[146] However, no further legal reasoning was provided.

Similarly, it was held that the destruction or damage of private housing, as well as private and public school establishments, did not reflect an adequate application of the principles of military necessity and proportionality, and as a result these attacks

[141] The final report listed the following ESC rights as relevant in this context: to adequate housing and not to be subjected to forced eviction, to health, and to adequate food and water. Report of the International Commission of Inquiry on Darfur to the United Nations Secretary General pursuant to Security Council resolution 1564 of 18 September 2004, 25 January 2005, para. 148.

[142] Report of the International Commission of Inquiry on Darfur to the United Nations Secretary General pursuant to Security Council resolution 1564 of 18 September 2004, 25 January 2005, paras. 318–321.

[143] Hundreds of homes were burnt to the ground. It was also reported that the attacks destroyed utensils, equipment for processing food, water containers, livestock, and other household items essential for the survival of villagers. Report of the International Commission of Inquiry on Darfur to the United Nations Secretary General pursuant to Security Council resolution 1564 of 18 September 2004, 25 January 2005, paras. 305 and 320.

[144] UN Commission of Inquiry on Lebanon, para. 321.

[145] UN Commission of Inquiry on Lebanon, para. 13 (emphasis added).

[146] UN Commission of Inquiry on Lebanon, para. 321. In its evaluation, the Commission referred inaccurately to the prohibitions contained in Arts. 35(3) and 55(1), API ('employing methods or means of warfare which are intended, or may be expected, to cause widespread, long-term and severe damage to the natural environment') because Israel is not party to those instruments. Recourse to customary law would have been more appropriate.

constituted a grave violation of IHL and human rights law.[147] The direct targeting of schools in areas outside occupied territory took place at a time when children were on summer holidays.[148] The Commission reported that 16 schools (public and private) were directly hit, causing major destruction of the facilities, and another 157 were seriously damaged, either following direct hits or in collateral damage from bombing on adjacent buildings.[149] The Commission concluded that it did not find any evidence as to the effective military contribution of attacking the buildings, the attacks 'constitute[d], therefore, a grave violation of international humanitarian law and human rights obligations'.[150] It further noted that, '[w]ithout any clear indication as to the military importance of these buildings, such attacks would constitute a grave violation of international humanitarian law, which may amount to war crimes'.[151] Although the Commission remained rather unclear and general in its legal qualification, there seems to be a presumption of ESC rights violations when structures and services essential for their enjoyment are attacked unlawfully under IHL.

UN Fact Finding Mission on the Gaza Conflict

The most detailed analysis has been done in relation to the armed conflict between Israel and Gaza in 2008–09.[152] In the report of the UN Human Rights Council Fact Finding Mission, various aspects of the ICESCR were included in the final report of the investigation, relating on the one hand to the actual military operations during the hostilities between Israel and Palestinian armed groups and, on the other, to the effect of the blockade by Israel on the civilian population living in Gaza.

Concerning the use of force by Israel, and the right to an adequate standard of living (Article 11), a similar assessment was made to the one conducted by the Commission of Inquiry on Lebanon. The military targeting against private houses, farms, water wells, pipe networks, and livestock that were not justified by any military necessity were found to be a violation of Article 11, ICESCR.[153] Generally, IHL was used to support an ESC rights' finding with respect to negative obligations.

[147] UN Commission of Inquiry on Lebanon, paras. 319 and 326.

[148] UN Commission of Inquiry on Lebanon, para. 230.

[149] UN Commission of Inquiry on Lebanon, para. 230.

[150] UN Commission of Inquiry on Lebanon, para. 326.

[151] ICC Statute, art. 8(2)(b)(ix) and e(iv). UN Commission of Inquiry on Lebanon, para. 232.

[152] *Operation Cast Lead* was launched by Israel and was started on 27 December 2008 with a week-long air attack and continued with ground operations until 18 January 2009. The mission was mandated by the Human Rights Council to 'investigate all violations of international human rights law and international humanitarian law that might have been committed at any time in the context of the military operations that were conducted in Gaza during the period from 27 December 2008 and 18 January 2009, whether before, during or after'. Report of the United Nations Fact Finding Mission on the Gaza Conflict, UN Doc. A/HRC/12/48, 15 September 2009, para. 1.

[153] Report of the United Nations Fact Finding Mission on the Gaza Conflict, UN Doc. A/HRC/ 12/48, 15 September 2009, paras. 957–958 and 996–1003. With regard to the destruction of water and sewage installation, reference was made to CESCR's General Comment No. 15 on the right to water.

With regard to certain use of weapons that could directly affect the right to health of the victims, the report observed the use of white phosphorus shells or Dense Inert Metal Explosive (DIME) or heavy metal shrapnel weapons.[154] Although these weapons are not prohibited as such under international law, and are currently used by many armed forces, the report stressed the very high risk of harming civilians when the weapons are used in built-up areas, which can have 'a particularly adverse impact on the enjoyment of the right to health of survivors, which would go beyond the impact generally associated with being affected by anti-personnel weapons in an armed conflict'.[155] However, the report did not expressly qualify whether the use of these weapons would amount to a violation of Article 12, ICESCR.

Moving to the blockade of the Gaza strip carried out by Israel since 2006, the report criticized the overall objectives and strategy and highlighted a wide range of adverse effects it has had on ESC rights, which can be more easily identifiable. The report concluded that the territory has remained under occupation, and as a result noted that Israel retains positive obligations under IHL towards the occupied population to ensure their civil life and welfare, including through the provision of food and medical supplies.[156]

The restriction on medical supplies, as well as power and fuel cuts, disrupted civil life on across a broad range of activities from business to education, health services, industry, and agriculture, but in particular, the functioning of hospitals, the standards of water and sanitation, things which were considered both a violation of the ICESCR as well as IHL rules.[157] To give two examples, restrictions on movement affected university students either planning to, or studying abroad, as well as impeding academics and scholars from travelling abroad on academic exchanges.[158] In addition, the restrictions imposed on goods resulted in a lack of educational material and equipment necessary for maintaining adequate teaching standards.[159]

[154] Report of the United Nations Fact Finding Mission on the Gaza Conflict, UN Doc. A/HRC/12/48, 15 September 2009, paras. 887– 910. See J. MacLeod and A.P.V. Rogers 'The Use of White Phosphorous and the Law of War', in T.L.H. McCormack (ed.), *Yearbook of International Humanitarian Law*, The Hague: Asser Press, 2009.

[155] Report of the United Nations Fact Finding Mission on the Gaza Conflict, UN Doc. A/HRC/12/48, 15 September 2009, para. 910.

[156] Report of the United Nations Fact Finding Mission on the Gaza Conflict, UN Doc. A/HRC/12/48, 15 September 2009, paras. 187 and 273–280. The relevant provisions relating to the duties of an occupying Power under GCIV include the obligations contained in Articles 50 (duty to facilitate the working of care and education institutions), 55 (duty to ensure food and medical supplies to the population), 56 (duty to ensure and maintain medical and hospital establishments and services), 59 (duty to agree on relief schemes if the occupied territory is not well supplied) and 60 (duty to continue performing obligations even if third parties provide relief consignments). Report of the United Nations Fact Finding Mission on the Gaza Conflict, UN Doc. A/HRC/12/48, 15 September 2009, para. 1301.

[157] Report of the United Nations Fact Finding Mission on the Gaza Conflict, UN Doc. A/HRC/12/48, 15 September 2009, paras. 1311, 1315, and 1729.

[158] Report of the United Nations Fact Finding Mission on the Gaza Conflict, UN Doc. A/HRC/12/48, 15 September 2009, para. 1270.

[159] This situation caused allegedly a decline in attendance and performance at governmental schools. Report of the United Nations Fact Finding Mission on the Gaza Conflict, UN Doc. A/HRC/12/48, 15 September 2009, para. 1269.

To sustain its claim, the mission relied on General Comment No. 8 on inter-state sanctions as a way to consider the argument put forward by the Israeli Government that the above restrictions are being imposed as a form of sanction because of the attacks coming from the Gaza strip and the continuing captivity of the Israel Defense Forces soldier Gilad Shalit by Palestinian armed groups.[160] On the economic sanctions and their effects, the CESCR held that:

> whatever the circumstances, such sanctions should always take full account of the provisions of the International Covenant on Economic, Social and Cultural Rights [and] it is essential to distinguish between the basic objective of applying political and economic pressure upon the governing elite of the country to persuade them to conform to international law, and the collateral infliction of suffering upon the most vulnerable groups within the targeted country. [161]

Regardless of the status of Gaza for the purpose of IHL, the effective control over the closure of the territory by Israel through its internal exercise of jurisdiction could be regarded as entailing extraterritorial human rights obligations on the basis of the foreseeable disproportionate effects this policy have on the enjoyment of ESC rights. The mission generally concluded that the restrictions imposed:

> subjected the local population to extreme hardship and deprivations that amounted to a violation of Israel's obligations as an occupying Power under the Fourth Geneva Convention. These measures led to a severe deterioration and regression in the levels of realization of economic and social rights of Palestinians in the Gaza Strip and weakened its social and economic fabric, leaving health, education, sanitation and other essential services in a very vulnerable position.[162]

This protracted policy of closure of Gaza depriving the civilian population of basic needs was qualified as a form of collective punishment in violation of IHL.[163]

D. General assessment

We have seen that IHL is sometimes relied on to support or even to qualify an ESC rights finding. In other instances ESC rights and IHL are examined in a separate manner for the same situation, and yet reference is made either to one or the other to assess a situation. In light of this rather disparate practice and particularly given the

[160] Report of the United Nations Fact Finding Mission on the Gaza Conflict, UN Doc. A/HRC/12/48, 15 September 2009, paras. 1336–1344.

[161] Report of the United Nations Fact Finding Mission on the Gaza Conflict, UN Doc. A/HRC/12/48, 15 September 2009, para. 1306. CESCR, General Comment No. 8, The relationship between economic sanctions and respect for economic, social and cultural rights, 1997, paras. 4 and 16. ICRC, 'Gaza closure: not another year!', News release 10/10314 June 2010, available at <http://www.icrc.org/web/eng/siteeng0.nsf/htmlall/palestine-update-1406104> (last accessed 21 November 2013). See: 'What goods does Israel bar from the Gaza Strip?', *The Economist*, 1 June 2010.

[162] Report of the United Nations Fact Finding Mission on the Gaza Conflict, UN Doc. A/HRC/12/48, 15 September 2009, para. 1931.

[163] Report of the United Nations Fact Finding Mission on the Gaza Conflict, UN Doc. A/HRC/12/48, 15 September 2009, para. 309.

absence of case law, the least that can be said is that the approach of the CESCR and the various commissions of inquiry are not consistent.

Taking this perspective on the relationship between ESC rights and IHL a few points are in order. First, it should be noted that the findings concerning violations of human rights have been formulated from a general viewpoint concerning a large group of victims and it cannot be expected to have a very elaborate legal reasoning. Second, this process of interpretation is not a mechanical exercise with a preconceived outcome. Each situation should be analysed on a case-by-case basis, bearing in mind that it may not be possible to articulate a comprehensive theory concerning the interaction between IHL and ESC rights. Third, for obvious reasons, international practice differs across judicial and quasi-judicial bodies that are often dependent on the jurisdictional limits imposed on the decision-maker.

In situations involving the conduct of hostilities, it seems that the applicable IHL rules are taken into the assessment of ESC rights. However, there is an important nuance to be made. Not all 'attacks' or forcible actions attributable to a party to a conflict against infrastructure or services—regardless of their lawfulness under IHL—can be characterized as violations of the obligation to respect ESC rights, no matter how disruptive they can be for the general well-being of a given community. Caution is called for on the causal link between the acts and the victims, since human rights law does not protect civil infrastructure or 'objects' as such. In fact, human rights law treaties, as opposed to IHL instruments, which also generally protect civilian objects and property, aim to protect and promote individuals' rights. As such, their provisions do not confer status on nor directly protect objects or buildings (for example, educational buildings). This being said, certain essential elements of socio-economic rights do require the existence, maintenance, and availability of physical structures.[164] The element of availability requires the state to ensure that facilities, goods, or services/programmes developed and implemented are available to all in sufficient quantity.[165] For example, under the right to education, states parties have to make available 'functioning educational institutions and programmes', or, under the right to health, ensure the 'functioning public health and health-care facilities, goods and services as well as programmes [...] in sufficient quantity'.[166] Since availability or access is a main element in these rights, logically their physical protection may be implied or presumed.

[164] See generally the AAAQ framework (availability, accessibility, acceptability, and quality of facilities, goods, services, and programmes) developed in the practice of the CESCR. CESCR, General Comment No. 4, The right to adequate housing (art. 11, para. 1, of the Covenant), 1991, para. 8. UN Special Rapporteur on the Right to Education, K. Tomaševski, Preliminary Report, UN Doc. E/CN.4/1999/49, 13 January 1999.

[165] CESCR, General Comment No. 14, The right to the highest attainable standard of health (art. 12 of the Covenant), 2000, para.12(a); similarly see General Comment No. 19, The right to social security, 2008, para.11; General Comment No. 18, The right to work (art. 6 of the Covenant), 2005, para.12(a); General Comment No. 15, The right to water (arts. 11 and 12 of the Covenant), 2002, para.12(a) and General Comment No. 13, The right to education (art. 13 of the Covenant). 1999, para. 6(a).

[166] CESCR, General Comment No. 14, The right to the highest attainable standard of health (art. 12 of the Covenant), 2000, para. 12(a); General Comment No. 13, The right to education (art. 13 of

Generally, when it comes to forcible actions affecting directly the physical integrity of individuals it may logically engage the right to health. As noted, the most straightforward example would be the use of certain prohibited weapons, such as chemical weapons (banned in all conflicts), against the civilian population.[167] This example is relatively easy as the weapons are prohibited under international law, but whether or not other weapons (such as white phosphorus shells or DIME) would also be sufficient to constitute a violation would require further assessment on the basis of IHL (for example, principle of distinction) and the right to health. Although, relevant practice has not provided a clear answer, we may advance the idea that if the weapons are used in an indiscriminate manner (that is, in populated areas) this may certainly constitute a violation of the right to health for the direct impact these weapons can have on the civilians.

Likewise, when it comes to environmental damage and the right to a healthy environment the relationship between IHL and ESC rights remains to be clarified. Contrary to the cautious assessment made by Kälin in Iraq relating to the destruction of oil wells, the UN Commission of Inquiry on Lebanon assumed that the pollution would violate the right to health. However, no legal reasoning was provided in relation to the effect of the attacks on the population in the areas and other possible long-term damage. Irrespective of its potential qualification as a war crime, the fact that the incident may represent potential threats to the well-being of the civilian population is clearly not sufficient to qualify a human rights violation.[168] In this respect, we have seen that in its General Comment No. 14 (2000) on the right to health, and No. 15 (2002) on the right to water, the CESCR integrated some environmental considerations and principles to define the scope of the right to health recognizing the right to a safe and healthy environment,[169] as well as relevant IHL provisions on the protection of the environment within the scope of

the Covenant). 1999, para. 6(a). In similar terms, the Committee considers that the core content of the right to adequate food implies 'the availability of food in a quantity and quality sufficient to satisfy the dietary needs of individuals, free from adverse substances, and acceptable within a given culture'. CESCR, General Comment No. 12, The right to adequate food (art. 11 of the Covenant), 1999, para. 8.

[167] In his *Dissenting Opinion* in *Legality of the Use by a State of Nuclear Weapons in Armed Conflict*, Judge Weeramantry took a similar approach. Referring to Art. 12 ICESCR the right to health, he stated that 'each state is under an obligation to respect the right to health of all members of the international community'. ICJ, *Legality of the Use by a State of Nuclear Weapons in Armed Conflict*, ICJ Reports, 1996, Vol. I, p. 144.

[168] Without qualifying the incident, the Commission referred to Article 8(2)(b)(iv) of the Rome Statute, which states that the intentional launching of an attack in the knowledge that such attack will cause widespread, long-term and severe damage to the natural environment is considered a war crime. UN Commission of Inquiry on Lebanon, para. 218.

[169] General Comment No. 14 states, for instance, that

> '[t]he Committee interprets the right to health, as defined in article 12.1, as an inclusive right extending not only to timely and appropriate health care but also to the underlying determinants of health, such as access to safe and potable water and adequate sanitation, an adequate supply of safe food, nutrition and housing, healthy occupational and environmental conditions, and access to health-related education and information'.

See also CESCR, General Comment No. 14, The right to the highest attainable standard of health, 2000, paras. 11 and 15.

the right to water.[170] However, even on this basis, it remains difficult to draw firm conclusions as to whether the destruction per se of oil wells could concurrently violate the right to health and the right to water. One would need to assess the direct impact the damages can have on the livelihood of the community affected and perhaps also the financial costs of cleaning up engaged for the territorial state, which can create a serious burden on the state's budget.

The main factor to be taken into consideration appears to be the impact the forcible measure has on victims, which indicates an element of immediacy. These examples show that deliberate attacks leading to the damage or destruction of infrastructure and services necessary for the enjoyment of certain ESC rights may lead to the violation of certain ESC rights in a number of cases relating to water, food, housing, and health. There is in fact a presumption that such destruction can negatively impact on the population, when it comes to objects indispensable to the civilian population, such as foodstuffs, crops, livestock, potable water, or housing, especially when they are destroyed or removed in large quantities. The complementary relationship between ESC rights and IHL would effectively broaden the legal scope of these rights.

Generally, it is accepted that IHL rules may play the role of 'explanatory' variable, providing criteria to determine the way the content of certain human rights should be identified in situations of armed conflict. However, the fact that disproportionate or excessive destruction and appropriation of protected property under IHL not justified by military exigencies can be a serious violation of IHL and may constitute a war crime in any armed conflict does not automatically qualify as a violation of socio-economic rights.[171] IHL rules may sometimes overlap with those rights but they are not necessarily coterminous with one another. For instance, the unlawful destruction or the arbitrary seizure of a private housing under IHL does not necessarily amount to an interference with the right to housing of an individual if the object does not correspond to her/his formal residence.[172] Similarly, unlawfully directing attacks against an educational building may constitute a war crime, but may not concurrently qualify as a violation of the *right* to education. This raises the question of what would be the exact threshold, the attack per se or the damaged caused? For instance, an unlawful attack on a school building,

[170] CESCR, General Comment No. 15, The right to water (arts. 11 and 12), 2002, para. 22.

[171] Art. 8(2)(b)(ix) of the Rome Statute, provide specific protection to educational facilities, which criminalizes acts of 'intentionally directing attacks against buildings dedicated to . . . education . . . provided they are not military objectives'. The crime of destruction of educational buildings as a war crime was considered by the ICTY as part of customary international law. *Kordić and Čerkez,* Appeals Judgment, 17 December 2004, para. 91. See also *Prosecutor v Naletilić and Martinović,* IT-98-34, 31 March 2003, paras. 604–605.

[172] See for instance, the *Loizidou* case concerning the alleged violation of the rights of a Cypriot land owner who was prevented by Turkish troops from returning to and enjoying her land in Northern Cyprus. While the lack of access of the applicant to her property amounted to a violation of the right to property (Art. 1 of Protocol No. 1 ECHR), there was no violation of the right to home (Art. 8), since the applicant did not have a home on the land in question. ECtHR, *Loizidou v Turkey*, Judgment (Merits), App. No. 15318/89, 18 December 1996, paras. 65–66.

amounting to a war crime may bring no destruction or only partial damage (for example, destruction of the sports facility). As a result, it is reasonable to consider the right to education not to be violated in this context.[173]

Perhaps we reach the limits of the humanitarian broadening phenomenon of ESC rights. ESC rights cannot provide all the answers and, as we have seen, in a spirit of complementarity, there are sufficient rules under IHL and international criminal law that are better adapted to regulate these situations. Having said this, it should be noted that the positive human rights obligations concerning the relevant rights remain. The territorial state (or the occupier in situations of belligerent occupation)[174] would be required to take all the reasonable and necessary measures to protect and fulfil socio-economic rights of the civilian population. If a school establishment has been damaged, a state would have the immediate positive duty to ensure that the children concerned continue to have access to the minimum essential level of education prescribed under the ICESCR either by repairing the school or by sending them to another establishment.[175]

6. Conclusion

This chapter has examined some aspects of the multifaceted relationship between ESC rights and IHL. The study has highlighted how IHL provides a detailed set of rules that are better adapted to address specific operational problems and threats that occur during the conduct of hostilities. When comparing respective norms, it becomes apparent that IHL rules seeks to protect, in practical terms, components essential for the enjoyment of socio-economic rights that are particularly endangered by armed conflicts. At the same time, ESC rights add protection to individuals in certain areas that are either not protected or fully protected by IHL, especially when a state exerts sufficient control over part of a territory both in internal armed conflict as well as in an occupied territory.

In the spirit of complementarity, the fact that ESC rights and IHL rules are different in nature does not imply that they are mutually exclusive. Reality simply cannot be compartmentalized the way that legal regimes can, and in certain circumstances there is no such thing as a pure human rights or humanitarian law issue. Therefore, armed conflict and its many situations are characterized by elements that could

[173] See generally, G. Giacca and T. Karimova 'Education as a "battleground" in conflicts in 2012, in S. Casey-Maslen (ed.), *War Report 2012* (Oxford: Oxford University Press, 2013), Ch. 6.

[174] See G. Giacca 'Economic, Social and Cultural Rights in Occupied Territories' in A. Clapham, P. Gaeta, and M. Sassòli (eds), *The 1949 Geneva Conventions: A Commentary* (Oxford: Oxford University Press, 2014) (forthcoming).

[175] See the discussion by the UN Commission of Inquiry on Lebanon concerning the positive obligations of the Government of Lebanon to take all necessary measures to ensure the protection of the civilian population. This included inter alia the reconstruction and repair of housing or schools and the provision of adequate healthcare to the victims. UN Commission of Inquiry on Lebanon, paras. 284–308.

warrant recourse either to both regimes, or to one or the other, if we are to afford the most effective and enhanced protection to an individual.

It follows that the arguments that are made that human rights guarantees may generally be suspended, or that, in contrast to IHL rules, ESC rights can only be implemented *progressively*—thus losing their normative relevance[176]—are no longer tenable. Although the term 'ESC rights' does not appear as such in the Geneva or Hague law, one can see how it has now entered the IHL discourse because of the influence exercised by international human rights law.[177]

[176] J. Pejic, 'The Right to Food in Situations of Armed Conflict: The Legal Framework' 83 *IRRC* (2001), 1097–1110. M. Dennis, 'Application of Human Rights Treaties Extraterritorially in Times of Armed Conflict and Military Occupation' 99 *AJIL* (2005), 140; Y. Arai-Takahashi, *The Law of Occupation: Continuity and Change of International Humanitarian Law, and its Interaction with International Human Rights Law* (Leiden/Boston: Martinus Nijhoff Publishers, 2009), 412–413.

[177] See further in G. Giacca 'Economic, Social and Cultural Rights in Occupied Territories' in A. Clapham, P. Gaeta, and M. Sassòli (eds.), *The 1949 Geneva Conventions: A Commentary* (Oxford: Oxford University Press, 2014) (forthcoming).

12

Economic, Social, and Cultural Rights

International Criminal Law's Blind Spot?

Larissa van den Herik

1. Introduction

The last two decades witnessed the spectacular promotion of international criminal law as a new sub-discipline of international law. The human rights movement constituted one of the strongest forces in this rise.[1] For instance, as is well known, it was a vigorous advocate in the campaign for a permanent International Criminal Court (ICC). In this dynamic, the ICC was perceived as an additional enforcement mechanism to address the most severe human rights violations. The involvement of human rights activists as driving forces in the ICC's establishment is illustrative of the close synergies that undeniably exist between human rights law and international criminal law. The historical kinship between international criminal law and human rights law has even led some scholars to claim that the sub-disciplines are both part of the same family of rules directly concerned with individuals.[2]

It is true that international criminal law and international human rights law share significant traits. However, the articulation between international criminal law and human rights law seems rather one-sided. International criminal law is primarily concerned with violations of civil and political rights. More concretely, the right to life and the right to physical and mental integrity are the central values shaping the register of international crimes. Economic, social, and cultural rights have, so far, less directly inspired the development of international criminal law, if at all. The bias against socio-economic and cultural rights might be explained by the traditional conceptualization of this generation of human rights as having the character of programmatic aspirations rather than justiciable rights. In a related vein, economic, social, and cultural rights are often characterized as entailing obligations of result rather than obligations of conduct.

[1] W.A. Schabas, *The International Criminal Court: A Commentary on the Rome Statute* (Oxford: Oxford University Press, 2010), 397. I am grateful to Adrian Plevin, LLM Advanced at Leiden University, for his excellent research assistance and insightful suggestions.

[2] R. Jennings, 'The Role of the International Court of Justice', 68 *British Yearbook of International Law* (1997), 1–63, 58.

Taking into account the alleged limited normative substance of economic, social, and cultural (ESC) rights, this chapter seeks to revisit the theoretical explanation for the disconnect between international criminal law and economic, social, and cultural rights. It addresses the following questions: does the special character of socio-economic and cultural human rights render them less easily reconcilable with the strict *mens rea* requirements that pervade international criminal law, or are socio-economic and cultural human rights less susceptible to international criminalization for another reason? Does the overall non-criminalization of violations of cultural and socio-economic rights in fact display a hidden sense of hierarchy despite the lofty promises of Vienna 1993?[3] In grappling with these questions, this chapter explores concrete examples and case scenarios in which international crimes prosecution could have a socio-economic or cultural dimension. This exercise will also identify limits of the current international crimes catalogue with regard to redressing second generation rights. I conclude with some thoughts on the instrumentality of international criminal justice as a means to protect economic, social, and cultural rights.

2. The Kinship between International Criminal Law and Human Rights Law

International criminal law and human rights law are two normative fields of international law that share core values with regard to human dignity and the autonomy of the individual. In contrast to other chapters of international law, such as treaty law or trade law, these two fields of law are primarily concerned not with relations between States but rather with the individual. The identification and rise of the individual as a new participant in international law was a movement that gained force in the aftermath of and in reaction to the Second World War. As both human rights law and international criminal law were part of this movement, it can be said that the two areas of law 'have a common base'.[4] However, while human rights have been steadily developed on the basis of post-war treaties and instruments, international criminal law came to a virtual standstill after the Nuremberg and Tokyo trials. Only in the 1990s—after the end of the Cold War—was this field of law reactivated with the foundation of the ad hoc Tribunals for the Former Yugoslavia (ICTY) and Rwanda (ICTR), and eventually the permanent International Criminal Court. In its revival, international criminal law was seen as a renewed promise to punish severe human rights violations that could potentially fill the gap of effective enforcement. Indeed, the Preamble of the Rome Statute evidences that ending impunity was one of the ICC's foundational values.[5] Yet the precise relationship

[3] UN World Conference on Human Rights, Vienna, 14–25 June 1993, UN Doc. A/CONF.157/23, adopted by 171 states, Vienna Declarations 1993, Part I, para. 5.

[4] R. Cryer, et al., *An Introduction to International Criminal Law and Procedure* 2nd edn (Cambridge: Cambridge University Press, 2010), 13.

[5] Preamble of the ICC Statute, para. 4.

and interaction between human rights law and international criminal law is both complex and elusive and, in fact, has mutated over time as international criminal law matured and its criminal law characteristics became more prominent.[6]

Although international criminal law is seen by some as the ultimate mechanism for ensuring compliance with human rights and, therefore, an extension of it, the ways in which the individual is central to both fields of law are diametrically opposed. Human rights law places obligations on states to treat individuals well. International criminal law, on the other hand, identifies the individual behind the state with the aim of prosecution. This takes place on the basis of the Nuremberg maxim that 'crimes against international law are committed by men, not by abstract entities, and only by punishing individuals who commit such crimes can the provisions of international law be enforced'.[7] This dichotomy of the two fields of law is further complicated by the fact that international criminal law itself is founded on a paradox whereby two contradictory aims have to be reconciled with each other. On the one hand, international criminal law as a form of criminal law is based upon principles of a classic liberal criminal law system which emphasizes respect for the independence of the individual, in particular the defendant. On the other hand, the human rights perspective, and possibly its very origin, focuses on the protection of victims. This paradox leads to a tension, in substantive international criminal law in particular, whereby it is difficult to reconcile strict methods and principles of interpretation, such as *in dubio pro reo*, with the teleological and more victim-oriented interpretation methods which are typical in human rights.[8]

In the construction phase of international criminal law that took place in the 1990s, the teleological approach prevailed and the ad hoc Tribunals had occasional recourse to human rights law to interpret the material elements of substantive crimes.[9] The paucity of precedent and the lack of a sufficiently fleshed out international criminal code stimulated references to human rights as a means to shape definitions and elucidate elements of crimes.[10] These practices were justified on the basis of similarities and synergies in goals, values, and terminology between international criminal law and human rights law.[11] In this spirit, definitions and

[6] On the nature of international criminal law and its relationship to human rights law, see generally, A. Clapham, 'Three Tribes Engage on the Future of International Criminal Law', 9 *Journal of International Criminal Justice* (2011), 689–695; C. Stahn and L. van den Herik, '"Fragmentation", Diversification and "3D" Legal Pluralism: International Criminal Law as the Jack-in-the-Box?', in L. van den Herik and C. Stahn (eds.), *The Diversification and Fragmentation of International Criminal Law* (Leiden: Martinus Nijhoff Publishers, 2012), 21–89.

[7] Trial of the Major War Criminals before the International Military Tribunal, Nürnberg, 14 November 1945 to 1 October 1946, published at Nürnberg, Germany (1947), 223.

[8] D. Robinson, 'The Identity Crisis of International Criminal Law', 21 *Leiden Journal of International Law* (2008), 925–963.

[9] T. Meron, 'Human Rights Law Marches into New Territory: The Enforcement of International Human Rights in International Criminal Tribunals (Marek Nowicki Memorial Lecture)', in T. Meron (ed.), *The Making of International Criminal Justice: A View from the Bench: Selected Speeches* (Oxford: Oxford University Press, 2011), 181–98, esp. 189–197.

[10] *Prosecutor v Kunarac*, Case No. IT-96-23-T & 92-23-1-T, Judgment of 22 February 2001 (ICTY), para. 467.

[11] *Prosecutor v Kunarac*, Case No. IT-96-23-T & 92-23-1-T, Judgment of 22 February 2001 (ICTY), para. 467.

concepts from the 1984 Torture Convention,[12] the 1926 Slavery Convention,[13] and other human rights treaties were given extra-conventional importance.[14] They were transposed to the international criminal law context to lend greater specificity to the statutory crime definitions of the ad hoc Tribunals. In this process, the ICTY recognized two crucial structural differences between human rights law and international criminal law, namely that human rights law establishes a list of protected rights and exclusively binds states, whereas international criminal law establishes a list of offences and is binding on the individual.[15] It thus acknowledged that there is a certain normative separation between the two areas of law beyond the mere fact that not all human rights violations are subject to international criminalization.

The relationship between human rights law and procedural international criminal law has its own intricacies. In fact, the first forms of actual interaction between the two fields of law concerned questions of procedural international criminal law and more specifically the right of the defendant to a fair trial. In one of its first rulings, the ICTY concluded that Article 6 of the European Convention of Human Rights (ECHR) was only relevant to a limited degree for the Tribunal because it operated on the basis on its own 'unique legal framework'.[16] It espoused that '[i]n international law, every tribunal is a self-contained system (unless otherwise provided)'.[17] More specifically, the Tribunal ruled that the shocking nature of the crimes and the special context in which the Tribunal was operating could justify a more flexible attitude to rules of evidence and the rights of the defendant.[18] It held that:

> the interpretation given by other judicial bodies to Article 14 of the ICCPR and Article 6 of the ECHR is only of limited relevance in applying the provisions of the Statute and Rules of

[12] *Prosecutor v Furundžija*, Case No. IT-95-17/1-T, Judgment of 10 December 1968 (ICTY), para. 162; *Prosecutor v Mucić and others*, Case. No. IT-96-21-T, Judgment of 16 November 1998 (ICTY), paras. 447–459.

[13] *Prosecutor v Kunarac*, Case No. IT-96-23-T & 92-23-1-T, Judgment of 22 February 2001 (ICTY), para. 519.

[14] In considering the existence of a right to freedom of expression under customary international law in *Bikindi*, Trial Chamber III referred to, among other things, the 1948 Universal Declaration of Human Rights, the 1966 International Convention on Civil and Political Rights, the 1966 Convention on the Elimination on All Forms of Racial Discrimination, the 1950 European Convention for the Protection of Human Rights and Fundamental Freedoms, the 1969 Inter-American Convention on Human Rights, and the 1981 African Charter on Human and Peoples' Rights. See *Prosecutor v Bikindi*, Case No. ICTR-01-72-T, Judgment of 2 December 2008 (ICTY), paras. 379–380.

[15] *Prosecutor v Kunarac*, Case No. IT-96-23-T & 92-23-1-T, Judgment of 22 February 2001 (ICTY), para. 470.

[16] *Prosecutor v Tadic*, Case No. IT-94-1-T, Decision on the Prosecutor's Motion Requesting Protective Measures for Victims and Witnesses, 10 August 1995 (ICTY), paras. 26–28.

[17] *Prosecutor v Tadic*, Case No. IT-94-1-T, Decision on the Defence Motion for Interlocutory Appeal on Jurisdiction, 10 August 1995 (ICTY), para. 11.

[18] The special context related to the fact that the Tribunal was operating while the conflict was still ongoing, and that the Tribunal did not have its own police force or witness protection programme, see also T. Meron, 'Human rights law marches into new territory: the enforcement of international human rights in international criminal tribunals' (Marek Nowicki Memorial Lecture), in T. Meron, *The Making of International Criminal Justice: A View from the Bench: Selected Speeches* (Oxford: Oxford University Press, 2011), 181–98, 185.

the International Tribunal, as these bodies interpret their provisions in the context of their legal framework, which do not contain the same considerations.[19]

In later jurisprudence, this heavily criticized position was modified and greater value was given to the ECHR and the jurisprudence of the European Court of Human Rights.[20] Nevertheless, the special circumstances in which the Tribunal operates can lead to adapted interpretations of certain aspects of the right to a fair trial. The issue here is not—as in the relationship between human rights and substantive international criminal law—one of tension in relation to the adapted interpretation method which works out either in favour of the victim or of the defendant. In procedural international criminal law the rights of the defendant correspond with human rights as protected in Article 6 of the ECHR. However, the question which arises in the dynamic between human rights law and procedural international criminal law is whether the human rights, which have been formulated to operate at the level of the state, can be directly applied in the context of international tribunals or whether a transposition should take place given the structural differences between national and international procedures. In his dissenting opinion in the *Erdemovic* case, Cassese has described these structural differences as follows:

> [...] international criminal courts are not part of a State apparatus functioning on a particular territory and exercising an authority of which courts partake. International criminal courts operate at the state level. They discharge their functions in a community consisting of sovereign States. The individuals over whom these courts exercise jurisdiction are under the sway and control of sovereign States.[21]

Taken all together, these examples show that the ICTY, as one of the most prominent international criminal tribunals before the ICC came into operation, has been inspired by human rights and more specifically by the jurisprudence of the ECHR. Nonetheless, the Tribunal was, to a certain extent, quite aware of the various structural differences between the two fields of law which impede a too mechanical transplantation of concepts and principles.

The ICC's creation and operation marked a momentum in international criminal law. In this new phase, the penal nature of international criminal law

[19] *Prosecutor v Tadic*, Case No. IT-94-1-T, Decision on the Prosecutor's Motion Requesting Protective Measures for Victims and Witnesses, 10 August 1995 (ICTY), para. 27.

[20] See, e.g. *Prosecutor v Jankovic*, Case No. IT-96-23/2-PT, Decision on Referral of Case under Rule 11 *bis*, 22 July 2005 (ICTY), paras. 28, 47–48, and 73; *Prosecutor v Delalić* et al., Case No. IT-96-21-A, Judgment of 20 February 2001 (ICTY), paras. 782–83; *Prosecutor v Furundžija*, Case No. IT-95-17/1-A, Judgment of 21 July 2000 (ICTY), para. 69; *Prosecutor v Furundžija*, Case No. IT-95-17/1-T, Judgment of 10 December 1968 (ICTY), para. 160; and *Prosecutor v Prlić* et al., Case No. IT-04-74-AR73.6, Decision on Appeals against Decision Admitting Transcript of Jadranko Prlić's Questioning into Evidence, 23 November 2007 (ICTY), paras. 51 and 53. Similar jurisprudence has come from the ICTR, see, e.g. *Barayagwiza v The Prosecutor*, Case No. ICTR-97-19-AR72, Decision of 3 November 1999 (ICTR), paras. 83–84 and 88–89; *Prosecutor v Kayishema*, Case No. ICTR-01-67-R11bis, Decision on Prosecutor's Request for Referral to the Republic of Rwanda, 22 February 2012, para. 30.

[21] *Prosecutor v Erdemovic*, Case No. IT-96-22-A, Judgment of 7 October 1997 (ICTY), para. 5.

increasingly gained prominence over its function as an enforcement mechanism of human rights norms. In this spirit, some scholars made the appeal for a more forceful divorce between international criminal law and human rights law, also advising against the use of human rights law as guidance for the interpretation of substantive criminal law.[22] Article 21 of the ICC Statute on applicable law and in particular the phrasing of the legality principle in Article 22(2), which includes the instruction to the ICC judiciary only to engage in strict interpretation of crime definitions, reflects this trend. Human rights are not mentioned as a direct source of international criminal law, but Article 21(3) does prescribe that the application and interpretation of international criminal law by the ICC judges must be 'consistent with internationally recognized human rights'.[23] This provision has been used in practice to bolster the rights of the accused and to some extent to flesh out procedural rights and notions in relation to victim participation.[24] The interpretational instruction of Article 22(2) combined with the elaborate definitions of crimes in the ICC Statute and the Elements of Crimes leaves considerably less space for direct recourse to human rights concepts in the realm of substantive criminal law.[25] This constellation might thus not be the most conducive for a further integration of socio-economic and cultural notions in international criminal law. On a deeper level, there may also be structural impediments which could be explanatory of the disconnect between international criminal law and ESC rights.

3. Revisiting the Disconnect between International Criminal Law and ESC Rights

The legal status of socio-economic rights and their alleged nature as aspirational, programmatic, or non-justiciable has been much discussed in scholarly writing.[26] It has also been asserted that the rights concerned are more political in nature.[27]

[22] G.P. Fletcher and J.D. Ohlin, 'Reclaiming Fundamental Principles of Criminal Law in the Darfur Case', 3 *Journal of International Criminal Justice* (2005), 539–561, 544.

[23] ICC Statute, Art. 21(3).

[24] W.A. Schabas, *The International Criminal Court: A Commentary on the Rome Statute* (New York: Oxford University Press, 2010), 397–401.

[25] The argument has been made that, even if unintentional, the sweeping language of Art. 21(3) could be used to broaden the ICC's competence by declaring certain Elements of Crimes incompatible with human rights. See M.H. Arsanjani, 'The Rome Statute of the International Criminal Court', 93 *American Journal of International Law* (1999), 22–43, 29. On the perplexity of this provision, see also, A. Pellet, 'Applicable Law', in A. Cassese et al. (eds.), *The Rome Statute for an International Criminal Court: A Commentary* (vol. 2, New York: Oxford University Press, 2002), 1051–1084, 1079–1082; G. Bitti, 'Article 21 of the Statute of the International Criminal Court and the Treatment of Sources of Law in the Jurisprudence of the ICC', in C. Stahn and G. Sluiter (eds.), *The Emerging Practice of the International Criminal Court* (Leiden: Martinus Nijhoff Publishers, 2009), 285–304.

[26] See, e.g. M.J. Dennis and D.P. Stewart, 'Justiciability of Economic, Social and Cultural Rights: Should there be an International Complaints Mechanism to Adjudicate the Rights to Food, Water, Housing and Health?', 98 *American Journal of International Law* (2004), 462–516.

[27] E.G. Vierdag, 'The Legal Nature of the Rights Granted by the International Covenant on Economic, Social and Cultural Rights', 9 *Netherlands Yearbook of International Law* (1978), 69–105, 103.

Alternatively, the argument could be made that even if the rights concerned have been codified in an international treaty and are binding as such, they do not specify concrete legal obligations and thus lack normative content.[28] These claims have been rebutted by human rights scholars.[29] Nevertheless, the question still arises whether the presumed softness that is inherent in socio-economic rights renders them incompatible with the legality concerns that permeate international criminal law. In addition, there may be other interrelated features of these second-generation rights that generate a certain unsuitability for international criminalization.

The legality principle underpins international criminal law as a system of *criminal* law.[30] This fundamental principle of criminal law encapsulates several dimensions. In addition to the prohibition of retroactivity, it also requires that crimes be prescribed with sufficient clarity and precision so as to provide fair warning to individuals of what constitutes criminal conduct. Such requirements contrast sharply with the relatively vague formulation of socio-economic rights, in particular, as they have been codified in the International Covenant on Economic, Social and Cultural Rights (ICESCR).[31] The imprecise wording, or softness, of socio-economic rights may thus present a certain technical barrier that hinders direct criminalization. It has been suggested that these considerations should not be exaggerated. First, the precise formulation of given rights differs per convention. In particular, the 1990 International Convention on the Protection of the Rights of All Migrant Workers and Members of Their Families evidences a more detailed and rights-oriented wording of concrete rights.[32] Furthermore, the Committees have instilled socio-economic provisions with greater normativity through their particularized General Comments.[33] In a more general fashion, the Committee on Economic, Social and Cultural Rights (CESCR) has presented the idea that, based on the *raison d'être* of the ICESCR, a certain minimum core of each right can be

[28] Such indeterminate treaty provisions may be called 'soft law'; see D. Shelton, 'Soft Law', in D. Armstrong (ed.), *Routledge Handbook of International Law* (London: Routledge, 2009), 68–80, 69. On this conception of soft law, see also J. d'Aspremont, 'Softness in International Law: A Self-Serving Quest for New Legal Materials', 19 *European Journal of International Law* (2008), 1075–1093.

[29] See, e.g. E. Riedel, 'International Law Shaping Constitutional Law: Realization of Economic, Social and Cultural Rights', in E. Riedel (ed.), *Constitutionalism: Old Concepts, New Worlds* (Berlin: Berliner Wissenschafts-Verlag, 2005), 105–120. Also see E. Riedel, 'New Bearings in Social Rights? The Communications Procedure under the ICESCR', in U Fastenrach et al. (eds.), *From Bilateralism to Community Interest: Essays in Honour of Bruno Simma* (Oxford: Oxford University Press, 2011), 574–589.

[30] G.P. Fletcher and J.D. Ohlin, 'Reclaiming Fundamental Principles of Criminal Law in the Darfur Case', 3 *Journal of International Criminal Justice* (2005), 539–561, 541.

[31] P. Alston, 'No right to complain about being poor: the need for an optional protocol to the Economic Rights Covenant', in A. Eide, and J. Helgesen (eds.), *The Future of Human Rights Protection in a Changing World* (Oslo: Norwegina University Press, 1991), 86.

[32] As noted by M. Scheinin, 'Economics and Social Rights as Legal Rights', in A. Eide, C. Krause, and A. Rosas (eds.), *Economic, Social and Cultural Rights: A Textbook* 2nd edn (Leiden: Martinus Nijhoff Publishers, 2001), 31.

[33] These comments are non-binding and, in the words of Boyle and Chinkin, they are part of a process of soft law formation, whose strength depends on levels of consistency and persuasiveness; see A. Boyle and C. Chinkin, *The Making of International Law* (Oxford: Oxford University Press, 2007), 154–157. See also chapter 1 in this book.

identified which must be respected regardless of available resources.[34] It cemented this idea by providing specific examples of minimum essential levels of each right that must be guaranteed. For instance, a state party may not deprive a significant number of individuals of essential foodstuffs, of essential primary healthcare, of basic shelter and housing, or of the most basic forms of education.[35] In particular, the deprivation of essential means of subsistence directly corresponds to the right to life and can thus be said to be sufficiently tangible to offer a primary norm that is susceptible to being criminalized.[36]

An intertwined second feature that characterizes socio-economic human rights conventions is that, at first glance, they primarily spell out positive obligations, that is, obligations of result. A violation of such obligations is mostly constituted by a failure to act. Conversely, criminal law is generally concerned with commission of acts rather than omission. This prima facie incompatibility between the nature of ESC rights and the scope of international criminal law is less pronounced than it seems, though. The nature of ESC rights has been refined through the application of the threefold typology which encompasses the obligation to respect, protect and fulfil.[37] The 1997 Maastricht Guidelines further specified that these obligations can each entail elements of obligation of conduct and of result.[38] The understanding of ESC rights as only entailing obligations of result thus lacks nuance. Moreover, the mere fact that a positive obligation is at stake does not necessarily exclude the potential for action in the domain of international criminal law.

The question to what extent a failure to act can indeed result in criminal liability has long occupied legal scholars and philosophers. Even if international criminal law is not entirely adverse to the idea of criminal omission or omission liability, as it has been codified through certain theories on individual responsibility such as the concept of command responsibility, the criminalization of omission remains an exception to the rule.[39] This is also exemplified by the intricate drafting discussions

[34] CESCR, General Comment No. 3, The nature of State Parties' Obligations, 14 December 1990, para. 10. For a critical appraisal, see, K. Young, 'The Minimum Core of Economic and Social Rights: A Concept in Search of Contents', 33 *Yale Journal of International Law* (2008), 113–175.

[35] CESCR, General Comment No. 3, The nature of State Parties' Obligations, 14 December 1990, para. 10.

[36] In the context of the right to self-determination, the right has also been formulated in absolutist terms. Art. 1(2) of both the ICCPR and the ICESCR reads: 'in no case may a people be deprived of its own means of subsistence'.

[37] Originally espoused by Henry Shue where he distinguished between the duties to avoid depriving; duties to protect from deprivation; and duties to aid the deprived; see H. Shue, *Basic Rights: Subsistence, Affluence and US Foreign Policy* (Princeton: Princeton University Press, 1980). This typology was further developed within the framework of a study on the normative content of the right to adequate food by Mr. Asbjorn Eide. See Report by Asbjorn Eide, The Right to Adequate Food as a Human Rights, UN Doc. C/CN.4/Sub.2/1987/23, 7 July 1987. CESCR, General Comment No. 12, The right to adequate food (Art. 11), 1999; General Comment No. 13, The right to education (Art. 13), 1999; and General Comment No. 15, The right to water (Arts. 11 and 12), 2002. The same typology in the ambit of civil and political rights is equally valid and is treated as such in the literature. See M. Nowak, *UN Covenant on Civil and Political Rights, CCPR Commentary* 2nd edn (Berlin: Kehl am Rhein, Engel, 2005), 37–41.

[38] Maastricht Guidelines on Violations of Economic, Social and Cultural Rights, 22–26 January 1997, para. 6

[39] See on commission and omission in international criminal law, E. van Sliedregt, *Individual Criminal Responsibility in International Law* (Oxford: Oxford University Press, 2012), 54–57.

and the subsequent codification of a policy requirement for crimes against humanity. This requirement is laid down in Article 7(2)(a) of the Rome Statute and further elaborated in the Elements of Crimes, which require that 'the State or organization actively promote or encourage such an attack against a civilian population'.[40] Interestingly, this specification is footnoted as:

> Such a policy may, in exceptional circumstances, be implemented by a deliberate failure to take action, which is consciously aimed at encouraging such attack. The existence of such a policy cannot be inferred solely from the absence of governmental or organizational action.[41]

This phrasing exhibits a delicate compromise through which, for instance, mass starvation in a famine could be captured but only if proven that there was a certain deliberateness involved.[42] Deliberate famines are less rare than one might think, or in the words of Amartya Sen, 'there has never been a famine in a functioning multiparty democracy'.[43] And even economic and social governmental policies that are not intentionally famin-inducing but that are continued despite clear indications of disastrous consequences might in certain circumstances amount to a policy as described in the ICC footnote.[44]

A palpable third impediment to direct criminalization relates to the different addressees of human rights law and international criminal law respectively. Human rights conventions postulate obligations for *states*, whereas international criminal law targets *individuals*. The mainstream position is that non-state actors, including individuals, are not directly legally bound by human rights law.[45] Therefore, this area of law cannot provide the primary norms of international crimes without a certain transposition.

Overall, the inherent nature of socio-economic rights renders *direct* criminalization impossible. However, this does not preclude that factual socio-economic misconduct and abuses can be captured by the existing international crimes repertoire, and conversely that socio-economic human rights provisions can be utilized as a source of inspiration and guidance. In addition, the international criminal judiciary could draw on another area of law that protects certain socio-economic values in both direct and more indirect ways; namely, international humanitarian law.

[40] Elements of Crimes, Crimes Against Humanity, Introduction, para. 3.

[41] Elements of Crimes, Crimes Against Humanity, Introduction, para. 3, fn. 6.

[42] See on famine causation and prevention, A. Sen, *Development as Freedom* (New York: Oxford University Press, 1999), esp. ch. 7.

[43] A. Sen, *Development as Freedom* (New York: Oxford University Press, 1999), 178.

[44] See, e.g. D. Marcus, 'Famine Crimes in International Law', 97 *American Journal of International Law* (2003), 245–281, connecting the great Twentieth Century famines in Ukraine (1930s) and Ethiopia (1980s), and the present North Korea famine to human agency. According to Marcus, these famines were possibly not only the consequence of recklessness behaviour by state leaders but rather of direct criminal intention. Also see S. Skogly, 'Crimes against Humanity—Revisited: Is There a Role for Economic and Social Rights?' 5 *International Journal of Human Rights* (2001), 58–80.

[45] J.H. Knox, 'Horizontal Human Rights Law', 102 *American Journal of International Law* (2008), 1–47. For a different view, see A. Clapham, 'Human Rights Obligations of Non-State Actors in Conflict Situations', 88 *International Review of the Red Cross* (2006), 491–523. On the relationship between ESC rights and international humanitarian law, see ch. 11 by G. Giacca in this book.

It is by including socio-economic criminal misbehaviour in international crime adjudication in particular that greater sensitivity can be created to the values underpinning socio-economic rights. Under certain circumstances socio-economic acts can fulfil existing substantive crime definitions. The ad hoc Tribunals have experimented with this potential to some extent. Former High Commissioner for Human Rights Louise Arbour has also advocated for a different vision of justice that is more inclusive of social justice. As discussed in chapter 18 of this book, there have been a few voices in the last decade to deplore the fact that ESC rights abuses have rarely been included within transitional justice processes and mechanisms.[46] Arbour insisted that the current neglect of socio-economic rights in mainstream justice must be corrected and urged to further explore and capitalize on the potential of international criminal law to address the socio-economic dimensions of conflict.[47]

4. Criminalizing the Socio-Economic and Cultural Dimensions of Conflict

As discussed in the previous sections, in the formative stages of international criminal law in the 1990s, similarities in normative content between human rights law and substantive international criminal law were recognized and exploited to give shape to the relatively loose definitions of crimes in the statutes of the ad hoc Tribunals. In this human rights-friendly environment, the Tribunals were not entirely antagonistic to the possibility of addressing socio-economic abuses through international criminal law. In particular, the broad crime definitions of persecution and other inhumane acts as crimes against humanity offered some leeway to import socio-economic human rights notions. In this vein, the Trial Chamber in the *Brdjanin* case considered that the cumulative denial of the right to employment, the freedom of movement, proper judicial process, and proper medical care, if committed on discriminatory grounds, could be qualified as a violation of fundamental rights fulfilling one of the elements of the crime of persecution.[48] Similarly, in the *Simić* case, the Trial Chamber found that when prisoners did not

[46] See ch. 18 by F. Haldemann and R. Kouassi in this book.

Commission on Human Rights, Final report on the question of the impunity for perpetrators of human rights violations (economic, social and cultural rights), prepared by Mr. El Hadji Guissé, pursuant to Sub-Commission resolution 1996/24, UN Doc. E/CN.4/Sub.2/1997/8, 27 June 1997; R. Mani, *Beyond Retribution: Seeking Justice in the Shadows of War* (Cambridge: Polity Press, 2002); C. Chinkin, 'The Protection of Economic, Social and Cultural Rights Post-Conflict', paper series commissioned by the Office of the High Commissioner for Human Rights, 2009, available at <http://www2.ohchr.org/english/issues/women/docs/Paper_Protection_ESCR.pdf> (last accessed 20 November 2013.

[47] L. Arbour, 'Economic and Social Justice for Societies in Transition', 40 *International Law and Politics* (2007), 1–27, 16.

[48] *Prosecutor v Brdjanin*, Case No. IT-99-36-T, Judgment of 1 September 2004 (ICTY), paras. 1031–1049. See also, *Prosecutor v Kupreškić and others*, Case No. IT-95-16-T, Judgment of 14 January 2000 (ICTY), paras. 605, 619; *Prosecutor v Kordić and Čerkez*, Case No. IT-95-14/2-T, Judgment of 26 February 2001 (ICTY), paras. 193 and 195; *Prosecutor v Krstić*, Case No. IT-98-33-T,

have sufficient food and water supply, were kept in unhygienic conditions, and had insufficient access to medical care; this, in combination with the findings that the prisoners were subjected to beatings, led to the conclusion that the prisoners were confined under inhumane conditions which constituted cruel and inhuman treatment as an act of persecution.[49] These examples portray an understanding that socio-economic acts can, in certain contexts, be qualified as persecution, or perhaps also as other acts that constitute a crime against humanity. In this construction there is no direct criminalization of socio-economic rights, but rather a pronounced appreciation of the socio-economic dimensions of crimes.

In the ICC setting, there is perhaps a slightly reduced opportunity to manoeuvre socio-economic narratives into crime charges. In addition to Article 22(2)'s interpretational instructions of strict construction, the drafters of the ICC Statute crafted more precise definitions of crimes, which were coupled with the elaborate Elements of Crimes. In reaction to the ICTY's creative use of the open-ended definitions of persecution and other inhumane acts, the Elements of Crimes specifically lift the standards for these two *actus rei* of crimes against humanity.[50] Yet even in this more refined constellation, there are criminal acts and crime headings that could possibly capture certain cultural and socio-economic features of international crime scenes. Alternatively, the commission of crimes will often have socio-economic consequences for the victims involved that are immediately destructive to their life, health, and dignity. It could serve the expressive and preventative value of international criminal law well if some more attention was paid to the socio-economic nature of these consequences.

A range of different socio-economic notions may be implicated. These are discussed in turn.[51] The relevant human rights protecting these notions serve as the starting point for the analysis, in full awareness that these are not directly applicable or transposable to the international criminal law setting. The idea is to identify the underlying value that these human rights aim to protect and in particular to zoom in on specific features of these rights as applicable in times of violence or armed conflict,[52] and subsequently to look for synergies with international criminal law both in statute and in practice. To this end, some concrete examples are given, where possible and relevant, of instances in which the ICC actors have or

Judgment of 2 August 2001 (ICTY), para. 535. Compare with *Prosecutor v Statić*, Case. No. IT-91-24-T, Judgment of 31 July 2003 (ICTY), para. 773.

49 *Prosecutor v Simić and others*, Case No. IT-95-9-T, Judgment of 17 October 2003 (ICTY), para. 775.

50 For instance for persecution, it must be established that the persecutory act was committed in connection with another crime in the jurisdiction of the ICC, Art. 7(1)(h), Element no. 4 and for other inhumane acts, it must be proven that the act was of a character similar to any other act that can constitute a crime against humanity in the definition of the ICC Statute, Art. 7(1)(k), Element no. 2.

51 For a comprehensive overview in relation to war crimes, see E. Schmid, 'War Crimes Related to Violations of Economic, Social and Cultural Rights', 71 *Heidelberg Journal of International Law* (2011), 523–540.

52 See generally, G. Giacca, *Economic, Social and Cultural Rights in Armed Conflict and other Situations of Armed Violence* (Oxford: Oxford University Press, 2014).

could have taken note of the socio-economic dimensions of the crimes they were prosecuting. The aim of this exercise is to explore the potential for international criminal law to engage with some cultural and socio-economic notions and, on the basis of a few pertinent examples, to engage with the underlying question whether international criminal processes are the most appropriate avenue to address cultural and socio-economic abuses and perhaps root causes of conflict.

A. Food

The right to adequate food is protected in Article 25 of the Universal Declaration of Human Rights (UDHR) and Article 11 of the ICESCR under the general heading of a right to adequate living standards. In General Comment No. 12, the CESCR elucidated that the right to food was inextricably linked to the inherent dignity of the human person.[53] It explicitly held that the prevention of access to humanitarian food aid during internal conflict could constitute a violation of the right to food.[54] In addition, international humanitarian treaties contain provisions specifically geared towards guaranteeing access to food during armed conflict for persons not participating in the hostilities.[55] In elaborating the basic humanitarian principle of distinction that applies during combat situations, the Additional Protocols prohibit starvation of civilians as a method of warfare.[56] The provisions specify that:

> it is prohibited to attack, destroy, remove or render useless for that purpose, objects indispensable to the survival of the civilian population such as food-stuffs, agricultural areas for the production of food-stuffs, crops, livestock, drinking water installations and supplies and irrigation works.[57]

The commentaries to these provisions explain that starvation can also result from omission if there is a deliberate decision not to take necessary measures.[58] They also explicate that a variety of verbs is used to make sure that all eventualities are covered, including pollution of water supplies by chemical agents or the destruction

[53] CESCR, General Comment No. 12, The right to adequate food (Art. 11), UN Doc. E/C.12/1999/5, 12 May 1999, para. 4.

[54] CESCR, General Comment No. 12, The right to adequate food (Art. 11), UN Doc. E/C.12/1999/5, 12 May 1999, para. 12.

[55] See generally, G. Giacca, *Economic, Social and Cultural Rights in Armed Conflict and other Situations of Armed Violence* (Oxford: Oxford University Press, 2014) and J. Pejic, 'The Right to Food in Situations of Armed Conflict: The Legal Framework', 83 *International Review of the Red Cross* (2001), 1097–1109.

[56] Additional Protocol I of 8 June 1977 to the Geneva Conventions of 12 August 1949, Art. 54; and Additional Protocol II of 8 June 1977 to the Geneva Conventions of 12 August 1949, Art. 14.

[57] Additional Protocol II of 8 June 1977 to the Geneva Conventions of 12 August 1949, Art. 14. Art. 54 of Additional Protocol I is phrased slightly differently and adds that the motive for which the starvation is undertaken, to starve out civilians or to cause to move them away or for any other motive, is irrelevant.

[58] Y. Sandoz, C. Swinarski, and B. Zimmerman (eds.), *Commentary on the Additional Protocols of 8 June 1977 to the Geneva Conventions of 12 August 1949* (International Committee of the Red Cross, Leiden: Martinus Nijhoff 1987), para. 4800.

of a harvest by defoliants.[59] Starvation of civilians as a war crime is included in the ICC Statute in Article 8(b)(xxv) but only for international armed conflict.

Outside the context of armed conflict, international criminal law also has the potential to capture severe and large-scale deprivation of food. For instance, it could be qualified as the genocidal act of 'deliberately inflicting on the group conditions of life calculated to bring about its physical destruction in whole or in part',[60] when all the other elements of crime are met. The footnotes in the Elements of Crime explain that the mentioned 'conditions of life' may include deliberate deprivation of resources for survival, such as food or medical services.[61] Similarly, extermination as a crime against humanity can cover food deprivation, as this is explicitly mentioned in Article 7(2)(b) and the Elements of Crime.[62]

These provisions recognize that food can be used as a deadly weapon, a fact well known in particular since 7 to 10 million Ukrainians perished in Europe's breadbasket under Stalin's rule in the famine of 1932–33. In the context of ICC situations, this was most pertinently noted in relation to Darfur. The Commission of Inquiry headed by Cassese found that access to food was curtailed for civilians in various severe ways during the conflict. During the destruction of villages, crops were burnt, implements for food processing wrecked, and cattle and other livestock looted.[63] Moreover, living conditions in the camps and settlements were dire, with inadequate access to food.[64]

Similarly, the ICC Prosecutor charged Al Bashir with indirect methods of killing as an integral part of an overall genocidal policy and of the commission of crimes against humanity. These methods included: (i) subjecting the group to destruction of their means of survival in their homeland; (ii) systematic displacement from their homes into inhospitable terrain where some died as a result of thirst, starvation and disease; (iii) usurpation of the land; and (iv) denial and hindrance of medical and other humanitarian assistance needed to sustain life in camps for internally displaced persons.[65] This policy of including slow-death measures in the

[59] Y. Sandoz, C. Swinarski, and B. Zimmerman (eds.), *Commentary on the Additional Protocols of 8 June 1977 to the Geneva Conventions of 12 August 1949* (International Committee of the Red Cross, Leiden: Martinus Nijhoff 1987), para. 4801.

[60] ICC Statute, Art. 6(c)

[61] Elements of Crime, Art. 6(c), Element 4, fn. 4.

[62] Elements of Crime, Art. 7(1)(b), Element 1, fn. 9.

[63] Report of the International Commission of Inquiry on Darfur to the United Nations Secretary-General, Pursuant to Security Council Resolution 1564 of 18 September 2004, Geneva, 25 January 2005, paras. 235 and 305. On issues relating to access to food in the context of the conflict in Darfur, see, e.g. UN Economic and Social Council, 'Situation of human rights in the Darfur region of the Sudan', Report of the United Nations High Commissioner for Human Rights and Follow Up to the World Conference on Human Rights, Sudanese Human Rights Organization, 'The Situation of Human Rights In Sudan', 26 March 2003; Sudanese Human Rights Organization, 'Report on the situation of Human Rights in Sudan, 1 October 2003–31 January 2004', 5 February 2004, Amnesty International, 'Sudan: No One to Complaint To: No Respite for the Victims, Impunity for the Perpetrators', 2 December 2004.

[64] Report of the International Commission of Inquiry on Darfur to the United Nations Secretary-General, Pursuant to Security Council Resolution 1564 of 18 September 2004, Geneva, 25 January 2005, para. 196.

[65] *Prosecutor v Al Bashir*, Case No. ICC-02/05-01/09, Second Decision on the Prosecution's Application for a Warrant of Arrest (ICC), 12 July 2010, para. 34.

charges presents a significant attempt to integrate socio-economic abuses in the overall crime picture and thus to take the socio-economic dimension into account at the ICC setting.

B. Water

The right to water is not recognized as such in the ICESCR and not even in the UDHR. In 2002, the CESCR did, however, adopt General Comment No. 15 on the Right to Water, which brought this right in the realm of Article 11(1) on adequate standards of living, stating that 'the right to water clearly falls within the category of guarantees essential for securing an adequate standard of living, particularly since it is one of the most fundamental conditions for survival'.[66] It further specified, 'an adequate amount of safe water is necessary to prevent death from dehydration, to reduce the risk of water-related disease'.[67]

The General Comment refers to a variety of international documents that have recognized the right to water, such as CEDAW and the CRC. The Committee also made use of the 1949 Geneva Conventions and the 1977 Additional Protocols to construe some of the corollaries of the right to water.[68] Reference to concrete obligations arising from international humanitarian law are accompanied by the following statement:

> during armed conflicts, emergency situations and natural disasters, the right to water embraces those obligations by which States parties are bound under international humanitarian law. This includes protection of objects indispensable for survival of the civilian population, including drinking water installations and supplies and irrigation works, protection of the natural environment against widespread, long-term and severe damage and ensuring that civilians, internees and prisoners have access to adequate water.[69]

Even if the affirmation, or perhaps creation, of the right to water has not remained undisputed, in spite of its recognition by the UN General Assembly,[70] these statements do recognize that the deprivation of safe water may, in the extreme, have direct repercussions for the life, health, and dignity of individuals—values that international criminal law purports to protect.

[66] CESCR, General Comment No. 15, The right to water (Arts. 11 and 12), 2002, UN Doc. E/C.12/2002/11, para. 3,.

[67] CESCR, General Comment No. 15, The right to water (Arts. 11 and 12), 2002, UN Doc. E/C.12/2002/11, para. 2. See E. Riedel, 'The Human Right to Water and General Comment No. 15 of the CESCR', in E. Riedel and P. Rothen (eds.), *The Human Right to Water* (Berlin: Berliner Wissenschaftsverlag, 2007), 19-36.

[68] Reference is made to Arts. 20, 26, 29, and 46, GCIII; Arts. 85 and 89, GCIV; Arts. 54 and 55, API; Arts. 5 and 14 APII; CESCR, General Comment No. 15, The right to water (Arts. 11 and 12), 2002, UN Doc. E/C.12/2002/11, para. 4.

[69] CESCR, General Comment No. 15, The right to water (Arts. 11 and 12), 2002, UN Doc. E/C.12/2002/11, para. 22. Relevant provisions include Art. 14 of Additional Protocol II of 8 June 1977 to the Geneva Conventions of 12 August 1949,

[70] The United Nations General Assembly explicitly recognized the human right to water and sanitation and acknowledged that clean drinking water and sanitation are essential to the realization of all human rights. UNGA, Resolution 64/292, 28 July 2010.

The Cassese Commission of Inquiry also recognized how water was used as a method of warfare in Darfur. Water pumps, wells, and containers were systematically destroyed and poisoned by dropping the carcasses of cattle into them.[71] Moreover, women who would go to fetch water outside the camps ran the continuous risk of being raped.[72] In the second Arrest Warrant against Al Bashir, which reinstated genocidal charges, it was explicitly acknowledged that, in furtherance of a genocidal policy, Sudanese state forces had contaminated the wells and water pumps of the town and villages which were primarily inhabited by the targeted tribal groups.[73] So even if the general existence of an overall right to water as a human right remains disputed, within the international criminal law context it is appreciated that severe deprivation may amount to an international crime. As was already indicated above, the charges against Al Bashir display a certain awareness that the socio-economic dimensions of violence may be of comparable gravity as more direct forms of killing and mistreatment.

C. Healthcare

The right to health is protected by Article 12 of the ICESCR as well as by other provisions in specialized human rights treaties.[74] General Comment No. 14 purports to provide an authoritative interpretation of this right.[75] In its Comment, the CESCR specifically refers to more concrete legal obligations for states in times of armed conflict arising from international humanitarian law. In this context, the CESCR explicitly specified that the obligation to respect the right to health includes an obligation for states to refrain from limiting access to health services as a punitive measure.[76] International humanitarian law does indeed provide a set of quite detailed rules on protecting health during armed conflict. In fact, the aim to collect and care for the wounded was one of the primary concerns that

[71] Antonio Cassese et al., *Report of the International Commission of Inquiry on Darfur to the United Nations Secretary General*, 25 January 2005, paras. 235 and 305; UN Economic and Social Council, 'Situation of human rights in the Darfur region of the Sudan', Report of the United Nations High Commissioner for Human Rights and Follow Up to the World Conference on Human Rights, Sudanese Human Rights Organization, 'The Situation of Human Rights In Sudan', 26 March 2003, para. 50.

[72] Antonio Cassese et al., *Report of the International Commission of Inquiry on Darfur to the United Nations Secretary General*, 25 January 2005, paras. 341 and 342.

[73] *Prosectuor v Al Bashir*, Case No. ICC-02/05-01/09, Second warrant of arrest issued by Pre-Trial Chamber I (ICC), 12 July 2010, para. 7.

[74] 1965 Convention on the Elimination of all forms of Racial Discrimination, Art. 5(e)(iv); 1979 Convention on the Elimination on all forms of Discrimination Against Women, Arts. 11(1) and 12; 1989 Convention on the Rights of the Child, Art. 24, ICESCR, Art. 11; 1981 African Charter on Human and Peoples' Rights, Art. 16 ACHPR, Additional Protocol on Economic and Social Rights to the 1969 Inter-American Convention on Human Rights, Art. 10; CESCR, General Comment 14, The right to the highest attainable standard of health (Art. 12), 2000, UN. Doc., E/C.12/2000/4, para. 2.

[75] See for an insightful overview of the international protection of the right to health, E. Riedel, 'Health, Right to, International Protection', in R Wolfrum (ed.), *Max Planck Encyclopedia of Public International Law* (New York: Oxford University Press, 2009).

[76] CESCR, General Comment 14, The right to the highest attainable standard of health (Art. 12), 2000, UN. Doc., E/C.12/2000/4, para. 34.

prompted Dunant to write about the *Battle of Solferino* and which underlies the entire Red Cross/Crescent movement.[77] In particular, the First and Second Geneva Convention of 1949 and Part II of Additional Protocol I of 1977 contain a great set of provisions regulating the protection and care of the wounded and sick and establishing a system of protection for medical personnel and equipment, hospitals, ambulances, and other medical transport. The Third and Fourth Protocols provide complementary medical protection for prisoners of war and civilians, and the Hague Regulations also contain some relevant provisions.[78]

Some of the primary norms laid down in these Geneva provisions have been transposed to international criminal law and codified as international crimes in the ICC Statute. These include for instance the prohibition of biological, medical, and scientific experiments.[79] The Elements of Crimes explain that the word 'health' refers to physical and mental health or integrity.[80] Other provisions specifically protect buildings dedicated to public health from attack,[81] as well as objects and persons using the Geneva Conventions emblem.[82] The deprivation of medicines or access to medical services may, if all other conditions are met, also arise to genocide or a crime against humanity, as stated.

In line with the rather articulated web of provisions protecting healthcare and medical assistance during armed conflict, several international prosecutions with a medical angle have been undertaken both at the ICTY and the ICC. Defendants Mrkšić, Radić, and Šljivančanin were jointly prosecuted at the ICTY in relation to an incident where Serb soldiers transferred approximately 300 Croats and non-Serbs who had sought refuge at the Vukovar Hospital to a Yugoslav People's Army barracks as a precursor to persecutions, extermination, murder, torture, inhumane acts, and cruel treatment.[83] At the ICC, the denial and hindrance of medical assistance was charged as part of a greater plan in the case against Al Bashir.[84] Furthermore, in the context of preliminary examinations in the situation of Afghanistan, attacks on hospitals and MEDEVAC helicopters were singled out as constituting an attack on protected objects.[85] These examinations have not

[77] H. Dunant, *A Memory of Solferino* (Geneva: ICRC, 1986).

[78] See, e.g. 1907 Regulations Concerning the Laws and Customs of War on Land, The Hague, Arts. 27 and 56.

[79] This is prohibited by Art. 13 of the Third Geneva Convention and Art. 32 of the Fourth Geneva Convention and Art. 11(2)(b) of Additional Protocol I. There is no specific prohibition for internal armed conflict, but the prohibition is understood to be covered by common article 3, see W.A. Schabas, *The International Criminal Court; A Commentary on the Rome Statute* (Oxford University Press, 2010), 217. The prohibition is criminalized in Arts. 8(2)(a)(ii), 8(2)(b)(x), and 8(2)(e)(xi) of the ICC Statute.

[80] Elements of Crimes, Art. 8(2)(a)(ii)-1, War Crime of Torture, para. 1, Art. 8(2)(a)(ii)-2; War Crime of Inhuman Treatment, para. 1, Art. 8(2)(b)(x)-1; War Crime of Mutilation, para. 1, Art. 8(2)(b)(x)-2; War Crime of Medical or Scientific Experiments, para. 1, Art. 8(2)(e)(xi)-1; War Crime of Mutilation, para. 1, Art. 8(2)(e)(xi)-2; War Crime of Medical or Scientific Experiments, para. 1.

[81] Arts. 8(2)(b)(ix) and 8(2)(e)(iv).

[82] Art. 8(2)(b)(xxv).

[83] *Prosecutor v Mrkšić and others*, Case No. IT-95-13/1 (ICTY).

[84] See section 4.A. 'Food'. *Prosecutor v Al Bashir*, Case No. ICC-02/05-01/09, Second Decision on the Prosecution's Application for a Warrant of Arrest, 12 July 2010 (ICC), para. 34.

[85] ICC Office of the Prosecutor, *Report on Preliminary Examination Activities*, 13 December 2011, para. 28; and ICC Office of the Prosecutor, *Report on Preliminary Examination Activities 2012*, 22 November 2012, para. 31.

led to actual prosecutions, but they do display a certain sensitivity on the part of the Prosecutor to the medical aspects of crime scenes. Perhaps a more intricate question is to what extent the ICC Prosecutor should engage with diseases that are the consequences of crime? In many situations where rape is used as a weapon of war, the additional consequences are that victims get infected with HIV/AIDS.[86] The ICC Prosecutor has included, on occasion, references to these consequences without necessarily making them part of the core charges.[87] Such references may serve as an acknowledgement to victims and perhaps on certain occasions these consequences may also be used to prove a given intent, or they may be invoked as aggravating factors for sentencing purposes. Even in situations where socio-economic consequences are not directly relevant to fulfil elements of crimes, they may thus be used in a variety of different ways linked to the criminal process.

D. Humanitarian assistance

The right to humanitarian assistance is not included as such in the ICESCR, but is encompassed by the obligation of states to ensure access to food and medicine.[88] International humanitarian law provides a more detailed set of rules applicable during armed conflict at both substantive and procedural levels, which translates operational issues into a normative system.[89] The Geneva Conventions of 1949 together with the Additional Protocols of 1977, comprise basic rules on the provision of relief to the civilian population, which reflect to a certain extent the corresponding customary rules.[90] Both the more explicit provisions regulating humanitarian assistance during international armed conflict, and the sparser provision for non-international armed conflict, regulate relief actions, but subject these

[86] See, e.g. M. Pratt et al., 'Sexual Terrorism: Rape as Weapon of War in Eastern Democratic Republic of Congo: An Assessment of Programmatic Responses to Sexual Violence in North Kivu, South Kivu, Maniema, and Orientale Provinces, January 9–16, 2004', USAID/DCHA Assessment Report, 18 March 2004; J. Kelly, 'Rape in War: Motives of Militia in the DRC', United States Institute of Peace, Special Report No. 243, June 2010.

[87] *Prosecutor v Bemba Gombo*, Case No. ICC-01/05-01/08, Public Redacted Version of Document Containing the Charges, 1 October 2008 (ICC).

[88] ICESCR, Arts. 11 and 12. See also, First Geneva Convention of 1949, Arts. 12 and 32; Second Geneva Convention of 1949, Art. 12; Third Geneva Convention of 1949, Arts. 26, 28, 30–31; Fourth Geneva Convention of 1949, Arts. 23, 55, 59, 76, 87, 89, and 91–92, Additional Protocol I of 1977 to the Geneva Conventions of 1949, Arts. 10–11, 54, and 69; Additional Protocol II of 1977 to the Geneva Conventions of 1949, Arts. 5, 7, 14, and 18. See generally, H.-J. Heintze and A. Zwitter (eds.), *International Law and Humanitarian Assistance: A Crosscut Through Legal Issues Pertaining to Humanitarianism* (Heidelberg: Springer, 2011). See also Tahmina Karimova's ch. 6 in this book, 'The Nature and Meaning of "International Assistance and Cooperation" under the International Covenant on Economic, Social and Cultural Rights'.

[89] For instance, it provides for the rules regulating the practical provision on the delivery of relief operations on free passage, or for the freedom of movement for authorized humanitarian relief personnel.

[90] ICRC Customary International Humanitarian Law Study, Rules 31, 32, 55, and 56.

to State consent.[91] In addition, Additional Protocol I contains a specific provision protecting relief personnel.[92]

This level of protection was increased with the ICC Statute's criminalization of intentional attacks against personnel, installations, material, units, and vehicles involved in humanitarian assistance or peace operations as a war crime both in international as well as in non-international armed conflict.[93] The UN Secretary-General has identified violence against humanitarian personnel as among the most severe and prevalent constraints in humanitarian access.[94] Through an analogous interpretation of Article 9 of the Convention on the Safety of the UN and Associated Personnel, abduction can also be regarded as an attack and thus come within the purview of the relevant ICC provisions on war crimes. As indicated by various scholars, this provision does not add much in terms of legal framework, since civilian personnel and objects already enjoyed a good level of protection. It has thus been argued that the provision is merely symbolic. Yet, the articulation that attacks against personnel and objects involved in humanitarian assistance missions are considered international crimes does serve the expressive function of international criminal law and sends a clear political message of the importance that the international community attaches to such undertakings.[95] The ICC Prosecutor has already brought charges on the basis of this provision.[96] These charges concerned peace operations rather than humanitarian assistance missions, but this practice does demonstrate that the mere symbolic value of the provision in legal terms is overtaken by its expressive potential in terms of the message that is being conveyed. In addition to this concrete protective provision, wilfully impeding relief supplies can also be a war crime under Article 8(2)(b)(xxv) if it is done with the intention to starve the civilian population. Again, the criminalization in this respect is limited to the context of international armed conflict.[97]

A distinct, but notable instance in which the actions of humanitarian organizations also played a role in the construction of legal realities concerned the Darfur situation. The Commission of Inquiry had the specific task of investigating whether

[91] See, e.g. Fourth Geneva Convention of 1949, Arts. 23, 30, 55, 59(1), 142; Additional Protocol I of 1977 to the Geneva Conventions of 1949, Arts. 68, 69, and 70(1)-(5); Additional Protocol II of 1977 to the Geneva Conventions of 1949, Art. 14(1)-(2). See further, J. Pejic, 'The Right to Food in Situations of Armed Conflict: The Legal Framework', 83 *International Review of the Red Cross* (2001), 1097–1109, 1102–1108.

[92] Art. 71 of Additional Protocol I of 1977.

[93] Arts. 8(2)(b)(iii) and (2)(e)(iii) of the ICC Statute.

[94] UNSG, Report of the Secretary-General on the protection of civilians in armed conflict, S/2009/277, 29 May 2009, Annex I, II, and III. Following the report of the UNSG, the UNSC in its Resolution 1894 (2009) on the protection of civilians in armed conflict underlined for its part 'the severity and prevalence of constraints on humanitarian access, as well as the frequency and gravity of attacks against humanitarian personnel and objects and the significant implications of such attacks for humanitarian operations', preamble, para. 11.

[95] W.A. Schabas, *The International Criminal Court; A Commentary on the Rome Statute* (New York: Oxford University Press, 2010), 229.

[96] See, e.g. *Prosecutor v Abu Garda*, Case No. ICC-02/05-02/09, Decision on Confirmation of Charges, 8 February 2010 (ICC), para. 21.

[97] See more elaborately, C. Rottensteiner, 'The denial of humanitarian assistance as a crime under international law', 835 *International Review of the Red Cross* (1999), 555.

acts of genocide had been committed in Darfur. It concluded that no genocidal policy could be established. One of the arguments that no genocidal intent could be found was that humanitarian organizations had been allowed to offer their assistance which undermined the theory that Sudanese state officials had acted with an intent to destroy the entire population.[98] Even if perverse, such reasoning might constitute an incentive to abusive authorities to allow humanitarian organizations access.[99] In sum, the current ICC constellation is not entirely insensitive to the need to protect humanitarian assistance.

E. Housing

The right to adequate housing is protected, among others, in Article 11(1) of the ICESCR as part of the right to adequate living standards. The ICESCR has further elaborated on this right in its General Comments 4 and 7.[100] Forced eviction is defined as 'the permanent removal against their will of individuals, families and/or communities from the homes and/or which they occupy, without the provision of, and access to, appropriate forms of legal or other protection'.[101] In General Comment No. 4, it states, inter alia, that forced evictions are prima facie incompatible with the Covenant provisions and can only be justified in the most exceptional circumstances. This statement has been further elaborated in General Comment No. 7 on Forced Evictions. These rules are complemented by specific provisions of international humanitarian law applicable in times of armed conflict.[102] The understanding of a need to protect adequate housing and shelter also resonates in several ICC crimes, such as deportation or forced displacement as a crime against humanity,[103] or a war crime,[104] attacks against

[98] Antonio Cassese et al., *Report of the International Commission of Inquiry on Darfur to the United Nations Secretary General*, 25 January 2005, para. 515.

[99] As set out in section 4.1, the ICC Prosecutor had a different vision on the reality on the ground and alleged that the denial and hindrance of humanitarian assistance in the IDP camps in fact constituted an element that proved genocidal intent.

[100] CESCR, General Comment 4, The right to adequate housing (Art. 11 (1)), 13 December 1991; CESCR, General Comment No. 7, The right to adequate housing (Art. 11.1): forced evictions, 20 May 1997. The practice of forced evictions may also result in violations of civil and political rights, such as the right to life, the prohibition of inhuman and degrading treatment, the right to security of the person, the right to non-interference with privacy, family and home and the right to the peaceful enjoyment of possessions. For instance, the Human Rights Committee, in interpreting the right of persons to be free from arbitrary or abusive interference with the home (Art. 17) of the International Covenant on Civil and Political Rights, proclaimed in its General Comment, that 'States Parties are under a duty themselves not to engage in interferences inconsistent with Art. 17 of the Covenant and to provide the legislative framework prohibiting such acts by natural or legal persons'. Human Rights Committee, General Comment No. 16, The right to respect of privacy, family, home and correspondence, and protection of honour and reputation (Art. 17), 4 August 1988, para. 9.

[101] CESCR, General Comment No. 7, The right to adequate housing (Art. 11.1): forced evictions, 20 May 1997, para. 3.

[102] Fourth Geneva Convention of 1949, Art. 49; Additional Protocol I of 1977 to the Geneva Conventions of 1949, Art. 85(3)(a); Additional Protocol II of 1977 to the Geneva Conventions of 1949, Art. 17.

[103] ICC Statute, Art. 7(1)(d).

[104] ICC Statute, Arts. 8(2)(a)(vii) and 8(2)(e)(viii).

civilian objects,[105] and the attack or bombardment of towns and villages as war crimes.[106]

Deportation and forced displacement were included at the ICTY.[107] In the context of Darfur, both the Commission of Inquiry and the ICC Prosecutor in various cases have exposed the massive displacement of the population and large-scale destruction of villages—two practices that directly impede the adequate housing of civilians. In the preliminary examinations of the situation of Afghanistan, the ICC Prosecutor investigated a different infringement of respect for adequate housing. In this instance, the Prosecutor looked at the use of human shields by forcing villagers to host and feed Taliban members and using civilian houses as military bases and checkpoints.[108] So even if the denial of adequate housing is not criminalized as such, there are a significant number of crimes that have direct repercussions for housing, which are included in the regular international crimes catalogue. Conversely, the violation of concrete ESC rights, such as deprivation of electricity, housing, and other rights that protect essential needs may also lead to the crime of forced displacement.

F. Education

The right to education is protected in Articles 13 and 14 of the ICESCR.[109] In General Comment No. 13, this right is described as a right of empowerment for economically and socially marginalized people, and in particular also for women and children.[110] International humanitarian law offers some complementary protection during armed conflict for buildings of science and education, but these provisions are relatively sparse in their contents.[111] Given this sparseness, two defendants at the ICTY, Kordić and Čerkez, challenged their conviction for wilful damage to institutions dedicated to education as a war crime, claiming that normal education institutions were not protected as such.[112] After lengthy and somewhat ambiguous reasoning, the ICTY Appeals Chamber decided that the war crime of destruction of educational buildings was part of customary international law.[113] This discussion was laid to rest with the ICC Statute, which

[105] ICC Statute, 8(2)b(ii). [106] ICC Statute, 8(2)b(v).

[107] See generally, J. Korner 'Criminal Justice and Forced Displacement in the Former Yugoslavia', International Centre for Transitional Justice (July 2012).

[108] ICC Office of the Prosecutor, *Report on Preliminary Examination Activities 2012*, 22 November 2012, para. 30.

[109] The right is also protected in Art. 26(2) of the UDHR, Art. 5(1)(a) of the UNESCO Convention against Discrimination in Education, Art. 28(1)(b) of the Convention on the Rights of the Child.

[110] CESCR, General Comment No. 13, The right to education (Art. 13), UN Doc. E/C.12/1999/10, 12 August 1999, para. 1.

[111] 1907 Regulations Concerning the Laws and Customs of War on Land, The Hague, Arts. 27 and 56.

[112] *Prosecutor v Kordić and Čerkez*, Case No. T-95-14/2-A, Judgment of 17 December 2004 (ICTY), para. 85

[113] *Prosecutor v Kordić and Čerkez*, Case No. T-95-14/2-A, Judgment of 17 December 2004 (ICTY), para. 92.

expressly penalizes intentional attacks against education buildings as war crimes in both international and non-international armed conflict in Articles 8(2)(b)(ix) and (e)(iv). Again, these provisions may not add much in legal terms to the more general protective provisions of civilian objects,[114] but they do send a political message and may provide some guidance to the ICC Prosecutor as to which civilian objects merit particular attention. In fact, in the situation of Afghanistan, the preliminary investigations of the ICC Prosecutor also focused on the unrelenting assaults on girls' schools by means of arson, armed attacks, and bombs.[115]

In addition, much attention has been paid to the phenomenon of child soldiers, and charges have been brought on this matter in various cases.[116] Similar to the discussion on HIV/AIDS as a consequence of rape, the question arises in this context to what extent the ICC Prosecutor should focus on socio-economic consequences of the crime in terms of lack of education and housing. On the one hand, the argument could be made that more attention for consequences reinforces the expressive and preventative value of international criminal law. On the other hand, the question is whether the courtroom is the proper place for such reflections and exercises. This discussion ties into broader reflections on the proper role and function of international criminal justice. The mainstream position currently is that international criminal trials are not the proper place for grand historical exercises which explain the economic, social, and other root causes of the conflict. Still, some attention for the societal consequences of criminal behaviour is not necessarily out of tune with the purposes of establishing the contours of criminal responsibility. Even if not directly formulated as part of the charges, the ICC Prosecutor may be well placed to shed more light on some tangible socio-economic consequences of concrete criminal behaviour.

G. Culture

Cultural rights are protected in Article 15 of the ICESCR. The normative content of this right is bolstered by General Comment No. 21, which provides some further detail to notions such as 'cultural life'.[117] Moreover, this General Comment

[114] According to Bothe, the provisions even carry the risk of creating unnecessary confusion, M. Bothe, 'War Crimes', in A. Cassese et al. (eds.), *The Rome Statute for an International Criminal Court: A Commentary, Volume I* (New York: Oxford University Press, 2002), 410.

[115] ICC Office of the Prosecutor, *Report on Preliminary Examination Activities*, 13 December 2011, para. 28; and ICC Office of the Prosecutor, *Report on Preliminary Examination Activities 2012*, 22 November 2012, para. 31.

[116] *Prosecutor v Lubanga*, Case No. ICC-01/04-01/06, Decision on Confirmation of Charges, 29 January 2007 (ICC); *Prosecutor v Katanga and Chui*, ICC-01/04-01/07, Decision on Confirmation of Charges, 30 September 2008 (ICC); *Prosecutor v Ntaganda*, ICC-01/04-02/06, Decision on Prosecutions', Application under Art. 58, 18 July 2012 (ICC); *The Situation in Uganda*, ICC-02/04, Warrant of Arrest for Okot Odhiambo, 8 July 2005 (ICC); *The Situation in Uganda*, ICC-02/04, Warrant of Arrest for Vincent Otti, 8 July 2005 (ICC); *The Situation in Uganda*, ICC-02/04-01/05, Warrant of Arrest for Joseph Kony, Issued on 8 July 2005 (ICC), as amended on 27 September 2005.

[117] CESCR, General Comment No. 21, Right of everyone to take part in cultural life (Art. 15. 1 (a))', 21 December 2009, paras. 10–13.

stipulates express obligations for states to respect and protect cultural heritage during times of armed conflict.[118] Similar obligations are laid down in more concrete and legally binding ways in international humanitarian law, such as Articles 27 and 56 of the Hague Regulations and Article 16 of Additional Protocol II. Attacking 'clearly-recognized historic monuments, works of art or places of worship which constitute the cultural or spiritual heritage of people' is a grave breach of Article 85(4)(d) of Additional Protocol I and a serious violation of Article 15 of the Second Protocol to the 1954 Hague Convention for the Protection of Cultural Property in the Event of Armed Conflict. Article 3(d) of the ICTY Statute includes the war crime of seizure, destruction, or wilful damage to institutions dedicated to religion, charity, education, arts and sciences (as well as works of arts and science), and historic monuments—and several charges based on this provision were brought forward in a variety of cases.[119] For example, the ICTY even found that wilful damage or destruction of institutions dedicated to Islam or Islamic education constituted persecution as a crime against humanity, since 'all of humanity is indeed injured by the destruction of a unique religious culture and its concomitant cultural objects'.[120]

The ICC pays equal tribute to the importance of culture for humanity. The opening paragraph to its preamble reflects a consciousness that 'all peoples are united by common bonds, their culture pieced together in a shared heritage', and a concern that 'this delicate mosaic may be shattered at any time'. In the ICC architecture, the two relevant and concrete provisions are Articles 8(2)(b)(ix) and (e)(iv), which also expressly criminalize such attacks when committed in internal armed conflict. In these more internal settings, the destruction of cultural heritage may not in any way be linked to military purposes but rather be inspired by religious considerations.[121] In the situation of Mali, which was referred to the ICC on 13 July 2012 and in which the Prosecutor started investigations on 16 January 2013,[122] the intentional attack on protected objects was one of the crimes within the purview of the Prosecutor's investigations. On 1 July 2012, she made an express statement that the attacks on the religious shrines in Timbuktu could constitute a war crime.[123]

[118] CESCR, General Comment No. 21, Right of everyone to take part in cultural life (Art. 15. 1 (a))', 21 December 2009, para. 50(a).

[119] *Prosecutor v. Blaškić* Case No. IT-95-14, Judgment of 3 March 2000 (ICTY), para. 185; *Prosecutor v. Naletilić*, IT-98-34, Judgment of 31 March 2003 (ICTY), paras. 603–605; *Prosecutor v Strugar*, IT-01-42, Judgment of 31 January 2005 (ICTY).

[120] *Prosecutor v Kordić and Čerkez*, Case No. T-95-14/2-T, Judgment of 26 Feburary (ICTY), para. 207.

[121] As was argued in relation to the destruction of the Bamiyan Buddhas by the Taliban in March 2001, F. Francioni and F. Lenzerini, 'The Destruction of the Buddhas of Bamiyan and International Law', 14 *European Journal of International Law* (2003) 619–651, 620.

[122] ICC Office of the Prosecutor, *Situation in Mali: Article 53(1) Report*, 16 January 2013, paras. 1 and 175.

[123] ICC, 'Prosecutor's statement on Mali, News, OTP Briefing, Issue No. 126, 20 June 2012–3 July 2012, available at <http://www.icc-cpi.int/NR/rdonlyres/B8B506C8-E2DE-4FF5-A843-B0687C28AA6C/284735/OTPBriefing20June3July2012.pdf> (last accessed 20 November 2013).

5. Conclusion

The nature of ESC rights is not necessarily incompatible with the strictures of international criminal law. The preceding discussion illustrates that there is ample opportunity to include socio-economic and cultural concerns in mainstream criminal justice modalities. Despite some modest efforts principally by the ICTY and the ICC to import such notions in the international criminal law architecture, scholarly critiques have exposed the neglect of the socio-economic dimensions of conflict in transitional justice processes.[124] It is argued that socio-economic grievances, such as systematic discrimination or unequal access to land, work, and housing, trigger conflict or exacerbate social tensions,[125] and that the current justice processes offer only a one-dimensional narrative that is focused on physical violence and in which economic structural root causes remain invisible.[126] In this vein, Mark Drumbl has observed that a greater emphasis on such dimensions in traditional criminal justice processes would serve in particular the expressive and preventative purposes of international criminal law.[127] However, he also noted the limitations of such processes,[128] which arise in part from international criminal law's individualized focus both in terms of perpetrators and victims. Indeed, other scholars also advocate integrating socio-economic concerns in broader transitional justice processes with perhaps slightly lesser focus on criminal law with its rigid legality requirements.[129] These processes include truth commissions,[130] human rights courts,[131] and a greater focus on housing, land reform, and property

[124] L. Arbour, 'Economic and Social Justice for Societies in Transition', 40 *International Law and Politics* (2007), 1–27; E. Schmid, 'War Crimes Related to Violations of Economic, Social and Cultural Rights', 71 *Heidelberg Journal of International Law* (2011), 523–540; S.C. Agbakwa, 'A Path Least Taken: Economic and Social Rights and the Prospects of Conflict Prevention and Peacebuilding in Africa', 47 *Journal of African Law* (2003), 38–64; M. A. Drumbl, *Accountability for Property Crimes and Environmental War Crimes, Prosecution Litigation, and Development*, International Centre For Transitional Justice, 2009.

[125] L. Arbour, 'Economic and Social Justice for Societies in Transition', 40 *International Law and Politics* (2007), 1–27, 8–9; S.C. Agbakwa, 'A Path Least Taken: Economic and Social Rights and the Prospects of Conflict Prevention and Peacebuilding in Africa', 47 *Journal of African Law* (2003), 38–64, 40.

[126] Z. Miller, 'Effects of Invisibility: In Search of the "Economic" in Transitional Justice', 2 *The International Journal of Transitional Justice* (2008), 266–291.

[127] M.A. Drumbl, *Accountability for Property Crimes and Environmental War Crimes, Prosecution Litigation, and Development*, International Centre For Transitional Justice, 2009, 21.

[128] M.A. Drumbl, *Accountability for Property Crimes and Environmental War Crimes, Prosecution Litigation, and Development*, International Centre For Transitional Justice, 2009, 22–25.

[129] Chapter 18. L. Arbour, 'Economic and Social Justice for Societies in Transition', 40 *International Law and Politics* (2007), 1–27, 14–16.

[130] L.J. Laplante, 'Note from the Field: Truth Commissions, Reparations and the Right to Development', 10 *Yale Human Rights and Development Law Journal* (2007), 141–177.

[131] For instance, the Inter-American Court of Human Rights has issued reparations for human rights violations occurring during conflict, see *Plan de Sanchez Massacre v Guatemala* Case, 2004 Inter-Am. Ct. H.R. (ser. C) No. 116, at 101 (Nov. 19, 2004), as cited by L. Arbour, 'Economic and Social Justice for Societies in Transition', 40 *International Law and Politics* (2007), 1–27, 16, fn. 44.

restitution programmes in peace agreements,[132] also with a view to embedding socio-economic rights in constitutional processes.

In this context, the role of international criminal law is rather marginal, but not necessarily redundant or inconsequential. Given the great social focus on international criminal processes and in particular the ICC, the attention paid to socio-economic abuses by the ICC Prosecutor can help to increase their visibility and to reduce the overall blind spot on socio-economic abuses. Without promoting a need for further convergence of the international criminal law and human rights law regimes, the argument can be made that there are no legal impediments to import certain socio-economic notions in the arena of international criminal law[133] and that there may be a policy argument to do so to some limited extent, with a view to shaping a more encompassing conflict discourse.[134] Such an argument depends on concrete perceptions and expectations that one has from international criminal law, either as an area of criminal law elevated to the international level or as an international form of crisis management.[135] If international criminal law is viewed and appraised through the strict lenses of criminal law with a focus primarily on individual cases, the need to integrate socio-economic notions might be overtaken by other prosecutorial considerations. If the mechanism of international criminal justice is, however, situated within broader reflections on post-conflict justice and peace management, the argument to pay attention to socio-economic and cultural dimensions of conflict, be it only limited, gains weight.

Even if international criminal law has matured and operates with greater respect to fundamental criminal law requirements than in its early years, a development to be applauded, it is argued here that a full analogy to the domestic level would belittle the precise role and function of international criminal law and the context in which it is applied. It may well be that at the international level, the expressive function of international criminal law carries more weight. It is also in this vein that the ICC Prosecutor has developed the concept of the 'shadow of the law' to determine ICC impact beyond the actual cases it adjudicates.[136] It is within the confines of this concept, which acknowledge the great symbolic or educational function of the ICC, that attention to socio-economic abuses may be encouraged, but only to the extent that this does not trespass the boundaries set for a criminal court.

[132] See generally, C. Bell, *Peace Agreements and Human Rights* (Oxford: Oxford University Press, 2000).

[133] As also made by E. Schmid, 'War Crimes Related to Violations of Economic, Social and Cultural Rights', 71 *Heidelberg Journal of International Law* (2011), 523–540, 540.

[134] See generally, Z. Miller, 'Effects of Invisibility: In Search of the 'Economic' in Transnational Justice', 2 *International Journal of Transitional Justice* (2008), 266–291.

[135] For an analysis on the duality of the ICC, see G.P. Fletcher and J.D. Ohlin, 'The ICC Two Courts in One?' 4 *Journal of International Criminal Justice,* (2006), 428–433.

[136] See ICC Prosecutor, Address, Council on Foreign Relations, 4 February 2010, 10; as also discussed in C. Stahn, How is the Water? Light and Shadow in the First Years of the ICC, 22 *Criminal Law Forum* (2011), 175–197.

V

CONCEPTS AND TOOLS TO MEASURE THE PROGRESSIVE REALIZATION OF ESC RIGHTS

13

Budget Analysis and Economic and Social Rights

Aoife Nolan

1. Introduction

Budget analysis is a hot topic. It is a subject of increasing interest to those concerned with monitoring the implementation of human rights, and of economic and social rights (ESR) in particular.[1] While until recently ESR-based budget work was being carried out by a relatively small number of organizations based primarily in Latin America and Sub-Saharan Africa, this work has since been taken up by a wide range of non-governmental, inter-governmental, national human rights institutions, academics, and expert bodies working on a broad spectrum of human rights issues in different national, regional, and international contexts.[2]

The growing focus on, and employment of, rights-based budget analysis is merely one manifestation of a broader move towards the integration of human rights and

[1] From 2008–10, the author was co-manager of the 'Budget Analysis and the Advancement of Economic and Social Rights in Northern Ireland'. This two-year project, which was based at the School of Law Queen's University Belfast, sought to evaluate the compliance of the devolved administration in Northern Ireland with its human rights obligations under the International Covenant on Economic, Social and Cultural Rights (ICESCR). Research produced by the Project is cited as appropriate in footnotes. For more information on Project outputs, see <http://www.law.qub.ac.uk/schools/SchoolofLaw/Research/HumanRightsCentre/ResearchProjects/BudgetAnalysis/Documents> (last accessed 16 November 2013).

[2] For an overview of key examples of existing work on ESR-based budget analysis, see R. O'Connell, A. Nolan, C. Harvey, E. Rooney, and M. Dutschke, *Applying and International Human Rights Framework to State Budget Allocations: Rights and Resources* (London: Routledge, 2014) ch. 2. For further discussion of a range of groups that have carried out such work, see chs. in M. Robinson (ed.), *Budgeting for the Poor* (Basingstoke: Palgrave MacMillan, 2008).

economics discourses at the academic,[3] advocacy, [4] and policy levels[5] The evolving congruence, or at least the emergent conversation, between these respective disciplines has accelerated as a result of the current economic crisis.[6] This is attributable to, first, increasing awareness of the role that neo-liberal, macroeconomic, and domestic economic policies and structures played in causing the crisis, and second, mounting concern about the implications of national and supranational responses thereto for the human rights enjoyment of the most vulnerable in society.[7] As Saiz noted in 2009, 'despite the obvious human rights dimensions of the crisis, human rights have barely figured in the diagnoses or prescriptions proposed by the international community'.[8] Indeed, there is clear evidence that crisis- (and crisis response-) driven cuts to budgetary allocation and expenditure have threatened ESR enjoyment in a range of countries.[9] The former Commissioner for Human Rights of the Council Europe has highlighted that this context renders human rights analysis of budgets 'particularly important'.[10]

[3] See, e.g. Nolan et al., *supra* note 2; R. Balakrishnan and D. Elson, *Economic Policy and Human Rights* (London: Zed Books, 2011); S. Hertel and L. Minkler (eds.) *Economic Rights: Conceptual, Measurement and Policy Issues* (New York: Cambridge University Press, 2010); T. Landman and E. Carvalho, *Measuring Human Rights* (New York: Routledge, 2010); D. Richards and K. Clay, 'Measuring Government Effort to Respect Economic, Social and Cultural Rights', Economic and Social Rights Working Paper Series, Human Rights Institute, University of Connecticut, No. 13 of 2010; and S. Randolph, S. Fukuda-Parr, and T. Lawson-Remer, 'Economic and Social Rights Fulfillment Index: Country Scores and Rankings', Economic and Social Rights Working Paper Series, Human Rights Institute, University of Connecticut, No. 11 of 2009; L. Minkler, 'Economic Rights and Political Decision Making' 31 *Human Rights Quarterly* (2009), 368–393.

[4] For a wide range of example of advocacy work demonstrating a preoccupation with the relationship between human rights enjoyment and economics (particularly budgets), see the website of the International Budget Project, available at <http://ww.internationalbudget.org> (last accessed 16 November 2013). See also, see A Blyberg, 'The Case of the Mislaid Allocation: Economic and Social Rights and Budget Work', 6 *SUR—International Journal on Human Rights* (2009), 123–140.

[5] One example of such integration at a policy level is the growing (albeit still limited) reference of international financial institutions to human rights in their conceptualization and implementation of macroeconomic policy and development policy. See, e.g. the adoption of 'safeguard' policies and the Inspection Panel by the World Bank.

[6] For a discussion of the differences between and the growing congruence between human rights and economics following the economic crisis, see ESCR-Net, AWID, Center for Economic and Social Rights, Center for Women's Global Leadership, *Bringing Human Rights to Bear in Times of Crisis: A Human Rights Analysis of Government Responses to the Economic Crisis* (March 2010), 1–3. For a more general discussion of the complementarity of human rights and economics as disciplines, see, e.g. D. Seymour and J. Pincus, 'Human Rights and Economics: The Conceptual Basis for their Complementarity', 26 *Development Policy Review* (2008), 387–405.

[7] See, e.g. ESCR-Net, AWID, Center for Economic and Social Rights, Center for Women's Global Leadership, *Bringing Human Rights to Bear in Times of Crisis: A Human Rights Analysis of Government Responses to the Economic Crisis* (March 2010), 1–3, available at <http://www.escr-net.org/usr_doc/HRResponsestoEconCrisis_Final.pdf> (last accessed 16 November 2013).

[8] I. Saiz, 'Rights in Recession? Challenges for Economic and Social Rights Enforcement in Times of Crisis', 1 *Journal of Human Rights Practice* (2009), 277–293, 280.

[9] See, e.g. the Committee on Economic, Social and Cultural Rights' Concluding Observations in relation to the most recent period state reports of Iceland and Spain: CESCR, Concluding Observations: Iceland, UN Doc. E/C.12/ISL/CO/4 (2012), and Concluding Observations: Spain, UN Doc E/C.12/ESP/CO/5 (2012).

[10] T. Hammarberg, 'State Budgets Reveal whether Governments are Committed to Human Rights' *Viewpoint* (3 August 2009).

Given the resource-dependent nature of many of the obligations imposed by ESR, budgetary decisions have a key role to play with regard to the realization or violation of such rights.[11] This was recognized in a 2009 report issued by OHCHR which emphasized that the budget 'as the instrument that determines the extent of the State's resources, their allocation and prospective expenditures' is of especial relevance to the realization of economic, social, and cultural rights.[12] Indeed, the budget is undoubtedly one of the most important of the 'legislative measures' that states are enjoined to take in order to ensure the full realization of Covenant rights in terms of Article 2(1) ICESCR.[13] More broadly, international human rights law obligations are binding on all branches of government of the states that have ratified the instruments containing them. Thus, those rights should necessarily be taken into account by the legislature and executive when it comes to determining budgetary allocations and expenditures. As such, all rights can be said to have 'budgetary' implications' in the sense that where such rights exist, budgetary decisions should not contravene them.

However, despite recent strides in terms of ESR-based budget analysis practice both internationally and comparatively, as well as growing recognition by international human rights actors of the importance of such work, important issues and challenges remain. These challenges must be addressed if ESR-based budget analysis is to contribute effectively to improved achievement and enjoyment of ESR. As such, they constitute the primary focus of this chapter.

In terms of structure, having opened with a discussion of what 'ESR-based budget analysis' actually is, I turn to the challenges that arise in relation to such activity. I begin by addressing the conceptual challenges that result from the current condition of the international ESR framework as set out in the International Covenant on Economic, Social and Cultural Rights (ICESCR) and interpreted by the Committee on Economic, Social and Cultural Rights (CESCR, or the Committee). The second category of challenges addressed is those of a practical or logistical nature that are faced by practitioners seeking to carry out budget analysis in the performance of such work. The final set of obstacles discussed relates to efforts to use budget analysis outputs for advocacy purposes. The chapter concludes with a consideration of the implications that the economic crisis and the international and domestic responses thereto have for the prospects of rights-based budget analysis as a tool to advance ESR.

[11] While neither ESR nor civil and political rights is either always cost-free or unfailingly requires the expenditure of resources, states' efforts to vindicate socio-economic rights are often more likely to entail the expenditure of resources than efforts to assure civil and political rights. This is due to the more directly resource-dependent nature of socio-economic rights, as well as the fact that the mechanisms necessary to ensure civil and political rights are more likely to already be in place.

[12] OHCHR, Report of the High Commissioner for Human Rights on Implementation of Economic, Social and Cultural Rights (8 June 2009), UN Doc. E/2009/90, para. 46.

[13] A. Nolan and M. Dutschke, 'Article 2(1) ICESCR and States Parties Obligations: Whither the Budget?', 3 *European Human Rights Law Review* (2010), 278–304, at 281.

2. ESR-Based Budget Analysis: A Term with Multiple Definitions

ESR-based budget analysis is a sub-aspect of human rights budget work. Human rights budget work has been described as 'human rights budgeting', 'budgeting or budget work from a human rights perspective' and 'budget analysis and ESC rights'.[14] Given this plethora of terminology, it is vital to clarify the parameters and content of 'ESR-based budget analysis'. I define such activity as the analysis of budgetary decisions using a framework premised on substantive ESR protections set out in international or domestic human rights instruments (for example, in human rights treaties, constitutions, domestic legislation). Ultimately all such analysis seeks to determine the impact of budgetary decisions on the implementation and enjoyment of ESR.

There is a wide range of potential variants within ESR-based budget analysis work. First, such analysis may be rights-thematic, group-based, or both. While some practitioners analyse budgets from the perspective of a particular ESR such as housing,[15] education,[16] or health,[17] others focus on the impact of budget decisions on the ESR of a particular group, for instance children.[18]

Second, ESR-based budget analysis may also vary in terms of the 'budget' (or 'budgetary aspect') being analysed. Budgetary allocation, expenditure, revenue, and international and domestic macroeconomic policy all have implications for the enjoyment of ESR. ESR-based budget analysis may thus focus on a range of different budgetary aspects. In practice, however, most practitioners have focused on the first two budgetary issues. [19] Furthermore, there is variety within ESR-based

[14] Blyberg, *supra* note 4, at 125.

[15] See, e.g. QUB Budget Analysis Project, *Budgeting for Social Housing in Northern Ireland: A Human Rights Analysis* (Belfast: Queen's University Belfast, 2010).

[16] For an example of guidance on how right to education-based budget analysis might be carried out, see IHRIP/International Budget Project, *Reading the books: Government budgets and the right to education* (Washington: IHRIP/IBP, 2010).

[17] See, e.g. Fundar, *Healthcare: A Question of Rights, Not Charity* (Fundar: Mexico, 2002).

[18] See, e.g. the work of the Indian-based HAQ Centre for Child Rights which produces analyses of the impact of national and state budgets from a child rights perspective, including ESR, available at <http://www.haqcrc.org> (last accessed 16 November 2013).

[19] Evidence for this point is provided by the QUB Budget Analysis Project's consideration of a range of key case studies and guidance on ESCR-based budget analysis. The study revealed that practitioners examined numerous dimensions of budgets: 'All documents refer to allocation of resources and past expenditure is discussed by 13 out of the 14 documents. Budget outcomes (the impact that the budget has on the enjoyment of ESR) are considered in 12. Budget outputs (the goods and services produced by the budget) are identified in nine reports, while budget revenue streams were cited in eight. Only four papers discuss the macroeconomics of the budget'. (QUB Budget Analysis Project, *Budget Analysis and Economic and Social Rights: A Review of Selected Case Studies and Guidance* (Belfast: Queen's University Belfast, 2010), at 6). For an example of a recently developed methodology designed to evaluate macroeconomic policies from an ESR perspective, see R. Balakrishnan, D. Elson, and R. Patel, *Rethinking Macroeconomic Strategies from a Human Rights Perspective (Why MES with Human Rights II)* (New York: Marymount Manhattan College/US Human Rights Network 2009).

budget analysis work in terms of the 'kind' of budget being considered, with actors focusing on national, sub-national, or local government level budgets.[20]

Finally, ESR-based budget analysis may either be static or dynamic: 'static analysis evaluates a given budget by itself. Dynamic analysis compares the evolution of budgets over time, looking at variations in allocations and spending over different periods'.[21] Dynamic analysis is particularly important when practitioners are seeking to evaluate the extent to which states are giving effect to their obligations to progressively realize ESR to the maximum extent of available resources in terms of Article 2(1) ICESCR.

Therefore, although all ESR-based budget analysis efforts will involve the employment of a framework premised on substantive ESR protections to analyse budgetary decisions, the framework chosen, the budgetary element analysed, the adoption of a group/rights-thematic approach, and the specific methodology employed will vary from case to case.

3. The Challenges with Budget Analysis

The 'state of play' is outlined with regard to ESR-based budget analysis and the key challenges faced by those seeking to carry out ESR-based budget analysis are discussed. These are, in turn, (a) conceptual, (b) logistical/practical, and (c) advocacy-related in nature.

A. Conceptual challenges related to the International ESR Framework[22]

Although not all ESR-based budget analysis practitioners premise their work on ICESCR, many do so. Of those that do not, many employ frameworks that are strongly influenced by that instrument and use the work of the CESCR to support their arguments.[23] As such, it makes sense to focus on this, the most established and best-known of ESR frameworks, when considering the conceptual challenges faced by those seeking to carry out budget analysis.

[20] A useful South African example of an organization carrying out ESR-based analyses of both national and sub-national budgets is IDASA, which has produced 'Budgetbriefs' analysing both national and provincial budgets from an ESR perspective.

[21] OHCHR, *supra* note 12, at 14.

[22] Much of the following section is derived from A. Nolan, 'Putting ESR-Based Budget Analysis into Practice: Addressing the Conceptual Challenges' in Nolan et al., *supra* note 2, at 46–56.

[23] Of the 14 studies considered by the QUB Budget Analysis Project in its review of existing guidance and case studies on ESR budget analysis, 11 referred to ICESCR and the General Comments of CESCR as points of reference. (QUB Budget Analysis Project, *supra* note 19, at 5. See also O'Connell et al., *supra* note 3, ch. 2.) The three IDASA-authored studies that did not premised their analysis on the South African Constitution, the formulation and the interpretation of ESR of which have been heavily influenced by ICESCR. On the role of international instruments in the formulation of the socio-economic rights provisions under the CRSA, see S. Liebenberg, Socio-Economic Rights', in M Chaskalson et al. (eds.), *Constitutional Law of South Africa* (Cape Town: Juta, 1996), 41.

A major issue faced by practitioners is that the substantive content of ESR duties such as 'maximum available resources' and 'minimum core obligation' is complex and subject to contestation.[24] Questions include: what resources come within the scope of Article 2(1)? How can/should one determine whether the state is making the fullest possible use of the wide range of resources available to it?[25] Is the minimum core an obligation of conduct or result? Is it relative or absolute?[26] Similarly, the tripartite typology of 'respect, protect and fulfil', which has been used by the Committee as an analytical tool in all its General Comments on substantive ESR since its 1999 General Comment on the Right to Adequate Food,[27] has been criticized for its indeterminacy and the overlap between the respective levels of obligation.[28] There are undoubtedly definite advantages to having ESR and the obligations they imposed sufficiently broadly phrased or conceptualized in order to ensure that they should be capable of general application to a variety of individual circumstances and different contexts over time.[29] However, where obligations are vague and overlapping this will have implications for the efficacy of budget analysis as a human rights monitoring methodology. How can one evaluate budgetary compliance with ESR standards if those standards are not clear?[30]

Until recently, only limited work had been done to link these different categories of obligation directly with budgetary processes. While the literature on this point has expanded,[31] important gaps remain in terms of the conceptualization and delineation of ICESCR obligations. Dealing with all of these would be impossible in the scope of a single chapter. Therefore, this consideration is limited to two issues that are especially relevant with regard to the causes, impacts, and responses to financial

[24] A discussion of the many debates surrounding these obligations is beyond the scope of this paper. For a general consideration of the debate surrounding these obligations and their interrelationship with budgetary processes, see QUB Budget Analysis Project, *Budgeting for Economic and Social Rights: A Human Rights Framework* (Belfast: Queen's University Belfast, 2010).

[25] For more the issues surrounding the obligation of 'maximum available resources' and other elements of Article 2(1) ICESCR from a 'budget perspective', see Nolan and Dutschke, *supra* note 13. For a useful discussion of how fiscal and monetary policy decisions influence the resources available for realising rights, see R. Balakrishnan, D. Elson, J. Heintz, and N. Lusiani, *Maximum Available Resources & Human Rights* (New Jersey: Center for Women's Global Leadership, 2011).

[26] For more on the contested nature of the minimum core, see K. Young, 'The Minimum Core of Economic and Social Rights: A Concept in Search of Content', 33 *Yale Journal of International Law* (2008), 113–175.

[27] CESCR, General Comment No. 12 on the right to adequate food (art. 11), UN Doc. E/C.12/1999/5 (1999). For more on the evolution of the tripartite typology and its application by the CESCR, see A Nolan, 'Addressing Economic and Social Rights Violations by Non-state Actors through the Role of the State: A Comparison of Regional Approaches to the 'Obligation to Protect', 9 *Human Rights Law Review* (2009), 225–255; I. Koch, 'Dichotomies, Trichotomies or Waves of Duties?', 5 *Human Rights Law Review* (2005), 81–103, 84–7.

[28] See O'Connell et al., *supra* note 3, Ch. 4; QUB Budget Analysis Project, *supra* note 23, at 48.

[29] A. Nolan, M. Langford, and B. Porter, 'The Justiciability of Social and Economic Rights: An Updated Appraisal' *NYU Centre for Human Rights and Global Justice Working Paper Series*, No.15 of 2007, at 14.

[30] This paragraph is taken from Nolan, *supra* note 22, at 46.

[31] Notable examples include QUB Project Analysis, *supra* note 23; IHRIP, 'Government Human Rights Obligations and Budget Work' (IHRIP, 2008); A. Blyberg, 'Notes from an International Roundtable Discussion on the Obligation to Use "Maximum of Available Resources"' (IBP/IHRIP, 2008).

and economic crises: retrogressive measures and the role of private (non-state) actors in the delivery of ESR-related goods and services.

In the context of delineating the different elements of the obligations imposed by Article 2(1) ICESCR, the Committee on Economic, Social and Cultural Rights' General Comment No. 3 makes it clear that a prohibition on taking deliberately retrogressive measures in terms of Covenant rights is implicit in the duty of progressive realization. According to the Committee,

> any deliberately retrogressive measures in that regard would require the most careful consideration and would need to be fully justified by reference to the totality of the rights provided for tine the covenant and in the context of the full use of the maximum available resources.[32]

Sepúlveda has argued that in budgetary terms, this includes unjustified reductions in public expenditure devoted to the implementation of ESR in the absence of adequate compensatory measures for the protection of injured individuals.[33]

Prior to the crises, the Committee had provided some limited guidance on the approach that it will adopt in evaluating the acceptability of retrogressive measures.[34] In a statement on 'An Evaluation of the Obligation to Take Steps to the "Maximum of Available Resources" under an Optional Protocol to the Covenant', the Committee highlighted that, should a state party use 'resource constraints' as an explanation for any retrogressive steps taken, the Committee would consider such information on a country-by-country basis in the light of 'objective criteria'.[35] Such criteria would include: the country's level of development; the severity of the alleged breach (in particular whether the situation concerned the enjoyment of the minimum core content of the Covenant); the country's current economic situation (in particular whether the country was undergoing a period of economic recession); (d) the existence of other serious claims on the state party's limited resources (for example, resulting from a recent natural disaster or from recent internal or international armed conflict); (e) whether the state party had sought to identify low-cost options; and (f) whether the state party had sought cooperation and assistance or rejected offers of resources from the international community for the purposes of implementing the provisions of the Covenant without sufficient reason.[36] The Committee did not, however, use this statement as an opportunity to define what a retrogressive measure actually is, apparently regarding the term as self-explanatory.

[32] CESCR General Comment No. 3, para. 9.

[33] M. Sepúlveda Carmona, *The Nature of the Obligations under the International Covenant on Economic, Social and Cultural Rights* (Antwerp, Intersentia, 2003), at 324.

[34] For more on the Committee's approach to retrogressive measures, see C. Courtis, 'The Prohibition of Retrogression in the Area of Economic, Social and Cultural Rights: An Introductory Outline', in A Nolan (ed.), *Economic and Social Rights after the Global Financial Crisis* (Cambridge: Cambridge University Press, forthcoming 2014).

[35] CESCR, An Evaluation of the Obligation to Take Steps to the "Maximum of Available Resources" under an Optional Protocol to the Covenant, UN Doc. E/C.12/2007/1 (2007), para. 10.

[36] CESCR, An Evaluation of the Obligation to Take Steps to the "Maximum of Available Resources" under an Optional Protocol to the Covenant, UN Doc. E/C.12/2007/1 (2007), para. 10.

The conception of a retrogressive measure thus remains nebulous. Among other things, the Committee has never addressed the difference between retrogressive measures that are 'deliberate' and those that are not. Nor has the Committee consistently engaged with, or attempted to delineate, the circumstances in which such a measure might be permissible in terms of concrete examples so as to build on the 'test' outlined in its General Comment No. 3, other than to comment in a number of other General Comments that states are required to ensure 'there has been the most careful consideration of all alternatives'.[37] A number of other General Comments have highlighted that the adoption of any retrogressive measures incompatible with the 'core obligations' under the Covenant would be impermissible.[38] In only one General Comment, however, has the Committee delineated detailed examples of the retrogressive measures.[39] Furthermore, it was only in General Comment No. 19, in the context of the right to social security, that the Committee proceeded to outline in detail some of the key factors it would employ in considering whether a retrogressive measure was justifiable in terms of the Covenant.[40]

The Committee has also failed to consider the notion of limitations on Covenant rights in terms of Article 4 ICESCR. According to that provision, states parties may only subject the rights set out in that instrument to such limitations 'as are determined by law' and 'only in so far as this may be compatible with the nature of these rights and solely for the purpose of promoting the general welfare in a democratic society'. Not only has the Committee failed to outline the scope of such limitations in any detail, it has also failed to address the relationship (if any) between Article 4 limitations and retrogressive measures.[41]

[37] CESCR General Comment No. 19, para. 42; CESCR General Comment No. 18, para. 21; CESCR General Comment No. 17, para. 27; CESCR General Comment No. 15, para. 19; CESCR General Comment No. 14, para. 32; and CESCR General Comment No. 13, para. 45.

[38] See CESCR General Comment No. 15, para. 42; CESCR General Comment No. 14, para. 48.

[39] See CESCR General Comment No.18 on the right to work (art. 6), UN Doc. E/C.12/GC/18 (2006), para. 34: 'As for all other rights in the Covenant, there is a strong presumption that retrogressive measures taken in relation to the right to work are not permissible. Such retrogressive measures include, inter alia, denial of access to employment to particular individuals or groups, whether such discrimination is based on legislation or practice, abrogation or suspension of the legislation necessary for the exercise of the right to work or the adoption of laws or policies that are manifestly incompatible with international legal obligations relating to the right to work. An example would be the institution of forced labour or the abrogation of legislation protecting the employee against unlawful dismissal. Such measures would constitute a violation of States parties' obligation to respect the right to work'.

[40] CESCR General Comment No.19, para. 42. Here, the Committee stated that with regard to the justifiability of retrogressive measures in the area of social security, it would look carefully at '(a) there was reasonable justification for the action; (b) alternatives were comprehensively examined; (c) there was genuine participation of affected groups in examining the proposed measures and alternatives; (d) the measures were directly or indirectly discriminatory; (e) the measures will have a sustained impact on the realization of the right to social security, an unreasonable impact on acquired social security rights or whether an individual or group is deprived of access to the minimum essential level of social security; and (f) whether there was an independent review of the measures at the national level'.

[41] For more on this point, see Nolan, *supra* note 22, at 49. For a variety of views of the inter-relationship (or not) between Arts. 4 and 2(1), see S. Leckie, 'Another Step Towards Indivisibility: Identifying the Key Features of Violations of Economic, Social and Cultural Rights', 20 *Human Rights Quarterly* (1998), 81–124, 98; P. Alston and G. Quinn, 'The Nature and Scope of State Parties' Obligations under the International Covenant on Economic, Social and Cultural Rights', 9 *Human Rights*

Given the ongoing spending cuts and austerity measures impacting ESR enjoyment globally, the Committee's failure to delineate clearly the parameters of permissible retrogressive measures or limitations in terms of ESR proved problematic for ESR advocates in the post-financial/economic crises era. In her 2011 annual report, the UN Independent Expert (now Special Rapporteur) on the Question of Human Rights and Extreme Poverty highlighted that a number of economic 'recovery measures' taken by states, such as cuts to social protection systems, may violate the prohibition of retrogressive measures.[42]

Given this continuing dearth of engagement with retrogression, the post-crises efforts of ESR advocates, including budget analysis practitioners, have been greatly aided by the Committee's work in this area since May 2012. That month saw the Chairperson of the Committee address a letter to states parties 'in relation to the protection of Covenant rights in the context of the economic and financial crisis'.[43] The letter stated that 'economic and financial crises, and a lack of growth, impede the progressive realization of ESC rights and can lead to retrogression in the enjoyment of those rights'[44] and highlighted that the Covenant provides 'certain important guideposts which can help States Parties to adopt appropriate policies that deal with the economic downturn while respecting economic, social, and cultural rights'.[45] This letter undoubtedly constituted progress on the part of the Committee in terms of addressing the issue of retrogression.

The most important part of the letter centres on the requirements that 'any proposed policy change or adjustment' in response to the crises has to meet the following requirements: first, the policy must be a *temporary* measure covering only the period of the crisis; second, the policy must be *necessary and proportionate*, in the sense that the adoption of any other policy, or a failure to act, would be more detrimental to economic, social, and cultural rights; third, the policy must not be *discriminatory* and must comprise all possible measures, including tax measures, to support social transfers and mitigate inequalities that can grow in times of crisis and to ensure that the rights of disadvantaged and marginalized individuals and groups are not disproportionately affected; and, finally, the policy should identify the *minimum core content of rights*, or a social protection floor, as developed by the International Labour Organization, and ensure the protection of this core content at all times.[46]

Quarterly (1987), 156–229, and A. Müller, 'Limitations to and Derogations from Economic, Social and Cultural Rights', 9 *Human Rights Law Review* (2009), 557–601.

42 M. Sepúlveda Carmona, Report of the Independent Expert on the question of human rights and extreme poverty on the human rights based approach to recovery from the global economic and financial crises, with a focus on those living in poverty, UN Doc. A/HRC/17/34, paras. 44 and 47.

43 CESCR, Letter from CESCR Chairperson to States Parties in the context of the economic and financial crisis, UN Doc. CESCR/48th/SP/MAB/SW, 16 May 2012, available at <http://www2.ohchr.org/english/bodies/cescr/docs/LetterCESCRtoSP16.05.12.pdf> (last accessed 25 November 2013).

44 CESCR, Letter from CESCR Chairperson to States Parties in the context of the economic and financial crisis, UN Doc. CESCR/48th/SP/MAB/SW, 16 May 2012, 1.

45 CESCR, Letter from CESCR Chairperson to States Parties in the context of the economic and financial crisis, UN Doc. CESCR/48th/SP/MAB/SW, 16 May 2012, 2.

46 For more on the concept of a 'social protection floor', see ILO Recommendation concerning National Floors of Social Protection, adopted by International Labour Conference on 14 June

This letter constituted a very useful first step on the part of the Committee with regard to delineating state responsibilities in the wake of the global financial meltdown, particularly in relation to austerity measures. However, it is notable that the words 'retrogressive measures' are not mentioned in it. Nor is there reference to the language of General Comment No. 3 with regard to the need for such measures to be 'fully justified by reference to the totality of the rights provided for in the Covenant and in the context of the full use of the maximum available resources'. Furthermore, while the letter is written on behalf of the Committee as a whole, it is not a General Comment. Indeed, it is highly unlikely that it has the status of even soft law.[47]

However, these issues have been addressed to a significant degree by the Committee's subsequent practice. A particularly positive feature of recent Concluding Observations on crisis-affected states parties is that the Committee applied the requirements outlined in the Chairperson's letter to specific national budget decisions and developments, most notably in the case of its Concluding Observations on state reports by New Zealand, Iceland, and Spain.[48] In addressing the New Zealand report, the Committee criticized the 'retrogressive nature and possible discriminatory impact of welfare reforms'.[49] Taking these together with the May 2012 letter, the Committee has advanced in terms of providing examples and standards to advocates who hope to evaluate and criticize retrogression on the part of states parties to address specific budget decisions that impact negatively on ESR enjoyment. The Committee has thus moved to answer many—if not all—of the questions surrounding the scope of impermissible retrogressive measures in terms of ICESCR.

Another example of the Committee failing to provide adequate elaboration of ICESCR—which remains unaddressed—arises in the context of the role of private actors and privatization.[50] Given the increasing global tendency towards the privatization of ESR-related services that have traditionally been delivered by states, as well as what the Committee has described as 'a corresponding increase in

2012, available at <http://www.ilo.org/ilc/ILCSessions/101stSession/reports/provisional-records/WCMS_183326/lang--en/index.htm> (last accessed 25 October 2013), and M. Sepúlveda Carmona and C. Nyst, *The Human Rights Approach to Social Protection* (Finland: Finland Ministry for Foreign Affairs, 2012), 9–10, available at <http://www.cdp-hrc.uottawa.ca/uploads/Human Rights ApproachToSocialProtection.pdf> (last accessed 16 November 2013).

[47] I am grateful to Professor Michael O'Flaherty for his useful insights on this point. (In conversation, 16 November 2012.)

[48] See CESCR, Concluding Observations: New Zealand, UN Doc. E/C.12/NZL/CO/3 (2012), para. 17; CESCR, Concluding Observations: Iceland, UN Doc E/C.12/ISL/CO/4 (2012), para. 6; and CESCR, Concluding Observations: Spain, UN Doc E/C.12/ESP/CO/5 (2012), para. 8.

[49] CESCR, Concluding Observations: New Zealand, UN Doc. E/C.12/NZL/CO/3 (2012), para. 17.

[50] By privatization, I mean 'a shift towards provision by nongovernmental organisations of certain classes or goods and services, or performance by those organisations of certain classes of functions, for the provision or performance of which, individuals have been accustomed to relying exclusively or mainly on government offices and agencies'. See F. Michelman, 'Constitutionalism, Privatisation and Globalisation: Whither the Constitution?' (2000), 21 *Cardozo L. Rev.*, 1063, at 1063.

the role and even responsibilities attributed to private actors',[51] it is vital that the Committee should engage adequately with this issue.[52]

In terms of budgetary processes, resources are directed to private actors by the state for the provision of ESR-related services in a range of different ways; for instance, through the payment of housing benefit to private landlords (whether directly or via the right-holder) or the funding of school tuition vouchers that can be used by students to attend private educational institutions from public funds.

One key way in which the private sector is involved in the provision of ESR-related goods and services is through the increasing use in many jurisdictions of public-private partnerships (PPP) for the delivery of housing[53] and health services.[54] The Northern Ireland social housing example is instructive in this instance. Social housing in that jurisdiction is financed through a PPP where the private partners are housing associations. These private partners do not operate on a profit-making basis. Rather, housing association surpluses are reinvested in housing. The reason for this choice of model was the belief that housing associations could raise additional finance while central government rules barred the state housing provider from doing so. It would thus be possible to assert that the employment of a PPP in this context would enable the generation of greater resources for the realization of the right to adequate housing. However, a study carried out by the QUB Budget Analysis Project found that, 'as housing association debt is repaid using revenue guaranteed or forgone by NIHE, the use of housing associations as a proxy for borrowing is primarily an exercise in creative accounting which keeps government debt off-budget'.[55] Furthermore, the use of housing associations resulted in a number of other costs in terms of both economic and other kinds of resources. In practice, housing associations are less likely than public sector bodies to access borrowing on advantageous terms, while the transfer to housing associations may have also involved a loss of skills and expertise in housing development and undermined economies of scale.[56] Thus, serious questions need to be asked about whether this model of ESR-provision has in fact resulted in the state complying with the 'maximum available resources' obligation set out in Article 2(1). These concerns are not specific to either Northern Ireland or the housing context.[57]

[51] CESCR, Globalisation and its impact on the enjoyment of economic, social and cultural rights, 18th session, UN Doc. E/1999/22-E/C.12/1998/26; ch. VI, section A, para. 515, para. 2.

[52] For an excellent example of an ESR-thematic expert addressing privatization in the context of ESR, see Independent Expert on the Issue of Human Rights Obligations Related to Access to Safe Drinking Water and Sanitation, Report on Human Rights Obligations Related to Non-State Service Provision in Water and Sanitation (June 29, 2010), UN Doc. A/HRC/15/31.

[53] For a discussion of the operation of such partnerships in the housing context, see various reports of the UN Special Rapporteur on the Right to Adequate Housing.

[54] For information on a range of European examples of PPP in a healthcare context, see I. Nikolic and H. Maikisch, *Public-Private Partnerships and Collaboration in the Health Sector: An Overview with Case Studies from Recent European Experience*, Health, Nutrition and Population (HNP) Discussion Paper (Washington: The World Bank, 2006).

[55] QUB Budget Analysis Project, *supra* note 15, at 68.

[56] QUB Budget Analysis Project, *supra* note 15, at 36–37.

[57] See R. Balakrishnan, D. Elson, J. Heintz, and N. Lusiani, *Maximum Available Resources and Human Rights: Analytical Report* (New Jersey: Center for Women's Global Leadership, Rutgers University, 2011), 8–9 for a broader discussion of the resource-related costs that PPPs may pose.

Admittedly—and commendably—the Committee has not ignored the role of private actors with regard to the realization of ESR. Indeed, as I have noted,[58] seven General Comments contain chapters explicitly addressing 'obligations of actors other than states'.[59] However, when focusing on the state's duty with regard to private actors, in the context of the tripartite typology, the Committee has generally based its analysis on the obligation to protect—that is to say, the state's duty to prevent third parties from interfering with ESR.[60] Similarly, much of the Committee's discussion of the role of the state vis-à-vis the satisfaction of ESR-related needs by private actors has centred on the issue of the regulation of such actors.[61] In doing so, the Committee has failed to pay adequate attention to the obligation to fulfil; namely, the duty of the state to adopt appropriate legislative, administrative, budgetary, judicial, promotional, and other measures towards the full realization of ESR.[62]

The furthest that the Committee has gone in terms of considering the issue of resources and privatization in its General Comments is its statement in its General Comment No. 4 on the right to adequate housing:

> While in some states public financing of housing might most usefully be spent on direct construction of new housing, in most cases, experience has shown the inability of Governments to fully satisfy housing deficits. The promotion by States parties of 'enabling strategies', combined with a full commitment to obligations under the right to adequate housing, should thus be encouraged. In essence the obligation is to demonstrate that, in aggregate the measures being taken as sufficient to realise the right for every individual in the shortest possible time in accorded with the maximum of available resources [...] Many of the measures that will be required will involve resource allocations and policy initiatives of a general kind.[63]

[58] See Nolan, *supra* note 22, at 54.

[59] See, General Comment No. 13 on the right to education (art. 13), UN Doc. E/C.12/1999/10 (1999), Ch. III; General Comment No. 14 on the right to the highest attainable standard of physical and mental health (art. 12), UN Doc. E/C.12/2000/4 (2000), Ch. V; General Comment No. 15 on the right to water (arts. 11 and 12), UN Doc. E/C.12/2002/11 (2003), Ch. VI; UN Doc. General Comment No. 17 on the right of everyone to benefit from the protection of the moral and material interests resulting from any scientific, literary or artistic production of which he or she is the author, UN Doc. E/C.12/GC/17 (2006); General Comment No. 18 on the right to work (art. 6), UN Doc. E/C.12/GC/18 (2006), Ch. VI; General Comment No. 19 on the right to social security, UN Doc. E/C.12/GC/19 (2008), Ch. VI; and General Comment No. 21, Ch. IV.

[60] See, General Comment No. 12, paras. 15 and 27; General Comment No.13, para. 50; General Comment No. 16, paras. 19–20; General Comment No. 17, para. 32; General Comment No. 18, para. 25; General Comment No. 19, paras. 45–46; and General Comment No. 21, para. 50(b).

[61] General Comment No. 19, para. 46; General Comment No. 5 on persons with disabilities, UN Doc. E/1995/22 (1994), para. 11; General Comment No. 7 on the right to adequate housing: forced evictions (art. 11 (1)), UN Doc. E/1998/22, annex IV, para. 9; General Comment No. 12 on the right to adequate food (art. 11), UN Doc. E/C.12/1999/5, para. 27; General Comment No. 13, para. 59; and General Comment No. 14, paras. 12(b)(iii), 26.

[62] Paraphrased from General Comment No. 14, para. 33. The Committee has only addressed the issue of privatization in the context of a discussion of the obligation to fulfil ESR twice—in General Comment No. 14 on the right to the highest attainable standard of health (para. 36) and General Comment No. 15 on the right to water (para. 27).

[63] General Comment No. 4, paras. 14 and 15.

Given that such measures can be understood to include privatization, the Committee's statement here can be taken as recognition that such a model will have resource implications. However, while this is a useful general guidance statement, models of privatization vary widely in terms of their form and the extent to which they result in the effective realization of ESR. These models will have different implications for budgetary decisions. Thus far, however, the Committee has failed to engage in any extensive discussion of privatization and ESR, whether in its General Comments or in Concluding Observations.

So, where do these conceptual challenges leave us? If ESR-based budget analysis is to be effective, then practitioners should not—indeed, cannot—ignore the conceptual challenges caused by gaps and confusions in the existing ESR framework. Where an element of the ESR framework being employed is ambiguous or unclear and the practitioner has settled upon a particular interpretation, this should be expressly recognized and the chosen approach justified. Some degree of divergence in interpretation of what are often rather broad standards is inevitable. However, it is notable—and worrying—that there has been relatively little consistency in the application of ICESCR principles and concepts to budgets by practitioners.[64] A failure to explain and justify the specific understanding of ESR concepts that are being employed in different analyses is similarly a feature of much ESR-based analysis work.[65] This will not just have a negative effect on the quality of the analysis presented in specific cases—it may also operate to limit the transferability of frameworks employed by different practitioners to different contexts.

B. Practical challenges in performing ESR-based budget analysis

I now turn to practical challenges faced by those seeking to carry out such work. The most frequent and potentially gravest problem faced by practitioners relates to data. There may be a lack of budgetary data, such data may be inaccessible, or they may not be recorded or presented in such a way as to render budget analysis possible. Blyberg highlights that 'of particular importance for human rights budget work are disaggregated data, that is, data broken down by key characteristics, such as ethnicity, gender and so on'.[66] An example of where a lack of disaggregated data operated as a significant obstacle to ESR-based budget analysis arose in the context of the QUB Budget Analysis Project's efforts to analyse the extent to which the state was giving effect the right to the highest attainable standard of mental health of children and adolescents.

There is extensive evidence of children and adolescents in Northern Ireland experiencing difficulties in accessing mental health patient care.[67] A seminal five-year review of Mental Health and Learning Disability commissioned by the Northern

[64] For examples of this, see, QUB Budget Analysis Project, *supra* note 19.

[65] QUB Budget Analysis Project, *supra* note 19.

[66] Blyberg, *supra* note 4, at 125.

[67] See, e.g. Northern Ireland Commissioner for Children and Young People, *Report by NICCY to the UN Committee on Economic, Social and Cultural Rights on the Implementation of ICESCR in Northern Ireland* (Belfast: NICCY, 2009).

Irish Department for Health, Social Services and Public Safety examined a range of aspects of mental health and highlighted that 'resources dedicated to mental health are often inadequate and inequitable compared to those available to other parts of the public sector, and this is reflected in poor access, neglect and discrimination'.[68] The Review made it clear that there were serious shortcomings with child and adolescent mental health services due to under-resourcing. Among other things, evidence presented to the Commission suggested that child and adolescent mental health represented 3 to 5 per cent of mental health expenditure compared to a UK average of 10 per cent, despite NI having a larger proportion of young people (27 per cent of Northern Ireland's population is aged between 0 and 17 years compared to 22 per cent of the English population).[69] The Review highlighted however, that there has historically been no clear budget line for child and adolescent mental health services.[70] There is thus a lack of clear budgetary data for allocations to this sector, despite the acknowledged vulnerability of this group. Therefore, despite the clear existence of problems arising in relation to the funding of services related to children and adolescent's right to the highest attainable standard of mental health, a lack of disaggregated data severely limits the scope for ESR-based budget analysis to serve as an effective basis for advocacy work on this issue in Northern Ireland.

Another major challenge in terms of 'the practice' of ESR-based budget analysis relates to the issue of capacity. Few human rights experts have a strong grasp of the tools of economic analysis and the same is true vice versa. While ESR-based budget analysis expertise on the part of human rights advocates is growing, skills development remains a key issue for those hoping to carry out such work. Indeed, the potential for such work to become more widespread is necessarily limited by a shortage of training opportunities, human and other resources, as well as time. It is important that those keen to take on such work acknowledge the level of expertise required for such work and that a lack of capacity will directly impact on the quality of the work produced and, subsequently, its efficacy in terms of advocacy aims. Addressing this challenge may entail the strengthening of in-house skills with the assistance of international budget analysis experts and/or the development of partnerships with existing economics think tanks who can perform the relevant analysis.

This latter approach is attractive in that, in theory at least, it involves the combination of complementary expertise. It poses its own challenges, however, given the fact that the growing conversation between human rights experts and economists is by no means always straightforward or successful. Just as human rights advocates will not necessarily have a strong grasp on economic analysis methodologies, nor will economists (even so-called 'progressive economists') find

[68] The Bamford Review of Mental Health and Learning Disability (Northern Ireland), *Mental Health Improvement and Well-being: a Personal, Public and Political Issue* (2006), at 121.

[69] QUB Budget Analysis Project, *Human Rights Obligations and Budgeting for Mental Health in Northern Ireland* (Belfast: Queen's University Belfast, 2012), at 37.

[70] Bamford Review, *supra* note 68, at 63.

it a simple task to employ and apply a human rights framework.[71] Nor will the aims of economists and human rights activists necessarily be the same when it comes to carrying out such work:

For many, particularly those coming from an activist perspective, the realisation of human rights is an end in itself [...] In contrast, mainstream economics has a largely consequentialist normative framework. Human welfare is generally viewed in terms of utility levels, preference satisfaction, etc. Therefore [...] some economists consider human rights to be a means (i.e., a tool) that can be instrumentalised to achieve less distorted or corrupt markets or more equitable development. These are two very different conceptions of human rights. For one group, they are an additional tool or method, to be adopted where they have practical value; for the other, human rights are a goal representing intrinsic values that should not be compromised. [72]

Understandings of key concepts such as 'efficiency' and 'sufficiency' are likely to vary significantly from economists to human rights activists, given the difference in aims that these respective actors attach to the budgetary decisions to which these concepts relate. Balakrishnan and others, for instance, argue that 'efficiency is often defined in terms of the financial costs of the inputs required to produce a particular outcome—greater efficiency implies that more can be produced with a given amount of financial resources'.[73] They point out that employment of narrowly defined concepts of efficiency must be done with care as they may not account for the full impact on social and economic rights; for example, efficiency may appear to improve if governments reduce compensation to public sector workers.[74] However, this will result in the ESR of those workers being compromised: '[i]f so, then such tactics will be less efficient than they appear to be, since the full impact on social and economic rights must take into account the impact on public sector workers'.[75] Thus, an 'ESR-influenced' understanding of 'efficiency' may necessarily be considerably more expansive than that employed by economists.

The potential disconnect between economists and human rights advocates also manifests itself at the methodological level. While there is significant scope for a range of different economic techniques to be employed to evaluate the human rights impact of budgetary decisions, such techniques may not reflect much or all of the full impacts of those decisions on human rights. For instance, in discussing a range of economic analysis methodologies that might be employed to 'appraise (and post-hoc evaluate) government expenditure programmes from a rights perspective',[76] Harvey and Rooney highlight that cost–benefit analysis (which they describe as

[71] For an explanation of these terms, see R. Balakrishnan and D. Elson, 'Introduction: Economic Policies and Human Rights Obligations', in R. Balakrishnan and D. Elson (eds.), *Economic Policy and Human Rights* (London: Zed Books, 2011), 2–3.

[72] ESCR-Net et al., *supra* note 6, at 1 (footnotes omitted). For more, see Seymour and Pincus, *supra* note 6.

[73] Balakrishnan et al., *supra* note 25, at 7.

[74] Balakrishnan et al., *supra* note 25, at 8.

[75] Balakrishnan et al., *supra* note 25, at 8.

[76] C. Harvey and E. Rooney, 'Integrating Human Rights? Socio-economic Rights and Budget Analysis', 3 *European Human Rights Law Review* (2010), 266, at 273.

identifying 'the net value of an expenditure programme by adding its anticipated benefits and subtracting its expected costs')[77] can

> encompass a comprehensive range of impacts [...] However it may also be overly reductionist if it results in the debasement of the concept of human dignity to monetary values [...] [Cost-effective analysis] does not require such monetisation but its focus on very specific outcomes may be too narrow to satisfy the holistic nature of rights.[78]

Thus, 'bridging the gap' between human rights experts and economists effectively may prove to be one of the most significant challenges to ESR-based budget analysis in practice.

C. Challenges in using budget analysis outputs for advocacy purposes

Every attempt to employ budget analysis outputs in advocacy will be faced with its own particular challenges in light of the specific context in which such work is to be carried out.[79] De Renzio and Krafchik argue that factors that shape the impact of budget work generally include the political environment, the legal and institutional framework, the role of international donors, budget literacy, and public interest in budget issues, as well as the relationships that budget work practitioners develop with other actors and stakeholders such as civil society, government, and the media.[80] This is all true of ESR-based budget analysis. Frequent broad obstacles that practitioners and others may face when seeking to employ ESR-based analysis outputs in advocacy include the risk of government resistance to rights-based arguments due to, among other things, the lack of a human rights culture or a historically conflicted relationship between civil society and government.

In this section, however, I will focus on the advocacy-related challenges faced by ESR-based budget analysis efforts that are carried out using an international instrument containing ESR in a jurisdiction where such rights have been excluded from domestic incorporation and/or where there is a prioritization of domestic human rights protections over international human rights protections.

Where governments have not chosen to domestically incorporate ESR, such rights are at particular risk of being ignored both in terms of budgeting processes. A useful example of this is the UK, where the principal human rights legislation, the Human Rights Act 1998 (HRA) has been accused of reflecting a 'distorted vision of human rights'.[81] This is due to the fact that the HRA gives domestic

[77] C. Harvey and E. Rooney, 'Integrating Human Rights? Socio-economic Rights and Budget Analysis', 3 *European Human Rights Law Review* (2010), 266, at 271.

[78] C. Harvey and E. Rooney, 'Integrating Human Rights? Socio-economic Rights and Budget Analysis', 3 *European Human Rights Law Review* (2010), 266, at 271.

[79] For a discussion of how to develop an advocacy strategy around ESR-based budget analysis, see FAO, 'Budget Work to Advance the Right to Food: Many a Slip...'. (Rome: FAO, 2009), 69–76.

[80] See, e.g. P. De Renzio and W. Krafchik, 'Implications for Policy and Practice', in M. Robinson (ed.), *Budgeting for the Poor* (New York: Palgrave MacMillan, 2008), 186.

[81] This criticism was made by Keith Ewing who has argued that, by failing to incorporate social rights into domestic law and hence 'dividing the indivisible', a constitutional hierarchy of rights has

effect to the European Convention of Human Rights—an instrument that accords only very limited protection to ESR.[82] The UK government has proved highly reluctant to contemplate the domestic incorporation of justiciable ESR, in either a national[83] or regional bill of rights.[84] The UK government has also sought to undermine efforts to strengthen ESR protection at the international level, most recently demonstrated by its contribution to the work of the Open-ended working group to consider options regarding the elaboration of an Optional Protocol to the International Covenant on Economic, Social and Cultural Rights. During the working group negotiations, UK representatives consistently sought to limit the scope of a potential Optional Protocol providing for a complaints mechanism in relation to ICESCR.[85]

Interestingly, the UK Treasury's guide to appraisal and evaluation ('the Green Book') states that a range of Conventions, including the ICESCR 'should inform the development of policy'.[86] There is no evidence that this occurs in practice, however. Certainly, the government has thus far resisted carrying out a human rights impact assessment of its post-economic crisis austerity measures—a fact that suggests a reluctance to 'build in' ESR into decision-making.[87] In turn, this bodes badly for advocates seeking to convince the UK of its budgetary obligations under

been created that did not exist prior to the HRA. (K. Ewing, 'The Unbalanced Constitution', in T. Campbell, K.D. Ewing, and A. Tomkins (eds.), *Sceptical Essays on Human Rights* (Oxford: Oxford University Press, 2001), 103, at 103–4).

[82] For more on the protection of ESR through the ECHR and the HRA, see E Palmer, *Judicial Review, Socio-Economic Rights and the Human Rights Act* (Oxford: Hart, 2007), 49–86.

[83] See, e.g. Department of Justice, *Rights and Responsibilities: Developing Our Constitutional Framework* (London: Stationary Office, 2009) in which the previous UK government outlined its vision of a Bill of Rights and Responsibilities of the UK. This report stated, 'some argue that economic, social and cultural rights should be guaranteed as "human rights", carrying the same status in domestic law as the civil and political rights in the European Convention. While many specific welfare entitlements are legally enforceable, the Government believes that such policy matters should generally be developed by democratically accountable elected representatives, rather than by the courts' (para. 3.48). See also the 2013 report of the UK Bill of Rights Commission, a majority of whom 'would be hesitant about' a Bill of rights for the UK containing ESR. (Commission on a Bill of Rights, 'A UK Bill of Rights? The Choice before Us', Vol. 1 (London: Ministry of Justice, 2012), para. 8.28.)

[84] In terms of regional bills of rights, governmental reluctance to domestically incorporate ESR was evidenced by the Secretary of State for Northern Ireland's rejection of the Northern Ireland Human Rights Commission's recommendations that a range of ESR be included in a Bill of Rights for Northern Ireland. Admittedly, the Secretary of State premised his views on the assertion that such rights 'are equally as relevant to the people of England, Scotland and Wales as they are to the people of Northern Ireland and, therefore, fall to be considered in a UK-wide context' (Secretary of State for Northern Ireland, *A Bill of Rights for Northern Ireland: Next Steps* (Belfast, Northern Ireland Office, 2009), para. 3.14).

[85] See, e.g. Report of the open-ended working group to consider options regarding the elaboration of an optional protocol to the International Covenant on Economic, Social and Cultural Rights on its 2nd session (2005), UN Doc. E/CN.4/2005/52, paras. 60 and 103; Report of the open-ended working group to consider options regarding the elaboration of an optional protocol to the International Covenant on Economic, Social and Cultural Rights on its 3rd session (2006), UN Doc. E/CN.4/2006/47, paras. 29 and 93.

[86] HM Treasury, *The Green Book: Appraisal and Evaluation in Central Government*, Annexe 5, 95.

[87] For more, see the statements of the Lord Chancellor and the Minister of Justice, in 'Human Rights Joint Committee—Minutes of Evidence: The Government's Human Rights Policy', 16 November 2010, HL Paper 131/HC 609-i.

ICESCR through the use of ESR-based budget analysis. Admittedly, it is not simply ESR that have not been factored into UK budgetary decisions (no meaningful human rights-based assessment has been carried out by the state).[88] However, it is strongly arguable that the recent cuts to social programmes in response to the economic crisis have greater implications for the enjoyment of ESR by vulnerable groups in the UK than for others' rights. As such, an ESR-based impact assessment is particularly important.

The UK context also serves to illustrate effectively another key issue arising in relation to the employment of ESR-based budget analysis outputs for advocacy purposes. Notably, while there is a growing move towards the employment of ESR-based budget analysis work in ESR-related litigation,[89] the scope for such legal strategy will be very limited where there are no domestic ESR protections on which to hook such litigation. This is evidenced by the fact that, while litigation has been brought in the UK challenging spending cuts that have implications for ESR, these have been premised on duties under equality legislation rather than ESR.[90] A majority of those strategic litigation efforts have not proved successful.[91] The potential for such strategy seems considerably broader in countries where ESR

[88] See, for instance, the UK parliamentary select committee on human rights' criticism of the failure of the Government to provide a full human rights memorandum for the key legislative element of welfare reform, the Welfare Reform Bill 2011. The Committee also bemoaned the Government's 'failure to carry out any detailed analysis of the compatibility of the proposals in the Bill with the UK's obligations under the UNCRC, the ICESCR and the UNCRDP'. (Human Rights Joint Committee, 'Legislative Scrutiny: Welfare Reform Bill', 6 December 2011, HL Paper 233/HC 1704, at 3.)

[89] See, e.g. the Argentinean litigation *Asociación Civil por la Igualdad y la Justicia c/Gobierno de la Ciudad de Buenos Aires* (Expte. No. 23360/0). See also, the use of budget-based argumentation by the applicants in the matter of *Mahlangu v Minister for Social Development & Ors,* Case No. 25754/05 (South African High Court, Transvaal Provincial Division). For an account of budget analysis informing an Indian High Court case which involved health services for pregnant women and children in government healthcare centres in a tribal or low-income area in Maharashtra, see P. Raymus, 'In India Budget Analysis Informs a High Court Case to Protect Local Health for Women and Children' (2011), 58 *International Budget Partnership e-Newsletter* 2, available at <http://internationalbudget.org/wp-content/uploads/2011/04/newsletter58.pdf> (last accessed 16 November 2013).

[90] See, e.g. the litigation brought by the Child Poverty Action Group challenging two of the cuts to Housing Benefit for private sector tenants due to be brought into force in April 2011. CPAG's argumentation is based, among other things, on general equality duties under the Race Relations Act 1976 and the Sex Discrimination Act 1975. In *Child Poverty Action Group v Secretary of State for Work and Pensions*, [2011] EWHC 2616 (Admin), The Upper Tribunal found against CPAG. (For more information, see <http://www.cpag.org.uk/content/court-rules-allow-discriminatory-impacts-housing-benefit-cuts> (last accessed 16 November 2013). On appeal, the case was joined with two others but these equality duties were not addressed by the Court of Appeal in any detail (although the prohibition on non-discrimination in Article 14 of the European Convention on Human Rights was). (For further discussion of that ruling, see discussion of *Burnip* at following fn. 91.) In August 2010, the Fawcett Society sought judicial review of the UK budget claiming that, in not assessing the way in which the budget would impact differently on women and men, the Treasury had not met the requirements of the Gender Equality Duty, under sections 76A and 76B of the Sex Discrimination Act 1975. Judicial review was refused on the grounds that (a) the society had delayed too long in making its application, and (b) the application was 'unarguable', and there was 'no prospect' of a court declaring the budget unlawful. ('Fawcett Society loses court challenge to legality of budget', *The Guardian*, 6 December 2010.)

[91] One notable exception is *Burnip, Trengove and Gorry v Secretary of State for Work and Pensions*, [2012] EWCA Civ 629, where a majority of the Court held that the appellants (tenants in the private sector) had established a prima facie case that the local housing allowance size criteria which was

protections are legally enshrined and the courts are prepared to give effect to them, even in contexts of resource constraint.[92]

The UK thus serves to demonstrate effectively the potential limitations of attempts to employ ESR-based budget analysis outputs to bring about the introduction or mainstreaming of ESR principles into legal and policy processes, where such rights have not been legally enshrined or accorded equal standing with their civil and political counterparts.

Of course, even in countries where ESR have been domestically incorporated, there will frequently be obstacles to budget analysis work. In some instance, this may be attributable to a reluctance on the part of the state to accept the implications of such rights for law and policy design, and implementation.[93] In other cases, there may be a lack of a receptive (political, social, or media) audience for such research: where there is strong societal prejudice to particular groups of right-holders, (for instance, ethnic or religious minorities, migrants), advocacy focusing on the rights of such groups may well fall on deaf ears. There is no doubt, however, that where ESR are not afforded adequate national protection, practitioners are also faced with having to outline why ESR that the state has not chosen to incorporate domestically should be taken into account in state budget decision-making at all. Admittedly, the Committee has highlighted that ICESCR does not formally oblige states to incorporate its provisions in domestic law.[94]

applied to quantify housing benefit discriminated against the three appellants on grounds of disability in terms of Art. 14 ECHR, by not including provision to meet their need for an additional room. This discrimination was unlawful as the Secretary of State had failed to establish objective and reasonable justification for the discriminatory effect of the statutory criteria. A more common approach is that taken by the Court in *MA and others (on the application of) v Secretary of State for Work and Pensions & Ors* [2013] EWHC 2213 (QB) (30 July 2013)—the so-called 'bedroom tax' case in which a challenge was brought against changes introduced to housing benefit regulations reducing the eligible rent for the purpose of the calculation of such benefit in the case of public sector rentals where the number of bedrooms in the property let exceeded the number permitted in terms of the regulations. It was argued that the new measures were discriminatory on the grounds of disability in terms of Art. 14 ECHR with regard to Art. 1 Protocol 1 on the right to property. Finding that there was no unlawful (i.e. unjustified) discrimination here, Laws LJ in High Court stated that the complainants' arguments 'amount to an attempt to persuade the Court to "micro-manage" the policymaking process' (para. 86), and cited previous Supreme Court dicta that a wide margin of appreciation is usually accorded to states in the areas of social and economic policy (paras. 16, 18, and 61): 'in context, it is a function of democratic rule' (para. 62).

92 See, e.g. Case 187/2013 of the Portuguese Constitutional Court which struck down a range of proposed budget-related austerity measures, including cuts to public sector salaries and pensions on the basis of constitutionally impermissible differential treatment of the public and private sectors in the context of the right to a salary and the right to social security (including a pension). For an overview of the varying willingness of courts in jurisdictions with domestically protected ESR to enforce ESR claims (or not) during times of financial or economic crisis, see A. Nolan (ed.), *Economic and Social Rights after the Global Financial Crisis* (Cambridge: Cambridge University Press, 2014). The Court held that the cuts were a violation of proportional equality and that the goal in question—that of reducing the public deficit did not provide adequate grounds for this.

93 A useful example of this is South Africa where, despite extensive constitutional and legislative protection of ESR, there has been a refusal on the part of a range of state actors to regard such rights as directive in the context of budget-related decision-making with regard to ESR-related areas, including housing and education.

94 General Comment No. 9 on the domestic application of the Covenant (1998), UN Doc. E/C.12/1998/24, para. 8.

However, it has made clear that such an approach is desirable.[95] This is certainly true when it comes to maximizing the effectiveness of Covenant ESR-based budget analysis advocacy.

4. Conclusion: Budget Analysis After the Economic Crisis

This chapter opened by highlighting the growing interest in ESR-based budget analysis as an advocacy tool, an interest that has been spurred by the economic crisis. I will conclude by considering the implications of that crisis and the responses thereto for the prospects of rights-based budget analysis as a tool to advance ESR. On the one hand, the harsh effects of the crisis and its 'solutions' have resulted in a broader societal awareness and concern about ESR and the impact of budgetary cuts on enjoyment of those rights. This is evidenced by the growing interest in ESR language and advocacy in jurisdictions such as the UK, US, and Ireland where advocates have historically shied away from, or been unaware of, the use of ESR. It has also created new partners for ESR-based budget analysis practitioners such as public sector workers and policymakers who are keen to engage with such work due to its value as a basis for argumentation in favour of 'shoring up' departmental budgets related to areas such as housing, education, or social welfare.

The economic crisis has also resulted in a greater global focus on 'progressive economics' or non-traditional forms of economics.[96] It might thus be expected that this will result in a greater openness on the part of economists and those responsible for the global economic 'reconstruction' to a new and more human rights-friendly financial and economic model. Indeed, commentators such as the UN Independent Expert on the Question of Poverty and Human Rights have argued that 'the challenge of recovering from successive crises presents a unique opportunity for States to formulate a transformative vision for the future aimed at the full realization of human rights'.[97] Panitch and Konings have highlighted that 'the politicisation of economic life at which the popular response to the current crisis has so far only hinted nevertheless invites the articulation of visions and strategies for social transformation that have not been seen for a generation'.[98] In practice, however, as discussed earlier, human rights have not been integrated in any meaningful

[95] General Comment No. 9 on the domestic application of the Covenant (1998), UN Doc. E/C.12/1998/24, para. 8.

[96] See, e.g. the work of groups such as the Political Economy Research Institute, University of Massachusetts, available at <http://ww.peri.umass.edu/> (last accessed 25 October 2013), and the Irish-based TASC, available at <http://www.tascnet.ie> (last accessed 25 October 2013). See also, R. Balakrishnan and D. Elson, *Economic Policy and Human Rights* (London: Zed Books, 2011).

[97] Independent Expert on the question of human rights and extreme poverty, *supra* note 42, para. 56.

[98] L. Panitch and M. Konings, 'Myths of Neoliberal Deregulation' (2009), 57 May–June, *New Left Review*, 67, at 83.

way to recovery efforts.[99] Nor does the dominance of individualistic, anti-statist, unregulated, free-market liberalism appear to have been displaced by the economic crisis.[100] Indeed, it is strongly arguable that by rescuing the financial markets through taxpayers' money, mainstream neoliberalism has actually produced an opportunity to *intensify* the dominance of individualistic, anti-statist, unregulated, free-market liberalism at the expense of other more 'human rights-friendly' economic models.[101] Thus, while the economic crisis appears to have heightened awareness of ESR as an advocacy tool, it has largely served to shore up existing power distributions and inequalities, to the detriment of ESR enjoyment. Returning to Panitch and Konings, there is clear evidence that 'social justice is necessarily trumped by the goal of returning to business-as-usual' following the crisis.[102]

The fact that international and domestic macroeconomic and microeconomic policy appears to have remained largely immune to ESR-related concepts or priorities will inevitably impact upon the prospects of rights-based budget analysis as a tool to advance ESR. Indeed, given the 'nation state'-centric nature of most human rights-based budget work, as well as the relatively nascent discussion on the extra-territorial obligations (ETOs) imposed by ESR generally,[103] the capacity of ESR-based budget analysis work in its current form to impact on—or even engage effectively with—with often supranational issues such as deregulation, international economic governance, and the role of non-state actor international financial

[99] Paul O'Connell has argued that the post-crisis austerity drive has little or nothing to do with objective, economic necessity, but instead is driven by an ideological and political project to further entrench neoliberal capitalism in a nutshell and should be understood as the natural order with respect to government attitudes to socio-economic rights. (P. O'Connell, 'Let Them Eat Cake: Socio-economic Rights in An Age of Austerity', in Nolan et al., *supra* note 2, 58).

[100] See, e.g. Persendorfer who highlights key challenges to a post-economic crisis paradigm shift from neoliberalism (which he defines as 'a plural set of ideas framed by beliefs of free market superiority (which is regularly criticised as market fundamentalism or market radicalism), individualism and -anti-statism in terms of opposition against social interventions') to alternative economic conceptions and Institutions. (D. Persendorfer, 'Goodbye Neoliberalism? Contested Policy Responses to Uncertain Consequences of the 2007–2009 Financial Crisis', in K. Alexander and R. Dhumale (eds.), *Research Handbook On International Financial Regulation* (London: Edward Elgar Publishing, 2012), ch. 19). For an entertaining and informative discussion of the 'zombie economics of market liberalism/neoliberalism' and an argument that economists need to return their attention to policies that will generate a more equitable distribution of income, see John Quiggin, *Zombie Economics: How Dead Ideas Still Walk among Us* (Princeton: Princeton University Press, 2010).

[101] I am grateful to Dr Ciaran O'Kelly for bringing this point to my attention. For examples of considerations of more human rights-friendly economic models, see, in the context of the right to housing, R. Rolnik and L. Rabinovich, 'Late-Neoliberalism: The Financialisation of Homeownership and the Housing Rights of the Poor', in Nolan (ed.), *Economic and Social Rights after the Global Financial Crisis* (Cambridge: Cambridge University Press, 2014). More broadly, see R. Balakrishnan, D. Elson, and R. Patel, *Rethinking Macroeconomic Strategies from a Human Rights Perspective (Why MES with Human Rights II)* (New York: Marymount Manhattan College/US Human Rights Network, 2009).

[102] Panitch and Konings, *supra* note 98, at 81.

[103] For a relatively recent, significant development in terms of the extra-territorial obligations imposed by ESR, see Maastricht Principles on Extraterritorial Obligations of States in the area of Economic, Social and Cultural Rights, a collection of guiding principles adopted by a range of human rights experts on 28 September 2011. These Principles do not explicitly refer to budgets or macroeconomic policy. However, if implemented, they would have significant implications for such. For more on the Principles, see O. De Schutter, A. Eide, A. Khalfan, M. Orellana, M. Salomon, and I. Seiderman, 'Commentary to the Maastricht Principles on Extraterritorial Obligations of States in

institutions in advancing a particular neo-liberal market-oriented economic model with serious implications for ESR is not great.[104] This will need to be borne in mind as ESR-based budget analysis work develops.

Where states (or, rather, budget decision-makers in states) are entrenched in economic models that are antithetical to ESR, they are unlikely to be receptive to argumentation based on such standards—whether based on economic data or not. It is important, however, not to overstate the limitations of ESR-based budget analysis in the contemporary economic and political context. Even in the absence of wholesale incorporation of ESR values into budgetary processes and policies, this methodology can play a vital role in analysing budgetary decisions and in holding governments to account in terms of their ESR obligations.

the area of Economic, Social and Cultural Rights' (2012), 34 *Human Rights Quarterly*, 1084. For a consideration of the ETOs imposed by ICESCR and outlined by the Committee, see W. Vandenhole, 'EU and Development Extraterritorial Obligations under the International Covenant on Economic, Social and Cultural Rights', in M.E. Salomon, A. Tostensen, and W. Vandenhole (eds.), *Casting the Net Wider: Human Rights, Development and New Duty-Bearers* (Intersentia, 2007), 85, at 86–98; and F. Coomans, 'The Extraterritorial Scope of the International Covenant on Economic, Social and Cultural Rights in the work of the United Nations Committee on Economic, Social and Cultural Rights' (2011), *Human Rights Law Review* 1.

[104] For more on this point, see M. Salomon, 'International Economic Governance and Human Rights Accountability', in Salomon et al., *supra* note 103, at 153, esp. pp. 165 and 177.

14

Human Rights Impact Assessments

Emerging Practice and Challenges

Simon Walker

1. Introduction

Interest in human rights impact assessment (HRIA) has grown considerably over the last 10 to 15 years. Today, an HRIA practice has emerged and interest among human rights practitioners and others appears to be growing steadily. Much of that practice has focused on examining impacts on economic, social, and cultural rights, although HRIA practice tends not to make a distinction between categories of rights, tending to focus on civil and political rights as well as economic, social, and cultural rights. This chapter looks at the existing HRIA practice, and discusses some of the concerns facing them. The chapter is divided into three main sections. The first identifies some of the main motivations behind undertaking HRIAs and sets out their basic elements and provides an illustration of a right to health impact assessment. The second raises some of the challenges confronting HRIA practice and explores these issues in greater depth. The third and final section identifies some areas for further study and practice to advance HRIAs.

2. Human Rights Impact Assessment

A. The emergence of HRIAs

Discussions about HRIAs began in the 1990s, spurred originally by the increasing focus on rights-based approaches to development as well as monitoring and evaluation by donors of their investments in human rights-related activities.[1] Today, a body of HRIA practice has emerged. The website of the Human Rights Impact Assessment Resource Centre includes a broad selection of impact assessment

[1] See, e.g. T. Landman, *Studying Human Rights* (Oxford: Routledge, 2006), 126.

methodologies and case studies, indicating a trend towards growth in this field.[2] Importantly, attention has moved beyond simply the development of tools and instruments to undertake HRIAs towards creating a body of practice demonstrating how such tools play out in reality. A review of the HRIA Resource Centre website suggests there are around twice as many HRIA case studies as tools.[3] While the numbers of both case studies and tools are relatively low, it nonetheless indicates that a body of knowledge on HRIA is developing.

HRIA practice has focused on a range of civil, cultural, economic, political, and social rights. However, it is fair to say that the growing interest in HRIAs has been propelled significantly by the parallel acknowledgement of economic, social, and cultural rights on the human rights agenda. While traditional human rights work has focused more on monitoring and reporting on situations (for example, conditions in prisons), or events (such as political demonstrations), the increased focus on economic, social, and cultural rights has led human rights reporting into newer areas—such as development, trade, investment, business practices, and so on—which tend to have multiple impacts that develop and change over time, requiring new tools and methodologies for monitoring. Impact assessment provides a means to understand these multiple impacts and how they develop and change. It is not surprising therefore that experts working in the field of economic, social, and cultural rights have been an important motor driving research into HRIAs. For example, special procedures of the UN as well as UN treaty bodies such as the Committee on Economic, Social and Cultural Rights have encouraged states and other actors to undertake HRIAs of trade and investment agreement on economic, social, and cultural rights.[4]

While their origins might have been in project monitoring and evaluation, a review of current practice demonstrates broader interest today and at least three motivations appear to underlie HRIAs. First, concern over the enjoyment of particular rights—often economic, social, or cultural rights—or specific people has motivated principally civil society organizations but also public authorities and intergovernmental organizations to undertake HRIAs. For example, one of the more widely implemented HRIA methodologies in this category is the Health

[2] In relation to 'tools and instruments' the website demonstrates a clear progressive interest in the development of HRIA methodologies: 2001 (1); 2005 (2); 2006 (3); 2007 (2); 2008 (3); 2009 (3); and 2010 (4). Human Rights Impact Assessment Resource Centre website, available at <http://www.humanrightsimpact.org/toolsinstruments> (last accessed 10 November 2013).

[3] Of the tools and instruments included on the HRIA website, 14 conformed to the definition of HRIA relied upon in this article. At the same time, 31 case studies conformed to the definition of HRIA. Human Rights Impact Assessment Resource Centre website, available at <http://www.humanrightsimpact.org/> (last accessed 10 November 2013).

[4] See, e.g. the Committee on Economic, Social and Cultural Rights recommendation to Switzerland in 2010 that it should undertake HRIAs of its trade policies to examine impacts on the economic, social, and cultural rights of populations of its partner countries. United Nations, Concluding Observations of Switzerland, Committee on Economic, Social and Cultural Rights, UN Doc. E/C.12/CHE/CO/2-3, para. 24; United Nations, Mission to the World Trade Organization, Report of the Special Rapporteur on the Right to Adequate Food, Olivier De Schutter, UN Doc. A/HRC/10/5/Add.2, para. 38, where the Special Rapporteur identifies that impact assessment is a useful tool to help a state understand the impacts of the trade agreements it is entering into.

Rights of Women Assessment Instrument (HeRWAI) developed by Aim for Human Rights.[5] Further, the Food and Agriculture Organization (FAO) has produced a right to food impact assessment checklist to help ensure that the right to food is respected in the development context.[6] At the same time, public authorities, particularly in the United Kingdom, have begun undertaking equality impact assessments of local authorities' policies on certain individuals and groups such as persons with disabilities, people who are lesbian, gay, bisexual, and transgender, ethnic and religious minorities, and older persons.[7]

A second motivation behind the development of HRIAs has been concern over the impact of certain *policies and projects*. Instead of focusing on protecting particular rights, this second category of HRIAs takes a specific intervention as a starting point and examines impact on an unspecified range of rights. Four significant subcategories of HRIAs have emerged under this heading. To start with, considerable practice exists in relation to examining the impact of business investments on the enjoyment of human rights. Civil society organizations such as Rights and Democracy as well as Nomogaia have developed methodologies in the field, as well as intergovernmental organizations such as the International Finance Corporation; business enterprises themselves, such as British Petroleum, have also commissioned HRIAs.[8]

Next, there is an increasing interest in the assessment of trade and investment agreements on the enjoyment of human rights, in particular rights to access essential medicines, adequate food, and affordable basic services, such as water, health, and education services. The Thai Human Rights Commission was the first to undertake an HRIA of a trade agreement, by considering the potential impact of the proposed Free Trade Agreement between Thailand and the US which includes

[5] S. Bakker and H. Plagman, *Health Rights of Women Assessment Instrument* rev.edn (Utrecht: Aim for Human Rights, 2006/2010).

[6] United Nations, *Right to Food Assessment Checklist: Assessing the Right to Food in the National Development Context* (Rome: Food and Agriculture Organization, 2009).

[7] See, e.g. Aberdeen City Council, *Equality and Human Rights Impact Assessment: The Guide* (2008), available at <http://www.aberdeencity.gov.uk/nmsruntime/saveasdialog.asp?lID=21290&sID=2603> (last accessed 10 November 2013); M.-A. Stephenson and J. Harrison, *Unravelling Equality?: A Human Rights and Equality Impact Assessment of the Public Spending Cuts on Women in Coventry* (A Joint Report of the Centre for Human Rights in Practice, University of Warwick and Coventry Women's Voices, 2011), available at <http://www2.warwick.ac.uk/fac/soc/law/chrp/projects/humanrightsimpactassessments/women> (last accessed 10 November 2013).

[8] Rights and Democracy, *Human Rights Impact Assessments for Foreign Investment Projects: Learning from Community Experiences in the Philippines, Tibet, the Democratic Republic of Congo, Argentina and Peru* (Montreal: International Centre for Human Rights and Democratic Development, 2009); Nomogaia, *A Methodology for Human Rights Impact Assessment*, available at <http://www.nomogaia.org/HRIA/Entries/2011/1/1_A_Methodology_for__Human_Rights_Impact_Assessment_files/Methodology%20for%20HRIA%202.0.pdf> (last accessed 10 November 2013); International Finance Corporation, International Business Leaders Forum and the Global Compact, *Guide to Human Rights Impact Assessment and Management* (2010), available at <http://www.ifc.org/wps/wcm/connect/8ecd35004c0cb230884bc9ec6f601fe4/hriam-guide-092011.pdf?MOD=AJPERES> (last accessed 10 September July 2013); G. Smith and B. Freeman, *Human Rights Impact Assessment of the Proposed Tangguh Project: Summary of Recommendations and Conclusions* (2002), available at <http://www.bp.com/liveassets/bp_internet/globalbp/STAGING/global_assets/downloads/I/hria_summary_Tangguh_HRIA_1736.pdf> (last accessed 10 November 2013).

a focus on economic, social, and cultural rights, such as the right to health.[9] Since then, the Ecumenical Advocacy Alliance (EAA) has commissioned studies of the impact of trade agreements on the right to food and a general methodology on HRIAs of trade agreements on human rights has been developed and illustrated in Costa Rica, with a particular focus on the right to health.[10] In the context of the Canada-Colombia Free Trade Agreement, the Canadian Parliament has required the Minister of International Trade to present annual reports to the Canadian Parliament concerning the impact of the agreement on human rights in Canada and Colombia over the previous year.[11]

Further, concern over the impact of development projects has given rise to HRIAs of development projects, one example being the methodological guidance prepared by the Norwegian Agency for Development Cooperation.[12] However, interest in impact assessment in the development field appears to have waned.[13]

Finally, laws and policies relating to anti-trafficking have motivated the development of HRIA methodologies to ensure that such policies have positive effects on the enjoyment of human rights.[14]

The third motivation behind the increased attention to HRIAs has been concern of certain actors, principally donors, that their investments in human rights are providing dividends—in other words, the focus is on assessing the impact of the *work of human rights organizations*. The concern among donors that their investments in human rights activities were paying off was a major initial motivator for impact assessments, and today many human rights organizations—whether civil society or intergovernmental—are under increasing pressure to demonstrate a positive correlation between donor contributions and human rights outcomes. To give just one example, the Office of the United Nations High Commissioner for Human Rights (OHCHR) has employed results-based budgeting techniques to develop and report on its Strategic Management Plan with impacts reflected in its Annual Reports.[15]

As can be seen, much of this practice relates to economic, social, and cultural rights. Trade and investment, development projects, and business investment often

[9] National Human Rights Commission of Thailand, *Report on Results of the Examination of Human Rights Violations* (2006, Ad-Hoc Coordinating Sub-Committee to Review and Examine the Establishment of the Thailand-United States Free Trade Area) on file with the author.

[10] A. Paasch, F. Garbers, and T. Hirsch (eds.), *Trade Policies and Hunger: The Impact of Trade Liberalization on the Right to Food of Rice Farming Communities in Ghana, Honduras and Indonesia*, Commissioned by the Ecumenical Advocacy Alliance (2007); S. Walker, *The Future of Human Rights Impact Assessments of Trade Agreements* (Brussels: Intersentia, 2009).

[11] *An Act to implement the Free Trade Agreement between Canada and the Republic of Colombia, the Agreement on the Environment between Canada and the Republic of Colombia and the Agreement on Labour Cooperation between Canada and the Republic of Colombia*, clause 15.1.

[12] Norwegian Agency for Development Cooperation (NORAD), *Handbook in Human Rights Assessment: State Obligations, Awareness and Empowerment* (Oslo: NORAD, 2001).

[13] J. Harrison, 'Human Rights Measurement: Reflections on Current Practice and Future Potential of Human Rights Impact Assessment', 3 *Journal of Human Rights Practice* (2011), 162–187.

[14] M. Wijers and L. Chew, *The Right Guide: A Tool to Assess the Human Rights Impact of Anti-Trafficking Laws and Policies* (The Netherlands: Aim for Human Rights, 2010).

[15] United Nations, *High Commissioner's Strategic Management Plan 2010–2011* (Geneva: Office of the High Commissioner for Human Rights, 2010).

focus on construction of infrastructure, food production, exchange of goods and services, employment creation, and so on, which in turn has significant social impacts relating to economic, social, and cultural rights. For example, the trade and investment assessments mentioned concentrate predominantly on the right to health, cultural rights, and the right to food. In turn, the HeRWAI and FAO methodologies relate primarily to the right to health and right to food respectively.

At the same time, HRIA methodology and practice has tended to reflect the interdependence and inter-relatedness of human rights and so has not been self-conscious in its focus on economic, social, and cultural rights. Instead, methodologies tend to examine impacts on those rights—whether civil and political or economic, social, and cultural rights—that are of most concern or are most likely to be affected by a change in policy or the introduction of a project or other intervention. Consequently, it is not uncommon to see impact statements on the right to health, alongside statements relating to the right to take part in public affairs and the right to a remedy in any tool or case study. So while economic, social, and cultural rights have perhaps been the motor behind HRIAs, the practice of HRIAs has underlined the difficulties of categorizing rights into unhelpful groups of civil and political rights or economic, social, and cultural rights. Looking at one right generally involves examining a range of other rights.

B. What is a human rights impact assessment?

There is no single or official definition of HRIAs. The HRIA Resource Centre, an online information source on HRIA methodologies and practice, has been an important source of grouping and structuring information and experience on HRIAs. The Resource Centre has described HRIAs in the following terms: 'Human rights impact assessment measures the impact of policies, programmes, projects and interventions on human rights'.[16] Several elements of this definition are relevant for particular focus.

1. *Timing of impact*

A key element of measuring impact is the time perspective. An *ex ante* assessment considers the potential future impact of a policy, programme, project, or intervention on human rights. In other words, it seeks to collect and analyse data with a view to predicting what the impact on human rights might be once the instrument under assessment is implemented at some later date. An *ex post* impact assessment considers the existing impacts that have resulted from the past implementation of

[16] Website of the Human Rights Impact Assessment Resource Centre, available at <http://www.humanrightsimpact.org/hria-guide/overview/> (last accessed 10 November 2013). Bakker et al. rely on a similar definition: S. Bakker et al., 'Human Rights Impact Assessment in Practice: The Case of the Health Rights of Women Assessment Instrument (HeRWAI), 1 *Journal of Human Rights Practice* (2009), 436–458, at 436.

a policy, programme, project, or intervention. Rather than being forward-looking, it looks backward in time to attempt to identify real impacts on human rights.

In reality, many HRIAs might be a combination of both *ex ante* and *ex post* assessments. For example, an impact assessment examining the existing impacts of a business investment on a local indigenous community might identify not only existing impacts (*ex post*) but also make recommendations for future directions of the business project which in turn should be assessed for their potential to affect the same community (*ex ante*).

It is interesting to note that there appears to be equal interest in *ex ante* and *ex post* impact assessments, with possibly slightly more interest in designing *ex post* methodologies.[17] In several cases, methodologies are consciously designed to serve the function of both *ex ante* and *ex post*. For example, the Health Rights of Women Assessment Instrument (HeRWAI) methodology has been developed to perform both functions, and case studies employing the methodology have been both *ex ante* and *ex post*.[18] In the trade and investment sphere, methodologies have tended to be either *ex ante* or *ex post*, with an equal interest in both. The assessment of the impact of Central American Free Trade Agreement (CAFTA) on the right to health relied on an *ex ante* methodology while the EAA methodologies on the impact of trade liberalization on the right to food and the methodology under development to assess the Canada–Colombia Free Trade Agreement are both *ex post*.[19]

An important question is whether the distinction between *ex ante* and *ex post* is in fact helpful as it could create a false distinction in HRIA theory and practice given that the steps required to undertake the assessment are often essentially the same.[20] It is important to bear in mind that the terms *ex ante* and *ex post* refer only to the timing of the assessment. However, a function of identifying the timing of the assessment will influence decisions on the choice of data collection and analysis methods and in turn, which steps should be followed to arrive at an impact statement. For example, participatory methods might be more important in *ex post* HRIAs so as to identify people's lived experience of a project or policy. For *ex ante* HRIAs, participatory methods might be relevant to identifying people's fears or concerns related to the projected introduction of a policy or project or as a means of mobilizing communities to debate and engage with a forthcoming change.

2. *Assessment of policies, programmes, projects, and interventions*

Another element of the definition is that the assessment concerns the impact of 'policies, programmes, projects, and interventions'. Policies, programmes, projects,

[17] A review of the 'tools and instruments' page on the HRIA Resource Centre website revealed 15 methodologies that clearly fell within the definition of an HRIA methodology as defined here; of which seven were *ex post* methodologies, four were *ex ante* methodologies, and four fulfilled both functions: *exante* and *ex post*.

[18] Bakker and Plagman, *supra* note 5.

[19] Walker, *supra* note 10; Paasch et al., *supra* note 10; Act of the Canadian Parliament, *supra* note 11.

[20] Question asked during the session 'New Tools to Monitor the Progressive Realization of Economic, Social and Cultural Rights', Expert Meeting on 'Contemporary Issues in the Realization of Economic, Social and Cultural Rights', Geneva, 10–11 February 2011, Notes of the Author.

and other interventions can have widely different scope and affects on different people. Existing impact assessment methodologies tend to fall into two main groups: on the one hand, policies; and on the other hand, programmes, projects, and other interventions—for shorthand, I will refer to the two groups as policy or project HRIAs.

In relation to scope, a policy tends to have wide reach that often, although not always, goes beyond the reach of projects. For example, a national policy can affect the entire population anywhere in the country while a policy of local government can affect an entire community. The methodologies and practice referred to above indicate a wide range of policies that have been subject to HRIA, from trade and investment agreements, to local authority policies, anti-trafficking policies, and health policies among others, many of which have significantly wide scope to affect a broad category of people.

In contrast, projects tend to be more defined both in terms of the population affected and the geographic scope, although this clearly depends on the nature of the project. Project HRIAs have focused principally on assessing the impacts of business investments, national and local development projects, and human rights activities. The impacts of a development programme or a business project often, although not always, affect a particular group, community, or geographic area. This makes it easier to identify the geographic scope as well as the people affected by the intervention. This can provide some relief to an assessment team, particularly where the assessment relies on participatory assessment techniques that require the examination of impacts on a representative selection of the population. In contrast, employing participatory techniques at a national level in relation to the impact of a policy might be considerably difficult and risky in terms of the reliability and validity of the data.

While impact assessments generally fall into these two groups of policy or project HRIAs, the inclusion of the general term 'other interventions' in the definition reminds us that an impact assessment could examine other instruments or actions. For example, while budget analysis is not necessarily the same as impact assessment, it nonetheless overlaps with impact assessment where analysis examines the real or likely impact of a budget allocation on human rights. Similarly, phenomena such as corruption or criminality are neither policies nor projects, yet could be subject to impact assessment.

3. *Intended and unintended impacts*

Many policies and projects can affect human rights in different ways and as a result of different intentions. Landman separates these different intentions into two groups: first, policies and projects that intend to have an impact on human rights; and, second, interventions that do not intend to affect human rights directly but nonetheless do. Interventions in the first group include human rights laws, bills of rights, policies, and projects, such as technical cooperation projects focusing on realizing human rights. A much wider group of interventions falls into the second group. This second group refers to the majority of interventions that have been subject to impact assessments, such as trade agreements, business investments, or development programmes. These outwardly seek, for example, to increase trade flows, construct a dam, or provide development assistance but, at the implementation stage, can unconsciously, or at least unintentionally, affect human rights. A trade agreement that strengthens intellectual property protection related to pharmaceuticals might outwardly seek to strengthen innovation and flows of essential medicines but also, albeit not expressly intentionally, affect universal access to medicines. Table 14.1 illustrates four categories of HRIAs.[21]

Table 14.1

	Intended impacts	Unintended impacts
Ex ante	Assessment of a policy or project that intends to affect human rights to determine the likelihood of those and other impacts occurring, e.g. HRIA of a draft labour code.	Assessment of a policy or project not expressly related to human rights but which nonetheless could have direct or indirect impacts on the human rights situation, e.g. HRIA of a free trade agreement under negotiation on access to medicines.
Ex post	Assessment/evaluation of human rights policies and projects for the extent to which they achieved their aim to improve enjoyment of human rights, e.g. HRIA of a technical cooperation programme to achieve affordable drinking water of good quality to a particular region.	Assessment/evaluation of the human rights outcomes of policies and projects that were not intended to change the human rights situation, e.g. HRIA of the impact of a business investment on the rights of an indigenous community living close to the project.

4. *Impacts on human rights*

HRIAs have to examine impacts of interventions on human rights. This might seem a fairly obvious observation; however, it has been noted that some impact assessments presented as HRIAs have not done so convincingly.[22] HRIAs are not simply about expressing social impacts in terms of human rights impacts. Instead, HRIAs should use human rights norms and standards as measures, and further, should also ensure that the HRIA methodology respects human rights in the process of undertaking the assessment. This can be referred to as a rights-based approach to impact assessment and recalls other areas where rights-based approaches have emerged, such as in relation to development cooperation and humanitarian assistance. The work on rights-based approaches can be adapted to provide a framework for HRIAs comprising three elements.[23]

[21] Landman, *supra* note 1, at 128.

[22] For example, the HRIA undertaken by the Thai NHRI referred to in section 3 (*supra* note 9) has been criticized for not clearly linking the analysis and outcomes to human rights standards. See Walker, *supra* note 10, at 30.

[23] United Nations, *The Human Rights Based Approach to Development Cooperation: Towards a Common Understanding Among UN Agencies* (New York: United Nations Development

First, HRIAs should express likely impacts by reference to human rights norms and standards, principally those found in human rights treaties or national human rights norms and standards, supplemented by authoritative statements of expert human rights bodies such as the General Comments of treaty bodies. To do so effectively, an HRIA should measure the impact of the intervention on both the respect for obligations as well as the fulfilment of rights. This comprises a focus on two distinct groups:

1. The HRIA should measure the likely or real impact of the intervention on the obligations on *states and others* to respect, protect, and fulfil human rights. This involves for example, an examination of the capacity of states to meet their human rights obligations in light of the introduction of the intervention under examination.
2. Similarly, it requires an examination of the impact of the intervention on the enjoyment of rights by *individuals and groups* as well as their capacity to deal with any negative impacts if and when it arises. For example, in the case of an assessment related to the right to health, the assessment would consider impacts of a policy or project on the availability, accessibility, acceptability, and quality of health goods, services, and facilities with regard to individuals and groups.

Second, the HRIA should ensure that process rights and human rights principles such as non-discrimination, participation, inclusion, and accountability, are respected in two respects.

1. The process of introducing the policy or project subject to the HRIA should respect process rights. In other words, the actor—government, business enterprise, or any other entity responsible for introducing the intervention—should ensure adequate consultation prior to and after introduction of the intervention, act without discrimination, provide adequate information, and ensure that grievance mechanisms exist to hold all actors accountable.
2. The other aspect of process is that the HRIA itself should respect process rights. Thus, not only should the process surrounding the introduction of the intervention be transparent, consultative, and accountable, the HRIA itself should as well. This can have important implications for the methodology such as the choice of data collection and analysis techniques.

The third element of the human rights approach has less to do with the measurement of impact itself. This element emphasizes the importance of engaging human rights actors and institutions in the process of measurement and in the outcome. Consequently, an HRIA should ensure that it draws on information of human

Group, 2003), available at <http://www.undg.org/archive_docs/6959-The_Human_Rights_Based_Approach_to_Development_Cooperation_Towards_a_Common_Understanding_among_UN.pdf> (last accessed 10 November 2013).

rights mechanisms such as reports of special procedures of the United Nations Human Rights Council—for example, the Special Rapporteur on the right to health or on the right to adequate food—as well as UN treaty bodies such as the Committee on Economic, Social and Cultural Rights. It should also draw upon the network of actors such as international and national human rights institutions and civil society organizations, for example, for follow-up on recommendations. This third element is clearly less definitive of an HRIA than the first two. An HRIA could feasibly still respect the first two elements without drawing on human rights institutions in the process. However, the HRIA can also have a role in strengthening the role of those institutions and also strengthening its own methodology by drawing in these national and international networks.[24]

5. *Measurement of impact*

It is important to highlight another aspect of the definition of HRIAs, namely the recognition that an HRIA should 'measure impact'. Measurement of impact calls to mind a precise method or process for moving from a starting point—namely, the introduction of a policy or project—towards an outcome, that is to say, the impact on human rights. I would argue that this distinguishes HRIAs from other methodologies with similar functions but that do not include this element of measuring impact. Take the example of human rights compliance models. A methodology designed to assist a business enterprise to identify whether its policies comply with human rights standards is, in my view, not an HRIA. This methodology is merely examining whether the various elements of the business policy are compatible with human rights standards. For example, does the policy prohibit the worst forms of child labour and include measures to protect against this practice through its suppliers? This is an important step to ensure that there will be no negative human rights impacts through faulty labour practices in the future, but it is only a measurement of compliance, not a measurement of impact. In the same case, a HRIA might examine what the likely impact would be of a business enterprise that did not have a policy on preventing the worst forms of child labour, given the surrounding context of the enterprise's operations and so on. Similarly, a methodology designed to help a donor or business enterprise identify the human rights sensitivities in a region or country prior to investing in a project measures risk rather than impact, although admittedly there is a fine line and measurement of risk is an important step in measuring impact in any *ex ante* HRIA.

Methodologies for undertaking measurement of impact have been developed for some decades in other areas of impact assessment, such as environmental impact assessment or social impact assessment. HRIA can benefit from this work, adapting those methodologies to the specific requirements of measuring impacts on

[24] To understand in greater detail how these three elements of the human rights framework affect impact assessment, see: S. Walker, 'The United States–Dominican Republic–Central American Free Trade Agreement and Access to Medicines in Costa Rica: A Human Rights Impact Assessment', 3 *Journal of Human Rights Practice* (2011), 188–213.

human rights. Three aspects of measurement are important: the step-by-step process used to arrive at a measurement; techniques for data collection and analysis; and human rights indicators' frameworks. Typically, the step-by-step process is as follows:

1. *Preparation*—The preparation steps clarifies: the objectives for investigating a policy or project; the overall context of the assessment based on an examination of the relevant legal, economic, environmental, social, and regulatory context; an identification of the people affected as well as those in positions of responsibility; and finally the resources available to undertake the assessment and whether other strategies might achieve the desired objectives better than an HRIA. Importantly, the preparation step might result in a decision not to proceed with the assessment.
2. *Screening*—The screening step narrows the areas of the policy or project under examination to those areas that are more likely to have significant impacts. The screening step therefore requires a preliminary elaboration of the policy or project, an identification of related sensitive human rights issues and a mini-assessment of the project's or policy's likely impacts (to be verified later in the assessment process).
3. *Scoping*—The scoping step describes in detail the elements of the policy or project selected for assessment during the screening step and identifies the potential impacts to be examined. On this basis, it is important to identify which data collection and analysis techniques and which indicators are to be relied upon to measure impact as well as the stakeholders to be consulted. A thorough baseline human rights assessment is undertaken at this stage so as to identify current enjoyment of human rights in relation to the indicators chosen. While the screening step is a narrowing process, the scoping step is a process that aims at broadening and deepening understanding of the pertinent aspects of the policy and project.
4. *Data Collection and Analysis*—This step employs the tools and techniques identified in the scoping step with a view to verifying or rejecting potential impacts. The analysis examines the likelihood of various impacts occurring and whether impacts might have cumulative effects as well as which stakeholders—rights-holders and duty-bearers—are more likely to be affected (*ex ante*) or have been more affected (*ex post*) by the policy or project.
5. *Conclusions and Recommendations*—This step sets out the overall statement of impact and also identifies the various factors that could intervene to modify impact. The assessment team should identify recommendations to remedy any arising human rights breaches, as well as measures to avert future problems while optimizing positive impacts identified.
6. *Monitoring and Evaluation*—The assessment should itself undergo its own assessment, to ensure that it has respected human rights principles. Stakeholders should be involved in this process. In addition, the results of the assessment should be monitored in the future and the HRIA should include a future monitoring plan.

In terms of data collection and analysis methods—assessment techniques—the HRIA practitioner should not try to reinvent the wheel but instead make the most of the many advances in social inquiry and economic analysis already available: participatory assessment methods, key informant interviewing guides, economic modelling, statistical methods, surveys, and many other techniques are available to assist with HRIAs.[25] The most important factor to bear in mind is that the rights-based approach to impact assessment encourages the combination of both quantitative and qualitative methods. Thus, an HRIA that relies entirely on statistical analysis, without any quantitative analysis of stakeholder concerns, might not meet the definition of HRIAs already discussed. Instead, an HRIA should rely on assessment techniques that allow collection of both qualitative and quantitative data. Similarly, the focus on participation in HRIA might require a particular emphasis on some types of techniques, particularly participatory techniques. The choice of data collection and analysis methods will respond to the requirements of the human rights framework as well as each individual assessment.

Closely linked to the choice of assessment techniques is the choice of indicators—those pieces of information which focus data collection and analysis and provide the basis for statements as to the level of enjoyment of rights. As with assessment techniques, the choice of impact indicators should encompass information that is both quantitative and qualitative in nature. The issue of indicators is a subject of disagreement among practitioners, in particular whether it is possible to identify a list of indicators in a methodology that is universally applicable.[26] I would argue against any attempt at identifying universally applicable indicators. Instead, methodologies should provide guidance to HRIA practitioners to enable them to identify HRIA-specific indicators that help identify those impacts most relevant to the policy or project at hand.

One such indicator framework had been developed by the Office of the High Commissioner for Human Rights (OHCHR) for use in the process of state party reporting to treaty bodies.[27] These indicators are explicitly linked to human rights standards in treaties and fall within three categories, namely: structural indicators that measure state commitment to the particular aspect of the right under examination; process indicators that measure state effort to achieve the particular right; and, outcome indicators that measure the result of that commitment and effort on individuals' enjoyment of the right.[28] Indicators falling in each of these three

[25] S. Walker, 'The United States–Dominican Republic–Central American Free Trade Agreement and Access to Medicines in Costa Rica: A Human Rights Impact Assessment', 3 *Journal of Human Rights Practice* (2011), 188–213.

[26] Berne Declaration, CCIC & Misereor, *Human Rights Impact Assessment for Trade and Investment Agreements* (Report of the Expert Seminar, Geneva, 23–24 June 2010).

[27] United Nations, *Report on Indicators for Promoting and Monitoring the Implementation of Human Rights* (HRI/MC/2008/3, Geneva: Office of the High Commissioner for Human Rights, 2008). See also: United Nations, *Human Rights Indicators: A Guide to Measurement and Implementation*, Office of the High Commissioner for Human Rights, United Nations (HR/PUB/12/5, 2012).

[28] United Nations, *Report on Indicators for Promoting and Monitoring the Implementation of Human Rights* (HRI/MC/2008/3, Geneva: Office of the High Commissioner for Human Rights, 2008). See

categories should be disaggregated as far as possible.[29] Model indicators have been developed covering a wide variety of civil, cultural, economic, political, and social rights.[30]

The OHCHR framework provides a useful guide which, although elaborated for state party reporting to treaty bodies, deserves more attention in the HRIA field. On the one hand, it is true that some aspects of OHCHR work in this area make it less relevant for HRIAs. For example, many of the indicators identified under the OHCHR framework for use by treaty bodies are quantitative in nature and so are not necessarily relevant to HRIA practice which requires a mix of both quantitative and qualitative data.[31] Similarly, the indicators identified using the framework are intended as universally applicable indicators to assist with global human rights monitoring and are not necessarily relevant to HRIAs that might require different categories of information related, for example, to the enjoyment of rights at the local and community level. However, in spite of these concerns, the OHCHR framework can be adapted for use in a variety of situations, not only global treaty reporting. For this reason, I suggest that the OHCHR framework, rather than the indicators identified under that framework, could provide a useful guide for HRIA practice. The framework is one that is solidly based in human rights law and helps identify information relating to both the level of state respect for human rights as well as individuals' enjoyment. The important factor to bear in mind is that the framework should act only as a guide and not as a straitjacket, allowing flexibility for practitioners to identify human rights indicators most relevant to the assessment at hand.

C. Illustration: a human rights impact assessment of the United States–Dominican Republic–Central American Free Trade Agreement and access to medicines in Costa Rica

It is helpful to examine these issues through an example. A human rights impact assessment of the United States–Dominican Republic–CAFTA was undertaken in 2009, with a particular emphasis on the impact of its patent provisions on access

also: United Nations, *Human Rights Indicators: A Guide to Measurement and Implementation*, Office of the High Commissioner for Human Rights, United Nations (HR/PUB/12/5, 2012) (Report on Indicators).

29 United Nations, *Report on Indicators for Promoting and Monitoring the Implementation of Human Rights* (HRI/MC/2008/3, Geneva: Office of the High Commissioner for Human Rights, 2008). See also: United Nations, *Human Rights Indicators: A Guide to Measurement and Implementation*, Office of the High Commissioner for Human Rights, United Nations (HR/PUB/12/5, 2012) (Report on Indicators).

30 United Nations, *Report on Indicators for Promoting and Monitoring the Implementation of Human Rights* (HRI/MC/2008/3, Geneva: Office of the High Commissioner for Human Rights, 2008). See also: United Nations, *Human Rights Indicators: A Guide to Measurement and Implementation*, Office of the High Commissioner for Human Rights, United Nations (HR/PUB/12/5, 2012) (Report on Indicators).

31 S. Bakker et al., 'Human Rights Impact Assessment in Practice: The Case of the Health Rights of Women Assessment Instrument (HeRWAI), 1 *Journal of Human Rights Practice* (2009), 436–458, at 439.

to medicines in Costa Rica.[32] The *ex ante* assessment was taken just prior to the entry into force of the trade agreement in Costa Rica with a view to predicting the future impact on access to medicines. The focus on CAFTA demonstrates an HRIA of a policy instrument that was not designed consciously to have an impact on human rights, but which nonetheless could well have unintended impacts given the relationship of its provisions on issues such as access to medicines. In addition to examining impacts of specific agreements on access to medicines, the assessment also considered how the process of negotiating and adopting the agreement respect human rights, in particular the right to take part in the conduct of public affairs.

The HRIA adopted the step-by-step methodology outlined. While the HRIA ultimately focused on intellectual property provisions and their impact on access to medicines, the screening stage examined the potential impact of the entire agreement on a range of human rights. With the help of secondary materials (articles, expert commentaries, media materials), the screening process identified that provisions concerning the agricultural sector might affect the right to an adequate standard of living and the right to food; the labour provisions might affect workers' rights; investment provisions might affect government regulatory capacity, particularly in areas of public health, that could in turn affect the enjoyment of human rights; and the insurance provisions might affect universal access to social security. Relying on those secondary materials, the screening process concluded that the potential impact of the agreement on access to medicines was the most pressing and this became the focus of the rest of the assessment.

The scoping stage then examined in detail the possible impacts that the intellectual property provisions might have on access to medicines, and also identified the various data collection and analysis tools to determine those impacts. Economic modelling was used as a way to forecast economic impacts of intellectual property provisions on access to medicines. This was accompanied by the use of expert judgment, made on the basis of a series of interviews with key stakeholders from government (Ministry of Health, Ministry of External Trade, the Social Security Institute, and the Patent Office) as well as civil society organizations, academics, and the National Human Rights Institution. In addition, legal analysis helped with the examination of the trade provisions and implementing legislation as well as national laws and case law relating to the right to health and how this might affect access to medicines in light of the new trade provisions.

Drawing from the OHCHR indicator framework previously discussed, the scoping stage also identified a series of structural, process, and outcome indicators relating to the right to health, and in particular, state obligations to prevent, treat, and control diseases (Article 12(2)(c) of the International Covenant on Economic, Social and Cultural Rights). It is not possible to refer to all the indicators here; however, an example of each type of indicator follows: date and entry into force and coverage of the right to health in the Constitution (structural); proportion of people covered by health insurance (process); and incidence of persons foregoing essential medicines (outcome).

[32] See Walker, 'The Future of Human Rights Impact Assessments', *supra* note 10.

On the basis of the results of the economic modelling, legal analysis, and expert judgment, the assessment identified impacts on both government capacity to ensure access to medicines and individuals' likely enjoyment of access to medicines in ten years' time. The assessment identified that the intellectual property provisions would increase prices of patented pharmaceuticals, which in turn would place pressure on the budget of the Social Security Institute in charge of administering the access to medicines regime. As a result, it was likely that the Social Security Institute would face the choice of either increasing its budget or decreasing the quality or quantity of medicines provided through the public system and these pressures were found to be likely to grow over time.

At the same time, the assessment concluded that the impact of these price increases might not have a significant impact on individuals' enjoyment of their right to health. This was due to the fact that the strong human rights framework in Costa Rica, including a justiciable right to health, could help many individuals avoid carrying the burden of increased prices of essential medicines. Specifically, an easy-to-access and low-cost complaints mechanism to protect the right to health before the Constitutional Court provided an important avenue to ensure continued access to medicines in spite of price increases. As a result, the real loser from CAFTA might be the Social Security Institute which would have legal obligations to ensure access to medicines while also facing increasing prices to pay for essential medicines as a result of the strong intellectual property protection.

The HRIA nuanced these results by identifying a series of variables that might mitigate or exacerbate the extent of the pressure of stronger intellectual property provisions on access to medicines. For example, aggressive protection of intellectual property rights by pharmaceutical companies might reduce the space for cheaper generic drugs on the Costa Rican market and therefore drive up prices of medicines. On the other hand, a strong push by civil society organizations and individuals to protect access to medicines through public interest litigation and lobbying of both government and pharmaceutical companies might have a downward effect on prices, at least of some key essential medicines.

As noted, the HRIA also examined the extent to which the negotiation process respected human rights. The assessment concluded that the negotiation and adoption of the trade agreement in many ways respected political rights. For example, Costa Rica held a national referendum to decide whether it would ratify the agreement which passed by a slim majority. Nonetheless, the assessment also found that the US required that it certify all laws implementing the trade agreement prior to adoption by the Costa Rican Parliament, which clearly undermines democratic processes in Costa Rica.

Finally, the assessment identified some recommendations focusing on strengthening government institutional capacity to mitigate potential impact of the CAFTA and identifying with greater clarity the human rights responsibilities of pharmaceutical companies. The assessment also recommended that the National Human Rights Institution should continuously monitor the impact of the trade agreement on access to medicines and that a full *ex post* impact assessment should be undertaken in 2020 to identify the real impacts of the agreement. The assessment also recommended that the government leave open the possibility of renegotiating the intellectual property provisions of the agreement in the future.

3. Some Contemporary Issues in Human Rights Impact Assessment

A. Introduction

The growing interest in HRIAs demonstrates a need among human rights practitioners—whether in civil society, academia, national human rights institutions, government, or intergovernmental organizations—to respond in a more systematic way to the real and potential impacts of policies and projects on the enjoyment of human rights. HRIAs, done properly, help to collect and analyse data in a structured way; help to empower rights-holders by making it easier to demonstrate the cause–effect relationships between policies, projects, and human rights outcomes; build human rights capacities of organizations undertaking HRIAs; and raise awareness of human rights, and the relationship between norms and standards and the daily work of the people and organizations involved in the HRIA.[33] The focus of HRIA on evaluating human rights practice can also be beneficial in questioning the appropriateness of human rights responses in a given situation, and in doing so, encouraging an internal examination that should ideally lead to better responses and solutions to problems. In short, HRIAs provide a means of moving beyond arguing for better policy on the basis of principle to reliance on evidence and good argumentation.

However, HRIAs also face challenges. Three are considered here. First, HRIAs are costly to do properly in terms of time and also human and financial resources. These technical challenges must be examined closely—both at the level of HRIAs generally as well as in relation to each individual HRIA—if we are to avoid overselling HRIAs and, as a result, simply disappointing by not living up to expectations. The second and third challenges are closely connected: the second challenge concerns the compatibility of the essentially political or partisan nature of the human rights framework with the principle of neutrality that underlies impact assessment generally; the third challenge relates to the threat of commercialization and bureaucratization of HRIAs when they are undertaken by business enterprises and government representatives.

B. Technical challenges to human rights impact assessments

A significant challenge to HRIAs, mirroring in many ways a similar challenge to other forms of impact assessment, is the fact that they are sometimes difficult to do properly. They require considerable human, time and financial resources, and those

[33] See Walker, 'The Future of Human Rights Impact Assessments', *supra* note 10, at 449.

undertaking HRIAs face challenges of understanding and applying the human rights framework.[34] Each assessment will require different resources depending on the subject matter of the assessment. For example, a project assessment might be more focused on a geographical and population sector narrowing the scope of assessment and therefore easing pressures on the methodology. On the other hand, some assessments might require in-depth participatory data collection methodologies, a factor that considerably increases the burden of data collection—and therefore human and financial resources.

Such technical challenges do not necessarily constitute an outright barrier to undertaking HRIAs; however, they do need to be understood and built into methodologies if HRIAs are to be undertaken effectively and sustainably.

To demonstrate the resources required to undertake an HRIA, I draw from the experience of the HRIA of the US-Dominican Republic–CAFTA on the right to health, as mentioned. The HRIA focused on only one sector in CAFTA, namely the impact of intellectual property protection on access to essential medicines.[35] Even this narrow focus required considerable effort. In terms of human resources, one lawyer undertook the assessment itself over a period of some three months. However, the fact that only one lawyer undertook the assessment was possible due to the fact that other actors were performing the economic modelling concurrently, which saved significant time and effort.[36] In determining real time and resource allocations, it would therefore be necessary to add an additional three months or more of work for an economist.[37] Ideally, a social scientist could have broadened the analysis through the use of more participatory data collection techniques. Consequently, even for the limited focus on one sector of a trade agreement, it is possible to consider three or even more months of work for three legal, economics, and social science professionals. If an HRIA of the entire trade agreement had been undertaken, considerably more time would have been necessary; up to six months or even a year.[38]

Of course, all impact assessments face such technical challenges, not only HRIAs. However, the human rights framework poses some specific difficulties. First, the nature of human rights requires both qualitative as well as quantitative methods, so that statistical evidence can be balanced with qualitative evidence about how individuals experience a particular situation and perceive their enjoyment of rights.[39] As noted in section 2, the human rights framework integrates human rights principles not only into the process of decision-making related to the policy or project under consideration, but also into the HRIA process itself. Consequently, reliance on qualitative participatory techniques for data collection and analysis is of great

[34] See Walker, 'The Future of Human Rights Impact Assessments', *supra* note 10, at 452.

[35] Walker, *supra* note 10, at 130.

[36] G. Hernández-González, M. Valverde, and C. Murillo, *Evaluación del Impacto de las Disposiciones de ADPIC+ en el Mercado Institucional de Medicamentos de Costa Rica* (Centro Internacional de Política Económica (CINPE) y International Centre for Trade and Sustainable Development (ICTSD) (2008) on file with the author).

[37] Walker, *supra* note 10, at 207.

[38] Walker, *supra* note 10, at 207.

[39] Walker, *supra* note 10, at 103; Harrison, *supra* note 13.

significance in the context of HRIAs.[40] This mixed methods approach requires a range of professional experience and data collection methods which adds to the burden of the assessment. Moreover, even with the requisite experience in the assessment team, in some cases participatory techniques might be hard to apply. In the case of an *ex ante* assessment of a policy that potentially applies to an entire country, it raises the question of how to choose a representative group of individuals to be subject to the HRIA.[41]

Second, the nature of human rights law as a framework for impact assessment requires some level of understanding of the human rights framework itself. On the one hand, not all people undertaking HRIAs have knowledge and understanding of the human rights framework. This is particularly the case with economic, social, and cultural rights which are still not widely understood, even among human rights practitioners. Harrison concludes that the complexity of the human rights framework leads to a risk that HRIA methodologies will either be ignored or followed half-heartedly, giving the example of the various UK equality impact assessments undertaken by relatively inexperienced assessors that have tended to overlook potentially grave human rights violations while highlighting more trivial impacts.[42] Bakker et al. raise a related issue, noting that HRIA methodologies can sometimes be too complicated for use by independent grassroots organizations. They suggest that, in such cases, the use of HRIA methodologies depends on the involvement of other organizations that have the required HRIA skills to involve grassroots organizations in the process.[43]

One way to deal with these factors is to build the effects of the resource requirements into the methodology so that methodologies balance technical purity with usability. Certainly, any human rights methodology must be accessible to a broad public, otherwise it risks excluding potential users, and potentially failing to live up to its own principles of participation and inclusion. One measure is to ensure that the methodology includes as a first step—the preparation step—the determination of the time, and human and financial resources required to undertake the assessment. On this basis, those undertaking the assessment should take a decision on the appropriateness of using HRIA as a strategy as opposed to other strategies, such as advocacy.

Similarly, methodologies can be designed for different levels of use—for example, quick assessments as well as detailed assessments. A quick assessment would rely primarily on secondary materials while more detailed assessments would rely on the combination of several data collection and analysis techniques. Simpler options detract from the reliability of the results and also deny options of public

[40] There are potentially some subjects of impact assessment for which participatory techniques might provide little additional data. In my case study on CAFTA and access to medicines, the negative impact of CAFTA, if it emerged, was more likely to fall on the government rather than individuals, given the various human rights protections in place in Costa Rica which should save negative impacts being passed on to rights-holders. That being the case, I argue that participatory techniques might have added little. Walker, *supra* note 10.

[41] Walker, *supra* note 10, at 207.

[42] Harrison, *supra* note 13.

[43] Bakker et al., *supra* note 5, at 452.

participation in the process; however, they provide a means to undertake the assessment with more limited resources. Lower resourced and potentially less reliable (in other words, less exact) HRIAs might at least provide a means of alerting policymakers or project managers to problems that had not yet been considered. Moreover, a quick assessment might also pave the way for a more detailed assessment to follow by raising concerns which in turn might mobilize resources. The important factor to bear in mind is that the conclusions openly acknowledge that a simpler methodology was chosen so that HRIA results do not over-represent risks or mislead.

C. A neutral or partisan process

HRIAs can be particularly challenging as they apply a framework that is essentially highly political and partisan to a science of impact assessment. This potential tension gave rise to an interesting discussion at a meeting in June 2010 on HRIAs in the context of trade and investment agreements. Some at the meeting argued that HRIAs should seek a level of 'neutrality' through implementation of a robust methodology that transcends ideological concerns; others argued that the human rights framework underlying HRIAs is not apolitical and assessors should not shy away from this fact.[44] I argued at the time for the importance of respecting the principle of neutrality as this is an important principle of social inquiry and impact assessment. Nonetheless, respecting the principle of neutrality while at the same time respecting the values underlying the human rights framework might be challenging in practice.

The human rights framework is 'political' in the sense that it does not perceive different actors in society as politically or economically neutral—on the contrary, it identifies them as actors with varying levels of power and with duties to act responsibly to individuals, including the marginalized. At least under international human rights law, the framework seeks to transform these power relations with a view to avoiding social exclusion. It places specific importance on protecting individual rights—particularly, the rights of those in vulnerable or marginalized situations. In this sense, the human rights framework is far from being neutral and takes sides—in favour of rights-holders and against a non-interventionist state (at least in certain situations, particularly in relation to economic, social, and cultural rights).[45]

On the other hand, impact assessment seeks to apply a scientific method to the collection of analysis and data so that it reveals evidence as to the real or likely impact of a policy or project as an objective means of influencing decision-making processes. It requires an element of detachment from the policy and project, and

[44] Berne Declaration et al., *supra* note 26, at 7.

[45] P. Gready, 'Reasons to be Cautious about Evidence and Evaluation: Rights-based Approaches to Development and the Emerging Culture of Evaluation', 1 *Journal of Human Rights Practice* (2009), 380–401, at 388.

the identification or real and likely impacts and, importantly, a rejection of bias.[46] Theory and ideology should be put to one side and the assessor should be open to contradiction and to being surprised. The partisan nature of the human rights framework raises the question of whether such neutrality is possible at all.

It is necessary to understand the 'partisan nature' of human rights and the 'neutrality' of impact assessment as applying to different aspects of the impact assessment process. The 'neutrality' of impact assessment applies to the objective process of undertaking the HRIA. In other words, the assessor should enter into the exercise with an open mind and be ready to acknowledge both positive and negative impacts and even be ready to question underlying assumptions about the policy at hand—for example, whether the assessor is ultimately in favour or against the adoption of free trade agreements might have to be put aside and the assessor should acknowledge that beneficial impacts arise. The impact assessment should assess, as objectively as possible, the capacity of states to meet their responsibilities under human rights law as well as the capacity of individuals to enjoy their rights and claim their entitlements. The assessor should seek to identify a causal chain of events from introduction of a policy or project and its impact on rights, and verify each of those steps through a transparent process of data collection and analysis.

However, this needs to be done by respecting the underlying principles of the human rights framework. For example, in seeking participation of rights-holders in the impact assessment, the human rights framework goes beyond participation as simply 'needs assessment' to encouraging advocacy and mobilization towards inclusive problem-solving and decision-making, and political activism.[47] The risk of identifying too closely with the position of 'rights-holders' will be present; however, there will undoubtedly be dissonant voices among 'rights-holders' and the assessor will have to maintain a neutral position in order to analyse such results as well. At the level of conclusions, a finding that a proposed development project will negatively affect an indigenous community must, using the human rights framework, be interpreted in relation to the rights of that community to property, to culture and with a view to ensuring that those human rights breaches do not occur. Yet the process for arriving at that conclusion should be scientific and transparent—neutral—and this should not preclude the formulation of conclusions in a way that is geared towards political mobilization beyond the assessment.

Scott-Samuel and O'Keefe appear to have arrived at a similar conclusion in the field of health impact assessment.[48] According to the authors, an underlying objective of health impact assessment should be to identify what they refer to as

[46] See, e.g. G. King, R.O. Keohane, and S. Verba, *Designing Social Inquiry* (Princeton: Princeton University Press, 1994); R.K. Yin, *Case Study Research: Design and Methods* 3rd edn (London: Sage Publications, 2003), 59, which states as one of the desired skills of a case study researcher that 'a person should be unbiased by preconceived notions, including those derived from theory. Thus, a person should be sensitive and responsive to contradictory evidence'.

[47] Gready, *supra* note 45, at 389.

[48] A. Scott-Samuel and E. O'Keefe, 'Health impact assessment, human rights and global public policy: a critical appraisal', 85 *Bulletin of the World Health Organization* (2007), 212–217, at 214.

'health-damaging concentrations of power and locations from which alternative power structures may have a feasible chance of emerging'.[49] Noting that health impact assessment promotes values of equity and participation of stakeholders, they argue that the application of these values should not be confused with partiality or bias. Their argumentation parallels directly with the reconciliation of the partisan nature of the human rights framework with the neutrality of impact assessment. Nonetheless, as the volume of HRIA practice increases, it will be crucial to observe the extent to which the scientific neutrality of impact assessment prevails in front of the human rights activism that seeks to mobilize and empower communities. The debate on this issue will no doubt continue.

D. Commercialization and bureaucratization

Another challenge to HRIAs relates to the potential for their appropriation and 'misuse' by commercial or bureaucratic interests. The risk of the commercialization of HRIAs was raised during the discussion related to this paper at the 10 February 2011 expert meeting.[50] Commercialization refers to the potential for an HRIA industry to arise, comprising consultants with little or no knowledge of the human rights framework who are prepared to 'deliver' an HRIA, principally to a business enterprise that is ready to pay. At best, roving consultants might not pursue the same eagerness for transformative change through the use of participatory assessment techniques as many of those advocating for impact assessment. At worst, commercialization could lead to the use of human rights language as a means of validating a business policy, with complete disregard for the principles underlying the human rights framework.

The risk of bureaucratization of HRIAs is more complex and potentially arises at three levels. First, bureaucratization might occur in situations where HRIAs are institutionalized within the internal practice of governments, business enterprises, or others and become tick-box or checklist exercises; another red-tape hurdle that must be jumped in order to arrive at pre-determined decisions to implement the policy or project being assessed. A second form of bureaucratization is closely linked to the first and relates to the situation where an HRIA is undertaken as a means only to validate certain policies or projects but not to question them in any serious way. Unlike the first form of bureaucratization where the HRIA is a tick-box exercise, under this scenario, the human rights framework is used as a morally and publicly acceptable language to justify the policy or project.[51] Third, bureaucratization might arise at the level of implementation of HRIA recommendations. A perfectly fine HRIA, undertaken independently and transparently, might identify recommendations which then get lost within the maze of bureaucratic decision-making

[49] A. Scott-Samuel and E. O'Keefe, 'Health impact assessment, human rights and global public policy: a critical appraisal', 85 *Bulletin of the World Health Organization* (2007), 212–217, at 214.

[50] Expert Meeting on Contemporary Issues in the Realization of Economic, Social and Cultural Rights, Geneva, 10–11 February, Session 3, notes on file with the author.

[51] Harrison, *supra* note 13.

where incompetence or special-interests groups might obstruct implementation.[52] The result is that HRIAs might become another exercise to perform with a worst case scenario being that they provide a means to white-wash potentially harmful, or at least questionable, policies and projects.

The extent to which the commercialization and bureaucratization of HRIAs is in fact occurring or likely to occur is difficult to determine. As long as the results of the HRIA are made public and the process is undertaken according to a transparent and objective methodology, it is arguable that the assessment is as good as its underlying methodology. Similarly, if consultants are too indulgent of the interests of those commissioning the assessment, the reputation of the consultants will come under scrutiny.

One response to the challenges of commercialization and bureaucratization lies in the professionalization of HRIAs.[53] The development and testing of a range of methodologies and the establishment of the website of the Human Rights Impact Assessment Resource Centre are important steps towards this end. Similarly, the move towards developing principles and guidelines for HRIAs should help to identify those HRIAs that are rigorous and independent and to isolate those that are overly subject to commercial or bureaucratic influences. Indeed, professionalization goes beyond dealing only with problems of commercialization and bureaucratization and goes to the heart of the future of impact assessment.

An initiative in this area has been the Guiding Principles for Human Rights Impact Assessment of Trade and Investment Agreements developed by the UN Special Rapporteur on the Rights to Adequate Food, Olivier de Schutter, to follow up on a seminar in June 2010 on the issue of HRIAs of trade and investment agreements.[54] The Guidelines should provide an authoritative guide and international benchmark to determine what constitutes a credible HRIA.

Finally, it is worth raising a word of caution in the context of professionalizing HRIAs. To the extent that professionalization leads to an overemphasis on the development of tools and methodologies and the application of various economic and social science techniques for data collection and analysis, this could detract from the transformative role of the human rights framework, focusing too much on ensuring scientific precision and issues of process and losing sight of the ultimate aim of HRIAs—to protect the rights of individuals and to ensure that governments respect their human rights responsibilities and have the capacity to do so. It risks privileging the professional over those who might have a deeper or different

[52] See (in relation to sustainability impact assessments commissioned by the European Commission), e.g. Federation Internationale de Droits de l'Homme, *Human Rights Impact Assessment of Trade and Investment Agreements Concluded by the European Union* (2008), Position Paper, available at <http://www.europarl.europa.eu/meetdocs/2009_2014/documents/droi/dv/droi_20100304_51fidh_/droi_20100304_51fidh_en.pdf> (last accessed 10 November 2013).

[53] Harrison, *supra* note 13.

[54] United Nations, Guiding Principles on Human Rights Impact Assessments of Trade and Investment Agreements, Special Rapporteur on the Right to Food, Addendum 5 to the Report of the Special Rapporteur to the Human Rights Council, UN Doc. A/HRC/19/59/Add.6; See also: Berne Declaration et al., *supra* note 26.

understanding of the issues under examination.[55] For example, an overemphasis on a scientific discussion on whether there is sufficient data to demonstrate with certainty a negative impact of a policy or project on the enjoyment of the right to health in a particular community might lose sight of the fact that individuals in that community might believe their right to health has suffered—whether or not this can be justified scientifically, it nonetheless is a real concern that requires action. Similarly, a human rights impact assessment, even if not methodologically sound, might nonetheless motivate a community and create awareness of rights and a basis for advocacy and action, again, a valid outcome even if the results of the assessment itself might be lacking. It would be ironic indeed if a move to professionalize HRIAs as a means of overcoming commercialization and bureaucratization in fact leads to their further bureaucratization.

4. Conclusion

There is clearly growing interest in HRIA among a range of actors, not only civil society organizations but also government representatives and business enterprises and HRIAs undoubtedly have a place within the growing toolbox of human rights methodologies. The increased focus on economic, social, and cultural rights by human rights practitioners since the 1990s has encouraged this interest, particularly given the fact that respecting these rights can be achieved through implementing a range of different projects and policies: HRIAs provide a means to examine which policies or projects are better and to monitor their multiple impacts over time.

A question I often ask in meetings on impact assessment to civil society representatives is whether they would consider undertaking an HRIA as a strategy to respond to a given policy or project instead of relying on more traditional options such as advocacy work. The response is, more often than not, affirmative and the interest lies in the potential of having evidence to support arguments which are otherwise based on values and principles. And not only civil society actors are concerned. In 2009, I expressed some scepticism as to whether government actors would undertake HRIAs, given the link between HRIAs and their own legal accountability.[56] That Switzerland recently refused a recommendation during its Universal Periodic Review before the Human Rights Council to undertake human rights impact assessments due to the methodological uncertainty of such assessments tends to support this position.[57] Yet the fact that the UK government is undertaking equality assessments of policies and Canada is undertaking an assessment of its free trade agreement with Colombia suggests that at least some governments are interested in undertaking HRIAs.

[55] Harrison, *supra* note 13. [56] Walker, *supra* note 10.

[57] United Nations, Report of the Working Group of the Universal Periodic Review: Switzerland, Addendum, Views on Conclusions and/or Recommendations, Voluntary Commitments and Replies Presented by the State party under Review, UN Doc. A/HRC/22/11/Add.1.

Given this context, the most important move forward is to build on the already growing body of HRIA practice. This should continue at the level of building methodologies—for example, identifying appropriate techniques for data collection and analysis, and human rights indicators—as well as undertaking HRIAs on the ground. Further, HRIA professionals should continue analysing experience, including in relation to some of the issues discussed in this chapter, asking questions such as: how useful was a particular HRIA in bringing about change? Could change have been achieved using another strategy? Were there secondary benefits related to undertaking an HRIA, for example, mobilization of local communities, human rights education? This in turn should help to feed into and fine-tune ongoing practice. Importantly, monitoring of HRIAs could also help identify whether problems such as commercialization or bureaucratization are emerging and help to expose such phenomena. Finally, the fact that HRIA practitioners are reaching out to the broader impact assessment community is also important as a means of sharing experience and professional standards and to consolidate HRIA's position within a broader community of professionals and impact assessment practice.

VI

TRENDS IN THE JUSTICIABILITY AND MONITORING OF ESC RIGHTS AT THE NATIONAL AND INTERNATIONAL LEVEL

15

Judicial Review in National Courts

Recognition and Responsiveness

Malcolm Langford

1. Introduction

The question of 'justiciability' has featured strongly in the struggle to legitimize economic, social, and cultural (ESC) rights.[1] It has consumed the energies of advocates for two principal reasons. Conceptually, establishing justiciability would overcome objections that ESC rights lack the necessary legal and determinate qualities for any putative human or citizen right.[2] Instrumentally, legal enforceability offered the promise of a concrete tool to tackle social injustice and balance a legal bias towards civil, political, and property rights.[3]

Thus far, this quest has been a qualified success. A gradual and reflexive transnational diffusion of the idea that social rights are, and should be, legally enforceable has accelerated in the last two decades. Enforceable ESC rights are prominent in a wave of new and revised constitutions and international treaties while jurisprudence has thickened in comparative and international law.[4]

[1] Justiciability is an 'unusually protean' term, manifesting itself in multiple forms: T. Barton, 'Justiciability: A Theory of Judicial Problem Solving', 24 *Boston College Law Review* (1983), 505–634, 506. For the purposes and remainder of this chapter, justiciability will be used in a rather narrow and legalistic sense to signify a doctrine or approach that courts, despite possessing formal jurisdiction, should find that certain legal provisions are non-self-executing (requiring ancillary legislation) or certain questions are unsuitable for adjudication. The bases for non-justiciability can vary greatly though, from technical legal criteria through to prudential concerns over institutional competence and democratic legitimacy.

[2] For a classical argument along these lines, see E.W. Vierdag, 'The legal nature of the rights granted by the international Covenant on Economic, Social and Cultural Rights', 9 *Netherlands Yearbook of International Law* (1978), 69–105.

[3] For a classical critique of the inability of law and rights to affect social justice and for a concern that social rights will not affect the conservative bias of the judiciary, see D. Kennedy, *Critique of Adjudication (fin de siècle)* (Cambridge: Harvard University Press, 1997).

[4] This is not to suggest that legal recognition has solely driven the jurisprudence. Other triggers of jurisprudence included the relative strength of civil society support structures, judicial culture and the availability of alternatives to litigation. See M. Langford, 'Domestic Adjudication of Economic, Social and Cultural Rights: A Socio-Legal Review' (2009) 11 *SUR—International Journal of Human Rights*;

It is possible now to cite a judgment for almost any dimension of an ESC right or duty.[5]

These developments have triggered an outbreak of optimism. Justice Sachs of South Africa predicted that the '21st-century jurisprudence will focus increasingly on socio-economic rights'.[6] The Optional Protocol to the International Covenant on Economic, Social and Cultural Rights (ICESCR)[7] has been heralded with similar sentiments.[8] The growing confidence in the judicial enforceability is equally evident in the posture of the UN Committee on Economic, Social and Cultural Rights (CESCR). In 1991, it articulated a somewhat classical and spatial position on justiciability: 'many component elements' of a Covenant right were justiciable.[9] By 1998, the Committee felt comfortable enough to emphasize that accountability was the standard: 'whenever a Covenant right cannot be made fully effective without some role for the judiciary, judicial remedies are necessary'.[10] Since then, it has strongly encouraged states to incorporate the Covenant in the domestic legal order[11] and even criticized specific states for failing to do so.[12]

Nonetheless, the emerging practice of social rights adjudication faces an array of issues and challenges.[13] They range from philosophical and normative debates[14]

V. Gauri and D. Brinks, *Courting Social Justice: Judicial Enforcement of Social and Economic Rights in the Developing World* (New York: Cambridge University Press, 2008).

[5] For a comparative overview with in-depth country chapters, see M. Langford (ed.), *Social Rights Jurisprudence: Emerging Trends in International and Comparative Law* (Cambridge: Cambridge University Press, 2008); R. Gargarella, P. Domingo, and T. Roux, *Courts and Social Transformation in New Democracies: An Institutional Voice for the Poor?* (Aldershot: Ashgate, 2006); and F. Coomans (ed.), *Justiciability of Economic and Social Rights: Experiences from Domestic Systems* (Antwerpen: Intersentia and Maastrict Centre for Human Rights, 2006). Global estimates of the total number of social rights judgments exceed half a million but this figure is inflated by individual *tutela* actions in Latin America.

[6] A. Sachs, 'Social and Economic Rights: Can They Be Made Justiciable?' (Southern Methodist University School of Law, 1999), 18.

[7] GA Res. 832, UN GAOR, 63rd Session, UN Doc A/RES/63/117 (2008).

[8] In 2008, the UN High Commissioner for Human Rights, an individual complaints and inquiry mechanism, by praising its 'singular importance' in 'closing a historic gap in human rights protection under the international system'. Statement by the High Commissioner for Human Rights, Ms Navanethem Pillay, *Official Records*, 65th Plenary meeting, UN Doc. A/63/PV. 66, Wednesday 10 December 2008, 3 p.m.

[9] General Comment No. 4, *The right to adequate housing* (6th session, 1991), UN Doc. E/1992/23, annex III, at 114 (1991) (CESCR), para. 17.

[10] General Comment No. 9, *The domestic application of the Covenant* (19th session, 1998), UN Doc. E/C.12/1998/24 (1998) (CESCR), para. 9.

[11] General Comment No. 9, *The domestic application of the Covenant* (19th session, 1998), UN Doc. E/C.12/1998/24 (1998) (CESCR), para. 8.

[12] See, e.g. Conclusions and recommendations of CESCR: United Kingdom of Great Britain and Northern Ireland—Dependent Territories, UN Doc. E/C.12/1/Add.79 (2002), para. 10.

[13] Many of these are not unfamiliar to the field of civil and political rights.

[14] For example, the status of social rights, the institutional competence of the judiciary, and the democratic legitimacy of judicial review. See, e.g. J. Waldron, 'Socio-Economic Rights and Theories of Justice', in T. Pogge (ed.), *Freedom from Poverty as a Human Right* (Paris: UNESCO, 2009); J.A. King, *Judging Social Rights* (Cambridge: Cambridge University Press, 2012); C.F. Sabel and W. Simon, 'Destabilization Rights: How Public Law Litigation Succeeds' (2004) 117 *Harvard Law Review* 1015; A.C. Hutchinson, 'A 'Hard Core' Case Against Judicial Review' (2008) 121 *Harvard Law Review* 57.

through to doctrinal,[15] empirical,[16] and strategic[17] questions. This chapter will confine itself to two issues that seem most pertinent to a volume that seeks to stocktake the progress of the enterprise of ESC rights. Both concern law and jurisprudence but the analytical lens will be socio-legal and external rather than doctrinal and internal.

The first is recognition, the degree to which ESC rights are formally enforceable by the judiciary. The last few decades have witnessed an explosion of constitutional guarantees, providing a handmaiden to the emerging practice of express ESC rights adjudication. Nonetheless, the legal opportunity structure for claimants remains a global patchwork. Its variance, causes, and consequences deserve greater attention. Section 2 therefore reviews the current constitutional recognition of ESC rights, with a particular focus on enforceability and legal standing.

The second is responsiveness, the extent to which national courts are willing to entertain petitions in good faith. The CESCR has expressed concern at the reluctance of some national courts;[18] critics have gone further and predicted that the story of ESC rights adjudication is likely to end not with a bang but a whimper.[19] These concerns are not without foundation and there is clear evidence of a judicial conservatism or avoidance in some states. However, the question is whether it is a systemic and permanent problem. If judicial behaviour is varied and conditional, it may be sensitive to institutional reform and calibrated litigation strategy. Section 3 takes up this question of responsiveness by analysing the theoretical contestation over its causes, the lessons learned from state-level right to education litigation in the United States, and the comparative picture of judicial responsiveness. In doing so, it also provides a picture of contemporary trends of ESC rights jurisprudence.

[15] For example, questions of jurisdiction, interpretation and discretion, scope of rights and duties, the question of resources, conflicts of rights and remedies. See, e.g. S Liebenberg, *Socio-Economic Rights: Adjudication Under a Transformative Constitution* (Claremont: Juta, 2010); and country chapters in references in fn. 4.

[16] For instance, the empirical debates concerning the causes of litigation, the judicial behaviour of courts, the patterns of judicial outcomes, compliance with judicial orders, and impact of litigation. See, e.g. B. Wilson, 'Rights Revolutions in Unlikely Places: Costa Rica and Colombia' (2009) 1 *Journal of Politics in Latin America* 59; Gauri and Brinks (fn. 4); A.E. Yamin and S. Gloppen, *Litigating Health Rights: Can Courts Bring More Justice to Health?* (Cambridge: Harvard University Press, 2011).

[17] Strategic debates exist over the sequencing and ambitions of claims, the use of civil and political rights as proxies, and the use of quantitative evidence. See, e.g, J. Cavallaro and S. Brewer, 'The Virtue of Following: The Role of Inter-American Litigation in Campaigns for Social Justice' (2008) 5 *SUR—International Journal on Human Rights* 8; B. Porter, 'The Crisis of ESC Rights and Strategies for Addressing It', in J. Squires, M. Langford, and B. Thiele (eds.), *The Road to a Remedy* (2005).

[18] General Comment No. 9, *The domestic application of the Covenant*, para. 11. The Committee addresses the Canadian courts directly, noting that they should 'take account of Covenant rights' where this is 'necessary to ensure' that a state acts consistently with its obligations and refers to a particular case of concern: Concluding Observations of CESCR: Canada UN Doc. E/C.12/CAN/CO/4-E/C.12/CAN/CO/5 (2006), para. 36.

[19] See Section 3.1.

2. Recognition

A. Constitutional jurisdiction

It is sometimes thought that the subject of ESC rights was unusual or peculiar to constitutions. Viewed in the aggregate, the constitutional history of ESC rights is not significantly different from civil and political rights. As Figure 15.1 reveals, by 1970 the general recognition of core rights for both sets of rights was similar. Moreover, subsequent constitutionalization has proceeded at similar rate.

What has distinguished the two sets of rights is judicial enforceability. Jurisdiction over civil and political rights was granted more often to the courts. This was achieved in two ways. In some constitutions, the sets of rights were divided into judicially enforceable and non-enforceable categories (for example South Asian and African constitutions). Alternatively, ESC rights tended to be more recognized in the constitutions but no rights were enforceable (for example many communist states but also countries such as the Netherlands and New Zealand). The principal exceptions to this pattern were a handful of European, Latin American, and Pacific island states.

The consequence of this constitutional architecture was that judicial enforcement of ESC rights proceeded largely through the frame of civil and occasionally political rights. A largely minimalist conception of ESC rights was integrated into rights such as life, dignity, property, equality, and a fair hearing.[20] This is

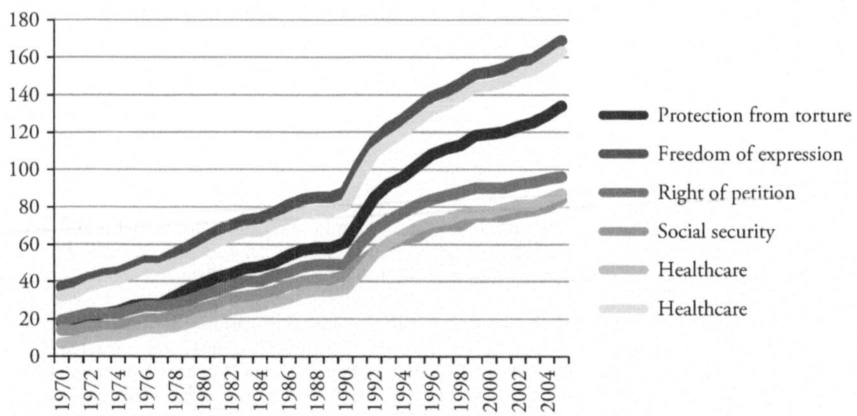

Figure 15.1 Trends in constitutional rights: 1970–2005*

* The source of the original data is the CCP Data Set, available at <http://www.comparativeconstitutionsproject.org/> (last accessed 27 October 2013) To transform it into times series data, it was determined for each year, whether a constitution (dated by its most significant recent reform—usually at a time of democratic or post-colonial transition) included the particular right. As the recognition of some rights could have been through earlier amendments to a constitution, there is likely to be a margin of error. However, the overall trend is fairly clear.

[20] However, note that in some of these jurisdictions, social rights were formally enforceable but courts chose to largely apply civil rights in concrete cases. The Netherlands, France, and the Inter-American Court on Human Rights are notable examples. See further discussion in Section 3.

particularly evident in jurisprudence in Germany, Switzerland, India, Colombia, Hungary, Pakistan, the Inter-American Court of Human Rights, and the European Court of Human Rights, and partly Canada and the United States.[21] To take the example of Germany, the right to human dignity and the directive principle of the *Sozialstaat* were subsumed and interpreted in the 1960s to establish a right to an *Existenzminimum*.[22] Accordingly, the state must ensure 'every needy person the material conditions that are indispensable for his or her physical existence and for a minimum participation in social, cultural and political life'.[23]

The 1980s, however, heralded a dramatic shift in this legal opportunity structure. Direct constitutionalization of ESC rights and the domestic incorporation of treaties such as the ICESCR proceeded apace.[24] Figure 15.2 shows the degree of formal judicial enforceability of 16 ESC rights in 146 countries (marked in dark grey).[25] For the sake of quantitative illustration, these rights are weighted equally

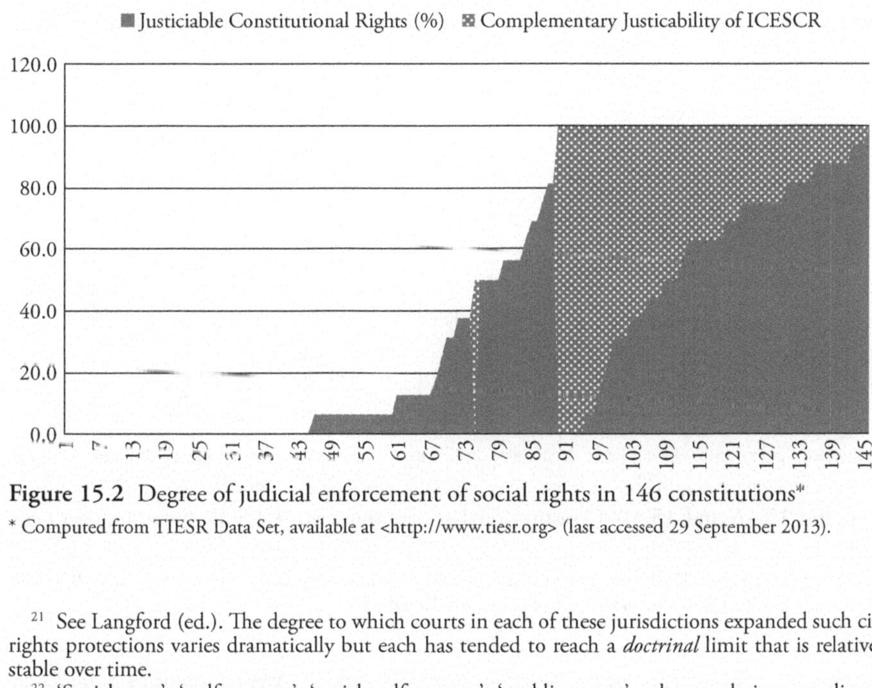

Figure 15.2 Degree of judicial enforcement of social rights in 146 constitutions*

* Computed from TIESR Data Set, available at <http://www.tiesr.org> (last accessed 29 September 2013).

[21] See Langford (ed.). The degree to which courts in each of these jurisdictions expanded such civil rights protections varies dramatically but each has tended to reach a *doctrinal* limit that is relatively stable over time.

[22] 'Social state', 'welfare state', 'social welfare state', 'enabling state'—the translations are diverse. See S.-I. Koutnatzis, 'Social Rights as a Constitutional Compromise: Lessons from Comparative Experience' (2005) 44 *Colombia Journal of International Law* 74, 113.

[23] 1 BvL 1/09, 1 BvL 3/09, 1 BvL 4/09. The Court usually abstains from setting such a minimum and takes instead the role of reviewing whether the state's legislation and benefits system etc meets the minimum requirements. It was first interpreted in the 1960s, for example, to include rights against taxation that threatened the sustenance minimum of families with children. BVerfGE 99, 246, (259).

[24] GA Res. 2200A (XXI), 21 UN GAOR Supp. (No. 16), at 49; UN Doc. A/6316 (1966), 993 UNTS 3, entered into force 3 January 1976.

[25] These constitutional rights compromise employment-related rights (fair wage, trade union rights, right to strike, leave, healthy work environment, social security) and general social rights (education, child protection, non-employment social security, health, land, housing, food and water,

(for example a score of 50 per cent corresponds to eight justiciable ESC rights). If the ICESCR is constitutionally incorporated and made justiciable,[26] a score of 100 per cent is given (light grey).[27] As can be seen, at least one ESC right is judicially enforceable in 100 of 146 sampled countries (69 per cent). All 16 rights are enforceable in 55 countries (38 per cent).[28]

Jung and Rosevear argue that this picture of the rising recognition of enforceable ESC rights is partly misleading. They claim that there was a slowdown in the period 1990–2004 as compared to 1974–89.[29] They attribute this to the rise of the Washington-based consensus, which reached its zenith in the later period. This statistical and causal interpretation is, however, questionable. An alternative picture might be preferred.

Using the same data, Figure 15.3A charts constitutional recognition of enforceable ESC rights on a continuous time scale (rather than with artificial time periods). It is clear that the general trend line is upwards. The graph reveals the surge of constitutionalization in a third wave of democratization (late 1980s, early 1990s) in Latin America and Eastern Europe, which was followed by another swell

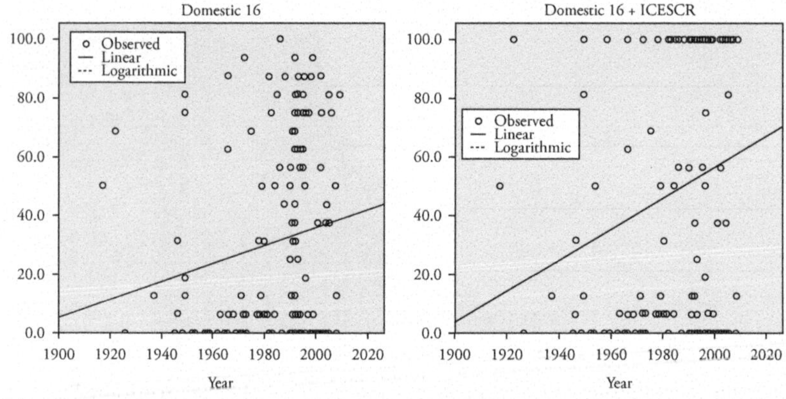

Figures 15.3A and 15.3B Constitutional recognition and ICESCR incorporation over time*

* Note that in Figure 15.3B, the year of constitutional adoption was presumed to be the year of ICESCR incorporation though this was adjusted in one case to a later date.

development, healthy environment). Note that the representation of Western countries is limited in relation to other regions. There are only 10 Western European countries included. Otherwise, there is a fair representation of other countries: Arab countries (21), Asia (24), Eastern and Central Europe (25), Latin America (22), and Sub-Saharan Africa (44). The Pacific region is completely excluded.

[26] Whether explicitly or through a monist doctrine of international law.

[27] In the case of Norway, a score of 50 per cent was given since the ICESCR was not incorporated at the constitutional level but as superior legislation.

[28] For a fuller analysis of regional, legal tradition and other patterns of justiciability in this dataset, see C. Jung and E. Rosevear, 'Economic and Social Rights Across Time, Regions, and Legal Traditions: A Preliminary Analysis of the TIESR Dataset' (2012) 30 *Nordic Journal of Human Rights*.

[29] Jung and Rosevear, *supra* note 28, at 381. Note that they use only the dataset of 136 countries minus the 10 Western countries. However, excluding these 10 countries does not change the results.

in the late 1990s in Asia and sub-Saharan Africa. Thus, the rise in recognition of constitutional social rights is both recent and concentrated. Moreover, if we include constitutional incorporation of the ICESCR, the upward trend becomes even clearer: see Figure 15.3B.[30]

However, this graph clearly reveals the underlying challenge: the equal persistence of the non-recognition of social rights. The weak correlation scores underline this wide variance. The R-squared results are respectively 0.03 and 0.05. What explains this variance? It is doubtful that the World Bank and the rise of neoliberalism accounts for constitutional reluctance. The causes are more likely to be region- and country-specific. For example, the variance across Eastern Europe can be partly explained by the struggle between a new political elite (often backed by the United States) and a populace worried about the erosion of social rights in the shift to a market democracy.[31] In Sub-Saharan Africa, legal concerns and worries over fiscal burdens have most likely dampened the enthusiasm for domestic recognition even though African governments have strongly promoted the rights in international affairs.

These numerous silent spaces of non-judicial enforceability of ESC rights highlight a particular constitutional challenge. The scope for formal judicial review of ESC rights is rather limited outside the use of civil rights or international mechanisms. This does not mean opportunities for change do not exist. Constitutional reform processes continue to emerge or erupt in unlikely places. In the last six years, ESC rights have been made judicially enforceable in new constitutions in Kenya, Egypt, Bolivia, Ecuador, and Zimbabwe; interim constitutions in Nepal, Libya, and Tunisia; and in official proposals for reformed constitutions in Norway and Fiji. However, a process to consider inclusion of enforceable civil and social rights in the Australian constitution did not lead to any result. Although, most of these processes are part of broader processes to reform constitutions or bills of rights (due to democratic transitions, political crises, or efforts to modernize constitutions). Only occasionally is the process driven by a demand for the constitutional recognition of specific ESC rights.[32]

It is also worth recalling the increased international pressure for judicial review of ESC rights. In General Comment No. 9, the CESCR called for the incorporation of the Covenant in the domestic legal order and, in its concluding observations on United Kingdom, the Committee stated, with some exasperation, that 'the Covenant has still not been incorporated in the domestic legal order' and reiterated its 'concern about the state party's position that the provisions of

[30] The trend would be even higher if we included recent constitutional reforms in Kenya, Egypt, Tunisia, Uruguay, and Fiji among other countries.

[31] On the clash between elites and the public, see W Sadurski, *Rights before Courts: A Study of Constitutional Courts in Postcommunist States of Central and Eastern Europe* (Dordrecht: Springer, 2005).

[32] For example, on 31 October 2004, over 64 per cent of Uruguayan voters approved the measure to recognize the right to water and end water privatisation. See D. Hall, E. Lobina, and R. De la Motte, *Making water privatisation illegal: New laws in Netherlands and Uruguay*, 31 November 2004, available at <http://www.waterjustice.org> (last accessed on 29 September 2013). A referendum to include the right to housing in the Geneva canton of Switzerland was also successful in 1992.

the Covenant, with minor exceptions, constitute principles and programmatic objectives rather than legal obligations that are justiciable'.[33] This would also apply to other international treaties containing ESC rights such as the CRPD[34] and CRC.[35] However, domestication of the ICESCR need not always involve constitutionalization. It can be achieved through the adoption of superior legislation.[36] Moreover, the incentives to domesticate judicial review of ESC rights may be enhanced in states that ratify the Optional Protocol to ICESCR. Governments could ensure that litigation must exhaust real remedies in domestic courts before proceeding to the international plane.[37]

B. Legal standing

Constitutional recognition represents only one dimension of jurisdiction or, in political science terms, the formal legal opportunity structure. The rules of standing may limit significantly the types of actors that may seek judicial relief or the circumstances under which it can be sought. As Ginsburg notes, 'Access to the court is perhaps the most important ingredient in judicial power'.[38] Jurisdictions vary significantly in which parties can seek review: from relatively restrictive systems (for example that only grant standing to an individual victim or parliamentary minority) through to more open systems (which grant access rights to organizations, collectives, parliamentarians, parliament, and judges). In some jurisdictions, legislation cannot be impugned in contentious proceedings and only ex ante abstract review is permitted. While common law systems were traditionally more restricted (along the lines of the British model) and continental systems more open (along the lines of the German model), there has been marked variance within and across jurisdictions over time. The same has continued in new constitutional democracies with restricted forms of review in approximately half of them.[39]

For ESC rights, this institutional dimension of jurisdiction is particularly important.[40] Standing to pursue non-victim based litigation can be crucial when individuals are disabled from litigating (by virtue of harassment, bribes, lack of

[33] Conclusions and recommendations of CESCR: United Kingdom of Great Britain and Northern Ireland—Dependent Territories, UN Doc. E/C.12/1/Add.79 (2002), para. 10.

[34] International Convention on the Protection and Promotion of the Rights and Dignity of Persons with Disabilities, GA Res. 61/106, Annex I, UN GAOR, 61st Sess., Supp. No. 49, at 65, UN Doc. A/61/49 (2006), entered into force 3 May 2008.

[35] Convention on the Rights of the Child, GA Res. 44/25, annex, 44 UN GAOR Supp. (No. 49) at 167, UN Doc. A/44/49 (1989), entered into force 2 Sept. 1990.

[36] See, e.g. Human Rights Act (1999), Norway. See also Section 2 of the Protection of Human Rights Act, 1993 of India,

[37] See Art. 3, Optional Protocol to the ICESCR.

[38] T. Ginsberg, *Judicial Review in New Democracies: Constitutional Courts in Asian Cases* (New York: Cambridge University Press, 2003), 37.

[39] T. Ginsberg, *Judicial Review in New Democracies: Constitutional Courts in Asian Cases* (New York: Cambridge, 2003), 36–38.

[40] This is not to assert that standing is the only institutional feature of jurisdictional interest. Access to legal representation and aid is as crucial: see A. Aurbach, 'The Right to Legal Aid in Social Rights Litigation', in M. Langford (ed.), *Social Rights Jurisprudence: Emerging Trends in International and Comparative Law* (Cambridge: Cambridge University Press, 2008). In addition, Dugard and Roux

legal assistance), there is no system of precedent (meaning the individual litigant and the court are not required to consider the collective dimensions of the issue) or collective enforcement agencies lack the power, means, or will to enforce constitutional rights and relevant legislation (for example, regulators, ombudsmen, national human rights institutions, public defenders). More broadly, collective action rights can allow marginalized groups to emerge as repeat-action litigation players rather than one-shotters; thus levelling the litigation playing field against well-organized government and corporate legal teams.[41] However, there are a significant number of jurisdictions in which such collective interest litigation is not possible.

Standing rights are not only determined by positive law; it is often a question of judicial interpretation.[42] Here, conceptions of the justiciability of ESC rights may figure prominently. The Inter-American Court provides a good illustration. The Court has first constructed Article 26 of the American Convention on Human Rights[43] in a rather narrow fashion, requiring only the 'growing coverage' of social rights 'over the entire population'.[44] Despite the wording of the provision being (ever so) slightly more ambiguous than the equivalent Article 2 of ICESCR, the Court interpreted it much more narrowly than the CESCR or some other courts faced with similar provisions. This reading limits the article to imposing general and collective obligations of result to the exclusion of conduct-related and respect-oriented duties.[45] Moreover and importantly, it has a knock-on effect on standing.[46] With the only exception of indigenous peoples, the Court has adopted a comparatively restrictive understanding of standing. It is limited to named individuals in a petition who have suffered harm.[47] As Article 26 had been completely

argue that direct access to apex courts should be permitted on the grounds of costs to applicants: J. Dugard and T. Roux, 'The Record of the South African Constitutional Court in Providing an Institutional Voice for the Poor: 1995–2004', in R. Gargarella, P. Domingo, and T. Roux (eds.), *Courts and Social Transformation in New Democracies: An Institutional Voice for the Poor?* (Aldershot/ Burlington: Ashgate, 2006).

[41] M. Galanter, 'Why the 'Haves' Come Out Ahead: Speculations on the Limits of Legal Change' in R. Cover and O. Fiss (eds.), *The Structure of Procedure* (London: Foundation Press, 1969).

[42] In a number of jurisdictions, e.g. USA and European Court of Human Rights, standing rules also vary over time to not only control the docket but allow a court to consider cases *it* considers important.

[43] The provision reads: 'Progressive Development. The States Parties undertake to adopt measures, both internally and through international cooperation, especially those of an economic and technical nature, with a view to achieving progressively, by legislation or other appropriate means, the full realization of the rights implicit in the economic, social, educational, scientific, and cultural standards set forth in the Charter of the Organization of American States as amended by the Protocol of Buenos Aires'.

[44] *Five Pensioners' Case* Judgment of 28 February, 2003, Inter-Am. HR (Ser. C) No. 8, (Inter-American Court of Human Rights), para. 147.

[45] For a discussion, see T. Melish, 'Inter-American Court of Human Rights: Beyond Progressivity', in Langford, *supra* note 5, 375.

[46] T. Melish, 'Inter-American Court of Human Rights: Beyond Progressivty', in Langford, *supra* note 5, 387. Even in cases concerning prison conditions, every applicant must be named.

[47] *International Responsibility for the Promulgation and Enforcement of Laws in Violation of the Convention (Arts. 1 and 2 of the American Convention on Human Rights)* Advisory Opinion OC-14/94, 9 December 1994, Inter-Am. Ct. HR (Ser. A) No. 14 (Inter-American Court of Human Rights). See discussion in J Pasqualacci, *The Practice and Procedure of the Inter-American Court of Human Rights* 2nd edn (Cambridge: Cambridge University Press, 2013), 133.

denuded substantively of any direct or indirect individual entitlement, it cannot be litigated in contentious proceedings. Thus, while the Court has enlarged the content of civil rights to include various social dimensions,[48] it could have plausibly interpreted Article 26 differently or partially relaxed its standing requirements.[49]

3. Responsiveness

A. Theoretical contestation

The second question is whether courts are sufficiently responsive to ESC rights claims. The idea that courts will be responsive is intrinsic to various justifications for judicial review of rights. Such justifications range from *epistemological* claims that judges are better suited to interpret the content of constitutional rights through to *functional* or political arguments that courts provide a forum of accountability or public deliberation.[50] These qualities are often critical in refuting claims that constitutional rights adjudication is democratically illegitimate or beyond the institutional competence of judges.

However, will courts play such a role in practice? The empirical assumptions embedded in the claim would appear reasonable within a traditional liberal and positivist framework. If social rights are incorporated in constitutional instruments, we assume courts will conform to their legal duty to apply them and provide rights-enhancing outcomes. This will be particularly so in more mature democracies when judges have sufficient independence and there is respect for the rule of law. As Altman puts it: [t]he rule of law can do this, according to liberal thought, because the law has the power to constrain, confine, and regulate the exercise of social and political power'.[51]

However, pointing to illustrative or hypothetical cases of judicial accountability is not sufficient. Sadurski remarks that Dworkin, a pre-eminent defender of judicial review, seems strangely undisturbed 'by cases implicating important issue of rights in which the legislature was more rights-protective than the [US] Supreme Court or when the legislature enhanced rights that had been affected by restrictive decisions of the Supreme Court'.[52] We need to ask, with the passage of time and jurisprudence, which branch of government on balance is better equipped in protecting and enhancing rights.[53]

[48] See generally Melish, *supra* note 46.

[49] For instance, the African Commission on Human and People's Rights has relaxed standing requirements in cases concerning systemic denials of both civil and social rights.

[50] See, e.g. R. Dworkin, *Taking Rights Seriously* (Cambridge: Harvard University Press, 1977); B. Friedman, *The Will of the People: How Public Opinion has Influenced the Supreme Court and shaped the Meaning of the Constitution* (New York: Farrar, Straus and Giroux, 2009).

[51] A. Altman, *Critical Legal Studies: A Liberal Critique* (Princeton: Princeton University Press, 1990), 13.

[52] W. Sadurski, 'Judicial Review and the Protection of Constitutional Rights', 22 *Oxford Journal of Legal Studies* (2002), 275, 278.

[53] W. Sadurski, 'Judicial Review and the Protection of Constitutional Rights', 22 *Oxford Journal of Legal Studies* (2002), 275, 279.

Some commentators claim that the answer is straightforward. Courts are not the place in which to find robust interpretation and implementation. *Institutional* critiques posit that concerns over justiciability, competence, or democratic legitimacy are likely to make courts wary of adjudicating ESC rights. The result is that high levels of deference are exercised, whether at the procedural, substantive, or remedial stages. Adjudication thus offers no prospect of social change or, even worse, legitimates problematic policies and diverts civil society energy away from political avenues.

Distributive critiques claim that adjudication will favour the advantaged rather than disadvantaged groups. A structural explanation for general distributive bias points to the ability of advantaged groups to secure better access to legal representation, to strategically maximize the benefits of repeat litigation, and to accommodate the institutional passivity and duration of court-based procedure.[54] Landau argues that this is accentuated in ESC rights adjudication. Judges will tend towards modes of adjudication that mimic classical civil rights litigation such as enforcement of individual (not collective) social rights and the obligation of non-retrogression.[55] While such approaches provide greater institutional comfort for courts, they may be most susceptible to middle-class capture as they protect the status quo, for example, pensions, health schemes, subsidized mortgages etc.

An alternative distributive explanation is ideological: courts are swayed by political subjectivism rather than legal formalism. O'Connell argues that these ideological preferences are usually invisible but nonetheless discernible.[56] For instance, he claims that whereas the judgments of the Supreme Court of Ireland in *Sinnott* and *TD* concerning the right to education in Ireland were formally deferential, they carried strong normative overtones and captured the economic and neoliberal *zeitgeist* of Ireland's elite.[57] Moreover, the Court had no qualms in enforcing the right to property when it had significant budgetary implications but was adverse to social rights adjudication on the grounds that it would impact budgetary allocations.[58]

However, distributive critics tend to be divided on the source of ideological conservatism. Hirschl identifies it as historical. In his view, the recognition of rights and establishment of judicial review is 'driven in many cases by attempts to maintain the social and political status quo'.[59] The judiciary enters a 'strategic tripartite pact' with political elites concerned with the 'vicissitudes of democratic politics' and economic elites 'who share a commitment to free markets'.[60] O'Connell takes almost the opposite point of departure and argues in sociological terms for a form

[54] Galanter, *supra* note 41.

[55] D. Landau, 'The Reality of Social Rights Enforcement' (2011), 53 *Harvard International Law Journal*, 401.

[56] P. O'Connell, 'The Death of Socio-Economic Rights', 74 *Modern Law Review* (2011), 532.

[57] P. O'Connell, 'The Death of Socio-Economic Rights', 74 *Modern Law Review* (2011), 542.

[58] P. O'Connell, 'The Death of Socio-Economic Rights', 74 *Modern Law Review* (2011), 552.

[59] R. Hirschl, *Towards Juristocracy: The Origins and Consequences of the New Constitutionalism* (Cambridge: Harvard University Press, 2004), 213–214.

[60] R. Hirschl, *Towards Juristocracy: The Origins and Consequences of the New Constitutionalism* (Cambridge: Harvard University Press, 2004), 214.

of contemporary norm acculturation: neoliberalism as the dominant force in constitutional interpretation.[61] Leading critical legal scholars tend to be more nuanced and emphasize that the textual ambiguity of law creates the space for ideology-based reasoning. Kennedy argues that 'The rule choices that emerge from [this] interaction should be understood neither as simply the implications of [legal] authority nor as the implications of the ideological projects, but as a compromise'.[62]

The question ultimately comes down to evidence. Are the liberal or transformatory expectations of courts borne out? Clearly, jurisprudential deference or rejection of certain cases is not a problem in itself. There may be good reasons for particular decisions or doctrines. These might include textual restraints and particular claims may be legally groundless, poorly substantiated, judicially unmanageable, or excessively interfere with the separation of powers. What is of concern are the general pattern and trends.

B. A future foretold? American education jurisprudence

When examining comparative jurisprudence on ESC rights for any particular trend, the analysis is customarily narrated through a tour of India, South Africa, and then selected Latin American, Asian, or European countries.[63] Curiously it overlooks a century of jurisprudence on the right to education in the United States. What is particularly interesting about US school litigation is that it provides an insight into how judiciary across multiple states wrestled at a much earlier stage with legal challenges (such as justiciability, institutional competence, and democratic legitimacy) and to what extent they provided an avenue for accountability and deliberation. In this respect, the US experience represents a forerunner of what has been comparatively witnessed elsewhere. This is not to deny some of the peculiarities of the American experience.[64] Nonetheless, it presents a useful comparative picture in itself that is worthy of initial examination.

In contrast to the US Federal Constitution, all 50 state constitutions contain a specific section on education.[65] The provisions range from a mere 'duty to promote this important object' (Maine) through to a 'paramount duty' to make 'ample provision for the education of all children' (Washington).[66] As part of a broader

[61] O'Connell, *supra* note 56. [62] Kennedy, *supra* note 3, at 19.

[63] See the complaint on this by P. Alston, 'Foreword', in Langford, *supra* note 5.

[64] This includes diversity in the wording of right to education provisions across states, an express commitment in many constitutions to publicly provided and sufficiently funded schooling, heavily entrenched political and tax inequalities, a generally more active judiciary, the direct election of judges in some states, and the failure of the United States to ratify the ICESCR.

[65] 'It is the only public function that has its own article in every single state constitution in this nation'. A. Hickrod, R. Chaudhari, G. Pruyne, and J. Meng, 'The Effect of Constitutional Litigation on Education Finance: A Further Analysis', in W. Fowler (ed.), *Selected Papers in School Finance 1995* (National Center for Education Statistics) (Washington: NCES, 1995), 51. Note that education is not the only social right included in US state constitutions. In the state of New York, the right to a minimum level of social security is enshrined as a justiciable right in the constitution. In *Tucker v Toia*, 43 N.Y.2d 1, 7 (1977), a court has found that there is 'a positive duty upon the state' to provide welfare payments to anyone considered indigent under the state's constitutional 'need standard'.

[66] Article 8, Main Constitution; Art. 9, Washington Constitution. See overview in *Pauley v Kelly* 225 s.E.2d 859 (1979) (Supreme Court of Appeals of West Virginia, United States), Appendix 1.

movement to first develop free public schools (initially based on local property taxes and then partly supported by state-level subsidies), the right to education was gradually recognized in state constitutions.[67] Between 1776 and 1834, roughly half the states included educational clauses in their constitutions, which tended to be more general in nature. The remainder were adopted between 1835 and 1912 and were more 'explicit' in regard to the 'establishment, funding and administration of free common school systems'.[68]

From the late 19th century onwards, courts responded with extreme caution to litigation based on these rights and duties. Two exceptions were made. The first was defensive: the rights were drawn upon to legitimate impugned state legislation that sought to raise taxes for financing education or diminish local funding disparities.[69] The second was to adopt a very thin standard of review: courts interpreted the provisions as providing binding positive duties to provide education of a certain standard[70] but indicated that they would only intervene if legislation was clearly irrational or arbitrary.[71] For the most part, courts subscribed to the view that '[t]o hold otherwise would be to substitute judicial opinion for the legislative will'.[72]

In the 1960s, the issue was revived in the wake of the *Brown v Board of Education.*[73] In laying down a prohibition on segregated schooling, the court proffered a more robust interpretation of the right to equal protection and articulated the importance of equal educational opportunity in particularly strong terms. Moreover, the socio-economic dimension of civil rights was receiving greater and favourable attention from courts, as they scrutinized more closely the impugned arbitrariness of state action and legislative schemes.[74] For instance, In *Goldberg v Kelly*, the US Supreme Court found that the summary or immediate denial of a welfare benefit to an individual violated their right to due process.[75]

[67] See discussion, e.g. in *Robinson v Cahill* 62 N.J. 473 (1973), (Supreme Court of New Jersey, United States), 507. In 1823, President Jefferson listed as one of his failures as a politician and attempt to secure an educational bill I the Virginia legislature that would fund education through a state tax and not through local financing: Hickrod, Chaudhari, Pruyne, and Meng, *supra* note 65.

[68] P. Trachtenberg, *Education Provisions in State Constitutions: A Summary of a Chapter for the State Constitutions for the Twenty-First Century Project*, 2 quoted in A. Shanor and C. Albisa, 'The Parameters of the Possible: Social Movements and the Right to Education in the United States', in M. Langford, C. Garavito-Rodriguez, and J. Rossi (eds.), *Making it Stick: Compliance with Social Rights Judgments in Comparative Perspective* (2014).

[69] See discussion in *Pauley v Kelly*, *5 and fn. 25 noting with embarrassment that West Virginia was the only state in which the courts that had consistently 'not given extra weight to the education mandate'.

[70] See, for example, *Landis v Ashworth (School District No. 44)* 57 NJL 509, 31 A. 1017 (1895) (Supreme Court of New Jersey, United States).

[71] *People ex rel. Russell v Graham*, 301 Ill. 446, 134 N.E. 57 (1922) (Supreme Court of illinois, United States), 452; *Mumme v Marrs* 120 Tex. 383 (1931) (Supreme Court of Texas, United States), 396; *Flory v Smith* 134 SE 360 (1926) (Supreme Court of Virginia, United States), 362.

[72] *Flory v Smith*, at 362.

[73] *Brown v Board of Education* 347 US 483 (1954) (Supreme Court of the United States).

[74] See generally C. Albisa and J. Schultz, 'The United States: A Ragged Patchwork', in Langford, *supra* note 5, 235; and C. Sunstein, *The Second Bill of Rights: FDR's Unfinished Revolution and Why We Need It More Than Ever* (New York: Basic Books, 2004), 159.

[75] 397 US 254, 264 (1970).

These developments held out the promise of rectifying dramatic inequality in school financing.[76] For almost two centuries, state legislatures had been largely resistant to reducing a heavy reliance on local taxes.[77] As reflected in a range of indicators, the quality of schooling was highly dependent on the average wealth in a municipality.[78] In the so-called first wave of school finance litigation, plaintiffs requested that statutes that authorized unequal educational expenditures be declared unconstitutional on the grounds that they denied the *civil right* of equal protection. *Federal* courts declined to uphold the claim. In *McInnes v Shapiro*, the court acknowledged that children in Illinois were receiving dramatically different levels of education.[79] The average per-pupil expenditures varied between $480 and $1,000 per pupil and by a factor of three for primary school. However, the claim was ruled non-justiciable: there were 'no judicially discoverable and manageable standards' by which 'a court can determine when the Constitution is satisfied and when it is violated' in respect of the right to equal protection.[80] This was because the 'only possible standard' for review was the 'rigid assumption that each pupil must receive the same dollar expenditures'. This could not be the 'exclusive yardstick of a child's educational needs',[81] as there might be good reasons for variations in expenditure.[82]

A subsequent shift by legal advocates away from a predetermined equality formula to a justification standard initially produced a more favourable federal judicial reception.[83] In the 1971 *Serrano v Priest* judgment, the California Supreme Court also rejected the idea that constitutional rights (whether education or equal treatment) required 'equal school spending' but found the claims justiciable on other grounds.[84] Finding that education was a 'compelling interest' and 'wealth' a suspect category, it stated that a 'strict scrutiny' standard was required for the right to equal protection. Highly unequal school financing must survive a closer and demanding inspection. The Court found that the two primary arguments by the state defendants for the existing system, namely local control and local priorities, were insufficient in meeting this burden of justification.[85] The Court returned the matter to the trial court for a full determination on the

[76] M. Heise, 'State Constitutions, School Finance Litigation, and the Third Wave: From Equity to Adequacy, Heise, Michael', 68 *Temple Law Review* (1995), 1151, 1154.

[77] At times, the resistance may have been justified. The Court in *Robinson v Cahill*, at 508, notes that wealthier communities complained that the rural areas 'deliberately' undervalued their taxable revenue in order to increase cross-subsidisation.

[78] H. Horowitz, 'Unseparate but Unequal—The Emerging Fourteenth Amendment Issue in Public School Education' (1965–1966) 13 *UCLA Law Review*, 1147.

[79] *McInnes v Shapiro* 293 F.Supp. 327 (1968) (District Court N. D. Illinois, United States). See also *Burress v Wilkerson* 310 F.Supp. 572 (1969) (District Court, WD Virginia, United States).

[80] *McInnes v Shapiro*, at 335. The argument that the financing formula was arbitrary on due process grounds was rejected on the grounds that legitimate 'rational' grounds could be found to explain all the variations.

[81] *McInnes v Shapiro*, at 335.

[82] *McInnes v Shapiro*, at 335.

[83] W.R. Andersen, 'School Finance Litigation: The Styles of Judicial Intervention', (1979–1980), 55 *Washington Law Review*, 137, 146.

[84] *Serrano v Priest* 5 Cal.3d 584 (1971) (Supreme Court of California, United States), Part II.

[85] *Serrano v Priest* 5 Cal.3d 584 (1971) (Supreme Court of California, United States), Part II, part C.

merits but noted that the need for remedies which provided time and space for the Californian state to develop an 'appropriate new system'.[86] This approach of only policing the boundaries of rights (articulating a general standard but not its detailed content) was to prove generally popular in the three waves of review as a means of avoiding charges of institutional incompetence and democratic illegitimacy. However, courts tended to become more involved in issuing more detailed orders when there was no or insufficient governmental reaction to decisions.[87]

This line of reasoning based on equal protection clauses was, nonetheless, short-lived. In *San Antonio School District v Rodriguez*, the US Supreme Court ruled that wealth could not be a suspect class in the domain of education like race; moreover, education, at least beyond the barest minimum, was not a federal constitutional right.[88] The result was that litigants turned to the express rights to education in state constitutions.

In the two subsequent waves of litigation, many, but not all, state courts rejected the earlier and restrictive justiciability doctrines concerning education rights. The judgment in *Seattle School District No. 1* contains perhaps the most considered dismissal.[89] Article 9 of the Washington Constitution provides that: '[i]t is the paramount duty of the state to make ample provision for the education of all children residing within its borders'. The Supreme Court of Washington first rejected a number of textual arguments that suggested the provision was merely 'preambular'; and claims that it was vague or hortatory: 'it does not merely seek to broadly declare policy, explain goals, or designate objectives to be accomplished. It is declarative of a constitutionally imposed *duty*'.[90] Second, the Court dismissed the claim that the provision was solely directed to the legislature and created no subjective rights. It noted that all constitutional rights possessed elements for which the legislature might be the sole 'guardian' but in this instance,[91] not only was a class of persons mentioned specifically ('all children') but individual interests were affected. Third, it rejected claims concerning the separation of powers. The Court noted that it was 'sensitive to the fact that our state government is divided into legislative, executive and judicial branches' but that the 'compartments of government are not rigid'.[92] Questions of separation of powers raised the possibility of judicial restraint rather than abstention and non-justiciability.

[86] *Serrano v Priest* 5 Cal.3d 584 (1971) (Supreme Court of California, United States), Part II, part C.

[87] Although D. Horowitz, *The Courts and Social Policy* (The Brookings Institution, 1977) argues that some judgments did have significant consequences for policymaking.

[88] *San Antonio Independent School District v Rodriguez* 411 US 1 (1973) (Supreme Court, United States).

[89] *Seattle School District No. 1 v Washington* 90 Wn.2d 476 (1978) (Supreme Court of Washington, United States).

[90] *Seattle School District No. 1 v Washington* 90 Wn.2d 476 (1978) (Supreme Court of Washington, United States), at 499.

[91] *Seattle School District No. 1 v Washington* 90 Wn.2d 476 (1978), (Supreme Court of Washington, United States), at 502.

[92] *Seattle School District No. 1 v Washington* 90 Wn.2d 476 (1978), (Supreme Court of Washington, United States), at 502.

In the landmark case for the second wave, the New Jersey Court ruled in 1973 that the system of school financing violated the right to a 'thorough and efficient' education, inserted in Article 9 of the state Constitution in 1875. This was the first decision in which a social right was the basis for a judicial assault on school financing. The New Jersey Court agreed with the Supreme Court that equal protection provisions were problematic, partly because it would be unmanageable. But their focus was much more on the implications of the reasoning for other public services:

> It has simply never been within the constitutional prerogative of this Court to nullify state-wide measures for financing public services merely because the burdens or benefits thereof fall unevenly depending upon the relative wealth of the political subdivisions in which citizens live.[93]

The Court also rejected an alternative and more ambitious legal construction by plaintiffs of the provision, based on the drafting history, which would have prohibited local taxation for schools or required only state-wide taxes for financing.

The legal standard was solely one of adequacy: did the system provide a 'thorough and efficient education' for all children?[94] The state was faced with achieving a particular result but there was considerable flexibility in the means to be applied: 'Whether the State acts directly or imposes the role upon local government, the end product must be what the Constitution commands'.[95] Turning to whether the state's action passed constitutional muster, the Court found that the test for review was whether New Jersey could demonstrate it has 'a plan which will fulfil the State's continuing obligation'.[96] The plan 'must define in some discernible way the educational obligation' and if local schools are tasked with financing, it 'must *compel* the local school districts to raise the money necessary to provide that opportunity'.[97]

As to the first prong, the Court was troubled by the fact the state had not defined the standards of what constitutes a 'thorough and efficient education'. It was at this point the Court used gross inequality in per-pupil spending as a proxy for a violation of this standard. This is because 'dollar input is plainly relevant' and the Court was 'shown no other viable criterion for measuring compliance with the constitutional mandate'.[98] As to the second prong, the Court noted new reform efforts but that the 'present scheme is a patchy product reflecting provincial contests rather than a plan sensitive only to the constitutional mandate'.[99] However,

[93] *Robinson v Cahill*, at 489.

[94] *Robinson v Cahill*, at 513.

[95] *Robinson v Cahill*, at 513.

[96] *Robinson v Cahill*, at 519. This is not dissimilar to the widely quoted reasonableness test of the 2000 *Grootboom* case in South Africa: See discussion in Section 3.

[97] *Robinson v Cahill*, at 519. This is not dissimilar to the widely quoted reasonableness test of the 2000 *Grootboom* case in South Africa: See discussion in Section 3.

[98] *Robinson v Cahill*, at 519. This is not dissimilar to the widely quoted reasonableness test of the 2000 *Grootboom* case in South Africa: See discussion in Section 3, at 515.

[99] *Robinson v Cahill*, at 519. This is not dissimilar to the widely quoted reasonableness test of the 2000 *Grootboom* case in South Africa: See discussion in Section 3, at 518.

the Court refused requests for supervisory jurisdiction or specific orders to the legislature and instead granted the state nine months to develop a new plan.[100]

In the third wave of litigation, there was a decisive shift from equity to adequacy. Courts began to articulate more clearly the basic contours of an adequate or minimum right to education. The proof was not limited to input or outcome disparities and increasingly evidence was provided that schools on average or in particular areas were failing to reach accepted standards. The cause for the shift was diverse. This included the particularities of constitutional provisions,[101] the perception than adequacy claims were more justiciable,[102] a recognition that finance inequities were recognized only one explanation of inadequate education and a public more attuned to standardized achievement, within and across states.[103]

In the most well-known third-wave case, *Rose v Council for Better Education*, the Supreme Court of Kentucky specified that the duty to provide an efficient system of education means providing each and every child with seven particular capacities.[104] Those included:

- sufficient oral and written communication skills to enable students to function in a complex and rapidly changing civilization;
- sufficient knowledge of economic, social, and political systems to enable the student to make informed choices;
- sufficient understanding of governmental processes to enable the student to understand the issues that affect his or her community, state and nation;
- sufficient self-knowledge and knowledge of his or her mental and physical wellness;
- sufficient grounding in the arts to enable each student to appreciate his or her cultural and historical heritage;
- sufficient training or preparation for advancing training in either academic or vocational fields so as to enable each child to choose and pursue life work intelligently; and
- sufficient levels of academic or vocational skills to enable public school students to compete favourably with their counterparts in surrounding states, in academics and the job market.[105]

[100] *Robinson v Cahill*, at 519. This is not dissimilar to the widely quoted reasonableness test of the 2000 *Grootboom* case in South Africa: See discussion in Section 3, at 480.

[101] M. McUsic, 'The Use of Education Clauses in School Finance Reform Litigation', 28 *Harvard Journal on Legislation* (1991), 307.

[102] Because it concerned adjudging minimum standards rather than more relative standards of equity. Practically at least, some variations in expenditure were necessary or not troublesome, see *Olsen v State* 554 P.2d 139 (Supreme Court of Oregon), and discussion in Heise, *supra* note 76, at 1161.

[103] Heise, *supra* note 76.

[104] *Rose v Council for Better Education* 790 SW2d 186 (1989) (Supreme Court of Kentucky, United States).

[105] *Rose v Council for Better Education* 790 SW2d 186 (1989) (Supreme Court of Kentucky, United States), 212–213.

The Court then cited a range of evidence suggesting the Kentucky system was inadequate, which included evidence of dramatically substandard performance on national benchmarks with 21 per cent of ninth graders failing to graduate from high school. The Court also examined the various financial and educational efforts to correct the system and found them wanting. In the end it made a single order declaring the 'entire system of common schools' unconstitutional and remitted the matter to the legislature for comprehensive reform.

Moreover, some cases have dealt with non-retrogression. In May 2011, the New Jersey Supreme Court found that cuts to a school budget sharply violated a previous court order requiring a proper education in poor districts.[106] The majority stated that the government cannot misuse its budgetary power 'to diminish' the right of students in poor areas to their constitutional right to a 'thorough and efficient education'. The Court had earlier relaxed its orders for these students when new legislation was introduced but found that this law could not be later used a shield to avoid constitutional responsibilities.

In this outline of the litigation, there are a number of important lessons to be drawn. The first is that courts have been able to overcome objections of *justiciability* and develop legal standards of review for a social right with clear positive obligations. This is significant since the debate on justiciability pushed by some commentators and courts around the world seems not to have caught up with a practice that first emerged almost five decades ago.[107] Arguments that the right to education was irrefutably vague and indeterminate did not establish subjective individual rights, or was bereft of judicially manageable standards of review (and thoroughly political) were brushed aside by a significant number of state courts. At the same time, in many leading cases, courts displayed a sensitivity to the constraints of their institutional competence and their legitimacy vis-à-vis the legislature as they developed the standards of review and crafted remedies. The jurisprudential record illustrates at least how legal methods can be developed, whether one agrees or disagrees with the particular balance that judges struck in particular cases. Moreover, it illustrates the potential for the use of social rights, including cases that directly implicate resource allocation.

The second distinctive feature is that the responsiveness of courts varies significantly between the state courts. In the equity-dominated period between 1972 and 1992, more than 60 lawsuits were filed in 41 states.[108] Complainants achieved success to varying degrees in more than half of them.[109] However, the success rate

[106] *Abbott v Burke* (M-1293-09), decided 24 May 2011.

[107] See, e.g. I.L. Backer, 'Ideals and Implementation—Ratifying another Complaints Procedure?', 27 *Nordic Journal of Human Rights* (2009), 91; C. Tomuschat, 'An Optional Protocol for the International Covenant on Economic, Social and Cultural Rights', in L. Dicke, S. Hobe, K.-U. Meyn, A. Peters, E. Riedel, H.-J. Schütz, and C. Tietje (eds.), *Weltinnenrecht: Liber amicorum Jost Delbrück* (2005); 18 June 2004, *LJN*:AP4680 (Central Court of Appeals, Netherlands); Rt. 2001–1006 (Supreme Court of Norway).

[108] A. Hickrod, E. Hines, G. Anthony, J. Dively, and G. Pruyne, 'The Effect of Constitutional Litigation on Education Finance: A Preliminary Analysis', 18 *Journal of Education Finance* (1992), 180.

[109] 'At present, 17 states have successfully defended their statutes against constitutional challenges and more will likely do so in the future': Hickrod, Chaudhari, Pruyne, and Meng, *supra* note 65, at 50.

improved in the first decade of the adequacy wave of litigation: from the early 1990s, 68 per cent of cases were successful.[110] Moreover, even when successful, there have been some important variances between state courts in their intensity of their review or their willingness to order strong remedies in the face of legislative intransigence. For instance, in some adequacy cases, courts have adopted a bare minimum of an educational standard while in others national or state benchmarks for particular grades have been adopted.

The lesson from this litigation is that the responsiveness of judges seems to be highly conditional and variable. The US jurisprudence suggests that excessive optimism over the possibility of judicial-led accountability for social rights or critical pessimism about the prospect of a responsive judiciary should be tempered. Both the legal jurisprudence (with similar courts reaching different decisions in roughly similar contests) and the political science research on the determinants of judicial behaviour in US state courts (which includes varying political preferences and constraints) suggests that an array of factors can influence eventual outcomes. The likelihood of judicial enforcement of the right to education increased over time (suggesting perhaps a glass half-full) but the chances of success have remained uncertain. As Hickrod notes: '[t]raditions of court deference to legislative bodies in this area are quite strong in a number of states'.[111]

C. Comparative doctrinal responsiveness

Moving beyond the United States, the emerging body of comparative law is significant but certainly not uniform in terms of responsiveness. Some jurisdictions demonstrate a form of judicial abdication in the face of justiciable socio-economic rights, others are prone to bouts of or sustained judicial activism, with a palette of approaches in between.

1. Conservative archetypes

In the case of formal doctrine, one conservative archetypal example of the institutional hypothesis is the Supreme Court of Ireland. In *Sinnott Minister for Education*, which concerned the right of a man with autism to primary education, the court established the principle that it should refrain from using its powers to enforce positive constitutional rights, unless there were very exceptional circumstances.[112] The leading judgment by Justice Hardiman cites all of the aforementioned institutional factors in coming to this conclusion: adjudicating social rights would force judges into 'ranking some areas of policy in priority to others', 'lead

Rebell found that 47 per cent of surveyed cases in this period were successful: M. Rebell, 'Fiscal Equity Litigation and the Democratic Imperative' (1998), 24 *Journal of Education Finance*, 23.

[110] Rebell, *supra* note 109, at 23. The sample size for the first period was 15 cases; the second period 22 cases.

[111] Hickrod, Chaudhari, Pruyne, and Meng, *supra* note 65, at 50.

[112] *Sinnott v Minister for Education* [2001] 2 IR 545 (Supreme Court of Ireland).

the courts into the taking of decisions in areas in which they have no special qualification or experience', result in the inappropriate use of individual-based adversarial procedures to solve 'issues of policy', and would permit courts to make decisions which 'they are not, and cannot be, democratically responsible for'.[113] Ultimately, such a practice would 'offend' the constitutional separation of powers since there is a 'proper sphere for both elected representatives of the people and the executive elected or endorsed by them in the taking of social and economic and legislative decisions, as well as another sphere where the judiciary is solely competent'.[114]

In taking such positions, the Irish court is not alone. In the Netherlands, international treaties are incorporated into domestic law and, since 1956, prevail over statutory law.[115] However, the Dutch courts have only exercised the power of judicial review in applying the ICCPR and ECHR. The self-executing character of the ICESCR and the European Social Charter has been consistently rejected.[116] The provisions are deemed (1) too indeterminate, and (2) void of subjective individual rights.[117] Authorities are simply obliged to recognize generally the treaty rights and take measures. For instance, in a 2000 case concerning asylum seekers, the District Court relied on the first ground to find that no minimum level could be inferred from the right to food in Article 11 of the ICESCR. Four years later, the Central Court of Appeals confirmed the latter ground—Article 11 contained no subjective or private rights.[118]

Likewise in France, civil and political rights have been deemed *droits-libertés* while social rights were labelled *droits-créances*, a right to claim a benefit or service.[119] In the main, the Constitutional Council has been only willing to employ the latter category as a principle (that might justify legislation or a restriction on a civil right) but not as direct and subjective justiciable rights.[120] The Cantonal

[113] *Sinnott v Minister for Education* [2001] 2 IR 545 (Supreme Court of Ireland), 710–711.

[114] *Sinnott v Minister for Education* [2001] 2 IR 545 (Supreme Court of Ireland), 710.

[115] Art. 94 of the Constitution provides that: 'Statutory regulations in force within the Kingdom shall not be applicable if such application is in conflict with provisions of treaties that are binding on all persons or of resolutions by international institutions'.

[116] The courts have though applied one provision in ILO Convention 102 and one in ILO Convention 118. F. Vlemminx, 'The Netherlands and the ICESCR: Why Didst Thou Promise such a Beauteous Day?', in F. Coomans (ed.), *Justiciability of Economic and Social Rights: Experiences from Domestic Systems* (Intersentia and Maastrict Centre for Human Rights, Antwerpen 2006), 60.

[117] *'Right to Strike Case'* 6 December 1983, NJ 1984, 557 (Supreme Court of Netherlands). In addition, the Court places emphasis on the explanation given by the Dutch government at the time of ratification as to whether a treaty is justiciable.

[118] See respectively, 6 September 2000, *Rawb* 2001, 55 (District Court of the Hague, Netherlands), In the 1990s, the Central Court of Appeals briefly flirted with the idea that the right to food in Art. 11 of the ICESCR might contain minimum obligations—although it never found a violation; 31 March 1995, *JB* 1995, 161 (Central Court of Appeals, Netherlands). See discussion in F. Vlemminx, 'The Netherlands and the ICESCR: Why Didst Thou Promise such a Beauteous Day?', in F. Coomans (ed.), *Justiciability of Economic and Social Rights: Experiences from Domestic Systems* (Intersentia and Maastrict Centre for Human Rights, Antwerpen, 2006), 50.

[119] See discussion in L. Pech, 'France: Rethinking *Droits-Créances*', in Langford, *supra* note 5.

[120] For examples of the exceptions, see *Loi portant diverses mesures relatives aux prestations de vieillesse* CC, May 28, 1983, No. 83-156DC (Constitutional Council, France); *Loi relative à la lutte contre le tabagisme et l'alcoolisme* CC, 8 January 1991, No. 90-283 DC (Constitutional Council, France). The

Court in Geneva, Switzerland, perhaps represents the high watermark of such an approach.[121] A referendum inserted a justiciable right to housing in the Geneva constitution in 1992. But despite this rather clear and contemporary democratic mandate, the court found that the right was non-justiciable. The result was a passionate public debate (with some claiming constitutionalization had not achieved anything) but the upshot was the insertion of greater detail on the right to housing in the constitution.[122]

2. *Progressive archetypes*

However, these jurisdictions provide only one picture of comparative constitutional jurisprudence. First, many of the jurisdictions in which justiciability has been formally rejected do not have constitutionally recognized rights: it is the approach of implied rights that has been rejected.[123] Second, there are a significant number of courts that take a decidedly more robust approach to social rights adjudications, displaying a more relaxed or nuanced attitude to institutional constraints. These courts keenly recognize and articulate their institutional limits but equally seek to establish protective doctrines and apply them in concrete cases. The archetype in this case would be the Colombian Constitutional Court. As previously discussed, this Court established a range of doctrines and procedures. First, the state 'must devise and adopt a plan of action for the implementation of the rights' even if obligations concerning social rights are progressive in character.[124] Second, it has intervened to immediately enforce such rights by broadly interpreting the right to life, dignity, and security, and enforcing 'minimum conditions for dignified life'. Procedurally, the court accepted that claims for violations by public or private actors of the minimum core of social rights could be litigated under the *acción de tutela*, which permits an individual to secure a summary proceeding and judgment within ten days of filing the writ.[125] Third, it has issued structural judgments where it finds an 'unconstitutional state of affairs'. If there are systematic and widespread violations of a number of constitutional rights, which cannot be attributed to only one state authority, the Court has stepped in to make wide-ranging orders.[126]

In this category, one could also include apex courts such as Costa Rica, Nepal, Portugal, Latvia, or local courts in Finland.[127] In these jurisdictions, courts have

Constitutional Council has though begun to shift over the last decade, increasingly recognizing the direct applicability of international treaty provisions. Moreover, the Council of State has begun to enforce the right to housing in some concrete cases: see, e.g. *Ministre de l'immigration c/M* Conseil d'État, Juge des référés, 13/08/2010, 342330, (Council of State, France).

[121] See, e.g. Cour de Justice du canton de Genève, Judgment No. 1472/2010, 13 December 2010.

[122] It is in Art. 38 of the new Constitution of the Canton of Geneva, which entered into force on 1 June 2013.

[123] For example, Ghana, Lesotho, and US Federal Supreme Court.

[124] SU-111/97 (Constitutional Court of Colombia).

[125] See discussion in M. Sepúlveda Carmona, 'Colombia: The Constitutional Court's Role in Addressing Social Injustice', in Langford, *supra* note 5, 146.

[126] See, e.g. T-760 of 2008 (Consitutional Court of Colombia).

[127] See, e.g. Wilson, *supra* note 16; M Langford and A Bhatterai, 'Constitutional Rights and Social Exclusion in Nepal', 18 *International Journal on Minority and Group Rights* 387; M Tushnet, *Weak*

strongly affirmed the justiciability of social rights and taken a relatively robust approach in their application. Not all cases have been successful for litigants but the reasoning of the courts in the cases demonstrates a sensitivity to both the effectiveness of rights as well as compelling arguments from the state. Take Nepal, for example, which has witnessed a slew of successful public interest litigation on civil, political, property, and ESC rights in the last decade. In *Prakashmani Sharma and Others*, the petitioners cited research which showed that the problem of uterus prolapse was affecting at least 600,000 women, especially in remote and poor districts.[128] After examining relevant health and reproductive rights in great detail, it took the view that the right to reproductive health requires effective protection and that the state must adopt the necessary laws and measures and create a satisfactory and conducive environment for fulfilment. The Court issued a directive order that required the Prime Minister and cabinet to hold consultations with health experts and civil society representatives and submit a Bill to the parliament as soon as possible. It also ordered social and health ministries to prepare special work plans, provide free consultation, treatment, health services, and facilities to the aggrieved women, set up various health centres, and initiate effective programmes with the aim of raising public awareness on the issue.

Another notable court is the Latvian Constitutional Court. The ICESCR is incorporated in the Constitution and the Court has ruled a number of times on the right to social security. Most recently, structural adjustment legislation that was enacted to fulfil terms of a loan bailout from the IMF and European Union in 2009 was found to have substantively violated the individual's right to social security,[129] and the principle of the rule of law.[130] In addition, and relevantly, the court also held that lawmakers had *too quickly approved* the package and had not carefully evaluated the alternatives.

3. *A mixed global picture*

Complicating this picture further are those courts that evince moderate approaches or appear to vary between cases or over time. The South African Constitutional Court provides a classificatory problem. In its landmark *Grootboom* judgment, the Court rejected the idea of enforcing an immediate minimum core obligation but

Courts, Strong Rights: Judicial Review and Social Welfare Rights in Comparative Constitutional Law (Princeton University Press, Princeton 2008); Langford, *supra* note 5.

128 *Prakash Mani Sharma & Ors v GON, Office of Prime Minister and Council of Ministers & Ors* (June 2008), Writ No. 064-WO-0230 (Supreme Court of Nepal). The key causes were the lack of nutritious food during pregnancy, lack of care and health services for lactating mothers, discriminatory social and cultural practices against women, lack of awareness on reproductive health, lack of access to health centres, poor availability of equipment and medical practitioners, unsafe abortion, poverty.

129 The ICESCR is incorporated in the constitution.

130 Case No. 2009-43-01 (On Compliance of the First Part of Section 3 of State Pensions and State Allowance Disbursement in 2009–2012) insofar as it Applies to State Old-Age Pension with Art. 1, Art. 91, Art. 105, and Art. 109 of the Satversme (Constitution) of the Republic of Latvia.

established the reasonableness test for the evaluation of governmental policy and action. In itself, this doctrine generated significant optimism. The BBC reported that while the judgment was unclear in 'practical terms', it 'could lead to a total overhaul of the government's housing policy';[131] the amicus curiae noted it was a 'watershed moment in our constitutional democracy' and showed 'the power of desperately poor people to leverage assistance from the state'.[132] The follow-up judgment in *Treatment Action Campaign* appeared to confirm this potency. The Court held that a policy which limited access to antiretroviral treatment that prevented mother-to-child transmission of HIV to a few pilot sites was irrational in light of medical evidence and the costs involved. The remedies ordered went beyond a declaration and the government was required to facilitate the extension of the programme throughout the country.

However, the two judgments have attracted their fair share of critics. The approach of the Court has been slated for failing to enforce a minimum core obligation,[133] avoiding the definition of the content of the rights,[134] or evincing a reticence to supervise implementation of the remedies.[135] Others, such as Brand, defend the Court on some of these grounds but argue that the institutional conservatism is apparent elsewhere.[136] Instead of substantively addressing the issues at stake, the Court adopts an overly depoliticized proceduralism in its reasoning. It looks principally for rational policymaking and due process and consequently mimics the neoliberal demands of 'good governance' rather than the constitutional promise of social transformation. These sceptical arguments appear vindicated by two recent cases. In *Mazibuko*, the Court found that the City of Johannesburg's policy of prepaid water meters did not constitute a form of 'disconnection or limitation', that the roll-out of these meters in exclusively poor black areas was not indirect discrimination, and that a policy of providing 25 litres per person per day (on the assumption that a household had eight persons) was reasonable even though it resulted in only 8 litres per person in large households and international standards pointed towards 50 litres per person per day. In *Nokotyana,* the Court rejected claims for a free-standing right to basic sanitation and access to ventilated improved pit latrines in informal settlements.[137]

[131] G. Barrow, *South African squatters win battle* (2000).

[132] LRC, *Annual Report for the Period 1 April 2000 to 31 March 2001* (Legal Resources Centre and Legal Resources Trust, Johannesburg 2002), 4.

[133] D. Bilchitz, *Poverty and Fundamental Rights: The Justification and Enforcement of Socio-Economic Rights* (Oxford: Oxford University Press, 2007).

[134] S. Wilson and J. Dugard, 'Constitutional Jurisprudence: The First and Second Waves', in M. Langford, B. Cousins, J. Dugard, and T. Madlingozi (eds.), *Symbols or Substance? The Role and Impact of Socio-Economic Rights Strategies in South Africa* (Cambridge: Cambridge University Press, 2013).

[135] C. Mbazira, 'Non-Implementation of court orders in socio-economic rights litigation in South Africa' (2008) 9 *ESR Review*, 2.

[136] D. Brand, *Courts, Socio-Economic Rights and Transformative Politics* (Stellenbsoch: Stellenbosch University Press, 2009). For instance, trying to strike a reasonable balance between individual and collective claims.

[137] *Nokotyana and Others v Ekurhuleni Municipality* 2010 (4) BCLR 312 (CC), paras. 29–31 and 45.

However, it is difficult to categorize definitively the South African court and some critics acknowledge that it may be too early to forecast the future pattern of jurisprudence.[138] The *Mazibuko* decision, for instance, was authored by the more classically liberal-leaning Justice O'Reagen in her last month of office and seems to reinterpret the *Grootboom* decision as a mere rationality test.[139] In the *Nokotyana* case, the applicant only raised the issue in the final hearing and the claim was not well-argued. In addition, the court has been very robust in cases concerning negative obligations for social rights. In the case of forced evictions,[140] the Court has found that forced evictions violate the right to housing;[141] forced eviction protections extend to debt defaulters[142] and occupiers of private land[143] and housing;[144] victims have the right to alternative accommodation,[145] which must meet minimum standards;[146] a municipality must meaningfully engage with a community before an eviction can proceed;[147] individuals have the right to restoration of shelters and return to land after a forced eviction;[148] and the authorities cannot roll back constitutional prohibitions on forced evictions through legislation.[149] As Wilson and Dugard conclude in their discussion of one these forced eviction cases: it reveals 'the power and the peculiarity of the interpretive approach the Court adopted in *Grootboom*'.[150]

Jurisprudential variation can also be found across different rights, time and court branches. An archetype of the first is the Supreme Court of India.[151] On the one hand, the Court has been relatively robust in its judgments on emergency and primary health care,[152] access to basic education,[153] elimination of exploitative child

[138] P Bond, *Fighting for the Right to the City: Discursive and Political Lessons from the Right to Water* (New York: Syracuse University 2010), 24.

[139] See para. 67. [140] For a deep analysis of this jurisprudence, see Liebenberg (2010).

[141] *Government of the Republic of South Africa v Grootboom* 2001 (1) SA 46 (CC) (*Grootboom*).

[142] *Jaftha v Schoeman; Van Rooyen v Scholtz* 2005 (2) SA 140 (CC) (*Jaftha*);

[143] *President of the Republic of South Africa v Modderklip Boedery (Pty) Ltd* 2005 (5) SA 3 (CC) (*Modderklip*).

[144] *City of Johannesburg Metropolitan Municipality v Blue Moonlight Properties* 39 (Pty) Ltd and Another (338/10) [2011] ZASCA 47 (30 March 2011) (Note that this is Supreme Court of Appeal judgment).

[145] In particular, sec *Port Elizabeth Municipality v Various Occupiers* 2005 (1) SA 217 (CC) (*Port Elizabeth Municipality*). 'A court should be reluctant to grant an eviction against relatively settled occupiers unless it is satisfied that a reasonable alternative is available, even if only as an interim measure pending ultimate access to housing in the formal housing programme' (para. 28).

[146] *Residents of the Joe Slovo Community, Western Cape v Thubelisha Homes and others* 2010 (3) SA 454 (CC) (*Thubelisha Homes*).

[147] *Occupiers of 51 Olivia Road Berea Township and 197 Main Street Johannesburg v the City of Johannesburg and others* 2008 (3) SA 208 (CC) (*Olivia Road*).

[148] *Tswelopele Non-Profit Organisation and Others v City of Tshwane Metropolitan Municipality*, 2007 SCA 70 (RSA) (Note that this is Supreme Court of Appeal judgment but was not appealed).

[149] *Abahlali BaseMjondolo v Premier of KwaZulu-Natal Province and others* 2010 (2) BCLR 99 (CC).

[150] J. Dugard and T. Roux, 'The Record of the South African Constitutional Court in Providing an Institutional Voice for the Poor: 1995–2004', in R. Gargarella, P. Domingo, and T. Roux (eds.), *Courts and Social Transformation in New Democracies: An Institutional Voice for the Poor?* (Aldershot/Burlington: Ashgate, 2006), 60.

[151] For an overview, see S. Muralidhar, 'India:the Expectations and Challenges of Judicial Enforcement of Social Rights', in Langford, *supra* note 5.

[152] E.g. *Paschim Banga Khet Majoor Samity v State of West Bengal* (1996) 4 SCC 37 (Supreme Court of India).

[153] E.g. *Unni Krishnan, JP v State of Andhra Pradesh* (1993) 1 SCC 645 (Supreme Court of India).

labour,[154] occupational health,[155] environmental rights, and,[156] in the last decade the right to food.[157] The relevant rights were recognized, implementation was scrutinized, and detailed orders were issued, with extensive supervision occurring in two cases concerning environmental pollution and starvation.

However, this Court has faced considerable criticism for its deference to the state in the area of housing, land and, to some extent, labour rights. In the much-cited decision in *Olga Tellis v Bombay Municipal Corporation*,[158] the Court opined that the right to life included the right to livelihood and found a violation of due process in the eviction process of pavement dwellers. Yet, it refused to find that eviction would deprive the most marginalized of urban residents of their livelihood and only weakly recommended the provision of alternative accommodation (which was not provided and the evictions were carried out in mid-winter).[159] This attitude towards to the urban poor continued in *Municipal Corporation of Delhi v Gurnam Kaur*, where the Court held that the municipality had no legal obligation to provide evictees with alternative space for livelihoods[160] and reaffirmed it in *Sodan Singh v NDMC*.[161] In rural and forest areas, the Courts have displayed a similar reluctance to halt or regulate displacement of millions of small farmers and indigenous peoples in dam catchment areas or in forests coming under environmental protection.[162] In the *Narmada Dam* case, the majority stated: 'whether to have an infrastructural project or not and what is the type of project to be undertaken and how it is to be executed, are part of policy-making process and the courts are ill-equipped to adjudicate on a policy decision so undertaken'.[163]

Second, there can be variation over time. Some courts have become more progressive. In Kenya, the adoption of a new constitution in 2010 and a period of judicial education have ushered in a new era of social rights jurisprudence. Slum communities and tenants traditionally lost in court,[164] but in a rush of recent cases they have found a more receptive judicial audience. In *Ayuma & Ors*, where the owner of a private housing estate wished to evict tenants for commercial

154 E.g. *M.C. Mehta v State of Tamil Nadu* (1996) 6 SCC 772 (Supreme Court of India).

155 E.g. *Consumer Education and Research Centre v Union of India* (1995) 3 SCC 42 (Supreme Court of India).

156 *M.C. Mehta v Union of India (Taj Trapezium Case)* WP 13381/1984 (1996.12.30) (Supreme Court of India).

157 E.g. *People's Union for Civil Liberties v Union of India* (2001) 5 SCALE 303 (Supreme Court of India). Note that a further 70-plus orders followed.

158 (1985) 3 SCC 545.

159 (1985) 3 SCC 579: 'No one has the right to make use of a public property for a private purpose without the requisite authorisation and, therefore, it is erroneous to contend that the pavement dwellers have the right to encroach upon pavements by constructing dwellings thereon... If a person puts up a dwelling on the pavement, whatever may be economic compulsions behind such an act, his use of the pavement would become unauthorised'.

160 (1989) 1 SCC 101.

161 (1989) 4 SCC 155.

162 E.g. *T.N.Godavarman Tirumulkpad v Union of India* (1997) 2 SCC 267 and *T.N.Godavarman Tirumulkpad v Union of India* (2000) 6 SCC 413 concerning eviction of forest dwellers.

163 *Narmada Bachao Andolan v Union of India* (2000) 10 SCC 664, (Supreme Court of India), 762. They also reference a conflict of rights between water and houses and agricultural rights (764).

164 See overview in O. Odindo, 'Litigation and Housing Rights in Kenya', in J. Squires, M. Langford, and B. Thiele (eds.), *The Road to a Remedy* (2005).

development, Justice Musinga noted that the Court must 'strive to reach an appropriate balance' between the human rights of the residents and the property rights of the land owners, taking into account the constitutional requirement to adopt interpretations that 'most favour the enforcement of a right' and promote the values of the Constitution.[165] After citing international standards on forced evictions and South African jurisprudence, the Court ordered an injunction against eviction.

In other countries it is possible to observe the reverse trend. In China, between 2001 and 2008, the Court issued 27 decisions in which it directly applied constitutional rights, including the right to education in the *Qi Yuling* case.[166] However, in 2008, seemingly under political pressure, the Court repealed their legal interpretation in all of these cases.[167] In the United States, from the 1960s, the Supreme Court appeared to be slowly moving towards the constitutional implication of some basic social rights. However, a wave of new appointments by Republican Presidents from 1974 put a stop to that development.[168]

Third, it is possible to find divergences between different courts in a country. For instance, in a number of countries, it is possible to find lower courts exhibiting higher degrees of conservatism under a new constitutional dispensation while the apex court can be more devoted to ushering in a new era of constitutional interpretation. However, this pattern can be then reversed as lower courts become more robust (possibly due to judicial reforms, direct exposure to evidence of rights violations) while higher courts may become more conscious of political pressure. South Africa, India, and Argentina would appear to fit this pattern to a certain extent. Even in the archetypal Irish case we see an interesting movement in lower courts in later cases despite the signals from the Supreme Court.[169]

D. Comparative distributive responsiveness

The more difficult question is assessing the *distributional* character of comparative jurisprudence. Even if doctrines are progressive on their face, who benefits? This question is challenging. Different benchmarks abound and no single or simple methodology exists. It is clear from the emerging literature that the measure for determining whether the 'disadvantaged' have 'gained' from ESC rights adjudication varies dramatically.

[165] *Satrose Ayuma & Ors v The Registered Trustees of the Kenya Railways Staff Retirement Benefits Scheme & Ors*, High Court of Kenya, Petition No. 65 of 2010, Judgment of 17 February 2011. Likewise, the same judge ordered an injunction against eviction in *Kariuki & Ors v The Town Clerk, Nairobi City Council & Ors*, High Court of Kenya, Petition No. 65 of 2010, Judgment of 17 February 2011.

[166] *'Qi Yuling', Interpretation (2001) No. 25 Official Reply of the Supreme People's Court on Whether the Civil Liabilities Shall be borne for the Infringement upon a Citizen's Fundamental Right to Education* (Supreme People's Court of China).

[167] Zhushi [2008] 15 (Supreme Peoples' Court of China).

[168] See discussion in Sunstein, *supra* note 74.

[169] See discussion in A. Nolan, 'Ireland: *The Separation of Powers Doctrine v Socio-economic Rights*', in Langford, *supra* note 5.

The *strongest* benchmark is radical equality: all benefits must accrue to the poorest. This is most apparent in the work of Ferraz: not only does he criticize Brazilian courts for granting access to medicines to the middle classes and authorities for distributing legal aid across many income deciles, he argues that all judicially generated benefits should accrue to the most disadvantaged.[170] An alternative and more flexible strong form is weighted equality, which would demand that the disadvantaged gain more than advantaged groups.[171] The middle class (and lower middle class) can share in judicial outcomes but it must not be the dominant winner.

Then, there are a range of *moderate* forms of equality, which are more agnostic as to the reduction of social disparities. Instead, they require at least equal shares (proportional), equal improvement over time (diachronic), or that the disadvantaged secure a baseline equality of opportunity or adequate standard of social rights (threshold).[172] A related but different measure might be labelled Rawlsian: inequalities are tolerated as long as the system of adjudication maximizes the position of the least advantaged among the different options for the most advantaged.[173] Some might even accept a very *weak* form of equality: the reduction of absolute poverty approach without a concern for comparison between different groups.

Parsing these measures, the radical equality demand seems too extreme: it ignores the moderately poor, the working poor, and the vulnerable working/middle class—even Marx did not ascribe to it.[174] Even strong social democratic and social citizenship approaches emphasize universalist modes of social policy which benefit both the poor and middle class. Interestingly, the South African court is one of the few courts that would come close to meeting the radical equality test. Almost all of its judgments *on social rights* have been targeted at the most disadvantaged, particularly slum-dwellers and those facing forced eviction. However, it has been heavily criticized for being unresponsive to claims for progressive realization of the rights for other groups.[175]

[170] O.L.M. Ferraz, 'Brazil: Health Inequalities, Rights and Courts', in A.E. Yamin and S. Gloppen (eds.), *Litigating Health Rights: Can Courts Bring More Justice to Health?* (Cambridge: Harvard University Press, 2011).

[171] J. Rawls, *A Theory of Justice* (Cambridge: Colombia University Press, 1971).

[172] For instance, Ferraz is critical of Brazilian courts for ordering expensive medicines for middle-class litigants while poorer litigants tend to use courts to secure very basic medicines and medical goods. This is problematic when viewed in the aggregate and in monetary terms and could be seen as enhancing inequality. But when looked at through the lens of basic capabilities or utility, the poor may have secured more. Note that this might actually mean a higher increase in utility for disadvantaged groups since they value the gains more highly.

[173] J. Rawls, *Justice as Fairness: A Restatement* (Cambridge: Harvard University Press, 2001), §16.1. The acceptable level of inequality may vary greatly across time and societies. The difference principle could support a very high or low level of inequality due to the contextual variance in possible social arrangements. If it results in a very high level of inequality though, Rawls simply states that the gap should be narrowed through intervention to prevent political dominance by the most advantaged.

[174] S. Gosepath, 'Equality' (2007) *Stanford Encyclopedia of Philosophy*.

[175] See discussion above on the *Mazibuko* case. However, this characterization of the South African court might change if we brought in equality rights to the frame. There the court has been quite

The weighted strong form is more reasonable and yet still transformational. It seems to raise though a legal problem. The recognition of social rights tends towards the achievement of thresholds rather than a reduction of disparities. However, the CESCR and many courts emphasize that efforts to realize social rights should give particular emphasis to the most disadvantaged. It would not seem unreasonable to hold courts to a similar standard. Moreover, some constitutional rights are explicitly concerned with reduction of disparities and it can be argued that courts should pay greater attention to the disparity concerns that often lie behind such standards (for instance, many of the US courts were able to identify this link between equity and adequacy).

Nonetheless, given that courts are more reactive than proactive, an expectation that courts can control their output in such a fashion may be too idealistic. While they do have control over doctrine (which does influence outcomes), institutional reforms may be required to address other factors such as to improve access to court. In this respect, moderate measures may represent a better evaluative standard since at least the most disadvantaged make significant gains. Moreover, if the gains for the middle class lay the basis for more a solid universalist social policy in the future that everyone can share in, rather than ever-widening disparities, then diachronic equality may be quite attractive from a strategic perspective.

Currently, no scholarly effort provides a systemic picture of the extent to which court rulings are distributively fair. Until recently, a common method has been to examine the *posture* of courts to different applicants longitudinally. Some courts display a consistency in the robustness of their responses to claims from the most disadvantaged. The Supreme Court of Nepal and Costa Rica Constitutional Court are perhaps the most notable in this respect.[176] However, it is clear that some courts with seemingly progressive credentials fail, at least, the moderate test on closer examination. A good example is Hungary. In terms of doctrine, the Constitutional Court has articulated a relatively modest and minimal vision of justiciability:

> Social rights are implemented both by the formation of adequate institutions and by the rights of the individual to have access to them, which rights are to be specified by the legislature. In a few exceptional cases, however, certain social rights to be found in the Constitution have an element of subjective (justiciable) right.[177]

These exceptional cases are: the absence of any necessary legislation, a failure to ensure a minimum level of the rights, or the imposition of disproportionate restrictions or arbitrary or discriminatory treatment in the exercise of the rights.[178]

responsive to groups, including middle-class dominated groups, to claims of discrimination in relation to social rights and goods.

[176] B.M. Wilson and J.C.R. Cordero, 'Legal Opportunity Structures and Social Movements: The Effects of Institutional Change on Costa Rican Politics', 39 *Comparative Political Studies* (2006), 325.

[177] Decision No. 28/1994, para. 29(b). See also discussion of the Court's approach on the justiciability of social rights by the former Chief Justice in S László, 'Introduction to the Decisions of the Constitutional Court', in L Sólyom and G Brunner (eds.), *László Constitutional Judiciary in a New Democracy: The Hungarian Constitutional Court* (Ann Arbor: University of Michigan Press, 2000).

[178] Decision No. 28/1994, para. 29(b). See further, Langford, *supra* note 5.

In practice though, the Court has not demonstrated consistency which has had distributive implications. It has taken a relatively robust approach to cases raising arbitrariness, discrimination, and unfair conditions for accessing social programmes.[179] But when confronted with claims concerning the levels of benefits its posture is distributionally questionable. In the 1995 *Social Benefits* case and related judgments,[180] the Court famously halted cuts to a range of universal benefits: maternity leave, family benefits, sickness benefits, and education supports. This was done on the basis of property rights and the right to legal certainty as the cuts did not interfere with the minimum core of the right.

However, the Court has been very deferential in cases that concern the minimum level of social rights and the enabling legislative framework. For instance, in Decision 42/2000, the Court was directly confronted with the question of whether there had been an unconstitutional omission by the state to legislate on account of its failure to create an adequate regulatory and institutional system to ensure sufficient access to housing. For example, local municipalities were tasked with managing social housing but resources were not evenly or adequately distributed to them or the beneficiaries. After dismissing the claim of an implied constitutional right to housing, the Court assessed compliance with the right to social security. It acknowledged that the state must organize and operate a system of social security and benefits although noted that this does not mean that 'citizens would have a subjective right to state support in acquiring a flat, nor is the state obliged to secure a *specific form and system* of support for housing'.[181] This may reduce the liberty of the legislature to define the tools in guaranteeing social security within 'the capacity of the national economy'. The majority did affirm, however, the importance of securing the minimum level of the right to social security that would guarantee human dignity. In the case of homelessness, there was a 'State obligation to provide support' which includes the 'provision of shelter when an emergency situation directly threatens human life'.[182]

Despite these strong formal affirmations, the substantive and remedial approach of the court was notable for its deferentialism. After briefly examining the relevant legislation, the Court acknowledged it was an 'extreme' situation but simply exhorted and encouraged the government to 'endeavour to increase the level of support and to expand the scope of social benefits in line with' economic capacity'.

[179] See, for example, Decision 21/1994 (16 April 1994) (quota on taxi licences found to violate right to work—failed proportionality test); Decision No. 39/1997 (excessive restrictions on registration of foreign doctors struck down—violated free choice of occupation). In Decision 47/1996 it found requirements for a social housing programme that included a deposit with their application and residence or employment in the city for ten years to be unreasonable, and in Decision 20/2000 that the conditions imposed in another municipality had no bearing on applicant's 'social, income and financial' situation. However, these latter cases were decided through statutory interpretation although the line of reasoning is consistent with the established constitutional principles.

[180] Decision 43/1995: 30 June 1995. For discussion, see A. Sajó, 'Social Rights as Middle-Class Entitlements in Hungary: The Role of the Constitutional Court', in R. Gargarella, P. Domingo, and T. Roux (eds.), *Courts and Social Transformation in New Democracies: An Institutional Voice for the Poor?* (Aldershot/Burlington: Ashgate, 2006).

[181] ABH 1995, 801, 803, in Decision No. 42/2000, Part IV.

[182] ABH 1995, 801, 803, in Decision No. 42/2000, Part IV.

Other cases studies tend to be more controversial. Some commentators have sought to puncture claims that the Colombian Constitutional Court has been a progressive force for social rights by pointing to the middle-class capture of the *tutela* system. Rueda notes that the combination of the minimum core doctrine and the right to an immediate constitutional remedy (*tutela* action) favoured the most disadvantaged in the 1990s. But during the economic crisis in the 2000s, the middle class were able to capture courts.[183] Some empirical evidence in health litigation reveals that in the 2000s judicial orders for medicines were increasingly for more expensive medicines, which provided less effect in terms of quality-adjusted life-years (QALYs).[184] However, these studies suffer from a longitudinal challenge. They underestimate the benefits gained in the 1990s but also the structural judgment of the Colombian Constitutional Court in 2008. The latter sought to address more directly the dysfunctionality of the health system and some of the unintended consequences of individual-based litigation.[185] Rodriguez-Garavito has also produced data that pours some cold water on claims that the middle class has achieved comparatively more.[186] This suggests that the Colombian system meets a moderate distributive test.

The quantitative approach to the Colombian debate has been undertaken elsewhere. One approach is to break down the litigant profiles. Gauri does this for the Indian Supreme Court.[187] He finds that more disadvantaged groups were more likely to attain success in the 1990s than advantaged groups while the reverse was the case in the 2000s. His conclusion is that ideological factors may be important in explaining this development (confirming perhaps McConnell's hypothesis). However, the Court's most extensive use of supervisory jurisdiction for social rights has been in the 2000s in the right to food case, which makes it difficult to treat cases before the court with equal weight.

In a review of distributive legal impact of social rights jurisprudence in five Southern countries, Gauri and Brinks also find significant variance. They chart a series of cases where only the middle class benefits (that is, weak) and then other decisions where the disadvantaged only or primarily benefit (that is, strong). Overall, they conclude that the jurisprudence is characterized by a balanced impact, which could be seen as proportional equality.

[183] P. Rueda, 'Legal Language and Social Change during Colombia's Economic Crisis', in J. Couso, A. Huneeus, and R. Sieder (eds.), *Cultures of Legality: Judicialization and Political Activism in Latin America* (Cambridge: Cambridge University Press, 2010)

[184] O.F. Norheim and S. Gloppen, 'How Can We Assess Impact on Health Outcomes?', in A.E. Yamin and S. Gloppen (eds.), *Litigating Health Rights: Can Courts Bring More Justice to Health?* (Cambridge: Harvard University Press, 2011).

[185] Judgment T-760/08 July 31, 2008 (Constitutional Court of Colombia).

[186] C. Rodríguez Garavito, 'The Judicialization of Health Care: Symptoms, Diagnosis, and Prescriptions' in R. Peerenboom and T. Ginsberg (eds.), *Law and Development of Middle-Income Countries: Avoiding the Middle-Income Trap* (New York: Cambridge University Press, 2014).

[187] See V. Gauri, 'Public interest litigation in India: overreaching or underachieving?', 1 *Indian Journal of Law and Economics* (2011).

4. Conclusion

The presence of ESC rights in national constitutions and jurisprudence continues to grow. The overwhelming majority of constitutions in the world now contain at least one justiciable social right. It gives comfort to efforts to promote the justiciability of ESC rights and enhance accountability and public deliberation over their implementation. However, a tempered approach is needed in the field with greater attention to be given to the broader legal opportunity structure for litigation as well as the absence of judicial enforceability in a significant number of countries.

Of more concern is perhaps the responsiveness of courts. Variance is the norm. It was clear in the formative period of US right to education jurisprudence and continues in contemporary comparative jurisprudence. On one hand, there is no ground for naïve constitutional optimism. Lawyers in particular need to be more sensitive to these concerns lest the agenda of ESC rights adjudication provide a mere hollow hope than an instrument of transformation or at least a wall of defence for the most marginalized. On the other hand, there is no case for a rampant constitutional pessimism. A significant number of courts have responded in a considered and robust fashion to claims of violations. This fact also suggests that the focus should be institutional reform of courts not an abandonment of the idea of judicial enforceability of social rights.

Ensuring courts are distributively fair is perhaps more challenging: it is difficult for courts to ensure over time that the disadvantaged are achieving most of the benefits or an appropriate share. Again, this might require intervention of other actors to correct such patterns. However, courts can also respond themselves to such evidence, and the Colombian Constitutional Court represents a court that is self-conscious of its expected role in ESC rights adjudication.

16

The Intersection of Economic, Social, and Cultural Rights and Civil and Political Rights

Ioana Cismas

1. Introduction

The African Commission on Human and Peoples' Rights (AfCHPR) handed down in 2010 its verdict in a communication dealing with a number of human rights violations alleged to have been committed by the Sudanese government and non-State actors in Darfur.[1] The Commission found a violation of the right to housing and of the prohibition of forced evictions despite the fact that the African Charter on Human and Peoples' Rights does not entail an explicit provision in this area.[2] Consistent with and expanding on its previous practice, it implied the right to housing and the prohibition of forced evictions by appeal to Article 14 of the Charter on the right to property.[3] Furthermore, in the eyes of the Commission, the implied housing rights violations amounted to an Article 5 breach, and thus to 'treatment [which] was cruel and inhuman and threatened the very essence of human dignity'.[4] To summarize: a hybrid right with economic and political elements was used to imply a socio-economic right, which was then used to find a breach of a legal prohibition of a right of a civil and political nature. This decision is paradigmatic for the chapter as it illustrates its premise: ESC and CP rights intersect not only at the normative level, on the basis of the interdependence principle but also, and more importantly, in practice. While adjudicated by national, regional, and international courts and monitored by various treaty bodies and Special Procedures, the intersection of these rights often reinforces the realization of ESC

[1] AfCHPR, *Sudan Human Rights Organisation & Centre on Housing Rights and Evictions (COHRE) v Sudan* (2010), Communication No. 279/03 & 296/05. See also B. Thiele, 'Applying the African Charter on Human and Peoples' Rights to Atrocities in Darfur', 7 *Housing and ESCR Quarterly* 3, September 2010, 1.

[2] See African Charter on Human and Peoples' Rights, adopted 28 June 1981, entered into force 21 October 1986.

[3] AfCHPR, *supra* note 1, paras. 191–205. See for previous practice AfCHPR, *The Social and Economic Rights Action Center and the Center for Economic and Social Rights v Nigeria* (2001), Communication No. 155/96.

[4] AfCHPR, *supra* note 1, para. 164.

and CP rights. It can, however, also weaken their advancement. Understanding the intricate ways of intersection and unearthing its consequences on the realization of ESC rights and CP rights is therefore the aim of this chapter.

As such, in the next section the term intersection, rooted in though not identical to its use in gender studies, will be explained. The third section will look at the intersection of ESC and CP rights at a normative-theoretical level, including as a result of the principle of interdependence of rights. This part will also draw upon changed and promising realities for human rights. The final section will focus on the intersection in practice as evident from the jurisprudence of courts and the monitoring work of international treaty bodies. Cases where the intersection of ESC and CP rights results in a weakening of rights, together with a discussion of the options to avoid such consequences, will also be addressed.

2. On Intersection

The term intersection originates in gender, sexualities, and post-colonial studies but was coined by a legal scholar with the intent to expose the 'single-axis framework that is dominant in antidiscrimination law [...] reflected in feminist theory and antiracist politics'.[5] According to Kimberle Crenshow, this single-axis viewpoint blinds the analysis in so far as it excludes black women's experiences not as women, or as black, but as black women.[6] In gender studies, intersection describes the interaction of different categories such as gender, race, ethnicity, class, and sexuality. 'Instead of merely summarizing the effects of one, two or three oppressive categories, adherents to the concept of intersectionality stress the interwoven nature of these categories and how they can mutually strengthen or weaken each other'.[7] Intersectionality has become a paradigm in gender studies[8] and has penetrated international law and the UN system via the human rights of women.[9]

The framework of intersection has a tremendous explanatory force in human rights law not only when applied to categories of exclusion, but also when applied to rights. This chapter will thus adapt the concept of intersection away from the interaction of 'oppressive categories' towards the interaction of constructed categories of rights, ESC rights, and CP rights. While adopting and adapting intersection,

[5] K. Crenshaw, 'Demarginalizing the Intersection of Race and Sex: A Black Feminist Critique of Antidiscrimination Doctrine, Feminist Theory and Antiracist politics', 1989 *University of Chicago Legal Forum* (1989), 139–167, 139.

[6] K. Crenshaw, 'Demarginalizing the Intersection of Race and Sex: A Black Feminist Critique of Antidiscrimination Doctrine, Feminist Theory and Antiracist politics', 1989 *University of Chicago Legal Forum* (1989), 140 and 149 ff.

[7] G. Winker and N. Degele, 'Intersectionality as Multi-level Analysis: Dealing with Social Inequality', 18 *European Journal of Women's Studies* 1 (2011), 51–66, 51.

[8] See K. Davis, 'Intersectionality as Buzzword: A Sociology of Science Perspective on What Makes a Feminist Theory Successful', 9 *Feminist Theory* 1 (2008), 67–85.

[9] See Commission on Human Rights, The Integration of the Human Rights of Women throughout the United Nations System, UN Doc. E.CN.4/2002/L.59; N. Yuval-Davis, 'Intersectionality and Feminist politics', 13 *European Journal of Women's Studies* 3 (2006), 193–209, 194.

the aim is not to estrange the concept but keep it rooted in its original mission of improving an analytical framework and perhaps a worldview. Crenshaw was concerned with the problematic consequence of the tendency to treat race and gender as mutually exclusive categories of analysis. By analogy, this chapter attempts to show that it is counterproductive for the human rights movement and beyond to treat ESC rights and CP rights as separate and mutually exclusive categories. For various reasons, which will be discussed later, ESC rights and CP rights have been treated as separated categories throughout the history of human rights, a categorization that still lingers on today. On the other hand, in theory and notably in practice ESC rights and CP rights intersect, and this intersection usually reinforces the realization of both ESC rights and CP rights, not only as ESC rights or as CP rights, but as human rights. At times, however, a weakening effect is at play. Understanding and exploring ways to avoid such weakening of human rights situates this adapted intersectionality framework closest to its original roots. It is here that the use of the concept resonates most strongly with that in gender studies.

The analytical value of the proposed framework gains in importance when examining previous attempts by legal scholars to propose concepts echoing intersectionality, although without fully managing to capture its essence. In 1989, Craig Scott developed the notion of permeability in order to give practical legal effect to the abstract doctrine of interdependence, which, in the words of the author, 'thus far in its lifespan, existed as little more than a rhetorical slogan'.[10] Permeability is understood as 'the openness of a treaty dealing with one category of human rights to having its norms used as vehicles for the direct or indirect protection of norms of another treaty dealing with a different category of human rights'.[11] Scott's specific aim was to subject economic rights to the supervisory jurisdiction of the Human Rights Committee (HRCttee), the treaty body receiving communications on alleged violations of the International Covenant on Civil and Political Rights (ICCPR).[12] Ultimately, his project was driven by a lack of similar communication procedures under the International Covenant of Economic, Social and Cultural Rights (ICESCR).[13] With the entering into force of the Optional Protocol to the ICESCR on 5 May 2013, reality might change. Hence, the concept of permeability although useful for encouraging the litigation of ESC rights violations by the HRCttee appears rather dated today. Moreover, intersection captures (better) the two-way flow: the fact that not only can CP rights be used to advance ESC rights, but also this process can occur vice-versa.

[10] C. Scott, 'Interdependence and Permeability of Human Rights Norms: Towards a Partial Fusion of the International Covenants on Human Rights', 27 *Osgoode Hall Law Journal* (1989), 769–878, 771.

[11] C. Scott, 'Interdependence and Permeability of Human Rights Norms: Towards a Partial Fusion of the International Covenants on Human Rights', 27 *Osgoode Hall Law Journal* (1989), 769–878, 771.

[12] International Covenant on Civil and Political Rights, adopted 16 December 1966, entered into force 28 March 1976.

[13] International Covenant on Economic, Social and Cultural Rights, adopted 16 December 1966, entered into force 3 January 1976.

In a 2005 article focusing on the Inter-American system, James Cavallaro and Emilie Schaffer strongly advocate for the 'less as more' doctrine as a strategy for the advancement of ESC rights. The conservative thesis more or less proposes an expansive interpretation of CP rights in preference to the development and direct adjudication of ESC rights themselves.[14] Cavallaro and Schaffer urge lawyers and activists to embrace the 'less as more' strategy in bringing cases before the Inter-American Commission and Court of Human Rights on the basis of one major presumption: the lack of enforceable duties of ESC rights.[15] In a critique of the proposed approach from a technical-jurisdictional perspective, Tara Melish discards the 'outmoded dichotomy' of categories of rights and emphasizes that 'it is not rights that are or are not justiciable; it is the *claims* crafted under them that fulfill, or fail to fulfill, the elements of a justiciable controversy'.[16] Where these jurisdictional predicates 'are not met, no claim may be "saved" by recasting it under a civil or political rights norm'.[17]

Melish also describes two litigation approaches—the integration and indirect approaches—that can advance ESC rights in practice[18] while explicitly refuting the idea that human rights are separated into normative categories or generations.[19] The integration approach involves the litigation of CP rights that entail an ESC rights dimension with the aim of protecting the latter.[20] The indirect approach relies on due process guarantees and the prohibition of discrimination to adjudicate ESC rights.[21] These two litigation strategies can be seen as conceptually close to the intersectionality framework.

Two main differences between, on the one hand, the intersectionality framework proposed in this chapter and, on the other, permeability, integration, and indirect approaches should be noted. First, the latter three approaches have an inbuilt single-axis mindset, which tends to obscure the full range of interactions between ESC and CP rights. They conceive of CP rights as the privileged group of rights and hence little attention is given to their advancement. However, in certain contexts that are elaborated in this study, CP rights can be in a weak or vulnerable position

[14] J.L. Cavallaro and E.J. Schaffer, 'Less as More: Rethinking Supranational Litigation of Economic and Social Rights in the Americas', 56 *Hastings Law Journal* 2 (2004), 218–282, 218.

[15] J.L. Cavallaro and E.J. Schaffer, 'Less as More: Rethinking Supranational Litigation of Economic and Social Rights in the Americas', 56 *Hastings Law Journal* 2 (2004), 225 and 268.

[16] See T.J. Melish, 'Rethinking the "Less as More" Thesis: Supranational Litigation of Economic, Social and Cultural Rights in the Americas', 39 *New York University Journal of International Law and Politics (JILP)* (2006), 173–343, esp. 237 and 211.

[17] See T.J. Melish, 'Rethinking the "Less as More" Thesis: Supranational Litigation of Economic, Social and Cultural Rights in the Americas', 39 *New York University Journal of International Law and Politics (JILP)* (2006), 211.

[18] See *infra* Part 4. for the dangers posed by an exclusive use of this litigation approaches.

[19] Melish, *supra* note 16, at 233–332.

[20] See T.J. Melish, 'Protecting Economic, Social and Cultural Rights in the Inter-American Human Rights System: A Manual on Presenting Claims' (New Haven: Center for International Human Rights, Yale Law School, 2002), 233–332.

[21] See T.S. Bulto, 'The Indirect Approach to Promote Justiciability of Socio-Economic Rights of the African Charter on Human and Peoples' Rights', in R. Murray (ed.), *Human Rights Litigation and the Domestication of Human Rights Standards in Sub-Saharan Africa*, vol. 3 (Nairobi: Kenyan Section of the International Commission of Jurists, 2009), 135–167.

vis-à-vis ESC rights.[22] The advantage of intersectionality is that it recognizes that CP rights can equally be boosted through ESC rights. A second difference between intersectionality and permeability, the integration and indirect approaches is one of scope; while the latter are designed as litigation strategies, intersectionality is construed as a framework applicable to litigation, monitoring, and advocacy. As shall be argued further it can also contribute to the de-categorization of human rights in practice and at normative-theoretical level.

It should be clearly stated at this point that intersectionality is not seen and cannot be seen as an alternative to the formal acceptance through legislation and the direct adjudication of ESC rights.

3. The History of a Separation Wall

A. The two Covenants and the categorization of human rights

The abominations of the two World Wars and especially of the Nazi regime have taught humankind and the then-leaders that safeguards for future generations ought to be put in place. These safeguards took an extra-systemic form by bestowing individuals (and groups) with rights; a departure from the purely state-centred paradigm.[23] Perhaps in the wake of tremendous catastrophes, the obvious does appear obvious and hence the new world was built on four pillars reflecting equally socio-economic and civil and political concerns: 'freedom of speech and belief and freedom from fear and want'.[24] It is perhaps ironic to note—in light of future developments—that the inclusion of ESC rights in the 1948 Universal Declaration of Human Rights (UDHR) on equal footing with CP rights is rooted in President Franklin D. Roosevelt's 'Four Freedoms Address' of 1941 which served as inspiration for a draft prepared by the American Law Institute; this latter document was one of the main sources for the drafting of the UDHR, together with other texts containing ESC rights and submitted, notably, by the West.[25] As Asbjorn Eide and Wenche Barthe Eide have demonstrated, historical evidence shows that ESC rights were included in the UDHR as a result of Western action, not as suggested by Cold War discourse by Socialist states.[26] In short, ESC rights appeared alongside CP rights in the UDHR, which conveyed a factual and symbolic indication of the interwoven nature of ESC and CP rights.

[22] See Section 3.C.2. in this ch.

[23] See for example L.B. Sohn, 'The New International Law: Protection of the Rights of Individuals Rather Than States', 32 *American University Law Review* (1982), 1–64.

[24] Universal Declaration of Human Rights, adopted 10 December 1948, Preamble, para. 2.

[25] A. Eide, and W.B. Eide, 'Article 25', in G. Alfredsson and A. Eide (eds.), *The Universal Declaration of Human Rights: A Common Standard of Achievement* (The Hague: Martinus Nijhoff Publishers, 1999), 523–550, esp. 527–528.

[26] A. Eide, and W.B. Eide, 'Article 25', in G. Alfredsson and A. Eide (eds.), *The Universal Declaration of Human Rights: A Common Standard of Achievement* (The Hague: Martinus Nijhoff Publishers, 1999), 528.

The responsibility of the Cold War East–West divide in the construction of a separation wall between ESC and CP rights has reached mythological proportions. The West is usually seen as being responsible for the rejection of ESC rights,[27] while the East for the refutation of CP rights. Whereas ideological divisions across the Cold War blocs certainly played a role, the *travaux préparatoires* of the International Covenants speak to a far more equally shared responsibility for the separation of human rights into two international legal documents.

The primary concern of the West, joined notably by developing States such as Egypt, India, Mexico, and Uruguay, is best summarized by the *Annotations on the Text of the Draft International Covenants on Human Rights*:

> Those in favour of drafting two separate covenants argued that that civil and political rights were enforceable, or justiciable, or of an 'absolute' character, while economic, social and cultural rights were not or might not be; that the former were immediately applicable, while the latter were to be progressively implemented; and that, generally speaking, the former were rights of the individual 'against' the State, that is, against unlawful and unjust action of the State, while the latter were rights which the State would have to take positive action to promote.[28]

Today, it is obvious that at stake was a conflation of the legal nature, the enforceability, and the justiciability of ESC rights.[29] Clarifying this misunderstanding has taken decades of effort by scholars, UN experts, courts, and NGOs and, indeed, it remains a work in progress.[30] Yet, it is again ironic to note that implementation of ESC rights was also the objection raised by the Eastern bloc. While being the advocates of ESC rights at a discursive level,[31] as the history of the Cold War period has revealed albeit only rarely, in practice communist States were among the most fervent opponents of a treaty regime of implementation, least of all one involving individual communications.[32] As such, proposals by Lebanon in

[27] For an article that regards this view as a 'preposterous lie', see J. Donnelly and D.J. Whelan, 'The West, Economic and Social rights, and the Global Human Rights Regime: Setting the Record Straight', 29 *Human Rights Quarterly* 4 (2007), 908–949. For a reply, which seeks to infirm or relativize the findings of the former article by critiquing the positivist method and exposing its pitfalls see T. Evans and A. Kirkup, 'The Myth of Western Opposition to Economic, Social, and Cultural Rights?: A Reply to Whelan and Donnelly', 31 *Human Rights Quarterly* 1 (2009), 221–237.

[28] Annotations on the Text of the Draft International Covenants on Human Rights, 1 July 1995, UN Doc. A/2929, para. 10. See also Scott, *supra* note 10, at 794.

[29] Michael Addo explains that '[e]nforcement of human rights deals with the identification of the entitlements and duties created by the legal regime which have to be maintained and executed. Justiciability [...] presupposes the existence of a review mechanism to determine non-compliance with the terms of the legal regime. [...] Justiciability is a juridical mechanism triggered off by the inadequacies in the enforceability or execution of human rights'. M.K. Addo, 'The Justiciability of Economic, Social and Cultural Rights', 14 *Commwealth Law Bulletin* (1988), 1425–1432 and 1425.

[30] See K. Arambulo, 'Drafting an Optional Protocol to the International Covenant on Economic, Social and Cultural Rights: Can an Ideal Become Reality', 2 *University of California Davis Journal of International Law and Policy* (1996), 111–136, 117–120. See also M.C.R. Craven, *The International Covenant on Economic, Social, and Cultural Rights: A Perspective on its Development* (New York: Oxford University Press, 2002), 10–16.

[31] For an explanation of the position of the Eastern bloc based on Marxist theory, see K. Arambulo, *Strengthening the Supervision of the International Covenant on Economic, Social and Cultural Rights: Theoretical and Procedural Aspects* (Antwerp: Intersentia, 1999), 10–11 and 17.

[32] P. Alston, 'Out of the Abyss: The Challenges Confronting the New UN Committee on Economic, Social and Cultural Rights', 9 *Human Rights Quarterly* (1987), 332–381, esp. 337 and 339; Scott, *supra* note 10, at 798.

1951,[33] France in 1954,[34] Italy[35] and the United States of America in 1966,[36] that ESC rights could be dealt with by a committee of independent experts have been opposed by the Eastern bloc and subsequently withdrawn one after another. Ultimately, while the West may have been responsible for the partition, it was the East that robbed the ICESCR of its expert monitoring and individual communication procedure. In the end, both blocs contributed to the separation wall and the image of non-justiciability of ESC rights.

B. The principle of interdependence and progress towards de-categorization

At the same time as the process of dividing human rights in two categories was underway, interdependence was becoming one of the basic principles of international human rights law. Interdependence found its main utility at a theoretical level,[37] emphasizing that ESC and CP rights are intrinsically linked and as a consequence realizing the former is related to the latter, and vice-versa. The concept of intersection goes beyond that of interdependence. Intersectionality explains the fact that the interaction between ESC and CP rights may result in a strengthening, but also a weakening of the rights. Interdependence does not capture the weakening aspect because, as we shall see, its mission was to focus only on the strengthening aspect, so as to first counter and later manage the separation of human rights in the two Covenants.

The drafting process of the International Covenants can also be read through the lens of the constant reaffirmation of the principles of interdependence and indivisibility of human rights. The interdependence principle was first mentioned in the *Unity* resolution of 1950 which called upon the Commission on Human Rights to draft a single International Covenant on Human Rights and thus to include 'a clear expression of economic, social and cultural rights in a manner which relates them to the civic and political freedoms proclaimed'.[38] Once it became evident that the objections to a unified international human rights instrument were insurmountable, the interdependence principle served to manage the compromise outcome as a constant reminder that all human rights are to be treated equally. The UN General Assembly insisted in its *Separation* resolution that 'enjoyment of civil and political rights freedoms and of economic, social and cultural rights is interconnected and interdependent' and that 'when deprived of economic, social and cultural rights, man does not represent the human person whom the Universal Declaration regards as the ideal of the free man'.[39] To underline the indivisibility, or

[33] UN Doc. E/CN.4/570 (1951).
[34] UN Doc. E/CN.4/L.388 (1954).
[35] UN Doc. A/C.3/L.1358 (1966).
[36] UN Doc. A/C.3/L.1360 (1966).
[37] See Scott's observation that interdependence found little utility beyond the theoretical level (*supra* note 10, at 771).
[38] General Assembly Resolution 421(V) of 4 December 1950, section E, paras. 2 and 7(b).
[39] General Assembly Resolution 543 (VI) of 5 February 1952, Preamble, paras. 2–3.

in its own words the 'unity of the aim in view', the Assembly also insisted that the two International Covenants contain as many similar provisions as possible, and asked for their simultaneous submission, approval, and opening for signature.[40]

In a nutshell, states have opted for the separation into two Covenants of ESC and CP rights—a decision based, as was pointed out on the assumption that ESC and CP rights represented two different categories of rights, while at the same time pledging to uphold all human rights equally. A compromise being struck between the two dominant ideologies of the time would be the realpolitik explanation for this paradoxical course of action. Another explanation, more naïve perhaps, but one on which the human rights movement has built, is suggested by Daniel J. Whelan and Jack Donnelly: 'Australia, China, France, Guatemala, Lebanon, Sweden, and Uruguay changed their votes because they were convinced that separate human rights conventions did not necessarily mean a violation of the principle of "indivisibility"'.[41] Consequently, the interdependence principle has been restated on several occasions after the end of the Cold War, notably in the Vienna Declaration and Programme of Action of 1993:

> All human rights are universal, indivisible and interdependent and interrelated. The international community must treat human rights globally in a fair and equal manner, on the same footing, and with the same emphasis… [I]t is the duty of States, regardless of their political, economic and cultural systems, to promote and protect all human rights and fundamental freedoms.[42]

Echoing the Vienna Declaration, on 10 December 2008 the UN General Assembly adopted the Optional Protocol to the ICESR establishing an individual communication procedure, and thereby rectifying a historic omission.[43] Over the years, a number of factors contributed to this significant development. The managing force of the interdependence principle was clearly among these factors. However, other important aspects—themselves interrelated and interdependent—must also be credited for the change in mind-set that enabled the adoption of the communication procedure.

The pioneering role of the gender movement in acknowledging that the livelihoods of women are significantly affected by violations of ESC rights and thus their insistence on an international treaty which addresses discrimination in respect to all human rights cannot be overstated. After the adoption of the Convention

[40] General Assembly Resolution 543 (VI) of 5 February 1952, Preamble, para. 1.

[41] J. Donnelly, and D.J. Whelan, 'The Reality of Western Support for Economic and Social Rights: A Reply to Susan L. Kang', 31 *Human Rights Quarterly* 4 (2009) 1030–1054 and 1049.

[42] World Conference on Human Rights, *Vienna Declaration and Programme of Action*, 25 June 1993, Art. 5.

[43] Optional Protocol to the International Covenant on Economic, Social and Cultural Rights, General Assembly Resolution A/RES/63/117 of 10 December 2008. See M. Langford, 'Closing the Gap? An Introduction to the Optional Protocol to the International Covenant on Economic, Social and Cultural Rights', 27 *Nordic Journal of Human Rights* (2009), 2–29; E. Riedel, 'New Bearings in Social Rights? The Communication Procedure under the ICESCR', in U. Fastenrath et al. (eds.), *From Bilateralism to Community Interest. Essays in Honour of Judge Bruno Simma* (Oxford: Oxford University Press, 2011), 574–589,

on the Elimination of All Forms of Discrimination against Women in 1979,[44] incorporating ESC rights in general human rights treaties alongside CP rights has become the norm.[45] Regional documents of more recent date have followed suit.[46] These instruments represent a gradual advance towards the de-categorization of human rights at a normative level, away from the generations approach towards a single genre.[47]

Today, international NGOs are embracing ESC rights alongside CP rights in their advocacy and strategic litigation campaigns. The opening towards ESC rights of Amnesty International is symptomatic: contested at the beginning from inside and outside,[48] the move has been emulated by other international NGOs.[49] Together, these organizations have put ESC rights on the international agenda reflecting the needs and realities on the ground. They have thus contributed to legitimizing the normative positioning of ESC rights on the same value plane as CP rights.

The adjudication of ESC rights by national and regional courts[50] and the monitoring by international treaty bodies, in particular the Committee on Economic, Social and Cultural Rights (CESCR)[51] and UN Special Procedures,[52]

[44] However, it should be underlined that not all ESC rights present in the UDHR also found their place in CEDAW. Notably the right to food is absent, although certain aspect can be implied by appeal to art. 12.

[45] See Convention on the Rights of the Child, adopted 20 November 1989, entered into force 2 September 1990 (hereafter CRC); International Convention on the Protection of the Rights of All Migrant Workers and Members of Their Families, adopted 18 December 1990, entered into force 1 July 2003; and the recent Convention on the Rights of Persons with Disabilities, adopted 13 December 2006, entered into force 3 May 2008.

[46] See the African Charter on Human and Peoples' Rights, adopted 28 June 1981, entered into force 21 October 1986; and the (Rev.) Arab Charter on Human Rights, adopted 22 May 2004, entered into force 15 May 2008.

[47] For the generations approach to human rights see C. Tomuschat, *Human Rights: Between Idealism and Realism* (New York: Oxford University Press, 2003), 24–28. See, however, also A. Eide and A. Rosas, 'Economic, Social and Cultural Rights: A Universal Challenge', in A. Eide, C. Krause, and A. Rosas (eds.), *Economic, Social and Cultural Rights. A Textbook* 2nd rev. edn (The Hague: Martinus Nijhoff, 2001), 3–7, 4.

[48] See for example 'Many Rights, Some Wrong: The World's Biggest Human Rights Organisation Stretches its Brand', *The Economist,* 22 March 2007, available at <http://www.economist.com/node/8888792> (last accessed 25 November 2013); K. Roth, 'Defending Economic, Social and Cultural Rights: Practical Issues Faced by an International Human Rights Organization', 26 *Human Rights Quarterly* 1 (2004), 63–73. And for a reply, see L.S. Rubenstein, 'How International Human Rights Organizations Can Advance Economic, Social and Cultural Rights: A Response to Kenneth Roth', 26 *Human Rights Quarterly* 4 (2004), 845–865.

[49] An excellent example is the recent work on ESC rights of the World Organization against Torture, an NGO traditionally orientated towards CP rights protection, available at <http://www.omct.org/escr> (last accessed 25 August 2013).

[50] See, for example, C. Golay, *Droit à l'alimentation et accès à la justice* (Bruxelles: Bruylant, 2011); M. Langford (ed.), *Social Rights Jurisprudence: Emerging Trends in Comparative and International law* (New York: Cambridge University Press, 2008); F. Coomans (ed.), *Justiciability of Economic and Social rights: Experiences from Domestic Systems* (Antwerp: Intersentia, 2006).

[51] See M. Sepúlveda Carmona, *The Nature of the Obligations under the International Covenant on Economic, Social and Cultural Rights* (Antwerp: Intersentia, 2003), 73–112.

[52] C. Golay, C. Mahon, and I. Cismas, 'The Impact of the UN Special Procedures on the Development and Implementation of Economic, Social and Cultural rights', 15 *The International Journal of Human Rights* (2011), 299–318.

have contributed to the clarification of the content of ESC rights and towards changing the perception of their non-justiciability. This development in the realm of judicial adjudication and monitoring echoes the prophetic words of Pierre Juvigny, one of the drafters of the International Covenants. Back in 1954, the French delegate argued that over time ESC rights 'tend to become semi-enforceable or even fully enforceable by judicial action'.[53]

C. Is intersection still needed today?

Given the promising current context, it is only legitimate to ask whether an intersectionality framework is still needed today. Alongside the direct adjudication of ESC rights, intersectionality may continue to play a significant role today in three areas: (1) the advancement of ESC rights; (2) the advancement of CP rights; and (3) in efforts towards the de-categorization of human rights.

1. Advancement of ESC rights

The current context is certainly much rosier for human rights than during the Cold War period, although we are far from living *la vie en rose*. The process of realigning ESC and CP rights towards an equal footing is underway, however, even with an operational Optional Protocol to the ICESCR[54], the process will not be finalized. Indeed, as Philip Alston contends, the name-calling phase has been outgrown, and we have entered a more mature and diverse phase where litigation and monitoring of ESC rights is being pursued in a wide range of jurisdictions, at national, regional, and international levels, and with a vast number of strategies in the litigators' toolbox.[55] As such, the traditional use of intersection, as a means to realize ESC rights via enforceable CP rights, in particular in national and regional jurisdictions where individuals and groups do not have direct access to justice for ESC rights violations, remains significant. It is worth noting, however, that such use of intersectionality should be understood as an additional strategy to one which advocates the direct justiciability of ESC rights.

The traditional use continues to be handy also at the normative level. Catarina de Albuquerque's attempt to carve out the right to sanitation through intersection is a telling example. The then-UN Independent Expert[56] illustrates that sanitation is an integral part of numerous socio-economic and CP rights—the rights to an adequate standard of living, adequate housing, health, education, water, work, life, physical security, the prohibition of inhuman or degrading treatment, gender equality, and the prohibition of discrimination—and that it has been identified

[53] As quoted in Alston, *supra* note 32, at 338.
[54] The Optional Protocol to the ICESCR entered into force on 5 May 2013. As of June 2013, the Protocol has ten state parties.
[55] P. Alston, 'Foreword', in Langford, *supra* note 50, at ix–x.
[56] Today, Special Rapporteur on the human right to safe drinking water and sanitation. See Human Rights Council resolution A/HRC/16/L.4 of 18 March 2011.

as such under various treaties, declarations, national constitutions and law, and international and domestic jurisprudence.[57] In her analysis, intersection operates in two ways. On the one hand, it has a legitimizing effect, in as much as the enumerated rights of which it is part give rise to binding obligations of states in respect to sanitation.[58] On the other hand, de Albuquerque uses these intersections as a foundation upon which she builds her argument for a distinct right. Encapsulating human dignity in a specific way, the right to sanitation has thus a life of its own and should be recognized as such.[59] It should be noted that the CESCR has taken up this interpretation in its Statement on Sanitation,[60] and the General Assembly and Human Rights Council have recognized the right to safe and clean drinking water and sanitation.[61]

2. *Advancement of CP rights*

While it remains under-explored, intersectionality as a strategy for the advancement in practice and at a normative level of CP rights via ESC rights can prove very useful in certain circumstances. Some governments are reluctant to engage on CP rights issues with UN experts who are mandated to monitor human rights. The reasons for this reluctance may vary: some countries remain faithful to the Cold War ideology or CP rights violations are a stain on their record. Visiting one such country, a UN Special Rapporteur engaged the authorities on the issue of the right to food for prisoners rather than on the right not to be subjected to inhumane and degrading treatment while in detention. It is believed that such, admittedly, unorthodox use of intersectionality may have contributed in that particular situation to improving the inhumane detention conditions, including, but not limited to nutrition.[62]

Related to this reluctance of some states, some UN mandate-holders working on CP rights have experienced difficulties in securing country visits. ESC rights Special Procedures appear to have been more successful in visiting some of those same countries, as their mandates were seen as less threatening. To counter this trend, joint missions of ESC and CP rights mandates are increasingly being explored. Joint missions would, in principle, increase the chances of accessing the country and monitoring all human rights and would implicitly reject the pick-and-choose strategy of states in relation to which Special Procedures they wish to host.

[57] Report of the independent expert on the issue of human rights obligations related to access to safe drinking water and sanitation, Catarina de Albuquerque, UN Doc. A/HRC/12/24, 1 July 2009, paras. 13–54.

[58] Catarina de Albuquerque, UN Doc. A/HRC/12/24, 1 July 2009, paras. 60–80.

[59] Catarina de Albuquerque, UN Doc. A/HRC/12/24, 1 July 2009, paras. 55–59, 81.a.

[60] CESCR, Statement on Sanitation, UN Doc. E/C.12/2010/1, 19 November 2010.

[61] UN General Assembly Res. 64/292 of 28 July 2010; Human Rights Council resolution, A/HRC/15/L.4 of 24 September 2010.

[62] See for an account of practice in relation to the right to food J. Ziegler, C. Golay, C. Mahon, and S.-A. Way, *The Fight for the Right to Food: Lessons Learned* (Hampshire: Palgrave Macmillan, 2011).

Traditionally seen as being (also) a CP right, the right to property is the major absentee from both the ICCPR and the ICESCR.[63] Thus far, the HRCttee has rejected communications dealing with the right to property given the absence of normative backing in the Civil and Political Covenant. In the context of the ideological rift characterizing the Cold War period, the right to property as stipulated by the UDHR could not represent more than an aspirational norm.[64] Eibe Riedel contended in 1991 that:

> All that remains to be done in such a situation is to climb down the ladder of norms of international law from the universal to the regional or even to the sub-regional level where more homogeneous conceptions about the contents of these norms may exist.[65]

Today, however, regional bodies are increasingly building on one another's case law in relation to the right to property and in order to construct a more coherent, cross-regional understanding of the content of this right.[66] The right to property has been used to advance the rights to food, housing, and social security.[67] It will be interesting to see whether, in its communications, the CESCR will draw on the jurisprudence at regional level in the inverse direction; that is, by advancing property rights through the prism of housing and social security rights.

Another example for the relevant use of intersectionality refers to reproductive rights. Abortion is often perceived to entail a dominant civil rights dimension, while in practice it has been advocated or adjudicated by relying upon a panoply of other rights: health, bodily integrity, liberty, privacy, and life.[68] Under the communication procedures, the CESCR will have the opportunity to adjudicate reproductive rights via the right to health, and potentially, advance the normative understanding of a right to abortion as well as the corresponding state obligations.

The intersection of ESC rights can further contribute to the recognition that the obligations to protect and fulfil—the latter at least related to the need to identify vulnerable groups—apply to CP rights as well, and that states are not only obliged, as the ingrained laissez-faire tradition dictates, solely to abstain from action. As Manfred Nowak notes a great number of CP rights perceived to require an abstention on the part of governments can be 'effectively guaranteed *only* by a combination

[63] See C. Golay and I. Cismas, 'Legal Opinion: The Right to Property from a Human Rights Perspective', *Rights and Democracy* (Montreal: Rights & Democracy, 2010), available at <http://ssrn.com/abstract=1635359> (last accessed 25 November 2013).

[64] E. Riedel, 'Standards and Sources. Farewell to the Exclusivity of the Sources Triad in International Law?', 2 *European Journal of International Law* 1 (1991), 58–84, 69–70.

[65] E. Riedel, 'Standards and Sources. Farewell to the Exclusivity of the Sources Triad in International Law?', 2 *European Journal of International Law* 1 (1991), 58–84, 69–70.

[66] See Golay and Cismas, *supra* note 63.

[67] See Golay and Cismas, *supra* note 63, 23–25 and 26–27 and *infra* 4.C.

[68] See C. Zampas and J.M. Gher, 'Abortion as a Human Right: International and Regional Standards', 8 *Human Rights Law Review* 2 (2008), 249–294; Report of the International Conference on Population and Development, Cairo, 5–13 September 1994, UN Doc. A/CONF.171/13/Rev.1 (1995), Chs. VII and VIII; Convention on the Elimination of All Forms of Discrimination against Women, adopted 19 December 1979, entered into force 3 September 1981 (CEDAW), arts. 10.h, 12.1, and 14.2.b.

of negative and positive State obligations'.[69] For instance, the right not to be tortured is a CP right placed firmly in the basket of negative state obligations. Such an interpretation, however, fails to recognize the protect and fulfil dimensions which permeate the text of the Convention Against Torture and Other Cruel, Inhuman or Degrading Treatment or Punishment.[70] The World Organization against Torture has understood the benefits of intersectionality and the need to insist on the positive obligations of states with respect to the prohibition of torture. It has embarked on a strategy that aims to prevent torture and other forms of violence by acting on the root causes identified in the failure of states to realize ESC rights.[71]

3. De-categorization

Closely related to the acknowledgement of a generally applicable respect, protect, and fulfil framework as a result of intersectionality is what we can call the de-categorization effect. Writing in 1987, Philip Alston and Gerard Quinn observed that:

> from a legal perspective, however, this controversy [related to the concept of ESC rights] should have been laid to rest by the adoption of the International Covenant on Economic, Social and Cultural Rights by the United Nations General Assembly in 1966, its entry into force in 1976, and the formal acceptance of the ensuing treaty obligations by 87 states.[72]

Today, after 160 ratifications and the entry into force of the Optional Protocol to the ICESCR, sadly the same observation continues to be valid. Legal scholarship is saturated with debates challenging the allegedly different nature of ESC rights and demonstrating that the 'intrinsic' lack of justiciability of ESC rights is not at all intrinsic, but constructed. Today there are few legal scholars that question ESC rights as human and legal rights.

Nonetheless, in several respectable governments of this world, ESC rights are still seen as 'non-rights': merely social goals or policy objectives.[73] Whether acknowledged

[69] M. Nowak, *UN Covenant on Civil and Political Rights: CCPR Commentary* 2nd edn (Kehl: N.P. Engel, 2005), XXI.

[70] Convention Against Torture and Other Cruel, Inhuman or Degrading Treatment or Punishment, adopted 10 December 1984, entered into force 26 June 1987, arts. 7, 10, 11, and 12. See also S.R. Marks and A. Clapham, *International Human Rights Lexicon* (Oxford: Oxford University Press, 2005), 370–376.

[71] See, for example, 'Implementation of the UN Convention against Torture. Uzbekistan. Shadow Report UN Committee Against Torture', *World Organization Against Torture* and *Rapid Response Group*, November 2007, available at <http://www.omct.org/files/2005/09/3070/uzb_report_un_cat_11_2007_eng.pdf> (last accessed 25 November 2013). More generally, see 'Preventing torture and other forms of violence by acting on their economic, social and cultural root causes. A Report on the implementation of OMCT's Project Addressing the Root Causes of Torture 2007–2010', *World Organization Against Torture,* available at <http://www.omct.org/files/2010/07/6146/report_escr2007_2010.pdf> (last accessed 25 November 2013).

[72] P. Alston, and G. Quinn, 'The Nature and Scope of States Parties' Obligations Under the International Covenant on Economic, Social and Cultural Rights', 9 *Human Rights Quarterly* 2 (1987), 156–229, 158.

[73] See, for example, *Discours de la Conseillère fédérale Micheline Calmy-Rey,* 2ème session du Groupe de travail sur l'Examen périodique universel, Conseil de droit d'homme des Nations Unies, 8 May

as rights or not, they are opposed in these circles as too costly and intrusive, and hence the old and erroneous juxtaposition is put forward: negative obligations attach to CP rights, positive obligations to ESC ones. And, indeed, many years after the fall of the Iron Curtain, ESC rights continued to be portrayed as symbols of socialism.[74] In this context, then, the intersection of ESC and CP rights at adjudication, monitoring, and advocacy levels may help concretely and practically to de-categorize ESC rights. By underlining the similarities between ESC and CP rights and their interrelationships, politicians, too, will in time escape the non-rights-non-justiciable paradigm. And, indeed, politicians are the ones adopting new constitutions, establishing policy priorities, and allocating budgets. They are also the addressees of courts when the latter employ judicial practices such as the deference to the executive or the margin of appreciation doctrine.

4. Intersection in Practice

The analysis in this section will focus on a selection of rights that intersect in various judicial and quasi-judicial jurisdictions and will attempt to unearth the particular consequences of these intersections for ESC and CP rights.

A. The right to life as an intersectional device

At a conceptual level one would have difficulties understanding how other rights, whether ESC or CP, can be meaningful 'without an effective guarantee on the right to life as an existence guarantee'.[75] In this context, litigators have sought to use the 'roof' right to life to advance a wide range of ESC rights.[76] However, precisely because it offers an easy avenue for adjudicating the violations of numerous ESC rights, the right to life intersectional device also poses some risks.

At the national level, the Indian example—where ESC rights are placed under Part IV of the Constitution and as directive principles of state policy 'shall not be enforceable by any court'[77] —is perhaps the most famous and as such relatively well explored. This mature jurisprudence allows us to illustrate the use of the right to life as an intersectional device as well as its pitfalls. Given the weak constitutional

2008. It should be noted that the Swiss Constitution supports this view. Art. 41 of the Constitution of the Swiss Confederation, adopted 1999.

[74] See, for example, 'Steele Calls Obama Health Plan "Socialism": Republican Party Chairman Accuses Democrats of Conducting a "Risky Experiment" ', *CBSNews*, 20 July 2009, available at <http://www.cbsnews.com/stories/2009/07/20/politics/main5174417.shtml> (last accessed 25 November 2013).

[75] See E. Riedel, 'The Right to Life and the Right to Health, in Particular the Obligation to Reduce Child Mortality', in C. Tomuschat, E. Lagrange, and S. Oeter (eds.), *The Right to Life* (Leiden: Brill, 2010), at 353.

[76] See E. Riedel, 'The Right to Life and the Right to Health, in Particular the Obligation to Reduce Child Mortality', in C. Tomuschat, E. Lagrange, and S. Oeter (eds.), *The Right to Life* (Leiden: Brill, 2010), at 353.

[77] Art. 37 of the Constitution of the Republic of India.

backing, the reading of the right to life by the Indian Supreme Court and some High Courts so as to include ESC rights is progress per se. The legal actions on to the rights to food,[78] education,[79] and health[80] are regarded as success stories of how the right to life can become a vehicle for realizing ESC rights in practice. There was a consensus among the judges—reflecting perhaps a wider societal consensus—in respect of the straightforward linkages between these rights and the right to life. Building upon this 'legitimate' intersection, the Court identified yardsticks for States' obligations and thus significantly contributed to the clarification of these 'implied' rights and in the case of the right to food to ongoing monitoring of state action.

Overall, the balance sheet of right to life litigation in India used to adjudicate ESC rights is more nuanced. With respect to the rights to work and housing,[81] including the prohibition of forced evictions, a weakening of afforded protection is noticeable. For instance, the right to life has been used to further the right to a clean and healthy environment, another directive principle of the Indian Constitution;[82] in *Bombay Environmental Action Group v A.R. Bharati* the latter was conflicting with the right to housing of another group. The public interest litigation resulted in the eviction of several thousand slum dwellers and the demolition of their huts in the Sanjay Gandhi National Park, while the proceedings discouraged and even barred access to justice of the evacuees.[83] This case reveals one limitation of the 'roof' right to life. In the absence of a formal recognition of ESC rights, the competition among these rights to make use of the same right to life as a justiciable device is important. And thus, 'queue jumping' in the interest of societal groups that are better off is facilitated.[84]

Beyond the Court's acknowledgement that the right to life included a right to livelihood, even the much-heralded *Olga Tellis v Bombay Municipal Corporation*

[78] The *People's Union for Civil Liberties* brought a public interest claim in 2001 arguing that the existing abundant food reserves should be used to prevent ravaging hunger and starvation. The Supreme Court instructed the Government to identify vulnerable groups nation-wide and include them in food schemes. The Court continued to monitor the implementation of its directives. See *People's Union for Civil Liberties v Union of India* (2001), *People's Union for Civil Liberties v Union of India* (2004); more recently, by the Delhi High Court *remlata w/o Ram Sagar & Ors v Government of NCT Delhi* (2010). See a collection of decisions in N.C. Saxena et al., *Right to food*, Human Rights Law Network, 2005; and C. Golay, 'The Right to Food and the Right to Life', in D. Fraser and G. Almeida Rodrigues (eds.), *Disrespect Today, Conflict Tomorrow: The Politics of Economic, Social and Cultural Rights* (Nottingham: CCC Press, 2009), 151–158, esp. 155–157.

[79] See *Mohini Jain v State of Karnataka* (1992) and *Unni Krishnan J.P. v State of A.P. and Others* (1993). The latter case paved the way for an amendment of the Indian Constitution introducing the right to education for children under 14 among the fundamental rights. Art. 21.A. of the Constitution of the Republic of India.

[80] *Paschim Banga Khet Majoor Samity v State of West Bengali* (1996); S. Muralidhar, 'Judicial Enforcement of Economic and Social Rights: the Indian Scenario', in Coomans, *supra* note 50, 237–268, at 244–246.

[81] See S. Muralidhar, 'The Expectations and Challenges of Judicial Enforcement of Social Rights', in Langford, *supra* note 50, 102–123, at 110–111.

[82] Art. 48.A. of the Constitution of the Republic of India.

[83] Muralidhar, *supra* note 81, at 113–114.

[84] See also C. Gonsalves, 'The Right to Housing: The Preserve of the Rich', 1 *Housing and ESC Rights Litigation Quarterly* 2 (2005), 1–3.

(1986) provides two other caveats concerning the use of this intersectional justiciability device. First, the right cannot stretch infinitely. The Court found in the case at hand that the eviction of the squatters from their pavement dwellings did not amount to a deprivation of their life, a deprivation of the right to livelihood being legally acceptable as long as it resulted from a just and fair procedure undertaken according to law.[85] Second, when an implied right clashes with another right—in this case, the right to property—the judiciary will seek to strike a balance orienting itself according to what is perceived as legitimate in society, including the political class.

Interestingly, the positive legacy of *Olga Tellisi* is to be found in a decision of the Supreme Court of Bangladesh from 1999.[86] Building on the findings of the Indian Court, the Bangladeshi judges derived through intersection the right to livelihood and shelter from the constitutional rights to life, respect for dignity, and equal protection of the law. The Court held that the livelihood of the evicted slum dwellers from Dhaka City had been severely impacted. As such, the Government was directed to put in place resettlement schemes, and in general to take into account a phasing of the process which would allow the evacuees to find alternative accommodation. These aspects would be in line with the interpretation provided by the CESCR in General Comment No. 7 on forced evictions.[87]

At the regional level, both the African and the Inter-American systems on several occasions read the right to life in an expansive way. For instance, in the Mauritania cases the AfCHPR found that in addition to burning (individuals) in sand and subjecting them to torture to the point of death, the denial of food and medical attention 'point to a shocking lack of respect for life, and constitute[s] a violation of article 4'.[88] Previously, in the *Ogoni* case the commissioners identified all rights in the African Charter as attaching the obligations to 'respect, protect, promote and fulfil'[89] and put forward an intersectional—if not sweeping—reading of the right to life:

> Given the wide spread violations perpetrated by the Government of Nigeria and by private actors (be it following its clear blessing or not), the most fundamental of all human rights, the right to life has been violated. The Security forces were given the green light to decisively deal with the Ogonis, which was illustrated by the wide spread terrorisations and killings. The pollution and environmental degradation to a level humanly unacceptable has made it living in the Ogoni land a nightmare. The survival of the Ogonis depended on their land and farms that were destroyed by the direct involvement of the Government. These

[85] See also Muralidhar, *supra* note 81, at 112–113, and M. Langford and A. Nolan, *Litigating Economic, Social and Cultural Rights* (Geneva: Centre on Housing Rights and Evictions, 2006), 277.

[86] *Ain o Salish Kendra v Government of Bangladesh* (1999).

[87] CESCR, General Comment No. 7, The right to adequate housing (Art.11.1): forced evictions, 05/20/1997.

[88] AfCHPR, *Malawi African Association and Others v Mauritania* (2000), Communication Nos. 54/91, 61/91, 98/93, 164/97 à 196/97 and 210/98, para. 120.

[89] AfCHPR, *Social and Economic Rights Action Center & the Center for Economic and Social Rights v Nigeria* (2001), Communication No. 155/96, para. 44.

and similar brutalities not only persecuted individuals in Ogoniland but also the whole of the Ogoni Community as a whole. They affected the life of the Ogoni Society as a whole.[90]

Consistent with its previous case law the Inter-American Court on Human Rights (IACtHR) has interpreted Article 4 of the American Convention on Human Rights (ACHR) as the 'life project'. A 2010 decision of the IACtHR in the *Xákmok Kásek Indigenous Community v Paraguay* case found violations of the right to life, including failure to provide access to water, food, medical assistance, and education, with the consequence of several deaths in the community.[91] The axiom on which the Court based its ruling is relevant to our argument that a gradual acceptance of the positive and negative obligations that both ESC and CP carry will contribute to a de-categorization of human rights. In the words of the Inter-American judges:

The observance of Article 4, in relation to Article 1(1) of the Convention, not only presumes that no one be deprived of their life arbitrarily (negative obligation), but also requires the States to take all appropriate measures to protect and preserve the right to life (positive obligation), in keeping with the obligation to ensure the full and free exercise, without discrimination, of the rights of all persons under their jurisdiction.[92]

The positive course on which the Court has embarked until today with respect to furthering ESC rights and strengthening the perception of interdependence with CP rights could result in increasing the understanding and acceptance in the Americas that all human rights are directly justiciable. The still dominant doctrine in the region ascribes different standards of state responsibility to claims of violations of CP as opposed to ESC rights, the first being seen as litigation-appropriate and the second one as inappropriate.[93] Melish argues, however, that the sole or over-reliance on intersectional mechanisms, in particular the right to life, could damage the protection of all human rights in the long term.[94] The IACtHR takes a conservatory, restrictive stance in respect to the *direct* adjudication of ESC rights by not judicially enforcing Article 26 of the Convention that readily offers them autonomous protection,[95] while taking a wide, expansive approach in their indirect litigation. Against this background, the breadth of the right to life could become infinite, and would result in the weakening of the norm, potentially making the obligations of states in relation to this right too abstract, too vague, too distant from the original understanding; while the Court's decisions would seem 'arbitrary, 'visionary', and lacking a 'basis in law', precisely the sort of cases that 'lead to legitimacy problems'.[96] A future move towards direct adjudication of

[90] AfCHPR, *Social and Economic Rights Action Center & the Center for Economic and Social Rights v Nigeria* (2001), Communication No. 155/96, para. 67.

[91] IACtHR, *Xákmok Kásek Indigenous Community v Paraguay* (2010), paras. 183–234.

[92] IACtHR, *Xákmok Kásek Indigenous Community v Paraguay* (2010), para. 187.

[93] T.J. Melish, 'The Inter-American Court on Human Rights: Beyond Progressivity', in Langford, *supra* note 50, 372–408, at 405.

[94] T.J. Melish, 'The Inter-American Court on Human Rights: Beyond Progressivity', in Langford, *supra* note 50, 372–408, at 405–408.

[95] See ACHR, adopted 22 November 1969, entered into force 18 July 1978, art. 26.

[96] Melish, *supra* note 16, at 327.

ESC rights alongside intersectional litigation when suitable would be a means to counter the still dominant doctrine, while steadily building legitimacy for direct justiciability.

The practice of the European Court of Human Rights (ECtHR) has long been to stress the importance of positive obligations of states, on a par with the negative ones.[97] In this context, then, there is an expectation that the Court would not shy away from adjudicating ESC rights when they intersect with Convention rights solely based on the 'name-calling' myths. Indeed, in *Cyprus v Turkey* the ECtHR found that:

> an issue may arise under Article 2 of the Convention where it is shown that the authorities of a Contracting State put an individual's life at risk through the denial of health care which they have undertaken to make available to the population generally. It notes in this connection that Article 2 § 1 of the Convention enjoins the State not only to refrain from the intentional and unlawful taking of life, but also to take appropriate steps to safeguard the lives of those within its jurisdiction.[98]

On intersection with Convention rights more generally, Luke Clemments and Alan Simmons assert that 'the Court's starting point is now an unequivocal acceptance of the view that the Convention protects a core irreducible set' of ESC rights.[99] Of course, the difficulty lies in deciding the boundaries of this core. Here, the two authors show moderate optimism: while still making use of the cherished margin of appreciation doctrine, the ECtHR is more open to looking at emerging international norms for inspiration.[100] Such a gradual and balanced approach by the ECtHR in addition to the work of the European Committee of Social Rights could prove useful over time in forging legitimacy and thus acceptability of ESC rights litigation in Europe.

The HRCttee has been reluctant to use an extensive definition of the right to life in the past. Nonetheless, in its concluding observations to monitoring states' reports, the Committee has raised questions related to infant mortality rates and life expectancy, nutritional matters, and issues related to HIV/AIDS in the context of the right to life.[101]

[97] See J.-F. Akandji-Kombe, *Positive Obligations under the European Convention on Human Rights: A Guide to the Implementation of the European Convention on Human Rights*, Human Rights Handbooks, No. 7 (Strasbourg: Council of Europe, 2007).

[98] ECtHR, *Cyprus v Turkey* (Judgment) (10 May 2001), Application no. 25781/94, para. 219.

[99] L. Clemens, and A. Simmons, 'The European Court of Human Rights: Sympathetic Unease', in Langford, *supra* note 50, 409–427, at 426–427.

[100] L. Clemens, and A. Simmons, 'The European Court of Human Rights: Sympathetic Unease', in Langford, *supra* note 50, 409–427, at 426–427.

[101] See Riedel, *supra* note 75, at 354–355; B.C.A. Toebes, *The Right to Health as a Human Right in International Law* (Antwerp: Intersentia, 1999). See also HRCttee, *Karen Noelia Llantoy Huamán v Peru*, Communication No. 1153/2003, UN Doc. CCPR/C/85/D/1153/2003 (2005), where the Committee found inter alia a violation of the prohibition on torture in a communication involving the denial to a minor of a therapeutic abortion of an anencephalic foetus. It did however not pronounce itself on art. 6.

B. Intersection of the prohibition of torture and cruel, inhuman and degrading treatment, the right to health, the right to housing, and children's rights

Estelle v Gamble, a case decided in 1976 by the US Supreme Court is deemed to be the milestone in the protection of the constitutional right of prisoners to healthcare in the United States.[102] Mr. Gamble, an inmate of the Texas Department of Corrections, was injured while performing a prison work assignment. He lodged a complaint against the head of the Department of Corrections, the warden of the prison, and the chief medical doctor arguing that they had subjected him to cruel and unusual punishment in violation of the Eighth Amendment of the US Constitution.[103] The Court found that the Eighth Amendment prohibiting torture and cruel and unusual punishment embodies 'broad and idealistic concepts of dignity, civilized standards, humanity, and decency' against which correctional measures in prison facilities must be evaluated.[104] The Supreme Court judges concluded that it is incumbent upon the Government to provide medical care for detainees and failure to do so may 'produce physical torture or a lingering death'.[105]

Despite having lost his case on the merits, Mr. Gamble's intersectional action is credited with having obtained the acknowledgement of three basic rights of prisoners in the USA: the right to access to healthcare, the right to care that is ordered, and the right to a professional medical opinion.[106]

The intersection of the right to humane treatment, including the prohibition of torture (Article 5 of the ACHR) and the rights to education and health, was at the centre of the *Juvenile Reeducation Institute v Paraguay* case. The IACtHR read Article 5 in conjunction with the rights of the child,[107] and to unearth the positive duties states have towards children held in re-education facilities.[108] The case at hand was especially suitable for an intersectional approach since it dealt with a recurrent, systemic pattern of violations of the ESC and CP rights of children placed in detention centres in Latin America.[109] The intersectional approach allowed the Court to demand an integrated systemic solution in the form of a state policy of short-, medium-, and long-term implementation in respect of children held in detention.[110]

[102] See W.J. Rold, 'Thirty Years after *Estelle v Gamble*: A Legal Retrospective', 14 *Journal of Correctional Health Care* 1 (2008), 11–20.

[103] *Estelle v Gamble* 429 U.S. 97 (1976), I.

[104] *Estelle v Gamble* 429 U.S. 97 (1976), sec. II.

[105] *Estelle v Gamble* 429 U.S. 97 (1976), sec. II.

[106] For an explanation of what these rights entail see Rold, *supra* note 102, at 14–15.

[107] Art. 19 of the ACHR.

[108] IACtHR, *Juvenile Reeducation Institute v Paraguay* (2004), paras. 157 *et seq.*

[109] For a similar observation see M. Tinta, 'Justicability of Economic, Social, and Cultural Rights in the Inter-American System of Protection of Human Rights: Beyond Traditional Paradigms and Notions', 29 *Human Rights Quarterly* 2 (2007), 431–459, 447–448.

[110] See IACtHR, *supra* note 108, paras. 135–190, section XIII on Reparations, in particular paras. 312–319.

Moldovan v Romania is a case crudely depicting the intersection of violations of human rights. The ECtHR shows that it has understood the plight of the Roma families who were subjected to a pogrom in 1993 and to ongoing institutional and societal discrimination ever since, while losing their houses, their belongings, and even their means of earning a decent living. In finding that the applicants had been subjected to degrading treatment, the Court enumerated aspects related to ESC and CP rights: 'the severely overcrowded and unsanitary environment and its detrimental effect on the applicants' health and well-being', 'the length of the period during which the applicants have had to live in such conditions', and 'the racial discrimination to which they have been publicly subjected by the way in which their grievances were dealt with by the various authorities'.[111] The Court's decision can be rightly read as factual evidence of the de-categorization of human rights.

Hajrizi Dzemajl et al. v Yugoslavia should be seen in the light of the same paradigm of de-categorization of human rights. The jurisprudence of the Committee against Torture reveals that ESC rights abuse can be used to find CP violations. In the case at hand, the Committee decided that the destruction and burning of houses constituted a violation of the prohibition of cruel, inhumane, and degrading treatment.[112] The Committee underlined the obligation of the state party to protect the complainants from attacks on their houses and held that the failure to do so amounted to the acquiescence of the police with the perpetrators. In addition, a series of positive obligations, such as information and training of law enforcement so as to prevent inhumane and degrading treatment, were fleshed out.[113]

C. The right to property as an intersectional device for the ESC rights of vulnerable groups

When referring to our intersectionality paradigm and its initial use in gender studies to emphasize discriminated versus privileged categories, the right to property would surely belong to the latter. Property has been a privilege of the few and served in the past as a means of excluding the large mass of 'non-possessors' from political life.[114] Today the concept is often associated with commercial rights protecting corporate ownership of goods, land, or scientific innovation.

In this context, it is interesting to examine the case law of the ECtHR to understand that property rights can be restricted to further social aims. In several cases, measures promoted by the state in order to fulfil the right to housing and achieve greater social justice have been accepted by the Court as having legitimate aims.[115]

[111] ECtHR, *Moldovan and Others v Romania* (Judgment) (12 July 2005) 41138/98; 64320/01, paras. 110–114.

[112] Committee against Torture, *Hajrizi Dzemajl et al. v Yugoslavia*, Case No. 161/2000, UN Doc. CAT/C/29/D/161/2000, para. 9.2.

[113] Committee against Torture, *Hajrizi Dzemajl et al. v Yugoslavia*, Case No. 161/2000, UN Doc. CAT/C/29/D/161/2000, para. 9.2.

[114] F. Cheneval, 'Property Rights as Human Rights', in H. de Soto and F. Cheneval, *Realizing Property Rights* (Zurich: Rueffer & Rub, 2006), at 11.

[115] Golay and Cismas, *supra* note 63, at 24.

For instance, in *Mellacher and others v Austria*, the applicants who were flat owners complained that the implementation of legislation which resulted in a reduction of rent infringed their right to property under Article 1 of Protocol No. 1. The ECtHR held that the aim of the interference was legitimate and the measure proportionate.[116] It thus appears that the Court is prepared to grant a wide margin of appreciation to states when they limit the right to property to fulfil the right to housing.[117]

The development of the right to property in the Inter-American and African systems reveals that the right (also) has an underprivileged mantra and can further the rights of the most discriminated and vulnerable groups. It is here that the right to property has become an intersectional vehicle for a number of ESC rights, such as the rights to food, and social security, and the *de lege ferenda* right to land of indigenous people.[118] The IACtHR has interpreted the right to property of indigenous people as giving rise to the positive obligations of the state to delimitate and demarcate the land, to protect *communal* rights to property so as to allow indigenous people to provide for their own means of subsistence.[119] The *Awas Tingni*,[120] *Yakye Axa*,[121] and the *Sawhoyamaxa*[122] cases are emblematic for the intersectional approach of the Court. In a decision involving the property rights of the *Endorois* indigenous community, the AfCHPR analysed the framework of states' obligations—respect, protect, fulfil—and made a case for the legality and indeed the requirement in certain contexts to redress imbalances through affirmative action.[123] According to the Commission, the ancestral land of indigenous people makes the object of a communal right to property and belongs to a special category of property. As such, 'the public interest test is met with a much higher threshold in the case of encroachment of indigenous land rather than individual private property'.[124]

[116] ECtHR, *Mellacher and others v Austria* (Judgment) (19 December 1989) Application Nos. 10522/83; 11011/84; 11070/84, paras. 47 and 51. See also ECtHR, *James and others v The United Kingdom* (Judgment) (21 February 1986) Application No. 8793/79, paras. 47 *et seq.*

[117] See also L. Clements and A. Simmons, 'The European Court of Human Rights: Sympathetic Unease', in Langford, *supra* note 50, 409–427, at 416.

[118] Golay and Cismas, *supra* note 63.

[119] F. MacKay, 'From "Sacred Commitment" to Justiciable Norms: Indigenous Peoples Rights in the Inter-American System', in A. Tostensen and W. Vandenhole (eds.), *Casting the Net Wider: Human Rights and Development in the 21st Century* (Antwerp: Intersentia, 2007), 371–394, 378–379.

[120] IACtHR, *The Mayagna (Sumo) Awas Tingni Community v Nicaragua* (Judgment) (31 August 2001).

[121] IACtHR, *Yakye Axa Indigenous Community v Paraguay* (Judgment) (17 June 2005).

[122] IACtHR, *Sawhoyamaxa Indigenous Community v Paraguay* (Judgment) (29 March 2006).

[123] AfCHPR, *Center for Minority Rights Development (Kenya) and Minority Rights Group International on behalf of the Endorois Welfare Council v Kenya* (2009) Communication No. 276/2003, para. 196.

[124] AfCHPR, *Center for Minority Rights Development (Kenya) and Minority Rights Group International on behalf of the Endorois Welfare Council v Kenya* (2009) Communication No. 276/2003, para. 212.

D. The intersectional obligation to prohibit discrimination

A correct reading of the prohibition of discrimination would not place this right in the category of CP or ESC rights, but at their intersection. The clearest indication is the similar wording contained in the two International Covenants prohibiting discrimination based on 'race, colour, sex, language, religion, political or other opinion, national or social origin, property, birth or other status'.[125] Moreover, anti-discrimination permeates the entire human rights treaty law system, equality clauses being pre-eminent in international and regional instruments that stipulate both CP and ESC rights.[126]

The right to equality is by its very nature and function an intersectional right. National jurisprudence, as well as international case law dealing with the right to equality, prove the utility of this clause in advancing ESC rights. At the same time, equality litigation facilitates the understanding that the cause of ESC rights violations is often to be found in historic and long-lasting exclusion and marginalization of certain groups. In Canada, the equality clause has on some occasions advanced claims related to housing, healthcare, and social assistance rights.[127] In Spain, the formal equality and the material equality principles have been, at times, successful in protecting labour rights, mainly in relation to gender discrimination.[128] In the Swiss context, in which most ESC rights are constitutionally stipulated as goals, as opposed to rights, the Federal Supreme Court found that the minimum conditions for life, including basic nutritional needs, are the right of everyone living within the boundaries of the country. In extending this right to non-citizens such as illegal immigrants and rejected asylum-seekers, the Court relied on the prohibition of discrimination.[129] At the international level the HRCttee would appear to have overcome its reluctance to approach ESC rights when the latter are related to discriminatory policies.[130]

The right to equality is an important monitoring and a powerful advocacy tool. However, the intersectionality of this right can advance ESC rights only that far. First, although of an intersectional nature, non-discrimination has finite flexibility when employed in legal actions to advance ESC rights. It cannot easily

[125] ICCPR, art. 2.1, art. 3, and art. 26; ICESCR, art. 2.2. See also HRCttee, General Comment 18: Non-discrimination (37th session, 1989), and General Comment No. 28: Equality of rights between men and women (art. 3) (68th session, 2000) UN Doc. CCPR/C/21/Rev.1/Add.10 (2000), both reprinted in Compilation of General Comments and General Recommendations Adopted by Human Rights Treaty Bodies, UN Doc. HRI/GEN/1/Rev.6 at 144 and 179 (2003); and CESCR, General Comment No. 20: Non-discrimination in economic, social and cultural rights (Art. 2, para. 2) UN Doc. E/C.12/GC/20, 2 July 2009.

[126] See, for example, CEDAW, art. 1; CRC, art. 2.1; African Charter on Human and Peoples' Rights, art. 2; ACHR, art. 1.1.

[127] D. Wiseman, 'Methods of Protection of Social and Economic Rights in Canada', in Coomans, *supra* note 50, 173–205, at 201.

[128] M.J. Añón and G. Pisarello, 'The Protection of Social Rights in the Spanish Constitutional System', Coomans, *supra* note 50, 67–96, 82–84.

[129] *V. gegen Einwohnergemeinde X. und Regierungsrat des Kantons Bern*, 1995, and see Golay, *supra* note 50.

[130] Concluding Observations of the Human Rights Committee, Israel, UN Doc. CCPR/C/ISR/CO/3, 29 July 2010, paras. 17 and 18.

accommodate aspects related to accessibility, availability, acceptability, adaptability, or quality, which are at the core of states' obligations with respect to ESC rights. Second, a case which presents itself as an ESC rights case without a discriminatory aspect is beyond the ambit of equality clauses. Third, as Daniel Wiseman suggests in the Canadian context—although the validity of the observation may be extrapolated to other jurisdictions—entrenched ideological or 'name-calling' motivations move judges to sacrifice the equality doctrine and dismiss intersectional ESC rights cases.[131] The non-discrimination principle, as is the case with judicial protection guarantees not discussed here,[132] are useful in advancing both ESC and CP rights through intersection. Even so, as these three limitations demonstrate the process guarantees are no panacea and no substitute for the direct judicial enforcement of ESC rights.

E. Intersection of freedom of religion and the rights to health and to education

Not the most intuitive association, the interaction between freedom of religion and ESC rights has created some controversies in recent years and merits scholarly attention.

In a recent case, a judge of the US District Court for the District of Columbia was faced with an innovative challenge to the Patient Protection and Affordable Care Act (PPACA), the healthcare reform passed by Congress in 2010. The claim based on the Freedom of Religion Restoration Act against the PPACA was brought by five individuals, three of whom refuse the use of medicine as being incompatible with their religion, while the others use holistic medicine that they contend will not be covered by insurance. The judge contended that '(1) [the individual mandate] does not place a substantial burden on the exercise of Plaintiffs' Christian faith, and (2), even assuming that it does, it is the least restrictive means of serving a compelling government interest'.[133] Given recent healthcare reform in the USA, it is not far-fetched to read a compelling interest of the Government in the realization of the right to health of Americans. Hence, the religious freedom challenge of the healthcare bill has paradoxically contributed to the legitimization of the right to health in the USA.[134]

The UK's House of Lords has, on several occasions, dealt with cases related to corporal punishment in public or private schools, which subsequently proceeded to the ECtHR. In 1982, two mothers objected to their children being subjected to corporal punishment in state schools based on Article 2, Protocol 1 of the European Convention. Under the heading of the right to education, the Article also provides for the right of parents to ensure such education and teaching in

[131] Wiseman, *supra* note 127, at 202.

[132] For a discussion, see Bulto, *supra* note 21, at 158–166.

[133] *Margaret Peggy Lee Mead et al. v Eric H. Holder Jr. et al.*, Civil Action No. 10-950 (GK), 2011.

[134] See also E.A. Friedman and E.Y. Adashi, 'The Right to Health as the Unheralded Narrative of Health Care Reform', 34 *Journal of the American Medical Association* 23 (2010), 2639–2640.

conformity with their own religions and philosophical convictions. The Court sided with the appellants finding, among other things, that the right to education of the child had been violated since the condition to access schooling—that is accepting corporal punishment—was unreasonable and fell outside the powers of regulation of the state.[135]

In 2005, the House of Lords was confronted with an application which reversed the 1982 claim. Parents who were supporting the use of corporal punishment as part of a Christian upbringing objected to the statutory ban in UK public and private schools.[136] Article 2, Protocol 1, as well as the right to freedom of religion (Article 9), were used in this case. The Lords missed the opportunity to fully engage in a discussion of the right to education of the child, which, although not part of the claim, was at the heart of the debate. They also omitted to draw on the work of the Special Rapporteur on the right to education regarding the unacceptability of corporal punishment in schools, an issue which she has tackled consistently in her reports.[137] Nonetheless, the Lords reached the conclusion that Article 9 and Article 1, Protocol 1 had not been violated, thereby upholding indirectly the right of education of the child.

In the much-publicized *Lautsi and Others v Italy* case a spectacular change of situation was registered, when the Grand Chamber of the ECtHR asserted that there was no violation of Article 2, Protocol 1, and that the decision whether or not to put crucifixes in classrooms fell within the state's margin of appreciation.[138] This effectively reversed the previous ruling from 2009, when Ms Lautsi brought her complaint under Article 9 and Article 2, Protocol 1.[139] Then, the Court held that the state 'has a duty to uphold confessional neutrality in public education, where school attendance is compulsory regardless of religion, and which must seek to inculcate in pupils the habit of critical thought'.[140] It is important to understand that several rights intersected in that case: on the one hand, the right to freedom *from* religion of Ms Lautsi and her children, her right to educate her children according to her beliefs, and the right of her children to acceptable education. At stake is also the right of the Italian state to protect the general interest, which here appears to have taken the contours of Catholicism. This case provides an example of the crucial role which context can play in the process of balancing human rights. Indeed, the context was calling on the Grand Chamber to take a stance on behalf of the freedom *of* religion, and much less *from* it. Had the Court considered the

[135] ECtHR, *Campbell and Cosans v United Kingdom* (1982) 4 EHRR 293, para. 41.

[136] *R v Secretary of State for Education and Employment and others (Respondents) ex parte Williamson (Appellant) and others* [2005] UKHL 15, 2005, para. 23.

[137] See K. Tomasevski, *Education Denied: Costs and Remedies* (London: Zed Books, 2003), and Report submitted by Ms Katarina Tomasevski, Special Rapporteur on the right to education, UN Doc. E/CN.4/2000/6/Add.1, 9 August 1999.

[138] ECtHR, *Case of Lautsi and Others v Italy* (Judgment) (18 March 2011) Application No. 30814/06.

[139] ECtHR, *Case of Lautsi and Others v Italy* (Judgment) (3 November 2009) Application No. 30814/06.

[140] ECtHR, *Case of Lautsi and Others v Italy* (Judgment) (3 November 2009) Application No. 30814/06, para. 56.

right of the two applicant children to education and engaged in a discussion of the legal standards developed by UN Special Procedures and the CESCR—availability, accessibility, acceptability, and adaptability—it may have avoided an over-reliance on extra-judicial, philosophical standards of what is and is not acceptable in a public educational institution. As it was, accepted ESC rights standards were not discussed nor did the right to education of the children play the role it should have in the Court's decision.

5. Conclusion

Starting from the premise that ESC and CP rights intersect at normative-theoretical level, as well as in practice through litigation, monitoring, and advocacy, this chapter has analysed the consequences of such interactions. At a normative level, a self-standing right to water and sanitation has been developed based on the intersection of a number of ESC and CP rights. Intersectional litigation has been mainly employed to further a panoply of ESC rights through CP rights, yet it has also led to an increased understanding that CP rights attach positive obligations alongside negative ones, therefore strengthening the rights regime in toto. Monitoring mechanisms of the UN have advanced the realization of CP rights by engaging authorities on ESC rights issues and international advocacy campaigns have relied heavily on the right to health to gain recognition for safe abortion and reproduction as human rights issues. As these and other discussed instances demonstrate, intersectionality can result in the advancement of both ESC and CP rights. The analysis has also shown that an over-reliance on indirect litigation of ESC rights through CP rights can lead to negative consequences, such as dilution of rights or neglecting the concerns of the most vulnerable in society. Furthermore, the risk of entertaining the perception that indirect litigation is the only way to adjudicate ESC rights should not be overlooked. In the end, intersectionality as an analytical framework has disclosed some additional means to further ESC and CP rights, while at the same time emphasizing that direct litigation and enforceability cannot be fully substituted if the wall of separation between rights is to fall.

17

Building Bridges

National Human Rights Institutions and Economic, Social, and Cultural Rights

Allison Corkery and Duncan Wilson

1. Introduction

With the elaboration of the International Covenants on Civil and Political and on Economic, Social and Cultural Rights (ICCPR and ICESCR)—binding agreements intended to implement the Universal Declaration on Human Rights—the 1960s marked the 'golden era of United Nations standard setting'. More recently, there have been moves towards a 'period of pragmatic implementation', with increasing focus on identifying means by which to anchor international obligations in the domestic context.[1] Although standard setting continues, establishing national level mechanisms has become a core priority on the international human rights agenda.[2] This chapter concerns one key official, independent mechanism for the promotion and protection of human rights: national human rights institutions (NHRIs).

While early notions that human rights should be enforced by specially mandated national committees date back to 1946, NHRIs remain a relatively new phenomenon.[3] Their proliferation followed the so-called third wave of democratization, coinciding with the end of the Cold War and the emergence of international actors such as the United Nations (UN) Office of the High Commissioner for Human Rights (OHCHR), which played a central role in their promotion.[4] As one study sharply observed 'if in the 1950s, the status symbol of a developing country was a

[1] J. Hucker, 'Bringing Rights Home: the Role of National Human Rights Institutions', in F. Butler (ed.), *Human Rights Protection: Methods and Effectiveness* (London: Kluwer Law International, 2002), 29–54, 31.

[2] See, e.g. J. Mertus, *Human Rights Matters: Local Politics and National Human Rights Institutions* (Stanford: Stanford University Press, 2009), 1; S. Cardenas, 'Adaptive States: The Proliferation of National Human Rights Institutions', Working Paper T-01-04 2004 (Carr Center of Human Rights Policy, 2004), 29.

[3] See A. Pohjolainen, *The Evolution of National Human Rights Institutions: The Role of the United Nations* (The Danish Institute for Human Rights, 2006), 30–33.

[4] See Cardenas, 'Adaptive States', *supra* note 2.

steel mill, in the 1990s, apparently, it was a human rights commission'.[5] The term 'national human rights institution' itself only acquired broad currency in 1991 when the First International Workshop on NHRIs was convened in Paris under the auspices of the UN. The Workshop adopted the *Principles Related to the Status of National Institutions for the Promotion and Protection of Human Rights* (the Paris Principles), which establish normative standards on the role, composition, status, and functions of these bodies.[6] As Richard Carver notes, this not only marked the first articulation of today's conceptual understanding of NHRIs, but was a turning point after which such institutions proceeded apace.[7] The Vienna Declaration and Programme of Action of the same year represented a further landmark, with states committing themselves to consider establishing NHRIs.[8] Twenty years later, the number of NHRIs has grown exponentially from fewer than 10 two decades ago, to more than 100 internationally accredited institutions.[9]

While their institutional design and mandate varies considerably from country to country, and region to region, they are generally defined as independent bodies with a specific mandate to promote and protect human rights.[10] They are administrative in nature (in the sense that they are neither judicial nor lawmaking) and have an 'on-going, advisory authority in respect of human rights at the national and international level'.[11] The Paris Principles require that NHRIs are established by a constitutional or legislative text; are independent and enjoy functional and structural autonomy; have a membership which reflects the principle of pluralism; have a broad mandate to promote and protect human rights; receive adequate funding; are accessible; and interact with national civil society organizations as well as regional and international bodies. It is with reference to compliance with these Principles together with other factors such as their effectiveness that NHRIs are accredited by their International Coordinating Committee (ICCtee).[12]

[5] Mertus, *supra* note 2, at 4 (quoting the South Asia Human Rights Documentation Center).

[6] The Paris Principles were subsequently adopted by the UN General Assembly (GA) in 1993. *National Institutions for the Promotion and Protection of Human Rights*, GA Res. 48/134, Annex, UN Doc. A/RES/48/134 (20 December, 1993).

[7] R. Carver, 'A New Answer to an Old Question: National Human Rights Institutions and the Domestication of International Law', 10 *Human Rights Law Review* (2010), 1–32, 6.

[8] World Conference on Human Rights, June 14 to 25, 1993, *Vienna Declaration and Programme of Action*, UN Doc. A/CONF.157/23 (12 July 1993).

[9] OHCHR, *Paris Principles: 20 years guiding the work of National Human Rights Institutions*, available at <http://www.ohchr.org/EN/NewsEvents/Pages/ParisPrinciples20yearsguidingtheworkofNHRI.aspx> (last accessed 7 November 2013).

[10] See, e.g. OHCHR, *National Human Rights Institutions: A Handbook on the Establishment and Strengthening of National Institutions for the Promotion and Protection of Human Rights*, Professional Training Series No. 4 (Geneva: OHCHR, 1995), 6.

[11] M. Parlevliet, 'National Human Rights Institutions and Peace Agreements: establishing national institutions in divided societies', Working Paper (Geneva: International Council for Human Rights Policy, 2006), at 2, available at <http://www.ichrp.org/files/papers/ 61/128_-_National_Human_Rights_Institutions_and_Peace_Agreements_Parlevliet__Michelle__ 2005.pdf> (last accessed 7 November 2013).

[12] See Sub-Committee on Accreditation, ICCtee, *Compilation of the Rules and Working Methods of the SCA* (2009), available at <http://nhri.ohchr.org/EN/AboutUs/ICCAccreditation/Documents/COMPILATION%20OF%20THE%20RULES%20AND%20WORKING%20METHODS%20OF%20THE%20SCA.doc> (last accessed 7 November 2013).

With few exceptions,[13] scant scholarly attention has been paid to the role of NHRIs specifically in relation to economic, social, and cultural rights (ESC rights). Nevertheless, there has traditionally been a perception that NHRIs have been less effective in relation to ESC rights than civil and political rights. For example, in its General Comment No. 10, the UN Committee on Economic, Social and Cultural Rights (CESCR) noted that while the establishment of an NHRI, if properly mandated, can be one means by which a state can take steps to achieve the progressive realization of Covenant rights, this role 'has too often either not been accorded to the institution or has been neglected or given a low priority by it'.[14] The 1998 Maastricht Guidelines similarly state that monitoring bodies, such as national ombudsman institutions and human rights commissions, 'should address violations of [ESC] rights as vigorously as they address violations of civil and political rights'.[15] OHCHR, too, has described the work of NHRIs in relation to ESC rights as 'uneven and sporadic', with NHRIs being 'less active than many other institutions and organizations'.[16]

The Paris Principles themselves do not mention ESC rights explicitly, merely stating that an NHRI 'shall be vested with competence to promote and protect human rights' and should have 'as broad a mandate as possible'.[17] However, while there is undoubtedly still an imbalance in their actions in favour of civil and political rights, NHRIs are increasingly engaging with ESC rights; a 2009 OHCHR study concluded that ESC rights were among the top priorities of NHRIs surveyed in all regions.[18]

To further the debate on the existing and potential role of NHRIs in relation to ESC rights, this chapter looks at how NHRIs address ESC rights. Specifically, we argue that their unique status and role, together with the broad range of functions they perform, should make them central actors in advancing ESC rights nationally, regionally, and internationally.

[13] See, e.g. M. Gomez, 'Social Economic Rights and Human Rights Commissions', 17 *Human Rights Quarterly* (1995), 155–196; C.R. Kumar, 'National Human Rights Institutions and Economic, Social, and Cultural Rights: Towards the Institutionalization and Developmentalization of Human Rights', 28 *Human Rights Quarterly* (2006), 755–779; E. Brems, G. de Beco, and W. Vandenhole (eds.), *National Human Rights Institutions and Economic, Social and Cultural Rights* (Mortsel: Intersentia, 2013).

[14] UN Economic and Social Council, Committee on Economic, Social and Cultural Rights [CESCR], General Comment No. 10, *The role of national human rights institutions in the protection of economic, social and cultural rights*, UN Doc. E/C.12/1998/25 (14 December 1998) [hereafter CESCR, General Comment No.10].

[15] *Maastricht Guidelines on Violations of Economic, Social and Cultural Rights*, Maastricht, 22 to 26 January 1997, para. 25, available at <http://www1.umn.edu/humanrts/instree/Maastrichtguidelines_.html> (last accessed 7 November 2013).

[16] OHCHR, *Economic, Social and Cultural Rights. Handbook for National Human Rights Institutions*, Professional Training Series No. 12 (OHCHR, 2005), viii.

[17] *Paris Principles, supra* note 6, at para. 2.

[18] OHCHR, *Survey on National Human Rights Institutions* (2009), available at <http://www.nhri.net/2009/Questionnaire%20-%20Complete%20Report%20FINAL-edited.pdf> (last accessed 7 November 2013).

2. The Institutional Significance of National Institutions

While a 'combination of broad ideological and diplomatic concerns' may bring states to the accession stage,[19] as Louis Henkin, notes, '[c]ompliance with international human rights obligations [...] is more responsive to domestic forces, to the domestic constitutional culture, than to any international culture pressing for compliance'.[20] This section explores how, as an element of that domestic constitutional culture, NHRIs advance state compliance with ESC rights by negotiating tensions between the international, national, and local levels. NHRIs fulfil a series of 'bridging' roles which, taken together, make them uniquely placed to pursue the national realization of ESC rights.

First, NHRIs bridge the divide between the national, regional, and international human rights systems, having formal recognition in all arenas. Their national legislative basis provides a legally defined relationship with the state—one which gives them specific duties and powers in relation to international human rights law. Likewise their accreditation by the ICCtee accords both international legitimacy, including standing rights before the UN Human Rights Council and enhanced domestic legitimacy. Further, as NHRIs take the UN human rights instruments as their core frame of reference, a 'triangular' relationship exists between the international human rights system, the state, and the NHRI.[21] In this relationship NHRIs act as both 'receptors and transmitters in the cycle of human rights activity'.[22]

As receptors, NHRIs can perform a crucial role in translating international obligations for domestic audiences. In states that have not incorporated the provisions of the ICESCR into domestic law, it is particularly important for NHRIs to perform this role, given that there may be less scope for the judiciary to do so. NHRIs can act as 'cultural translators', interpreting international human rights standards for a local audience, to influence the way people form their identity as rights claimants or duty bearers.[23] By invoking international standards, NHRIs can both elucidate the *content* of ESC rights and, through appeal to international standards, extend the *scope* of the ESC rights applicable nationally.[24] Furthermore, NHRIs can mediate between the universal claims of the international human rights regime and national contexts.[25] For example, the Human Rights Commission of

[19] P. Eldridge, 'Emerging Roles of National Human Rights Institutions in Southeast Asia', 14 *Pacific Review* (2002), 209–226, 211.

[20] Quoted in Hucker, *supra* note 1, at 33.

[21] Carver, *supra* note 7, at 20.

[22] Hucker, *supra* note 1, at 29, 34.

[23] Cultural translators are individuals 'deeply rooted in a particular local social and political context but with extensive connections to international and transnational communities'. B. Simmons, *Mobilizing for Human Rights: International Law in Domestic Politics* (New York: Cambridge University Press, 2009), 141, citing S.E. Merry, *Human Rights and Gender Violence: Translating International Law into Local Justice* (Chicago: University of Chicago Press, 2006).

[24] Carver, *supra* note 7, at 16.

[25] N. Shawki, 'A New Actor in Human Rights Politics? Transgovernmental Networks of National Human Rights Institutions', in N. Shawki and M. Cox (eds.), *Negotiating Sovereignty and Human*

Malaysia has appealed to the government's strong desire to achieve full economic development, 'cajoling the state into complying with the international human rights regime by using the language of development'.[26]

As transmitters, NHRIs can contribute significantly to the work of the UN human rights mechanisms, providing authoritative alternative information to balance 'formalistic' or 'self-serving' reports from states.[27] If genuinely independent, the information provided by them should carry considerable authority to either corroborate or challenge the state's interpretation of its performance. At the same time, states should be more receptive to international critique underpinned by information gathered by an official process at the national level. Further, as international mechanisms lack effective follow-up procedures at the national level, this triangular relationship is also important in promoting the implementation of their recommendations.[28]

NHRIs' interaction with the UN human rights system—particularly in relation to ESC rights—is in some respects still maturing.[29] However, CESCR itself has increasingly included references to NHRIs in its concluding observations,[30] and in 1998 issued a General Comment on NHRIs.[31] Likewise, a number of UN special procedure mandate holders have noted their positive engagement with NHRIs on ESC rights, particularly in the context of country visits. As one noted:

> The Special Rapporteur has found [NHRIs] key actors in promoting the integrated human rights approach as well as merging legal and extralegal methods of human rights protection. The Special Rapporteur has found her cooperation with [NHRIs] particularly useful, whether in Indonesia or Northern Ireland.[32]

Second, NHRIs bridge the divide between government and civil society.[33] As independent mechanisms with a formal human rights mandate, NHRIs have the

Rights: Actors and Issues in Contemporary Human Rights Politics (London: Ashgate, 2009), 41 to 57, 52 to 53.

[26] A. Whiting, 'Situating Suhakam: Human Rights Debates and Malaysia's National Human Rights Commission', 39 *Stanford Journal of International Law* (2003), 59–98, 97.

[27] Hucker, *supra* note 1, at 32.

[28] See C. Heyns and F. Viljoen, 'The Impact of the United Nations Treaties on the Domestic Level', 23 *Human Rights Quarterly* (2001), 483–535, 529 (suggesting that NHRIs should include information on what has been done by government in respect of concluding observations and individual complaints in their yearly reports).

[29] In 2009 OHCHR reported that the level of NHRI participation in UN treaty bodies' processes was 'moderate', while engagement with CESCR was slightly less common than with most others. *OHCHR Survey, supra* note 18, at 43.

[30] See, e.g. CESCR, Ireland, Concluding Observations, UN Doc. E/C.12/1/Add.77 (5 June 2002) (calling on governments to report on the activities of NHRIs on ESC rights); CESCR, New Zealand, Concluding Observations, UN Doc. E/C.12/1/Add.88 (23 May 2003) (recommending NHRIs prioritize ESC rights, including in National Human Rights Action Plans); and CESCR, Paraguay, Concluding Observations, UN Doc. E/C.12/PRY/CO/3 (23 Nov. 2007) (welcoming the attention some NHRIs have given to ESC rights).

[31] CESCR, *supra* note 14.

[32] Report of the Special Rapporteur on the Right to Education, Katarina Tomaševski, submitted to the Commission on Human Rights pursuant to Commission on Human Rights resolution 2002/23, UN Doc. E/CN.4/2003/9 (2003), para. 31.

[33] *See* A. Smith, 'The Unique Position of National Human Rights Institutions: A Mixed Blessing?', 28 *Human Rights Quarterly* (2006), 904–946.

potential to convene effective interactions between duty bearers, civil society, and rights holders, providing human rights defenders and victims of violations with an important ally inside the state system.[34] Thus, as Okafor and Agbakwa argue, the value of an NHRI comes not just from 'what it does', but also from 'what other agents are able to do with it'.[35]

Innumerable examples exist of cooperative but independent working between NHRIs, civil society, and public bodies. One example is the work of the Ghanaian Commission on Human Rights and the Administration of Justice (CHRAJ) to tackle harmful traditional practices, such as the practice of banishment and forced labour of women suspected of witchcraft by traditional village authorities, where they engaged with local chiefs and other traditional authorities through the Centre for National Culture and the House of Chiefs. These efforts to work constructively with an often overlooked constituency were lauded by Human Rights Watch, which noted that CHRAJ 'legitimized and strengthened' the advocacy of local NGOs by sending a message that a state institution would not condone traditional practices that violate constitutional and international law.[36]

Third, NHRIs bridge the artificial divide between civil and political and ESC rights. This should be a matter of both mandate and practice. NHRIs are regularly required to deal with issues that 'defy the conventional divisions' between civil and political and ESC rights.[37] In New Zealand, for example, the Human Rights Commission monitored the government's response to the Canterbury earthquake, with a particular focus on the right to adequate housing. Community members raised particular concerns about procedural rights including the limited amount of information about how decisions were made—for example, on zoning land, on insurance claims, and on the prioritization of repairs—and about how Canterbury residents could voice their concerns or make appeals.[38] Using a human rights lens to analyse recovery-related policies empowered the community to demand greater accountability for decisions made about the rebuilding of the city.

Finally, NHRIs clearly bridge what might be seen as the 'tactical divide' in human rights. As will be discussed in the following sections, the functions NHRIs perform combine 'naming and shaming', reactive, violations-based, or oppositional approaches, with proactive, and constructive approaches. The International Council on Human Rights Policy (ICHRP) considered that, despite the trend towards asserting the justiciability of ESC rights, it may be the 'broader and

[34] See, Cardenas, 'Adaptive States', *supra* note 2, at 6.

[35] O.C. Okafor and S. Agbakwa, 'On Legalism, Popular Agency and "Voices of Suffering": the Nigerian National Human Rights Commission in context', 24 *Human Rights Quarterly* (2002), 662–720, 688–689.

[36] Human Rights Watch (HRW), *Protectors or Pretenders? Government Human Rights Commissions in Africa* (New York: HRW, 2001), 65.

[37] International Council on Human Rights Policy (ICHRP), *Performance and Legitimacy: National Human Rights Institutions* (Geneva: ICHRP, 2004), 76.

[38] New Zealand Human Rights Commission, *Canterbury Earthquake Recovery*, available at <http://www.hrc.co.nz/key-projects/canterbury-earthquake-recovery> (last accessed 7 November 2013).

conciliatory powers enjoyed by most NHRIs [that] make them, in practice, well-suited to promote and protect these rights'.[39]

3. The Promotion and Protection Functions of National Institutions

NHRIs' functions can broadly be divided into those which promote awareness, understanding and implementation of human rights, and those which seek to protect rights by 'eliciting conformance with international norms and rules'.[40] In this section we elaborate how NHRIs' promotion and protection roles can advance ESC rights.

A. The promotion functions of national institutions

NHRI action to promote human rights can include advisory, capacity building, educational, or awareness-raising work. The purpose tends to be either: (1) empowering the population, particularly those who are marginalized or vulnerable, to know and be able to claim their rights; or (2) increasing duty bearers' awareness of their obligations and their ability to respect, protect, and fulfil human rights in their operations.

Promoting respect for ESC rights can be undertaken through either of these means. Raising awareness among the population on their ESC rights can be pursued through the broad range of approaches to human rights education, including more innovative and participatory approaches such as the 'Public Hearings on the Right to Health Care' that were held in India.[41] Work to promote respect for ESC rights among duty bearers can include the development of practical tools for their use, such as drafting eviction guidelines to prevent forced evictions in Kenya.[42]

NHRIs promotional work can also serve to develop understanding of the expectations on other duty bearers, aiding the state in meeting its obligation to protect ESC rights. In the Edinburgh Declaration, which resulted from their

[39] ICHRP, *Assessing the Effectiveness of National Human Rights Institutions* (Geneva: ICHRP, 2005), 18.

[40] S. Cardenas, 'Emerging Global Actors: the United Nations and National Human Rights Institutions', 9 *Global Governance* (2003), 23–42, 25–26.

[41] See, e.g. Hon. Dr Justice A.S. Anand, Chairperson, National Human Rights Commission, speech to the Valedictory Session of the National Public Hearing on the Right to Health Care, New Delhi (17 Dec. 2004), available at <http://nhrc.nic.in/speeches.htm#17%20December%202004> (last accessed 7 November 2013). The hearings were co-organized by the Indian NHRC and the People's Health Movement (Jan Swasthya Abhiyan).

[42] See, e.g. Statement of the Kenya National Commission on Human Rights before the 19th session of the Human Rights Council during the presentation of the report of the Special Rapporteur on Internally Displaced Persons on his mission to Kenya to examine the current situation of all IDPs (6 March 2012), available at <http://nhri.ohchr.org/EN/IHRS/HumanRightsCouncil/19/SR%20on%20IDPs/Statement%20delivered%20by%20the%20KNCHR%20(long%20version).pdf> (last accessed 7 November 2013).

10th International Conference, for example, NHRIs committed themselves to integrating business and human rights in all of their work including through education and awareness raising and advising all relevant actors on how to prevent and remedy corporate abuses of human rights.[43] Promoting the state's duty to protect human rights in the procurement of services or in the granting of licenses to provide services is an increasing area of NHRI activity, for example. In 2009 the South African Human Rights Commission (SAHRC) made a submission to the National Energy Regulator on the impact a proposed electricity price increase by the largest energy company would have on ESC rights.[44] Similarly, the European Network of NHRIs has contributed to the review of the European Commission Directives on procurement, to encourage clarification on their interrelation with the states' duty to protect human rights.[45]

The work of the Colombian *Defensoría del Pueblo* provides interesting examples of NHRI activity to promote the respect, protection, and fulfilment of ESC rights.[46] To advance understanding, awareness, and respect for the emerging right to water, the NHRI has developed a number of publications outlining the scope of the right and related obligations. To promote the protection of the right to health, the NHRI has undertaken a multi-annual review of the use of *tutela* actions to uphold that right, including through raising awareness that such actions can relate to failures to act, or omissions by the state.[47] Finally, to promote the fulfilment of that right, the NHRI has undertaken a significant evaluation of health providers. The evaluation was based on user feedback, assessed through the availability, accessibility, acceptability, and quality framework of the CESCR,[48] and resulted in substantial recommendations for reform, leading the Parliament to invite the institution to play a role in a formal review of health law.

In seeking to promote the ability of public authorities to fulfil ESC rights, NHRIs go beyond the identification of bad practice (often the domain of NGOs) and beyond expounding the requirements of the latest judicial decisions (often the domain of academics). Many were established with the explicit aim of supporting the development of a human rights culture, pursued through dual mechanisms

[43] 10th International Conference of National Human Rights Institutions, *The Edinburgh Declaration* (10 October 2010), available at <http://www.scottishhumanrights.com/international/biennial/edinburghdec> (last accessed 7 November 2013).

[44] South African Human Rights Commission (SAHRC), *Comment to NERSA on Eskom's Proposed 45% Tariff Increase* (30 November 2009), available at <http://www.sahrc.org.za/home/21/files/Reports/Subs%20to%20legislations/FinalCommentsNERSAEskomsProposedtariff%20Hike_30%20Nov%202009.pdf> (last accessed 7 November 2013).

[45] European Group of National Institutions for the Promotion and Protection of Human Rights' European Union Members: *Consultation Response: European Commission's Green Paper on the Modernisation of EU Public Procurement Policy—Towards a More Efficient European Procurement Market* (April 2011), available at <http://www.europarl.europa.eu/meetdocs/2009_2014/documents/droi/dv/701_ecprocurement2011_/701_ecprocurement2011_en.pdf> (last accessed 7 November 2013).

[46] Defensoría Del Pueblo, *Evaluación de los Servicios de Salud que brindan las Empresas Promotoras de Salud 2009*, available at <http://www.defensoria.org.co/red/anexos/publicaciones/evaluacionEps2009.pdf> (last accessed 7 November 2013).

[47] The action of *tutela* is a writ for the protection of constitutional rights.

[48] CESCR, General Comment No. 14, The right to the highest attainable standard of health (art. 12) UN Doc. E/C.12/2000/4 (11 August 2000).

of practical tools such as the 'human rights-based approach' and the identification and sharing of good practice. In an example of this approach, the Scottish Human Rights Commission undertook an independent evaluation of the practice of a high-security mental health institution that had sought to implement a human rights-based approach.[49] The process and outcome evaluation was based on both civil and political as well as ESC rights. In this way NHRIs are well placed to act as catalysts for the structural integration of human rights across all mechanisms of the state.[50]

B. The protection functions of national institutions

NHRIs' protection roles can be pursued both through actions that engage the government, parliament, or the judiciary to improve the legal protection of human rights and through actions undertaken independently by the NHRI to protect those rights. NHRIs are routinely involved in reviewing existing or proposed legislative or administrative provisions. They can also assist victims to seek legal redress, refer cases to competent tribunals, or participate in legal proceedings as amicus curiae. Functions NHRIs undertake independently include reporting on the national human rights situation or on more specific human rights violations, conducting inquiries, and submitting parallel reports to UN treaty bodies. Many NHRIs also have quasi-judicial competence, in that they are able to hear and make recommendations on complaints submitted by individuals.[51] As can be seen in the following examples, in carrying out these functions to advance compliance with the obligations to respect and protect and, increasingly, to fulfil ESC rights NHRIs seek to strike a balance between responding to individualized cases and tackling systemic issues.

1. The obligations to respect and protect

A significant number of NHRIs have the power to review individual or group complaints alleging ESC rights abuses.[52] This can provide an important non judicial mechanism to advance accountability and the right to an effective remedy for violations of ESC rights. While such mechanisms should of course not exist in isolation from a fully functioning justice system with the possibility of review of

[49] Scottish Human Rights Commission (SHRC), *Human Rights in a Healthcare setting: making it work for everyone, an evaluation of the human rights based approach adopted at The State Hospital* (2009), available at <http://www.scottishhumanrights.com/application/resources/documents/HRHCSFINALVERSION.pdf> (last accessed 7 November 2013).

[50] The Human Rights Commission of the Maldives, for example, provides an orientation programme for human rights focal points in all Government departments. SHRC, *Monitoring States' obligations to fulfil ESC rights: methodologies for national institutions, workshop report* (7–10 October 2010), available at <http://www.scottishhumanrights.com/application/resources/documents/CESR%20ICC_sideevent_report.pdf> (last accessed 7 November 2013).

[51] Cardenas, 'Emerging Global Actors', *supra* note 40, at 26.

[52] *OHCHR Survey, supra* note 18, at 53.

any alleged rights abuse by a properly constituted independent tribunal,[53] the forms of non-judicial complaints resolution offered by many NHRIs can provide a more accessible and less adversarial opportunity for victims to have some form of consideration of the alleged violation of their rights. NHRIs' complaints portfolio can include a significant number of ESC rights concerns. The Annual Report of the *Defensoría de Argentina*, for example, indicates that it investigated over 10,000 complaints related to social rights in 2012 alone.[54] The range of issues addressed is also broad; from forced evictions,[55] to employment disputes, landlord and tenant disputes,[56] and welfare.[57]

Some NHRIs have also used mediation where they have identified violations of ESC rights. In Peru, for example, the *Defensoría* reportedly mediated between affected communities, service providers, and the national water regulator to address a series of complaints related to access to water, prompting a review of the complaints procedure.[58]

Such mechanisms are often imperfect, however, and some have questioned whether responding to individual complaints is really the most effective use of NHRIs' generally scarce resources. OHCHR's survey on NHRIs noted: 'a number of respondents from all regions commented that complaints handling systems were underdeveloped or inadequate and that resources were insufficient to respond to high caseloads'.[59] Thus, while responding to actual human rights concerns is, of course, key to NHRIs' legitimacy,[60] their focus may be better served by addressing underlying systemic problems which abuses expose, and failures to ensure effective remedies. Where the investigation of complaints does not address systemic factors, that is clearly a concern.[61]

Among the most significant powers enjoyed by many NHRIs, beyond the power to review individual complaints, is the formal power of inquiry or investigation into systemic human rights concerns. This can often include a statutory power to

[53] See CESCR, General Comment No. 9, The domestic application of the Covenant, UN Doc. E/C. 12/1998/24 (3 December1998), para. 9.

[54] Defensoría Del Pueblo de la Nación, *Informe Anual 2012* (Buenos Aires: 2013), available at <http://www.dpn.gob.ar/informes_anuales/ianual2012.pdf> (last accessed 7 November 2013).

[55] The UN Special Rapporteur on the right to adequate housing has referred to such complaints investigations by NHRIs in, among others, Afghanistan, Nigeria, Sri Lanka, and Uganda. See OHCHR, *Special Rapporteur on Adequate Housing*, available at <http://www.ohchr.org/EN/Issues/Housing/Pages/HousingIndex.aspx> (last accessed 7 November 2013).

[56] See ICHRP, *supra* note 37, at 14. In relation to CRHAJ, ICHRP noted that only 'a small proportion comprise human rights matters as conventionally understood'.

[57] National Commission on Human Rights Indonesia, *Annual Report 2000* (Jakarta: 2001), 69, 226.

[58] C. de Albuquerque and V. Roaf, *On the Right Track: Good Practices in Realizing the Rights to Water and Sanitation* (Lisbon: 2012), 192.

[59] *OHCHR Survey, supra* note 18, at 53.

[60] ICHRP, *supra* note 37, foreword by Dr Kamal Hossain.

[61] ICHRP notes a number of examples where NHRIs have been criticized for failure to address systemic issues which fuel abuses. ICHRP, *supra* note 13, 71–72. In contrast, the Federación Iberamericano de Ombudsmen notes a trend among NHRIs in the region to identify and address systemic issues. See also Federacion Iberoamericana de Ombudsman, *IV Informe sobre Derechos Humanos, Protección de la Salud* (2006).

subpoena information which imposes a corresponding duty on state departments to cooperate.[62] Accordingly, many NHRIs can access information that civil society organizations may not be able to in order to conduct more large scale investigations. In 2005, for example, the Kenya National Commission on Human Rights (KNCHR) released a report entitled *Living Large: Counting the Cost of Official Extravagance in Kenya.* Drawing on its powers to issue subpoenas, the Commission was able to obtain information about the purchase of luxury cars by government departments.[63] It found that the amount spent on cars would have been sufficient to ensure eight years of education for 25,000 children or provide antiretroviral treatment to 147,000 people for a year.[64]

NHRIs have also used their protection powers in relation to non-state actors.[65] In a separate use of its inquiry powers, for example, KNCHR investigated allegations of human rights violations surrounding salt manufacturing in Malindi,[66] following repeated allegations of breaches of labour laws. After a five-day public inquiry, where it received oral and written evidence from the communities, salt manufacturing companies, local and national authorities, and experts, KNCHR found evidence of corruption, denial of communal land rights, and impact on community members' right to an adequate standard of living. The Commission recommended the participation of the community in the design of interventions, accountability of public and private actors for their human rights impact, non-discrimination, and a linkage to the rule of law. Outcomes of the investigation reportedly included workers' mobilization, the provision of safety equipment to workers, and increased attention from relevant government and other public bodies to issues of labour, health, and environmental protection.[67] Elsewhere, the National Commission on Human Rights of Indonesia has investigated allegations of human rights abuses associated with a mud flow, apparently connected to drilling for oil and gas in East Java issuing findings of violations in 2008,[68] and the Peruvian *Defensoría del Pueblo* has investigated the process and outcomes of granting concessions for gas extraction in Camisea. The *Defensoría* pointed to

[62] See *OHCHR Survey, supra* note 18, at 26.

[63] Kenya National Commission on Human Rights (KNCHR), *Living Large: Counting the Cost of Official Extravagance in Kenya* (2005), 22–24.

[64] Kenya National Commission on Human Rights (KNCHR), *Living Large: Counting the Cost of Official Extravagance in Kenya* (2005), 9–10.

[65] Over 70 per cent of respondents to the OHCHR Survey indicated that they could receive complaints against individuals and businesses. *OHCHR Survey, supra* note 18, at 27. See also, OHCHR, *Business and Human Rights: a Survey of NHRI Practices* (2008), available at <http://www.business-humanrights.org/Links/Repository/708317/jump> (last accessed 7 November 2013).

[66] KNHCR, *The Malindi Inquiry Report: Economic Interests Versus Social Justice: Public Inquiry into Salt Manufacturing in Magarini, Malindi District* (2006), available at <http://www.knchr.org/LinkClick.aspx?fileticket=rC6jaKn3zxk%3D&tabid=56&portalid=0&mid=477> (last accessed 7 November 2013).

[67] KNHCR, *The Malindi Inquiry Report: Economic Interests Versus Social Justice: Public Inquiry into Salt Manufacturing in Magarini, Malindi District* (2006), available at <http://www.knchr.org/LinkClick.aspx?fileticket=rC6jaKn3zxk%3D&tabid=56&portalid=0&mid=477> (last accessed 7 November 2013), 185–191.

[68] Asia Pacific Forum, *Indonesia: Rights body intensifies mudflow probe*, <http://www.asiapacificforum.net/news/indonesia-rights-body-intensifies-mudflow-probe.html> (last accessed 7 November 2013).

shortcomings in impact assessment processes, which had failed to identify risks to life and health of isolated communities of indigenous peoples, and criticized the lack of a baseline assessment to enable an evaluation of the actual impact.[69]

For the most part, NHRIs lack the power to enforce their recommendations. As a consequence NHRIs have also sought to advance access to justice for violations of ESC rights through other channels. In pursuit of this goal NHRIs have taken a number of approaches. First, NHRIs have participated in the development of new constitutions and foundational human rights laws, seeking to incorporate ESC rights. The Northern Ireland Human Rights Commission is perhaps the clearest example of this, as it was mandated in the Belfast (Good Friday) Agreement to develop a Bill of Rights for Northern Ireland. The Commission's recommendations, including substantial provisions on ESC rights, were published on 10 December 2008. At the time of writing, however, the future of the Bill remains uncertain, although the NHRI has used the Universal Periodic Review process to press for its adoption.[70]

NHRIs also seek to influence the development of legislation in a wider range of public policy areas. The role played by national human rights bodies in the recognition of the right to food in domestic law in Guatemala, for example, was described as 'decisive'.[71] As a result the NHRI (the *Procurador de los Derechos Humanos*) has been mandated to monitor the implementation of the law and the relevant government departments are required to adopt policies that respond to its annual recommendations on how to respect, protect, and fulfil the right to food.[72]

NHRIs also engage in the judicial enforcement of ESC rights, either directly as a party, indirectly as third-party interveners or amicus curiae, or as monitors of implementation of court orders. The Argentinean *Defensoría* offers an interesting example in this regard. It has been involved in social rights litigation for some time, including in the 1996 hearing and subsequent monitoring of a case requiring the preparation of a vaccine for a type of fever which was unique to Argentina.[73] More recently in a 2008 case involving environmental degradation of an important river basin the Supreme Court mandated the *Defensoría* to coordinate a committee to oversee the development and implementation of a Clean-up Plan.[74] Other NHRIs, including the Indian and South African commissions have been mandated to monitor the implementation of ESC rights court decisions.[75]

[69] FIO, *Salud, supra* note 61.

[70] See, e.g. Northern Ireland Human Rights Commission (NIHRC), *A Bill Of Rights For Northern Ireland: Next Steps Response to the Northern Ireland Office* (Belfast: NIHRC, 2010).

[71] Report of the Special Rapporteur on the right to food, Jean Ziegler Addendum Mission to Guatemala, UN Doc. E/CN.4/2006/44/Add.1, para. 32 (18 January 2006).

[72] The PDH issues annual monitoring reports. See, e.g. PDH, *IV Informe del Procurador de los Derechos Humanos en seguimiento a la Política Nacional de Seguridad Alimentaria y Nutricional del Gobierno de Guatemala* (2011).

[73] FIO, *Salud, supra* note 61.

[74] *Mendoza Beatriz Silva y otros c. Estado Nacional y otros s/daños y perjuicios (daños derivados de la contaminación ambiental del Río Matanza—Riachuelo)*. Expediente M. 1569. XL, available at <http://www.escr-net.org/docs/i/1469153> (last accessed 7 November 2013).

[75] See B.C. Patel, 'The role of NHRC in protecting and promoting the economic and social rights of vulnerable groups in India', and K. Quashigah, 'The monitoring role of the Ghana Commission on

2. The obligation to fulfil

Although the Paris Principles themselves do not use the term human rights 'monitoring', the 'active collection, verification, and use of information to address human rights problems' is central to NHRIs' effective performance of their protective functions.[76] As an ongoing activity that 'systematically uses information in order to measure the achievement of defined targets and objectives within a specified time frame',[77] it is particularly appropriate for NHRIs engaged in holding the state to account for its obligation to fulfil ESC rights. The obligation to achieve progressively the full realization of ESC rights requires the state to 'demonstrate that it is making *measurable progress* toward the full realization' of the rights in question.[78] The development of appropriate indicators which are measureable over time is therefore key.

CESCR has increasingly called for states to monitor their own progress towards the realization of Covenant rights.[79] OHCHR has shown increasing interest in the development of standardized international indicators to support this.[80] It has advocated the development of country-owned monitoring mechanisms, in which an independent institution takes a lead in interpreting available information from a human rights perspective and possibly also coordinating assessment. This institution, they suggest, 'could well be a NHRI'.[81]

This suggestion seems to have some force. While NHRIs may have resource and capacity considerations, their legally mandated role as a bridge between international human rights law and domestic practice should enable them to act as a catalyst for the development of nationally relevant indicators for the fulfilment of ESC (and other) rights, through a participatory process, involving both duty bearers and rights holders. Some NHRIs, such as the Procurador de Derechos Humanos de Guatemala, the National Human Rights Commission of Nepal, the (Great Britain) Equality and Human Rights Commission, and the Scottish Human Rights Commission have played key roles in developing national human rights measurement frameworks, drawing from OHCHR's framework.[82] The fact that NHRIs generally lack the requisite capacity and expertise to act alone in

Human Rights and Administrative Justice in the protection of economic, social and cultural rights, in G. de Beco et al. (eds.), *supra* note 13.

76 OHCHR, *Training Manual on Human Rights Monitoring,* Professional Training Series No. 7 (Geneva: OHCHR, 2001), para. 28.

77 OHCHR, Report of the High Commissioner for Human Rights on implementation of economic, social and cultural rights delivered to the Economic and Social Council, UN Doc. E/2009/90 (8 Jun. 2009), para. 8.

78 *Maastricht Guidelines, supra* note 15, at para. 8 (emphasis added).

79 See generally 'The Development of Economic, Social, and Cultural Rights in International Law', *Eibe Riedel, Gilles Giacca, and Christophe* Golay, ch. 1.

80 OHCHR, *Human Rights Indicators, a Guide to Measurement and Implementation* (Geneva: OHCHR, 2012).

81 OHCHR, *Human Rights Indicators, a Guide to Measurement and Implementation* (Geneva: OHCHR, 2012), 135.

82 OHCHR, *Human Rights Indicators, a Guide to Measurement and Implementation* (Geneva: OHCHR, 2012), 105, 115, and 117.

developing and using quantitative methodologies for monitoring ESC rights may in fact be a strength requiring that they work in partnership with other organizations to this end. In Nepal, for example, the National Human Rights Commission has coordinated a national working group on ESC rights, which is looking at the question of indicators.[83]

In addition, as institutions with a statutory base and security of tenure (according to the Paris Principles), NHRIs ought to be well placed to track issues over extended periods to identify trends and progress or retrogression in the realization of ESC rights.[84] Some NHRIs already conduct regular reporting on the state of ESC rights fulfilment. For example, the Afghan Independent Human Rights Commission has produced series of monitoring reports on economic and social rights in Afghanistan based on information obtained through structured interviews with more than 7,500 individuals annually, as well as through meetings and consultations with stakeholders throughout the country. The information is assessed against indicators on selected ESC rights.[85] SAHRC also routinely reports on the state of ESC rights based on a constitutional mandate.[86] The Aboriginal and Torres Strait Social Justice Commissioner, who is a member of the Australian Human Rights Commission, has published annual Social Justice Reports on the 'enjoyment and exercise' of human rights by Aborigines and Torres Strait Islanders including recommendations for action to ensure the enjoyment of rights since 2001, as mandated under the Commission's Act.[87]

Experience from Australia also demonstrates the importance of provisions that require an institution's reports to be tabled before parliament. In this way, reports go on the public record and where there is open debate on their findings and recommendations this can prompt a formal or informal response from the government. It may be that a government's acceptance of an NHRI's finding can amount to a commitment to take action which then forms a reference point against which to compare indicators. This was the case with *Close the Gap*, a campaign to close the 17-year gap in life expectancy between Indigenous and non-Indigenous Australians. The campaign originated with the Commissioner's 2005 Social Justice Report, which recommended that the Government adopt the following targets: 25 years to achieve equality in life expectancy; and 10 years to achieve equal

[83] OHCHR, *Human Rights Indicators, a Guide to Measurement and Implementation* (Geneva: OHCHR, 2012), 117.

[84] See Center for Economic and Social Rights, *A New Frontier in Economic and Social Rights Advocacy? Using Quantitative Data for Human Rights Accountability* (Madrid: CESR, 2009), available at <http://www.cesr.org/downloads/A%20new%20frontier%20in%20ESC%20advocacy.pdf> (last accessed 7 November 2013).

[85] Afghan Independent Human Rights Commission (AIHRC), *Fifth Report on the Situation of Economic and Social Rights in Afghanistan* (November/December 2011), 17–18.

[86] Section 184(3) of the South African Constitution states, 'Each year the Human Rights Commission must require relevant organs of state to provide the Commission with information on the measures that they have taken towards the realization of the rights in the Bill of Rights, concerning housing, health care, food, water, social security, education and the environment'.

[87] Australian Human Rights Commission Act, 1986, Section 46C(1) (Aus.). Under Section 46C(4) (a) the Commissioner must have regard to, inter alia, the ICESCR in fulfilling this function.

opportunity to access to primary health care and to infrastructure that supports health.[88] Following the launch of the report, a coalition of 40 Indigenous bodies and NGOs worked with the Commissioner to develop the campaign,[89] which culminated in the National Indigenous Health Equality Summit in March 2008. There, the Prime Minister and other government ministers, as well as leaders of health bodies, committed to achieving equality in life expectancy by 2030 and to measure, monitor, and report on their joint efforts against a range of supporting sub-targets and benchmarks.[90] The Indigenous Health Equality Targets were then developed through expert working groups to be integrated into a variety of existing government monitoring frameworks. Since 2009, the federal government has submitted annual reports to Parliament on its progress on closing the gap, with the Australian Human Rights Commission providing its own 'shadow' report.[91]

Such regular reporting can support NHRIs to meet their Paris Principles duty to contribute to periodic reporting under human rights treaties, as well as form baseline studies for the development of National Action Plans for the promotion and protection of human rights, as envisaged in the Vienna Declaration and Programme of Action.[92] The New Zealand Human Rights Commission (NZHRC), for example, undertook an extensive baseline assessment of the state of civil, political, economic, social, and cultural rights in the country in 2004.[93] This laid the basis for a consultation on the development of a National Action Plan for Human Rights 2005–2010. The variety of steps that have been taken to improve access to infant and maternal healthcare for those on low incomes as a result of the Action Plan illustrates the positive impact of this approach for the progressive realization of ESC rights.[94] Similarly, in 2012 the Scottish Human Rights Commission published a report on the state of realization of human rights following a three-year research project. The report, which addressed ESC rights as well as civil and political rights, forms a baseline for the development of the country's first National Action Plan for Human Rights, expected to launch in 2013.[95]

[88] Australian Human Rights Commission (AHRC), *Aboriginal and Torres Strait Islander Social Justice Report 2005* (2005), 96.

[89] AHRC and Standing Committee for Indigenous Health Equality, *National Indigenous Health Equality Targets: Outcomes from the National Indigenous Health Equality Summit Canberra, March 18–20, 2008* (2008), 7.

[90] AHRC and Standing Committee for Indigenous Health Equality, *National Indigenous Health Equality Targets: Outcomes from the National Indigenous Health Equality Summit Canberra, March 18–20, 2008* (2008), 7–8.

[91] See, AHRC, *Close the Gap: Indigenous Health Campaign*, available at <http://www.humanrights.gov.au/social_justice/health/index.html> (last accessed 7 November 2013).

[92] 'The World Conference on Human Rights recommends that each State consider the desirability of drawing up a national action plan identifying steps whereby that State would improve the promotion and protection of human rights'. *Vienna Declaration, supra* note 8, at para. 71.

[93] NZHRC, *Human Rights in New Zealand Today, Nga Tika Tangata O Te Motu* (2004).

[94] See, e.g. NZHRC, *New Zealand Action Plan for Human Rights: Mid-term Review of Progress* (2008), at 6.4.6; *Human Rights in New Zealand 2010* (2010), 167.

[95] See SHRC, *Scotland's National Action Plan*, available at <http://www.scottishhumanrights.com/actionplan> (last accessed 7 November 2013).

4. Effectiveness of NHRIs

NHRIs can be, and in many cases already are, key actors to promote and protect ESC rights, but it must be recognized that the context varies, often drastically, from country to country. In its seminal reviews of NHRIs, the ICHRP noted challenges to their effectiveness ranging from limitations of resources, mandate, capacity and independence. Many others, including a range of UN Special Rapporteurs, have pointed to similar concerns in relation to individual institutions.[96] Such limitations have led some to go so far as to suggest NHRIs can be 'double-edged' phenomena,[97] a label that reflects the concern that NHRIs not sufficiently empowered to meet the social demands they generate may be 'mere straw men', ineffective, or worse, complicit in violations.[98] Cardenas notes that while many NHRIs are relatively successful in promoting human rights norms domestically, as social awareness rises, so too do demands for actual protection, which NHRIs are not always able or willing to provide.[99]

It is broadly recognized that mere compliance with the Paris Principles will not in itself guarantee an NHRI's effectiveness. As Julie Mertus concludes, NHRIs are ultimately 'only as good as the local political and economic context permits them to be'.[100] The particularities of local context impact on NHRIs in two interlinked and overlapping ways: first, on the internal (organizational) dynamics of the institution; and second, on the external (relational) dynamics it has with other actors. These relationships move, to use Anne Smith's terminology, 'downwards' to partners, beneficiaries, and supporters, and 'upwards' to government, legislatures, and funders.[101]

In relation to the internal dynamics of the institution, not all NHRIs, particularly the earlier established ones, have an explicit mandate to address ESC rights. Many have therefore adopted a 'creative' interpretation of their mandate, now reflected in international best-practice guidance.[102] The definition of human rights contained

[96] Among many examples, commenting on a review of the Benin NHRI in the report of his mission to that country, the UN Special Rapporteur on the right to food noted, that '[t]he Commission has been of very limited effectiveness to date, notably because it does not receive any public funding'. UN Doc. A/HRC/13/33/Add.3, paras. 11, 13 (December 2009); commenting on the Zambian NHRI following her mission to that country the Independent Expert on Extreme Poverty and Human Rights noted, that '[w]hile the Commission benefits from a fairly broad mandate, the expert is concerned that its capacity and effectiveness is limited by a lack of funds and enforcement powers, as well as hesitancy in addressing abuses that are politically sensitive and follow up on initial recommendations when these have been rejected by the Government'. UN Doc. A/HRC/14/31/Add.1 (11 May, 2010).

[97] S. Cardenas, 'National human rights commissions in Asia', in J.D. Montgomery and N. Glazer (eds.), *Sovereignty Under Challenge: How Governments Respond* (New Brunswick: Transaction Publishers, 2002), 55–82, 57.

[98] A.H.M. Kabir, 'Establishing National Human Rights Commissions in South Asia: A Critical Analysis of the Processes and the Prospects', 2 *Asia-Pacific Journal of Human Rights and Law* (2001), 1–53, 4.

[99] Cardenas, 'Emerging Global Actors', *supra* note 40, at 38.

[100] Mertus, *supra* note 2, at 2.

[101] Smith, *supra* note 33, at 906.

[102] Commonwealth Secretariat, *National Human Rights Institutions, Best Practice* (London: Commonwealth Secretariat, 2001), 33–34 (counselling to NHRIs adopt an expansive and creative interpretation of their mandates including in inquiries related to the advancement of ESC rights).

in Section 3 of the *Australian Human Rights Commission Act 1986*, for example, does not include the ICESCR.[103] Nevertheless, under Section 10A(1) of the Act, the Commission is required to perform its functions 'with regard for the indivisibility and universality of human rights', which it has interpreted as permitting it to indirectly address ESC rights when they arise in relation to civil and political rights.[104] In India, Section 2(d) of the *Protection of Human Rights Act 1993* defines 'human rights' to mean 'the rights [...] guaranteed by the Constitution or embodied in the International Covenants *and enforceable by courts in India*' (emphasis added).[105] The only rights enforceable in Indian courts are the 'fundamental rights' enshrined in the Constitution. Nevertheless, the Supreme Court has recognized that one enshrined right, the right to life, encompasses a broader range of ESC rights articulated as 'directive principles' in the Constitution that assure the dignity of the individual. The Indian National Human Rights Commission has followed this approach in interpreting its mandate.[106] The Northern Ireland Human Rights Commission too has taken an expansive interpretation of its human rights mandate. As former Chief Commissioner Brice Dickson explains:

> The legislation governing the NIHRC simply says (in summary) that its role is to promote and protect human rights in Northern Ireland. The term 'human rights' is defined as including the rights in the European Convention on Human Rights. The Commission has decided to adopt a more expansive definition: by its Mission Statement it undertakes to measure laws, policies and practices in Northern Ireland against internationally recognized rules and principles for the protection of human rights.[107]

Second, even where an NHRI does have a mandate to address ESC rights in a general sense, its powers to promote and to protect these rights may be more vaguely defined than for civil and political rights.[108] SAHRC is a clear example of an NHRI vested with specific functions that relate to ESC rights. Under Article 84(3) of the Constitution of the Republic of South Africa, the SAHRC is empowered to request that national and state government bodies report to it annually on the measures they have taken towards the realization of the rights protected in the Bill of Rights, including rights to housing, healthcare, food, water, social security, education, and the environment.

[103] The definition of human rights is 'rights and freedoms recognized in the Covenant, declared by the Declarations or recognized or declared by any relevant international instrument'. 'Relevant international instruments' are declared as such by the Minister as has happened with the Convention on the Rights of the Child and the Convention on the Rights of Persons with Disabilities, but not the International Covenant on Economic, Social and Cultural Rights (ICESCR).

[104] See B. Burdekin, *National Human Rights Institutions in the Asia-Pacific Region* (Leiden: Martinus Nijhoff Publishers, 2007), 112–116 (discussing public inquiries carried out by the Commission on homelessness and mental health).

[105] Section 2(f) of the Act defines 'international covenants' as the International Covenant on Civil and Political Rights and the ICESCR.

[106] See Gomez, *supra*, note 13, at 157.

[107] Council of Europe, *3rd European Meeting of National Institutions* (2000), at 21, available at <http://www.nhri.net/pdf/4th-European-Meeting-NHRI/NHRI(2002)012%20E%20-%20Compilation%20of%20speeches.pdf> (last accessed 7 November 2013).

[108] Eldridge, *supra* note 19, at 210.

By contrast, the powers of the Commission on Human Rights of the Philippines (CHRP) illustrate how more specific protections can be accorded to civil and political rights than to ESC rights. Article XIII, Section 18(1) of the Constitution of the Republic of the Philippines gives the CHRP powers to 'investigate on its own or on complaint of any party all forms of human rights violations involving *civil and political rights*' (emphasis added). The Supreme Court has ruled that this provision gives the CHRP the power to investigate political rights only.[109] However, in response the CHRP has adopted a system of 'investigative monitoring', which enables it to respond to the large number of complaints it receives alleging violations of ESC rights by drawing on its other powers.[110]

Third, the organizational capacity to deal with ESC rights varies significantly from institution to institution depending on the availability of resources and staff expertise. A number of NHRIs have incorporated ESC rights into their institutional structure by establishing committees or working groups, or dedicating staff to work in this area. Nevertheless, OHCHR have expressed concern that many NHRIs lack an 'understanding of the legal nature and content' of these rights.[111] While staff may recognize the importance of the indivisibility and interdependence of all human rights, they are often insufficiently trained to deal with ESC rights issues.[112]

In particular, developing new methodologies for monitoring the obligation to fulfil ESC rights has generally proved to be a challenge for NHRIs. Few institutions are producing regular, comprehensive reports on ESC rights fulfilment in their countries. This may be because traditional approaches that NHRIs have adopted to monitor the state's obligation to respect and protect ESC rights are not as helpful in addressing the state's obligation to fulfil these rights. The fact that complex socio-legal and economic structures that give rise to violations of the obligation to fulfil ESC rights means that such violations are often not readily attributable to single incidents or particular perpetrators. It is therefore crucial that NHRIs identify appropriate supplementary methodologies and approaches in addressing these rights—including competencies in community consultation, policy assessment, collecting and analysing primary and secondary data, and analysing economic, including budgetary, information—and prioritize their implementation.[113]

[109] *Simon v Commission on Human Rights*, G.R. No. 100150 (S.C. January 5, 1994). P. Quisumbig, 'The Protection Role of the Philippines Human Rights Commission', in B. Ramcharan (ed.), *The Protection Role of National Human Rights Institutions* (Leiden: Martinus Nijhoff Publishers, 2005), 155–164, 161.

[110] *Simon v Commission on Human Rights*, G.R. No. 100150 (S.C. January 5, 1994). P. Quisumbig, 'The Protection Role of the Philippines Human Rights Commission', in B. Ramcharan (ed.), *The Protection Role of National Human Rights Institutions* (Leiden: Martinus Nijhoff Publishers, 2005). Section 18 of the Constitution also grants the CHRP a number of other powers relating to human rights more broadly, including 'to monitor the Philippine government's compliance with the international treaty obligations on human rights', which does include the ICESCR.

[111] *OHCHR Handbook, supra* note 16, at viii.

[112] Members of the Asia Pacific Forum of National Human Rights Institutions (APF) identified the ICESCR as the third highest priority area for training. APF, *Assessment of the Training Needs of Member Institutions of the Asia Pacific Forum of National Human Rights Institutions* (March 2010), 12.

[113] See A. Corkery, *National Human Rights Institutions as Monitors of Economic, Social and Cultural Rights* (Madrid: Center for Economic and Social Rights, 2011).

Of course, such concerns do not relate to all NHRIs. Many benefit from extensive mandates and additionally from extensive experience on ESC rights. Two reports by the FIO demonstrate the wealth of experience on ESC rights that exists in a large number of Latin American NHRIs, for example.[114]

In relation to an institution's external dynamics, the independence of an NHRI is widely recognized as one of the most important preconditions for its effective functioning and credibility. However, funding structures for most NHRIs create an ongoing tension in maintaining the conceptual space from which to critique 'the hand that feeds you'.[115] Underfunding is a persistent problem.[116] In some cases budget cuts have apparently resulted from an NHRI's criticism of government, overtly or covertly.[117] For NHRIs that receive financial support from international donor agencies, there is the added complexity of potentially competing priorities, which 'may reorient accountability upward, away from the grassroots, supporters and staff',[118] and mean that ESC rights issues fall through the cracks.[119]

NHRIs in federal or otherwise decentralized administrations may face further challenges in managing external dynamics. In countries where responsibility for the development or implementation of a range of social and economic policy areas falls within the competence of sub-state administration this can add an additional layer of complexity in terms of engagement on the promotion and protection of ESC rights.

5. Responding to Current Contexts

In the 20 years since the adoption of the Paris Principles and the Vienna Declaration and Programme of Action both the number of NHRIs and the context in which they operate has changed dramatically. Changes in global environmental and demographic trends, as well as in the economic and geopolitical climate, have necessitated enhanced engagement with ESC rights. The capacity of states to respect, protect, and fulfil their human rights obligations is shaped and constrained by an international economic order in which new regional powers are emerging and in which non-state actors are increasingly influential. The global financial crisis—which threw many industrialized countries into recession and had knock-on effects in developing and emerging economies—highlighted structural inequalities and

[114] See FIO, *Salud, supra* note 61 and FIO, *Educación, VI Informe sobre Derechos Humanos* (2008).

[115] Smith, *supra* note 33, at 920.

[116] *OHCHR Survey, supra* note 18, at 15 (nearly half of the survey respondents in all regions—and slightly higher in Africa—indicated that their budget is insufficient).

[117] Smith, *supra* note 33, at 920. [118] Smith, *supra* note 33, at 922.

[119] For an example of the apparent challenges for NHRIs in relying on international agencies for financial support, see G. Nicolau, *Ombudsman for Human Rights: The Case of Timor-Leste*, HURIGHTS OSAKA, available at <http://www.hurights.or.jp/asia-pacific/047/02.html> (last accessed 7 November 2013).

accountability gaps in the international economy that impede sustainable, inclusive development.

In response to these emerging issues, NHRIs are increasingly recognizing the importance of adopting an indivisible approach to human rights, as well as diversifying the issues and the actors they address in their work. For example, responding to the increasing international consensus on reproductive rights, encompassing a constellation of civil and political and ESC rights, NHRIs in the Asia Pacific region have expressed their commitment to more effectively integrate these rights into their ongoing work.[120] NHRIs have also supported and responded to the global consensus on the importance of business responsibilities for human rights, committing to action in this area at their 2010 International Conference.[121] Likewise, NHRIs are increasingly active in advancing a human rights-based response to climate change. The 2010 Annual Report of the Zambian Human Rights Commission, for example, focused on human rights and the environment,[122] and the Australian, Egyptian, and Mexican institutions, as well as the Asia Pacific Forum, also contributed to OHCHR's 2009 study on climate change and human rights.[123] A number of trends can be observed which follow or facilitate the work of NHRIs on such emerging issues.

First, NHRIs, like NGOs, are increasingly mobilizing in transnational networks, as commentators have highlighted.[124] Through activities such as accrediting members, facilitating technical assistance, and promoting education and training opportunities; these networks, in Mertus' words, contribute to establishing 'acceptable standards and patterns of behaviour [...] that help socialize states into the NHRI fold'.[125] These networks can exert a type of 'soft' power that influences how NHRIs go about fulfilling their mandate. Notably, it is through these international and regional networks that NHRIs have increasingly committed to strengthening their capacity and increasing their action and effectiveness on ESC rights. [126]

[120] See APF and UNFPA, *Integrating Reproductive Rights into the Work of National Human Rights Institutions in the Asia Pacific: a preliminary study of the current views and practices, challenges and opportunities* (2011), available at <http://asiapacific.unfpa.org/public/pid/7515> (last accessed 7 November 2013).

[121] *Edinburgh Declaration*, supra note 43.

[122] Zambian Human Rights Commission, *2010 State of Human Rights Report in Zambia: Human Rights & the Environment* (Lusaka: 2010), available at <http://cfnhri.org/wp-content/uploads/2012/03/state_of_human_rights_report_2010.pdf> (last accessed 7 November 2013).

[123] See OHCHR, *OHCHR Study: submissions and reference documents received*, available at <http://www.ohchr.org/EN/Issues/HRAndClimateChange/Pages/Submissions.aspx> (last accessed 7 November 2013).

[124] See Shawki, *supra* note 25; A. Byrnes, A. Durbach, and C. Renshaw, 'Joining the Club: The Asia Pacific Forum of National Human Rights Institutions, the Paris Principles, and the Advancement of Human Rights Protection in the Region', 14 *Australian Journal of Human Rights* (2008), 63–98.

[125] Mertus, *supra* note 2, at 129.

[126] See, e.g. *International Round Table on National Institutions Implementing Economic, Social and Cultural Rights, New Delhi, India, 29 November to 1 December 2005, Report of the Proceedings*, available at <http://nhrc.nic.in/Documents/Reports/misc_ESCR.pdf> (last accessed 7 November 2013); Eleventh International Conference of National Human Rights Institutions, *Amman Declaration and Programme of Action* (7 November 2012) paras. 6–14, available at <http://www.asiapacificforum.net/working-with-others/icc/icc-international-conference> (last accessed 7 November 2013).

Thematic working groups established through these networks, such as the ICCtee Working Group on Business and Human Rights[127] and the Working Group on Climate Change of the Commonwealth Forum of NHRIs,[128] enable NHRIs to gain confidence through sharing experiences in their work on ESC rights.

These networks also present new opportunities for collective advocacy from NHRIs. The European Network of NHRIs, for example, has begun to engage the European Union bodies in discussions on the impact of austerity measures on human rights, notably in Greece, Ireland, Portugal, and Spain.[129] Similarly, at the international level the ICCtee published an open letter calling on the Rio Plus 20 conference to recognize the importance of linking efforts to tackle climate change with human rights.[130] The outcomes from the Rio Conference did indeed recognize the importance of human rights to the development of sustainable development goals (SDGs).[131] Collective action has also extended to influencing standard setting including in supporting the ultimately successful efforts to draft an Optional Protocol to the ICESCR.[132]

Increasing NHRI involvement in norm development has seen more recognition of their role in recent conventions. In the development of the UN Convention on the Rights of Persons with Disabilities, for example, NHRI involvement helped secure innovative mechanisms to pursue national implementation, including an explicit reference to their potential role in independent national mechanisms to promote, protect, and monitor the implementation of the Convention.[133] Some surveys suggest that practice may in fact vary significantly between states in the nomination of NHRIs to the independent mechanisms.[134] Where they do play this role, however, NHRIs are necessarily engaging with ESC rights in each of these areas. For example, the European Network of NHRIs Working Group on the CRPD is considering the development of indicators to monitor the convention.[135]

[127] See ICCtee, *Business and Human Rights,* available at <http://nhri.ohchr.org/EN/Themes/BusinessHR/Pages/Home.aspx> (last accessed 7 November 2013) (information on the ICCtee Business and Human Rights Working Group, established in 2009).

[128] CFHRI, *Climate Change and Human Rights,* available at <http://cfnhri.org/working-groups/climate-change-and-human-rights/> (last accessed 7 November 2013).

[129] SHRC, *Austerity and Human Rights in Europe*, available at <http://www.scottishhumanrights.com/application/resources/documents/AusterityandHuman%20Rights13JuneBrussels(2).pdf> (last accessed 7 November 2013).

[130] ICCtee, *ICCtee Open Letter to the United Nations Conference on Sustainable Development,* 2 April 2012, available at <http://www.institut-fuer-menschenrechte.de/fileadmin/user_upload/PDF-Dateien/Sonstiges/icc_open_letter_to_the_united_nations_conference_on_sustainable_development.pdf> (last accessed 7 November 2013).

[131] Report of the UN Conference on Sustainable Development, Rio de Janeiro, Brazil (20–22 June 2012) UN Doc. A/CONF.216/16.

[132] See, e.g. Report of the Open-ended Working Group on an optional protocol to the International Covenant on Economic, Social and Cultural Rights on its 5th session (Geneva, 4–8 February and 31 March–4 April 2008), UN Doc. A/HRC/8/7 (23 May 2008).

[133] UN Doc. A/61/611 (2006), art. 33(2).

[134] See, e.g. OHCHR Europe Regional Office, *Study on the Implementation of Article 33 of the UN Convention on the Rights of Persons with Disabilities in Europe* (Brussels: OHCHR, 2012), 6.

[135] See, e.g. Deutsches Institut fuer Menschenrechte, *Monitoring* (in German), available at <http://www.institut-fuer-menschenrechte.de/de/monitoring-stelle.html> (last accessed 7 November 2013)

The Convention also requires independent mechanisms to involve disabled people in their work. While there has yet to be a global review of how NHRIs are approaching this work, a seminar for NHRIs and disabled peoples organizations from Burundi, Kenya, Rwanda, South Sudan, Tanzania, and Uganda provides a useful example of how NHRIs have established common action plans to discharge this mandate.[136]

Looking ahead, there are some indications that the process of developing a new sustainable development framework to follow the Millennium Development Goals (MDGs) when they expire in 2015 may provide enhanced opportunities for NHRIs to engage more actively with national development and climate change programming. One of the central issues in the post-2015 framework is the question of accountability; the absence of meaningful accountability mechanisms in the MDGs has been one of the main reasons that progress has been so limited. Within the UN system, both UNDP and OHCHR increasingly recognize a role for NHRIs in ensuring a human rights-based approach to delivering development outcomes.[137] OHCHR, for example, cites NHRIs as potentially a key component in national accountability systems for the post-2015 international development goals.[138] NHRIs, too, recognize that they can have an important role in 'nationalizing' global goals, ensuring that national targets and indicators are consistent with human rights standards and principles.[139] Examples of existing initiatives to link national efforts to achieve the current MDGs and human rights have demonstrated that the 'bridging' roles, already described, position NHRIs uniquely to strengthen the mutually reinforcing aspects of the MDGs and human rights. In particular, NHRIs should prioritize marginalized and excluded groups; facilitate community participation in decision-making; promote human rights in policy decisions and resource allocation; and ensure accountability and remedies for human rights violations—all key elements of a human rights-based approach to the MDGs.[140]

(discussing the role of the German Institute for Human Rights in the national CRPD monitoring body).

[136] Commonwealth Forum of National Human Rights Institutions, *National Human Rights Institutions and Disabled People's Organisations Working Together to Promote and Protect the Rights of People with Disability*, Workshop, Kampala, Uganda, 15–17 May 2012, available at <http://cfnhri.org/wp-content/uploads/2012/06/FINAL_ReportUgandaWorkshop_2012.pdf> (last accessed 7 November 2013).

[137] See, e.g. UNDP, *Human Rights and the Millennium Development Goals, making the link* (Oslo: UNDP, 2007), 24 (noting that NHRIs have the capacity to be much more involved in monitoring progress on the MDGs and ensuring strategies are consistent with human rights).

[138] OHCHR, Center for Economic and Social Rights, *Who Will Be Accountable? Human Rights and the Post-2015 Development Agenda* (New York and Geneva: 2013), 42–43.

[139] International Coordinating Committee of NHRIs, 26th Annual Meeting, Concept Note, Theme 4: Post 2015 Development Agenda (Geneva: 2013), available at <http://nhri.ohchr.org/EN/ICC/AnnualMeeting/26/Meeting%20Documents/Post%202015%20Development%20Agenda_APF_EN.docx> (last accessed 7 November 2013).

[140] A. Corkery, 'National Human Rights Institutions', in *Accelerating Achievement of MDGs by Ways and Means of Economic and Social Rights* (Bangkok: UNDP, 2012).

Nevertheless, even as recognition and demand for NHRIs roles in promotion and protection of ESC rights have increased, their funding has not been immune from the effects of the global financial crisis and many face significant budget pressures.[141] Uncertainty over resources makes it difficult for NHRIs to advance more ambitious, forward-looking, inter-disciplinary projects, which, as discussed, are important in addressing failures to fulfil ESC rights.

In this climate many NHRIs have looked to supplement their core funding with additional support from grant-making bodies or international donors. Such an approach can risk fragmentation or distortion in the institution's planning and prioritization. The Palestinian NHRI, however, provides an example of the potential for greater harmonization among donors to mitigate this risk. In that context, bilateral donors to the Independent Commission for Human Rights have signed a Joint Financial Agreement, enabling the Commission to align activities and projects over the next three years to its strategic plan.[142]

In the light of these trends, increasing UNDP support to NHRIs is a welcome development. In January 2008, 94 UNDP country offices reported that they were working with NHRIs, providing resources, capacity, and expertise—including legal and management expertise. In many cases, this occurred in partnership with OHCHR and/or with the ICCtee or regional coordinating committee.[143] There is increasing evidence of an enhanced coordination between NHRIs and the UN system, with the ICCtee considering that 'in recent years it has become increasingly noticeable that the role of NHRIs as natural partners at a domestic level to the United Nations has become more systematically institutionalised'.[144]

It is to be hoped that these developments will help to clarify the approach of the UN which has at times sent a confusing message to NHRIs. OHCHR, for example, has counselled NHRIs to prioritize 'core protection issues, such as the prevention of torture and degrading treatment, summary executions, arbitrary detention and disappearances, or the protection of human rights defenders',[145] to the potential detriment of their role in the promotion and protection of ESC rights.[146] A more

[141] See, e.g. Council of Europe Commissioner for Human Rights, *National Human Rights Structures can help mitigate the effects of austerity measures*, Human Rights Comment (31 May 2012) citing examples of NHRIs in Great Britain, Greece, Ireland, and Latvia.

[142] ICHR, *ICHR Signs Joint Financial Agreement*, available at <http://www.ichr.ps/en/2/20?d=2011> (last accessed 7 November 2013).

[143] H. Clark, UNDP Administrator, Address to the 23rd Session of the International Coordinating Committee of National Institutions for the Promotion and Protection of Human Rights (23 Mar. 2010), available at <http://content.undp.org/go/newsroom/2010/march/helen-clark-address-to-the-committe-for-the-protection-and-promotion-of-human-rights.en;jsessionid=a_uQBb7raV47> (last accessed 28 October 2013).

[144] ICCtee, *26th Annual Meeting, Concept Note, 20 years—the Vienna Declaration, Paris Principles and the ICCtee—planning for the future* (Geneva: 2013), available at <http://nhri.ohchr.org/EN/ICC/AnnualMeeting/26/Meeting%20Documents/20%20years%20_VD%20and%20PP%20-%20EN.doc> (last accessed 7 November 2013).

[145] OHCHR, *OHCHR and NHRIs*, available last at <http://www.ohchr.org/en/countries/nhri/pages/nhrimain.aspx> (last accessed 7 November 2013).

[146] The potential for core protection issues to side-line development-related issues is recognized by UNDP and OHCHR. See UNDP-OHCHR, *Toolkit for Collaboration with National Human Rights Institutions* (2010), 86.

harmonized approach has the potential to strengthen NHRIs' capacity to engage in framing national development agendas and poverty reduction strategies, including in relation to the post-2015 sustainable development framework, infusing such processes with a human rights approach.

6. Conclusion

As NHRIs grow in number, experience, and stature, they are coming to be recognized as unique bodies in the human rights community. They have been the subject of increasing interest among human rights practitioners and academics who have focused on explaining their rapid proliferation, on highlighting their current and potential added value in the human rights system, and on identifying challenges to their performance and legitimacy. Nevertheless there has been far less focus on their role in the promotion and protection of ESC rights.

This chapter has sought to make the case that NHRIs can, and in many cases already do, play a key strategic role in ensuring states' compliance with their obligations to respect, protect, and fulfil ESC rights. Specifically, we have argued that NHRIs' ability to bridge gaps between the national and international human rights systems, between government and civil society, between civil and political and ESC rights, and between reactive and proactive approaches to the promotion and protection of ESC rights makes them unique institutional actors in this area. In this way NHRIs can help to establish a holistic human rights culture, empowering people to know and claim their ESC rights, as well as supporting duty bearers if they are unable to comply with their obligations or to hold them accountable if they are unwilling to do so.

Current examples of NHRIs integrating ESC rights across their promotion and protection functions range from monitoring court decisions in Argentina, to developing National Action Plans for human rights in New Zealand, to conducting national inquiries in Kenya. In addition, NHRIs are increasingly engaging with ESC rights as they tackle emerging opportunities—from their specified role in the UN Disability Convention, to the increasing recognition that dominant global themes such as development, business activity, and climate change demand analysis through a human rights lens. Each of these factors has contributed to an identifiable trend where increasing numbers of NHRIs are embedding ESC rights issues across their operations, and advocating for structural changes that build a human rights culture within the state.

However, NHRIs, along with other actors, continue to face challenges to taking effective proactive action on ESC rights. Most significantly, a key remaining practical challenge is the development of new mechanisms and methodologies for NHRIs to address in a pragmatic fashion broader issues of resource allocation and socio-economic policy that are so central to the progressive fulfilment of ESC rights. Nevertheless, with institutional strengthening where needed, and appropriate partnerships, NHRIs can and should play a role in these issues; acting as national focal points as catalysts for national participatory processes to identify relevant indicators, agree on benchmarks, and independently monitor their achievement.

There is clear cause for optimism on the role of NHRIs as both promoters and protectors of ESC rights and efforts to strengthen their capacity to monitor ESC rights fulfilment should help them fully achieve that potential.

18

Transitional Justice Without Economic, Social, and Cultural Rights?

Frank Haldemann and Rachelle Kouassi

1. Introduction

'Human rights begin with breakfast'. This much-quoted quip from the former president of Senegal, Léopold Senghor, is never more appropriate than in the context of societies torn apart by prolonged conflict and political crisis. Stuck in patterns of political violence that are costly and often repetitive, these are typically low-income countries plagued by long-term malnutrition, low life expectancy and high infant mortality.[1] It is when our attention turns to such mass poverty phenomena that the so-called 'full belly thesis' acquires new cogency.[2] It is difficult to deny, after all, that basic well-being must be secured before people can indulge in the 'luxury' of being concerned about their political freedoms.

It is all the more surprising, therefore, how little attention economic, social, but also cultural rights (ESC rights) have received among scholars and practitioners of what is commonly termed 'transitional justice'—the study of how societies emerging from civil strife or repression should deal with past human rights abuses. By now a firmly established field of scholarly and policy inquiry, transitional justice has tended to focus on civil and political rights as well as notions of individual and especially criminal accountability, thus largely neglecting concerns of social and economic justice. How unsatisfactory such a narrow focus may be is aptly captured in the following comment by Ruben Carranza, a former Philippine defence ministry official, recounting a visit to East Timor in early 2000:

> The boys told me that they were cousins whose families had fled to the mountains when the post-referendum violence was happening [...] Many of their siblings and cousins never made it back. Some of their family members had died earlier, during the occupation. 'Died of what?' I asked. I had thought the answer would be that they were killed by Indonesian

[1] See P. Collier, *The Bottom Billion: Why the Poorest Countries Are Failing and What Can Be Done About It* (Oxford: Oxford University Press, 2008) identifying civil war as one of the main factors that 'trap' the world's poorest people—the 'bottom billion'—in poverty.

[2] See R. Howard, 'The Full Belly Thesis: Should Economic Rights Take Priority Over Civil and Political Rights? Evidence from Sub-Saharan Africa', 5: 4 *Human Rights Quarterly* (1983), 467–490.

forces, massacred by militias, tortured to death or simply forcibly disappeared. But one of the boys said, 'No, they died of hunger.'[3]

It is with such scenarios in mind that Louise Arbour and others have advanced what we will refer to in this chapter as the 'ESC rights thesis'—the claim that ESC rights (such as the right to food, housing, healthcare, and education) should be treated as an integral part of, rather than a peripheral diversion from, the transitional justice agenda.[4] The advocates of this thesis argue forcefully for an expanded understanding of transitional justice, one that transcends the traditional divide between civil and political rights (CP rights) on the one hand and socio-economic and cultural rights on the other.

This proposal, if taken seriously, is not just another addition to the growing literature on transitional justice and related topics; it is an effort to rethink the field of transitional justice as conventionally understood, marking anew its boundaries and priorities. Clearly, this is a radical project, one that fundamentally challenges transitional justice in its current form, and we must raise the question of whether it can be justified at all, not only in theory but also in practice. How central are ESC rights to the task of dealing with the aftermath of civil war or the fall of a repressive regime? What are the practical difficulties that potentially arise in such contexts of converting social justice claims into legal rights, and thus of involving courts in controversial questions about how to distribute scarce resources? Is the human rights vocabulary, with its emphasis on the individual, appropriate as a framework for responding to deep-rooted and complex patterns of social deprivation? Can the ESC rights thesis, in short, deliver on its promise?

Questions such as these must be asked and addressed if we are to advance the debate beyond rhetoric and hyperbole. In what follows a critical analysis of Arbour's ESC rights thesis in the light of current transitional justice debates will be undertaken. To do so, in the next section, the larger conceptual terrain where the debate about the incorporation of ESC rights into transitional justice discourses takes place will be outlined. Then, in the third section, the main threads of arguments commonly advanced to explain why and how ESC rights matter in contexts of mass violence and political transition will be drawn together. In the fourth section, a series of objections that may be raised against such arguments will be taken up, and whether and how these objections may be met or avoided will be discussed. In thus debating the ESC rights thesis, an approach to ESC rights that is

[3] R. Carranza, 'The Right to Reparations in Situations of Poverty', *ICTJ Briefing* (September 2009), 1–5, at 1, available at <http://ictj.org/sites/default/files/ICTJ-Global-Right-Reparation-2009-English.pdf> (last accessed 10 November 2013).

[4] See L. Arbour, 'Economic and Social Justice for Societies in Transition', 40 *International Law and Politics* (2007), 1–27. See also, for instance, S.C. Agbakwa, 'A Path Least Taken: Economic and Social Rights and the Prospects of Conflict Prevention and Peacebuilding in Africa' 47 *Journal of African Law* (2003), 38–64; C. Chinkin, 'The Protection of Economic, Social, and Cultural Rights Post-Conflict,' paper series commissioned by the Office of the High Commissioner for Human Rights, 2009, available at <http://www2.ohchr.org/english/issues/women/docs/Paper_Protection_ESCR.pdf> (last accessed 10 November 2013); L. Hecht and S. Michalowski, 'The Economic and Social Dimension of Transitional Justice', ETJN Concept Paper, available at <http://www.essex.ac.uk/tjn/documents/TheeconomicandsocialdimensionsofTJ.pdf> (last accessed 10 November 2013).

committed *and* realistic, attentive to the potential gap between 'law in books' and 'law in action', will be investigated.

2. Framing the Debate

The history of transitional justice remains to be written. Coined during the 1990s, the term 'transitional justice' has now become, to quote a prominent voice in the field, 'some sort of term of art' widely used to describe the process by which 'societies leave behind a legacy of massive and systematic human rights violations and start on the path to a more humane dispensation of rights and a more democratic society'.[5] The term 'transitional justice' itself, however, is not unproblematic, as it focuses too narrowly on just one component of dealing with the past: justice. Other concepts, such as the German '*Vergangenheitsaufarbeitung*' (meaning to 'come to terms with' or 'work through' the past),[6] may perhaps better capture the complexity of the task and the variety of forms it may take.

This is not the place to quibble over terminology, however. The term 'transitional justice' has, in any case, grown so popular and mainstreamed that any attempt to replace it would be like tilting at windmills. And what matters more than words, after all, is what is made of them. Now, both in theory and practice, the approach usually taken to transitional justice has been notoriously narrow-gauged, centred as it has been on four main responses to collective violence: criminal investigations and prosecutions; truth telling and seeking in the form of truth commissions; the granting of reparations to victims through complaints filed in courts or specially crafted administrative schemes; and institutional reform, particularly the removal of categories of people from public office.[7] These four fields of action can be connected, at least loosely, to state obligations commonly recognized under international human rights law: namely, the duty to investigate human rights violations effectively; to take action against those allegedly responsible; to provide effective remedies to victims; and to take appropriate measures to prevent future violations.[8]

[5] J. Méndez, 'Lou Henkin, Transitional Justice and the Prevention of Genocide', 38 *Columbia Human Rights Review* (2007), 477–485, 479.

[6] The term was made famous by Frankfurt School thinker T.W. Adorno, 'What Does Coming to Terms with the Past Mean?', in G.H. Hartmann (ed.), *Bitburg in Moral and Political Perspective* (Bloomington: Indiana University Press, 1986), 114–129. See also T. Garton Ash, 'The Truth about Dictatorship', *The New York Review of Books* (19 February 1998), 35–40.

[7] See Report of the Secretary-General on 'The rule of law and transitional justice in conflict and post-conflict societies', 23 August 2004, UN Doc. S/2004/616. See also P. de Greiff, 'Transitional Justice, Security, and Development', *Security and Justice Background Paper for the World Development Report 2011* (29 October 2010), at 2 (speaking of 'core elements that a transitional justice policy minimally must include').

[8] See, in particular, Principle 3 of the 'Basic Principles and Guidelines on the Right to a Remedy and Reparation for Victims of Gross Violations of International Human Rights Law and Serious Violations of International Humanitarian Law', UN Doc. A/RES/60/147. See also the landmark decision of the Inter-American Court of Human Rights in *Velásquez Rodríguez v Honduras (Merits)* (1988), 4, ser. C, 29 July 1988, para. 174.

The predominant view of transitional justice as 'inherently short-term, legalistic and corrective' and focused 'on accountability for gross violations of civil and political rights'[9] can be explained, at least partly, by the intellectual history of transitional justice as a field of academic inquiry and human rights activism.[10] But there are other factors, too, that have certainly contributed to the 'thinness' of dominant transitional justice discourses and practices.[11] Not least among these is the fact that transitional justice discourse has been strongly informed by human rights and by that discipline's long-standing bias towards social and economic rights. Moreover, transitional justice practice and theory have been heavily influenced by the rise of international criminal law with its emphasis on individual accountability, as distinct from collective patterns and structural causes of injustice.

In the course of the last decade, the dominant transitional justice script has increasingly come under attack, however. A change of mood is reflected with particular clarity in a 2008 collection edited by Irish transitional justice scholars Kieran McEvoy and Lorna McGregor. Published under the telling title, *Transitional Justice from Below*, this collection presents a powerful challenge to the mainstream of scholarship and praxis by suggesting an enriched, 'bottom-up' understanding of transitional justice. The declared aim, shared by the contributors to the collections, is to reach beyond a narrow, 'legalistic' perspective and encompass a community-based, 'thicker' version of transitional processes—particularly through a greater consideration of the socio-economic dimensions of dealing with the past.[12] Much of this, it should be noted, echoes an argument advanced earlier by Rama Mani. In her 2002 book, *Beyond Retribution*, she argued for a multi-dimensional approach to peace-building, aimed not only at rebuilding the rule of law and repairing past abuses but also at addressing socio-economic or cultural injustices as potential underlying causes of conflict.[13]

Most recently, this idea of expanding the framework of transitional justice to issues of socio-economic justice has gained new traction in the context of the 'Arab Spring' of 2011. Erupted largely in response to youth unemployment, income inequality, corruption, and nepotism, the upheavals that began in Tunisia and spread to Egypt and elsewhere in the Middle East were closely linked to calls for 'greater social justice' and 'less corruption', thus reaching far beyond the conventional boundaries of transitional justice.[14]

[9] L. Waldorf, 'Anticipating the Past: Transitional Justice and Socio-Economic Wrongs', 21 *Social & Legal Studies* (2012), 171–185, 179.

[10] See A. Paige, 'How "Transitions" Shaped Human Rights: A Conceptual History of Transitional Justice', 31 *Human Rights Quarterly* (2009), 321–367.

[11] On this and the following, see Waldorf, *supra* note 9, at 173.

[12] See, in particular, K. McEvoy, 'Letting Go of Legalism: Developing a "Thicker" Version of Transitional Justice', in K. McEvoy and L. McGregor (eds.), *Transitional Justice from Below: Grassroots Activism and the Struggle for Change* (Oxford: Hart, 2008), 14–45.

[13] R. Mani, *Beyond Retribution: Seeking Justice in the Shadow of War* (Cambridge: Polity, 2002).

[14] See R. Abou-El-Fadl, 'Beyond Conventional Transitional Justice: Egypt's 2011 Revolution and the Absence of Political Will', *The International Journal of Transitional Justice* (2012), 1–13. On the economic roots of the uprisings sweeping the Arab world, see L. Noueihed and A. Warren, *The Battle for the Arab Spring: Revolution, Counter-Revolution and the Making of a New Era* (New Haven: Yale University Press, 2012), 24–43.

The ESC rights thesis can, thus, be seen as part of a broader critical engagement with the conventional transitional justice discourse and its sweeping tendency to sideline issues of social justice. What is somewhat distinctive about this thesis, however, is that it draws extensive support from, and is firmly rooted in, international human rights law. This focus on human rights is hardly surprising, of course. Invoking human rights is, after all, a powerful strategy for winning arguments and, perhaps, changing social realities. If we live, as is sometimes suggested, in an 'Age of Human Rights', where 'human rights have become an ethical shibboleth or test of right, indeed of righteousness',[15] then playing the 'human rights card' can be very persuasive as a way of justifying one's claims.

Yet the application of human rights law to post-conflict settings, and especially low-income war-torn societies, may raise concerns. Does the language of human rights provide an adequate framework for addressing structural causes of malnutrition, poverty, or disease that permeate a society's economic structure? How can ESC rights be 'made real' under conditions of institutional and economic scarcity? Is access to justice and the judicial enforcement of ESC rights only a hollow hope for the poor? How can numerous claims be accommodated within a traditional, case-by-case court structure? And to what extent, if any, should unelected judges involve themselves with controversial issues of economic and social policy and, thus, interfere with the liberty of democratically elected governments to determine their own spending priorities? Issues such as these cannot be wished away if we are to move beyond mere 'human rights rhetoric'. However, first it is necessary to take a closer look at the ESC rights thesis, as an entry point for critical debate.

3. Unpacking the ESC Rights Thesis

Should ESC rights be an integral part of the transitional justice framework? In a 2006 lecture, Louise Arbour—the then-UN High Commissioner for Human Rights—tackled this question head-on, leaving her audience in no doubt about where she stood. A sweeping, oft-quoted statement made at the beginning of Arbour's speech set the stage for what we will refer to, in shorthand, as the ESC rights thesis:

> I believe that transitional justice, without losing its raison d'être, is poised to make the significant leap that would allow justice, in its full sense, to contribute as it should to societies in transition. [...] Transitional justice must have the ambition to assist the transformation of oppressed societies into free ones by addressing the injustices of the past through measures that will procure an equitable future. It must reach to—but also go beyond—the crimes and abuses committed during the conflict that led to the transition, and it must address the human rights violations that pre-dated the conflict and caused and contributed to it. With these aims so broadly defined, transitional practitioners will very likely expose a great number of discriminatory practices and violations of economic, social, and cultural rights.[16]

[15] S. Marks, 'Human Rights in Disastrous Times', in J. Crawford and M. Koskenniemi (eds.), *The Cambridge Companion to International Law* (Cambridge: Cambridge University Press, 2012), 309–326, 314.

[16] Arbour, *supra* note 4, at 2.

Transitional justice dilemmas, in this view, cannot be fitted into the conventionally tight, sleek framework heavily focused on CP rights, because it excludes too much that is important about rebuilding or building from scratch the social fabric of war-torn societies. To realize its full potential, transitional justice must embrace rather than ignore social justice by actively protecting and promoting ESC rights—this is, in essence, the thesis that the proponents of this approach undertake to defend. In making their argument, they appropriately distinguish two separate, but complementary, issues: (1) *why* should ESC rights be integrated into the framework of transitional justice? and (2) *how* can this be done?

A. The case for ESC rights

In making their case for integrating socio-economic rights in the transitional justice framework, the advocates of the ESC rights thesis tend to rely on two lines of argument: one based on the historical and conceptual origins of international human rights law, and one based on what Arbour calls 'instrumental reasons'.[17] The first line of argument is familiar enough. It involves calling into question the traditional divide between CP rights and ESC rights. This rigid division stemming from the Cold War is, indeed, largely overstated. Not only does the enjoyment of CP rights crucially depend on the realization of ESC rights,[18] it also—contrary to still widespread misconceptions—entails bundles of positive obligations and frequently demands significant amounts of state resources.[19] The boundaries between CP rights and ESC rights, then, are much more blurred than is conventionally thought; and these different types of rights are, therefore, best seen as being complementary, equally valuable partners in the struggle against injustice, and especially mass atrocities.[20] This, at any rate, is the basic assumption underlying the ESC rights thesis.

This line of argument is taken further by its proponents, even at the risk of entering far more controversial territory. They contend that ESC rights are not merely 'aspirational principles' but legally enforceable ('justiciable') claims, amenable to judicial review. We open Pandora's Box when we explore arguments against ESC rights adjudication, and the advocates of the ESC rights thesis critically address some of them. In particular, they rightly take issue with the assumption that the realization of socio-economic rights is, by definition, costlier and more burdensome than that of political and civil rights.[21] But unfortunately, Arbour and

[17] Arbour, *supra* note 4, at 8.

[18] For example, the effective exercise of the right to vote depends, among other things, on a basic level of education, namely literacy.

[19] Again the right to vote illustrates this well: it requires the state to take positive steps to make sure that elections are held at periodic intervals, which in turn entails considerable state expenditure.

[20] The idea commonly finds expression in the concept of the 'indivisibility' and 'interdependence' of human rights, famously articulated by the United Nations World Conference on Human Rights held in Vienna in 1993. See Vienna Declaration and Programme of Action (12 July 1993), art. 5, UN Doc. A/CONF.157/23.

[21] One can think of several examples to demonstrate the wrongheadedness of that assumption, if taken in full generality. For example, ensuring a 'classical' civil and political right such as the right to

other supporters of ESC rights tend to skip largely over some major arguments against the judicial enforceability of such rights—namely, the claim that judges have neither the democratic legitimacy nor the capacity to decide debatable issues of resource allocation that, as a matter of fact, affect the interests of virtually every citizen and involve complex, 'polycentric' questions of social policy.[22] This neglect of central objections to social rights adjudication may be indicative of a deeper weakness in the ESC rights thesis, and this is a point to which we will return in the next section.

According to the proponents of the ESC rights thesis, there is a second line of argument that should persuade scholars and practitioners to integrate socio-economic rights into their conception of transitional justice. The kind of argument they have in mind is 'instrumentalist' in the sense that it focuses on ESC rights as a means to a valuable end. If the broader aim of transitional justice is to prevent the recurrence of human rights atrocities and to stabilize post-conflict peace, then the socio-economic root causes of conflict need to be identified and addressed. The essence of the argument is this: deep-rooted patterns of exclusion and exploitation can be like 'powder kegs', ready to explode if unaddressed.[23] Where, as in Darfur, houses and villages were systematically burnt and the population forcibly displaced, 'no transition to a just peace will be possible [...] without putting into place an equitable, non-discriminatory framework of access to land and oil'.[24] In this picture, then, transitional justice is not only a story about physical violence and individual perpetrators committing gross violations of CP rights; it is—or should be—also a story about 'structural' violence, systematic discrimination, and great inequality of access to resources, land, work, and housing.[25]

B. Translating ESC rights into practice

It is one thing to explain *why* socio-economic rights should be integrated in the transitional justice framework; it is quite another to address the question of *how* this could be done. This is a crucial issue. If the ESC rights thesis is to be more than an empty abstraction, one should be able to describe the ways and means of putting it into practice. In approaching this matter, it is appropriate to distinguish two questions: what role, if any, can conventional transitional justice measures and instruments play in responding to ESC rights violations? In addition, how can

a fair trial involves a positive duty on the part of the state (creating legal institutions through which citizens can enforce their rights) that is likely to amount to a similarly large investment as providing compulsory, free primary education or accessible healthcare for all.

[22] See J. King, *Judging Social Rights* (Cambridge: Cambridge University Press, 2012), 3–8 (giving an overview of common arguments against constitutional social rights).

[23] See also I. Muvingi, 'Sitting on Powder Kegs: Socioeconomic Rights in Transitional Societies', 3 *The International Journal of Transitional Justice* (2009), 163–182.

[24] Arbour, *supra* note 4, at 9.

[25] This view of transitional justice is much in line with that proposed by the 'critical' literature mentioned earlier. See also Z. Miller, 'Effects of Invisibility: In Search of the "Economic" in Transitional Justice', 2 *The International Journal of Transitional Justice* (2008), 266–291.

ESC rights be built into the legal system of transitional societies so as to ensure respect for these rights in the future? The first question is about the *inclusion* of ESC rights in current transitional justice strategies, the second is about the legal and institutional *foundation* for such rights.

The discussion of the 'inclusion' issue tends to focus on three tools, each of which has become established as an undisputed part of the transitional justice repertoire: truth commissions, trials, and reparations. Each of these institutions and practices offers the potential for advancing ESC rights. This is particularly true of truth commissions. These commissions, the most prominent of which is perhaps the South African Truth and Reconciliation Commission, are typically set up to examine the principal causes and consequences of broad patterns of severe violence and to make recommendations for their redress and prevention in the future.[26] As such, they 'lend themselves particularly well', as Arbour puts it, 'to the investigation and protection of economic, social and cultural rights'.[27] The practice of various truth commissions is revealing in this regard. Particularly noteworthy is Timor-Leste's truth commission, which dedicated a whole chapter of its final report to ESC rights violations;[28] but truth commissions have dealt with patterns of socio-economic injustice elsewhere as well—namely in Liberia,[29] Sierra Leone,[30] and Guatemala.[31]

Furthermore, and more controversially, proponents of ESC rights typically argue for a strong judicial role in realizing these rights. Special attention, it is claimed, should be paid to the judicial enforcement of ESC rights in criminal settings. The upshot of the argument here is that many gross ESC rights violations (including deliberate starvation and violent forced evictions) fall within the category of 'international crimes' and that the still widespread lack of prosecution of such violations is legally unjustified, especially from the perspective of international criminal law.[32] Another way of securing ESC rights that is considered important is via human rights litigation. More use, it is claimed, should be made of domestic but also supranational human rights tribunals, and especially the Inter American Court

[26] See M. Freeman, *Truth Commissions and Procedural Fairness* (Cambridge: Cambridge University Press, 2006), 18; P.B. Hayner, *Unspeakable Truths: Transitional Justice and the Challenge of Truth Commissions* 2nd edn (New York: Routledge, 2011), 11–12.

[27] Arbour, *supra* note 4, at 14.

[28] See Timor-Leste Commission for Reception, Truth and Reconciliation (CAVR), Chega!, Report, Dili, April 2006, Ch. 7.9, available at <http://www.cavr-timorleste.org/chegaFiles/finalReportEng/07.9-Economic-and-Social-Rights.pdf> (last accessed 10 November 2013).

[29] See Republic of Liberia, Truth and Reconciliation Commission, Vol. II: Consolidated Final Report, June 2009, especially at 321 and 385, available at <http://trcofliberia.org/resources/reports/final/volume-two_layout-1.pdf> (last accessed 10 November 2013).

[30] See Sierra Leone Truth & Reconciliation Commission, Witness to Truth, Report, Vol. 1, 2004, at 38, para. 54, available at <http://www.sierra-leone.org/Other-Conflict/TRCVolume1.pdf> (last accessed 10 November 2013).

[31] See Comisión de Verdad y Reconciliación, Final Report (2003), Vol. VIII, available at <http://www.cverdad.org.pe> (last accessed 10 November 2013).

[32] For extensive arguments along these lines, see E. Schmid, 'War Crimes Related to Violations of Economic, Social and Cultural Rights', 71 *Heidelberg Journal of International Law* (2011), 523–540; S.I. Skogly, 'Crimes against Humanity—Revisited: Is There a Role for Economic and Social Rights?'

of Human Rights,[33] to increase respect for ESC rights and promote social justice. The basic idea behind such calls for judicial enforcement is plain enough: if ESC rights are 'real' human rights rather than mere goals, their enforcement is primarily, or at least to a significant degree, a matter for judges. Sceptics, however, may object that focusing on such a judge-centred approach is ineffective, perhaps even counterproductive, especially in contexts of mass deprivation. Supporters of the ESC rights thesis do little, if anything, to dispel such concerns.

This discussion is taken up in the next section, and the third avenue for actualizing socio-economic rights that advocates of ESC rights can point to is explored: reparation programmes. Most reparation programmes have dealt exclusively with gross violations of CP rights, but several such programmes have moved beyond that narrow focus to encompass reparation measures related to breaches of ESC rights, especially forced dislocation and dispossession of land and property. Examples include, of course, restitution campaigns arising from Nazi looting but also more recent efforts to return abusively confiscated dwellings, namely in post-Communist Eastern European countries such as Bulgaria and the Czech Republic,[34] South Africa,[35] Colombia,[36] and Mozambique.[37] Moreover, truth commissions have increasingly recommended the usage of reparations as a means of dealing with previous violations of socio-economic rights. Supporters of the ESC rights thesis mention approvingly the approach taken by Morocco's Equity and Reconciliation Commission. Not only did the Commission recommend quite far-reaching measures of socio-economic redress, it also insisted on the importance of communal reparations, the beneficiaries of which are communities and regions.[38] The adoption of such broad measures, it is argued, is essential, because

5 *The International Journal of Human Rights* (2001), 58–80. See also L. van den Herik, 'Economic, Social, and Cultural Rights: International Criminal Law's Blind Spot?', ch. 12 of this book.

[33] The Inter-American Court and Commission of Human Rights have repeatedly ordered ESC rights-related remedies, ranging from scholarships for higher education to medical treatment for carriers of HIV/AIDS to measures for providing members of indigenous communities with adequate living conditions. See *Cantoral-Benavides v Peru*, 2001 Inter-Am. Ct. H.R. (ser. C), No. 88, para. 80 (3 December 2001); *Jorge Odir Miranda Cortez* et al. *v El Salvador*, Case 12.249, Report No. 29/01 (2000), OEA/Ser. L/II.111 Doc. 20 re. at 284; *Yakye Axa Indigenous Community v Paraguay*, 2005 Inter-Am. Ct. HR (ser. C), No. 125, para. 221 (20 June 2006).

[34] See 'Summary of Property Restitution in Central and Eastern Europe' (Berlin: United States Diplomatic Mission to Germany, 2002), available at <http://germany.usembassy.gov/germany/img/assets/8497/property.pdf> (last accessed 10 November 2013).

[35] South Africa Restitution Act, as amended by Land Restitution and Reform Laws Amendment Act 63 of 1997. See also section 25(7) of the South African Constitution (stating that '[a] person or community dispossessed of property after 19 June 1913 as a result of past racially discriminatory laws or practices is entitled, to the extent provided by an Act of Parliament, either to restitution of that property or to equitable redress').

[36] In 2011, Colombia passed an ambitious reparation law which entitles those who were displaced to the restitution of their lands or, if that goal cannot be met, to equivalent land or monetary compensation. See 'Ley de Víctimas y Restitución de Tierras y sus Decretos Reglamentarios', Ley 1448 DE 2011, arts. 72 and 105(7).

[37] See J. Unruh, 'Property Restitution Law in a Post-War Context: The Case of Mozambique', 3 *African Journal of Legal Studies* (2005), 147–165.

[38] Kingdom of Morocco Justice and Reconciliation Commission, National Commission for Truth, Justice and Reconciliation, Summary of the Final Report, 2006, at 6 (explaining that the Commission primarily focused on communal reparation when dealing with damage inflicted upon communities

an approach solely focused on individual victims 'will never substitute for more broad-based and longer term socio-economic policies that aim to redress and prevent widespread inequalities and discrimination'.[39]

To consider the 'foundation issue': what is an effective way of incorporating socio-economic rights into the legal and institutional framework of newly emerging, transitional societies? The answer that comes immediately to mind is 'constitutionalization'. South Africa's post-apartheid constitution is probably the best-known example of a bill of rights that enshrines a comprehensive set of ESC rights, all of which are enforceable by the courts.[40] But there are many other examples of 'transitional' states that have entrenched ESC rights in their constitutions, including Namibia, Uganda, and Ghana.[41] Especially noteworthy is Kenya's most recent constitution, adopted in 2010, which includes a range of socio-economic rights (among which are the rights to 'the highest attainable standard of health', 'adequate food of acceptable quality', and 'social security').[42] This all looks perfect on paper, but is constitutional entrenchment really an effective way to advance social justice? To approach that question adequately, it must be kept in mind that there are different ways of putting social rights into constitutions. The Swiss Constitution, for instance, recognizes a variety of socio-economic rights, but with the explicit understanding that these are judicially unenforceable policy directives;[43] this will hardly satisfy those who fear that without judicial enforcement, ESC rights guarantees will be mere 'manifesto rights', empty rhetorical gestures.[44] South Africa's Constitution, by contrast, empowers courts to adjudicate, and thus to become 'deliverers' of, constitutional ESC rights; and this, in turn, is bound to attract criticism from those who reject such strong judicial interventions as undemocratic, inefficient, or even harmful to the interests of the victims, an issue that will be discussed later.

Another way of incorporating ESC rights into the legal and institutional framework of post-conflict or post-authoritarian societies is through peace agreements. Since the end of the Cold War, interstate conflicts have been increasingly settled through peace agreements that incorporate human rights values and commitments.[45] Typically and unsurprisingly, the focus of such references is on CP rights,

and recommended 'the adoption of socio-economic and cultural development projects serving the interest of cities and regions').

[39] Arbour, *supra* note 4, at 20.

[40] Constitution of the Republic of South Africa, no. 108 of 1996. The ESC rights enshrined in the Bill of Rights include the right to 'fair labour practices' (s. 23), 'housing' (s. 26), 'health care, food, water and social security' (s. 27), 'education' (s. 29), and 'language and culture' (s. 30). Under sec. 38 of the Constitution, assorted individuals and groups are conferred standing for Bill of Rights claims and may be granted 'appropriate relief'.

[41] See J.C. Mubangizi, 'The Protection of Socio-Economic Rights in Selected African Countries: A Comparative Evaluation', 2 *African Journal of Legal Studies* (2006), 1–19.

[42] The Constitution of Kenya, 28 August 2010, art. 43, available at <http://www.wipo.int/wipolex/fr/text.jsp?file_id=207672> (last accessed 10 November 2013).

[43] See Federal Constitution of the Swiss Confederation of 18 April 1999, art. 41(4); available at <http://www.admin.ch/ch/e/rs/1/101.en.pdf> (last accessed 10 November 2013).

[44] See J. Feinberg, *Social Philosophy* (Englewood Cliffs: Prentice-Hall, 1973), 95.

[45] See C. Bell, *On the Law of Peace: Peace Agreements and the Lex Pacificatoria* (Oxford: Oxford University Press, 2008). See also S. Aroussi and S. Vandeginste, 'When Interests Meet Norms: The

but some peace agreements make explicit mention of ESC rights. The Sudan Peace Agreement of 2006, for instance, provides for a number of ESC rights, including the right to 'free and compulsory primary education' (Article 51) and 'a clean and diverse environment' (Article 50).[46] Such agreements can be instrumental in indicating exit routes from violent conflict and outlining a path towards 'positive peace',[47] and the protection of ESC rights may be essential in this process. But even granting this, peace agreements should be seen for what they are—little more than roadmaps; signposts on a road towards peace that is often long and arduous, cut by thousands of obstacles and rife with frustration.[48]

A third avenue for translating ESC rights into the domestic legal order is ordinary legislation, and that avenue is perhaps the least controversial.[49] Indeed, even staunch critics of judicially enforceable ESC rights may find it unproblematic, if not beneficial, to use ordinary law to support measures and policies that are essential for the socio-economic or cultural well-being of individuals and communities.[50] In such legislative processes, after all, the decision-making authority is left in the hands of democratically elected representatives, while the courts are no more than secondary actors involved in guaranteeing the delivery of what the legislature has committed itself to providing. The same cannot be said, of course, for constitutional ESC rights adjudication, where judges become the primary deliverers of rights. It is all the more pressing, then, to ask whether judicially enforceable ESC rights offer a real advantage towards helping to promote social justice, especially in transition settings.

4. Debating the ESC Rights Thesis

Proponents of the ESC rights thesis offer a significant critical reflection on the state of the field, one that encourages us to look beyond the boundaries we have come to take for granted and to ask whether transitional justice is really where it can and should be. This should be welcomed, especially in a field which, some find (perhaps justifiably so), has become a bit too complacent, stuck in a self-congratulatory mode of 'toolbox' thinking.

Relevance of Human Rights for Peace and Power-Sharing', 17 *The International Journal of Human Rights* (2013), 183–203.

[46] Eastern Sudan Peace Agreement, Asmara, 19 June 2006, available at <http://www.sd.undp.org/doc/Eastern_States_Peace_Agreement.pdf> (last accessed 10 November 2013).

[47] We borrow the term 'positive peace' from Johan Galtung, who used it to describe the absence of 'structural violence'. See J. Galtung, 'Violence, Peace, and Peace Research', 6 *Journal of Peace Research* (1969), 167–191.

[48] See UN Secretary-General, In Larger Freedom: Towards Development, Security and Human Rights for All, UN Doc. A/59/2005 (21 March 2005), para. 114 (noting that about half the countries where peace agreements are negotiated lapse back into violence after five years).

[49] See Arbour, *supra* note 4, at 24–26.

[50] See, for instance, C. Gearty, 'Against Judicial Enforcement', in C. Gearty and V. Mantouvalou (eds.), *Debating Social Rights* (Oxford: Hart, 2011), 1–84, 55–58.

There is much to be said for the criticism of mainstream approaches to transitional justice and their neglect of social and economic justice issues. To begin with, it is hard to reject one of the core assumptions underlying the ESC rights thesis, namely, that socio-economic rights such as the right to subsistence and basic healthcare are as essential to the well-being of people as established political and civil rights.[51] Arbour and other proponents of ESC rights are correct in challenging head-on the traditional assumption that ESC and CP rights are conceptually distinct. That distinction is indeed overdrawn, and many arguments made in its support fail upon closer inspection. They are right, too, in stressing the importance of socio-economic redistribution for transitional societies. If it is to be socially meaningful, transitional justice requires more than a 'quick fix'. Rather, it requires a long-term, multifaceted, transformative process, aimed first and foremost at restoring (or creating) minimal social decency in 'a bombed and flattened moral landscape'.[52] The satisfaction of basic needs is integral, rather than marginal or accidental, to that process.

However, if the ESC rights thesis is not to be merely an abstract ideal without practical import, it must provide a realistic view of how to make it 'work' in the world as it is; and it is here that one would have wished a more critical and nuanced discussion, attentive to the special challenges arising in transitional and, especially, post-conflict societies which are often faced with extreme poverty and scarcity of resources. Although proponents of the ESC rights thesis discuss practical avenues for realizing ESC rights in transitional settings, there is often something disturbingly artificial about that discussion, as it fails, to a large extent, to seriously engage with debates about such rights that are far from settled.

A. The hedgehog and the fox

This is perhaps a common problem of human rights activism, its 'dark side', as David Kennedy would put it.[53] In itself, there is, of course, nothing wrong with being deeply passionate about human rights, about their potential for human progress and emancipation. Sticking to one's human rights ideals and vigorously giving voice to them is something we should value, to be sure; and there is no doubt that the international human rights movement has done a great deal of good by holding governments or other actors accountable for their human rights record. But focusing in this way on human rights does not come without costs. By viewing the world exclusively through the human rights lens, we risk losing sight of its complexity.

[51] For such an argument, see V. Mantouvalou, 'In Support of Legalisation', Gearty and Mantouvalou, *supra* note 50, at 85–171.

[52] We take the expression from S. Hampshire, *Innocence and Experience* (Cambridge: Harvard University Press, 1989), 68. For a helpful reflection on the notion of minimal decency, see R. Bhargava, 'Restoring Decency to Barbaric Societies', in R.I. Rotberg and D. Thompson (eds.), *Truth v Justice: The Morality of Truth Commissions* (Princeton: Princeton University Press, 2000), 45–67.

[53] See D. Kennedy, *The Dark Sides of Virtue: Reassessing International Humanitarianism* (Princeton: Princeton University Press, 2004).

Oxford philosopher Isaiah Berlin's metaphor of the hedgehog and the fox comes to mind. Hedgehogs, Berlin suggests, 'relate everything to a single central vision, one system, less or more coherent or articulate, in terms of which they understand, think and feel'.[54] The foxes, by contrast, 'pursue many ends, often unrelated and even contradictory'; 'their thought', Berlin says, 'is scattered or diffused, moving on many levels', and they do not seek 'any unitary inner vision'.[55] Like the hedgehog thinker, the human rights activist is tempted to rely on 'one single system', human rights, to answer any moral and political question; and it is this search for a universal, unitary vision that reduces the possibility for a larger, more nuanced, 'fox-like' view of political action and the context of action.

An illustration of this is Arbour's case for criminal law enforcement of ESC rights. Viewed abstractly, the idea of applying the (international) criminal law framework to ESC rights-related atrocities has much going for it, both morally and legally.[56] But the problem lies elsewhere, namely in a certain 'hedgehog-like' inclination to idealize the criminal law and what it can achieve in post-conflict settings, at the expense of a more realistic, cautious account of the difficulties of 'delivering criminal justice' in such politically and socially volatile contexts. Can one reasonably expect the ideal of criminal justice to 'work' in conflict-ridden and institutionally weak societies, where the existence of an independent and professional judiciary cannot be simply assumed? What role, if any, can international criminal tribunals usefully or properly play in contexts of transitional justice?[57] Should amnesty never be an option, even at the risk of prolonging violent conflict and human suffering?[58] Are restorative justice initiatives valuable alternatives for 'doing justice', especially in instances of widespread group-based harm?[59] Questions such

[54] I. Berlin, 'The Hedgehog and the Fox: An Essay on Tolstoy's View of History', in H. Hardy and A. Kelly (eds.), *Russian Thinkers* 2nd edn (London: Penguin Classics, 2008), 24–92, at 24.

[55] I. Berlin, 'The Hedgehog and the Fox: An Essay on Tolstoy's View of History', in H. Hardy and A. Kelly (eds.), *Russian Thinkers* 2nd edn (London: Penguin Classics, 2008), 24–25.

[56] Many people, after all, will share the strong moral intuition that gross violations of ESC rights such as mass starvation and the systematic denial of access to healthcare constitute 'unimaginable atrocities that deeply shock the conscience of humanity' and, therefore, ought to be 'of concern to the international community as a whole' (as stated in the preamble to the ICC Rome Statute). See Rome Statute of the International Criminal Court, UN Doc. A/CONF. 183/9*(1998), reprinted in 37 ILM (1998) 999, paras. 2 and 9 to the Preamble. See A. Duff, 'Authority and Responsibility in International Law', in S. Besson and J. Tasioulas (eds.), *The Philosophy of International Law* (Oxford: Oxford University Press, 2010), 601–602 (discussing the idea that the perpetrators of some kinds of wrongs should have to answer to 'humanity'); on the potential overlap between ESC rights-related atrocities and international crimes, see the literature in *supra* note 32.

[57] For a critical discussion of the impact of international criminal law on transitional processes, see M. Drumbl, *Atrocity, Punishment and International Law* (Cambridge: Cambridge University Press, 2007) (noting disconnects between aspirations of punishment and realities of sentence in the practice of international criminal courts); A. Branch, *Displacing Human Rights* (Oxford: Oxford University Press, 2011), 179–215 (criticizing the role of the ICC in Northern Uganda). See also L. van den Herik, ch. 12 of this book.

[58] For a critical legal discussion of this issue, see W. Schabas, *Unimaginable Atrocities: Justice, Politics, and Rights at the War Crimes Tribunals* (Oxford: Oxford University Press, 2012), 199–221.

[59] See, for instance, E. Kiss, 'Moral Ambition Within and Beyond Political Constraints', in R.I. Rotberg and D. Thompson (eds.), *Truth v Justice* (Princeton: Princeton University Press, 2000), 69–98 (discussing the concept of restorative justice in the context of the South African Truth and Reconciliation Commission).

as these are at the heart of current debates, but proponents of the ESC rights thesis tend to sidestep them.

Something similar can be said about the case for constitutional ESC rights. In making such a case, advocates of the ESC rights thesis tend to assume (rather than argue for) the proposition that putting such rights in the constitution and giving judges broad powers to enforce them is a good way to advance social and economic justice, especially in transitional societies. That conception is far from uncontroversial, however. ESC rights sceptics tend to be sceptics of judicial enforcement. Courts, they contend, are inappropriate avenues for securing such rights. Some critics even go so far as to claim that for socio-economic rights to work effectively in the advancement of social, economic, and cultural justice, they need to be kept as far away as possible from the courts. Conor Gearty puts the point provocatively when he claims that:

> [t]he least effective way of securing social rights is via an over-concentration on the legal process, with the constitutionalisation of such rights being an especial disaster wherever it occurs. Such a move turns the whole subject over to its falsest of false friends, the lawyers, a community which (in this context and however generally well-meaning) amounts to little more than an array of pseudo-politicians on the look-out for short-cuts to difficult questions and for ways of plying their trade that are more agreeable to their ethical selves.[60]

This is certainly a blunt statement; and some of those who care about constitutional ESC rights may take offence. Yet Gearty's argument should be seen for what it is (and what it is not). It is clearly not intended to deliver a knock-out blow against 'social rights talk' per se. Gearty acknowledges the value of the ESC rights language as a potentially powerful (cosmopolitan, morally loaded, urgent) way of expressing a commitment to care about others. What Gearty takes issue with is rather what he describes, in his characteristically outspoken style, as 'a hankering after the quick-fix of a judicial *Deus ex machina*'.[61] If we really want to make the world a socially more responsible place, Gearty argues, we should rely on political action as a continuous and progressive process,[62] supported (rather than replaced) by reliance on human rights as a powerful source of social critique and mobilization. Turning over the struggle for social change to the lawyers and, particularly, the judges is, on this account, not only 'politically insensitive and socially illiterate'; it is also 'a dangerous and indeed counter-productive move'.[63]

B. The limits of judicial enforcement

Along these lines, critics have offered a variety of arguments against constitutional social rights adjudication, some stronger than others. One of the most common

[60] Gearty, *supra* note 50, at 1. [61] Gearty, *supra* note 50, at 27.

[62] As Gearty notes (*supra* note 50, at 27–33), this idea of 'progressive realization' is built into the ICESCR. See, most significantly of all, art. 2(1) ICESCR, which requires that each state party undertake 'steps [...] to the maximum of its available resources, with a view to achieving progressively the full realization of the rights recognized in the present Covenant by all appropriate means, including particularly the adoption of legislative measures'.

[63] Gearty, *supra* note 50, at 2 and 55.

arguments against ESC rights adjudication is the claim that it is undemocratic. By enabling the courts to enforce ESC rights, so the argument goes, too much power is handed over to unelected judges on social policy matters that affect the interests of nearly everyone and, therefore, should be dealt with by a representative legislature.

This is a powerful objection, and courts have tried to respond to it by adopting innovative models of 'weak judicial review'.[64] An oft-noted example is the South African Constitutional Court's ruling in the *Grootboom* case.[65] The claimant, Irene Grootboom, and other applicants in the case had been evicted from an illegal squatter camp and had moved onto an adjacent sports field, with little more than plastic sheets for protection. In its judgment, the Court ruled that the political branches of South Africa had violated the Constitution by failing to develop an appropriate housing plan to address the needs of emergency shelter. The Court, however, refused to recognize a right 'to shelter or housing immediately upon demand'.[66] Adopting the so-called 'reasonableness model', the Court merely held that the state had the obligation to devise a 'coherent housing programme' and to devote 'a reasonable part of the national housing budget' to meeting the immediate needs of the poorest and most desperate.[67] Prominent constitutionalists lauded the decision as a promising approach to social rights enforcement, attentive to both the value of democratic self-governance and the limited nature of public budgets.[68]

Other arguments against ESC rights adjudication should also be seriously considered and discussed, but this is surely not the place to do so.[69] In what follows, we shall confine the discussion to one kind of argument that is of particular relevance here: the claim that ESC rights litigation is largely ineffective as a medium for advancing social justice, especially with respect to impoverished and marginalized social groups. It may well be true that ESC rights are no longer mere 'paper rights', since courts around the world are now actively enforcing them. But does ESC rights adjudication deliver what it promises? Does it really serve the interests of poor and marginalized groups, as is generally assumed?

In a recent article, constitutional law theorist David Landau challenges, quite fundamentally, the common view of ESC rights litigation as a powerful medium for social transformation. Drawing on extensive fieldwork in Colombia and on evidence from other countries, he argues that such litigation tends to benefit the middle or upper classes rather than the poor. 'Courts', Landau concludes, 'are far more likely to protect pension rights for civil servants or housing subsidies for the

[64] See, for instance, M. Tushnet, *Weak Courts, Strong Rights: Judicial Review and Social Welfare Rights in Comparative Constitutional Law* (Princeton: Princeton University Press, 2008), 18.

[65] *Government of the Republic of South Africa v Grootboom and Others*, 2000 (11) BCLR 1169.

[66] *Government of the Republic of South Africa v Grootboom and Others*, 2000 (11) BCLR 1169, para. 95.

[67] *Government of the Republic of South Africa v Grootboom and Others*, 2000 (11) BCLR 1169, paras. 41 and 66.

[68] See, especially, C. Sunstein, *Designing Democracy: What Constitutions Do* (Oxford: Oxford University Press, 2001), 221–237.

[69] For an extensive critical assessment of arguments against social rights, see J. King, *supra* note 22, at 3–8.

middle class than they are to transform the lives of marginalised groups'.[70] Octavio Luiz Motta Ferraz is equally critical about health litigation in Brazil. Empirical research demonstrates, he asserts, that social rights adjudication in this field has 'clearly not benefitted the poor'.[71] Virgílio Afonso da Silva is even harsher in his assessment of the Brazilian courts' role in promoting social justice. 'Empirical data has shown', he insists, 'that an effective access to the judicial system in Brazil is almost exclusively reserved for the financially well-resourced litigants. *Courts are actually an institutional voice for the rich*'.[72] According to Roberto Gargarella, the phenomenon applies to other Latin American countries as well. He speaks of 'the Latin American legal paradox': while Latin American countries tend to provide for social rights-rich constitutions, the underprivileged find it difficult to access a judicial system that is 'too far removed from the people'.[73]

It is tempting to regard this as an epiphenomenon, a sort of 'Latin American hiccup'. But that would be too simple. As Jeff King notes with respect to constitutional adjudication in the United Kingdom, 'only a fool would disregard the substantial barriers faced in access to justice by impecunious claimants in their quest for justice in the welfare state'.[74] In response to such scepticism, proponents of judicial enforcement of ESC rights tend to invoke the (supposedly promising) experience in India and South Africa. In both countries, the judiciary has indeed taken innovative approaches to the judicial protection of socio-economic rights, and several studies found that there is evidence of a positive impact of litigation for the poor and disadvantaged. The fact remains, however, that the ranks of the poor are still shockingly vast in India.[75] As for South Africa, it is one of the most unequal societies in the world.[76] This should give pause even to the most zealous advocates of ESC rights litigation.

All told, then, caution is required about what ESC rights adjudication can achieve, especially with respect to deep-rooted social injustices in low-income, conflict-ridden societies. The answer to the question of whether courts can be useful vehicles for achieving social justice cannot, of course, be determined in the abstract. Much depends on the political and social conditions prevailing in the

[70] D. Landau, 'The Reality of Social Rights Adjudication', 53 *Harvard International Law Journal* (2012), 402–459, 402 (emphasis omitted).

[71] OLM Ferraz, 'Harming the Poor through Social Rights Litigation: Lessons from Brazil', 89 *Texas Law Review* (2011), 1643–1668, 1667.

[72] V.A. da Silva, 'Taking from the Poor to Give to the Rich' (his emphasis), available at <http://www.enelsyn.gr/papers/w13/Paper%20by%20Prof.%20Virgilio%20Afonso%20da%20Silva.pdf> (last accessed 10 November 2013).

[73] R. Gargarella, '"Too Far Removed from the People"—Access to Justice for the Poor: The Case of Latin America', UNDP Issue Paper (Bergen: Chr. Michelsen Institute, 2002).

[74] King, *supra* note 22, at 85.

[75] According to a recent World Bank Report, one-third of the world's poorest live in India. See World Bank, 'The State of the Poor: Where Are the Poor and Where Are They Poorest?', 2, available at <http://www.worldbank.org/content/dam/Worldbank/document/State_of_the_poor_paper_April17.pdf> (last accessed 10 November 2013).

[76] South Africa's Gini index measure—the best known measure of inequality, in which 0 represents the most equal and 100 the least—was 63.1 in 2009. See also 'Over the Rainbow', *The Economist* (London, 20 October 2012).

political community at which the argument about judicial ESC rights is directed. Arguably, ESC rights adjudication works best when there is a reasonably independent and well-functioning judiciary and a good-faith political commitment to promoting social rights; conditions that cannot simply be taken for granted in transitional societies, especially poor and war-ridden ones.[77] Moreover, and significantly, a lack of institutional resources, a common problem in such contexts, is likely to widen the gap between the constitutional guarantees of ESC rights and the actual enforcement of these rights.[78] A certain degree of modesty about what can be achieved is, therefore, in order.

5. Conclusion: The Case for Legal Humility

The neglect of ESC rights in the dominant 'script' of transitional justice is rarely explicitly defended. Much of it, we suspect, has to do with some old shibboleths about the (supposedly sharp) analytical division between CP and ESC rights. The matter is too important to be left unattended, however, and this is why the ESC rights thesis as a substantial contribution to the topic should be welcomed. The question of whether social, economic, and cultural concerns should be an integral part of transitional justice discourses is, after all, more than a sideline issue; it involves a debate about the fundamentals of transitional justice, about its meaning and aspirations.

When they take an explicit stance, advocates of a narrow reading of transitional justice usually make an instrumental case for excluding ESC rights. By expanding transitional justice to broad social and economic concerns, they argue, we risk freighting it with expectations so overstretched and impractical as to make the whole project meaningless. In this view, particularly aptly defended by Lars Waldorf, transitional justice is best seen as an 'inherently short-term, legalistic and corrective' enterprise, essentially focused on accountability for gross violations of CP rights.[79]

While there is good reason to sympathize with such an attempt to offer a realistic view of transitional justice, it risks losing track of what is believed to be the 'core' concern of efforts at 'coming to terms with the past': to restore, or build from scratch, a minimally decent social order in the face of large-scale atrocity. Without due consideration of basic social rights, understood as entitlements to social goods that are essential for human welfare (food, decent housing, health, etc.), any such project is doomed from the start. Or as Amélie Oksenberg Rorty puts it, somewhat more succinctly: 'First let's eat and then talk of right and wrong'.[80]

77 See King, *supra* note 22, at 10–12.

78 For an illustrative example, see E. Skaar and JOS Van-Dúnem, 'Courts under Construction in Angola: What Can They Do for the Poor?', in R. Gargarella, P. Domingo, and T. Roux (eds.), *Courts and Social Transformation in New Democracies: An Institutional Voice for the Poor?* (Farnham: Ashgate, 2006), 213–232 (suggesting that the failure to enforce socio-economic rights in Angola is largely due to a lack of human and technical resources within the justice system itself).

79 Waldorf, *supra* note 9, at 179.

80 A. Oksenberg Rorty, 'From Decency to Civility by Way of Economics: "First Let's Eat and Then Talk of Right and Wrong" ', 64 *Social Research* (1997), 112–130.

From this perspective, ESC rights are integral rather than marginal to the transitional justice project. However, for all its value, 'social rights talk' provides no panacea, no quick fix, for the challenges of creating the conditions for social decency, civility, and even justice in the aftermath of political violence. Transitional justice, as we understand it, is a slow and messy business. The road to change is often difficult and winding, filled with genuine dilemmas and real costs, and there is surely no recipe, no algorithm, for deciding how best to deal with a particular society's violent past. The language of ESC rights, or human rights *tout court*, has certainly a great potential to inspire social transformation in such contexts; but it is necessary to resist the temptation of getting wrapped up in a kind of 'absolutist' human rights rhetoric that tends to obscure, rather than illuminate, the hard choices of transitional governance and ultimately inhibit the art of compromise and broader dialogue about what is realistically achievable, here and now.

At times, the proponents of the ESC rights thesis risk falling into just this trap. This is especially true regarding the issue of judicial enforcement. Much of the case for ESC rights adjudication reflects, it can be argued, what Conor Gearty describes somewhat provocatively but aptly as 'the activist's desire for a "quick fix"' and 'the lawyer's partiality for the legal'.[81] Not only do advocates of ESC rights tend to assume—all too uncritically, perhaps—that courts can provide an effective avenue for advancing social justice; they will generally pay little, if any, attention to the backdrop of social and political conditions which, especially in contexts of fragile transitions and limited resources, may render the judicial enforcement of socio-economic rights prone to all sorts of distorted outcomes.

Paradoxically enough, the South African *Grootboom* case provides an illustration of how the judicial enforcement of ESC rights can prove stubbornly difficult, especially in grossly unequal societies.[82] The word 'paradoxically' is used because proponents of ESC rights have spoken enthusiastically of 'an extraordinary decision by the South African Constitutional Court', lauding its approach to the right to adequate housing as 'novel and exceedingly promising'.[83] And yet, in August 2008 the affair came to a sad end. Irene Grootboom, the named plaintiff in the case, died 'homeless and penniless', in her 40s, while waiting for a decent house eight years after winning the case.[84] True, the case led to expansive legislative reforms, but this was hardly a consolation for the one who spent the rest of her life in a shack. Something, a deeply felt sense of injustice, was lost along the way.

Giving effect to ESC rights is no simple task, of course; and there are real questions about whether courts are well positioned to enforce such guarantees. But beyond that debate, the *Grootboom* case is perhaps best seen as an illustration of the deep dilemmas and trade-offs involved in realizing—making 'real'—ESC rights

[81] Gearty, *supra* note 50, at 35.

[82] *Government of the Republic of South Africa v Grootboom, supra* note 65.

[83] Sunstein, *supra* note 68, at 221.

[84] P. Joubert, 'Grootboom dies homeless and penniless', *Mail* and *Guardian* (Johannesburg, 8 August 2008), available at <http://mg.co.za/article/2008-08-08-grootboom-dies-homeless-and-penniless> (last accessed 10 November 2013).

in transitional societies haunted by the spectre of systemic, deep-rooted violence in the form of socio-economic mal-distribution and cultural misrecognition. Simplistically, absolute formulations will not do. What is needed, rather, is a kind of 'legal humility' that enables 'a more honest acknowledgement of the limitations of legal thinking and practice that aren't grounded in "the real world" '.[85] Here, as elsewhere, one should take seriously Berlin's advice: beware the hedgehog, follow the fox.[86]

[85] McEvoy, *supra* note 12, at 44. [86] Berlin, *supra* note 54.

Index